THIRD EDITION

HANDBOOK OF RESEARCH DESIGN AND SOCIAL MEASUREMENT

DELBERT C. MILLER

David McKay Company, Inc.
New York

611009

To
F. STUART CHAPIN *and* GEORGE A. LUNDBERG
Pioneers in Sociometric Scaling

Handbook of Research Design and Social Measurement

COPYRIGHT © 1964, 1970, AND 1977 BY DAVID McKAY COMPANY, INC.

Third Edition, 1977

Manufactured in the United States of America

Developmental Editor: Edward Artinian
Editorial and Design Supervisor: Nicole Benevento
Design: Pencils Portfolio, Inc.
Production and Manufacturing Supervisor: Donald W. Strauss
Composition: Automated Composition Service, Inc.
Printing and Binding: Hamilton Printing Company

Library of Congress Cataloging in Publication Data

Miller, Delbert Charles, 1913–
    Handbook of research design and social measure-
ment.

    Bibliography: p.
    Includes index.
    1. Social science research. 2. Sociometry.
I. Title
M62.M44 1977   301'.07'2   77-128
ISBN 0-679-30311-1 pbk.
ISBN 0-679-30312-X

Preface to the Third Edition

The third edition attempts to make the handbook a professional guide that will be equally helpful to teachers, researchers, and students. For the teachers, the book incorporates features that provide the framework through which the logic of research and theory may be viewed as each research step is taken. For professional researchers, the book is a reference guide to which they can turn when they wish to check their knowledge or find new material quickly. There are five major areas where aids are commonly required. These are in research functions associated with *research design and sampling*; *collection of data*; *statistical analysis*; *selection of sociometric scales or indexes*; and lastly, *research funding, costing, and reporting*. Accordingly, the handbook is organized around these functions. For students, the book provides the simplest step by step guidance to each phase of the research process.

No handbook can replace the training required for qualified research. This book is a compilation of resources organized to provide reference to the essential materials needed in the overall design of research. Designed research refers to the planned sequence of the entire process involved in conducting a research study. The steps of this sequence are shown in Guide 1.1 as:

1. Selection and definition of a sociological problem
2. Description of the relationship of the problem to a theoretical framework
3. Formulation of working hypotheses
4. Design of the experiment or inquiry
5. Sampling procedures
6. Establishment of methods of gathering data
7. Preparation of a working guide
8. Analysis of results
9. Interpretation of results
10. Publication or reporting of results

The handbook provides guides to accompany all of these steps.

A major purpose has motivated the development of this guidebook. The author seeks to advance a major goal of all research progress, i.e., to improve research and to expedite the design and other operational phases of research. Investigations into leading sociological journals show that replication of research is infrequent. Measures of sociological variables, except for such demographic variables as age, sex, religion, race, and the like are not used uniformly. Researchers often tend to ignore the scales available and to construct new ones.

Thus, it is impossible to make careful comparisons with previous research and it is also difficult to build an accumulation of empirically verified relationships. Some exceptions show what might be accomplished. Social researchers have made wide use of the *Bogardus Social Distance Scale, Moreno's Sociometry Measures, Chapin's Social Participation Scale, Edwards' Social-Economic Grouping of Occupations*, and other instruments included in this handbook. The psychologists have some relatively standard instruments in the *Minnesota Multiphasic Personality Inventory* and in the *F-Scale* to measure *Authoritarian Personality*. These scales have led to replication which has produced accumulative research findings.

This handbook seeks to bring together social scales that have, or promise to have, wide utility and validity. It is expected that new scales will continue to be constructed by the hundreds. Certainly, many new and better scales are needed. Meanwhile, we need an inventory and storage house for selected measures that ought to be used unless there are compelling reasons to the contrary. If the scales included herein are not the most useful and valid, then the author invites communication. The handbook should constantly improve as consensus among experts is achieved. Meanwhile, if the selection helps increase replication and speeds research operations, a major goal of this book will have been achieved.

Another possible outcome of this handbook may be its capacity to suggest new research. The student who is looking for a research problem should begin by examining the section containing the sociometric scales and indexes. These are generally measures of the dependent variables of greatest interest to social researchers. Any one of these scales can suggest to a researcher a new hypothesis requiring a test of a relationship not yet carefully demonstrated in a given population. In many ways, the sociometric scales in the storehouse of knowledge constitute the best seedbed for new research ideas and endeavors. The student can play an important role in replicating good research designs of professional researchers. Graduate students now exceed professional researchers in numbers. They represent manpower of such scope that their combined efforts could make a substantial contribution to verified social science knowledge.

Empirical social research is now being actively encouraged not only in all of the traditional social sciences but also in the professional schools of business, education, public administration, social work, and law. Newcomers also include criminal justice administration, hospital administration, health and housing administration, recreational administration, schools of communication, library administration, hotel administration, and many others. This edition has tried to incorporate materials to serve research needs as widely as possible.

New materials appear in every part of the book. Part 1 retains the guide for the overall research design and adds a guide for a research grant proposal. Blalock's description of the language of theory and research is new and contains valuable knowledge about bridging the gap between theory and research. The role of models in research design summarizes an important development. Factors jeopardizing the validity of research designs are described to prevent researchers from introducing unforeseen error.

In part 2 the most important additions are guides to the U.S. Census and research reports of the Bureau of Labor Statistics, a guide to private professional services for the social researcher, and a list of important international research associations and institutes.

Part 3 has a new section on causation and multivariate analysis that includes an introduction to the computer, path analysis, and factor analysis.

Part 4 offers sections on social indicators, measures of organizational structure, evaluation research, and organizational effectiveness. The inventory of sociometric measures utilized in the *American Sociological Review* has been extended so that the analysis covers the years 1965 to 1974.

Part 5 presents updated material on research funding and pre- and post-doctoral opportunities, a new guide to research budgeting, new guides to sociological and related journals and to major journals in all the social sciences and many applied fields, how and where sociologists get published, professional communication, and reporting to professional meetings.

I am especially indebted to David Long and Mort Seindenfeld for their efforts in assembling material. I am grateful to Diane Nelson, Susan Headley, Teresa Packard, Janet Barrett, and Linda Roberts for secretarial assistance. The Institute of Social Research at Indiana University also provided valuable information and staff assistance.

Delbert C. Miller

Contents

General Description of the Guides to Research Design and Sampling

PART 1 contains guides to accompany the first five steps in the sequence of a planned research proposal. These are (1) selection and definition of a sociological problem, (2) description of the relationship of the problem to a theoretical framework, (3) formulation of working hypotheses, (4) design of the experiment or inquiry, and (5) sampling procedures. The brief treatments of these subjects may be enriched by use of the bibliography placed at the end of part 1.

Instructions for Use of Guide 1.1

This outline for the design of social research lists the essential considerations in designing a research project. It is recommended that all steps be planned before field or laboratory work is undertaken. Each of the guides in part 1 has been selected to aid in planning the first five steps shown in the outline. Other guides in parts 2, 3, and 4 are available to assist the researcher in most of the steps shown.

I. The Sociological Problem
  1. Present clear, brief statement of the problem with concepts defined where necessary.
  2. Show that the problem is limited to bounds amenable to treatment or test.
  3. Describe the significance of the problem with reference to one or more of the following criteria:
    a. Is timely.
    b. Relates to a practical problem.
    c. Relates to a wide population.
    d. Relates to an influential or critical population.
    e. Fills a research gap.
    f. Permits generalization to broader principles of social interaction or general theory.
    g. Sharpens the definition of an important concept or relationship.
    h. Has many implications for a wide range of practical problems.
    i. May create or improve an instrument for observing and analyzing data.
    j. Provides opportunity for gathering data that is restricted by the limited time available for gathering particular data.
    k. Provides possibility for a fruitful exploration with known techniques.
II. The Theoretical Framework
  1. Describe the relationship of the problem to a theoretical framework.
  2. Demonstrate the relationship of the problem to previous research.
  3. Present alternate hypotheses considered feasible within the framework of the theory.
III. The Hypotheses
  1. Clearly state the hypotheses selected for test. (Null and alternate hypothesis should be stated.)
  2. Indicate the significance of test hypotheses to the advancement of research and theory.
  3. Define concepts or variables (preferably in operational terms).
    a. Independent and dependent variables should be distinguished from each other.

---

*Based on Russell L. Ackoff, *The Design of Social Research* (Chicago: University of Chicago, 1953). Adapted by Delbert C. Miller.

        b. The scale upon which variables are to be measured (quantitative, semiquantitative, or qualitative) should be specified.

    4. Describe possible mistakes and their consequences.

    5. Note seriousness of possible mistakes.

IV. Design of the Experiment or Inquiry

    1. Describe ideal design or designs with especial attention to the control of interfering variables.

    2. Describe selected operational design.

        a. Describe stimuli, subjects, environment, and responses with the objects, events, and properties necessary for their specification.

        b. Describe how control of interfering variables is achieved.

    3. Specify statistical tests including dummy tables for each test.

        a. Specify level of confidence desired.

V. Sampling Procedures

    1. Describe experimental and control samples.

        a. Specify the population to which the hypotheses are relevant.

        b. Explain determination of size and type of sample.

    2. Specify method of drawing or selecting sample.

        a. Specify relative importance of Type I Error and Type II Error.

        b. Estimate relative costs of the various sizes and types of samples samples allowed by the theory.

VI. Methods of Gathering Data

    1. Describe measures of quantitative variables showing reliability and validity when these are known. Describe means of identifying qualitative variables.

    2. Include the following in description of questionnaires or schedules, if these are used.

        a. Approximate number of questions to be asked of each respondent.

        b. Approximate time needed for interview.

        c. The schedule as it has been constructed to this time.

        d. Preliminary testing of interview and results.

    3. Include the following in description of interview procedure, if this is used.

        a. Means of obtaining information, i.e., by direct interview, all or part by mail, telephone, or other means.

        b. Particular characteristics interviewers must have or special training that must be given them.

    4. Describe use to be made of pilot study, pretest, or trial run.

        a. Importance of and means for coping with unavailables, refusals, and response error.

VII. Working Guide

    1. Prepare working guide with time and budget estimates.

        a. Planning.

        b. Pilot Study and Pretests.

        c. Drawing sample.

        d. Preparing observational materials.

        e. Selection and training.

        f. Trial plan.

        g. Revising plans.

      h. Collecting data.

      i. Processing data.

      j. Preparing final report.

    2. Estimate total man-hours and cost.

VIII. Analysis of Results

    1. Specify method of analysis.

      a. Use of tables, calculator, sorter, computer, etc.

      b. Use of graphic techniques.

      c. Specify type of tables to be constructed.

  IX. Interpretation of Results

    1. Discuss how conclusions will be fed back into theory.

    X. Publication or Reporting Plans

    1. Write these according to department and graduate school requirements.

    2. Select for journal publication the most significant aspects of the problem in succinct form (probably not in excess of fifteen typewritten pages double spaced). Follow style and format specified by the journal to which the article will be submitted.

A GENERAL STATEMENT TO GUIDE THE BASIC RESEARCHER IN THE FORMULATION OF RESEARCH PROBLEMS   *1.2*

Instructions for Use of Guide 1.2

The first step in the design of research is the selection of a fruitful problem. The range of potential topics for social research is as broad as the range of social behavior. This fact does not aid the researcher in making a *choice*. And the choice is the most important step. It becomes a commitment of time, money, and energy. It is not unusual for a researcher to give six months to a year finding the specific problem and formulating it for research study; it may take many years to conduct and publish his research.

The significance of a problem rests upon its probable contribution to knowledge. How can this significance be foreseen for research not yet undertaken and tested? The answer is that this is, to a great extent, an art; but there is little mystery about it. The master researcher knows the research literature and where the cutting edges of current research are. A rich array of theory and methodology is available against which to cast the proposed problem. To this is added a creative imagination, which provides the master contribution.

The student is led through this process during training and can develop mastery by finding a personal path. A progress chart that provides suggestions for maximizing effectiveness in finding a dissertation topic and research design follows:

1. Choosing begins with the first course.

    a. The art of raising questions is cultivated.

    b. The research implications of these questions are explored.

2. Choice of Field. Consider:

    a. your interest.

    b. your capacity.

    c. your potential growth and future career.

    d. ability of professor.

    e. ability to work with professor.

As you continue course work.

3. Grow thru seminars.

    a. Examine carefully how others have tackled research problems.

    b. Initiate small research projects in direction of your interests.

4. Begin discussion and work on a given topic.

    a. *Which* large, unexplored areas of the field should be studied?

    b. Define and delineate specific areas.

    c. Investigate previous research in one or more areas.

    d. Make a review of pertinent theory as it bears upon the specific areas.

    e. Set up hypotheses. Formulate theoretical background. Review all research pertaining.

    f. Feasibility of Testing Hypotheses.

        i. Time required.

        ii. Money required.

        iii. Availability of data.

        iv. Promise of fruitful contribution to general field.

    g. Fix experimental design.

        a. Progress chart with time schedule.

    h. "Pretest" design by setting up dummy tables.

        b. Check scales of measurement, statistics.

    i. Prepare your dissertation proposal by following outline guide 1.1.

It is well to recognize that this plan rests on the assumption that the student is planning for a future career and not simply to "knock out a thesis" (a plan of short-run expediency). From a thesis may emerge the published articles that will provide the base for the researcher's reputation in the field and the springboard for future growth and contributions.

For the young researcher seeking to be a master researcher there are no shortcuts to this process except that he or she may perform an important role by replicating some outstanding research models on different populations and in different settings. Social science needs this kind of research badly in acquiring cumulative evidence. The student may utilize secondary data (see part 2.7, Guide to Bodies of Collected Data for the Social Science Researcher: Data References and Data Archives) to enrich research and minimize time and money.

A few suggestions of value for selecting important problems may be found in some books now especially written for students.* The final formulation of the problem determines its potential for the growth of knowledge.

Guide 1.2 was formulated by a group of researchers to indicate those criteria that should be considered in ensuring that a research proposal will be significant. This guide may be most valuable to the professional researcher, but graduate students should use it as a standard by which to gauge their work. At the same time, the criteria of significance shown in guide 1.1 should be carefully considered.

---

*Jacqueline P. Wiseman and Marcia S. Aron, *Field Projects for Sociology Students* (Cambridge, Mass.: Schenkman, 1970); Editors of Arco Books, *1000 Ideas for Term Papers for Sociology Students* (New York: Arco, 1970).

Suggested Criteria for Research Problems*

1. A concern with basic concepts and relationships of concepts, as distinguished from local, particularized, or exclusively applied research, to the end that the knowledge produced may be cumulative with that from other studies.
2. The development, refinement, and testing of theoretical formulations. At present the theories appropriate as research guides will be more limited in scope than the comprehensive, speculative systems prominent in the early history of social science.
3. Superior research design, including careful specification of the variables involved and use of the most precise and appropriate methods available.
4. A probable contribution to methodology by the discovery, development, or refinement of practicable tools, techniques, or methods.
5. Full utilization of relevant concepts, theories, evidence, and techniques from related disciplines.
6. The integration of any single study in a planned program of related research to the end that the results become meaningful in a broad context.
7. Adequate provision to train additional research scientists.
8. Provision, wherever feasible, to repeat or check related research of other persons in order to provide a check on the generality of conclusions. A special aspect of this characteristic would be the repetition of studies in more than one culture group.

Decisions Ahead: Some Alternatives of Sociological Research Design

Even in the choosing of the problem, there must be some evaluation of the total research design. Obviously, no problem, however valuable, is a good choice if the required research cannot be carried out. Some considerations may be classified and used as a preliminary check list.**

Type of Underlying Theory	General theory
	Middle-range theory
	Suppositions
Study Design	Experimental group after
	Experimental group before and after
	Experimental and control group after
	Experimental and control group before and after
	Other
Access to Organization and Respondents	Requires permission of individual respondents only
	Requires permission of organizational officials
	Requires permission of organizational and labor officials

*From *Report of the Study for the Ford Foundation on Policy and Program* (Detroit: Ford Foundation, November 1949).

**I am indebted to Matilda White Riley for the idea of "alternatives of sociological research design." See her treatment on the cover page of *Sociological Research: A Case Approach* (New York: Harcourt, Brace & World, 1963).

	Requires permission of organizational and labor officials and respondents
Researcher Control over the Social System to Be Studied	No control Partial control Complete control
Data for Test of Hypotheses	Case and observational studies only Quantitative analysis only Quantitative supplemented with case and observational studies Other (historical, cross cultural, etc.)
Type of Datum	Personal (fact predicated about single individual) Unit (fact predicated about aggregate of persons)
Temporal Dimension	Cases from a single society at a single period (cross-sectional) Cases from a single society at many periods (time series or longitudinal) Cases from many societies at a single period (comparative cross-cultural) Cases from many societies at different periods (comparative longitudinal)
Sample or Universe to Be Studied	Individual in a role within a group Pair of interrelated group members (dyad) Primary group (30 or less) Secondary group (31 or more) Tertiary group (crowd, public, etc.) State, nation, or society
Number of Cases	Single or few cases Small sample of selected or random cases (under 30) Large sample of selected or random cases (31–5000 or more)
Source of Data	New data collected specifically by researcher Secondary data to be secured Secondary data already in hand
Method of Gathering Data	Direct observation with researcher as observer Participant observation with researcher as participant Interviewing by personal contact of researcher Interviewing by use of assistants or agents Mailed questionnaire Combined observation and interviewing Other

Number of Variables Involved	One Two More than two
Type of Variables Involved	Nominal Ordinal Variable
Selection of Scales for Measurement	None available; requires researcher to construct Scales available but relatively untested Scales of proved utility with high reliability and validity
Character of Distribution of Variables	Normal (allowing for parametric statistics) Nonnormal (requiring nonparametric statistics)
Treatment of Data	Hand calculation Machine calculation Computer
Time Required for Study	Less than one year Two years More than two years
Funding Required	Personal funds sufficient Partial support required Full support required
Availability of Funds	Assured Local funds available requiring competitive application National funds available requiring competitive application

In the pages that follow, guides have been provided for many of these design decisions.

THE BEARING OF SOCIOLOGICAL THEORY ON EMPIRICAL RESEARCH

1.3

Instructions for Use of Guide 1.3

To advance knowledge, both theory and substantive bodies of fact must be progressively interrelated. Robert K. Merton describes the bearing of theory on empirical research. He says that the "...notion of directed research implies that, in part, empirical inquiry is so organized that if and when empirical discoveries are made, they have direct consequences for a theoretic system." Note the functions of theory that he sets forth. The researcher must often formulate "middle range" or miniature theories that will link hypotheses to a more inclusive theory. Zetterberg has written that miniature theories delineate convenient research problems. "Granted that our ultimate purpose is a general theory and that this general theory will in part be made up by means of miniature theories, experimental evidence supporting a miniature theory will support also the inclusive theory of which the miniature theory is a special case."[1]

Milton Friedman has listed the following criteria for significant theory: "A theory is 'simpler' the less initial knowledge is needed to make a prediction within a given field of phenomena; it is the more 'fruitful' the more precise the resulting prediction, the wider the area within which the theory yields predictions, and the more additional lines for further research it suggests. . . . The only relevant test of the validity of a hypothesis is comparison of prediction with experience."[2]

Notes

1. Hans L. Zetterberg, *On Theory and Verification in Sociology* (New York: Tressler Press, 1954), p. 15.
2. Milton Friedman, "The Methodology of Positive Economics," *Essays in Positive Economics* (Chicago: University of Chicago Press, 1953), p. 10.

EMPIRICAL GENERALIZATIONS IN SOCIOLOGY*

Robert K. Merton

Not infrequently it is said that the object of sociological theory is to arrive at statements of social uniformities. This is an elliptical assertion and hence requires clarification. For there are two types of statements of sociological uniformities that differ significantly in their bearing on theory. The first of these is the empirical generalization: an isolated proposition summarizing observed uniformities of relationships between two or more variables.[1] The sociological literature abounds with such generalizations that have not been assimilated to sociological theory. Thus, Engel's "laws" of consumption may be cited as examples. So, too, the Halbwachs' finding that laborers spend more per adult unit for food than white-collar employees of the same income class.[2] Such generalizations may be of greater or less precision, but this does not affect their logical place in the structure of inquiry. The Groves-Ogburn finding, for a sample of American cities, that "cities with a larger percentage engaged in manufacturing also have, on the average, slightly larger percentages of young persons married" has been expressed in an equation indicating the degree of this relationship. Although propositions of this order are essential in empirical research, a miscellany of such propositions only provides the raw materials for sociology as a discipline. The theoretic task, and the orientation of empirical research toward theory, first begins when the bearing of such uniformities on a set of interrelated propositions is tentatively established. The notion of directed research implies that, in part,[3] empirical inquiry is so organized that if and when empirical uniformities are discovered, they have direct consequences for a theoretic system. Insofar as the research is directed, the rationale of findings is set forth before the findings are obtained.

*Reprinted with permission of the publisher from Robert K. Merton, "The Bearing of Sociological Theory on Empirical Research," *Social Theory and Social Structure* (rev. ed.; Glencoe. Ill.: Free Press, 1957), pp. 95–99. Copyright 1949 by The Free Press, copyright 1957 by The Free Press, A Corporation.

Sociological Theory

The second type of sociological generalization, the so-called scientific law, differs from the foregoing inasmuch as it is a statement of invariance derivable from a theory. The paucity of such laws in the sociological field perhaps reflects the prevailing bifurcation of theory and empirical research. Despite the many volumes dealing with the history of sociological theory and despite the plethora of empirical investigations, sociologists (including the writer) may discuss the logical criteria of sociological laws without citing a single instance that fully satisfies these criteria.[4]

Approximations to these criteria are not entirely wanting. To exhibit the relations of empirical generalizations to theory and to set forth the functions of theory, it may be useful to examine a familiar case in which such generalizations were incorporated into a body of substantive theory. Thus, it has long been established as a statistical uniformity that, in a variety of populations, Catholics have a lower suicide rate than Protestants.[5] In this form the uniformity posed a theoretical problem. It merely constituted an empirical regularity that would become significant for theory only if it could be derived from a set of other propositions, a task that Durkheim set himself. If we restate his theoretic assumptions in formal fashion, the paradigm of his theoretic analysis becomes clear:

1. Social cohesion provides psychic support to group members subjected to acute stresses and anxieties.
2. Suicide rates are functions of *unrelieved* anxieties and stresses to which persons are subjected.
3. Catholics have greater social cohesion than Protestants.
4. Therefore, lower suicide rates should be anticipated among Catholics than among Protestants.[6]

This case serves to locate the place of empirical generalizations in relation to theory and to illustrate the several functions of theory.

1. It indicates that theoretic pertinence is not inherently present or absent in empirical generalizations but appears when the generalization is conceptualized in abstractions of higher order (Catholicism–social cohesion–relieved anxieties–suicide rate) that are embodied in more general statements of relationships.[7] What was initially taken as an isolated uniformity is restated as a relation, not between religious affiliation and behavior, but between groups with certain conceptualized attributes (social cohesion) and the behavior. The *scope* of the original empirical finding is considerably extended, and several seemingly disparate uniformities are seen to be interrelated (thus differentials in suicide rates between married and single persons can be derived from the same theory).

2. Once having established the theoretic pertinence of a uniformity by deriving it from a set of interrelated propositions, we provide for the *cumulation* both of theory and of research findings. The differentials-in-suicide-rate uniformities add confirmation to the set of propositions from which they—and other uniformities—have been derived. This is a major function of *systematic theory*.

3. Whereas the empirical uniformity did not lend itself to the drawing of diverse consequences, the reformulation gives rise to various consequences in fields of conduct quite remote from that of suicidal behavior. For example, in-

quiries into obsessive behavior, morbid preoccupations, and other maladaptive behavior have found these also to be related to inadequacies of group cohesion.[8] The conversion of empirical uniformities into theoretic statements thus increases the *fruitfulness* of research through the successive exploration of implications.

4. By providing a rationale, the theory introduces a *ground for prediction* that is more secure than mere empirical extrapolation from previously observed trends. Thus, should independent measures indicate a decrease of social cohesion among Catholics, the theorist would predict a tendency toward increased rates of suicide in this group. The atheoretic empiricist would have no alternative, however, but to predict on the basis of extrapolation.

5. The foregoing list of functions presupposes one further attribute of theory that is not altogether true of the Durkheim formulation and which gives rise to a general problem that has peculiarly beset sociological theory, at least, up to the present. If theory is to be productive, it must be sufficiently *precise* to be *determinate*. Precision is an integral element of the criterion of *testability*. The prevailing pressure toward the utilization of statistical data in sociology, whenever possible, to control and test theoretic inferences has a justifiable basis, when we consider the logical place of precision in disciplined inquiry.

The more precise the inferences (predictions) that can be drawn from a theory, the less the likelihood of *alternative* hypotheses that will be adequate to these predictions. In other words, precise predictions and data serve to reduce the *empirical* bearing upon research of the *logical* fallacy of affirming the consequent.[9] It is well known that verified predictions derived from a theory do not prove or demonstrate that theory; they merely supply a measure of confirmation, for it is always possible that alternative hypotheses drawn from different theoretic systems can also account for the predicted phenomena.[10] But those theories that admit of precise predictions confirmed by observation take on strategic importance since they provide an initial basis for choice between competing hypotheses. In other words, precision enhances the likelihood of approximating a "crucial" observation or experiment.

The internal coherence of a theory has much the same function, for if a variety of empirically confirmed consequences are drawn from one theoretic system, this reduces the likelihood that competing theories can adequately account for the same data. The integrated theory sustains a larger measure of confirmation than is the case with distinct and unrelated hypotheses, thus accumulating a greater weight of evidence.

Both pressures—toward precision and logical coherence—can lead to unproductive activity, particularly in the social sciences. Any procedure can be abused as well as used. A premature insistence on precision at all costs may sterilize imaginative hypotheses. It may lead to a reformulation of the scientific problem in order to permit measurement with, at times, the result that the subsequent materials do not bear on the initial problem in hand.[11] In the search for precision, care must be taken to see that significant problems are not thus inadvertently blotted from view. Similarly, the pressure for logical consistency has at times invited logomachy and sterile theorizing, inasmuch as the assumptions contained in the system of analysis are so far removed from empirical referents or involve such high abstractions as not to permit of empirical inquiry.[12] But warrant for these criteria of inquiry is not vitiated by such abuses.

Notes

1. This usage of the term "empirical" is common, as Dewey notes. In this context, *"empirical* means that the subject-matter of a given proposition which has existential inference, represents merely a set of uniform conjunctions of traits repeatedly observed to exist, without any understanding of *why* the conjunction occurs; without a theory which states its rationale." John Dewey, *Logic: The Theory of Inquiry* (New York: Henry Holt, 1938), p. 305.

2. See a considerable collection of such uniformities summarized by C. C. Zimmerman, *Consumption and Standards of Living* (New York: Van Nostrand, 1936), pp. 55 ff.

3. "In part," if only because it stultifies the possibilities of obtaining fertile new findings to confine researches *wholly* to the test of predetermined hypotheses. Hunches originating in the course of the inquiry that may not have immediately obvious implications for a broader theoretic system may eventuate in the discovery of empirical uniformities that can later be incorporated into a theory. For example, in the sociology of political behavior, it has been recently established that the larger the number of social cross-pressures to which voters are subjected, the less interest they exhibit in a presidential election (P. F. Lazarsfeld, Bernard Berelson, and Hazel Gaudet, *The People's Choice* [New York: Duell, Sloan & Pearce, 1944], pp. 56–64). This finding, which was wholly unanticipated when the research was first formulated, may well initiate new lines of systematic inquiry into political behavior, even though it is not yet integrated into a generalized theory. Fruitful empirical research not only tests theoretically derived hypotheses; it also originates new hypotheses. This might be termed the "serendipity" component of research, i.e., the discovery, by chance or sagacity, of valid results that were not sought for.

4. E.g., see the discussion by George A. Lundberg, "The Concept of Law in the Social Sciences," *Philosophy of Science* 5 (1938): 189–203, which affirms the possibility of such laws without including any case in point. The book by K. D. Har, *Social Laws* (Chapel Hill: University of North Carolina, 1930), does not fulfill the promise implicit in the title. A panel of social scientists discussing the possibility of obtaining social laws finds it difficult to instance cases. Herbert Blumer, *An Appraisal of Thomas and Znaniecki's The Polish Peasant in Europe and America* (New York: Social Science Research Council, 1939), pp. 142–50.

5. It need hardly be said that this statement assumes that education, income, nationality, rural-urban residence, and other factors that might render this finding spurious have been held constant.

6. We need not examine further aspects of this illustration, e.g. (1) the extent of which we have adequately stated the premises implicit in Durkheim's interpretation; (2) the supplementary theoretic analysis that would take these premises not as given but as problematic; (3) the grounds on which the potentially infinite regression of theoretic interpretations is halted at one rather than another point; (4) the problems involved in the introduction of such intervening variables as social cohesion that are not directly measured; (5) the extent to which the premises have been empirically confirmed; (6) the comparatively low order of abstraction represented by this illustration; and (7) the fact that Durkheim derived several empirical generalizations from this same set of hypotheses.

7. Thorstein Veblen has put this with typical cogency: "All this may seem like taking pains about trivialities. But the data with which any scientific inquiry has to do are trivialities in some other bearing than that one in which they are of account," *The Place of Science in Modern Civilization* (New York: Russell & Russell, 1961), p. 42.

8. See, e.g., Elton Mayo, *Human Problems of an Industrial Civilization* (New York: Macmillan, 1933), pp. 113 and passim. The theoretical framework utilized in the studies of industrial morale by Whitehead, Roethlisberger, and Dickson stemmed appreciably from the Durkheim formulations, as the authors testify.

9. The paradigm of "proof through prediction" is, of course, logically fallacious: If *A* (hypothesis), then *B* (prediction).

B is observed.

Therefore, *A* is true.

This is not overdisturbing for scientific research, inasmuch as other than formal criteria are involved.

10. As a case in point, consider that different theorists had predicted war and internecine conflict on a large scale at midcentury. Sorokin and some Marxists, for example, set forth this prediction on the basis of quite distinct theoretic systems. The actual outbreak of large-scale conflicts does not in itself enable us to choose between these schemes of analysis, if only because the observed fact is consistent with both. Only if the predictions had been so *specified*, had been so precise, that the actual occurrences coincided with the one prediction and not with the other, would a determinate test have been instituted.

11. Stuart A. Rice comments on this tendency in public opinion research; see *Eleven Twenty-six: A Decade of Social Science Research*, ed. Louis Wirth (Chicago: University of Chicago, 1940), p. 167.

12. It is this practice to which E. Ronald Walker refers, in the field of economics, as "theoretic blight." *From Economic Theory to Policy* (Chicago: University of Chicago, 1943), chap. 4.

Additional Readings

GREER, SCOTT. *The Logic of Inquiry*. Chicago: Aldine, 1969.

HANSON, N. R. *Patterns of Discovery: An Inquiry into the Conceptual Foundations of Science*. Cambridge, Eng.: Cambridge University, 1958. See chap. 4, "Theories."

HEMPEL, CARL G., and OPPENHEIM, P. "Studies in the Logic of Explanation." *Philosophy of Science* 15 (1948): 135–75.

KAPLAN, ABRAHAM. *The Conduct of Inquiry, Methodology for Behavioral Science*. San Francisco: Chandler, 1964. See chap 8, "Theories."

STEPHENS, WILLIAM N. *Hypotheses and Evidence*. New York: Crowell, 1968.

WESTIE, FRANK R. "Toward Closer Relations between Theory and Research: A Procedure and an Example," *American Sociological Review* 22 (April, 1957): 149–54.

ZETTERBERG, HANS L. *On Theory and Verification in Sociology*. 3rd ed. rev. Totowa, N.J.: Bedminster Press, 1965.

1.4 BRIDGING THE GAP BETWEEN THE LANGUAGES OF THEORY AND RESEARCH*

Hubert M. Blalock, Jr.

1. Owing to the inherent nature of the scientific method, there is a gap between the languages of theory and research. Causal inferences belong on the theoretical level, whereas actual research can only establish covariations and temporal sequences.

2. As a result, we can never actually demonstrate causal laws empirically. This is true even where experimentation is possible. Causal laws are working assumptions of the scientist, involving hypothetical statements of the if-then variety.

3. One admits that causal thinking belongs completely on the theoretical level and that causal laws can never be demonstrated empirically. But this does not mean that it is not helpful to think causally and to develop causal models that

*Reprinted with permission from Hubert M. Blalock, Jr., *Causal Inferences in Nonexperimental Research* (Chapel Hill: University of North Carolina Press, 1961, 1964), pp. 172–73, 6–7, 26.

have implications that are indirectly testable. In working with these models it will be necessary to make use of a whole series of untestable simplifying assumptions, so that even when a given model yields correct empirical predictions, this does not mean that its correctness can be demonstrated.

Reality, or at least our perception of reality, admittedly consists of ongoing processes. No two events are ever exactly repeated, nor does any object or organism remain precisely the same from one moment to the next.[1] And yet, if we are ever to understand the nature of the real world, we must act and think as though events are repeated and as if objects do have properties that remain constant for some period of time, however short. Unless we permit ourselves to make such simple types of assumptions, we shall never be able to generalize beyond the simple and unique event.

4. The point we are emphasizing is that no matter how elaborate the design, certain simplifying assumptions must always be made. In particular, we must at some point assume that the effects of confounding factors are negligible. Randomization helps to rule out some of such variables, but the plausibility of this particular kind of simplifying assumption is always a question of degree. We wish to underscore this fact in order to stress the underlying similarity between the logic of making causal inferences on the basis of experimental and nonexperimental designs.

Note

1. This particular point is emphasized in Karl Pearson's classic, *The Grammar of Science* (1957 ed.; New York: Meridian, 1957), chap. 5.

CRITERIA FOR JUDGING USABLE HYPOTHESES*

1.5

Instructions for Use of Guide 1.5

The formulation of usable hypotheses is of central importance. The entire study rests upon the potential significance of the hypotheses. In this guide, William J. Goode and Paul K. Hatt prescribe step-by-step methods for evaluating hypotheses against criteria. Note again the emphasis given to the criterion that a hypothesis should be related to a body of theory. It is also important to anticipate the verification problem. Zetterberg has stated three criteria for the acceptance of a working hypothesis: (1) that the empirical data were found to be arranged in the manner predicted by the working hypothesis; (2) that we have disproved the null hypothesis with a certain probability; and (3) that we have disproved alternate hypotheses to the one tested.

FROM *METHODS IN SOCIAL RESEARCH*

William J. Goode and Paul K. Hatt

1. *The hypotheses must be conceptually clear.* The concepts should be clearly defined, operationally if possible. Moreover, they should be definitions that are

*By permission from William J. Goode and Paul K. Hatt, *Methods in Social Research* (New York: McGraw-Hill, 1952), pp. 68–73. Copyright 1962 by McGraw-Hill Book Company, Inc.

commonly accepted and communicable rather than the products of a "private world."

What to do: One simple device for clarifying concepts is to write out a list of the concepts used in the research outline. Then try to define them (*a*) in words, (*b*) in terms of particular operations (index calculations, types of observations, etc.), and (*c*) with reference to other concepts to be found in previous research. Talk over each concept with fellow students and other researchers in the field. It will often be found that supposedly simple concepts contain many meanings. Then it is possible to decide which is the desired referent.

2. *Hypotheses should have empirical referents.* It has also been previously pointed out that scientific concepts must have an ultimate empirical referent. No usable hypothesis can embody moral judgments. Such statements as "criminals are no worse than businessmen," "women should pursue a career," or "capitalists exploit their workers" are no more usable hypotheses than is the familiar proposition that "pigs are well named because they are so dirty" or the classical question, "How many yards of buttermilk are required to make a pair of breeches for a black bull?" In other words, while a hypothesis may involve the study of value judgments, such a goal must be separated from a moral preachment or a plea for acceptance of one's values.

What to do: First, analyze the concepts that express attitudes rather than describe or refer to empirical phenomena. Watch for key words such as "ought," "should," "bad," etc. Then transform the notions into more useful concepts. "Bad parents" is a value term, but the researcher may have a definite description in mind: parents who follow such practices as whimsical and arbitrary authoritarianism, inducing psychic insecurity in the child, failure to give love, etc. "Should" is also a value term, but the student may simply mean, "If women do not pursue a career, we can predict emotional difficulties when the children leave home, or we can predict that the society will not be able to produce as much goods," etc. When, instead, we find that our referent is simply a vague feeling and we cannot define the operations needed to observe it, we should study the problem further and discover what it is that we really wish to investigate.

3. *The hypotheses must be specific.* That is, all the operations and predictions indicated by it should be spelled out. The possibility of actually testing the hypothesis can thus be appraised. Often hypotheses are expressed in such general terms, and with so grandiose a scope, that they are simply not testable. Because of their magnitude, such grand ideas are tempting because they seem impressive and important. It is better for the student to avoid such problems and instead develop his skills upon more tangible notions.

By making all the concepts and operations explicit is meant not only conceptual clarity but a description of any indexes to be used. Thus, to hypothesize that the degree of vertical social mobility is decreasing in the United States requires the use of indexes. [At present there are many operational definitions of the status levels that define mobility. Therefore, the hypothesis must include a statement of the index that is to be used; see part 4 for available indexes.]

Such specific formulations have the advantage of assuring that research is practicable and significant, in advance of the expenditure of effort. It furthermore increases the validity of the results, since the broader the terms the easier it is to fall into the trap of using selective evidence. The fame of most prophets and fortune-tellers lies in their ability to state predictions so that almost any occurrence can be interpreted as a fulfillment. We can express this in almost statistical terms: the more specific the prediction, the smaller the chance that the prediction will actually be borne out as a result of mere accident. Scientific predictions or hypotheses must, then, avoid the trap of selective evidence by being as definite and specific as possible.

What to do: Never be satisfied with a general prediction, if it can be broken into more precise subhypotheses. The general prediction of war is not enough, for example: we must specify time, place, and participants. Predicting the general decline of a civilization is not a hypothesis for testing a theory. Again, we must be able to specify and measure the forces, specify the meaning and time of decline, the population segments involved, etc. Often this can be done by conceptual analysis and the formulation of related hypotheses: e.g., we may predict that urbanization is accompanied by a decline in fertility. However, we gain in precision if we attempt to define our indexes of urbanization; specify which segments will be affected, and how much (since in the United States the various ethnic and religious segments are affected differently); specify the amount of fertility decline, and the type (percentage childless, net reproduction rate, etc.). Forming subhypotheses (1) clarifies the relationship between the data sought and the conclusions; and (2) makes the specific research task more manageable.

4. *Hypotheses should be related to available techniques.* Earlier, the point was repeatedly made that theory and method are not opposites. The theorist who does not know what techniques are available to test his hypotheses is in a poor way to formulate usable questions.

This is not to be taken as an absolute injunction against the formulation of hypotheses that at present are too complex to be handled by contemporary technique. It is merely a sensible requirement to apply to any problem in its early stages in order to judge its researchability.

There are some aspects of the impossible hypothesis that may make its formulation worth while. If the problem is significant enough as a possible frame of reference, it may be useful whether or not it can be tested at the time. The socioeconomic hypotheses of Marx, for example, were not proved by his data. The necessary techniques were not available either then or now. Nevertheless, Marxian frameworks are an important source of more precise, smaller, verifiable propositions. This is true for much of Emile Durkheim's work on suicide. His related formulations concerning social cohesion have also been useful. The work of both men has been of paramount importance to sociology, even though at the time their larger ideas were not capable of being handled by available techniques.

Furthermore, posing the impossible question may stimulate the growth of technique. Certainly some of the impetus toward modern developments in technique has come from criticisms against significant studies that were considered inadequate because of technical limitations. In any serious sociological discussion, research frontiers are continuously challenged by the assertion that various problems "ought" to be investigated even though the investigations are presently impossible.

What to do: Look for research articles on the subject being investigated. Make a list of the various techniques that have been used to measure the factors of importance in the study. If you are unable to locate any discussion of technique, you may find it wiser to do a research on the necessary research techniques. You may, instead, decide that this lack of techniques means your problem is too large and general for your present resources.

Some items, such as stratification or race attitudes, have been studied by many techniques. Try to discover why one technique is used in one case and not in another. Note how refinements in technique have been made, and see whether one of these may be more useful for your purposes. Look for criticisms of previous research, so as to understand the weaknesses in the procedures followed.

Again, other problems may have been studied with few attempts at precise measurement. Study the literature to see why this is the case. Ascertain whether some subareas (for example, of religious behavior) may be attacked with techniques used in other areas (for example, attitude measurement, stratification measures, research on choice making, etc.).

5. *The hypothesis should be related to a body of theory*. This criterion is one which is often overlooked by the beginning student. He is more likely to select subject matter that is "interesting," without finding out whether the research will really help to refute, qualify, or support any existing theories of social relations. A science, however, can be cumulative only by building on an existing body of fact and theory. It cannot develop if each study is an isolated survey.

Although it is true that the clearest examples of crescive theoretical development are to be found in the physical and biological sciences, the process can also be seen in the social sciences. One such case is the development of a set of generalizations concerning the social character of intelligence. The anthropological investigations at the end of the nineteenth century uncovered the amazing variety of social customs in various societies, while demonstrating conclusively that there were a number of common elements in social life: family systems, religious patterns, an organization of the socialization process, etc.

The French school of sociology, including Lucien Lévy-Bruhl, Emile Durkheim, Marcel Mauss, Henri Hubert, and others, formulated a series of propositions, at the turn of the century, which suggested that the intellectual structure of the human mind is determined by the structure of the society. That is, perception and thought are determined by society, not alone by the anatomical structure of our eyes, ears, and other senses. Modes of thought vary from society to society. Some of these formulations were phrased in an extreme form that need not concern us now, and they were often vague. Nevertheless, the idea was growing that the intelligence of a Polynesian native could not be judged by European standards; his thinking was qualitatively, not merely quantitatively, different.

At the same time, however, better techniques were being evolved for measuring "intelligence," which came to be standardized in the form of scores on various IQ tests. When these were applied to different groups it became clear that the variation in IQ was great; children of Italian immigrants made lower grades on such tests, as did Negroes. Northern Negroes made higher grades than whites from many Southern states. American children of Chinese and Japanese parents made rather high scores. Since it was generally assumed that these tests measured "innate intelligence," these data were sometimes generalized to suggest that certain "racial" groups were by nature inferior and others superior.

However, such conclusions were opposed on rational grounds, and liberal sentiments suggested that they be put to the test. There were, then, two major sets of conclusions, one suggesting that intelligence is in the main determined by social experience, the other suggesting that the IQ is innately determined. To test such opposing generalizations, a research design was needed for testing logical expectations in more specific situations. If, for example, it is true that the intelligence of individuals who are members of "inferior" groups is really determined biologically, then changes in their environments should not change their IQ. If, on the other hand, the social experience is crucial, we should expect that such changes in social experience would result in definite patterns of IQ change.

Further deductions are possible. If identical twins are separated and are placed in radically different social experiences at an early age, we might expect significant differences in IQ. Or, if a group of rural Negro children moves from the poor school and social experience of the South to the somewhat more stimulating environment of the North, the group averages would be expected to change somewhat. Otto Klineberg, in a classic study, carried out the latter research. He traced Negro children of various ages after they had moved to the North and found that, in general, the earlier the move to the North occurred, the greater the average rise in the IQ. The later the move, the smaller the increase. Even if one assumes that the "better," more able, and more daring adult Negroes made this move, this does not explain the differences by time of movement. Besides, of course, the subjects were children at the time of the migration.[1]

In this research design a particular result was predicted by a series of deductions from a larger set of generalizations. Further, the prediction was actually validated. In justice to the great number of scholars who have been engaged in refining and developing IQ tests, it should be mentioned that other tests and investigations of a similar order have been carried out by many anthropologists, sociologists, and social psychologists. They do not invalidate the notion that IQ is based in part on "innate" abilities, but they do indicate that to a great extent these abilities must be stimulated by certain types of experience in order to achieve high scores on such tests.

From even so sketchy an outline of a theoretical development as the foregoing is, it can be seen that when research is systematically based upon a body of existing theory, a genuine contribution in knowledge is more likely to result. In other words, to be worth doing, a hypothesis must not only be carefully stated, but is should possess theoretical relevance.

What to do: First, of course, cover the literature relating to your subject. If it is impossible to do so, then your hypothesis probably covers too much ground. Second, try to abstract from the literature the way in which various propositions and sets of propositions relate to one another (for example, the literature relating to Sutherland's theory of differential association in criminology, the conditions for maximum morale in factories, or the studies of prediction of marital adjustment). Third, ascertain whether you can deduce any of the propositions, including your own hypothesis, from one another or from a small set of major statements. Fourth, test it by some theoretical model, such as Merton's "Paradigm for Functional Analysis in Sociology" (*Social Theory and Social Structure*, pp. 50-54), to see whether you have left out major propositions and determinants. Fifth, especially compare your own set of related propositions with those of some classic author, such as Weber on bureaucracy or Durkheim on suicide. If you find this task of abstraction difficult, compare instead with the propositions of these men as explained by a systematic interpreter such as Talcott Parsons in his *Structure of Social Action*. What is important is that, whatever the source of your hypothesis, it must be logically derivable from and based upon a set of related sociological propositions.

Note

1. Otto Klineberg, *Negro Intelligence and Selective Migration* (New York: Columbia University Press, 1935).

1.6 SCIENCE: OBSERVATIONAL, EXPERIMENTAL, HISTORICAL

Instructions for Use of Guides to Study Design: Guides 1.6, 1.7, 1.8

The study design involves such decisions as that of whether a historical analysis, statistical sampling survey, qualitative structured observation, or controlled experimentation is needed. In the following, Raymond Siever, a physical scientist, describes varieties and styles of science and stresses the importance of the problem and its relation to scientific method.

SCIENCE: OBSERVATIONAL, EXPERIMENTAL, HISTORICAL*

Raymond Siever

A question that has concerned many scientists for about as long as sciences started to differentiate from each other is, "Are there different sciences or is there just one science?" A related question can be put, "Is there *a* scientific method, or are there many scientific methods?" Discussion of these points is usually obfuscated by the speaker's background, in particular, what science he happens to be doing at the moment. It also, of course, is characteristically confused by mixing subject matter with the way in which an investigation is carried out. I will give my idea of how the different conventional groupings of sciences relate to each other and propose some answers to the question of whether there is just one science or many. It is not that these ideas are new. It is more that we need to remind ourselves of our philosophical underpinnings, especially now that branches of science have become more specialized and yet at the same time have joined together in attacks on complex systems.

Observational versus Experimental

The distinction between an observational science and an experimental science is often made. In this context in some people's language, the word "observational" is associated with the thought "solely descriptive" and the word "experimental" is usually associated with an analytical approach. There is an extension of these associations by which some scientists, thereby qualifying themselves as superior, imply that there is "good" or "bad" science by linking observational with bad and experimental with good. This choice of terms is dictated by diplo-

*Reprinted from *American Scientist* 56, no. 1 (1968): 70–77. Copyright by *Sigma Xi*, Princeton, N.J.

macy within the scientific community, for it is not good policy to refer to work that one's colleagues in another field are doing as bad; it is much better simply to call it "descriptive." We all know that there are appropriate uses for the words bad and good, but properly only as applied to an individual piece of work.

There are, of course, other terms that we are familiar with. There are the "hard" sciences and, by implication I suppose, the "soft" sciences. We also know that a good many other words have been juxtaposed to distinguish between "two cultures" within science (table 1). Without trying to wreck diplomacy, it is worthwhile to point out just how these words, observational, descriptive, experimental, analytical, are being used.

It must be taken as given, I think, that all sciences observe and describe. An example is one product of science that has been with us for a long time, the heat flow equation, an equation that is fundamentally based on simple observation. The laws that Newton first formulated for heat flow are simpler than the more elegant mathematical statements that we now use. But this elegant formulation with which we are able to do so much rests on rather elementary kinds of observations. So it is silly to speak of a nonobservational or a nondescriptive science.

There are said to be scientists who describe things and do not wish to make any analysis of them. They say description for its own sake is worthwhile science. It is true, of course, that many sciences in their early stages of development are characterized by an extraordinarily high ratio of data collecting to data analysis. This rarely implies that those who accumulate the data are not thinking about what they are describing or trying to integrate it into some pattern. It is obvious that those who describe are making a choice of what to describe and that analysis is involved in the selection of the object to be described. We ordinarily do not consider it science for somebody to observe everything that could be catalogued about a particular process, phenomenon, object, or other, though the point may be argued, and probably will be when the first man lands on the moon.

There is no denying that the scientific population includes some who do describe for its own sake, who admit that description is their only goal. As such they bear the same relationship to science as the inventory-taker does to business. But most who solely describe will say that they are only temporarily so engaged, that they are always working toward the goal of analysis (usually put off to some future time).

Table 1 *Words That Have Been Used in Characterizing Differences among the Sciences*

Analytical	Descriptive
Experimental	Observational
Soft	Hard
Non-mathematical	Mathematical
Good	Bad
Interesting	Dull
"Stamp Collecting"	Crucial experimentation
Classical	Modern
The general equation	The encyclopedic monograph
Rigorous	Inexact
Easy	Difficult
Exploding	Mined-out

If it is true that description for its own sake, without any analysis of what to describe or how to integrate it after description, is not what we usually call science, then we really cannot speak of a descriptive or nondescriptive science. When some scientists say of another scientist's work or of another field within science, "It's descriptive," they really mean that it is not science.

The kind of statement made above may also be interpreted to mean, with good grace, that the proportion of description to analysis is high compared to those in some other field. The proportion varies, of course, with the stage of development of the field and it varies, obviously, with the person. Even within a field that is largely beyond the stage where description is in a high ratio to analysis, the invention of a new instrument can lead to new kinds of observations, temporarily producing a great abundance of data relative to analysis.

If one of the major objects of scientific endeavor is to make general laws from specific observations, then it must also be granted that the endeavor is more or less difficult. Physics has come to be, by and large, the domain of those who work where generalizations are relatively easy to make from limited data (though no one would claim physics as an easy field in terms of mental effort). Another way to put it is that the data have small variance and the generalizations are very good. It is also true that in certain fields, of which perhaps the social sciences are the most obvious example, the data have such high variance that the generalizations are either difficult or almost impossible to make. This inevitably leads to differences in the overall logical structure of disciplines. A great many parts of physics are tied together with a strong interconnecting network of fundamental physical theory from which all other parts can be derived, so-called first principles. On the other hand we have fields, such as some areas of engineering, where empiricism is the order of the day simply because there is no generally valid group of first principles from which to operate.

Experiment and Science

Experiments have always been associated with science, and have rightly been considered the most powerful tools of science. Our vision of experiment is largely based on those that have been done in physics and chemistry. But there are a number of ways in which one can look at experiments. They can be divided into controlled and uncontrolled experiments. Alternatively, we can formulate experimentation as either natural or artificial. The artificial experiment we all know about; one chooses the starting materials and conditions of the experiment, then one observes the process in action or the final results.

The natural experiment we are somewhat less familiar with, except for those of us whose primary interest lies in biology, the earth sciences, or astronomy. We may ask what would have happened had Newton one day seen the mythical apple on the ground, somewhat overripe, partly eaten, and decayed. From such as observation, could he have extracted a generalization on gravity? I think it not improbable that he might have, but perhaps at a much greater cost in time and effort and with much less assurance. Many geochemists, for example, have to go about analyzing chemical processes on the earth in a special way. It would be as if someone who wanted to find out what was going on in an elementary chemistry laboratory would go to the laboratory when no one was in it, analyze what he found in the sink, and analyze what he found in the sewer leading from the laboratory. Noting how the laboratory is equipped he could make some deductions as to the experiments that were performed and guess what the starting reagents might have been. So natural experimentation has built into it restricted control and limited information on the nature of the starting materials. Natural experimentation, of course, has the same restrictions as artificial experimentation; one must pick the right observational parameters.

The natural experiment can be refined by looking at separable parts of it or by choosing the chance event that has resulted in a specially controlled or restricted experiment. In a multivariate situation we look for the occasional place or time when the variables are fewer. Those who have spent a good deal of time looking for controlled natural experiments can speak with feeling about the rarity or impossibility of finding the perfectly controlled natural experiment. They all have defects. And so those who work with such data seem always to be trying to draw some generalizations from rather poor experiments.

Restrictions on artificial experimentation possibilities in science are many. The first restriction is the largeness of some systems. Scaling factors are not always available or adequate to reduce the system in size for examination in the laboratory. The two most notable sciences in this regard are astronomy and geology. Here again, restricted bits and pieces of these large systems can be removed and taken to the laboratory, but the interrelatedness of the system itself cannot be reproduced.

The complexity and interrelatedness of some systems restrict the experiment. Warren Weaver (1955) applied the words "strongly coupled" and "weakly coupled" to the sciences. Weaver applied these terms to differentiate the natural from the social sciences, but I think the point can equally be taken to differentiate among the natural sciences. Some aspects of the study of the oceans, for example, the general oceanic circulation, appear to be relatively weakly coupled, in that one considers a few interactions between the motion of the planet, its atmosphere, and the heat budget of the earth and the oceans. Another branch of oceanography, ecology, is a very strongly coupled science. Ecology in the ocean is so strongly coupled that it is difficult even to distinguish the variables from each other. It appears that most natural phenomena of large scale on the earth's surface are rather strongly coupled in the sense that the variables are not separable either for experimental or analytical purposes.

There are, of course, large-scale artificial experiments that have been done and have revealed a great deal of information. I would class the modern air and water pollution disaster as an obvious, though socially evil, experiment. I can offer more examples: Bomb-C^{14} spread through the atmosphere and exchanged with the ocean to give us a much better picture of the circulation of CO_2 and its equilibrium between the ocean and the atmosphere than we had had previously. Attempts to counter the current pollution of the Great Lakes may be an experiment in reversibility; we have the social hope but scientific uncertainty that the Lakes can be cleaned up. Whether reversible or not, the pollution and the counter measures are certainly giving us a good deal of scientific (or engineering?) information.

In the past, social taboos have prevented a whole class of experiments, but it now seems that even these have broken down at some times, most notably with Nazi so-called "experimentation" in some concentration camps. There have been suggestions that warfare in Viet Nam involves certain experimental tests of new equipment and ideas. But it is still largely true that, for scientists, areas considered important in biological experimentation are taboo for what we consider good and sufficient social reasons.

Simulated or "hypothetical" experiments and systems analysis have been used to circumvent social control or for large systems that cannot be taken to the laboratory. But such "experiments" are only as good as the first principles that allow them to be carried on in the mind alone. Theoretical physics is a clear choice for the field in which such experiments have great value. But in most of the world of scientific practice, scientists use hypothetical experiments as a prelude to actual experimentation or further observation. One does not perform hypothetical experiments for their own sake. We grant that as teachers we have frequent recourse to such devices. As research workers in science they are of little value of and for themselves.

It appears then, that experimental science is of many different kinds, that though the nature of experiment is the same no matter where one sees it, the controls may vary and the ability to observe different parts of the experiment may be limited, and finally that there are experiments that simply cannot be done for social reasons.

Historical versus Nonhistorical Science

This topic, a recurring theme in the dialogue on the nature of science (Nagel, 1952), has been explored recently by G. G. Simpson (1963) and R. A. Watson (1966). It appears to me that there is no fundamental difference between historical and nonhistorical science except as it may be economically profitable or culturally desirable to determine as exactly as possible what happened at a certain place and time. Thus we really do not care, as Watson puts it, exactly how the Grand Canyon of the Colorado River was formed. We only care how the generic class of Grand Canyons forms and has formed in the past, assuming that canyon-cutting was not a unique event. This is true in the same way that a chemist does not care what the particular numbers of an individual experiment are. His only concern is in repeating and generalizing that experiment so that the results from his or anybody else's operation of the same kind will fall into the same pattern. In fact, one rarely sees the particular numbers of any experiment. The raw data are of little interest except as an intermediate stage in the calculation of the quantities that are usually of true interest, quantities the significance of which has been established by earlier scientific studies. So, though we measure a particular mass and volume, we quote the important number as the density.

We may differentiate the historical sciences from the so-called nonhistorical sciences by the time scale of the processes involved. Though a chemical reaction has a "history," that history is usually faster than most processes we consider "historical." Even slow chemical reactions are extraordinarily fast compared to geological processes. In astronomy, too, a great many processes are very slow, although there are others that are fast. But even the history of a chemical reaction can be of major importance, for the study of chemical kinetics is just this. Again, though it is a historical event, the chemist studying the course of a reaction is rarely interested in any particular one performed at any particular time in his laboratory, but rather in the general repeatable experiment that anyone can do.

What is different about historical sciences is that many times only one natural experiment is observable, or so few that generalization is difficult if not impossible. We have on this earth, apparently, only one example of organic macro-evolution. The general appearance of oxygen in the earth's primitive atmosphere probably happened only once. In modern times, the change in our lives caused by the development of the atomic bomb could happen only once. If the essence of experiment, whether artificial or natural, is that it be repeatable and that one needs at least one degree of freedom in order to make an average or to generalize, then we are destroyed by the uniqueness of some events. This is not to say, of course, that they are unique in the universe; they are only unique as far as our observational capabilities are concerned. It is for this reason that there is interest among biologists about the possibilities of some form of life on the moon or on Mars. They are simply seeking the additional experiment. Almost worse than the unique experiment is the availability of a very few experiments with a high variance. We have on the Earth only a few continents. In the development of the structure of the North American continent there have been only a few major evolutionary patterns of geosynclines and mountain chain evolution on the borders of the continent. There are only a few terrestrial planets. The social sciences to some extent are plagued by the same. There are as yet only a few nations that have atomic bombs.

Styles in Science

Each scientist selects the discipline he works in for variety of reasons, but many styles can be found in all. I use the word "style" because, as has already become apparent, I reject the notion that there are different kinds of science, or scientific disciplines. There are many different personalities that go into science, and each of these personality types has his own way of doing things, as pointed out by Kubie (1953) and Eiduson (1962). Though there may be some correlation between personality and the discipline selected, I do not wish to discuss that issue.

Style is a word that has many meanings, ranging from a particular historical "school" in any subject (for example, "classical style") to a designation of a particular approach to any intellectual effort that is the product of the interaction of a personality with his time and his subject. It is the latter meaning of the word that I will use exclusively. Styles are probably related to personality, but they are always modified by the field in which that person works. An obvious recent example of different styles is that given by the contrast in the addresses of two recent Nobel laureates in physics, Richard Feynman (1966) and Julian Schwinger (1966). Here two men working in the same field of physics reveal very different styles of tackling the same kind of problem and writing about it.

We can recognize and tag some of the more distinctive styles that are common to all fields. We recognize that some of these are cross-coupled and one may indulge in several styles at different periods or as the mood strikes:

The rigorous formalist
The brilliant phenomenologist
The painstaking laboratory methodologist and his equivalent, the careful, detailed field observer

The quick and dirty cream skimmer
The niche-lover or horizontal monopolist
The subgeneralist or vertical monopolist
The dilettante and his brother, the versatile virtuoso, separated by the difference
  between success and failure
The older, wiser generalist

This is a parlor game that anyone can play and apply to his friends and colleagues.

Value judgments are usually made about the relative worth of various stylists' contribution. But it is probably so that all of these styles are necessary for science to advance, for everyone leans on everyone else. There is some danger at the present time that there will be too much emphasis on certain styles in picking the leaders of science, and that style will be confused with discipline and with fundamental ability of the individual to make advances in science. Pluralism and diversity make for more interest in science as they do elsewhere in life. But let us have differences in style and subject and recognize that invidious distinctious between "kinds" of science serve only to build hierarchies of position and privilege.

References

EIDUSON, BERNICE T. *Scientists: Their Psychological World*. New York: Basic Books, 1962.
FEYNMAN, RICHARD P. "The Development of the Space-Time View of Quantum Electrodynamics." *Science* 153 (1966): 699–708.
KURIE, L.S. "Problems of the Scientific Career." *Scientific Monthly* 74 (1953). Reprinted in H. FEIGLE and M. BRODBECK, *Readings in the Philosophy of Science*. New York: Appleton-Century-Crofts, 1953. Pp. 688–700.
SCHWINGER, JULIAN. "Relativistic Quantum Field Theory." *Science* 153 (1966): 949–53.
SIMPSON, G.G. "Historical Science." In *The Fabric of Geology*, edited by C.C. Albritton, Jr. Reading, Mass.: Addison-Wesley, 1963. Pp. 24–27.
WATSON, R.A. "Is Geology Different: A Critical Discussion of 'The Fabric of Geology.'" *Philosophy of Science* 33 (1966): 172–85.
WEAVER, WARREN. "Science and People." *Science* 122 (1955): 1255–59.

Guides for Design, Model Building, and Large-Scale Research

At this point one must decide the nature of proof desired, taking into consideration the level of one's hypotheses, the size of one's budget, the amount of personnel and their skills, the time required, etc. It is now generally accepted that the model of the controlled experiment is always a valuable guide even if, in practice, deviation is necessary. "Some Observations on Study Design" (1.7) by Samuel A. Stouffer is regarded as the single most useful statement of design requirements for social investigation.

Hans L. Zetterberg explains the problems facing the researcher who wishes to use controlled observation and explains how alternative hypotheses can be tested with pseudo-experimental designs. See 1.8, an excerpt from *On Theory and Verification in Sociology*.

Model building has become an integral part of scientific work. "The Role of

Models in Research Design" (1.9) describes various types of models in current use.

Edward Suchman in 1.10 has listed some "General Considerations of Research Design." These are realistic appraisals often needed when ideal plans must be compromised. The professional researcher keeps these guides before him.

Factors affecting the validity of the research design are described in 1.11. Large-scale group research has grown in volume and in scope. Delbert C. Miller has written "The Shaping of Research Design in Large-Scale Group Research" (1.12) to provide a case study for the team research proposal. The breaking down of the problem into manageable parts is illustrated. The importance of individual differences among researchers is highlighted. Note also the progression of research stages. This guide is for the guidance of design in large-scale research only.

SOME OBSERVATIONS ON STUDY DESIGN*

1.7

Samuel A. Stouffer

We must be clear in our own minds what proof consists of, and we must, if possible, provide dramatic examples of the advantages of relying on something more than plausibility. And the heart of our problem lies in study design *in advance*, such that the evidence is not capable of a dozen alternative interpretations.

Basically, I think it is essential that we always keep in mind the model of a controlled experiment, even if in practice we may have to deviate from an ideal model. Take the simple accompanying diagram.

	Before	After	After—Before
Experimental group	x_1	x_2	$d = x_2 - x_1$
Control group	x_1'	x_2'	$d' = x_2' - x_1'$

The test of whether a difference d is attributable to what we think it is attributable to is whether d is significantly larger than d'.

We used this model over and over again during the war to measure the effectiveness of orientation films in changing soldiers' attitudes. These experiences are described in Volume III of our *Studies in Social Psychology in World War II*.[1]

One of the troubles with using this careful design was that the effectiveness of a single film when thus measured turned out to be so slight. If, instead of using the complete experimental design, we simply took an unselected sample of men and compared the attitudes of those who said they had seen a film with those who said they had not, we got much more impressive differences. This was more rewarding to us, too, for the management wanted to believe the films were

*Reprinted from Samuel A. Stouffer, "Some Observations on Study Design," *American Journal of Sociology* 55 (January 1950): 356–59. Copyright 1950 by the University of Chicago.

powerful medicine. The gimmick was the selective fallibility of memory. Men who correctly remembered seeing the films were likely to be those most sensitized to their message. Men who were bored or indifferent may have actually seen them but slept through them or just forgot.

Most of the time we are not able or not patient enough to design studies containing all four cells as in the diagram above. Sometimes we have only the top two cells, as in the accompanying diagram. In this situation we have two observations of the same individuals or groups taken at different times. This is

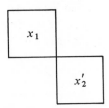

$$d = x_1 - x_2$$

often a very useful design. In the army, for example, we would take a group of recruits, ascertain their attitudes, and restudy the same men later. From this we could tell whose attitudes changed and in what direction. (It was almost always for the worse, which did not endear us to the army!) But exactly what factors in the early training period were most responsible for deterioration of attitudes could only be inferred indirectly.

The panel study is usually more informative than a more frequent design, which might be pictured thus:

$$x_1$$
$$x'_2$$

Here at one point in time we have one sample, and at a later point in time we have another sample. We observe that our measure, say, the mean, is greater for the recent sample than for the earlier one. But we are precluded from observing which men or what type of men shifted. Moreover, there is always the disturbing possibility that the populations in our two samples were initially different; hence the differences might not be attributable to conditions taking place in the time interval between the two observations. Thus we would study a group of soldiers in the United States and later ask the same questions of a group of soldiers overseas. Having matched the two groups of men carefully by branch of service, length of time in the army, rank, etc., we hoped that the results of the study would approximate what would be found if the same men could have been studied twice. But this could be no more than a hope. Some important factors could not be adequately controlled, for example, physical conditions. Men who went overseas were initially in better shape on the average than men who had been kept behind; but, if the follow-up study was in the tropics, there was a chance that unfavorable climate already had begun to take its toll. And so it went. How much men overseas changed called for a panel study as a minimum if we were to have much confidence in the findings.

A very common attempt to get the result of a controlled experiment without paying the price is with the design that might be as shown in the accompanying diagram. This is usually what we get with correlation analysis. We have two or more groups of men whom we study at the same point in time. Thus we have

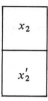

men in the infantry and men in the air corps and compare their attitudes. How much of the difference between x_2' and x_2 we can attribute to experience in a given branch of service and how much is a function of attributes of the men selected for each branch we cannot know assuredly. True, we can try to rule out various possibilities by matching; we can compare men from the two branches with the same age and education, for example. But there is all too often a wide-open gate through which other uncontrolled variables can march.

Sometimes, believe it nor not, we have only one cell:

When this happens, we do not know much of anything. But we can still fill pages of social science journals with "brilliant analysis" if we use plausible conjecture in supplying missing cells from our imagination. Thus we may find that the adolescent today has wild ideas and conclude that society is going to the dogs. We fill in the dotted cell representing our own yesterdays with hypothetical data, where x_1 represents us and x_2 our offspring. The tragicomic part is that most of the public, including, I fear, many social scientists, are so acculturated that they ask for no better data.

I do not intend to disparage all research not conforming to the canons of the controlled experiment. I think that we will see more of full experimental design in sociology and social psychology in the future than in the past. But I am well aware of the practical difficulties of its execution, and I know that there are numberless important situations in which it is not feasible at all. What I am arguing for is awareness of the limitations of a design in which crucial cells are missing.

Sometimes by forethought and patchwork we can get approximations that are useful if we are careful to avoid overinterpretation. Let me cite an example:

In Europe during the war the army tested the idea of putting an entire platoon of Negro soldiers into a white infantry outfit. This was done in several companies. The Negroes fought beside white soldiers. After several months we were asked to find out what the white troops thought about the innovation. We

found that only 7 percent of the white soldiers in companies with Negro platoons said that they disliked the idea very much, whereas 62 percent of the
white soldiers in divisions without Negro troops said they would dislike the idea
very much if it were tried in their outfits. We have:

	Before	After
Experimental		7%
Control		62%

Now, were these white soldiers who fought beside Negroes men who were
naturally more favorable to Negroes than the cross section of white infantry-
men? We did not think so, since, for example, they contained about the same
proportion of southerners. The point was of some importance, however, if we
were to make the inference that actual experience with Negroes reduced hostility from 62 to 7 percent. As a second-best substitute, we asked the white soldiers in companies with Negro platoons if they could recall how they felt when
the innovation was first proposed. It happens that 67 percent said they were
initially opposed to the idea. Thus we could tentatively fill in a missing cell and
conclude that, under the conditions obtaining, there probably had been a
marked change in attitude.

Even if this had been a perfectly controlled experiment, there was still plenty
of chance to draw erroneous inferences. The conclusions apply only to situations closely approximating those of the study. It happens, for example, that
the Negroes involved were men who volunteered to leave rear-area jobs for
combat duty. If other Negroes had been involved, the situation might have been
different. Moreover, they had white officers. One army colonel who saw this
study and whom I expected to ridicule it because he usually opposed innovations,
surprised me by offering congratulations. "This proves," he said, "what I have
been arguing in all my thirty years in the army—that niggers will do all right if
you give 'em white officers!" Moreover, the study applied only to combat
experiences. Other studies would be needed to justify extending the findings to
noncombat or garrison duty. In other words, one lone study, however well
designed, can be a very dangerous thing if it is exploited beyond its immediate
implications.

Now experiments take time and money, and there is no use denying that we in
social science cannot be as prodigal with the replications as the biologist who can
run a hundred experiments simultaneously by growing plants in all kinds of
soils and conditions. The relative ease of experimentation in much—not all—of
natural science goes far to account for the difference in quality of proof de-
manded by physical and biological sciences, on the one hand, and social scientists, on the other.

Though we cannot always design neat experiments when we want to, we can
at least keep the experimental model in front of our eyes and behave cautiously
when we fill in missing cells with dotted lines. But there is a further and even

more important operation we can perform in the interest of economy. That lies in our choice of the initial problem.

Note

1. Carl I. Hovland, Arthur A. Lumsdaine, and Fred D. Sheffield, *Experiments on Mass Communication* (Princeton, N.J.: Princeton University Press, 1949).

ON THE DECISIONS IN VERIFICATIONAL STUDIES*   *1.8*

Hans L. Zetterberg

The advantages of the experimental design, however, rest with the possibility of a random assignment of cases to the experimental and control groups and on the possibility of producing what the working hypothesis terms the cause. Unfortunately, in sociology we rarely have these possibilities.

Certainly many factors are intentionally introduced into society by politicians, educators, welfare agencies, etc. But these phenomena are seldom or never produced, because they are termed causes in a scientific social theory. Furthermore, when compulsory education, socialized medicine, public housing projects, etc., are introduced into a society, the very complexity of the new phenomena does not make them suitable as indicators of concepts of a theory.

In the second place, we can rarely introduce randomization of the persons supposed to enjoy these intentionally produced phenomena without violating strong moral sentiments. As to the social programs of the welfare state Chapin makes the comment:

> The conventional method of equalizing factors that are known and also unknown (by R. A. Fisher's design of experiment) is to select at random both the experimental group that receives treatment and the control group that serves as a reference group for comparison. In social research the program of social treatment cannot be directed toward a randomly selected group because the prevailing mores require that this treatment be directed to a group of individuals who are eligible because of greater *need*. Thus precise control of unknown is impossible and the only factors that can be controlled are factors that are known to be in the particular social situation because of previous studies.[1]

It seems that this inability to satisfy the conditions for a profitable use of the experimental design would definitely curtail the sociologist's prospect to verify his theories. However, the situation is by no means disastrous: sciences like meteorology and astronomy have verified theories without the employment of the experimental method.

For control of alternative hypotheses, the sociologist is to a large extent dependent on what might be called *pseudoexperimental* designs. These designs control propositions known as alternative ones, but, unlike the experimental designs, these designs cannot control unknown alternatives.

The most commonly used method in sociology for control of known alternative propositions is multivariate analysis, which has been formalized by Paul Lazarsfeld.[2] Skill in its use has become essential for most sociological research;

---

*From H. L. Zetterberg, *On Theory and Verification in Sociology* (2nd ed. rev.; Totowa, N.J.: Bedminster Press, 1963), pp. 61–66.

those who know how to use it deserve to be called "modern sociologists." The technique controls alternative propositions by testing the hypothesis in sub-samples that are homogeneous with respect to the determinants specified by the alternative propositions. It can be used to control all known alternative deter-minants provided the sample used is large enough.

The simplest relation between two variates X and Y is a fourfold table:

	X	non-X
Y		
non-Y		

To discover whether a third variable, Z, accounts for any of the relations found in such a table, we break it into two parts:

	X non-X			Z			non-Z	
				X non-X			X non-X	
Y		$=$	Y		$+$	Y		
non-Y			non-Y			non-Y		

If the relation between X and Y still holds in all subclasses of Z, we may retain, for the time being, our trust in the proposition that X affects Y. To this kind of design many new alternative determinants can be added, and it works equally well for qualitative and quantitative varieties.

However, the advantages do not end here. We can tabulate:

	X non-X			Y			non-Y	
				X non-X			X non-X	
Z		$=$	Z		$+$	Z		
non-Z			non-Z			non-Z		

and also:

	Y non-Y			X			non-X	
				Y non-X			Y non-Y	
Z		$=$	Z		$+$	Z		
non-Z			non-Z			non-Z		

The purpose of these tabulations is to discover the actual linkage between the three variables. It would carry us far to review all the rules of interpretation involved here. However, if certain assumptions about the time lag between the variates can be made, it is possible to use such tabulations to disentangle a wide variety of causal chains, as shown in the diagram (below) adapted from Dahlström.[3]

Another method of pseudoexperimental control is that of *matching*, advocated by F. S. Chapin.[4] An experimental group and a control group are made equal on some criteria by discarding cases in one group for which no "twin" can be found in the other group. One disadvantage of this procedure is that the matched groups so obtained are not representative of the original groups. When this way of matching is employed, we do not quite know to what population the results can be generalized.

Control in pseudoexperimental design can be obtained through the use of other statistical adjustments. Various applications of the *multiple regression* approach can be made, provided variables fitting the rather rigid assumptions are used. The most common methods are those of partial correlation and analysis of covariance. These methods become rather laborious if the number of factors to

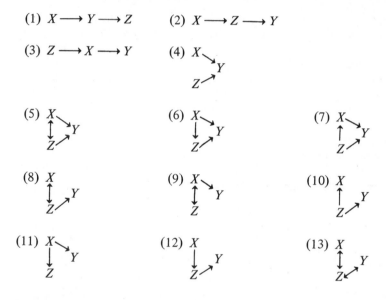

be controlled is more than three or four.

Experimental designs and pseudoexperimental designs may be cross-sectional or longitudinal. We have already pointed out that longitudinal designs are more effective than cross-sectional designs and that experimental designs are more effective than pseudoexperimental designs. We can now reach a typology of designs:

		The test of the null-hypothesis	
		Cross-sectional	Longitudinal
The control of alternative hypotheses	No control		
	Pseudoexperimental		
	Experimental		

The closer a design comes to the longitudinal experimental, the better it is. However, we know little or nothing about how to evaluate crosswise combinations of the two criteria. We have no way in which to tell whether a pseudoexperimental longitudinal design (such as a panel with multivariable analysis) is as effective as the cross-sectional experimental design (the conventional laboratory experiment).

Notes

1. F. Stuart Chapin, "Experimental Designs in Social Research," *American Journal of Sociology* 55 (1950): 402.
2. Paul F. Lazarsfeld, "Interpretation of Statistical Relations as a Research Operation," in *The Language of Social Research*, ed. Paul F. Lazarsfeld and Morris Rosenberg (Glencoe, Ill.: Free Press, 1955), pp. 115–25.
3. Edmund Dahlström, "Analys av surveymaterial," in *Sociologiska metoder*, ed. Georg Karlsson et al. (Stockholm: Svenska Bokförlaget, 1961), p. 193.
4. F. Stuart Chapin, *Experimental Designs in Sociological Research* (New York: Harper, 1947).

For further reading the advanced student should see F. Stuart Chapin, *Experimental Designs in Sociological Research* (rev. ed.; New York: Harper, 1955); Ernest Greenwood, *Experimental Sociology: A Study in Method* (New York: King's Crown, 1945); Claire Selltiz, Marie Jahoda, Morton Deutsch, and Stuart W. Cook, *Research Methods in Social Relations* (rev., 1 vol.; New York: Henry Holt, 1959), chap. 4; Russell L. Ackoff, *The Designs of Social Research* (Chicago: University of Chicago, 1953), chap. 3; Abraham Kaplan, *The Conduct of Inquiry* (San Francisco: Chandler, 1964).

1.9   THE ROLE OF MODELS IN RESEARCH DESIGN

Instructions for Use of Guide 1.9

Model building has been an integral part of social science for a long time. The work of Herbert Spenser and his followers based on a biological model of society would fill a small library. Physics has also served to encourage social scientists to seek social analogues. August Comte often used the term *social physics* to describe modern sociology.

Model building has been accentuated and accelerated by many forces in contemporary life. Models seem appropriate to the new world of computers, automation, and space technology; and they have conferred new status on the scientist in government, industry, and the military. Model building has become "modeling," and the language of social science now includes such terms as game models (gaming), simulation models, mathematical models, trend models, stochastic models, laboratory models, information and cybernetic models, causal and path models, and many more. Even theory itself is being fractionalized into "theoretical models." All these terms stand for a closed system from which are generated predictions (or hypotheses) that, when made, require some kind of empirical test.

In trying to bring some order out of the variety of models, it is soon discovered much overlapping and widely different usages exist. There is no common agreement on the classification of models. In the following description five categories of models and their variants are set out.[1] Don't hesitate to use models if they assist in identifying significant variables in such a way that tests of hypotheses can be defined more sharply.

I. Physical Models

A physical model is a concrete object fashioned to look like the represented phenomena. These objects incorporate static or structural properties. Examples include skeletons, organs, molecules, atoms, small-scale buildings, airplanes, and air tunnels. Perhaps the most famous model in contemporary science is the double-helix model showing the structuring of the DNA code gene that governs human reproduction. Pilot operating models introduce dynamic systems patterns to represent functioning mechanisms in many fields.

A cognitive function is performed by the physical model in almost every field of science and branch of technology from sewing to architecture and aeronautical engineering. Sociology has made limited use of physical models, but F. S. Chapin has experimented with models to demonstrate institutions and social space and D. C. Miller with models of group and power relations. Many possibilities present themselves.

Basic Reading

CHAPIN, F. S. "A Theory of Social Institutions." In *Contemporary American Institutions*. New York: Harper & Bros., 1935. Pp. 319-52.

MILLER, DELBERT C. "The Research, Administrative, and Teaching Uses of Sociological Models in Depicting Group Relations." *Proceedings of the Pacific Sociological Society* 19 (June 1951): 98-102.

II. Theoretical Models

The term *model* is often used loosely to refer to any scientific theory phrased in symbolic, postulational, or formal styles. If there is any value in using "theory" and "model" as synonymous, it probably exists when a theory is set forth as a set of postulations with the relations among the parts clearly specified or exhibited. Thus Talcott Parsons and Charles Ackerman argue that the "Social System is a theoretical device which maximizes analytical attention to its connectedness and it does so in a disciplined manner."[2]

Basic Reading

DUBIN, ROBERT. *Theory Building, A Practical Guide to the Construction and Testing of Theoretical Models*. New York: Free Press, 1969.

III. Mathematical Models

Applied in the social sciences, a mathematical model refers to the use of mathematical equations to depict the behavior of persons, groups, communities, states, or nations. Common use of mathematics can be observed in trend, causal, path, and stochastic models.

Trend models refer to the fitting of time-series data to equations or curves postulated as change principles or laws.

Research Examples

COLEMAN, JAMES S. *The Mathematics of Collective Action*. Chicago: Aldine, 1973.

DODD, STUART CARTER. "Testing Messages Diffusion in Controlled Experiments: Charting the Distance and Time Factors in the Interactance Hypothesis." *American Sociological Review* 18 (August 1952): 410-16.

HART, HORNELL. "Logistic Social Trends." *American Journal of Sociology* 50 (March 1945): 337–52.

HERNES, GUDMUND. "The Process of Entry into First Marriage." *American Sociological Review* 37 (April 1972): 173–82.

STOUFFER, SAMUEL A. "Intervening Opportunities: A Theory Relating Mobility and Distance." *American Sociological Review* 5 (December 1940): 845–67.

Causal and path models involve the construction of a simplified model of social reality in which variables are presumed to act in a causal or processual sequence. The most important variables affecting some dependent (outcome) variable or criterion are sought and arranged according to their influence or impact. *All* other variables entering into the causal system are regarded as residuals.

Research Examples

DUNCAN, O. D. "Path Analysis: Sociological Examples." *American Journal of Sociology* 72 (July 1966): 1–16.

DUNCAN, O. D., and BLAU, PETER. "The Process of Stratification." In *The American Occupational Structure*. New York: John Wiley, 1967. Pp. 163–77.

SEWELL, WILLIAM H.; HALLER, ARCHIBALD O.; and OHLENDORF, GEORGE W. "The Educational and Early Occupational Status Attainment Process: Replication and Revision." *American Sociological Review* 35 (December 1970): 1014–27.

A *stochastic model* refers to a probability construction in which a sequence of behavioral events occurs in time and to which are assigned probabilities for the joint occurrence of such events. Such models deal with "stochastic processes."

Research Examples

DODD, S. C. "Diffusion Is Predictable: Testing Probability Models for Laws of Interaction." *American Sociological Review* 20 (August 1955): 392–401.

HUNTER, ALBERT. "Community Change: A Stochastic Analysis of Chicago's Local Communities, 1930–60," *American Journal of Sociology* (January 1974): 923–47.

Basic Reading

BARTHOLOMEW, D. J. *Stochastic Models for Social Processes*. 2nd ed. New York: Wiley-Interscience, 1974.

COLEMAN, JAMES S. *Introduction to Mathematical Sociology*. New York: Free Press of Glencoe, 1964.

FARARO, THOMAS J. *Mathematical Sociology*. New York: Wiley-Interscience, 1973.

KEMENY, JOHN G., and SNELL, LAURIE. *Mathematical Models in the Social Sciences*. Cambridge, Mass.: MIT Press, 1962.

LAZARSFELD, PAUL F. *Mathematical Thinking in the Social Sciences*. Glencoe, Ill.: Free Press, 1954.

TUFTE, EDWARD R. *Data Analysis for Politics and Policy*. Englewood Cliffs, N.J.: Prentice-Hall, 1974.

IV. Mechanical Models

In social science mechanical models use concepts from physics to provide analogues for social behavior. Mathematics was to be the handmaiden for building the field and bringing new rigor and validity. Increasingly, interest has grown in machine models; these are an extension of the concern with mathematical models since they are based on mathematical language and symbolic logic. The computer is the focus of the machine model, and the term *computer simulated model* or *electronic simulated model* is current. The game model is clearly related.

The *computer simulated model* is focused on the use of a computer programmed to provide a test of a set of constructs that are internally consistent and have presumed explanatory power in order to derive generalizable propositions from the coded empirical data. Electronic computers are increasingly used to substitute for mathematical derivations in formal models. The postulates of the model can be programmed onto the computer (making the computer program the theory), and the computer will calculate the behavior that the program (i.e., theory) dictates.

Research Examples

BESHERS, JAMES M. *Computer Methods in the Analysis of Large Scale Social Systems.* Cambridge, Mass.: MIT Press, 1965.

COHEN, KALMAN J., and CYERT, RICHARD M. "Simulation of Organizational Behavior." In *Handbook of Organizations*, edited by James G. March. Chicago: Rand McNally, 1965. Pp. 305-34.

GULAHORN, JOHN T. and JEANNE E. "Some Computer Applications in Social Science." *American Sociological Review* 30 (June 1965): 363-65.

HARE, PAUL A.; RICHARDSON, R.; and SCHEIBLECHNER, HARTMAN. "Computer Simulation of Small Group Decisions." Wien: Institute for Hohere Studies, February 1968.

ROBY, THORNTON B. "Computer Simulation Models for Organization Theory." In *Methods of Organizational Research*, edited by Victor H. Vroom. Pittsburgh: University of Pittsburgh Press, 1967. Pp. 171-211.

Basic Reading

BRIER, ALAN, and ROBINSON, IAN. *Computers and the Social Sciences.* London: Hutchinson & Co., 1974.

DYKE, BENNETT, and MACCLUER, JEAN WALTERS. eds. *Computer Simulation in Human Population Studies.* New York: Academic Press, 1973 [1974].

Game models rest on a mathematical theory that pertains to the determination of optimum strategies in a competitive situation (game of strategy) involving two or more individuals or parties. Games of strategy, in contrast to games where the outcome depends only on chance, are games in which the outcome depends also, or entirely, on the moves chosen by the individual players.

Research Examples

GAMSON, WILLIAM A. *SIMSOC: Simulated Society.* 2nd ed. New York: Free Press, 1972.

SHIRTS, R. GARY. *Star Power.* La Jolla, Calif: Simile II, 1969.

SHUBICK, MARTIN. *The Uses and Methods of Gaming*. New York: Elsevier, 1975.

SINGLETON, ROBERT R., and TYNDALL, WILLIAM F. *Games and Programs: Mathematics for Modeling*. San Francisco: W. H. Freeman, 1974.

WINTERS, P. R. *The Carnegie Tech Management Game; An Experiment in Business Education*. Homewood Ill.: Irwin, 1964.

YATES, DAVID JULES. *Community Interaction Game*. Cambridge, Mass.: Simulmatics, 1967.

Basic Reading

BARTON, RICHARD F. *A Primer on Simulation and Gaming*. Englewood Cliffs, N.J.: Prentice-Hall, 1970.

DUKE, RICHARD. *Gaming, The Future's Language*. New York: Halsted Press, 1974.

GREENBLAT, C., and DUKE, R., eds. *Gaming-Simulation: Rationale, Designs, and Applications*. New York: Halsted Press, 1975.

INBAR, MICHAEL, and STOLL, CLARENCE S. *Simulation and Gaming in Social Science*. New York: Free Press, 1972.

SHUBICK, MARTIN. *Games for Society, Business, and War*. New York: Elsevier, 1975.

V. Symbolic Interactionist Models

Symbolic interactionist models address themselves to the meanings that actors give to the symbols they use or encounter. In social interaction cues to behavior are transmitted by word and gesture. Behavior is constantly changing as transactions occur. There are many nuances of meaning too subtle to be treated as mechanical phenomena. Some symbolic interactionist models are simple constructs involving few persons. Others are more elaborate and use the computer to seek out patterns and generalizations. All models tend to be simulation models, i.e., they are based on contrived situations or structured concepts that are isomorphic to reality situations.

Laboratory models refer to contrived situations simulating groups or organizations in which actors play roles that are either structured or unstructured according to the design of the researcher. Generally such behavior is observed in a closed environment where observation and recording devices can be employed. Well-known examples can be cited from the small-group laboratory. Somewhat less attention has been given to the *organization* in the laboratory, but research is increasing rapidly.

Research Examples

BALES, ROBERT F. *Interaction Process Analysis: A Method for the Study of Small Groups*. Cambridge, Mass.: Addison-Wesley, 1950.

BURKE, PETER J. "The Development of Task and Social-emotional Role Differentiation." *Sociometry* 30 (December 1968): 379–92.

SLATER, PHILIP E. "Role Differentiation in Small Groups." *American Sociological Review* 20 (June 1955): 300–310.

WEICK, KARL E. "Laboratory Experimentation with Organizations." In *Handbook of Organizations*, edited by James G. March. Chicago: Rand McNally, 1965. Pp. 194–260.

WEICK, KARL E. "Organizations in the Laboratory." In *Methods of Organizational Research*, edited by Victor H. Vroom. Pittsburgh: University of Pittsburgh Press, 1967. Pp. 1–56.

Basic Reading

BALES, ROBERT F. "Interaction Process Analysis." In *International Encyclopedia of Social Sciences*, edited by D. L. Sills. New York: Macmillan, Free Press, & Colliers Encyclopedia, 1968.

BALES, ROBERT F. *Personality and Interpersonal Behavior*. New York: Holt, Rinehart & Winston, 1970.

HARE, PAUL A. *Handbook of Small Group Research*. 2nd ed. New York: Free Press of Glencoe, 1975.

Information and cybernetic models depict information inputs, flows, and outputs within communication systems. Models may range from mechanical to symbolic interactionist, where meaning becomes more significant. The computer may or may not be a useful adjunct. Models may treat with noise, redundancy, looping, and feedback. The most common analog is human intelligence and the functioning of the brain. The scientific base is the information-scientific principle as explained by Pieter J. vanHeerden:[4]

The Information-Scientific Principle of Intelligence

We have a black box with an input signal $f(t)$ which is a function of the time t only, and an output signal $g(t)$; both are binary time series:

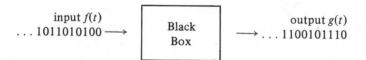

Figure 1. Basic Model of Artificial Intelligence

The black box is the analogy of the brain of living intelligent beings. The input signal forms the analogy of the psychological drives, while the output is analogous to the command, from the brain, through the nerves, to the muscles of hands, feet, mouth, etc. In a machine, the input series would be any information with which we want to disturb the machine and cause it to react; the output would operate any physical means we may wish to make available to it. A simple example would be an intelligent machine which operates a number of elevators, and the input would be formed by the buttons people push, and the complaints they utter, translated in a binary code.

Research Examples

DeFLEUR, MELVIN L., and LARSEN, OTTO N. *The Flow of Information: An Experiment in Mass Communication*. New York: Harper, 1958.

DODD, S. C. "Diffusion Is Predictable: Testing Probability Models for Laws of Interaction." *American Sociological Review* 20 (August 1955): 392–401.

SINGER, BENJAMIN D. *Feedback and Society*. Lexington, Mass.: D. C. Heath, 1973.

Basic Reading

FUCHS, WALTER R. *Cybernetics for the Modern Mind*. New York: Macmillan, 1971.

KLÍR, JIRI, and VALACH, MIROSLAV. *Cybernetic Modeling*. Princeton, N.J.: Van Nostrand, 1967.

MCKAY, DONALD. *Information, Mechanism, and Meaning*. Cambridge, Mass.: MIT Press, 1969.

WEINER, NORBERT. *Cybernetics*. New York: John Wiley, 1948.

Notes

1. Cf. Charles A. Lave and James G. March, *An Introduction to Models in the Social Sciences* (New York: Harper & Row, 1975).

2. Gordon J. DiRenzo, ed., *Concepts, Theory and Explanation in the Behavior Sciences* (New York: Random House, 1967), pp. 6–27.

3. These concepts are often used interchangeably. Information theory is concerned with the making of representations (i.e., symbolism in its most general sense) and of measuring changes in knowledge. Norbert Wiener, often called the father of cybernetics, said the term *cybernetics* would be used to cover "the entire field of control and communication theory whether in the machine or in the animal." Norbert Weiner, *Cybernetics* (New York, John Wiley, 1948), p. 8.

4. Pieter J. van Heerden, *The Foundation of Empirical Knowledge with a Theory of Artificial Intelligence* (Wassenar, The Netherlands: N. V. Uitoererij Wistik, 1968).

1.10   GENERAL CONSIDERATIONS OF RESEARCH DESIGN*

Edward A. Suchman

I. It seems to us futile to argue whether or not a certain design is "scientific." The design is *the plan of study* and, as such, is present in all studies, uncontrolled as well as controlled and subjective as well as objective. It is not a case of scientific or not scientific, but rather one of good or less good design. The degree of accuracy desired, the level of "proof" aimed at, the state of existing knowledge, etc., all combine to determine the amount of concern one can have with the degree of "science" in one's design.

2. The proof of hypotheses is never definitive. The best one can hope to do is to make more or less plausible a series of alternative hypotheses. In most cases multiple explanations will be operative. Demonstrating one's own hypotheses does not rule out alternative hypotheses and vice versa.

3. There is no such thing as a single, "correct" design. Different workers will come up with different designs favoring their own methodological and theoretical predispositions. Hypotheses can be studied by different methods using different designs.

4. All research design represents a compromise dictated by the many practical considerations that go into social research. None of us operates except on limited time, money, and personnel budgets. Further limitations concern the

---

*From *An Introduction to Social Research*, edited by John T. Doby with the assistance of Edward A. Suchman, John C. McKinney, Roy G. Francis, and John P. Dean, pp. 254–55. By permission of Edward A. Suchman and the Stackpole Company, 1954. The statements above are from chap. 10, "The Principles of Research Design."

availability of data and the extent to which one can impose upon one's subjects. A research design must be *practical*.

5. A research design is not a highly specific plan to be followed without deviation, but rather a series of guideposts to keep one headed in the right direction. One must be prepared to discard (although not too quickly) hypotheses that do not work out and to develop new hypotheses on the basis of increased knowledge. Furthermore, any research design developed in the office will inevitably have to be changed in the face of field considerations.

FACTORS JEOPARDIZING INTERNAL AND EXTERNAL VALIDITY OF RESEARCH DESIGNS

1.11

Campbell and Stanley list twelve factors jeaopardizing the validity of various experimental designs.

FROM *EXPERIMENTAL AND QUASI-EXPERIMENTAL DESIGNS FOR RESEARCH**

Donald T. Campbell and Julian C. Stanley

Fundamental to this listing is a distinction between *internal validity* and *external validity*. *Internal validity* is the basic minimum without which any experiment is uninterpretable: Did in fact the experimental treatments make a difference in this specific experimental instance? *External validity* asks the question of generalizability: To what populations, settings, treatment variables, and measurement variables can this effect be generalized? Both types of criteria are obviously important, even though they are frequently at odds in that features increasing one may jeopardize the other. While *internal validity* is the *sine qua non*, and while the question of *external validity*, like the question of inductive inference is never completely answerable, the selection of designs strong in both types of validity is obviously our ideal.

Relevant to *internal validity*, eight different classes of extraneous variables will be presented; these variables, if not controlled in the experimental design, might produce effects confounded with the effect of the experimental stimulus. They represent the effects of:

1. *History*, the specific events occurring between the first and second measurement in addition to the experimental variable.
2. *Maturation*, processes within the respondents operating as a function of the passage of time per se (not specific to the particular events), including growing older, growing hunger, growing more tired, and the like.
3. *Testing*, the effects of taking a test upon the scores of a second testing.
4. *Instrumentation*, in which changes in the calibration of a measuring instrument or changes in the observers or scores used may produce changes in the obtained measurements.

*Reprinted from Donald T. Campbell and Julian C. Stanley, *Experimental and Quasi-Experimental Designs for Research* (Chicago: Rand McNally, 1966), pp. 5–6. By permission of American Educational Research Association.

5. *Statistical regression*, operating where groups have been selected on the basis of their extreme scores.
6. Biases resulting in differential *selection* of respondents for the comparison groups.
7. *Experimental mortality*, or differential loss of repondents from the comparison groups.
8. *Selection-maturation interaction*, etc., which in certain of the multiple-group quasi-experimental designs is confounded with, i.e., might be mistaken for, the effect of the experimental variable.
    The factors jeopardizing *external validity* or *representativeness* are:
9. The *reactive* or *interaction effect* of *testing*, in which a pretest might increase or decrease the respondent's sensitivity or responsiveness to the experimental variable and thus make the results obtained for a pretested population unrepresentative of the effects of the experimental variable for the unpretested universe from which the experimental respondents were selected.
10. The *interaction* effects of *selection* biases and the *experimental variable*.
11. *Reactive effects of experimental arrangements*, which would preclude generalization about the effect of the experimental variable upon persons being exposed to it in nonexperimental settings.
12. *Multiple-treatment interference*, likely to occur whenever multiple treatments are applied to the same respondents, because the effects of prior treatments are not usually erasable. This is a particular problem for one-group designs.

The value of such a list is that it gives the researcher some cautions before finalizing a design. To increase the degree of accuracy desired, these factors cannot be ignored. What is put into a research design directs what will come out after the data are collected and analyzed.

1.12 THE SHAPING OF RESEARCH DESIGN IN LARGE-SCALE GROUP RESEARCH*

Delbert C. Miller

This paper examines some of the problems and opportunities in the shaping of research design posed by a large-scale group research project undertaken by the University of Washington for the U.S. Air Force.

*Reprinted from *Social Forces* 33 (May 1955): 383–90. This paper is based on the conclusions of the writer as director of the Air Site Project. Other members of the project have contributed in many different ways to the experiences described. Appreciation is acknowledged to Orvis F. Collins (Southern Illinois University), Edward Gross (University of Washington), F. James Davis (Illinois State University at Normal, Illinois), Glenn C. McCann (North Carolina State College), Nahum Z. Medalia (Oakland University at Rochester, Michigan), Charles D. McGlamery (University of Alabama at Birmingham), professional sociologists; David S. Bushnell, Donald L. Garrity, Robert Hagedorn, John Hudson, Harold Kant, Alvin S. Lackey, Robert Larson, Herman Loether, Duane Strinden, Wes Wager, Shirley Willis, and David Yaukey, research fellows; all are now professional sociologists in the United States.
    The research was supported in part by the U.S. Air Force under contract number AF-33-038-26823, monitored by the Human Resources Research Institute, Air Research and Development Command, Maxwell Air Force Base, Alabama. Permission is granted for repro-

   The project began in June 1951 under a contract with the Human Resources Research Institute calling for an exploration of human relations problems of air force personnel manning isolated Air Defense radar stations "with reference to job requirements, morale factors, and leadership under stressful noncombat conditions and to develop methods for improving effectiveness." The contract was concluded in December 1953. During the thirty-two months of active research, the project moved from exploration to descriptive and diagnostic study. Some cross-sectional experimental studies were undertaken in the final phase. The full research program included a national survey of the U.S. Air Defense Command Aircraft Control and Warning Stations, a study of the Japan Air Defense Command (A. C. and W.), and numerous investigations in the 25th Division of the Pacific Northwest. All these undertakings centered about personnel problems and squadron efficiency.

   It is the theme of this paper that research design in a group project is a product of a social process. That process is influenced by a number of organizational demands as well as by the dynamic interplay of personalities and experiences that are encountered by the group as research penetration continues. It is believed that it is entirely fallacious to consider group research as individual research simply grown big.

   Research design for group research must be sensitive to needs of individual researchers, to organizational demands, and to research growth through contact with the problem. Indeed, it should be clearly recognized that individual researchers do not become group researchers merely by joining group research. The problem of research design becomes one of wedding the logic of scientific method to the social pressures of many internal and external considerations. Four major factors affected research design on the Air Site Project. These were: (I) the characteristic imperatives of group research, (II) the personal wants of researchers, (III) the demands of education, and (IV) the accumulation of empirical and theoretical knowledge.

I. The Characteristic Imperatives of Group Research

A. *The Restrictions of Interdependent Research Relationships.* The individual researcher confronting group research is asked to change many research habits that he may value highly. The change in habits may be experienced as a set of onerous restrictions. He may find that he cannot choose his problem, and the problem assigned to him may require collaboration with others that reduces still further his area of free movement. He discovers that he has come to live in a web of interrelationships in which his work is intertwined. His own methods of work undergo close scrutiny of the group. He is subordinate to the final approval of a research director. Status and craft comparisons may clearly become causes of interpersonal conflict.[1] If the researcher does not or cannot adjust to this new social environment, conflict processes are intensified and spread to the group. In this atmosphere, even interpretation of words can

duction, translation, publication, and disposal in whole and in part by or for the U.S. government.

   I am especially indebted to the continuous encouragement of Dr. Raymond V. Bowers, director of the Institute from 1949–52, and to Dr. Abbott L. Ferriss, chief of the Human Relations Division, whose administrative efforts made possible our access to many research fields.

become a serious source of wrangling.[2] Learning to live together in close inter-dependence does not come easy. And in group research for a client, many additional pressures are added.

B. *The Demands of a Time Schedule.* Group research for a client usually has a number of deadlines. Our military client required quarterly, interim, and final reports on given dates. No longer could researchers regard as indefinite the date for concluding a study. The demand for a report often meant intensified work, and this brought to some workers a sense of frustration that quality had been sacrificed for lack of time to do one's best.

C. *Conciliation of Other Pressures.* The client—or, as in our project, the monitoring agent—may offer suggestions and instructions as the research proceeds. These are usually accepted as persuasions to modify or intensify work in a given direction. These come to the project director and are transmitted through his actions or instructions to the group researchers. Sometimes the reason is not understood, or it may be understood but resented as an outside idea, foreign to the group process, and emotionally rejected.

Scientific canons of rigor may be opposed by demands for exploratory or applied research on problems for which hypotheses and measurement tools cannot be readied. A researcher whose pride system has incorporated strict and rigid standards of craftsmanship may quail before problems whose solution requires simple exploration or vulgar practicality (especially if he does not see how he can get a published paper from it).

The requirements of expense accounts, security clearances, permission for entry to the research field, "logistic support," and numerous matters of red tape are often further irritations—a headache to researchers and director alike.

The airmen and officers in the research field also exert subtle pressure on the researchers. The questions, "What's this all about? What are you trying to find out?" are continuous and require some kind of answer. The challenge, "You won't be able to do any good" is even more difficult to meet. It can undermine the feeling of acceptance and make fieldwork a resented rather than a welcome experience.

All these new elements call for personal adjustments. It is apparent that a number of strains must be borne by group researchers who have not confronted these factors before. Who are these researchers that come into the group and what do they want?

II. The Personal Wants of Researchers

A. *Motivations of Researchers.* Young researchers are attracted to group research. If they are graduate students, the prospect of funds and a thesis presents an opportunity both to do research and to eat. Young Ph.D.s see opportunity for publication, promotion, and freedom from teaching. Both of these groups are seeking to build research reputations through publication. This motive serves to make the burdens of fieldwork sufficiently acceptable to get the necessary data collecting done, but marriage, parenthood, and sedentary proclivities all contrive to make absence from the home an increasing burden.

B. *Security Needs of Researchers.* Research staffs are often recruited from among those persons who are seeking permanent employment. When contracts are on a year-to-year basis with no fixed guarantee as to their duration, a job insecurity is added to the social influences that bear upon the researchers' morale and productivity. As individual contracts begin to approach termination, personal insecurities mount and are intensified by group interaction. The feelings of insecurity are expressed in many different ways, which may include demands for more say in both policy and administrative decisions, safeguards for individual publication rights, and almost single-minded preoccupation with the acquisition of the *next* research contract.

A research design is under the stress of individual wants, for group thinking is colored every step of the way by these personal concerns. Each person wants to know what part of the design he can claim for his research publications. Each person wants to have an opportunity to guide his fieldwork in such a way as to minimize its burdens. Each wants the maximum opportunity to determine his working conditions.

C. *Role of the Research Director.* The research director takes his place in the center of all the forces that have been described. His role is to direct group processes, ascertain group sentiment, and make decisions so that research can be designed and executed with harmony and efficiency. He must see that role definitions for each member are clearly outlined. He must interpret the external demands on the project and relate them to his research personnel so that appropriate action is taken. He must come to recognize that he will get little opportunity to do field research himself. And he must accept the fact that some interpersonal friction will accompany his most valiant efforts to make group research palatable, especially during the early period when a number of individual researchers are learning to live together as group researchers. He will come to understand that each member of the group is concerned with his reputation as the result of his membership. He wants to have his say as to what others do when he feels his own standards are being violated. This is at once a source of group power and of group conflict. The director will often be challenged as to how these group motivations can be channeled.

A research director who wishes to manage by the use of democratic methods must know the dilemmas of leadership in the democratic process and find his own way to cope with them.[3] Softhearted, inexperienced democratic leadership rivals autocratic blindness in creating poor conditions for efficiency and morale.

III. The Demands of Education

The major problem facing organization of group research within a university is to secure opportunity for each researcher to have maximum freedom to apply his talents to a project whose major problems have been outlined in a contract for him. This is no little task. A professional researcher, we have said, wants to choose his problem, be given the proprietary right of publication for his work, and have control over his working conditions. The university is concerned that graduate students receive broad research training and not be employed at mere clerical tasks. The research design must be constructed in recognition of these concerns and the staff organized in optimum-size working groups so that the best combination of professional staff and graduate students may be obtained.

The basic research unit of the Air Site Project was made up of a professional sociologist and two graduate students; in 1952–53, there were four such units in the Project. Graduate students alternated fieldwork and classwork so that both types of training were secured. In the close association of professional sociologist and graduate student, both educational and research functions were served.

IV. The Accumulation of Empirical and Theoretical Knowledge

Research progress on a central problem usually proceeds through stages—first, exploration of the social setting of the problem, the factors involved, and the criteria that may be used to measure or appraise the problem; then descriptive and diagnostic study may be possible. Hypotheses are set up, factors are isolated, measured, and relationships ascertained. Still later, experimental studies may be undertaken. Research design keeps changing as hypotheses are modified, eliminated, and substituted. Each stage of research requires the use of new skills, the recasting of theory, the introduction of new revised factors, and perhaps reinterpretation of results.[4]

A. *Exploratory Study*. The Air Site Project began as a military requirement to investigate the morale and personnel problems of air force personnel in radar squadrons. We agreed to go to the research field and discover the personnel problems and personnel needs. At the same time we were to find the most significant problems for basic research into morale and motivation. Three professional sociologists developed a plan of sampling and interviewing and devoted three months between July and October 1951 to field visits and analysis of seven squadrons in one Air Defense division.[5] Detailed interviews were held with a representative sample of air force personnel in each squadron. We lived with and observed the operations and leisure activities of each squadron for a number of days. From our interviews and notes a common record was prepared by the research team for each squadron. This record ranked the major personnel problems as reported to us in each squadron, the needs as expressed by air force personnel, and research clues that we determined through our experiences in the field. Table 1 gives a record of major personnel needs and research clues for one air force squadron.

Interviews were coded and an analysis of major personnel problems was made to determine possible associations with age, martial status, education, length of service, and isolation of site. Various tables were constructed to show analyses of interview data—Analysis of Management Problems, Impact of Isolation on Operating Problems, and Personnel Needs as Defined by Site Personnel. All these tables were prepared especially for top military leaders and were presented in briefing sessions to them for their guidance. On the basis of these facts and others, new facilities were subsequently made available to the squadrons.

Meanwhile, research clues were combed to find the most significant research problems. General clusters of factors that we called research sectors were set forth as the ones we believed to be most directly related to the adjustment of air force personnel.[6] We selected (1) The Job and the Career, (2) Organization and Communication, (3) Leadership, and (4) Morale and Motivation. We pressed forward without an overall theory;[7] rather, research teams were formed and these teams selected a research sector, set up hypotheses, and began field research in the fall of 1951.

B. *Descriptive and Diagnostic Study*. In January 1952, six months after the initiation of the project, the research design was composed of the parts shown on page 48. The central problem had become the adjustment of the person to a military organization. Morale, motivation, and management or personnel problems had been chosen as the principal objects of study. Guttman scaling techniques were being applied to the study of various attitude areas. Nonverbal indices, such as rate of promotion, were being developed. Later, as a squadron

Table 1 *Major Personnel Needs and Research Clues for One Air Force Squadron*

Problems encountered

1. Recreational outlets on the base.
2. Access to city or large town.
3. Degree of supervision.
4. Housing for the married man and his family.
5. Living on Indian Reservation and adjustment to Indian people.
6. Restrictions imposed on minors.
7. Career misassignment.
8. Pressures from division and group commands.
9. Irritations from GI regulations.
10. Inequities in promotions and advancements.
11. Supply problems.
12. Access to weapon and monotony of tracking.
13. Organizational change to larger unit.
14. Relative deprivation.
15. Organizational cleavages.

Basic research clues for possible future study

1. Study relationship between humor and tension. Compare a tense and relaxed site, watching for differences.
2. Study of emotional outbursts as manifested in attitude and in behavior such as AWOL, chewing out, or fighting.
3. Time sampling study of a group of highly motivated and poorly motivated personnel.
4. A study of newcomers over an extended time period to watch acculturation.
5. A study of the effect of increasing size on organizational and morale changes.
6. Relations of age, marital status, military experience, and residence and education to adjustment of highly and poorly adjusted persons.
7. A validation of relative deprivation.
8. A study of language functions, especially jargon and argot.
9. Socialization of the civilian to military culture.
10. Description of military culture.
11. The relation of job satisfaction to civilian training, experience, and goals.
12. Extent to which realization alone of choice of job is related to job satisfaction.

Observation clues for possible future measurement

1. Evaluate condition of uniform and military bearing at spot point.
2. Number of persons found in various places—barracks, dayroom, mess hall (goldbricking).
3. Count number who leave camp every day—check those who leave on 2-day-off periods.
4. Turnover as a generalized aspect of military organizations.
   —among officers (upward mobility involves spatial mobility).
   —among airmen (stay only 18 months in a site).
5. What is relation of high turnover to problem of morale, organization, and leadership, to identification with the site, fellows, CO?

efficiency rating system was developed by the officers of one air division (assisted by the Air Site Project), this criterion was introduced. Against these criteria we sought to determine the relationship of many social and social-psychological variables.

The illustration on page 48, Basic Generalities of Social Organization, became our overall design. It was based essentially on the importance of studying certain difficult sociological problems *intensively* while ascertaining the full scope of other problems *extensively*. The six research sectors that received intensive study were those of Personal History, Job Adjustment, Group Integration, Leadership, Organization, and Family and Community. In these sectors researchers at-

BASIC GENERALITIES OF SOCIAL ORGANIZATION

Relationships Validated in the
Air Defense Command

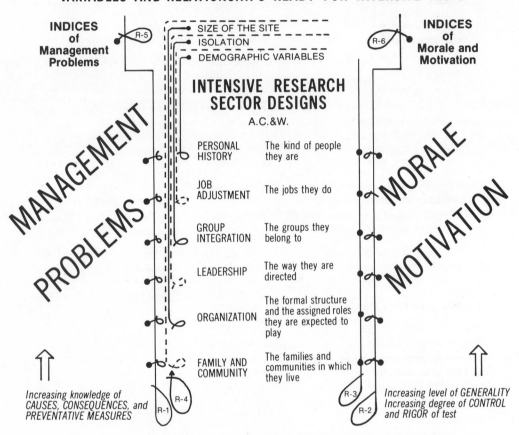

The general research design of large-scale investigation into the human factors affecting morale, motivation, and efficiency of radar sites.

tempted to find relationships in areas where it was difficult to secure the relevant data and in which understanding could come only through patient, skillful, and persistent study. Such study was usually confined to one or two sites.[8] As crucial variables were identified and quantitative measures were developed, these variables were considered ready for extensive intersite test. The intersite design called for a testing of variables on a selected sample of air force men in all (or representative sample of all) sites in the population studied. Here, the criteria of morale, personnel problems, and efficiency were measured by the most refined measures that could be constructed or utilized. Selected social, demographic, and ecological variables were employed as independent variables to determine significant relationships to criteria measures. Intersite questionnaires were administered in twelve sites of one division[9] (May 1952), and in the Japan Air Defense Command[10] (August–September 1952); and a national survey of the Air Defense Command was executed in April and May 1953.

The design reflects the twofold objectives: (1) to carry on basic research in morale (or personal adjustment) at the descriptive level, and (2) to work on personnel problems at the diagnostic level. The design thus reflects both the canons of basic research and the requirements of the client for operational results. The balance between these two foci was often beset by subtle pressures deriving from professional standards, on the one hand, and the practical concerns of the military officials, on the other. The research director who seeks to advance knowledge must see that the research work is so designed that the long-run concerns of basic science are carried along while, at the same time, good diagnostic studies of operational problems are produced that convince his client that research can be of service to him on the problems he faces *now*. He must persuade his staff of the importance of these twin demands, and he must protect them so that there is ample opportunity to achieve both basic and operational research. The basic research design of the Air Site Project grew out of these pressures, and it sought to satisfy them.

But more than this, the design must be understood as an expression of the researcher's desire for freedom to attack his problem in his own way. Some researchers took to the field at once to explore their problem. Others began to devise measuring instruments and to work out sampling plans. Some planned much observational work in the field; others planned fieldwork only to make pretests of questionnaires and scales. These differences seemed to be explained sometimes by differences in research approach (interactionists versus statistical testers) and sometimes by different adjustments to fieldwork. The deprivations of fieldwork and the new role relationships of a fieldworker (in contrast to those of the classroom teacher and library researcher) presented adjustment problems to all staff members. Some found field contact exciting and satisfying; others found absence from home and from customary routines of office a deprivation and sought to center their research in the university. It has already been suggested that the home plays an influential role in shaping the attitudes of the field researcher and thus indirectly the research work itself.

C. *Experimental Study.* Samuel Stouffer has written that "the necessary condition for dealing with a collection of variables is to isolate and identify them and, in addition, it is useful if they can also be measured. Until the relevant variables can be identified, empirical tests of a conceptual scheme involving these variables hardly can be expected."[11]

In the Air Site Project we identified the objects of study and were able to measure some of them. We ascertained many relationships between our criteria and social, demographic, and ecological factors. Many hypotheses were tested by field teams. Experimental work of a cross-sectional type was carried out.[12] Perhaps one of the most important relationships tested was that between morale in a squadron and the efficiency of the squadron. It is widely believed that good human relations are related positively to high efficiency. However, only a few tests have been made under experimental conditions involving a control group.[13]

The assignment of air force men is made according to the training specialty of available personnel and according to organizational needs. The assignment of men who are drawn out to fill quotas results in near stratified-random selection. As a result it is possible to find squadrons that have almost identical characteristics as to mean age, length of service, marital status, education, rank structure, degree of isolation, work conditions, and living conditions. In one division we studied twelve squadrons. Efficiency ratings of these squadrons were made each quarter by the responsible division officials. We constructed Guttman-type scales or items measuring such areas of morale as satisfaction with air site, satisfaction with air force, job satisfaction, and acceptance of mission goals. The relationship of morale to efficiency under controlled conditions was ascertained in our population. Because of the randomization in the squadron populations, control by frequency distribution could be employed. Squadrons were selected from the total universe (one division) and matched on variables believed to affect efficiency. The significance of differences between means was determined. Replication of this design was made on our larger universe of squadrons from all divisions.[14]

D. *Projected Experimentation.* Plans had been made for moving to the stage of true experimental study by taking before and after measures of experimental and control groups under controlled conditions. This would have consummated the direction of research movement. Unfortunately, the sharp curtailment of funds for human relations research in 1953 made it impossible to proceed into this type of experimentation. Projected experiments were not undertaken earlier because needed measures of morale, leadership, and efficiency had to be constructed first. Moreover, a high degree of confidence and cooperation from line military officers had to be earned before such work would have been possible. This is a hard social fact that cannot be ignored.

Four major factors influenced the shaping of research design on one large-scale group research project. These were: the characteristic imperative of group research, the personal wants of researchers, the demands of education, and the accumulation of empirical and theoretical knowledge.

These factors created both problems and opportunities. Problems have been considered in much of this paper, but opportunities were also abundant. Adequate financing of research brings professional, clerical, and technical assistance, permitting a rapid increase in the quantity and quality of research. Access to the research field and cooperation within it opens a new wealth of social data. A long-standing weakness of social science research has been the inability to get enough individual cases or organizational units so that relationships could be validated through replication. This is possible in large-scale group research. These opportunities can be capitalized, but only as the social processes of group research are marshaled. Social processes ever blend with scientific thinking to mold research design. As an end product of group research, it is a precipitate of personal feelings, thoughts, habits, and hopes.

Notes

1. Joseph W. Eaton, "Social Process of Professional Teamwork," *American Sociological Review* 16 (October 1951): 707–13; Alfred M. Lee, "Individual and Organizational Research in Sociology," *American Sociological Review* 16 (October 1951): 701–7.

2. Urie Bronfenbrenner and Edward C. Devereux, "Interdisciplinary Planning for Team Research on Constructive Community Behavior," *Human Relations* 5 (1952): 187–203; William Caudill and Bertram H. Roberts, "Pitfalls in the Organization of Interdisciplinary Research," *Human Organization* 10 (Winter 1951): 12–15.

3. Chester I. Barnard, "Dilemmas of Leadership in the Democratic Process," *Organization and Management* (Cambridge, Mass.: Harvard University, 1949), pp. 24–50.

4. Robert K. Merton, "The Bearing of Empirical Research upon the Development of Social Theory," *American Sociological Review* 13 (October 1948): 505–15.

5. Squadrons varied in size from approximately 100 to 300 men, depending on type and function of the station.

6. For a full report of this exploratory survey see F. James Davis, Edward Gross, and Delbert C. Miller, *Survey Report on Military Management Problems in Aircraft Control and Warning Stations in the Air Defense Command* (Human Resources Research Institute, Air University, Maxwell Air Force Base, Ala., 1951).

7. This was a source of much concern to some of our researchers, and we held many staff meetings groping for such a theory. Some members of the staff believed we should not set out at all until a fully-developed theory was in hand. Others believed theory should wait until the research and field experience were more advanced.

8. For published reports of this work see: F. James Davis, "Conceptions of Official Leader Roles in the Air Force," *Social Forces* 32 (March 1954): 253–58; F. James Davis and Robert Hagedorn, "Testing the Reliability of Systematic Field Observations," *American Sociological Review* 19 (June 1954): 345–48; F. James Davis, Robert Hagedorn, and J. Robert Larson, "Scaling Problems in the Study of Conceptions of Air Force Leader Roles," *Public Opinion Quarterly* 18 (Fall 1954): 279–86; Edward Gross, "Some Functional Consequences of Primary Controls in Formal Work Organizations," *American Sociological Review* 18 (August 1953): 368–73; Edward Gross, "Primary Functions of the Small Group," *American Journal of Sociology* 60 (July 1954): 24–29; Herman J. Loether, "Propinquity and Homogeneity as Factors in the Choice of Best Buddies in the Air Force," *Pacific Sociological Review* 3 (Spring 1960): 18–22; C. D. McGlamery, "Developing an Index of Work Group Communications," *Research Studies, State College of Washington* 21 (1953): 225–30; Nahum Z. Medalia, "Unit Size and Leadership Perception," *Sociometry* 17 (February 1945): 64–67; Nahum Z. Medalia, "Authoritarianism, Leader Acceptance, and Group Cohesion," *Journal of Abnormal and Social Psychology* 51 (September 1955): 207–13.

9. The Human Resources Research Institute published interim reports in 1952.

10. A final report has been prepared for Human Resources Research Institute by Edward Gross and Orvis Collins, *American Air Sites in Japan: An Analysis of Human Relations in A. C. & W. Detachment Within the Japan Air Defense Force* (12 January 1953).

11. Samuel A. Stouffer et al., *The American Soldier* (Princeton, N.J.: Princeton University Press, 1949), 1:34.

12. Stouffer writes, "I would trade a half dozen army-wide surveys on attitudes toward officers for one good controlled experiment. Keeping the model of the controlled experiment as an ideal, it is sometimes possible for one to approximate it. . . . Ingenuity in locating ready-made situations is much needed. In any program of future research, I would put far more emphasis on this than ever has been done in the past." Robert K. Merton and Paul

F. Lazarsfeld, eds., *Studies in the Scope and Method of "The American Soldier"* (Glencoe, III.: Free Press, 1950), p. 211.

13. See Daniel Katz, Nathan Maccoby, and Nancy C. Morse, *Productivity, Supervision and Morale in an Office Situation*, pt. 1 (Ann Arbor: Institute for Social Research, University of Michigan, 1950); Daniel Katz, Nathan Maccoby, Gerald Gurin, and Lucretia G. Floor, *Productivity, Supervision, and Morale Among Railroad Workers* (Ann Arbor: Survey Research Center, University of Michigan, 1951); Irving R. Weschler, Murray Kahane, and Robert Tannenbaum, "Job Satisfaction, Productivity and Morale: A Case Study," *Occupational Psychology* 1 (January 1952): 1–14; Gunner Westerlund, *Group Leadership, A Field Experiment* (Stockholm: Nordisk Rotogravyr, 1952).

14. This research is described by Nahum Z. Medalia and Delbert C. Miller in "Human Relations Leadership and the Association of Morale and Efficiency in Workgroups: A Controlled Study with Small Military Units," *Social Forces* 33 (May 1955): 348–52. See also D. C. Miller and N. Z. Medalia, "Efficiency, Leadership, and Morale in Small Military Organizations," *Sociological Review* 3 (July 1955): 93–107; Edward Gross and D. C. Miller, "The Impact of Isolation on Worker Adjustment in Military Installations of the United States and Japan," *Estudios de Sociologia*, Buenos Aires, 1 (Fall 1961): 70–86; Glenn C. McCann, Nahum Z. Medalia, and Delbert C. Miller, "Morale and Human Relations Leadership as Factors in Organizational Effectiveness," in *Studies of Organizational Effectiveness*, ed. R. V. Bowers (Washington, D.C.: Air Force Office of Scientific Research, 1962), pp. 85–114.

1.13   THE SAMPLING CHART

Instructions for Use of Guide 1.13

A sample is a smaller representation of a larger whole. The use of sampling allows for more adequate scientific work by making the time of the scientific worker count. Instead of spending much of his time analyzing a large mass of material from one point of view, he can use that time to make a more intensive analysis from many points of view. The researcher can also save much time and money by sampling, thus making possible investigations that could not otherwise be carried out.

The sampling problems may be divided into those that affect (1) the definition of the population, (2) the size of the sample, and (3) the representativeness of the sample. In regard to the definition of the population, the important problem is to decide the group about which the researcher wishes to generalize his findings. In regard to size of sample, consideration must be given to the persistent disappearance of cases in a breakdown analysis. This disappearance should be foreseen as clearly as possible. Dummy tables help provide for such planning. The third and perhaps most intricate sampling problem arises in connection with the method of securing a representative sample. The essential requirement of any sample is that it is as representative as possible of the population or universe from which it is taken.

Three methods of sampling are commonly used. These are *random sampling*, *stratified sampling*, and *judgmental* or *"purposive" sampling*.

Random sampling. A random sample is one that is drawn in such a way that every member of the population has an equal chance of being included. The most rigorous method of random sampling employs a table of random numbers. In this method, a number is assigned to each member of the population. Those members are included in the sample whose numbers are taken from the table of random numbers in succession until a sample of predetermined size is drawn. A more common method is to write the names or numbers of the members of a population on cards or discs, shuffling these, and then drawing. A convenient method, known as systematic sampling, which is not exactly equivalent to random sampling, but is often close enough for practical purposes, is to take every n^{th} item in the population, beginning at some random member in the population.

Stratified sampling. The aforementioned methods assume that the composition of the total group is not known, and that a representative sample will be best approximated by a strictly random selection or a selection by regular intervals. In some cases the more or less exact composition of the total group with respect to some significant characteristics is known before we select our sample. For example, we may know the exact ratio of men to women in the population and that sex differences are related to the variables we wish to test. In such cases we can increase the chances of selecting a representative sample by selecting subsamples proportionate in size to the significant characteristics of the total population. Thus, we can select a sample that is mathematically absolutely representative with regard to some significant characteristics. There are numerous forms of stratified random sampling techniques as shown in the Ackoff Sampling Chart, which follows on pages 54–55.

Judgment or "purposive" sampling. When practical considerations preclude the use of probability sampling, the researcher may seek a representative sample by other means. He looks for a subgroup that is typical of the population as a whole. Observations are then restricted to this subgroup, and conclusions from the data obtained are generalized to the total population. An example would be the choice of a particular state or county as a barometer of an election outcome, relying upon the results of past elections as evidence of the representativeness of the sample for the nation or state. Sampling errors and biases cannot be computed for such samples. For this reason judgmental sampling should be restricted to the following situations: (1) when the possible errors are not serious and (2) when probability sampling is practically impossible. Data from judgmental samples at best suggest or indicate conclusions, but in general they cannot be used as the basis of statistical testing procedures.

These three forms of sampling do not exhaust the range of sampling procedures. The Ackoff Sampling Chart lists such types as multistage random sampling, cluster, stratified cluster, and repetitive sampling. A description of these forms may be found in Russell Ackoff, *The Design of Social Research* (copyright 1953 by the University of Chicago Press), pp. 123–26. He writes:

> From practical as well as purely scientific purposes it is necessary to use selection procedures whose errors are measurable. A procedure should be capable of characterization relative to bias and variability. The fundamental procedure satisfying these conditions is simple random sampling, a method in which each individual has an equal chance of being selected. Simple random sampling is performed with the aid of random numbers, while systematic sampling is a variation which proceeds from a random start to select elements at a preset interval.
>
> By breaking the population into subgroups, we may select a sample in stages. If a random sample is selected at each stage, we have a multistage random sample. If a complete count of sampling units is taken at one stage other than the last, we have a stratified sample. If a complete count is made at the last stage, we have a cluster sample. The probability of selecting any subgroup may

Sampling Chart *

Type of sampling	Brief description	Advantages	Disadvantages
A. Simple random	Assign to each population member a unique number; select sample items by use of random numbers	1. Requires minimum knowledge of population in advance 2. Free of possible classification errors 3. Easy to analyze data and compute errors	1. Does not make use of knowledge of population which researcher may have 2. Larger errors for same sample size than in stratified sampling
B. Systematic	Use natural ordering or order population; select random starting point between 1 and the nearest integer to the sampling ratio (N/n); select items at interval of nearest integer to sampling ratio	1. If population is ordered with respect to pertinent property, gives stratification effect, and hence reduces variability compared to A 2. Simplicity of drawing sample; easy to check	1. If sampling interval is related to a periodic ordering of the population, increased variability may be introduced 2. Estimates of error likely to be high where there is stratification effect
C. Multistage random	Use a form of random sampling in each of the sampling stages where there are at least two stages	1. Sampling lists, identification, and numbering required only for members of sampling units selected in sample 2. If sampling units are geographically defined, cuts down field costs (i.e., travel)	1. Errors likely to be larger than in A or B for same sample size 2. Errors increase as number of sampling units selected decreases
1. With probability proportionate to size	Select sampling units with probability proportionate to their size	1. Reduces variability	1. Lack of knowledge of size of each sampling unit before selection increases variability
D. Stratified 1. Proportionate	Select from every sampling unit at other than last stage a random sample proportionate to size of sampling unit	1. Assures representativeness with respect to property which forms basis of classifying units; therefore yields less variability than A or C 2. Decreases chance of failing to include members of population because of classification process 3. Characteristics of each stratum can be estimated, and hence comparisons can be made	1. Requires accurate information on proportion of population in each stratum, otherwise increases error 2. If stratified lists are not available, may be costly to prepare them; possibility of faulty classification and hence increase in variability
2. Optimum allocation	Same as 1 except sample is proportionate to variability within strata as well as their size	1. Less variability for same sample size than 1	1. Requires knowledge of variability of pertinent characteristic within strata.
3. Disproportionate	Same as 1 except that size of sample is not proportionate to size of sampling unit but is dictated by analytical considerations or convenience	1. More efficient than 1 for comparison of strata or where different errors are optimum for different strata	1. Less efficient than 1 for determining population characteristics; i.e., more variability for same sample size

Sampling Chart—Continued

Type of sampling	Brief description	Advantages	Disadvantages
E. Cluster	Select sampling units by some form of random sampling; ultimate units are groups; select these at random and take a complete count of each	1. If clusters are geographically defined, yields lowest field costs 2. Requires listing only individuals in selected clusters 3. Characteristics of clusters as well as those of population can be estimated 4. Can be used for subsequent samples, since clusters, not individuals, are selected, and substitution of individuals may be permissible	1. Larger errors for comparable size than other probability samples 2. Requires ability to assign each member of population uniquely to a cluster; inability to do so may result in duplication or omission of individuals
F. Stratified cluster	Select clusters at random from every sampling unit	1. Reduces variability of plain cluster sampling	1. Disadvantages of stratified sampling added to those of cluster sampling 2. Since cluster properties may change, advantage of stratification may be reduced and make sample unusable for later research
G. Repetitive: multiple or sequential	Two or more samples of any of the above types are taken, using results from earlier samples to design later ones, or determine if they are necessary	1. Provides estimates of population characteristics which facilitate efficient planning of succeeding sample, therefore reduces error of final estimate 2. In the long run reduces number of observations required	1. Complicates administration of fieldwork 2. More computation and analysis required than in nonrepetitive sampling 3. Sequential sampling can only be used where a very small sample can approximate representativeness and where the number of observations can be increased conveniently at any stage of the research
H. Judgment	Select a subgroup of the population which, in the basis of available information, can be judged to be representative of the total population; take a complete count or subsample of this group	1. Reduces cost of preparing sample and fieldwork, since ultimate units can be selected so that they are close together	1. Variability and bias of estimates cannot be measured or controlled 2. Requires strong assumptions or considerable knowledge of population and subgroup selected
I. Quota	Classify population by pertinent properties; determine desired proportion of sample from each class; fix quotas for each observer	1. Same as above 2. Introduces some stratification effect	1. Introduces bias of observers' classification of subjects and nonrandom selection within classes

*Reprinted from Russell L. Ackoff, *The Design of Social Research* (Chicago: University of Chicago, 1953), p. 124. By permission of The University of Chicago Press. Copyright 1953 by The University of Chicago.

be made proportionate to some function of the size of the subgroup, and the number of units selected from any subgroup may also be made proportionate to some such function. Proportionate sampling tends to reduce sampling errors. Stratification and clustering can be combined to yield efficient samples, particularly where stratification and/or clustering is based on geographic properties (i.e., in area sampling). Area sampling reduces the complexity of preparing sampling lists and permits the clustering of subjects so that they come in bunches.

In double sampling a first sample can be used to provide information which can in turn be used to design an efficient second sample. Such sampling can also be used to reduce the number of observations required, on the average, for coming to a conclusion. When double sampling is generalized, it yields sequential sampling, a method of drawing one item or set of items at a time and using the data obtained to decide whether to continue sampling or not.

—The ultimate basis for selecting a sampling procedure should be minimization of the cost of getting the sample and the expected cost of errors which may result from using the method. Expert assistance should be employed in making such evaluations.

The sampling chart summarizes in a very brief way the description, advantages, and disadvantages of the various sampling procedures discussed.

1.14   THE RESEARCH-GRANT PROPOSAL

Each funding agency has its own rules for the applicant of a grant. Some seek very short statements, perhaps limited to five to ten pages; others prefer longer statements. Some provide forms that prescribe precisely what is wanted; others encourage latitude. The reseacher must bend to meet the requirements.

Whatever the differences between agencies or foundations, all are greatly concerned with elements of the research design. In general, they include those shown in the handbook in the "Outline Guide for the Design of a Social Research Problem" (pp. 3–5).

There are a few useful guides that are especially appropriate to grant applications:

1. A clearly written abstract is especially helpful. The review committee may be examining many proposals over a busy weekend. An abstract makes it possible to grasp, define, and retain the proposal for a comparative judgment.
2. A statement of previous work serves to validate the ability of the applicant to get into his or her research quickly without false starts and to carry out the proposed research successfully.
3. Availability of the research population is important. An indication from pretests which have shown that the population is responsive adds weight.
4. Availability of research facilities is likewise important. If matching funds or supporting facilities are needed, it is important for the committee to know that they are forthcoming.
5. Clear, professionally defined budgets over the time period are imperative. The committee must be convinced that the size of the grant is appropriate and that the money will be spent wisely. They want to know if the applicant is realistic.*

*See "Guide to Research Costing" and "Guide to Research Budgeting" in part 5.

6. Supporting evidence which convinces the committee the applicant is able and will carry the research to fruition is especially important. Such evidence may include a biographical sketch, a statement of ongoing research, current support letters of recommendation, and published material relevant to the proposal.

Space does not permit the publication of a complete proposal; however, the outline of a successful proposal to the National Science Foundation is appended. Those interested in more detailed advice on proposal writing are referred to D. R. Krathwohl, *How to Prepare a Research Proposal* (Syracuse, N.Y.: Syracuse University Press, 1965).

After you have written your proposal, imagine that you are a member of a review board. What questions would you have? Check carefully "Specifications for Sociological Report Rating" on page 485. Will you receive a superior rating on all specifications? If not, start again.

Guide for a Research-grant Proposal

Section

Abstract
1. Objective and Expected Significance
   a. Objective
   b. Significance
2. Previous Work
3. Theoretical Perspective and Hypotheses
   a. Perspective
   b. Hypotheses
4. Methods of Procedure
   a. Overview
   b. Estimated time schedule
   c. Selection of population to be studied
   d. Operationalization of variables
   e. Analysis
5. Available Research Facilities
6. References and Selected Bibliography
7. Biographical Sketch
8. Budget
9. Current Support and Pending Applications
10. Supporting Evidence
    a. Six letters from concerned officials
    b. Recent articles by applicant relevant to proposed research

Specific Cautions About Pitfalls and What You Can Do About Them in the Proposal

No one can foresee all the contingencies and conflicts that may arise in a research project. The sociology of research is a neglected area of study. There is not space in journals to detail all the problems encountered in each piece of published research. But it can be assumed that every researcher encounters some unanticipated problems. Some problems can be so severe that it is not possible to complete the research. In other cases the end result is agonizing conflict until a resolution is reached. A few books are now available to provide the kind of forewarnings that may be helpful.[1] And certain procedures can be followed to protect the researcher when dealing with a granting agency.

One important matter is the protection of the reseacher against the claims of the granting or monitoring agent after the research is under way. For example, there is the confidentiality of the data. One researcher found himself pressed by a granting agency to display his data after he had promised complete confidentiality to his respondents. He will not accept future grants without an explicit legal statement on confidentiality.[2]

The use of repondents in the research design may cause special problems when the research calls for concealing from the respondents certain treatments needed to conduct a successful test of the hypotheses. This has usually emerged as a legal question in the last decade because of abuses with research on the physical and psychological effects of drugs. Even in sociological research, however, the question of psychological injury may arise in such areas as role playing, group dynamics, and stress research. Criminologists and educational sociologists are directly involved because of their work with special groups. Sex researchers are also on warning. The U.S. Department of Health, Education, and Welfare has expressed its concern with research on human subjects in areas involving their privacy; the need for informed consent; and protection against physical, psychological, sociological, or legal risks. If the grant proposal involves human subjects, the research applicant is required to do the following:

1. Describe the requirements for a subject population and explain the rationale for using in this population special groups such as prisoners, children, the mentally disabled, or groups whose ability to give voluntary informed consent may be in question.
2. Describe and assess any potential risks—physical, psychological, social, legal or other—and assess the likelihood and seriousness of such risks. If methods of research create potential risks, describe other methods, if any, that were considered and why they will not be used.
3. Describe consent procedures to be followed, including how and where informed consent will be obtained.
4. Describe procedures (including confidentiality safeguards) for protecting against or minimizing potential risks and an assessment of their likely effectiveness.
5. Assess the potential benefits to be gained by the individual subject, as well as benefits which may accrue to society in general as a result of the planned work.
6. Analyze the risk-benefit ratio.[3]

Statements submitted by the applicant are subject to review by the local organization's review committee. The responsibility then shifts to the organizational review committee and the HEW staff and advisory committees. Any changes in the researcher's procedures must be reported.

Obviously, this means that all parties should get their agreements in hand so that no barriers can be thrown in the path of the researcher once the work is under way.

A guarantee of publication rights should be clearly spelled out. The problem can arise with any contract research agency of the federal government. Most applied-research contracts contain either a "rights in data" clause or a copyright clause. Two propositions, partially incompatible, must be reconciled. One states that everything done under a government contract belongs to the government, to do with as it sees fit. The second holds that the work done under a government contract should be freely available to the public. In actual practice this usually means that the government reserves exclusive license over the product of the study but interposes no objection to the publishing of results by the investigator as long as he or she *first secures the permission of the contracting officer.*

Academic researchers must recognize that a grant and a contract have two different sets of rules with respect to publication. The grant carries the right of publication; indeed, the National Science Foundation assures researchers that it encourages publication and distribution of the results of research conducted under its grants. Under contract research, the investigator cannot go off on his own and publish articles from the study.[4] Many applied-research agencies are uninterested in generating publications. Instead, the agency will insist upon reports that fit the specifications that meet its internal needs. It is up to the investigator to work out an understanding on publication rights. In dealing with a military funding agency, this is especially important; it is possible that the military will clamp a censorship or restraining order on research publication as the uncertain winds of military security blow across the Pentagon.

If none of the possible sources of conflict has frightened you against the research life, you are ready to enter or renew the exciting quest for knowledge. If you are the "academic man," you will probably seek "clean" money, i.e., a grant to do basic research with no strings attached. But you may find such a posture automatically removes you from many research opportunities. Basic research amounts to only about one-third of federal spending for applied research.[5]

Notes

1. Gunnar Boalt, *The Sociology of Research* (Carbondale, Ill.: Southern Illinois University Press, 1969); Richard O'Toole, ed., *The Organization, Management, and Tactics of Social Research* (Cambridge, Mass.: Schenkman, 1971). Refer also to part 1.12 of this handbook, "The Shaping of Research Design in Large-scale Research."

2. Robert F. Boruch, "Maintaining Confidentiality of Data on Educational Research: A Systematic Analysis," *American Psychologist* 26 (May 1971): 413–30; James R. Craig and Sandra C. Reese, "Retention of Raw Data: A Problem Revisted," *American Psychologist* 28 (August 1973): 723; R. W. Johnson, "Retain the Original Data," *American Psychologist* 19 (1964): 350–51; L. Wolins, "Responsibility for Raw Data," *American Psychologist* 17 (1962): 657–58.

3. These regulations follow from Sec. 212 of the National Research Act, Public Law 93–348, and were made effective 1 July 1974.

4. Keith Baker, "A New Grantsmanship," *American Sociologist* 10 (November 1975): 212–13.

5. Ibid., p. 206.

ACKOFF, RUSSELL L. *The Design of Social Research*. Chicago: University of Chicago Press, 1953.

ACKOFF, RUSSELL L., and EMERY, FRED E. *On Purposeful Systems*. Chicago: Aldine, 1972.

ARMER, MICHAEL, and GRIMSHAW, ALLEN, eds. *Comparative Social Research: Methodological Problems and Strategies*. New York: Wiley, 1973.

BLALOCK, HUBERT M., JR., ed. *Causal Models in the Social Sciences*. Chicago: Aldine, 1971.

BLALOCK, HUBERT M., JR., ed. *Quantitative Sociology: International Perspectives on Mathematical and Statistical Modeling*. New York: Academic Press, 1975.

BORGATTA, EDGAR F., ed. *Sociological Methodology*. San Francisco: Jossey-Bass, 1969.

BOUDON, RAYMOND. *The Logic of Sociological Explanation*. Harmondsworth: Penguin Education, 1974.

BROSS, IRWIN D. J. *Design for Decision*. New York: Macmillan, 1953.

CAMPBELL, DONALD T., and STANLEY, JULIAN C. *Experimental and Quasi Experimental Design*. Chicago: Rand McNally, 1966.

CANNON, WALTER BRADFORD. *The Way of an Investigator*. New York: Hafner, 1961.

CHURCHMAN, C. W. *Theory of Experimental Inference*. New York: Macmillan, 1948.

COCHRAN, W. G., and COX, G. N. *Experimental Designs*. 2nd ed. New York: John Wiley, 1957.

COHEN, MORRIS, and NAGEL, E. *An Introduction to Logic and Scientific Methods*. Rev. ed. New York: Harcourt, Brace & World, 1960.

DENZIN, NORMAN. *The Research Act*. Chicago: Aldine, 1973.

DIRENZO, GORDON J., ed. *Concepts, Theory, and Explanation in the Behavioral Sciences*. New York: Random House, 1967. See especially Paul F. Lazarsfeld, "Concept Formation and Measurement," pp. 144–202.

DUBIN, ROBERT. *Theory Building, A Practical Guide to the Construction and Testing of Theoretical Models*. New York: Free Press, 1969.

EDWARDS, ALLEN L. *Experimental Design in Psychological Research*. New York: Holt, Rinehart & Winston, 1960.

FICHTER, JOSEPH H. *One-Man Research, Reminiscences of a Catholic Sociologist*. New York: Wiley-Interscience, 1973.

FISHER, R. A. *The Design of Experiments*. 7th rev. ed. New York: Hafner, 1960.

FORCESE, DENNIS P., and RICHER, STEPHEN, eds. *Stages of Social Research: Contemporary Perspectives*. Englewood Cliffs, N.J.: Prentice-Hall, 1970. Forty-one authors describe such stages as the Scientific Approach, Conceptualization, Measurement, Research Format, Sampling, Data Collection, Data Analysis and Interpretation.

GIBBS, JACK. *Sociological Theory Construction*. Hinsdale, Ill.: Dryden, 1972.

GLASER, BARNEY G., and STRAUSS, ANSELM L. *The Discovery of Grounded Theory*. Chicago: Aldine, 1967.

GLOCK, CHARLES Y. *Survey Research in the Social Sciences*. New York: Russell Sage Foundation, 1967.

GOODE, WILLIAM J., and HATT, PAUL K. *Methods in Social Research*. New York: McGraw-Hill, 1952.

GREER, SCOTT. *The Logic of Social Inquiry*. Chicago: Aldine, 1969.

HAMMOND, P. E., ed. *Sociologists at Work: Essays on the Craft of Social Research.* New York: Basic Books, 1964.

HYMAN, HERBERT. *Survey Design and Analysis: Principles, Cases, and Procedures.* Glencoe, Ill.: Free Press, 1955.

KAPLAN, ABRAHAM. *The Conduct of Inquiry.* San Francisco: Chandler, 1964.

KERLINGER, FRED N. *Foundations of Behaviorial Research.* New York: Holt, Rinehart, & Winston, 1964.

KISH, LESLIE. *Survey Sampling.* New York: John Wiley, 1965.

LAVE, CHARLES A., and MARCH, JAMES G. *An Introduction to Models in the Social Sciences.* New York: Harper & Row, 1975.

LAZARSFELD, PAUL F., and REITZ, JEFFREY G. *An Introduction to Applied Sociology.* New York: Elsevier, 1975. See especially chap. 4, "Translating a Practical Problem into Research," pp. 66–97.

NORTHROP, F. S. C. *The Logic of the Sciences and the Humanities.* New York: Macmillan, 1947.

PHILLIPS, BERNARD S. *Social Research: Strategy and Tactics.* New York: Macmillan, 1966.

POPPER, KARL R. *The Logic of Scientific Discovery.* New York: Basic Books, 1959.

RILEY, MATILDA WHITE. *Sociological Research: A Case Approach.* New York: Harcourt, Brace & World, 1963.

SANDERS, WILLIAM B. *The Sociologist as Detective: An Introduction to Research Methods.* New York: Praeger, 1974.

SKIDMORE, WILLIAM. *Theoretical Thinking in Sociology.* Cambridge, England: Cambridge University Press, 1975.

SMITH, H. W. *Strategies of Social Research: The Methodological Imagination.* Englewood Cliffs, N.J.: Prentice-Hall, 1975.

STOUFFER, SAMUEL. *Social Research to Test Ideas.* New York: Free Press, 1962.

SUCHMAN, EDWARD A. *Evaluative Research, Principles, and Practice in Public Service and Social Action Programs.* New York: Russell Sage Foundation, 1968.

WALLACE, WALTER R. *The Logic of Science in Sociology.* Chicago: Aldine, 1971.

WHITEHEAD, ALFRED N. *A Philosopher Looks at Science.* New York: Philosophical Library, 1965.

ZETTERBERG, HANS L. *On Theory and Verification in Sociology.* 3rd rev. ed. Totowa, N.J.: Bedminister Press, 1965.

Guides to Methods and Techniques of Collecting Data in Library, Field, and Laboratory; Social Science Data Libraries and Research Centers

THE collection of data is the crucial operation in the execution of a good research design. The quality of the research rests upon the quality of the data. In this section the methods and techniques of social research are presented according to their common situs of research: library, field, and laboratory. Advantages and disadvantages of principal methods are pointed out. Guides to the construction of questionnaires, interviews, and scales are described.

A listing of social science data libraries is given. These social science archives are available to research scholars and offer many excellent opportunities for research. The collection of data is expensive, and the ability to use data previously collected offers the possibility of superior research at a greatly lowered cost. The guide to the U.S. Census and Bureau of Labor Statistics is especially thorough, to make known and usable the rich mine of data available to social researchers.

Finally, directories of social science research centers in the United States, England, and throughout the world are provided to aid the researcher. A list of important research associations and institutes affiliated with the International Sociological Association may be valuable contact points to determine the status of current research and to determine comparative research advances in various fields.

The collection of data occurs in a designed inquiry only after a long series of steps including:

1. The definition of the problem
2. The construction of the theoretical framework
3. The stating of hypotheses
4. The establishment of the design of inquiry
5. The determination of sampling procedures

This section introduces the most common methods of social science research and presents a brief set of instructions for the construction of questionnaires, interviews, and scales. These instructions will assist the researcher in evaluating the appropriate method for his problem. He should consult methods books for a thorough explanation of each method or technique.

Methods are handmaidens of designed inquiry. It is important to distinguish carefully between four terms: methodology, situs, methods, and techniques.

Methodology is a body of knowledge that describes and analyzes methods, indicating their limitations and resources, clarifying their presuppositions and consequences, and relating their potentialities to research advances. In this part the methods of social science are first examined in order to set forth the advantages and disadvantages of each method. The aim is to help the researcher to understand the process of gathering data and what his choice of method entails.

Situs refers to the place in which the data is gathered. For most sciences, the most used situses are the library, the field, and the laboratory.

Method refers to the means of gathering data that are common to all sciences or to a significant part of them. Thus methods include such procedures as the making of observations and measurements, performing experiments, building models and theories, or providing explanations and making predictions. The social sciences use documentary analysis, the mailed questionnaire, and the personal interview most frequently.

Techniques refer to specific procedures that are used in a given method. For example, the field method worker may employ such techniques as use of sociometric scales to measure social variables and personality inventories to identify personal traits. The research worker such as a demographer may draw heavily on statistical documents and use various statistical techniques to describe relationships or gain statistical control over the data.

The following aids first present an outline of methods and techniques as employed in the three situses: library, field, and laboratory. Then aids are presented for the most common methods and techniques. A list of reference books is given which describes various methods and techniques in detail.

Situs	Methods	Techniques
Library	1. Analysis of historical records: primary records—letters, diaries, etc.; secondary interpretations of events 2. Analysis of documents: statistical and nonstatistical records of formal agencies 3. Literature search for theory and previous research in books, journals, and monographs	Recording of notes Content analysis Tape and film listening and analysis Statistical compilations and manipulations Reference and abstract guides Content analysis
Field	1. Mail questionnaire	Identification of social and economic background of respondents Use of sociometric scales to ascertain such variables as social status, group structure, community and social participation, leadership activity, and family adjustment Use of attitude scales to measure morale, job satisfaction, marital adjustment, etc.
	2. Personal interview Structured interview schedule	Interviewer uses a detailed schedule with open and closed questions Sociometric scales may be used
	3. Focused interview	Interviewer focuses attention upon a given experience and its effects; he knows in advance what topics or questions he wishes to cover
	4. Free story interview	Respondent is urged to talk freely about the subjects treated in the study
	5. Group interview	Small groups of respondents are interviewed simultaneously; any of the above techniques may be used
	6. Telephone survey	Used as a survey technique for information and for discerning opinion May be used for follow-up of a questionnaire mailing to increase return
	7. Case study and life history	For case study, cross-sectional collection of data for intensive analysis of a person emphasizing personal and social factors in socialization For life history, longitudinal collection of data of intensive character also emphasizing socialization over an extended period of time
	8. Nonparticipant direct observation	Use of standard score cards and observational behavior scales
	9. Participant observation	Interactional recording; possible use of tape recorders and photographic techniques
	10. Mass observation	Recording mass or collective behavior by observation and interview using independent observers in public places
Laboratory	Small group study of random behavior, play, problem solving, or stress behavior of individuals and/or groups; organizational and role analysis	Use of contrived and nonconstructed situations, use of confederates; use of audio-visual recording devices; use of observers behind one-way mirror.

Statistical Sourcebooks

The social science researcher commonly uses reference books to assist him.
Among the most useful are:

U.S. Bureau of the Census. *Historical Statistics of the United States: Colonial
    Times to 1957.* A Statistical Abstracts Supplement. Washington, D.C.: U.S.
    Government Printing Office, 1960. 801 pp.

Arranged in twenty-six chapters: population; vital statistics and health and medical care;
migration; labor; prices and price indexes; national income and wealth; consumer income
and expenditures; social statistics; land, water, and climate; agriculture; forestry and
fisheries; minerals; construction and housing; manufactures; transportation; communication; power; distribution and services; foreign trade and other international transactions;
business enterprise; productivity and technological development; banking and finance;
government; colonial statistics. Index of names and subjects. Clothbound.

U.S. Bureau of the Census. *Historical Statistics of the United States: Colonial
    Times to 1957—Continuation to 1962 and Revisions.* A Statistical Abstract
    Supplement. Washington, D.C.: U.S. Government Printing Office, 1965.
    158 pp.

Arranged in two parts: continuation of series in "historical statistics"; revisions of series in
"historical statistics." Source notes. Paperbound.

U.S. Bureau of the Census. *Statistical Abstract of the United States, 1974.* 95th
    ed. Washington, D.C.: U.S. Government Printing Office, 1974. 1051 pp.

Arranged in thirty-three sections: population; vital statistics, health, and nutrition; immigration and naturalization; education; law enforcement, federal courts, and prisons;
area, geography, and climate; public lands, parks, recreation, and travel; labor force, employment, and earnings; national defense and veterans affairs; social insurance and welfare
services; income, expenditures, and wealth; prices; elections; federal government finances
and employment; state and local government finances and employment; banking, finance,
and insurance; business enterprise; communications; power; science; transportation—land;
transportation—air and water; agriculture—farms, land, and finances; agriculture—production, marketing, and trade; forests and forest products; fisheries, mining and mineral
products; construction and housing; manufactures; distribution and services; foreign commerce and aid; outlying areas under the jurisdiction of the United States; comparative
international statistics. Three appendixes. Index of names and subjects. Clothbound.

United States Census of Population by States. Washington, D.C.: U.S. Govern-
    ment Printing Office, 1973.

Contains the following information for most urban places of 2500 or more: size of population by sex; major occupational groups by sex; income for stated year of total families
and unrelated individuals; major industry groups by sex; color of population by sex; age of
population by sex; years of school completed; marital status of males and females, fourteen years and above; country of birth of foreign born white (a decennial publication).

*This guide was originally assembled by John Pease, University of Maryland; additions
have been made in the revised editions by the author.

World Handbook of Political and Social Indicators by Russett, Bruce M.; Alker, Hayward R., Jr.; Deutsch, Karl W.; and Lasswell, Harold D. New Haven: Yale University Press, 1964.

An extensive compilation of seventy-five variables for one hundred thirty-three states and colonies based on indices covering human resources, government and politics, communication, wealth, health, education, family and social relations, distributions of wealth and income, and religion. A matrix of intercorrelation is presented for the seventy-five variables and an analysis of trends and patterns is presented showing how the data can be used to investigate a wide variety of political and social questions.

Revised 2nd edition is now available. See Taylor, Charles Lewis, and Hudson, Michael C. *World Handbook of Political and Social Indicators.* New Haven: Yale University Press, 1972.

City Directories

Often useful in giving a wide range of information about industries and social organizations of the community. Contains alphabetical lists of persons and typically lists occupation and address of each adult.

The County and City Data Book. Washington, D.C.: U.S. Government Printing Office.

Lists numerous tables for each county and cities of 25,000 or more. Contains such tables as labor force, income, elections, banking and finance, buisness enterprises, and education.

The Municipal Year Book. Chicago: International City Managers' Association. (Issued yearly.)

Authoritative reference book on municipal governments. Facts available about the role of city governments including education, housing, welfare, and health make it possible to compare any city with other cities on hundreds of items.

For specialized purposes consult:

U.S. Census of Manufacturers, Area Statistics
U.S. Census of Population, Census Tract Bulletin
Poor's Register of Directors and Executives
Rand McNally's International Bankers' Directory
Moody's Industrial Manual
Editor and Publisher Market Guide
Sales Management, Survey of Buying Power
Fortune Magazine Directory of 500 Largest Corporations
The Economic Almanac
Labor Fact Book
Directory of National and International Labor Unions in the United States
Who's Who in America, Who's Who in the East, Who's Who in the Midwest, Who's Who in the South and Southwest, Who's Who on the Pacific Coast
Directory of Scholars, Social and Behavioral Sciences
Who's Who in Commerce and Industry
Who's Who in Labor

Abstracts

Abstracts of the Papers of the Annual Meetings of the American Sociological Association. Sociological Abstracts, Inc., 2315 Broadway, New York, New York 10024.

1961. Annually. Table of contents. Abstracts. Author index. Published as a supplement to *Sociological Abstracts.*

Catholic University of America Studies in Sociology Abstract Series. Catholic University of America Press, 620 Michigan Avenue, N. W., Washington, D.C. 20017.

1950. Irregularly. Abstracts of dissertations in sociology from the Catholic University of America.

Sociological Abstracts. Sociological Abstracts, Inc., 2315 Broadway, New York, New York 10024.

1952. Octannually. Classified table of contents. List of abbreviations. Abstracts arranged in twenty-four major information areas: methodology and research technology; sociology—history and theory; social psychology; group interactions; culture and social structure; complex organizations (management); social change and economic development; mass phenomena; political interactions; social differentiation; rural sociology and agricultural economics; urban structures and ecology; sociology of the arts; sociology of education; sociology of religion; social control; sociology of science; demography and human biology; the family and socialization; sociology of health and medicine; social problems and social welfare; sociology of knowledge; community development; planning, forecasting, and speculation. Author index. Cumulative index for each volume is published as the last (eighth) issue and includes: table of contents; subject index; periodical index; monograph index; author index; list of abbreviations. *Abstracts of the Papers of the Annual Meetings of the American Sociological Association* is published annually as a supplement and includes: table of contents; abstracts; author index.

Sociology of Education Abstracts. School of Education, University of Liverpool, 19 Abercromby Square, Liverpool 7, England.

1965. Quarterly. Education study areas index. Sociological study areas index. List of abstractors.

Almanacs

GENDELL, MURRAY, and ZETTERBERG, HANS L., eds. *A Sociological Almanac for the United States.* 2nd ed. New York: Charles Scribner's Sons, 1964. 109 pp.

Three essays—"The United States Summed Up by Browsing in a Sociological Almanac," "The Organization of a Sociological Almanac," and "How to Read a Table"—and ninety-six tables about American society organized in terms of nine major topics: human resources; non-human resources; polity and order; economy and prosperity; science and knowledge; religion and sacredness; art and beauty; ethics and virtue; community—local and national. Paperbound.

BRITTAIN, J. MICHAEL, and ROBERTS, STEPHEN A. *Inventory of Information Resources and the Social Sciences.* Lexington, Mass.: D. C. Heath, 1975.

This book provides a detailed list of specialized information resources and services in the social services and related fields in Western Europe, Scandinavia, Canada, and Japan. The inventory covers query answering and referral centers, bibliography sources, and ongoing research into information systems. For each resource listed, details are given of the full name and address, range of subjects covered and information handled, availability of services and relevant changes. Comprehensive title, subject, and geographical indexes are provided; these, together with headings in the text and the editorial introduction, are given in French and English.

Bibliographies

International Bibliography of the Social Sciences—Sociology. Aldine Publishing
Co., 320 West Adams Street, Chicago, Ill. 60606.

1952-1954, volumes 1-4 published in *Current Sociology;* 1955-1959, volumes 5-9 published as *International Bibliography of Sociology*, 1960. Annually. List of periodicals consulted. Classification scheme. Bibliography. Author index. Subject index.

Dictionaries and Glossaries

BOGARDUS, EMORY S. "Selected Sociological Concepts for Beginning Students
in Sociology." *Sociology and Social Research* 44 (January–February 1960):
200–208.

A brief definition of and discussion about fifty-two sociological concepts which are
recommended to beginning sociology students.

FAIRCHILD, HENRY PRATT, ed. *Dictionary of Sociology.* New Students Outline
Series. Paterson, N.J.: Littlefield, Adams, 1961. 350 pp.

This is a reprint, unchanged, of the original edition that first appeared in 1944. Paperbound.

GOULD, JULIUS, and KOLB, WILLIAM L., eds. *A Dictionary of Social Science.*
New York: Free Press, 1964. 777 pp.

Each entry outlines a brief history of usage and discusses the variations in current usage.
Foreward by the Secretariat of UNESCO. Clothbound.

MIHANOVICH, CLEMENT S.; MCNAMARA, ROBERT J.; and TOME, WILLIAM N.,
eds. *Glossary of Sociological Terms.* Milwaukee, Wis.: Bruce, 1957. 40 pp.

MITCHELL, G. DUNCAN, ed. *A Dictionary of Sociology.* Chicago: Aldine, 1968.
232 pp.

Especially prepared to introduce students to the language of the discipline.

THEODORSON, GEORGE A., ed. *Modern Dictionary of Sociology.* New York:
Thomas Y. Crowell, 1969.

Encyclopedias

SELIGMAN, EDWIN R. A., and JOHNSON, ALVIN, eds. *Encyclopedia of the
Social Sciences.* New York: Macmillan, 1930–35. 15 vols. (Now issued in an
8-volume set.)

Volume 1, in addition to regular articles, includes twenty-three essays in two introductory
sections: "The Development of Social Thought and Institutions," and "The Social Sciences as Disciplines." Volume 15, in addition to regular articles, includes a complete
index.

SILLS, DAVID L., ed. *International Encyclopedia of the Social Sciences.* New
York: Macmillan and Free Press, 1968. 17 vols.

Foreword by Alvin Johnson. Volume 17 is a complete index. Comprehensive, thorough,
authoritative. Succinct information on all important subjects in one source.

Guides to the Literature

BLAU, PETER M., and MOORE, JOAN W. "Sociology." In *A Reader's Guide to
the Social Sciences*, edited by Bert F. Hoselitz. Glencoe, Ill.: Free Press, 1959;
rev., 1975. Chap. 6, pp. 158–87.

Arranged in two major sections. The first section, "The Development of Sociology," includes early social philosophy, the separation of state and society, inevitable evolutionary forces, concern with social reform, history and sociology, the scientific study of social facts, implications and reactions. The second section, "Contemporary Sociological Literature in Selected Areas," includes social theory, interviewing surveys, social psychology, demography and human ecology, social differentiation in community and nation, formal and informal organization.

LEWIS, PETER R. "Sociology." *The Literature of the Social Sciences: An Introductory Survey and Guide*. London: Library Association, 1960. Chap. 10, pp. 183–203.

Arranged in five parts: bibliographies, guides, and reference books; sociological theory; sources on social conditions; social services; libraries and library problems.

MUKHERJEE, A. K. "Sociology, Social Psychology, and Allied Topics." *Annotated Guide to Reference Materials in the Human Sciences*. London: Asia Publishing House, 1962. Pt. 2, chaps. 4, 5, and 6, pp. 177–256.

Chapter 4 is arranged in eight parts: dictionary, encyclopedia, year book, directory, handbook, bibliography, abstract and index, historical material. Chapter 5 covers "Specialized Journals." Chapter 6 is arranged in sixteen parts: basic source material and standard treatise—sociology, rural and urban sociology, social change, social problems, family and kinship, social survey and methodology, social case work, race problems, social psychology, culture and personality, personality study, ethno-psychology, somato-psychology, author index, subject index.

ZETTERBERG, HANS L. "Sociology." In *Sources of Information in the Social Sciences: A Guide to the Literature*, edited by Carl M. White with an annotated bibliography by Thompson M. Little and Carl M. White. Totowa, N.J.: Bedminster Press, 1964. Chap. 4, pp. 183–228.

Zetterberg's essay is arranged in twenty parts, organized under four major headings: general orientation, sociological theory, topics of sociology, methods of sociology. Little and White's bibliography is organized under the following fourteen headings: guides to the literature; reviews of the literature; abstracts and digests; bibliographies—current; bibliographies—retrospective; dictionaries; encyclopedias and encyclopedic sets; directories and biographical information; atlases and pictorial works; handbooks, manuals, compendia; yearbooks; statistical sources; sources of scholarly contributions; sources of unpublished information.

Handbooks, Sourcebooks, and Reviews

BART, PAULINE, and FRANKEL, LINDA. *The Student Sociologist's Handbook*. Morristown, N.J.: General Learning Press, 1971.

BLUMER, HERBERT, ed. "Special Semicentennial Issue." *American Journal of Sociology* 50 (May 1945): 421–548.

An editorial foreword and fourteen articles especially prepared for this issue and arranged in four parts: developments in the last fifty years, fifty years of sociology in the United States, the proximate future of American sociology, trends in sociology.

FARIS, ROBERT E. L., ed. *Handbook of Modern Sociology*. Chicago: Rand McNally, 1964. 1096 pp.

A collection of twenty-seven articles written especially for this volume and aimed at summarizing "all major growing research areas of modern sociology." Each article includes an extensive bibliography. Index of names. Index of subjects. Clothbound.

GITTLER, JOSEPH B., ed. *Review of Sociology: Analysis of a Decade.* New York: John Wiley, 1957. 597 pp.

A collection of fourteen articles and five bibliographical appendixes especially prepared for this volume and aimed at "presenting and evaluating the significant literature in American Sociology" during the decade 1945–55. Clothbound.

GOULDNER, ALVIN, and MILLER, S. M., eds. *Applied Sociology: Opportunities and Prospects.* Glencoe, Ill.: Free Press, 1964.

Experts describe application of sociology to numerous fields of activity.

HOSELITZ, BERT F. ed. *A Readers Guide to the Social Sciences.* Rev. ed. New York: Free Press, 1975.

General introduction and guide to the literature of the social sciences. Covers historical development of sociology, psychology, anthropology, geography, and economics with appraisals of the classics in the field, systematic review of current output, and critical comments on present trends and directions. Bibliography.

HANDY, ROLLO, and KURTZ, PAUL. "Sociology." *A Current Appraisal of the Behavioral Sciences.* Great Barrington, Mass.: Behavioral Research Council, 1964. Chap. 2, pp. 25–34.

Arranged under the following nine headings: working specification of the field, other specifications of the field; schools, methods, techniques; results achieved; contemporary controversy; problems of terminology; comment and evaluation; selected bibliographies; germane journals.

LAZARSFELD, PAUL F.; SEWELL, WILLIAM H.; and WILENSKY, HAROLD L., eds. *The Uses of Sociology.* New York: Basic Books, 1967. 913 pp.

Introduction and thirty-one other articles written especially for this volume and arranged in six parts: sociological perspectives, the uses of sociology in the professions, the uses of sociology in establishments, social problems and formal planning, rapid social change, institutional problems in applied sociology. Index of names. Index of subjects. Cothbound.

LIPSET, SEYMOUR MARTIN, and SMELSER, NEIL J., eds. *Sociology, the Progress of a Decade: A Collection of Articles.* Englewood Cliffs, N.J.: Prentice-Hall, 1961. 646 pp.

Introduction and sixty-four other articles arranged in four parts: the discipline of sociology; the major boundaries of social systems; the production and allocation of wealth, power, and prestige; the balance between stability and change in society. Clothbound.

MADGE, JOHN. *The Origins of Scientific Sociology.* New York: Free Press of Glencoe, 1962.

A review of selected work by outstanding sociologists who have contributed to the building of a scientific sociology.

MERTON, ROBERT K.; BROOM, LEONARD; COTTRELL, LEONARD S., JR., eds. *Sociology Today: Problems and Prospects.* New York: Basic Books, 1959. 658 pp.

Introduction and twenty-five other articles written especially for this volume and arranged in five parts: problems in sociological theory and methodology, problems in the sociology of institutions, the group and the person, problems in demographic and social structure, selected applications of sociology. Index of names and subjects. Clothbound. (This is also available in a two-volume paperbound set from Harper & Row of New York.)

MITCHELL, G. DUNCAN. *A Hundred Years of Sociology.* Chicago: Aldine, 1968.

A concise history of the major ideas, figures, and schools of sociological thought.

PARSONS, TALCOTT, ed. *American Sociology: Perspectives, Problems, Methods.* New York: Basic Books, 1968. 368 pp.

Introduction and twenty-four other essays especially prepared for this volume and arranged in six parts and a conclusion: components of social systems; methods of investigation; functional subsystems; sociology of culture; strain, deviance, and social control; total societies and their change; conclusion. Index of names of subjects. Clothbound.

GUIDES FOR SELECTION AND CONSTRUCTION OF QUESTIONNAIRES AS UTILIZED IN FIELD RESEARCH

2.3

The mail questionnaire is a list of questions for information or opinion that is mailed to potential respondents who have been chosen in some designated manner. The respondents are asked to complete the questionnaire and return it by mail.

This means of gathering information is very popular because it promises to secure data at a minimum of time and expense. The popularity of the method is often defeating because many respondents are overburdened by the number of questionnaires that reach them. In the competition for their time, respondents increasingly examine the purpose of the study, the sponsorship, the utility of findings to them, the time required to fill it out, the clarity and readability of the type, and perhaps, the quality of the paper.

Decision-making criteria: Every researcher who chooses the mail questionnaire should consider its value in a highly competitive environment in which the majority of respondents will probably not complete and return the questionnaire. The researcher should examine carefully the advantages and disadvantages described below. The disadvantages are shown first to emphasize their importance. If the advantages override these disadvantages, and if the method fits the study, then the questionnaire is appropriate. A guide to questionnaire construction follows that should prove useful. Also note the guide to techniques for increasing percentage of returns.

Disadvantages of the Mail Questionnaire*

1. MAJOR WEAKNESS: Problem of nonreturns.
   a. Most ordinary studies as conducted by private and relatively unskilled persons yield only from 10 to 25 percent of returns.
   b. The questionnaire must be short to have a greater probability of return.
      i. Norton found 78.5 percent returned with less than five questions.
      ii. Stanton reported 28.3 percent returned a three-page questionnaire while 50.2 percent answered a double postcard containing a single question that could be answered by making a single check.
   c. Sletto found an altruistic appeal increased returns to 67 percent in a college-trained population.
   d. Shuttleworth found a questionnaire containing a 25-cent coin prompted a return of 52 percent; questionnaires without the coin produced 19 percent returns.
   e. The percentage of returns is about double for a regular stamped envelope over the business-reply envelope.

*Cf. David Wallace, "A Case For—and Against—Mail Questionnaires," *Public Opinion Quarterly* 18 (1954): 40–52.

2. Those who answer the questionnaires may differ from the nonrespondents, thereby biasing the sample.
3. Validity depends on the ability and willingness of the respondent to provide information.
4. Possibility of misinterpretation of the question.
5. No follow-through on misunderstood questions or evasive answers; no observation of apparent reluctance or evasiveness.

Advantages of Mail Questionnaire

1. Permits wide coverage for minimum expense both in money and effort.
2. Affords wider geographic contact.
3. Reaches people who are difficult to locate and interview.
4. Greater coverage may yield greater validity through larger and more representative samples.
5. Permits more considered answers.
6. More adequate in situations in which the respondent has to check information.
7. More adequate in situations in which group consultations would give more valid information.
8. Greater uniformity in the manner in which questions are posed.
9. Gives respondent a sense of privacy.
10. Affords a simple means of continual reporting over time.
11. Lessens interviewer effect.

Guide to Questionnaire Construction*

A. Reclarify the relation of the method to problem and hypotheses. Obtain a thorough grasp of the area to be studied and a clear understanding of the objectives of the study and the nature of the data needed.

   In a *descriptive* inquiry the investigator is seeking to estimate as precisely and comprehensively as possible a problem area; in an *explanatory* inquiry of a theoretical type the investigator is seeking to test some particular hypothesis about the determinants of a dependent variable or factor. In either type, economy and efficiency are important criteria. The rule is: Gather the data you need but not more than is needed. Know how you will use and analyze your data. Make your dummy tables now if possible and challenge their adequacy for describing the possible distributions or relationships that are related to your problem or hypotheses.

B. Formulate questions.

   1. Keep the language pitched to the level of the respondent.

      Interviews given only to specialized respondents can use the terminology with which they are familiar. But interviews given to the general public must use language with more common usage.

   2. Try to pick words that have the same meaning for everyone.

      A questionnaire involving American and British respondents might ask,

---

*Cf. Paul F. Lazarsfeld, *Qualitative Analysis: Historical and Critical Essays* (Boston: Allyn & Bacon, 1972), chap. 8.

"How often do you have tea?" To the American, tea would refer to a drink. To the British, tea would refer to a light meal.

3. Avoid long questions.

    When questions become long they often become ambiguous and confusing.

4. Do not a priori assume that your respondent possesses *factual* information, or firsthand opinions.

    A mother may be able to report what books her child reads, but a child himself must be questioned to know how he feels about reading those books.

5. Establish the frame of reference you have in mind.

    Don't ask: How many magazines do you read?

        Ask: Which magazines do you read?

6. In forming a question, either suggest all possible alternatives to the respondent or don't suggest any.

    Don't ask: Do you think the husband should help with dressing and feeding the small children when he's home?

        Ask: Do you think the husband should help with dressing and feeding the small children when he's home, or do you think it's the wife's job in any case?

        Or: Who should dress and feed the children when the husband is home?

7. Protect your respondent's ego.

    Don't ask: Do you know the name of the chief justice of the Supreme Court?

        Ask: Do you happen to know the name of the chief justice of the Supreme Court?

8. If you're after unpleasant orientations, give your respondent a chance to express positive feelings first so that he or she is not put in an unfavorable light.

    Ask: What do you like about X?

    Then: What don't you like about X?

9. Decide whether you need a direct question, an indirect question, or an indirect followed by a direct question.

        Direct: Do you ever steal on the job?

      Indirect: Do you know of anyone ever stealing on the job?

    Combination: Do you know of anyone ever stealing on the job? Have you ever taken anything from the job?

10. Decide whether the question should be open or closed.

    Open: It is believed that some people in this community have too much power. Do you think this is true? Who are they?

    Closed: It is believed that some people in this community have too much power. Is this statement ☐ True. ☐ False. ☐ Don't know. If true, who are they? ☐ Negroes. ☐ Jews. ☐ Poles. ☐ Italians. ☐ _____ .

11. Decide whether general or specific questions are needed.

    It may be enough to ask: How well did you like the book?

    It may be preferable to also ask: Have you recommended the book to anyone else?

12. Avoid ambiguous wording.
    Don't ask: Do you usually work alone?
        Ask: ☐ No, I never work alone. ☐ Yes, I work alone less than half the time. ☐ Yes, I work alone most of the time.
13. Avoid biased or leading questions.
    Don't ask: Did you exercise your right as an American citizen to vote in the last election?
        Ask: Did you vote in the last election?
14. Phrase questions so that they are not unnecessarily objectionable.
    Instead of: Did you graduate from high school?
        Ask: What is the highest grade in school you completed?
15. Decide whether a personal or impersonal question will obtain the better response.
    Impersonal: Are working conditions satisfactory or not satisfactory where you work?
    Personal: Are you satisfied or dissatisfied with working conditions in the plant where you work?
16. Questions should be limited to a single idea or a single reference.
    Don't ask: Do you favor or oppose increased job security and the guaranteed annual wage?
        Ask: Do you favor or oppose increased job security?
        And: Do you favor or oppose the guaranteed annual wage?

C. Organize the questionnaire.
  1. Start with easy questions that the respondent will enjoy answering.
     Don't start with age, occupation, or marital status.
     Ask questions to arouse interest.
  2. Don't condition answers to subsequent questions by preceding ones.
     a. Go from the general to the specific.
        How do you think this country is getting along in its relations with other countries?
        How do you think we are doing in our relations with Russia?
     b. Go from the easy to the difficult.
  3. Use the sequence of questions to protect the respondent's ego. Save the personal questions such as income for later.
  4. Decide whether one or several questions will best obtain the information for a given objective.
  5. With free-answer questions, it is sometimes helpful to have the questions in pairs, asking for the pros and cons of a particular issue.
  6. Open-ended questions which require most thought and writing should be kept to a minimum. Generally, these should be placed at the end to assure that the closed questions will be answered.
  7. The topics and questions should be arranged so that they make the most sense to the respondent. The aim is to secure a sequence that is natural and easy for the respondent.

D. Pretest the questionnaire.
  1. Select a number of respondents representative of those you expect to survey and interview them. Encourage them to ask any questions that they have as they respond to your items. Watch for misunderstanding,

ambiguity, and defensiveness. Ask them how they would restate a question that is difficult to understand or to answer.

2. Never omit pretesting!

E. Select paper and type carefully. The use of type-print can produce a mimeographed questionnaire on good paper that looks like a printed copy.

F. Consider how you can present the strongest possible sponsorship. The person, persons, or group that will support your efforts through a covering letter is important. Note the increase of 17 percent return reported in the technique guide for increasing percentage of returns.

G. Examine each of the techniques for increasing return of the questionnaire and decide which will maximize returns for you.

Techniques for Increasing Percentage of Returns

Method	Possible increase of total % of returns	Optimal conditions
Follow-up*	50%	More than one follow-up may be needed. If possible, returns may be increased by using double postcards with the most important questions on follow-ups. The telephone can often be used effectively for follow-up. Researcher should find out if respondent needs another copy of the questionnaire (it may have been destroyed or misplaced). Sewell and Shaw report a 87.2% return on 9007 from parents of Wisconsin high school students using 3 waves of mailed questionnaires and final telephone interview. *American Sociological Review* 33 (April 1968): 193.
Sponsor	17%	John K. Norton found that people the respondent knew produced the best results. A state headquarters received the second best rate. Others following in order were: a lower-status person in a similar field, a publishing firm, a college professor or student, and a private association or foundation.
Length	22%	If a questionnaire is short, then the shorter the better. A double postcard should produce the best results. However, if the questionnaire is over 10 pages at the minimum, length may cease to be a factor. Sewell and Shaw used a double postcard in the study reported.
Introductory letter	7%	An altruistic appeal seems to have better results than the idea that the respondent may receive something good from it.
Type of questions	13%	Questionnaires asking for objective information receive the best rate, and questionnaires asking for subjective information receive the worst.

Techniques for Increasing Percentage of Returns (Continued)

Method	Possible increase of total % of returns	Optimal conditions
Inducements	33%	Shuttleworth found that a questionnaire containing a 25-cent coin produced better results than one without. However, the population and the type of questionnaire could make such inducements unnecessary. Consider promise of report to respondent.
Method of return	Not known	A regular stamped envelope produces better results than the business-reply envelope.
Time of arrival	Not known	The questionnaire, if sent to the home, should arrive near the end of the week.
Format	Not known	Sletto found a need for an aesthetically pleasing cover, a title that would arouse interest, an attractive page format, a size and style of type easily readable under poor illumination and by people with poor vision, and photographs to illustrate the questionnaire.

Selection of respondents**	Respondent selection can rarely increase returns to above a total of 80%	**1.** Nonreaders and nonwriters are excluded from participation.
		2. Interest in, or familiarity with, the topic under investigation is a major factor in determining the rate of return.
		3. The better-educated are more likely to return questionnaires.
		4. Professionals are more likely to return questionnaires.
		One of the highest returns reported in the research literature is that by Rensis Likert. In a study of the League of Women Voters (commissioned by the League) a cross-sectional sample of 2905 League members and officers showed the following percent of return:
		    79% of members
		    95% of board members
		    100% of chapter presidents
		(Rensis Likert, *New Patterns of Management*, p. 145)

*The Bureau of Social Science Research, Inc., 1200 Seventeenth St. N.W., Washington, D.C. 20036, has compiled completion rates in mail surveys undertaken by BSSR. Data compiled by Lenore Reid. They report a 65 to 90% return with as many as four follow-ups. Covering letter from institutional sponsor is believed very important.

**For differential response by business, labor, political, religious, and civic leaders see Delbert Miller, *Leadership and Power in Bos-Wash Megapolis* (New York: Wiley, 1975), p. 380.

H. Examine the sample page from a questionnaire designed by Raymond F. Sletto. Note how attention has been given to appearance, spacing, ease of response. Note how the open and closed questions are presented, how the data are recorded.

YOUR EXPERIENCES

Please give your answers to the following questions by writing in the appropriate spaces or by marking an X in the blanks as indicated.

1. What is your present job, or last job if unemployed? (Please be specific so that responses can be accurately classified. For example, wholesale hardware salesman, retail sales clerk in department store, high school teacher of English, owner of drug store, housewife, etc.)

   Clinic Nurse & technician

   Housewife

2. What was your first full-time job after leaving the University? _____

   Medical technician

3. How did you obtain this first full-time job? (you may check more than one.)

   ☒ By direct application   ☐ Through University Employment Office
   ☐ Through friends   ☐ Through other University assistance
   ☐ Through relatives   ☐ Through other employment office
   ☐ Approached by employer   Other, please specify:
   ☐ By financial investment   _____
   ☐ Through an advertisement   _____

4. How did you obtain your present job? (You may check more than one.)

   ☒ By direct application   ☐ Through an employment office
   ☐ Through friends   ☐ Through previous employer
   ☐ Through relatives   Other, please specify:
   ☐ By financial investment   _____
   ☐ Through an advertisement   _____

5. How many hours per week on the average do you spend on your job? __*38*__

6. How closely related is your present job to your chosen field of specialization at the University?

   ☐ Same field   ☒ Related field   ☐ Different field

GUIDE FOR INCREASING RETURNS OF MAILED QUESTIONNAIRES, EXPECTED RESULTS, AND COSTS

2.4

Response rates to mailed questionnaires are typically low, usually not exceeding 50 percent. Recent research indicates that much better return rates can be achieved by skilled use of questionnaire construction and follow-up procedures. Four researchers are so sure of their methods that they assert "with a mail methodology available which will consistently provide a high response, poor return rates can no more be excused than can inadequate theory or inappropriate statistics."[1]

The effectiveness of a particular method for eliciting response to lengthy questionnaires (85–165 items) was tested on large statewide samples of the general public in Arizona, Indiana, North Carolina, and Washington. The methods utilized produced response rates of from 69.7 percent to 75.2 percent. They were equally effective in rural and urban regions. The quality of the data was uniformly high throughout the items.

Increasing Returns of Mailed Questionnaires

The method of achieving such results can be detailed in successive steps:

1. Prepare questionnaire as a booklet by photo reduction and multilithing. (This makes it seem less formidable.)
2. Make the cover page attractive and eye-catching.
3. Use straightforward, unambiguous questions carefully ordered and presented in a visually attractive manner. (See 2.3 for sample page of a questionnaire.) Questions in the first pages should be designed largely to attract respondents' interest in order to increase the likelihood that important questions of limited interest and appeal will be answered.
4. Prepare a cover letter and emphasize the social usefulness of the study and the individual importance of each respondent to the success of the study.
5. Make full use of personalization procedures.[2] Address salutation by name of respondent, not *Dear Sir* or *Madam*; sign your name; etc.
6. Mail questionnaire as first-class mail.
7. Use postcard follow-up one week later.
8. Prepare letter with replacement questionnaire and send at the end of the third week.
9. Send final letter with replacement questionnaire by certified mail after seven weeks.[3]

Table 1 shows the cumulative response rates to the four mailings used in each study.[4]

Table 1   *Cumulative Response Rates to Four Mailings Used in Each Study* *

Mailing	Time	Washington 1970 N = 4137[1]	Washington 1971 N = 4175[1]	North Carolina 1973 N = 4470[1]	Arizona 1973 N = 2021[1]	Indiana 1973 N = 7558[1]	Overall Mean
1. First mailing	Week 1	27.0%	26.3%	20.6%	26.5%	18.6%	23.8%
2. Postcard follow-up	Week 2	45.7	51.1	35.1	41.6	36.5	42.0
3. First replacement questionnaire	Week 4	59.2[2]	67.6	53.0	60.1	55.3	59.0
4. Second replacement questionnaire sent by certified mail	Week 7	75.0	75.2	69.7	71.3	70.9	72.4

[1]N = number of *potential* respondents. This is slightly less than the original mailing. Those dropped included persons (1) who had moved from the state so were no longer eligible, (2) to whom a questionnaire could not be delivered (usually because of moving and either leaving no forwarding address or leaving one that expired), (3) who had died, or (4) who were physically incapable of responding (usually due to infirmities of old age). The first two categories accounted for approximately three-fourths of the drops. The numbers (and percent of the original mailing) dropped in each state are as follows: Washington 1970, 363 (8.1%); Washington 1971, 325 (7.2%); North Carolina, 612 (12.0%); Arizona, 229 (10.2%); Indiana, 479 (5.9%).

[2]In this study the third mailing did not include a replacement questionnaire.

*Used with permission of the author and the American Sociological Association.

Expected Results

Note that the final response rates for the four states vary just over five percentage points from highest to lowest. Since there was high similarity in content, there is evidence that the topic per se made no difference.

The table reveals the importance of intensive follow-ups. Without the final two mailings, the probable final response rates would have been less than 50 percent for four of the five studies. The third mailing increased returns by an average of 17.0 percent. The fourth mailing (the final mailing) was only slightly less productive with a 13.4 percent return.

Cost of Data Collection Process

Low cost is one of the major advantages of the mail survey compared with personal interviews. Costs are incurred in such categories as labor, postage, printing, and supplies. What researchers have at their disposal can make a big difference in unit costs. Needless to say, costs do not stabilize; they continue to rise. The four state researchers, each working with different facilities in four state universities, present table 2 showing their unit costs.[5] The data reported in the table do not include the salaries of the principal investigators but do include costs for material, postage, and labor. These turn out to be quite similar on a per completed questionnaire basis. The researchers believe that all five studies would have cost about $1.60 per potential respondent if mailing costs had been the same. The Washington studies were conducted when 6-cent stamps were acceptable, not the 8-cent stamps required in the other studies. The North Carolina study enjoyed a franking privilege, which cut costs below the others. Still, there was only a 40-cent difference between the least and most expensive studies.

Table 2 *Cost of Data Collection Process**

	Costs				
	Washing-ton 1970 $N = 4500^1$	Washing-ton 1971 $N = 4500^1$	North Carolina 1973 $N = 4500^1$	Arizona 1973 $N = 2250^1$	Indiana 1973 $N = 8037^1$
Actual labor costs per potential respondent in original sample	$ .52	$ .57	$ .63	$ .42	$ .28
Actual cost of materials and postage per potential respondent	.49[2]	.45[2]	.11[3]	.61	.84
Total cost per potential respondent	1.01	1.02	.74	1.03	1.13
Total labor, materials, and postage cost per completed questionnaire	1.46	1.44	1.21	1.62	1.60
Actual cost of complete data collection and processing onto computer tape per completed questionnaire	2.84	2.84	1.79	1.94	1.60[4]

[1]Number of questionnaires sent in first mailing.
[2]Minimum first-class postage rate was 6 cents instead of 8 cents except for the last mailing of the 1971 study.
[3]Postage was not a direct cost, as the franking privilege was utilized.
[4]This figure and the one immediately above are the same inasmuch as the procedures used did not allow the costs to be separated.
*Used with permission of the author and the American Sociological Association.

Note that when all costs are considered, including data processing to the point of analysis, the range was quite large. Nonetheless, the cost per completed questionnaire in no case exceeded $3.00, a figure that is very small when compared with the cost of securing personal interviews. The subsequent increase in mailing and interviewer rates require an upward adjustment in estimating all costs today.

The writers conclude with the statement:

> There are still many unanswered questions about the limits of mail questionnaires. By demonstrating that a particular method can consistently produce completed questionnaires of a good quality from nearly three-fourths of the potential respondents, we hope to stimulate research aimed at finding these limits. Upgrading the status of mail questionnaires seems the necessary first step.[6]

Notes

1. Don A. Dillman, James A. Christensen, Edwin H. Carpenter, and Ralph M. Brooks, "Increasing Mail Questionnaire Response: A Four State Comparison," *American Sociological Review* 39 (October 1974): 755.
2. Don A. Dillman and James H. Frey, "The Contribution of Personalization to Mail Questionnaire Response as an Element of a Previously Tested Method," *Journal of Applied Psychology* 59, no. 3 (1974): 297–301. Cf. E H. Carpenter as cited in bibliography.
3. Dillman et al., "Increasing Questionnaire Response." Adapted from p. 746.
4. Ibid., p. 748.
5. Ibid., p. 754.
6. Ibid., p. 756.

References

American Statistical Association Conference on Surveys of Human Population. "Report on the ASA Conference on Surveys of Human Populations." *American Statistician* 28 (February 1974): 30–34.

BOYD, W., JR., and WESTFALL, RALPH. *Marketing Research: Text and Cases.* Rev. ed. Homewood, Ill.: Irwin, 1964.

BRUNNER, JAMES A., and BRUNNER, G. ALLEN. "Are Voluntarily Unlisted Telephone Subscribers Really Different?" *Journal of Marketing Research* 8 (February 1971): 121–24.

CARPENTER, EDWIN H. "Personalizing Mail Surveys: A Replication and Reassessment." *Public Opinion Quarterly* 38 (Winter 1974): 614–20.

CHRISTENSON, JAMES A. "A Procedure for Conducting Mail Surveys with the General Public." *Journal of Community Development Society* 6 (Spring 1975): 135–45.

DILLMAN, DON A. "Increasing Mail Questionnaire Response in Large Samples of the General Public." *Public Opinion Quarterly* 36 (Summer 1972): 254–57.

DILLMAN, DON A. *Mail and Telephone Data Collection Methods.* New York: Wiley-Interscience, 1976.

DILLMAN, DON A., and FREY, JAMES H. "The Contribution of Personalization to Mail Questionnaire Response as an Element of a Previously Tested Method." *Journal of Applied Psychology* 59 (1974): 297–301.

HELMSTADTER, G. C. *Research Concepts in Human Behavior. Education, Psychology, Sociology.* New York: Appleton-Century-Crofts, 1970.

KERLINGER, FRED N. *Foundations of Behavioral Research.* 2nd ed. New York: Holt, Rinehart & Winston, 1973.

LEIK, ROBERT K. *Methods, Logic and Research of Sociology*. Indianapolis: Bobbs-Merrill, 1972.

LEUTHOLD, DAVID A., and SCHEELE, RAYMOND J. "Patterns of Bias in Samples Based on Telephone Directories." *Public Opinion Quarterly* 35 (Summer 1971): 249–57.

LIU, BEN-CHIEH. *The Quality of Life in the United States*. Kansas City: Midwest Research Institute, 1973.

PERRY, JOSEPH, JR. "A Note on the Use of Telephone Directories as a Sample Source." *Public Opinion Quarterly* 32 (Fall 1968): 691–95.

SLOCUM, W. L.; EMPEY, L. T.; and SWANSON, H. S. "Increasing Response to Questionnaires and Structured Interviews." *American Sociological Review* 21 (April 1956): 221–25.

GUIDES FOR SELECTION AND USE OF PERSONAL INTERVIEWS AS UTILIZED IN FIELD RESEARCH

2.5

The interview represents a personal contact between an interviewer and a respondent usually in the home or office of the respondent. The interview can range from a highly structured situation with a planned series of questions to a very informal talk with no structure except for some areas of discussion desired by the interviewer. The degrees of freedom represent opportunity and danger: opportunity to explore many subjects with intensity but with the danger that the interview may not yield the appropriate data. It is often not susceptible to codification and comparability.

The researcher may not appreciate that every open-ended question will take considerable interview time. The analysis of open-ended questions requires a code guide and careful independent observers to establish the validity and reliability of the coding for each question. In general the rule is: Present closed rather than open-ended questions. If you must employ open-ended questions, choose a few with care and with the precise aims of the study in mind. If hypotheses are to be tested, make sure that the questions bear directly upon them. Open-ended questions are appropriate and powerful under conditions that require probing of attitude and reaction formations and ascertaining information that is interlocked in a social system or personality structure.

In general, keep the interview within a 45-minute time span. Public-opinion interviewers have reported that most respondents begin to weary and show less interest in the interview at this point. It is true that some respondents will "warm up" as the interview proceeds and there are examples of six- and eight-hour interviews in the literature. (Robert Dahl with community leaders in New Haven, Connecticut, and Neal Gross in planned interviews with Massachusetts School Superintendents in Cambridge, Massachusetts).[1] These long interviews are exceptional and can only occur under specially prepared conditions.

The interview may be identified in three forms: (1) The Structured Interview Schedule, (2) The Focused Interview, and (3) The Free Story. These forms and their characteristics are shown in the Outline Guide to Situses, Principal Methods, and Techniques of the Social Science Researcher (p. 66). Common techniques that may be employed include inclusion of scales to measure social factors, attitudes, and personality traits. Secret ballots and panel techniques are often employed.

The guide that follows lists advantages and disadvantages of the interview. Use it as a check list noting with a plus mark those advantages that are important or essential; mark a minus for the disadvantages that will affect your use of the interview. You now have an adequate base for your choice or rejection of the personal interview.

Other field methods are available including the group interview, telephone interview, case study and life history, direct observation, participant observation, and mass observation. Guides have not been prepared for these methods, but a list of reference books is appended to this part describing in detail all the methods and techniques.

Guide for Appraisal of Personal Interview for Data Collection

The researcher should check the advantages important for his study. Then check the disadvantages that cannot be overcome. Appraise the choice. Reconsider documentary analysis, mail questionnaire, observation, or other methods suggested in the Outline Guide to Situses, Principal Methods, and Techniques of the Social Science Researcher.

Advantages of Personal Interview

1. The personal interview usually yields a high percentage of returns, for most people are willing to cooperate.
2. It can be made to yield an almost perfect sample of the general population because practically everyone can be reached by and can respond to this approach.
3. The information secured is likely to be more correct than that secured by other techniques since the interviewer can clear up seemingly inaccurate answers by explaining the questions to the informant. If the latter deliberately falsifies replies, the interviewer may be trained to spot such cases and use special devices to get the truth.
4. The interviewer can collect supplementary information about the informant's personal characteristics and environment that is valuable in interpreting results and evaluating the representatives of the persons surveyed.
5. Scoring and test devices can be used, the interviewer acting as experimenter to establish accurate records of the subject.
6. Visual material to which the informant is to react can be presented.
7. Return visits to complete items on the schedule or to correct mistakes can usually be made without annoying the informant. Thus greater numbers of usable returns are assumed than when other methods are employed.
8. The interviewer may catch the informant off guard and thus secure more spontaneous reactions than would be the case if a written form were mailed out for the informant to mull over.
9. The interviewer can usually control which person or persons answer the questions, whereas in mail surveys several members of the household may confer before the questions are answered. Group discussions can be held with the personal interview method if desired.
10. The personal interview may take long enough to allow the informant to

become oriented to the topic under investigation. Thus recall of relevant material is facilitated.

11. Questions about which the informant is likely to be sensitive can be carefully sandwiched in by the interviewer. By observing the informant's reactions, the investigator can change the subject if necessary or explain the survey problem further if it appears that the interviewee is about to rebel. In other words, a delicate situation can usually be handled more effectively by a personal interview than by other survey techniques.

12. More of the informant's time can be taken for the survey than would be the case if the interviewer were not present to elicit and record the information.

13. In cases where a printed schedule is not used (cf. disadvantage 2, below), the language of the survey can be adapted to the ability or educational level of the person interviewed. Therefore, it is comparatively easy to avoid misinterpretations or misleading questions.

Disadvantages of Personal Interview

1. The transportation costs and the time required to cover addresses in a large area may make the personal interview method unfeasible.

2. The human equation may distort the returns. Interviewers with a certain economic bias, for example, may unconsciously ask questions so as to secure confirmation of their views. In opinion studies especially, such biases may operate. To prevent such coloring of questions, most opinion surveyors instruct their interviewers to ask the question *exactly* as printed on the schedule.

3. Unless the interviewers are properly trained and supervised, the data recorded may be inaccurate and incomplete. A few poor enumerators may make a much higher percentage of returns unusable than if the informants filled out and mailed the interview form to survey headquarters.

4. The organization required for selecting, training, and supervising a field staff is more complex than that needed for surveys conducted by other methods.

5. It is usually claimed that costs per interview are higher when field investigators are employed than when telephone or mail surveys are used. This may not be true if the area to be covered is not too great. If the general public in a community is to be surveyed, the costs of securing a *representative* sample by telephone or mail inquiries will probably equal or exceed the cost by the personal interview method, since in the end personal follow-up will be necessary to round out the sample.

6. The personal interview usually takes more time than the telephone interview providing the persons who can be reached by telephone are a representative sample of the type of population to be covered by the survey. However, for a sample of the general public, a telephone inquiry is not a substitute for a personal interview. The lowest-income groups often do not have telephones.[2]

7. If the interview is conducted in the home during the day, the majority of the informants will be housewives. If a response is to be obtained from a male member of the household, most of the field work will have to be done in the evening or on weekends. Since only an hour or two can be used for evening interviewing, the personal interview method requires a large staff for studies requiring contacts with the working population.

Notes

1. Robert A. Dahl, *Who Governs* (New Haven: Yale University Press, 1961), p. 334. Neal Gross, Ward S. Mason, and Alexander W. McEachern, *Explorations of Role Analysis: The Superintendency Role* (New York: John Wiley, 1958), p. 85.

2. Robert L. Kahn and Robert M. Groves of the Survey Research Center, University of Michigan, are making a major study to evaluate interviewing by telephone. They claim about 90% of all adults can be reached by phone.

2.6   GUIDES FOR THE SELECTION AND CONSTRUCTION OF SOCIAL SCALES AND INDICES

Scaling techniques play a major role in the construction of instruments for collecting standardized, measurable data. Scales and indices are significant because they provide quantitative measures that are amenable to greater precision, statistical manipulation, and explicit interpretation. However, before constructing a new scale, it is exceedingly important that a very careful survey of the literature be made to ascertain if an appropriate scale is already available to measure the dependent or independent variables in a given study. The general rule is: Use the available scale if it has qualities of validity, reliability, and utility (and in that order of priority). With such a scale comparative and accumulative research is possible. The need to develop a new scale can almost be considered a disciplinary failure unless the variable represents a factor never before considered as open to measurement. We shall begin, therefore, at the point at which the literature has not revealed an appropriate scale and the researcher decides to construct an index or scale.

How does one "think up" a number of indicators to be used in empirical research?

This question is answered by Paul F. Lazarsfeld and Morris Rosenberg as follows:

> The first step seems to be the creation of a rather vague image or construct that results from the author's immersion in all the detail of a theoretical problem. The creative act may begin with the perception of many disparate phenomena as having some underlying characteristic in common. Or the author may have observed certain regularities and is trying to account for them. In any case, the concept, when first created, is some vaguely conceived entity that makes the observed relations meaningful. Next comes a stage in which the concept is specified by elaborate discussion of the phenomena out of which it emerged. We develop "aspects," "components," "dimensions," or similar specifications. They are sometimes derived logically from the overall concept, or one aspect is deduced from another, or empirically observed correlations between them are reported. The concept is shown to consist of a complex combination of phenomena, rather than a simple and directly observable item. In order to incorporate the concept into a research design, observable indicators of it must be selected.[1]

Indices and scales are often used interchangeably to refer to all sorts of measures, absolute or relative, single or composite, the product of simple or elaborate techniques of measurement.

Indices may be very simple. For example, one way to measure morale is to ask the direct question, "How would you rate your morale? Very good, good, fair, poor, very poor." This might be refined slightly so that the responses are placed on a numerical scale. Note that there are nine points on the following scale.

How Would You Rate Your Morale?								
Very good		Good		Fair		Poor		Very poor
1	2	3	4	5	6	7	8	9

The basis for construction is logical inference and the use of a numerical scale requires the assumption of a psychological continuity which the respondent can realistically act upon in self-rating. Face validity is usually asserted for such a scale although it would be possible to make tests of relations with criteria such as work performance, absenteeism, lateness, amount of drinking, hours of sleep, etc.

A composite index is one or a set of measures, each of which is formed by combining simple indexes. For example, morale may be considered as a composite of many dimensions.

Four measures can be combined by such questions as

How satisfied are you with your job?
How satisfied are you with your company or organization?
How satisfied are you in your personal life?
How satisfied are you with your community?

Response choices of very good, good, fair, poor, and very poor may be offered for each question with weights of 5, 4, 3, 2, and 1. A range from 4 to 20 points is possible. Such a composite index may improve precision, reliability, and validity.

Rigor is introduced as greater attention is paid to tests of validity and reliability. At a certain point a given means of measurement reaches its limit of improvement and a more refined technique becomes necessary for greater precision. Many scaling techniques concern themselves with linearity and equal intervals or equal-appearing intervals. This means that the scale follows a straight line model and that a scoring system is devised, preferably based on interchangeable units and subject to statistical manipulation. This is a major attribute of the Thurstone attitude scaling technique.

Unidimensionality or homogeneity is another desired attribute assuring that only one dimension is measured and not some mixture of factors. This is a prime concern of the Guttman scaling technique. Reproducibility is a characteristic that enables the reseacher to predict the pattern of a respondent's answers by knowing only the total scale score. This attribute is built into Guttman scaling techniques.

The intensity of feeling is introduced in the Likert technique. The respondent is usually asked to indicate his feelings on a five-point scale ranging from strongly agree to strongly disagree. Tests of item discrimination are applied.

There is no single method that combines the advantages of all of them.[2] It is, therefore, important that we understand their respective purposes and the differences between them.

Notes

1. Paul F. Lazarsfeld and Morris Rosenberg, eds., *The Language of Social Research: A Reader in the Methodology of Social Research* (Glencoe, Ill.: Free Press 1962), p. 15.

2. The Scale Discrimination Technique developed by Allen Edwards makes an excellent attempt to secure a combination of the Thurstone, Likert, and Guttman features. See the following pages. Cf. Allen L. Edwards and Kathryn Claire Kenney, "A Comparison of the Thurstone and Likert Techniques of Attitude Scale Construction," *Journal of Applied Psychology* 30 (1946): 72–83.

2.6.a. THURSTONE EQUAL-APPEARING INTERVAL SCALE

NATURE: This scale consists of a number of items whose position on the scale has been determined previously by a ranking operation performed by judges. The subject selects the responses that best describe how he feels.

UTILITY: This scale approximates an interval level of measurement. This means that the distance between any two numbers on the scale is of known size. Parametric and nonparametric statistics may be applied. See part 3, guide 5 of this handbook.

CONSTRUCTION:

1. The investigator gathers several hundred statements conceived to be related to the attitude being investigated.
2. A large number of judges (50–300) independently classify the statements in eleven groups ranging from most favorable to neutral to least favorable.
3. The scale value of a statement is computed as the median position to which it is assigned by the group of judges.
4. Statements that have too broad a spread are discarded as ambiguous or irrelevant.
5. The scale is formed by selecting items that are evenly spread along the scale from one extreme to the other.

Example: Brayfield and Roethe's Index of Job Satisfaction. This index is reproduced in part 4, section I. The Thurstone technique is used in the initial development of the scale to provide equal-appearing intervals. The full scale contains eighteen items with Thurstone scale values ranging from 1.2 to 10.0 with approximately .5 step intervals. Some items from the scale representing the job satisfaction continuum are:

My job is like a hobby to me.
I am satisfied with my job for the time being.
I am often bored with my job.
Most of the time I have to force myself to go to work.

RESEARCH APPLICATIONS: Scales have been constructed to measure attitudes toward war, the church, capital punishment, the Chinese, blacks, whites, and institutions.

2.6.b. LIKERT-TYPE SCALE

NATURE: This is a summated scale consisting of a series of items to which the subject responds. The respondent indicates agreement or disagreement with each item on an intensity scale. The Likert technique produces an ordinal scale that generally requires nonparametric statistics. See part 3, guide 5 of this handbook.

UTILITY: This scale is highly reliable when it comes to a rough ordering of people with regard to a particular attitude or attitude complex. The score includes a measure of intensity as expressed on each statement.

CONSTRUCTION:

1. The investigator assembles a large number of items considered relevant to the attitude being investigated and either clearly favorable or unfavorable.
2. These items are administered to a group of subjects representative of those with whom the questionnaire is to be used.
3. The responses to the various items are scored in such a way that a response indicative of the most favorable attitude is given the highest score.
4. Each individual's total score is computed by adding his or her item scores.
5. The responses are analyzed to determine which items differentiate most clearly between the highest and lowest quartiles of total scores.
6. The items that differentiate best (at least six) are used to form a scale.

Example: Rundquist and Sletto Scales of Morale and General Adjustment. See the Minnesota Survey of Opinions (long and short form) as reproduced in part 4, section I. The scales to measure morale and general adjustment, and also inferiority, family, law, and economic conservatism, are examples of the Likert attitude scale technique. A significant characteristic is that each selected statement has been carefully researched to determine its discrimination through a criterion of interval consistency. A second feature is the addition of the intensity dimension to each statement as follows:

The Future Looks Very Black
Strongly agree[5] Agree[4] Undecided[3] Disagree[2] Strongly disagree[1]
Most People Can Be Trusted
Strongly agree[1] Agree[2] Undecided[3] Disagree[4] Strongly disagree[5]

2.6.c. GUTTMAN SCALE-ANALYSIS

NATURE: The Guttman technique attempts to determine the unidimensionality of a scale. Only items meeting the criterion of reproducibility are acceptable as scalable. If a scale is unidimensional, then a person who has a more favorable attitude than another should respond to each statement with equal or greater favorableness than the other.

UTILITY: Each score corresponds to a highly similar response pattern or scale type. It is one of the few scales where the score can be used to predict the response pattern to all statements. Only a few statements (five to ten) are needed to provide a range of scalable responses. Note the analysis below showing how fourteen subjects responded (yes) to several statements and how scores reflect a given pattern of response.

Respondent	Item 7	Item 5	Item 1	Item 8	Item 2	Item 4	Item 6	Item 3	Score
7	yes	yes	yes	yes	yes	yes	yes	–	7
9	yes	yes	yes	yes	yes	yes	yes	–	7
10	yes	yes	yes	yes	yes	yes	–	–	6
1	yes	yes	yes	–	yes	yes	–	yes	6
13	yes	yes	yes	yes	yes	yes	–	–	6
3	yes	yes	yes	yes	yes	–	–	–	5
2	yes	yes	yes	yes	–	–	–	–	4
6	yes	yes	yes	yes	–	–	–	–	4
8	yes	yes	yes	–	–	yes	–	–	4
14	yes	yes	yes	yes	–	–	–	–	4
5	yes	yes	yes	–	–	–	–	–	3
4	yes	yes	–	–	–	–	–	–	2
11	–	–	–	–	yes	–	–	–	1
12	yes	–	–	–	–	–	–	–	1

CONSTRUCTION:

1. Select statements that are felt to apply to the measurable objective.
2. Test statements on a sample population (about 100).
3. Discard statements with more than 80 percent agreement or disagreement.
4. Order respondents from most favorable responses to fewest favorable responses. Order from top to bottom.
5. Order statements from most favorable responses to fewest favorable responses. Order from left to right.
6. Discard statements that fail to discriminate between favorable respondents and unfavorable respondents.
7. Calculate coefficient of reproducibility.
   a. Calculate the number of errors (favorable responses that do not fit pattern)

   b. Reproducibility $= 1 - \dfrac{\text{Number of errors}}{\text{Number of responses}}$

   c. If reproducibility equals .90, a unidimensional scale is said to exist.
9. Score each respondent by the number of favorable responses.

Example: This handbook reproduces two scales constructed by the Guttman attitude scaling technique. These are the Guttman Scales of Military Base Morale (part 4, section I) and a Guttman Scale for Measuring Women's Neighborliness (part 4, section G). The statements must permit a range of opinions and evoke a definite feeling. Note the statements that scaled on air force personnel reflecting their satisfaction with the air force.

I have a poor opinion of the air force most of the time.
Most of the time the air force is not run very well.
I am usually dissatisfied with the air force.
The air force is better than any of the other services.
If I remain in military service I would prefer to remain in the air force.

2.6.d. SCALE-DISCRIMINATION TECHNIQUE

NATURE: This technique seeks to develop a set of items that meet the requirements of a unidimensional scale, possess equal-appearing intervals, and measure intensity. Aspects of the construction of Thurstone's equal-appearing intervals, Likert's summated scales, and Guttman's scale analysis are combined in this technique of Edwards and Kilpatrick.

UTILITY: Three distinct advantages of separate scaling techniques are combined. The interval scale quality of the Thurstone technique can be achieved. The discriminability between respondents and the addition of an intensity measure are derived from the Likert technique, and unidimensionality from the Guttman technique. Caution: Item analysis will eliminate items in the middle of the scale.

CONSTRUCTION:

1. Select a large number of statements that are thought to apply to the attitude being measured.
2. Discard items that are ambiguous or too extreme.
3. Give the statements to judges and have them judge the favorableness of each statement and place it in one of eleven categories.
4. Discard half the items with the greatest scatter or variance.
5. Assign scores to the remaining items as the median of the judges' scores.
6. Formulate the statements in the form of a summated scale and give to a new set of judges.
7. Perform an item analysis to determine which questions discriminate best between the lowest and highest quartiles.
8. Select twice the number of items that are wanted in the final scale. Select from each scale interval the statements that discriminate best.
9. Divide these statements in half.
10. Submit halves to separate test groups.
11. Determine coefficients of reproducibility for each test group and use if .90 or above.

2.6.e. RATING SCALES

NATURE: This technique seeks to obtain an evaluation or a quantitative judgment of personality, group, or institutional characteristics based upon personal judgments. The rater places the person or object being rated at some point along a continuum or in one of an ordered series of categories; a numerical value is attached to the point or the category.

UTILITY: Rating scales can be used to assess attitudes, values, norms, social activities, and social structural features.

CONSTRUCTION:

1. Divide the continuum to be measured into an optimal number of scale divisions (approximately 5–7).
2. The continuum should have no breaks or divisions.
3. The positive and negative poles should be alternated.

4. Introduce each trait with a question to which the rater can give an answer.
5. Use descriptive adjectives or phrases to define different points on the continuum.
6. Decide beforehand upon the probable extremes of the trait to be found in the group in which the scale is to be used.
7. Only universally understood descriptive terms should be used.
8. The end phrases should not be so extreme in meaning as to be avoided by the raters.
9. Descriptive phrases need not be evenly spaced.
10. Pretest. Ask respondents to raise any questions about the rating and the different points on the continuum if they are unclear.
11. To score, use numerical values as assigned.

Example: Miller's Scale Battery of International Patterns and Norms reproduced in part 4, section J, contains twenty rating scales to ascertain important norms and patterns within national cultures. The significant feature is the meaningful continuum that can be developed with approximately worded statements or adjectives for each point on the continuum. The scale can be designed so that the researcher or the respondent may make the rating. An example of a rating scale is item 7, Moral Code and Role Definitions of Men and Women, taken from the Miller Scale Battery of International Patterns and Norms.

7. Moral Code and Role Definitions of Men and Women

1	2	3	4	5	6
Single code of morality prevails for men and women. Separate occupational and social roles are not defined for men and women. Similar amounts and standards of education prevail.		Variations between moral definitions for men and women exist for certain specified behaviors. Occupational and social role definitions vary in degree. Varying educational provisions for the sexes.		Double code of morality prevails. Separate occupational and social roles for men and women exist and are sharply defined. Amount and standards of education vary widely between the sexes.	

2.6.f. LATENT DISTANCE SCALES

NATURE: A technique for scalogram analysis based on a probability model, that attempts to apply to qualitative data the principles of factor analysis providing ordinal information. The basic postulate is that there exists a set of latent classes such that the manifest relationship between any two or more items on a questionnaire can be accounted for by the existence of these latent classes and by these alone.

UTILITY: Unlike scalogram analysis, this technique includes imperfect scale types in the analysis without considering them as mistakes.

CONSTRUCTION:

1. List questions believed to be related to the latent attitude.

2. Dichotomize answers to questions in terms of positive-negative, favorable-unfavorable, etc.
3. Calculate proportion of respondents who demonstrate latent attitude in each response.
4. Arrange items in terms of their manifest marginals.
5. Compute the latent class frequencies through inverse-probability procedures.
6. Rank response patterns in terms of average latent position or use an index to characterize each response pattern.

Example: Latent Distance Scale on Neurotic Inventory

1. Have you ever been bothered by pressure or pains in the head?
   Positive answer: Yes, Often or Yes, Sometimes or No
   Answer   13.8%
2. Have you ever been bothered by shortness of breath when you were not exercising or working hard?
   Positive answer: Yes, Often or Yes, Sometimes or No
   Answer   30.7%
3. Do your hands ever tremble ever enough to bother you?
   Positive answer: Yes, Often or Yes, Sometimes or No
   Answer   43.1%
4. Do you often have trouble in getting to sleep or staying asleep?
   Positive answer: Very Often or No Answer   57.1%

Complete Analysis of Latent Distance Scale on Neurotic Inventory

Response pattern 1 2 3 4	Percent of each pattern in latent class					Fitted total	Actual total
	n_I	n_{II}	n_{III}	n_{IV}	n_V		
+ + + +	94.9%	4.2%	0.8%	0.1%	0.0%	100%	76.8	75
+ + – +	90.0	3.9	0.7	4.6	0.8	100%	14.6	10
+ + + –	90.4	4.0	0.7	0.1	4.8	100%	5.8	8
+ – + +	66.8	2.9	24.5	5.0	0.8	100%	16.3	14
– + + +	2.5	79.3	14.7	3.0	0.5	100%	108.3	110
– – + +	0.3	8.8	73.5	14.9	2.5	100%	145.4	141
– + – +	1.3	38.9	7.2	45.1	7.5	100%	39.7	49
+ – – +	24.5	1.1	9.0	56.1	9.3	100%	8.0	11
– – – +	0.0	1.4	11.9	74.3	12.4	100%	161.9	161
+ + – –	36.7	1.6	0.3	1.9	59.5	100%	2.6	3
– + + –	1.3	40.7	7.6	1.5	48.9	100%	15.2	11
+ – + –	25.9	1.2	9.5	1.9	61.5	100%	3.0	8
– – + –	0.1	1.5	12.8	2.6	83.0	100%	60.2	64
– + – –	0.1	2.5	0.5	2.9	94.0	100%	44.0	41
+ – – –	1.3	0.0	0.5	3.0	95.2	100%	10.9	9
– – – –	0.0	0.1	0.5	3.0	96.4	100%	287.3	285
Total in each class	109.9	129.5	161.3	181.4	417.9		1,000.0	1,000

The above items were taken from a neurotic inventory presented by Samuel A. Stouffer, *The American Soldier: Measurement and Prediction* (Princeton, N.J.: Princeton University Press, 1949), 4: 445. Consult the book for instruction in this technique or see section 2.9 of this handbook. The bibliography on Index and Scale Construction will prove useful. Paul F. Lazarsfeld developed latent structure analysis. See Lazarsfeld, "Recent Developments in Latent Structure Analysis," *Sociometry* 18 (December 1955): 647–59.

2.6.g. PAIRED COMPARISONS

NATURE: This technique seeks to determine psychological values of qualitative stimuli without knowledge of any corresponding respondent values. By asking respondents to select the more favorable of a pair of statements or objects over a set of several pairs, an attempt is made to order the statements or objects along a continuum. It is sometimes called the forced-choices technique. Note how it is applied in the Neal and Seeman Powerlessness Scale reproduced in part 4, section J.

UTILITY: The ordering by paired comparisons is a relatively rapid process for securing a precise and relative positioning along a continuum. Comparative ordering generally increases reliability and validity over arbitrary rating methods.

CONSTRUCTION:

1. Select statements that relate to the attribute being measured.
2. Combine statements in all possible combination of pairs. $\dfrac{N(N-1)}{2}$
3. Ask judges to select which statement of each pair is the more favorable.
4. Calculate the proportion of judgments each statement received over every other statement.
5. Total the proportions for each statement.
6. Translate the proportions into standardized scale values.
7. Apply an internal consistency check by computing the absolute average discrepancy.
8. Present statements to respondents and ask them to indicate favorableness or unfavorableness to each statement.
9. Respondent's score is the median of his favorable responses.

Example: Hill's Scale of Attitudes Toward Involvement in the Korean War*

Item set favorable to U.S. involvement in Korea	Paired comparison scale score
1. I suppose the United States has no choice but to continue the Korean war.	0.00
2. We should be willing to give our allies in Korea more money if they need it.	0.74
3. Withdrawing our troops from Korea at this time would only make matters worse.	0.98
4. The Korean war might not be the best way to stop communism, but it was the only thing we could do.	1.07
5. Winning the Korean war is absolutely necessary whatever the cost.	1.25
6. We are protecting the United States by fighting in Korea.	1.46
7. The reason we are in Korea is to defend freedom.	1.71

*From Richard J. Hill, "A Note on Inconsistency in Paired Comparison Judgments," *American Sociological Review* 18 (October 1953): 564–66. Richard Ofshe and Ronald E. Anderson have translated Hill's Korea items to Vietnam and the Vietnam scale is described in "Testing a Measurement Model," in *Sociological Methodology*, ed. Edgar F. Borgatta (San Francisco: Jossey-Bass, 1969).

2.6.h. SEMANTIC DIFFERENTIAL

NATURE: The semantic differential seeks to measure the meaning of an object to an individual. The subject is asked to rate a given concept (e.g., "Negro," "Republican," "wife," "me as I would like to be," "me as I am") on a series of seven-point, bipolar rating scales. Any concept, whether it is a political issue, a person, an institution, or a work of art, can be rated. The seven-point scales include such bipolar scales as the following: (A) fair–unfair, clean–dirty, good–bad, valuable–worthless; (B) large–small, strong–weak, heavy–light; (C) active–passive, fast–slow, hot–cold. The rating is made according to the respondent's perception of the relatedness or association of the adjective to the word concept. Osgood and his colleagues have inferred that the three subgroups (A), (B), and (C) measure the following three dimensions of attitude:

A—the individual's *evaluation* of the object or concept being rated, corresponding to the favorable–unfavorable dimension of more traditional attitude scales.

B—the individual's perception of the *potency* or power of the object or concept.

C—his perception of the *activity* of the object or concept.

The authors suggest that the measuring instrument is not grossly affected by the nature of the object being measured or by the type of persons using the scale. For further information see the developers of the semantic differential: Charles E. Osgood, George J. Suci, and Percy H. Tannenbaum, *The Measurement of Meaning* (Urbana: University of Illinois Press, 1957).

UTILITY: A 100-item test can be administered in about ten to fifteen minutes. A 400-item test takes about one hour. The semantic differential may be adapted through choice of concepts and scales to the study of numerous phenomena. It may be useful in constructing and analyzing sociometric scales.

CONSTRUCTION:

1. Prepare a list of concepts appropriate to the theory guiding the variable to be measured.
2. Pairs of polar adjectives are selected on a priori grounds.
3. Selection of adjectives are determined empirically by asking different groups (comparative or experimental-control design) to take prescribed orientations in responding to an adjective-rating task. For example, one group of respondents is asked to rate as it believes a person would rate the concept if he held a positive attitude; another group of respondents is asked to rate as it believes a person would rate the concept if he held a strong negative attitude.

   Respondents are given the standard instructions for using the semantic differential form (Osgood, Suci, and Tannenbaum, *Measurement of Meaning*). Analyze data and select adjective pairs that distinguish clearly between the groups.
4. Select new groups of respondents who take prescribed orientations in rating the concepts. Analyze data. For guidance, again see Osgood, Suci, and Tannenbaum.

A SAMPLE OF A SEMANTIC DIFFERENTIAL SCALE*

Fifteen concepts:

Love, Child, My Doctor, Me, My Job, Mental Sickness, My Mother, Peace of Mind, Fraud, My Spouse, Self-control, Hatred, My Father, Confusion, Sex

Each concept was rated on the following ten scales:

valuable	___:___:___:___:___:___:___	worthless
clean	___:___:___:___:___:___:___	dirty
tasty	___:___:___:___:___:___:___	distasteful
large	___:___:___:___:___:___:___	small
strong	___:___:___:___:___:___:___	weak
deep	___:___:___:___:___:___:___	shallow
fast	___:___:___:___:___:___:___	slow
active	___:___:___:___:___:___:___	passive
hot	___:___:___:___:___:___:___	cold
tense	___:___:___:___:___:___:___	relaxed

*This sample Semantic Differential was used in a study reported by Charles E. Osgood and Zella Luria, "A Blind Analysis of a Case of Multiple Personality Using the Semantic Differential," *Journal of Abnormal and Social Psychology* 49 (1954): 579–91.

2.6.i. MULTIDIMENSIONAL SCALING

The majority of scaling techniques that have been described produce one-dimensional scales, i.e., the scales consist of a single continuum along which are located a succession of the opinion items. Multidimensional scaling is a technique that is increasingly of interest to the social sciences. In psychophysics multidimensional scaling has been utilized for some time.[1] In the study of attitudes, however, there is a dearth of satisfactory methods, but there is nothing to prevent the adoption of the multidimensional method to the attitude domain. The key concept involved is that of social or psychological distance. Social distance is well known; see, for example, the Bogardus scale and the research cited in part 4. Psychological distance is a concept employed in approach and avoidance gradient theory[2] and in Lewin's field theory.[3]

If social or psychological distance can be analyzed as though it were physical distance, it would be possible to draw a "map" of the way in which an individual structures the similarities and differences among attitudes (or behavioral or organizational characteristics) in a given domain. On such a map, short distances would represent similarity or agreement, and long distances would represent dissimilarity or disagreement. Multidimensional scales based upon the interpretation of dissimilarities or disagreements as distances have already been constructed with nonpsychological stimuli.[4]

For students interested in multidimensional scaling, a good model is that of

Robert P. Abelson, "A Technique and a Model for Multi-Dimensional Attitude Scaling," *Public Opinion Quarterly* (Winter 1954–55): 405–18. Also reprinted in Martin Fishbein, ed., *Readings in Attitude Theory and Measurement* (New York: John Wiley, 1967), pp. 147–56.

Students interested in applying multidimensional scaling to social characteristics should see Joel H. Levine, "The Sphere of Influence," *American Sociological Review* 37 (February 1972): 14–27. Levine describes an analysis of a network of interlocking directorates, specifically the network in which the boards of major banks interact with the boards of major industrials in the United States. He constructs maps showing "spheres of influence." The sectors of the sphere represent similarly linked corporations, and the relations among the sectors represent the relations among bank industrial communities. Smallest-space analysis is utilized.

Another very interesting application of multidimensional scaling can be found in Edward O. Laumann, "The Social Structure of Religious and Ethnoreligious Groups in a Metropolitan Community," *American Sociological Review* 3, 4 (April 1969): 182–97. The relatively new technique of smallest-space analysis is used to analyze the formation of friendship relations among 15 religious and 27 ethnoreligious groups. Indexes of Dissimilarity of friendship choices are computed, and three dimensional solutions are mapped.

Good treatments of multidimensional scaling for advanced students are Clyde H. Coombs, *A Theory of Data* (New York: John Wiley, 1967), pp. 444–95; and Warren S. Torgerson, *Theory and Methods of Scaling* (New York: John Wiley, 1960), pp. 247–97.

Notes

1. M. W. Richardson, "Multidimensional Psychophysics," *Psychological Bulletin* 35 (1938): 659–60.
2. N. Miner, "Comment on Theoretical Models," *Journal of Personality* 20 (1951): 82–100.
3. Kurt Lewin, *Principles of Topological Psychology* (New York: McGraw-Hill, 1936).
4. F. L. Klingberg, "Studies in Measurement of the Relations Among Sovereign States," *Psychometrika* 6 (1941): 335–52; C. E. Osgood and G. J. Suci, "A Measure of Relations Determined by Both Mean Difference and Profile Information," *Psychological Bulletin* 49 (1952): 251–62.

GUIDE TO BODIES OF COLLECTED DATA FOR THE SOCIAL SCIENCE RESEARCHER: DATA REFERENCES AND DATA ARCHIVES   2.7

Instructions for the Use of Guide 2.7

Two major kinds of information resources are important to the researcher. The first contains bibliographic *references* to documents that contain data; the second consists of *collected data* such as population characteristics, public opinion, or voting records. The modern researcher explores both sources before embarking on the expensive task of collecting new data. Today great stores of data are available, often at no cost or limited cost. Data seldom are exhaustively analyzed by the original research effort, although the initial collection may have cost hundreds of thousands of dollars. It may be an unexplored gold mine of data for the problem a researcher wishes to investigate. A review of data sources is now as important as a review of the research literature.

Data References

Directory of Data Bases in the Social and Behaviorial Sciences, edited by Vivian Sessions. Science Associates/International, Inc., 23 East 26 Street, New York, N.Y. 10010. 1974. 300 pp.

Contains references for some 1500 groups of data files from over 650 organizations throughout the world, representing the data holdings of governmental, academic, and commercial organizations. Information on data files includes major subject field, title, time frame of data, geographic coverage, data sources, and data collection agency. Also contains profiles of reporting organizations. Completely indexed.

The National Archives and Statistical Research, edited by Meyer H. Fishbein. Ohio University Press, Athens, Ohio 45701. 1973. 255 pp.

Proceedings of a conference held May 27 and 28, 1968, cosponsored by the National Archives and Records Service and the National Academy of Science. Examines statistical data available in the records of the National Archives; discusses uses by economists, historians, geographers, political scientists, sociologists, and statisticians; and discusses current production of conventional and electronic statistical source records as well as criteria for preserving records for future research.

The Review of Public Data Use. Data Use and Access Laboratories (DUALabs), Suite 900, 1601 North Kent Street, Arlington, Va. 22209.

This is an interdisciplinary journal published by a nonprofit corporation and devoted to the spectrum of intellectual activity associated with public data access and use. It publishes primary articles and current awareness information on social science research and methodology using publicly available data bases as well as planning and research in state and local government fields. In addition, it covers computer software for accessing statistical data files, information technology, technical problems of data file use, legislation and administrative actions affecting public access, and foreign developments.

S S Data. Newsletter of Social Science Archival Acquisitions, 321A Schaffer Hall, University of Iowa, Iowa City, Iowa 52242. Published quarterly in September, December, March, and June by the Laboratory for Political Research of the University of Iowa.

Its purpose is to communicate information on the current acquisitions of social science data archives to social science researchers. More than 40 archives are now cooperating in providing information about the original data collection agency and principal investigator, the time period of the data, the population covered, and a paragraph describing the substance of the study.* The information received is classified under Sociology, Political Science, History, Public Opinion Surveys, and Miscellaneous. The newsletter also publishes descriptions of the archives participating in the project and information on new technical developments that enhance the use of machine-readable data for research and instruction.

1975 Directory of Computerized Data Files and Related Software Available from Federal Agencies. National Technical Information Service, Springfield, Va. 1975. This directory is a product of the National Technical Information Service (NTIS) of the U.S. Department of Commerce.

This is essentially a bibliographic project. A few of the 72 subject fields are consumer affairs, elections, immigration, price statistics and price indexes, state and local government finance, and international relations. Although originally weak in the "soft sciences," the system is now more heavily committed to the social sciences, and to the urban area in

*See List of Cooperating Archives as shown in this Handbook, pp. 101–3.

particular. NTIS, for those who are unfamiliar with it, offers numerous bibliographic information services: a weekly index to documents wholly or partially funded by federal money in just about every aspect of human endeavor, a weekly abstract service for the most significant documents in specialty areas, information retrieval services either in batch mode through direct query to NTIS or on-line through both the Lockheed and the Systems Development dial-up systems, and physical access to the documents themselves in either microform or hard copy. Each NTIS reference to a data file has an identifying title, a date, name of the generating agency, the distributing agency (if different), notes about the number of tapes in each file, the density of the tapes, the number of tracks, and the coding structure. There is also an abstract of about 100 words describing the contents of the file as to subject, kinds of variables, and the number of records in the file. The subject index, in addition to providing subject access to the contents of the 530 computerized data files listed in this edition of the *Directory*, is also a good source of terminology for others who are faced with the problem of analyzing the contents of data files. (This description is drawn from Vivian S. Sessions, *Public Data Use* 3 [January 1975] : 3.) Of special interest to the social scientist is the weekly *Behavior and Society*, containing government abstracts of social research projects.

University On-Line Computer Searches for Social Scientists

An increasing number of universities are providing their own on-line bibliographic search. For example, Indiana University has a contract with the Lockheed Retrieval Service which furnishes the following data references:

Sociological Abstracts On-Line.

Over 60,000 citations from the world's sociological literature. Coverage is from 1963 to present. File is updated quarterly.

Social Scisearch On-Line.

Equivalent to printed *Social Sciences Citation Index*. Journal literature and books in the social and behavioral sciences. Covers from 1972 to present. Updated monthly. Growth is 80,000 items per year.

Social Science Data Archives in the United States*

This section contains two lists of sources for collected social data. The first contains members of the original Council of Social Science Data Archives. The type of data and subject matter are shown. The second list contains those archives currently cooperating with the Laboratory for Political Research, University of Iowa. There is overlap but together the two lists represent a fairly exhaustive bibliography of social data. For employment of data banks those researchers described by Hymans demonstrate how productive use can be made of such archival data.** Deutsch's statement about comparisons across time, space, concepts, and methods illustrate that the surface of prospects for data bank use is barely scratched.†

*Assembled and described by David Nasatir, asst. research sociologist, Survey Research Center, University of California, Berkeley, Calif. *The American Sociologist* 2 (November 1967): 207–12.

**Herbert Hyman, *Secondary Analysis of Sample Surveys* (New York: Wiley, 1972).

†Karl W. Deutsch, "The Impact of Complex Data Bases on the Social Sciences," in *Data Bases, Computers and the Social Sciences*, ed. Ralph Bisco (New York: Wiley, 1970), pp. 19–41.

Table 1. *Members of the Council of Social Science Data Archives*[1]

Name of data library	Address	Type of data	Subject matter
Archive on Political Elites in Eastern Europe	Dept. of Political Science 1028 H Cathedral of Learning University of Pittsburgh Pittsburgh, Pa. 15123	Biographical information	Political elites in Eastern Europe
Archive on Comparative Political Elites	Dept. of Political Science University of Oregon Eugene, Ore. 97403		
Bureau of Applied Social Research	Columbia University 605 West 115 Street New York, N.Y. 10025	Sample surveys	Health and welfare occupations and professions, mass communications, politics, education, organizations
Bureau of Labor Statistics[2]	United States Department of Lab.		
Carleton University, Social Science Data Archive	Dept. of Political Science Carleton University Colonel By Drive Ottawa 1, Canada	Sample surveys, Biographies, Election statistics, Census data	Politics and public opinion
Center for International Studies Data Bank	Mass. Inst. of Technology E53-365, Hermann Building Cambridge, Mass. 02139	Sample surveys	Politics, social behavior, public opinion
Columbia University School of Public Health and Administrative Medicine Research Archives	630 West 168 Street New York, N.Y. 10032	Sample surveys, Operational data	Administrative medicine, public health
Council for Inter-Societal Studies	Northwestern University 1818 Sheridan Road Evanston, Ill. 60201		
National Opinion Research Center	University of Chicago 6030 South Ellis Avenue Chicago, Ill. 60637	Sample surveys	Health and welfare, mass communication, community problems
Political Science Research Library and Political Data Program	Yale University 89 Trumbell Street New Haven, Conn. 06520	Sample surveys	Studies from Roper ICPR in political science
Public Opinion Survey Unit	Research Center, School of Business & Public Administ. University of Missouri Columbia, Mo. 65201	Sample surveys	Politics and public opinion in Missouri, U.S.
Project Talent Data Bank	132 North Bellefield Avenue Pittsburgh, Pa. 15213	Sample surveys	High school student attitudes surveys, career plans, aptitude tests
Roper Public Opinion Research Center[2]	Williams College Williamstown, Mass. 01267	Sample surveys	Politics, economics, business, education, public opinion
Social Science Data and Program Library Service[2]	Social Systems Research Inst. Rm. 4451, Social Science Bldg. University of Wisconsin Madison, Wis. 53703	Sample surveys	Economics, demography

Table 1. *(Continued)*

Name of data library	Address	Type of data	Subject matter
Survey Research Laboratory	437 David Kinley Hall University of Illinois Urbana, Ill. 61801	Sample surveys, Statistics	Politics, economics, public opinion
UCLA Political Behavior Archive	Dept. of Political Science University of California Los Angeles, Calif. 90024		
Yale Growth Center	Yale University 52 Hillhouse Avenue New Haven, Conn. 06520	National accounts	Country analysis of under-developed nations
Graduate School of Industrial Administra-tion	Carnegie Inst. of Technology Pittsburgh, Pa. 15213	Ecological statistics, Sample surveys	French cantons: election and demographic statistics
Human Relations Area Files	Yale University P.O. Box 2054 Yale Station New Haven, Conn. 06520	Some machine-readable data, reports, bibliog-raphies, texts	Social structure, organiza-tion: diet practices, kinship
International Data Library and Reference Service[2]	Survey Research Center 2220 Piedmont Avenue University of California Berkeley, Calif. 94720	Sample surveys	Politics, communication, social behavior. Em-phasis on Asia, Latin America
International Develop-ment Data Bank	Michigan State University 322 Union Building East Lansing, Mich. 48823		List of Archive holdings is available
Inter-University Consortium for Political Research[2]	University of Michigan P.O. Box 1248 Ann Arbor, Mich. 48106	Sample surveys	Political behavior Public opinion
Laboratory for Political Research	Dept. of Political Science University of Iowa Iowa City, Iowa 52240	Sample surveys, Voting studies	Politics; biography data on American and Argentine legislators
Louis Harris Political Data Center[2]	Dept. of Political Science University of North Carolina Cardwell Hall Chapel Hill, N.C. 27514	Public-opinion surveys	Politics in individual states in U.S.

[1]This is not an exhaustive list of data archives as it contains only those who had affiliated with the Council of Social Science Data Archives. The Council itself is not currently active. The List of Archives Cooperating with the Laboratory for Political Research, University of Iowa (below) provides a fuller list.

[2]General purpose, service-oriented libraries. Materials in these libraries are routinely available to the entire community of social scientists.

Table 2. List of Archives Cooperating with the Laboratory for Political Research, University of Iowa*

Project TALENT Data Bank
AMERICAN INSTITUTES FOR RESEARCH
P.O. Box 1113
Palo Alto, Calif. 94302

Evert Brouwer, Manager
AMSTERDAMS SOCIAALWETENSCHAPPELIJK DATA ARCHIEF
University of Amsterdam
Room 143 - Roetersstraat 15
Amsterdam, Netherlands

William Klecka, Director
BEHAVIORAL SCIENCES LABORATORY
University of Cincinnati
Cincinnati, Ohio 45221

Philippe Laurent
BELGIAN ARCHIVES FOR THE SOCIAL SCIENCES
Van Evenstraat 2A, Room 04-05
3000 Louvain, Belgium

Table 2. *(Continued)*

Data Archivist
BUREAU OF APPLIED SOCIAL RESEARCH
Columbia University
New York, N.Y. 10025

Arthur S. Banks, Director
CENTER FOR COMPARATIVE POLITICAL RESEARCH
State University of New York
Binghampton, N.Y. 13901

Alice Robbin
DATA & PROGRAM LIBRARY SERVICE
4451 Social Science Building
University of Wisconsin
Madison, Wis. 53706

David Amos
DATA LIBRARY
Computing Centre
University of British Columbia
Vancouver 8, British Columbia
Canada

Librarian
Information Documentation Center
DUALABS, INC.
1601 North Kent Street, Suite 900
Arlington, Va. 22209

Stein Rokkan, Director
EUROPEAN CONSORTIUM FOR POLITICAL RESEARCH
Data Information Service
Gamel Kalvedalsveien 12
N-5000 Bergen, Norway

Thomas Atkinson, Director
Data Bank
INSTITUTE FOR BEHAVIORAL RESEARCH
York University
4700 Keele Street
Downsview, Ontario
Canada

Data Librarian
INTERNATIONAL DATA LIBRARY & REFERENCE SERVICE
Survey Research Center
University of California
Berkeley, Calif. 94720

Survey Research Archive
Historical Archive
International Relations Archive
INTER-UNIVERSITY CONSORTIUM FOR POLITICAL RESEARCH
P.O. Box 1248
Ann Arbor, Mich. 48106

ISR SOCIAL SCIENCE ARCHIVE
P.O. Box 1248
Ann Arbor, Mich. 48106

Manuel J. Carvajal, Director
LATIN AMERICAN DATA BANK
Room 471 International Studies Building
University of Florida
Gainesville, Fla. 32601

Charles Dollar, Chief
Machine-readable Archives Division (NNR)
NATIONAL ARCHIVES AND RECORDS SERVICE
Washington, D.C. 20408

Patrick Bova
NATIONAL OPINION RESEARCH CENTER
University of Chicago
6030 South Ellis Avenue
Chicago, Ill. 60637

Lorraine Borman
NORTHWESTERN UNIVERSITY INFORMATION CENTER
Vogelback Computing Center
Northwestern University
Evanston, Ill. 60201

Eugene J. Watts
OHIO DATA ARCHIVES
Ohio Historical Society
Ohio Historical Center
Columbus, Ohio 43211

Richard Hofstetter
POLIMETRICS LABORATORY
Department of Political Science
Ohio State University
Columbus, Ohio 43210

Elizabeth Powell, Associate Director
POLITICAL SCIENCE DATA ARCHIVE
Department of Political Science
Michigan State University
East Lansing, Mich. 48823

Ronald Weber, Director
POLITICAL SCIENCE LABORATORY AND DATA ARCHIVE
Department of Political Science
248 Woodburn Hall
Indiana University
Bloomington, Ind. 47401

Philip K. Hastings
ROPER PUBLIC OPINION RESEARCH CENTER
P.O. Box 624
Williams College
Williamstown, Mass. 02167

SOCIAL DATA EXCHANGE ASSOCIATION
333 Grotto Avenue
Providence, R.I.

James Grifhorst
SOCIAL SCIENCE DATA ARCHIVE
Laboratory for Political Research
321A Schaeffer Hall
University of Iowa
Iowa City, Iowa 52242

Lucinda Conger
SOCIAL SCIENCE DATA ARCHIVE
Social Science Library
Yale University
Box 1958 Yale Station
New Haven, Conn. 06520

Daniel Amick
SOCIAL SCIENCE DATA ARCHIVE
Survey Research Laboratory
414 Kinley Hall
Urbana, Ill. 61810

Peter C. Tolos
SOCIAL SCIENCE DATA ARCHIVE
UCLA Survey Research Center
Los Angeles, Calif. 90024

Tony Falsetto
SOCIAL SCIENCE DATA ARCHIVES
Department of Sociology
Carleton University
Ottawa 1, Canada

Everett C. Ladd, Jr.
SOCIAL SCIENCE DATA CENTER
University of Connecticut
Storrs, Conn. 06268

Neal E. Cutler
SOCIAL SCIENCE DATA CENTER
University of Pennsylvania
3508 Market Street—Suite 350
Philadelphia, Pa. 19104

Sue A. Dodd
SOCIAL SCIENCE DATA LIBRARY
University of North Carolina
Room 10, Manning Hall
Chapel Hill, N.C. 27514

SOCIAL SCIENCE INFORMATION CENTER
621 Social Science Bldg.
University of Pittsburgh
Pittsburgh, Pa. 15213

Judith S. Rowe
SOCIAL SCIENCE USER SERVICE
Princeton University Computer Center
87 Prospect Avenue
Princeton, N.J. 08540

Jack Elinson
SOCIOMEDICAL RESEARCH ARCHIVES
Columbia University School of Public Health
Black Research Building
630 West 168th Street
New York, N.Y. 10032

Director
SSRC SURVEY ARCHIVE
University of Essex
Colchester
England

William E. Bicker, Director
Neal McGowan, Senior Programmer
STATE DATA PROGRAM
Institute of Governmental Studies
109 Morse Hall
University of California
Berkeley, Calif. 94720

Cees P. Middendorp
STEINMETZ ARCHIVES
Information and Documentation Centre for the Social Sciences
Royal Netherlands Academy of Arts and Sciences
Keizersgracht 569-571
Amsterdam, Netherlands

ZENTRALARCHIV FUR EMPIRISCHE SOZIALFORSCHUNG
Universitat zu Koln
5 Koln
Bachemer Str. 40
Germany

*List as shown in *S.S. Data*, Newsletter of Social Science Archival Acquisitions 4 (March 1975): 15–16.

Recently Established Washington Base for Archives of Institutional Change

An organization has been formed in Washington, D.C., to survey the social responses of institutions devoted to the advancement and application of knowledge. The Archives of Institutional Change is a nonprofit documentation center that collects reports and published findings of studies of educational and research institutions, libraries, learned and professional societies, museums, experimental social services, and comparable establishments, primarily in North America. In cooperation with Acropolis Books of Washington, D.C., the Archives has published a number of institutional studies in a series with the overall title of *Prometheus*. The titles of the first four books were as follows: *The Bankruptcy of Academic Policy; Scientific Institutions of the Future; Talent Waste—How Institutions of Learning Misdirect Human Resources;* and *Documenting Change in the Institutions of Knowledge—A Prometheus Bibliography.*

Inquiries are invited and may be addressed to the Archives of Institutional

Change, Georgetown Office Service Center, 3160 O Street, N.W., Washington, D.C. 20007.

2.8 GUIDE TO THE U.S. CENSUS AND BUREAU OF LABOR STATISTICS: DATA REFERENCES AND DATA ARCHIVES

Instruction for the Use of Guide 2.8

The U.S. Census is one of the richest sources of primary data for the social scientist. The data are collected at ten-year intervals as a national enumeration of the U.S. population. Various survey samples of many different kinds are taken at intervals between the decennial censuses. Because of its magnitude and importance, a special section has been prepared. Data references are first shown and then the character of the data bank is described. Almost every field of sociology can draw upon this magnificent collection, and the U.S. Census staff are anxious to help the researcher.

The Bureau of Labor Statistics in the Department of Labor is an excellent complement to the U.S. Census. It gathers a large amount of information on occupations and the changes affecting them. It is a major source of data about cost of living, wages, strikes, and industrial relations generally. The Bureau reports are topically presented with data and interpretation. The Bureau will cooperate with researchers seeking data relevant to the responsibilities of the office.

Data References: General and Specialized Guides to the U.S. Census

The Bureau of the Census has prepared a number of guides to the Census including the following:

Bureau of the Census Catalog

Descriptions of all Census Bureau materials, published and unpublished. Indexes to subjects, states, and local areas. Quarterly, cumulative to annual, with monthly supplements.

Bureau of the Census Catalog of Publications, 1790–1972

Bibliographic guide to the content and development of all census publications. Comprehensive subject index; geographic index since 1945.

Census Data for Community Action

Simple instructions for using 1970 census data.

Guide to Foreign Trade Statistics

Examples of tables from each report.

Guide to Programs and Publications, Subjects and Areas

Content of programs and reports in outline form. Indexes to subjects and to geographic areas.

Guide to Recurrent and Special Government Studies, GSS-62

Examples of tables from each report.

Mini-Guide to the 1972 Economic Censes

Concise reference guide to census information on business, construction, industry, and transportation.

1970 Census Users' Guide: Part 1

Definitions of terms and applications of population and housing data. Indexes to programs and concepts.

Each of the Guides reports on some aspects of the Bureau's data files. The *Bureau of the Census Catalog*, issued quarterly, publishes reports and data files currently available. Since 1964 each issue has had a section on Data Files and Special Tabulations. A current issue describes the data held and available to users.

U.S. Census Data Files and Special Tabulations

The Bureau of the Census publishes only essential and widely useful data in its printed reports of censuses and surveys, but much more information is available to the public. The Bureau maintains data files that can be processed to provide almost unlimited subject cross-classifications and area tabulations. Some of these tape and punchcard files, which do not contain confidential individual records, may be purchased and used by the purchaser for making tabulations. All files, under appropriate circumstances, can be used by the Bureau to prepare tabulations specified by customers. Special tabulations can also be prepared directly from files of filled-in questionnaires. Tabulations made from individual records are subject to review to make certain that the results are in such summary form that no individual information is disclosed. Some unpublished nonstatistical information is also available, including maps, computer programs, and address directories of public officials.

The materials are arranged according to major subject field. Within each field, the items generally are separated into two groups, Data Files and Selected Special Tabulations, with the occasional use of a third category, Other Materials. Under Data Files are listed the large machine-readable files that have become available during the period covered by this issue of the *Catalog*; the contents of each are described, and the description indicates whether the files are for sale or may be used only by the Census Bureau to prepare tabulations for individual customers. Under Selected Special Tabulations are listed examples of tabulations prepared during the current period for individual users. Under Other Materials are maps and computer programs as well as materials that have become available during the period covered by this issue of the *Catalog*.

A section describing available machine-readable materials first appeared in the 1964 *Catalog*. It provided information on many data files of the 1960 Censuses of Population and Housing, the 1959 Census of Agriculture, the 1958 Census of Business and Manufactures, the 1962 Census of Governments, the *County and City Data Book*, and other series which have not been repeated in later issues of the Catalog. The 1969 edition of *Guide to Census Bureau Data Files and Special Tabulations* provides a cumulative inventory of items still available for the period 1958 through 1968.

For detailed information about any item listed, write to the Chief of the Division named at the beginning of each section. When inquiring about a file or special tabulation, please specify the catalog item number.

The Bureau's data files are of two basic types: (1) those containing the basic records on the individual respondents (i.e., the returns for each person, establishment, and the like), and (2) those containing statistical totals (i.e., summarizations for small areas or for detailed subject classifications). The description of each file indicates whether it is for sale or may be used only by the Census Bureau for preparation of special tabulations for the buyer.

Basic record tapes. The tapes containing basic individual records are in nearly all cases confidential; therefore the Bureau cannot sell them but can prepare special tabulations from them. However, certain sets of nonconfidential individual records on tapes and punchcards (as described in the *Guide to Census Bureau Data Files and Special Tabulations* mentioned above) can be purchased from the Bureau. The Bureau has prepared for sale tape files containing 1/100, 1/1,000, and 1/10,000 samples of individual records from the 1960 and 1970 Censuses of Population and Housing by removing all information that might make possible identification of any person, household, or housing unit. The Bureau also makes available the nonconfidential returns from some of the public agencies that report on their activities for the Bureau's surveys, for example, information from each building permit-issuing jurisdiction is available on computer tapes.

Summary tapes. Some summary tapes are available; these contain small-area totals that were subsequently added together by the computer to obtain the results required for the published tables. Summary tapes are generally useful for further machine processing to obtain totals for areas not shown separately in the published reports or for preparing derived measures (averages, ratios, etc.) for specific geographic areas. The data on these tapes can also be obtained as printouts of the tape content. Such displays are accompanied by technical memoranda explaining the content and organization of the display and supplying identification for the totals.

In addition to the data described above, some files contain the same statistics found in published reports; these files are made available for users who wish to summarize further or to rearrange the published data. Examples of such data files are the computer tape "copies" of all editions of the *County and City Data Book*, which are also available on punchcards on a special-order basis.

Punchcard files. All punchcards are of the 80-column type.

Documentation furnished with tapes and punchcard files. Furnished with all purchases of computer tapes and punchcard files are descriptions of the data, a layout of the record format, the code structure used, and other needed technical documentation.

Data Archive: The U.S. Census as a Data Bank

The U.S. Census is a gold mine of data for the social science researcher. The 1970 census content and coverage shown below indicates the scope of information gathered in the decennial census.

Table 1. *Population and Housing Items, 1970 U.S. Census*

Population items	Sample percentages
Relationship to head of household[1]	100%
Color or race	100
Age (month and year of birth)	100
Sex	100
Marital status	100
State or country of birth	20
Years of school completed	20

Population items	Sample percentages
Number of children ever born	20
Employment status	20
Hours worked last week	20
Weeks worked last year	20
Last year in which worked	20
Occupation, industry, and class of worker	20
Activity 5 years ago	20
Income last year:	
Wage and salary income	20
Self-employment income	20
Other income	20
Country of birth of parents	15
Mother tongue	15
Year moved into this house	15
Place of residence 5 years ago	15
School or college enrollment (public or private)	15
Veteran status	15
Place of work	15
Means of transportation to work	15
Mexican or Spanish origin or descent	5
Citizenship	5
Year of immigration	5
When married	5
Vocational training completed	5
Presence and duration of disability	5
Occupation-industry 5 years ago	5

Housing items	Sample percentages
Number of units at this address	100%
Telephone	100
Access to unit[2]	100
Complete kitchen facilities[3]	100
Rooms	100
Water supply	100
Flush toilet	100
Bathtub or shower	100
Basement	100
Tenure[4]	100
Commercial establishment on property	100
Value	100
Contract rent	100
Vacancy status	100
Months vacant	100
Components of gross rent	20
Heating equipment	20
Year structure built	20
Number of units in structure and whether a trailer	20
Farm residence (acreage and sales of farm products)	20
Source of water	15
Sewage disposal	15
Bathrooms	15
Air conditioning	15

Table 1. *(Continued)*

Housing items	Sample percentages
Automobiles	15
Stories, elevator in structure	5
Fuel—heating, cooking, water heating	5
Bedrooms	5
Clothes washing machine	5
Clothes dryer	5
Dishwasher	5
Home food freezer	5
Television	5
Radio	5
Second home	5

[1]Such as wife of head, other relative of head, or not related to head.
[2]Direct access or access through other living quarters.
[3]"Complete kitchen facilities" is defined as including a sink with piped water, a range or cook stove, and a refrigerator.
[4]Owner occupied or renter occupied.

The information on population items is generally of most interest to the social scientist. The tables that follow show details of general characteristics of the population, social characteristics of the population, labor-force characteristics of the population, and income characteristics of the population.

Table 2. *Published Census Tract Report—Population Data**

Table P-1. General characteristics of the population	Table P-2. Social characteristics of the population
Census Tracts	**Census Tracts**
RACE	**NATIVITY, PARENTAGE, & COUNTRY OF ORIGIN**
All persons	**All persons**
White	Native of native parentage
Negro	Native of foreign or mixed parentage
Percent Negro	Foreign born
AGE BY SEX	**Foreign stock**
Male, all ages	United Kingdom
Under 5 years	Ireland (Eire)
3 and 4 years	Sweden
5 to 9 years	Germany
5 years	Poland
6 years	Czechoslovakia
10 to 14 years	Austria
14 years	Hungary
15 to 19 years	U.S.S.R.
15 years	Italy
16 years	Canada
17 years	Mexico
18 years	Cuba
19 years	Other America
20 to 24 years	All other and not reported
20 years	Persons of Spanish language
21 years	Other persons of Spanish surname
25 to 34 years	Persons of Spanish mother tongue
35 to 44 years	Persons of Puerto Rican birth or parentage

Table P-1.   General characteristics of the population

Table P-2.   Social characteristics of the population

Census Tracts

AGE BY SEX

Male, all ages
45 to 54 years
55 to 59 years
60 to 64 years
65 to 74 years
75 years and over

Female, all ages
Under 5 years
  3 and 4 years
5 to 9 years
  5 years
  6 years
10 to 14 years
  14 years
15 to 19 years
  15 years
  16 years
  17 years
  18 years
  19 years
20 to 24 years
  20 years
  21 years
25 to 34 years
35 to 44 years
45 to 54 years
55 to 59 years
60 to 64 years
65 to 74 years
75 years and over

RELATIONSHIP TO HEAD OF HOUSEHOLD

All persons
In households
  Head of household
    Head of family
    Primary individual
  Wife of head
  Other relative of head
  Not related to head
In group quarters
Persons per household

TYPE OF FAMILY AND NUMBER OF OWN CHILDREN

All families
With own children under 18 years
  Number of children

Husband-wife families
With own children under 18 years
  Number of children
    Percent of total under 18 years

Census Tracts

SCHOOL ENROLLMENT

Enrolled persons, 3 to 34 years old
Nursery school
  Public
Kindergarten
  Public
Elementary
  Public
High school
  Public
College
Percent enrolled in school by age:
  16 and 17 years
  18 and 19 years
  20 and 21 years
  22 to 24 years
  25 to 34 years
Percent 16 to 21 years not high school graduates and not enrolled in school

YEARS OF SCHOOL COMPLETED

Persons, 25 years old and over
No school years completed
Elementary: 1 to 4 years
              5 to 7 years
              8 years
High school: 1 to 3 years
               4 years
College: 1 to 3 years
              4 years or more
Median school years completed
Percent high school graduates

CHILDREN EVER BORN

Women, 35 to 44 years old ever married
Children ever born
  Per 1,000 women ever married

RESIDENCE IN 1965

Persons, 5 years old and over, 1970
Same house as in 1970
Different house:
  In central city of this SMSA
  In other part of this SMSA
  Outside this SMSA
    North and West
    South
Abroad

MEANS OF TRANSPORTATION AND PLACE OF WORK

All workers
Private auto: Driver
               Passenger
Bus or streetcar
Subway, elevated train, or railroad

Table 2. (*Continued*)

Table P-1. General characteristics of the population	Table P-2. Social characteristics of the population

Census Tracts

TYPE OF FAMILY AND NUMBER OF OWN CHILDREN

    Families with other male head

With own children under 18 years

  Number of children

    Percent of total under 18 years

Persons under 18 years

MARITAL STATUS

    Male, 14 years old and over

Single

Married

  Separated

Widowed

Divorced

    Female, 14 years old and over

Single

Married

  Separated

Widowed

Divorced

Census Tracts

MEANS OF TRANSPORTATION AND PLACE OF WORK

    All workers

Walked to work

Worked at home

Other

Inside SMSA

  A city central business district

  Balance of A city

  Balance of A County

  B County

  C County

  D County

  E County

  F County

  G County

  H County

  I County

  J County

  K County

Outside SMSA

Place of work not reported

Table P-3. Labor force characteristics of the population	Table P-4. Income characteristics of the population

Census Tracts

EMPLOYMENT STATUS

    Male, 16 years old and over

Labor force

  Percent of total

  Civilian labor force

    Employed

    Unemployed

    Percent of civilian labor force

Not in labor force

  Inmate of institution

  Enrolled in school

  Other under 65 years

  Other 65 years and over

    Male, 16 to 21 years old

Not enrolled in school

  Not high school graduates

    Unemployed or not in labor force

    Female, 16 years old and over

Labor force

  Percent of total

  Civilian labor force

    Employed

    Unemployed

    Percent of civilian labor force

Census Tracts

INCOME IN 1969 OF FAMILIES AND UNRELATED INDIVIDUALS

    All families

Less than $1,000

$1,000 to $1,999

$2,000 to $2,999

$3,000 to $3,999

$4,000 to $4,999

$5,000 to $5,999

$6,000 to $6,999

$7,000 to $7,999

$8,000 to $8,999

$9,000 to $9,999

$10,000 to $11,999

$12,000 to $14,999

$15,000 to $24,999

$25,000 to $49,999

$50,000 or more

Median income

Mean income

Families and unrelated individuals

  Median income

  Mean income

Unrelated individuals

  Median income

  Mean income

| Table P-3.   Labor force characteristics of the population | Table P-4.   Income characteristics of the population |

Census Tracts

EMPLOYMENT STATUS

Female, 16 years old and over
Not in labor force
Married women, husband present
  In labor force
  With own children under 6 years
  In labor force

OCCUPATION

Total employed, 16 years old and over
Professional, technical, and kindred workers
  Health workers
  Teachers, elementary and secondary schools
Managers and administrators, except farm
  Salaried
  Self-employed in retail trade

Sales workers
  Retail trade
Clerical and kindred workers
Craftsmen, foremen, and kindred workers
  Construction craftsmen
  Mechanics and repairmen
Operatives, except transport
Transport equipment operatives

Laborers, except farm
Farm workers
Service workers
  Cleaning and food service workers
  Protective service workers
  Personal and health service workers
Private household workers

Female employed, 16 years old and over
Professional, technical, and kindred workers
  Teachers, elementary and secondary schools
Managers and administrators, except farm
Sales workers
Clerical and kindred workers
  Secretaries, stenographers, and typists

Operatives, including transport
Other blue-collar workers
Farm workers
Service workers, except private household
Private household workers

INDUSTRY

Total employed, 16 years old and over
Construction
Manufacturing
  Durable goods
Transportation
Communications, utilities, and sanitary services

Census Tracts

TYPE OF INCOME IN 1969 OF FAMILIES

All families
With wage or salary income
  Mean wage or salary income
With nonfarm self-employment income
  Mean nonfarm self-employment income
With farm self-employment income
  Mean farm self-employment income
With Social Security income
  Mean Social Security income
With public assistance or public welfare income
  Mean public assistance or public welfare income
With other income
  Mean other income

RATIO OF FAMILY INCOME TO POVERTY LEVEL

Percent of families with incomes:
  Less than .50 of poverty level
  .50 to .74
  .75 to .99
  1.00 to 1.24
  1.25 to 1.49
  1.50 to 1.99
  2.00 to 2.99
  3.00 or more

INCOME BELOW POVERTY LEVEL

Families
  Percent of all families
Mean family income
Mean income deficit
Percent receiving public assistance income
Mean size of family
With related children under 18 years
  Mean number of related children under 18
    years
With related children under 6 years
  Mean number of related children under 6 years
Families with female head
  With related children under 18 years
    Mean number of related children under 18
      years
  With related children under 6 years
    Percent in labor force
    Mean number of related children under 6
      years

Family heads
  Percent 65 years and over
  Civilian male heads under 65 years
    Percent in labor force

Table 2. (*Continued*)

Table P-3. Labor force characteristics of the population	Table P-4. Income characteristics of the population

Census Tracts

INDUSTRY

Total employed, 16 years old and over
Wholesale trade
Retail trade

Finance, insurance, and real estate
Business and repair services
Personal services
Health services
Educational services
Other professional and related services
Public administration
Other industries

CLASS OF WORKER

Total employed, 16 years old and over
Private wage and salary workers
Government workers
  Local government workers
Self-employed workers
Unpaid family workers

Census Tracts

INCOME BELOW POVERTY LEVEL

Unrelated individuals
    Percent of all unrelated individuals
  Mean income
  Mean income deficit
  Percent receiving public assistance income
  Percent 65 years and over
Persons
  Percent of all persons
  Percent receiving Social Security income
  Percent 65 years and over
    Percent receiving Social Security income
  Related children under 18 years
    Percent living with both parents
Households
  Percent of all households
  Owner occupied
    Mean value of unit
  Renter occupied
    Mean gross rent
  Percent lacking some or all plumbing facilities

Table P-5. General and social characteristics of the Negro population: 1970	Table P-6. Economic characteristics of the Negro population: 1970

Census Tracts With 400 or More Negro Population

AGE BY SEX

Male, all ages
Under 5 years
  3 and 4 years
5 to 9 years
  5 years
  6 years
10 to 14 years
  14 years
15 to 19 years
  15 years
  16 years
  17 years
  18 years
  19 years
20 to 24 years
  20 years
  21 years
25 to 34 years
35 to 44 years
45 to 54 years
55 to 59 years
60 to 64 years
65 to 74 years
75 years and over

Census Tracts With 400 or More Negro Population

EMPLOYMENT STATUS AND OCCUPATION

Male, 16 years old and over
Labor force
  Civilian labor force
    Employed
    Unemployed
Not in labor force

Female, 16 years old and over
Labor force
  Civilian labor force
    Employed
    Unemployed
Not in labor force
Married women in labor force, husband present
  With own children under 6 years

Total employed, 16 years old and over
Professional, technical, and kindred workers
Managers and administrators, except farm
Sales workers
Clerical and kindred workers
Craftsmen, foremen, and kindred workers
Operatives, except transport
Transport equipment operatives
Laborers, except farm

Table P-5. General and social characteristics of the Negro population: 1970	Table P-6. Economic characteristics of the Negro population: 1970

Census Tracts With 400 or More Negro Population

AGE BY SEX
  Female, all ages
Under 5 years
  3 and 4 years
5 to 9 years
  5 years
  6 years
10 to 14 years
  14 years
15 to 19 years
  15 years
  16 years
  17 years
  18 years
  19 years
20 to 24 years
  20 years
  21 years
25 to 34 years
35 to 44 years
45 to 54 years
55 to 59 years
60 to 64 years
65 to 74 years
75 years and over

RELATIONSHIP TO HEAD OF HOUSEHOLD
  All persons
In households
  Head of household
    Head of family
    Primary individual
  Wife of head
  Other relative of head
  Not related to head
In group quarters
Persons per household

TYPE OF HOUSEHOLD
  All households
Male primary individual
Female primary individual
Husband-wife households
Households with other male head
Households with female head

SCHOOL ENROLLMENT
  Persons, 16 to 21 years old
Not attending school
  Not high school graduates
    Percent of total

Census Tracts With 400 or More Negro Population

EMPLOYMENT STATUS AND OCCUPATION
    Total employed, 16 years old and over
Farm workers
Service workers, except private household
Private household workers
    Female employed, 16 years old and over
Professional, technical, and kindred workers
Managers and administrators, except farm
Sales workers
Clerical and kindred workers
Operatives, including transport
Other blue-collar workers
Farm workers
Service workers, except private household
Private household workers

FAMILY INCOME IN 1969
  All families
Less than $1,000
$1,000 to $1,999
$2,000 to $2,999
$3,000 to $3,999
$4,000 to $4,999
$5,000 to $5,999
$6,000 to $6,999
$7,000 to $7,999
$8,000 to $8,999
$9,000 to $9,999
$10,000 or more
Median income: Families
                Families and unrelated individuals

RATIO OF FAMILY INCOME TO POVERTY LEVEL
Percent of families with incomes:
  Less than .50 of poverty level
  .50 to .74
  .75 to .99
  1.00 to 1.24
  1.25 to 1.49
  1.50 to 1.99
  2.00 or more

INCOME BELOW POVERTY LEVEL
Families
  Percent of all families
  Mean family income
  Mean income deficit
  Percent receiving public assistance income
  Mean size of family
  With related children under 18 years
    Mean number of related children under 18 years
  With related children under 6 years
    Mean number of related children under 6 years

Table P-5. General and social characteristics of
the Negro population: 1970

Table P-6. Economic characteristics of the Negro
population: 1970

**Census Tracts With 400 or More Negro
Population**

YEARS OF SCHOOL COMPLETED

Persons, 25 years old and over
No school years completed
Elementary: 1 to 4 years
              5 to 7 years
              8 years
High school: 1 to 3 years
              4 years
College: 1 to 3 years
              4 years or more
Median school years completed
Percent high school graduates

RESIDENCE IN 1965

Persons, 5 years old and over, 1970
Same house as in 1970
Different house:
  In central city of this SMSA
  In other part of this SMSA
  Outside this SMSA
    North and West
    South
Abroad

**Census Tracts With 400 or More Negro
Population**

INCOME BELOW POVERTY LEVEL

Families
  Families with female head
    With related children under 18 years
      Mean number of related children under 18
      years
    With related children under 6 years
      Percent in labor force
      Mean number of related children under 6
      years

Family heads
  Percent 65 years and over
  Civilian male heads over 65 years
    Percent in labor force

Unrelated individuals
  Percent of all unrelated individuals
  Mean income
  Mean income deficit
  Percent receiving public assistance income
  Percent 65 years and over

Persons
  Percent of all persons
  Percent receiving Social Security income
  Percent 65 years and over
    Percent receiving Social Security income
  Related children under 18 years
    Percent living with both parents

Households
  Percent of all households
  Owner occupied
    Mean value of unit
  Renter occupied
    Mean gross rent
  Percent lacking some or all plumbing facilities

*Source: *1970 Census Users' Guide, Part I.* Washington, D.C.: U.S. Government Printing Office, 1970, pp. 147–49.

Also available are other census tract reports, which include: General and Social Characteristics of Persons of Spanish Language, 1970; Occupancy, Utilization, Financial Characteristics of Housing Units; Structural, Equipment, and Financial Characteristics of Housing Units; Occupancy, Utilization, and Financial Characteristics of Housing Units with Negro Head of Household; Characteristics of Housing Units with Household Head of Spanish Language.

Geographic Areas

Geographic areas from which census data is reported are shown in figure 1. Note that these include standard metropolitan statistical areas and such component

Figure 1.   Geographic Areas in 1970 Census Reports

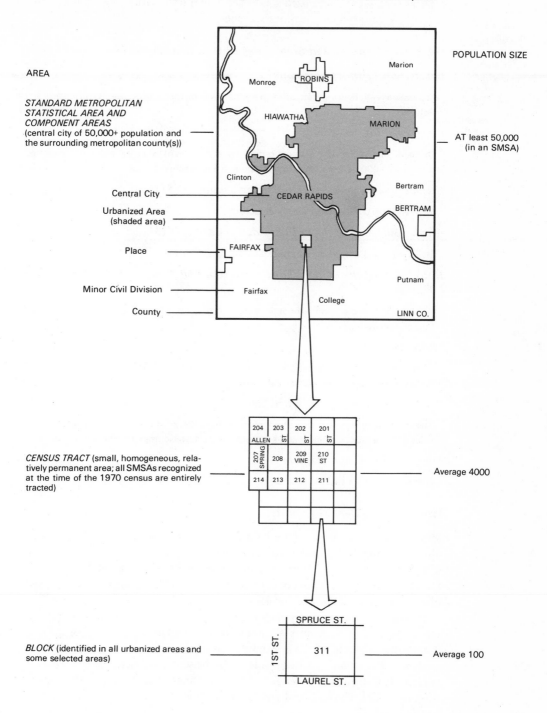

AREA

*STANDARD METROPOLITAN
STATISTICAL AREA AND
COMPONENT AREAS*
(central city of 50,000+ population and
the surrounding metropolitan county(s))

Central City

Urbanized Area
(shaded area)

Place

Minor Civil Division

County

POPULATION SIZE

AT least 50,000
(in an SMSA)

CENSUS TRACT (small, homogeneous, relatively permanent area; all SMSAs recognized
at the time of the 1970 census are entirely
tracted)

Average 4000

BLOCK (identified in all urbanized areas and
some selected areas)

Average 100

areas as central city, urbanized area, place, minor civil division, and county; also, for SMSAs, census tract and block statistics.

General and Specialized Summaries of U.S. Census Data

Congressional District Data Book

Population and housing data with maps for each district; votes cast for President and Congress.

County and City Data Book

Demographic, social, and economic data for states, counties, cities, and unincorporated places of 25,000 or more, and for metropolitan and urbanized areas.

Graphic Summary of the 1970 Housing Census, HC(S1)-16

Maps and charts excerpted from final reports.

Graphic Summary of the 1970 Population Census, PC(S1)-55

Maps and charts excepted from final reports.

Historical Statistics of the United States, Colonial Times to 1970—Bicentennial Edition

Demographic, social, and economic trends. Analytical text and detailed source notes. Comprehensive index.

Pocket Data Book, U.S.A.

A condensation of the *Statistical Abstract*, simplified for ready reference, with charts on current trends. Index and glossary of terms.

Statistical Abstract of the United States

The standard annual summary of statistics on the social, political, and economic characteristics of the nation. Extensive guide to public and private sources. Comprehensive index.

Subject and U.S. Area Reports

U.S. summaries for specific censuses.

Where to Find Census Reports

Most college and university libraries contain census reports. Many public libraries obtain the principal census reports for their communities; if your branch library does not, try the main library. The city planning office, city government library, mayor's office, chamber of commerce, or similar public and private agencies also often have census reports on hand.

A community-action group may discover that it has frequent need to refer to census reports. If so, copies are available at a reasonable cost. Department of Commerce field offices in forty-three cities stock many of the reports for their cities and surrounding areas, or orders may be sent directly to the U.S. Superintendent of Documents. Order forms may be obtained by writing to the Publications Services Division, Social and Economic Statistics Administration, Washington, D.C. 20233.

Where to Find Research Assistance

A number of data products and services have been developed in connection with the 1970 census that are primarily of interest to census users who have substantial and frequent need for census data. Of greatest importance is the availability of 1970 census data on computer tape. The data are statistics, like those found in census reports, for blocks, tracts, cities, and other areas. Because of the compact nature of storing data on tape, however, much more data can be put on tape than can be published in reports, including data for some areas not found in reports, such as enumeration districts.

Anyone may purchase these tapes. Many organizations, both public and private, buy census tapes and offer data services such as preparing printouts and suggesting ways to apply the statistics. A public listing of these organizations, called Summary Tape Processing Centers, is maintained by the Census Bureau.

The Census Bureau has published a great deal of descriptive information about 1970 census programs. For example, the two-volume *1970 Census Users' Guide* is a comprehensive reference resource. Also, there are occasional pamphlets and bulletins (*Data Access Descriptions* and *Census Users' Bulletins*), a monthly newsletter (*Small-Area Data Notes*), and a quarterly *Bureau of the Census Catalog.*

If you would like to discuss the use of census data in your community activities or have questions about Census Bureau products and services, contact the Data Access and Use Laboratory, Data Users Services Office, Bureau of the Census, Washington, D.C. 20233. This office can provide the names of more than 175 organizations (public, private, governmental, and academic) that the Bureau of the Census recognizes as Summary Tape Processing Centers. These organizations file a statement with the Bureau indicating their intention to service the needs of census data users outside their organization and specifying their planned activities. *Data Access News* reports these activities within its pages. The centers are not franchised, established, or supported by the Bureau of the Census. Each processing center establishes its own cost structure for services and may serve any interested client according to its own procedures.

The professional social scientist probably would want the *1970 Census Users' Guide* for his immediate search of user information. The *Guide* is a two-part publication designed to furnish most of the information data users will need for effective access and use of 1970 census data products.

Part 1 of the *Guide* (standard paperbound edition) includes the text and three appendixes. The text covers such subjects as the collection and processing of 1970 data, data delivery media (computer tapes, microfilm, and printed materials), maps, and information on how to obtain census materials. The appendixes are:

1970 Census Users' Dictionary: defines concepts associated with population and housing tabulations and geographic areas relevant to the collection and publication of data.

Comparison of Printed Reports and Summary Tapes summarizes and compares the contents of the reports and tapes.

Glossary: defines many terms used in connection with collecting, processing, and publishing census data, and lists many abbreviations relevant to the census.

Part 2 of the *Guide* (prepunched for three-ring binder) contains appendixes specifically related to the use of census summary tapes and the Address Coding Guide.

Technical Conventions and Character Set: presents information on the physical characteristics, format, and languages associated with tapes released by the Bureau.

1st–4th Count Technical Documentation: describes the arrangement of geographic codes and census data on the first four series of summary tapes.

Addressing Coding Guide Technical Documentation: furnishes information on the format and content of ACGs.

Many data users will find both parts of great value. Part 1, with its comprehensive coverage of the decennial census program, data products, and related services, is an important instructional and reference tool. Part 2, concerned exclusively with computer tape products, is designed particularly for those who plan to obtain tapes or who want complete information on the data content of the summary tapes.

Part 1 only of the *1970 Census Users' Guide* is $2.10 per copy:* c3.6/2:c33/2/ 970-2/PT.1. Part 2 only of the *1970 Census Users' Guide* is $3.70 per copy: c3.6/2:c33/2/970-2/PT.2. Write to: Superintendent of Documents, U.S. Government Printing Office, Washington, D.C. 20402.

Community leaders will find *Census Data for Community Action* suitable for their use. Several examples are provided of the types of community problems the solution of which begin with analysis of census statistics. In one, the census results are used to evaluate the impact of alternate routes for an expressway on various neighborhoods in a community. Another shows how census data on age, education, and other population characteristics can establish the need for adult education programs. A third indicates how census data can help in assessing a community's need for day-care centers. Income figures, households headed by a woman, and the number of children under five years of age are all utilized in this analysis.

Copies of the booklet, which is priced at 50 cents and contains 23 pages, may be obtained from the Publications Distribution Section, Social and Economic Statistics Administration, Washington, D.C. 20233. Checks should be made payable to the Superintendent of Documents (U.S. Government Printing Office).

For more detailed research activity in the local area, the *Census Use Study* is the required resource.

The *Census Use Study* was established by the U.S. Bureau of the Census to explore the current uses and future needs for small-area data, and data handling and display techniques in local, state, and federal agencies. There is a growing need to improve the system for relating census data with local agency data. Linking of data from census and local sources is essential for enhancing the analysis of various urban problems and trends of change. For example, in the study of crime and delinquency statistics, agencies are interested in linking incident reports prepared by law-enforcement agencies with neighborhood socioeconomic data available from the Census Bureau. Similarly, in transportation planning, local data on land use and travel patterns must be related to specific

---

*All prices are of course subject to change.

demographic and social characteristics for small areas such as traffic zones. Trip generation rates as related to the socioeconomic characteristics of study areas can then be computed and used to estimate future transportation facility requirements. Other areas of interest include educational planning, health planning, housing and redevelopment planning, public safety planning, and various subjects of concern to commerce and industry such as studies of telephone and bank service users in relation to the socioeconomic characteristics of small groups of the population.

A special census of New Haven, Connecticut, was conducted in April 1967 to test proposed 1970 census procedures. Local agencies cooperated by making available certain data from their own records to enable testing of data handling techniques. Research was carried out in the following areas: geographic base systems, record matching, computer mapping, special data tabulations, local data user interests and needs, and special sample surveys of family health and area travel patterns. One of the most apparent needs identified through this effort was the desire of users for data tabulated by the smallest feasible geographic area, particularly data at the block level in metropolitan areas.

The first twelve reports listed below are directly based on the *New Haven Census Use Study*. Others indicate the growing scope of the studies undertaken. For further information write to the Publications Distribution Section, Bureau of the Census, Washington, D.C. 20233.

CENSUS USE STUDY DOCUMENTATION

Census use study reports

1. General Description
2. Computer Mapping
3. Data Tabulation Activities
4. The DIME Geocoding System
5. Data Interests of Local Agencies
6. Family Health Survey
7. Health Information System
8. Data Uses in Health Planning
9. Data Uses in Urban Planning
10. Data Uses in School Administration
11. Area Travel Survey
12. Health Information System—II
13. Geocoding with ADMATCH—A Los Angeles Experience

Southern California regional information study reports

1. Computer Graphics
2. ACG-DIME Updating System—A First Look
3. ACG-DIME Updating System—An Interim Report

4. ACG-DIME Updating System— The Long Beach, California Experience
5. Research Notes—1970-1971

Computer program packages

1. ADMATCH: An Address Matching System
2. ADMATCH/OS: An Address Matching System
3. GRIDS—A Computer Mapping System
4. DIME: A Geographic Base File Package
5. CARPOL—An Approach to Large-Scale Carpooling

Social and health indicators system reports

1. Mount Bayou, Mississippi: Part I
2. Mount Bayou, Mississippi: Part II
3. Los Angeles
4. Atlanta: Part I
5. Atlanta: Part II
6. Phoenix: Part I

Miscellaneous publications

1. 1970 Census User Conference Illustrations
2. A Geographic Base File for Urban Data Systems
3. Unified Statistical Evaluation Study—Report No. 2 (Preliminary)
4. Handbook for Manpower Planners—Part I
5. First International DIME Colloquium: Conference Proceedings
6. DIME Workshop: An Interim Report
7. CARPOL—An Overview
8. Everything You Always Wanted to Know About CARPOL* . . . And More
9. ADMATCH Adventures
10. Data Uses in the Private Sector

Selected papers

UNIMATCH—A Computer System for Generalized Record Linkage Under Conditions of Uncertainty, by Matthew A. Jaro
Composite Social Indicators for Small Areas—Census Use Study—Recent Developments in Methodology and Uses, by Samuel P. Korper, John C. Deshaies, Leo Schuerman, and Ronald Crellin

Public Use Samples of the U.S. Census* could prove especially valuable to social scientists who want to perform detailed analyses that would exhaust samples of the usual size of 1500 to 3000. For example, detailed cross-tabulation of race, sex, and occupation become quite feasible with the public use sample (PUS). The U.S. Bureau of the Census has released a collection of samples of the U.S. population as of April 1, 1970, which contains data on individuals and their households. The *Public Use Samples of Basic Records* from the 1970 census come from the sample questionnaires administered to the population as part of the decennial census. No names, addresses, or other identifying information are included in the data, but all other data collected through the sample question-naire are coded onto computer-readable magnetic tapes. These individual and household data are a major resource for social science research, for they provide flexibility in analysis that the aggregate (tabulated) data released by the Bureau cannot provide. PUS is a collection of six statistically independent samples, each reporting data from a 1 percent sample of households permitting a pooling of approximately 12 million observations (or 6 percent of households). An inter-esting application of the PUS is described by Richard C. Rockwell, "Applica-tions of the 1970 Census Public Use Samples in Affirmative Action Programs," *American Sociologist* 19 (February 1975): 41–46.

For users of small-area statistics, *Data User News* is valuable. This publication is issued monthly by the Social and Economic Statistics Administration of the Department of Commerce, Washington, D.C. For information, write Larry W. Hartke, Editor, Data User Services Division, Bureau of the Census, Washington, D.C. 20233. The issue for January 1975 has a complete directory of all special-ists in the Bureau of the Census. Data users will find the name and telephone

*U.S. Bureau of the Census, *Public Use Samples of Basic Records from the 1970 Census: Description and Technical Documentation* (Washington, D.C.: Government Printing Office, 1972).

numbers of each specialist assigned to some one hundred demographic, economic, geographic, and user service fields.

Data Access Descriptions are intended as a means of access to unpublished data of the Bureau of the Census for persons with data requirements not fully met by the published reports. These are published as occasional reports when various kinds of data become available. *Data Access Description*, U.S. Bureau of the Census, Washington, D.C. 20233.

Data Access News is published by the Clearinghouse and Laboratory for Census Data (CLCD) six to eight times a year. The CLCD also publishes a quarterly *Review of Public Data Use.* The CLCD is operated by Data Use and Access Laboratories with a grant from the National Science Foundation. CLCD offices: Suite 900, 1601 North Kent Street, Arlington, Virginia 22209. These are significant references for current information about research and data for behavioral sciences.

Current Population Reports represents a data resource of great value to demographers and social scientists generally. In addition to the findings of the Census of Population, conducted every few years, the Bureau of the Census publishes continuing and up-to-date statistics on population counts, characteristics, and other special studies on the American people. Data are issued under eight subject areas and released under the general title *Current Population Reports.* The eight categories are:

P-20 Population Characteristics
P-23 Special Studies
P-25 Population Estimates and Projections
P-26 Federal-State Cooperative Program for Population Estimates
P-27 Farm Population
P-28 Special Censuses
P-60 Consumer Income
P-65 Consumer Buying Indicators

Of these, P-20 Population Characteristics and P-23 Special Studies have most general utility to the social scientist.

The P-20 series began in September 1947. Since then, approximately ten reports a year have been issued covering current national and, in some cases, regional data on geographic residence and mobility, fertility, education, school enrollment, marital status, numbers and characteristics of household and families, and so on. Almost three hundred reports have appeared. A few more recent titles indicate range:

Social and Economic Characteristics of Students: October 1972 (No. 260)
Educational Attainment in the United States: March 1973 and 1974 (No. 274)
Marital Status and Living Arrangements: March 1974 (No. 271)
Voting and Registration in the Election of November 1972 (No. 253)

Mobility of the Population of the United States: March 1970 to March 1973 (No. 262)

Fertility Histories and Birth Expectations of American Women: June 1971 (No. 263)

The P-23 series, Special Studies, is a collection of frequent reports on methods, concepts, or specialized areas. The first study appeared in 1949 and the initial title of the series was Technical Studies. The change to the present title was made in 1970. More than fifty studies have now been published. A few more recent titles include:

The Social and Economic Status of the Black Population in the United States, 1973 (No. 46)

Characteristics of American Youth, 1972 (No. 44)

Population of the United States, Trends and Prospects 1950–1990 (No. 49)

Female Family Heads (No. 50)

Illustrative Projections of Money Income Size Distributions for Families and Unrelated Individuals (No. 47)

Census Bureau Methodological Research is available to researchers interested in methodological problems centered on census surveying and data processing. This annual publication is an annotated list of papers and reports on the status of methodological research within the Bureau of the Census. The first list covered the years 1963–66; the list has been issued annually since then. Sections include Statistical Theory and Sampling Methods; General Planning and Procedures for Censuses and Surveys; Measurement of Coverage and Response Error; Census of Population and Housing Evaluation Projects; Data Processing; Concepts and Techniques of Analysis; Data Access and Use; Other Documents of Methodological Interest; Selected Methodological Reports Conducted in Past Years.

Bureau of Labor Statistics

The Bureau of Labor Statistics is a fact-finding agency engaged in the collection, interpretation, and dissemination of economic information. It conducts research on employment, manpower, prices, wages and industrial relations, productivity, safety and health, and economic growth. In many of these areas the Bureau has experience dating back to 1884. A description of the Bureau's current activity may be found in *Major Programs* (published annually), U.S. Department of Labor, Bureau of Labor Statistics, Washington, D.C. 20212.

Publications include the *Monthly Labor Review, Occupational Outlook Quarterly, Handbook of Labor Statistics* (annually), *B.L.S. Handbook of Methods,* and *Publications of the Bureau of Labor Statistics,* a semiannual annotated catalog listing all current Bureau publications.

Of particular interest to social scientists are the *Special Labor Force Reports.* These have such potential value to researchers that the list of all reprints since February 1970 is appended. Copies may be obtained from the Bureau of Labor Statistics in Washington, D.C., or at any of its regional offices. In your library the reports will be filed under U.S. Bureau of Labor Statistics, Special Labor Force Reports, Government Classification No. L. 2.98.

Number
140 Educational Attainment of Workers, March 1971
141 Work Experience of the Population in 1970
142 Employment and Unemployment in 1971
143 Usual Weekly Earnings of American Workers, 1971
144 Marital and Family Characteristics of the Labor Force, March 1971
145 Employment of High School Graduates and Dropouts, October 1971
146 An Analysis of Unemployment by Household Relationship
147 Employment of School-Age Youth, October 1971
148 Educational Attainment of Workers, March 1972
149 The Employment Situation of Vietnam Era Veterans, 1972
150 Jobseeking Methods Used by Unemployed Workers
151 Employment of Recent College Graduates, October 1971
152 Changes in the Employment Situation in 1972
153 Marital and Family Characteristics of the Labor Force, March 1972
154 Children of Working Mothers, March 1973
155 Employment of High School Graduates and Dropouts, October 1972
156 The U.S. Labor Force: Projections to 1990
157 Job Losers, Leavers, and Entrants: Traits and Trends
158 Young Workers; in School and Out
159 Going Back to School at 35
160 Education of Workers: Projections to 1990
161 Educational Attainment of Workers, March 1973
162 Work Experience of the Population in March 1972
163 Employment and Unemployment in 1973
164 Marital and Family Characteristics of the Labor Force in March 1973
165 Children of Working Mothers, March 1973
166 Multiple Jobholding, May 1973
167 Job Situation of Vietnam-era Veterans
168 Employment of High School Graduates and Dropouts, 1973
169 Employment of Recent College Graduates, October 1972
170 Employment of School-Age Youth, October 1973
171 Work Experience of the Population, 1973
172 Job Tenure of Workers, January 1973
173 Marital and Family Characteristics of the Labor Force, March 1974
174 Children of Working Mothers, March 1974
175 Educational Attainment of Workers, March 1974
176 Occupational Mobility of Workers
177 Multiple Jobholders in May 1974
178 Employment and Unemployment in 1974
179 Trends in Overtime Hours and Pay, 1969–74
180 Students, Graduation, and Dropouts in the Labor Market, October 1974
181 Work Experience of Population in 1974
182 Multiple Job Holders in May 1975

The Department of Labor has a unique set of longitudinal data on labor-force behavior and work attitudes, which is available to interested users for a fee. The opportunities are described in Herbert S. Parnes, "The National Longitudinal Surveys: New Vistas for Labor Market Research," *American Economic Review*

65, no. 2 (May 1975): 244–49. The Department of Labor may support research using data from the tapes either by (1) small grants for dissertion research by doctoral candidates on manpower-related subjects or (2) contracts or grants for research that is likely to have significant implications for manpower policies or programs. Write Howard Rosen, Director, Office of Manpower Research and Development, Patrick Henry Building, 601 D. Street N.W., Washington, D.C. 20213. Challenging problems in this area may be found in Willard Wirtz, *The Boundless Resource: A Prospectus for an Education/Work Policy*, The New Republic Book Co. Inc., 1220 19 Street N.W., Washington, D.C. 20036.

2.9 GUIDE TO PRIVATE PROFESSIONAL SERVICES FOR THE SOCIAL RESEARCHER

This guide is not a complete directory, but rather a selected compilation of certain services that are available at various prices. They are services rendered by universities, government, and private companies. Perhaps the NORC General Social Survey of the National Opinion Research Center is the most valuable commercial social data service, bringing to fruition an idea long nurtured by researchers, i.e., to provide a nationwide sample of data available on an annual basis such that time-series analysis might be possible. Such a sample was also needed by sociologists to make selected data available that, for various reasons, could not be delivered by the U.S. Census.

Other services provide research in progress within specified fields, such as designing a sample, developing questionnaires or interview schedules, collecting data by mail or personal interview, and completing analysis. The researcher can even get help on budgeting and funding.

NORC also provides a variety of services for the social survey researcher. These include sample design, questionnaire construction, pretesting of questionnaires, coding, data processing, and analyses. NORC has had twenty-five years' experience in data collection maintaining a national probability sample and a staff of trained and experienced interviewers.

For information, write: National Opinion Research Center, University of Chicago, 6030 South Ellis Avenue, Chicago, Ill. 60637.

The NORC General Social Survey

This is a program of social indicators research and a data diffusion system. The data come from annual personal interviews administered to national cross sections of about 1500 adults, using a standard questionnaire repeated each year. The questionnaire content covers a broad spectrum of sociological interests. Distribution of GSS data sets is handled by the Roper Public Opinion Research Center, Williams College, Williamstown, Mass. 01267. The 1972 survey costs $50 plus postage. The 1973 and 1974 surveys cost $100 each.* Users do *not* have to belong to the Roper Center to obtain GSS data.

The basic idea of GSS is to provide a nationwide sample of data so that time-series data of high quality is available on an annual basis. The rationale for the enterprise stems from NORC's opinion that the field of sociology shows a num-

*The 1975 survey is also available now. Check distributor for price.

ber of research weaknesses when compared to other social science disciplines. An unhealthy division exists between a handful of investigators associated with major research institutes and the great majority of sociologists who can obtain national data only on a hand-me-down basis after the original investigation or when Uncle Sam is tired of the materials. It is hoped this resource will stimulate research and make available high-quality national data.

Given the scope of the questionnaire, a variety of analyses can be performed. For example:

1. Replicating findings from previous studies, perhaps introducing variables that were not available to the original author.
2. Testing one's own hypotheses.
3. Studying small population groups by merging studies across years. (This is possible because of the repetition of questions.)
4. Studying trends over time by comparing current results with those in the various baseline studies. The codebooks give references to the original study for each item drawn from a previous national sampling.
5. Since respondent age is reported to the year, one can use the cohort method in studying age trends for variables reported by age in the original study.

The data can also be used in classwork in a number of ways:

6. Students can use the data to test hypotheses derived from readings and lectures.
7. Methods classes can use the data for practice in analyses. Many content areas have enough items for exercises on scale and index construction.
8. Teachers can run data to bring their lectures up to date.

Reference

CITRO, CONSTANCE F., with the assistance of JAMES A. DAVIS. "The NORC General Social Survey." *Public Data Use* 2 (October 1974): 28–31.

National Opinion Research Center. "The NORC General Social Survey: Questions and Answers." All questionnaire items classified by broad content type and causal stage. Revised and updated, March 1974.

Broadly speaking, the measures of the GSS survey fall into the following content scheme:

1. Ecology
2. Family and life cycle
   a. Age
   b. Marriage and family structure
   c. Sex (gender, behavior, and roles, especially employment)
   d. Children and fertility
   e. Miscellaneous
3. Socioeconomic status
   a. Occupational level
   b. Education
   c. Income
   d. Class consciousness

4. Primordial groups
    a. Ethnicity
    b. Religion
    c. Race
    d. Politics
5. Social psychology
    a. Interaction
    b. Social integration
    c. Other
6. Miscellaneous
    a. Deviance
    b. Health
    c. Other

Response Analysis

This organization, like NORC, offers a full range of research services. It will collect data, design a sample, consult on questionnaire development, or do analysis. Response Analysis advertises the advantages of its services as follows:

> We can undertake any kind of study, anywhere. We have developed our own national probability sample and also possess expertise in the design and implementation of local and regional studies. We have a national resident staff of over 500 personally trained interviewers, including specially trained elite interviewers.
>   We are cost-efficient. We insist on quality work, but we do it efficiently for reasonable budgets.
>   We get the job done when you need it, and have developed a special field control system toward that end.

For further information, write: Response Analysis, Research Park, Route 206, Princeton, N.J. 08540.

Smithsonian Science Information Exchange (SSIE) (Research Retrieval)

The SSIE is a nonprofit corporation of the Smithsonian Institution. It calls itself the national source for information on research in progress.

By maintaining a data base of information about ongoing or recently completed research projects, the SSIE has been serving research investigators and managers in the social sciences since 1963. The SSIE receives project information from over 1300 federal and other organizations that support research, indexes it, and stores it in a computerized file. Exchange scientists conduct searches of this file upon requests from users in government agencies and research laboratories in universities and private industry. Information is collected at the time a project is funded and is usually available for retrieval well before reports are made at professional meetings or articles appear in the published literature.

The current data base, which covers ongoing research and research initiated and completed between July 1973 and the present, contains information on more than 8000 projects in all areas of the social sciences. This research is sponsored by organizations such as the National Science Foundation; the U.S. Department of Health, Education, and Welfare; the Social Science Research Council; and many other public and private groups.

For further information, write Ann Riordan, Chief, Social Sciences Branch, Smithsonian Science Information Exchange, Room 300, 1730 M Street N.W., Washington, D.C. 20036.

NEXUS, a Baker and Taylor Information Service (Literature Retrieval)

Nexus is a data storage and retrieval firm specializing in research tools to serve the academic community throughout the English-speaking world. The word *nexus* means "a link," a link between modern computer technology and traditional research methods to furnish speedy, efficient access to large bodies of published scholarly source materials.

NEXUS promises an individually tailored resource list and describes its services as follows:

> *Preliminary Bibliographies with Enlightening Speed.* We have on computer the authors and abstracted titles of all articles ever printed in any of 534 history, political science and sociology journals (see list inside) published the world over, obscure and well-known both, since these journals began—more than 350,000 articles in all, going back to 1834. We'll search the file by computer on any topic you select, furnishing a bibliography individually tailored to your needs. The computer will dig out citations either by a specific author *or* about a specific subject (your choice).
>
> *Periodical Guide.* In effect, we're a computerized periodical literature guide covering pertinent (sometimes esoteric) journals of most interest to the serious researcher. Based on your own "key word" choices, our bibliography homes in directly on your specific research target. With one search, it can cover the entire 140-year archive. In the handy form of computer printouts, our source lists are easily tucked into a notebook or pocket and carried along with you.

For further information, write: NEXUS, P.O. Box 1517, Costa Mesa, Calif. 92705.

Institute for Scientific Information (Literature Retrieval)

The Institute offers an individualized weekly service of reporting on any of 68 topics in the social and behavioral sciences as they appear in the world's leading professional journals. ASCATOPICS is a computer system to locate articles relevant to the topics the researcher selects.

For further information, write: Institute for Scientific Information, 325 Chestnut Street, Philadelphia, Pa. 19106.

Academic Media (Literature Search)

This organization searches for directories, fact books, almanacs, and other sources for information desired by the researcher. For further information, write: Academic Media, 14852 Ventura Blvd., Sherman Oaks, Calif. 91403.

Inventory Services Available in Public Institutions

For examples of inventories and of their great variety in format and content, the following are illustrations: *A Guide to Resources and Services of the Inter-University Consortium for Political Research, 1972–73* (Ann Arbor: Institute for Social Research, University of Michigan); *Canadian Social Science Data Catalog* (Institute for Behavioral Research, York University, April 1974); and Latin American Data Bank, *File Inventory* (Gainesville: Center for Latin American Studies, University of Florida, August 1974).

Clearinghouses Offer Sociologists Variety of Services

Several clearinghouses that are operating in this country can be usefully employed by sociologists to keep posted on research projects, to conduct literature searches, to maintain currency with the existing information, and to circulate their products.

Content of the clearinghouses ranges from broad, general topics such as mental health to narrow, limited topics such as commuting students.

Among the services provided by clearinghouses are computer-generated bibliographies tailored to specific requests; notification of new literature in the field through the mailing of concise summaries of abstracts; specialized bibliographies on selected subjects of wide interest, a variety of publications, including books, monographs, newsletters, digests and directories; and referrals to other sources that have more complete information. Many services are provided free of charge. For more information write to the clearinghouses whose addresses are presented below.

National Clearinghouse for Mental Health Information, 5600 Fishers Lane, Rockville, Md. 20852.

National Clearinghouse for Alcohol Information, P.O. Box 2345, Rockville, Md. 20852.

National Clearinghouse for Drug Abuse Information, P.O. Box 1908, Rockville, Md. 20850.

National Criminal Justice Reference Service, Law Enforcement Assistance Administration, U.S. Dept. of Justice, Washington, D.C. 20530.

Child Abuse and Neglect Clearinghouse Project, Herner and Company, 2100 M Street, NW, Suite 316, Washington, D.C. 20037.

National Female Offender Resource Center, 1705 DeSales Street, NW, Washington, D.C. 20036.

Clearinghouse, Bureau of Research and Training (MH), Eastern Pennsylvania Psychiatric Institute, Henry Avenue and Abbottford Road, Philadelphia, Pa. 19129.

National Clearinghouse on Revenue Sharing, 1785 Massachusetts Ave., NW, Washington, D.C. 20036.

National Clearinghouse for Commuter Programs, 1211 Student Union, University of Maryland, College Park, Md. 20742.

Association for the Development of Religious Information Systems, Dept. of Sociology and Anthropology, Marquette University, Milwaukee, Wisc. 53233.

The National Agricultural Library, 10301 Baltimore Blvd., Beltsville, Md. 20705.

National Library of Medicine, 8600 Rockville Pike, Bethesda, Md. 20014.

2.10   DIRECTORIES OF SOCIAL RESEARCH CENTERS IN THE UNITED STATES, ENGLAND, AND THE WORLD

Research Centers in the United States

Research Centers Directory. Gale Research Co., Detroit, Mich. 48226, 1975. 5th edition.

Lists 3200 research centers in the following:

1. Agriculture, Home Economics, and Nutrition

2. Astronomy

3. Business, Economics, and Transportation
4. Conservation
5. Education
6. Engineering and Technology
7. Government and Public Affairs
8. Labor and Industrial Relations
9. Law
10. Life Sciences
11. Mathematics
12. Physical and Earth Sciences
13. Regional and Area Studies
14. Social Sciences, Humanities, and Religion

> A total of 376 centers are listed including Anthropology, Communications, Human Development, Population, Religion, Sociology, History, Ethnic Folklore, Linguistics, Journalism, Creativity, Family Study, Behavior, Race Relations.

15. Multidisciplinary Programs
16. Research Coordinating Offices

A typical entry shows the information given:

2750 Columbia University
BUREAU OF APPLIED SOCIAL RESEARCH
605 West 115th Street
New York, New York 10025
Dr. Allen H. Barton, Director   Phone (212) 280-4034
                                  Founded 1937

Integral unit of graduate faculties of Columbia University. Supported by parent institution, U.S. Government, state and local agencies, foundations, non-profit social organizations, and industry. Staff: 18 research professionals, 6 supporting professionals, 20 graduate research assistants, 15 others, plus research fellows, interns, and part-time student interviewers, coders, and statistical clerks.

Principal Fields of research: Public and elite opinion formation; political behavior; international comparative studies; manpower and populations; sociology of professions; formal organizations; community studies and evaluation of social programs. Also collects cases of application of social research to practical problems, codifies social research methods, develops new methods for study of aggregate aspects of mass social behavior, and provides empirical social science research training for graduate students and visiting foreign scholars. Maintains its own IBM data processing equipment.

Research results published in books, monographs, professional journals, project reports, and graduate student doctoral dissertations. Publication: *Bureau Reporter* (bimonthly). Holds periodic seminars on sociological problems and application of social science research methodology.

World Directory of Research Institutes

The World of Learning. Europe Publications, Ltd., 18 Bedford Square, London, England. 1974-75. 25th edition.

A compilation, for all countries of the world, of academies, learned societies, research institutes, libraries, museums, art galleries, and universities (including lists of faculty) in all fields of knowledge. This coverage is excellent for most purposes but often fails to include research organizations within academic departments and the university generally.

In the United States the Gale *Research Centers Directory* is superior. For additional information, consult the Social Science Research Council, 230 Park Avenue, New York, N.Y. 10017.

International Organizations in the Social Sciences

Consult UNESCO reports and papers in the Social Sciences No. 21: *International Organizations in the Social Sciences.* 1964. Revised edition.

2.11 **LIST OF IMPORTANT RESEARCH ASSOCIATIONS AND INSTITUTES AFFILIATED WITH THE INTERNATIONAL SOCIOLOGICAL ASSOCIATION**

This guide should assist research scholars who wish to communicate with other sociological researchers across the world. The list is not definitive. Not all research organizations are affiliated with the International Sociological Association. Many members belong to the older International Institute of Sociology, and a scholar should try to contact their members to have a more complete channel of communication. *The World of Learning* cited in the previous guide will be helpful.

Collective Members Directory of the International Sociological Association, 1975

MEMBERS IN CATEGORY A: NATIONAL SOCIOLOGICAL ASSOCIATIONS:

Africa

EGYPT	Egyptian Sociological Association National Center for Sociological & Criminological Research Gezira P.O., Cairo
GHANA	Ghana Sociological Association Department of Sociology University of Ghana Legon, Accra
MOROCCO	Centre Universitaire de la Recherche Scientifique Université du Maroc Avenue Ibn Batota B.P. 447 Rabat
NIGERIA	Nigerian Anthropological and Sociological Association Department of Sociology University of Ibadan Ibadan

TUNISIA	Institut de Planification Statistique et d'Etudes Juridiques, Economiques et Sociales 23, rue d'Espagne Tunis

Asia

CYPRUS	Cyprus Sociological Association P.O. Box 4688 Nicosia
INDIA	Indian Sociological Society Centre for the Study of Social Systems Jawaharlal Nehru University New Delhi 110057
IRAN	Institute for Social Studies and Research Faculty of Social Sciences and Cooperative Studies University of Tehran P.O. Box 13 1155 Tehran
ISRAEL	Israel Sociological Society Department of Sociology Hebrew University Jerusalem
KOREA	Korean Sociological Association Department of Sociology Korea University Seoul
JAPAN	Japan Sociological Society Department of Sociology Faculty of Letters University of Tokyo Bunkyo-ku, Tokyo
MONGOLIA	Academy of Sciences of the Mongolian People's Republic Institute of Philosophy, Sociology and Law Str. Peace, Building "B" 54 Ulan-Bator
TAIWAN	Chinese Sociological Association Department of Agricultural Extension National Taiwan University Taipei
Australia and New Zealand	Sociological Association of Australia and New Zealand Department of Sociology La Trobe University Bundoora, Victoria 3083

Eastern Europe

BULGARIA

Bulgarian Sociological Association
27B Moskowska Street
Sofia

CZECHOSLOVAKIA

Czechoslovak Sociological Society
Ul. 1, Listopadu
Nouzove stavby cp. 804
Praha 4–Nusle

DDR

Nationalkomitee für Soziologische Forschung bei
    der Akademie der Wissenschaften der Deutschen
    Demokratischen Republik
Otto-Nuschke-strasse 22/23
108 Berlin

HUNGARY

Institute of Sociology
Hungarian Academy of Sciences
Uri Utca 49
Budapest 1

POLAND

Polish Sociological Association
Warsaw University
Department of Sociology
72 Nowy Swiat
Warsaw 00 330

RUMANIA

Comitetul National de Sociologie
Academy of Social and Political Sciences
Str. Onesti Nr. 11, Sectorul 1
Bucharest

USSR

Soviet Sociological Association
Novocheremushkinskaya 46
Moscow 117418

Western Europe

AUSTRIA

Österreichische Gesellschaft für Soziologie
Fleischmarkt 3-5
A-1010 Wien

BELGIUM

Belgian Sociological Society
Van Evenstraat 2C
B-3000 Louvain

DENMARK

Danish National Institute of Social Research
Borgergade 28
DK-1300 Copenhagen K

FRG

Deutsche Gesellschaft für Soziologie
Universität Mannheim
Lehrstuhl fur Soziologie
Schloss, 68 Mannheim 1

FINLAND	The Westermarck Society PL 85 00511 Helsinki 51
FRANCE	Société Française de Sociologie 82 rue Cardinet 75017 Paris
GREAT BRITAIN	British Sociological Association 13, Endsleigh Street Skepper House London W.C. 1
GREECE	Hellenic Sociological Association "Alexander Papanastassiou" 1, Pesmajoglou Str. Athens 121
IRELAND	The Economic and Social Research Institute 4 Burlington Road Dublin 4
ITALY	Asociazione Italiana di Scienze Sociali Istituto di Sociologia Facolta di Magistero Universita di Torino 10100 Torino
NETHERLANDS	Nederlandse Sociologische en Antropologische Vereniging Mauritsweg 26A Rotterdam 3002
NORWAY	Norsk Sosiologforening P.O. Box 41 Blindern Oslo 3
SWEDEN	Sveriges Sociologforbund Sociologiska Institutionen Drottninggatan 1A S-752 20 Uppsala
SWITZERLAND	Société Suisse de Sociologie Case 152 1000 Lausanne 24
YUGOSLAVIA	Yugoslav Sociological Association Studentski trg. 1 11000 Beograd

Latin America*

CUBA	Universidad de la Habana Relaciones Internacionales La Habana

*For further information see Gunther Remmling, *South American Sociologists: A Directory*. Austin: Institute of Latin American Studies, University of Texas, 1966.

MEXICO	Asociacion Mexicana de Sociologia Providencia 330 Col. del Valle Mexico 12, D.F.
VENEZUELA	Asociacion Venezolana de Sociologia Apdo. 80044 Caracas 108

North America

CANADA	Canadian Sociology and Anthropology Association P.O. Box 878 Montreal, P.Q.
	Association Canadienne des Sociologues et Anthropologues de Langue Française Dépt. de Sociologie Université de Montréal C. P. 6128 Montréal, P.Q.
U.S.	American Sociological Association 1722 N. Street, N.W. Washington, D.C. 20036
	The Society for the Study of Social Problems Executive Office: Social Problems P.O. Box 533 Notre Dame, Ind. 46556

MEMBERS IN CATEGORY B: INTERNATIONAL AND MULTINATIONAL REGIONAL ASSOCIATIONS OF SOCIOLOGISTS

Western Europe

FRANCE	International Council for Research in Cooperative Development 7, avenue Franco-Russe Paris 7
	Association Internationale des Sociologues de Langue Française 17, rue de la Sorbonne Paris 5
	European Association of Experimental Social Psychology Université de Provence 13100 Aix-en-Provence
FRG	Arbeitsgemeinschaft Sozialwissenschaftliches Institut Plittersdorfer Str. 21 53 Bonn-Bad Godesberg

	European Society for Rural Sociology
	Nussallee 21
	Bonn
SWITZERLAND	Institut International de Sociologie
	Palais Wilson
	C.P. 7
	1211 Genève 14

Africa

SOUTH AFRICA	Association for Sociology in Southern Africa
	Centre for Intergroup Studies
	University of Cape Town
	Rondebosch 7700

MEMBERS IN CATEGORY C: RESEARCH INSTITUTES AND UNIVERSITY DEPARTMENTS

Africa

MOZAMBICO	Course of Economics
	University of Lourenço
	Marques
	Lourenço Marques
DAHOMEY	Département de Sociologie
	Centre de Recherches Appliquées du Dahomey
	B.P. 6
	Porto-Novo
REPUBLIQUE DU NIGER	Institut de Recherche en Sciences Humaines
	Université de Niamey
	B.P. 318
	Niamey
SUDAN	Department of Social Anthropology and Sociology
	Faculty of Economic and Social Studies
	University of Khartoum
	Khartoum
	Economic and Social Research Council
	P.O. Box 1166
	Khartoum
SOUTH AFRICA	Centre for Intergroup Studies
	c/o University of Cape Town
	Rondebosch 7700
	Department of Sociology and Criminology
	University of Fort Hare
	Private Bag 314
	Alice 5700
	The School of Social Sciences
	University of Cape Town
	Department of Sociology
	Private Bag, Rondebosch, C.P.

New Zealand	Department of Sociology University of Auckland Private Bag Auckland

Asia

CYPRUS	Social Research Centre Charalambides Building Grivas Dighenis Avenue Nicosia
HONG KONG	Social Research Centre Chinese University of Hong Kong 545 Nathan Rd. On Lee Building, 10/F Kowloon
INDIA	Indian Statistical Institute 203, Barrackpore Trunk Rd. 35 Calcutta

Western Europe

AUSTRIA	Institut für Musiksoziologie und Musikpädagogische Forschung Lothringerstrasse 18 A-1030 Wien
BELGIUM	Sociologische Onderzoeksinstituut Katholieke Universiteit Leuven Van Evenstraat 2B 3000 Louvain
	Centre de Recherches Sociologiques Université Catholique de Louvain Van Evenstraat 2B 3000 Louvain
FRANCE	Centre d'Etudes Sociologiques Centre National de la Recherche Scientifique 82, rue Cardinet 75017 Paris
	Centre de Recherches Sociologiques de Toulouse Faculté des Lettres et des Sciences Humaines 56, chemin du Mirail 31 Toulouse
FRG	Forschungsinstitut für Soziologie der Universität Köln Zulpicher strasse 182 5 Köln–Sulz
	Institut für Marxistische Studien und Forschungen Liebigstrasse 6 6 Frankfurt/Main

Zentralarchiv für Empirische Sozialforschung der
  Universität zu Köln
D-5000 Koln 41 (Lindenthal)
Bachemer Strasse 40

Institut für Soziologie der Rheinisch-Westfälischen
  Technischen Hochschule
Kopernikusstrasse 16
51 Aachen

GREECE   Centre National de Recherches Sociales
1, rue Sophocleous
Athens 122

ITALY   Istituto di Sociologia
Facolta di Magistero
Via S. Ottavio 20
10124 Torino

Istituto di Studi Sociali
Facolta di Scienze Politiche
Universita degli Studi di Perugia
06100 Perugia

Centro Nazionale di Prevenzione e Difesa Sociale
Piazza Castello 3
20121 Milano

Istituto per gli studi di servizio sociale
Via Arno 2
Roma 00198

Istituto di Socialogia
Facolta di Scienze Politiche
Universita degli Studi di Milano
Via Conservatorio 7
20122 Milano

Dipartimento di Sociologia e de Scienze Politica
Universita della Calabria
Arcavacata
87100 Cosenza

Servizio Richerche Sociologiche e Studi sull' Org.
  della Ing. C. Olivetti & Co.
Via Jervis 24
10015 Ivrea

SPAIN   Instituto "Balmes" de Sociologia
4 Duque de Medinaceli
Madrid 14

Instituto de Estudios Politicos
Plaza de la Marina Espanola 8
Madrid 13

SWITZERLAND   Département de Sociologie
Université de Genève, C.P. 141
1211 Genève 24

Latin-America

ARGENTINA	Centro de Investigaciones Sociales del Instituto Torcuato di Tella Superi 1502 Buenos Aires
	Asociacion de Graduados en Sociologie de la Facultad de Ciencias Sociales Universidad del Salvador Callao 542 Buenos Aires
BRAZIL	Departmento de Ciencias Sociales e Filosofia Universidade Federal do Ceara C.P. 1257 Fortaleza 60000 Ceara
CHILE	Instituto de Sociologia Universidad Catolica de Chile Casilla 1114-D Santiago
DOMINICAN REPUBLIC	Escuela de Sociologia Universidad Nacional Pedro Henriquez Urena Santo Domingo
HAITI	Centre Haïtien d'Investigation en Sciences Sociales rue Bonne Foi, 23 B.P. 1294 Port-au-Prince
PARAGUAY	Centro Paraguayo de Estudios Sociologicos Eligio Ayala 973 Asuncion
VENEZUELA	Centro de Investigaciones en Ciencias Sociales Apartado 12863 Caracas 101
WEST INDIES	Department of Sociology Faculty of Social Sciences University of the West Indies St. Augustine Trinidad
	Department of Economics University of the West Indies Cave Hill Campus G.P.O. Box 64 Barbados

North America

CANADA	Queen's University Department of Sociology Kingston, Ontario
U.S.	Rural Sociological Society 306A Comer Hall Auburn University Auburn, Ala. 36830
	Sociological Abstracts Inc. P.O. Box 22206 San Diego, Ca. 92122

MEMBERS IN CATEGORY E: SUPPORTING ORGANIZATIONS AND INSTITUTIONS

FRG	Forschungsgruppe für Gerontologie Am Bergwerkswald 16 63 Giessen
	Lehrstuhl für Betriebswirtschaftslehre Universitat Munchen Amalienstrasse 73 8 München 73
GREAT BRITAIN	National Documentation Centre for Sport, Physical Education and Recreation University of Birmingham P.O. Box 363 Birmingham B15 2TT

A BIBLIOGRAPHY OF METHODS GUIDES   *2.12*

Documents

ALLPORT, GORDON. *The Use of Personal Documents in Psychological Science.* New York: Social Science Research Council, 1942.

GOTTSCHALK, L.; KLUCKHOHN, C.; and ANGELL, R. *The Use of Personal Documents in History, Anthropology, and Sociology.* New York: Social Science Research Council, 1945.

THOMAS, W. I., and ZNANIECKI, F. *The Polish Peasant in Europe and America.* New York: Dover Publications, 1958.

WEBB, EUGENE J.; CAMPBELL, DONALD T.; SCHWARTZ, RICHARD D.; and SECHREST, LEE. *Unobtrusive Measures: Nonreactive Research in the Social Sciences.* Chicago: Rand McNally, 1966. See chaps. 3 and 4.

Content Analysis

BERELSON, BERNARD. *Content Analysis in Communication Research.* New York: Free Press, 1952.

HOLSTI, OLE R. *Content Analysis for the Social Sciences and Humanities.* Reading, Mass.: Addison-Wesley, 1969.

Direct Observation

BALES, ROBERT F. *Interaction Process Analysis.* Reading, Mass.: Addison-Wesley, 1949. Cf. his revised work, *Personality and Interpersonal Behavior.* New York: Holt, Rinehart & Winston, 1970.

DUNPHY, DEXTER C. *The Primary Group: A Handbook for Analysis and Field Research.* New York: Appleton-Century-Crofts, 1972.

RILEY, MATILDA, and NELSON, EDWARD E., eds. *Sociological Observation: A Comparative Strategy for New Social Knowledge.* New York: Basic Books, 1974.

WEBB, EUGENE J.; CAMPBELL, DONALD T.; SCHWARTZ, RICHARD D.; and SECHREST, LEE. *Unobtrusive Measures: Nonreactive Research in the Social Sciences.* Chicago: Rand McNally, 1966. See chaps. 5 and 6.

Participant Observation

BRUYN, SEVERYN T. *The Human Perspective in Sociology: The Methodology of Participant Observation.* Englewood Cliffs, N.J.: Prentice-Hall, 1966.

FRIEDRICKS, J. and LUDTKE, H. *Participant Observation Theory and Practice.* Lexington, Mass.: D. C. Heath, 1975.

JACOBS, GLENN, ed. *The Participant Observer.* New York: G. Braziller, 1970.

POWDERMAKER, HORTENSE. *Stranger and Friend, The Way of An Anthropologist.* New York: W. W. Norton, 1966.

Questionnaire Construction

LAZARSFELD, PAUL F., and BARTON, ALLEN. "Some General Principles of Questionnaire Classification." In *The Language of Social Research*, edited by Paul F. Lazarsfeld and Morris Rosenberg. Glencoe, Ill.: Free Press, 1962. Pp. 83–92.

OPPENHEIM, A. N. *Questionnaire Design and Attitude Measurement.* New York: Basic Books, 1966. See chaps. 2 and 3.

Interview

CANNELL, CHARLES F.; LAWSON, SALLY A.; and HAUSSER, DORIS L. *A Technique for Evaluating Interviewer Performance: A Manual for Coding and Analyzing Interviewer Behavior from Tape Recordings of Household Interviews.* Ann Arbor, Mich.: Institute of Social Research, University of Michigan, 1975.

HYMAN, HERBERT H., et al. *Interviewing in Social Research.* Chicago: University of Chicago Press, 1954; reissued 1975.

KAHN, ROBERT L., and CANNELL, CHARLES F. *The Dynamics of Interviewing.* New York: John Wiley & Sons, 1957.

MERTON, ROBERT K., et al. *The Focused Interview: A Manual of Problems and Procedures.* Glencoe, Ill.: Free Press, 1956.

GORDEN, RAYMOND L. *Interviewing: Strategy, Techniques, and Tactics.* Rev. ed. Homewood, Ill.: Dorsey Press, 1975.

Staff of the Survey Research Center. *Interviewer's Manual.* Rev. ed. Ann Arbor, Mich.: Institute for Social Research, University of Michigan, 1976.

Index and Scale Construction

BAUER, RAYMOND A., ed. *Social Indicators.* Cambridge, Mass.: MIT Press, 1966.

COMBS, CLYDE H.; DAWES, ROBIN M.; and IVERSKY, AMOS. "Scaling and Data Theory." In *Mathematical Psychology: An Elementary Introduction.* Englewood Cliffs, N.J.: Prentice-Hall, 1970.

EDWARDS, ALLEN. *Technique of Attitude Scale Construction.* New York: Appleton-Century-Crofts, 1957.

LAND, KENNETH C., and SPILERMAN, SEYMOUR, eds. *Social Indicator Models.* New York: Russell Sage Foundation, 1975.

MARANELL, GARY M. ed. *Scaling: A Sourcebook for Behavioral Scientists.* Chicago: Aldine, 1974.

OPPENHEIM, A. N. *Questionnaire Design and Attitude Measurement.* New York: Basic Books, 1966. See chap. 5.

RILEY, MATILDA W.; RILEY, JOHN W.; and TOBY, JACKSON. *Sociological Studies in Scale Analysis.* New Brunswick, N.J.: Rutgers University Press, 1954.

SHAW, MARVIN E., and WRIGHT, JACK M. *Scales for the Measurement of Attitudes.* New York: McGraw-Hill, 1967.

SHELDON, ELEANOR B., and MOORE, WILBERT E. *Indicators of Social Change: A Symposium on Concepts and Measures.* New York: Russell Sage Foundation, 1968.

STOUFFER, SAMUEL, et al. *The American Soldier: Measurement and Prediction,* vol. 4. Princeton, N.J.: Princeton University Press, 1949. See chaps. on Scaling and on Latent Structure Analysis.

TORGERSON, W. *Theory and Methods of Scaling.* New York: John Wiley & Sons, 1958.

The Sample Survey (Vehicle for Data Collection)

HYMAN, HERBERT. *Survey Design and Analysis: Principles, Cases, and Procedures.* Glencoe, Ill.: Free Press, 1955.

HYMAN, HERBERT. *Secondary Analysis of Sample Surveys; Principles, Procedures, and Potentialities.* New York: John Wiley & Sons, 1972.

SUDMAN, SEYMOUR, and BRADBURN, NORMAN M. *Response Effects in Surveys: A Review and Synthesis.* Chicago: Aldine, 1974.

WARWICK, DONALD P. *The Sample Survey.* New York: McGraw-Hill, 1975.

Use of Panels

LAZARSFELD, PAUL F.; PASANELLA, ANN K.; and ROSENBERG, MORRIS, eds. *Continuities in the Language of Social Research.* Rev. ed. of *Language of Social Research.* New York: Free Press of Macmillan, 1975. See section on Panel Analysis.

Use of Informants

SEIDLER, JOHN. "On Using Informants: A Technique for Collecting Quantitative Data and Controlling Measurement Error in Organizational Analysis." *American Sociological Review* 39 (December 1974): 816–31.

Field Methods for Studying Social Organizations

HABENSTEIN, ROBERT W., ed. *Pathways to Data: Field Methods for Studying Ongoing Social Organizations.* Chicago: Aldine, 1970.

HAMMOND, PHILLIP E., ed. *Sociologists at Work.* New York: Basic Books, 1964; reprinted in 1970 as Doubleday Anchor Book.

part 3

Guides to Statistical Analysis

THIS part includes guides that should prove useful to researchers as they seek statistical tools to test hypotheses. They may find it necessary to reformulate initial hypotheses in order to use the most precise statistical test. Qualitative and quantitative variables require appropriate statistics to provide tests of association or of significant differences between groups. In part 3 the researcher will find statistical tests organized to deal with these two kinds of variables. Also the question of the probability of normal distribution of the data forces the researcher to make a distinction between parametric and nonparametric statistics in drawing inferences from samples. These distinctions are set forth in the description of the statistics presented.

Statistical planning is an integral part of designed research. The sooner attention can be given to this part of research the better. After the problem, the theory, study design, and hypotheses are chosen, the time has arrived. Researchers should not wait until they are in the process of gathering or analyzing data. This is especially true for young researchers who wish to avoid mistakes, but all researchers will have better research designs if their statistical designs are prepared before fieldwork begins.

Causal analysis refers to the depicting of the causal relationships of the variables. Zetterberg listed thirteen possible causal chains for three variables.[1] The selection of an appropriate chain is an important first step in designing statistical analysis.

Example: Two major determinants influencing the productivity or effectiveness of a work group are leadership behavior and the morale of workers. The causal relationship is often assigned to the chain that identifies Leadership Behavior as the independent variable(x), Morale as an intervening variable(y), and Productivity as the outcome (or dependent) variable(z). The causal chain can be diagrammed as $x \longrightarrow y \longrightarrow z$. The statistical tests of hypotheses now are given form, and appropriate techniques are applied. Alternate assumptions about the causal relationships of these three variables would call for different treatments.

A multivariate problem with many interacting variables poses more elaborate constructions. A *path model* is important if many independent and intervening variables are involved in measuring relationships with a dependent variable.

Example: Path analysis is discussed in 3.8.d where a path diagram is shown. This model diagrams the interrelationships of variables believed to influence the son's current occupation. Father's occupation and father's education are shown as independent variables, son's education and son's first job as intervening variables. The algebraic representation of the causal scheme now rests on a system of equations rather than the single equation often employed in multiple regression analysis.

Dummy statistical tables become the statistical plan for qualitative data. These tables represent the actual tables to be used for analysis when data are collected and frequencies or values are inserted within them. By setting up dummy tables in advance, a careful appraisal of the appropriate statistics can be made and a selection of the best technique chosen. If the researcher wants help from a statistician, these tables are a necessity. With them decisions can be made as to the statistic, techniques, and confidence that may be entertained. Perhaps a recasting of the data collection process may be called for. Or different types of data are needed. This is the stage at which the researcher needs this kind of information. Later it may not be possible, and valuable time and money may be lost.

Example: Note how Allen Barton in 3.3, "The Idea of Property Space in Social Research," has prepared dummy tables for dichotomous and trichotomous attributes in two-, three-, and four-dimensional space. The variables involve relationships of father's occupation, father's political party with son's occupation and political party. The dummy tables are particularly useful in permitting the effects of the various background variables to be compared, holding the others constant in each case.

Skeleton primary tables are tables proposed for future display of the published data. The scientific worth of the tables depends upon the soundness of the reasoning underlying the classifications and associations of the data. The originator of a set of tables should ask:

What important fact or facts should this table emphasize?
How can these facts be made most evident?
Is the form adapted for the vehicle of publication?[2]

Example of a Skeletal Primary Table:

Product-Moment Correlations between Socioeconomic Status and Sentence Length for Crime Categories in Three States[3]

	New York r r^2 N	Colorado r r^2 N	Mississippi r r^2 N
2nd Degree murder	— — —	— — —	— — —
Forcible rape	— — —	— — —	— — —
Burglary	— — —	— — —	— — —
Embezzlement	— — —	— — —	— — —
Drug offenses	— — —	— — —	— — —

This table will show the product-moment correlation (Pearsonian r) between the socioeconomic status level of defendants and the sentences received for specific crimes within three states. Also to be shown is the proportion of variance(r^2) in one variable that is explained by the other, as well as the sample size (N) for each crime category. Levels of statistical significance for computed correlation coefficients will be shown where relevant.[4]

Reluctance to take these steps in statistical design means that the research is placed under greater risk. The execution of these steps means the heart of the completed product is projected in advance for appraisal and evaluation. Improvements can be made and risks of failure minimized.

No limited set of guides can replace a good text in statistics. However, the researcher can find an array of concepts so organized here that he may be able to survey the dimensions of his problem. Computation guides have been included for the use of the most commonly used statistical measures.

A section on causation and multivariate analysis includes an introduction to the computer, path analysis, and factor analysis.

The bibliography at the end of this part has been selected to provide additional information on statistics, tables, and graphic presentation. Each reference enables the reader to follow step-by-step explanations.

Notes

1. See Hans L. Zetterberg, "On the Decisions in Verificational Studies," p. 33 of this book.

2. For further information about construction of such tables, see Mary Louise Mark, *Statistics in the Making*, Bureau of Business Research Publication 92 (Columbus, Ohio: College of Commerce and Administration, Ohio State University, 1958), pp. 156–79.

3. The suggestion for this table is drawn from Theodore G. Chiricos and Gordon P. Waldo, "Socioeconomic Status and Criminal Sentencing: An Empirical Assessment of a Conflict Proposition," *American Sociological Review* 40 (December 1975): 760.

4. For presentation of the data in graphic form, see Calvin F. Schmid, *Handbook of Graphic Presentation* (New York: Ronald, 1954). For a brief description of graphic presentation, see Pauline V. Young, *Scientific Social Surveys and Research* (3rd ed.; Englewood Cliffs, N.J.: Prentice-Hall, 1956), pp. 360–405.

William Lurie

Instructions for Use of Guide 3.1

This article should sharpen researchers' awareness of the dimensions of their hypotheses as they prepare to test them. As Lurie puts it: "It is the scientist's responsibility to decide exactly what his hypotheses are, what these hypotheses are about, and how sure he wants to be of their correctness. . . . And the more the scientist becomes aware of his responsibilities, and takes them into account in his work, so much more accurate and valid will his conclusions be, and so much more properly related to the reality with which he deals."

Prologue

It has become fashionable to ornament science with statistical embellishments. No equation is complete without at least a double summation sign somewhere in it, sub-ij's attach themselves to familiar Xs, Ys and Zs; and phrases like "poly-modal distribution," "inverse reciprocal correlation," and "multivariate deviations" now can be seen on practically every other page of "The Journal of the Society for Thus-and-So," "The Transactions of the Association for Such-and-Such," and "The Proceedings of the Symposium on Etc., Etc."

But in addition to providing mathematical and linguistic ornamentation for these publications, the statistician, if he is really to assist the scientist, must perform a necessary, but irritatingly annoying task: he must ask the scientist impertinent questions. Indeed, the questions, if bluntly asked, may appear to be not only impertinent but almost indecently prying—because they deal with the foundations of the scientist's thinking. By these questions, unsuspected weaknesses in the foundations may be brought to light, and the exposure of weaknesses in one's thinking is a rather unpleasant occurrence.

The statistician will, then, if he is wise in the ways of human beings as well as learned in statistics, ask these questions diplomatically, or even not ask them as questions at all. He may well guide the discussion with the scientist in such a way that the answers to the questions will be forthcoming without the questions having been even explicitly asked.

And if happily the scientific and statistical disciplines reside within one mind, and it is the scientist's statistical conscience that asks him these questions, instead of impertinent questioning there is valid scientific soul-searching.

Regardless, then, of whether these questions arise inside or outside the scientist's own mind, what are they? These:

1. With respect to the experiment you are performing, just what are your ideas?
2. With respect to the scientific area to which these ideas refer, just what are they about?
3. How sure do you want to be of the correctness of these ideas?

American Scientist 46 (March 1958): 57–61.

In order to understand the statistician's reasons for asking these questions, let us first see how the scientist's activities look to the statistician.

From the statistician's point of view, what the scientist does, is: performs experiments and/or makes observations to obtain data relating to *an idea he has* about the organization of *that portion of the world he is interested in*, so that he can decide *whether his idea was correct or not.*

For each of these italicized aspects of the scientist's activity, there is a corresponding question.

Let us, then, examine each of these aspects of the scientist's activities, and the purpose for and consequences of the question concerning it.

An Idea He Has

The impertinent questioner must take the risk of appearing to imply that the scientist is not thinking clearly. And, of course, even an implication to this effect is not calculated to endear the implier to the heart of the implyee. But it is exactly this implication that, perhaps innocently, is associated with the question, "Just what are your ideas?"

Why does the statistician ask this impertinent question? Because it is a precondition for the statistician's being able to help the scientist accomplish his objective. A hazily formulated idea not only can be discussed, at best, with difficulty, but further, it is practically impossible to test its correctness. Therefore, the statistician has a rule, his name for which is: EXPLICIT HYPOTHESIZATION. This rule expresses the requirement that the idea, whose correctness is to be determined by the experiment, should be stated in as clear, detailed, and explicit form as possible, preferably before the experiment is conducted. This idea can relate either to the influence of one factor or to the influence of several factors, or to the numerical characterization of a property (or properties) of whatever is being experimented on. In the early stages of an investigation, where what are being sought are the influential factors (i.e., those which, when they are at varying levels, give rise to sufficiently varied results), the idea (or hypothesis) need not be specific, but it must be explicit. The hypothesis can be broad, but it must be explicitly broad:—that is, even though it is not a hypothesis about details, its boundary must be sharply delineated.

For example, "Factors, A, B, C, and D individually influence the results," "Factors A and B, acting in conjunction, influence the results differently than would be expected from the effects of A alone and B alone," "Factors A, B, and C, acting in conjunction, etc., etc." Or later in the investigation, and more specifically, "The measurement of the effect of factor A at level a_1, will result in the numerical value $N \pm n$."

To emphasize unmistakably the requirement for explicit hypothesization, let us use an obviously exaggerated example dealing with a particular subject: the task of an industrial psychologist who has been given the job of finding out why the accounting clerks are making too many errors in addition. (The problem of deciding how many errors are "too many" is another statistical problem, which will not be considered here.)

The psychologist, for the purposes of this example, may say to himself: "My training as a psychologist tells me that the situation in which a person operates affects his behavior. So let me find out what the situation is that is causing the clerks to make these errors." If the formulation of the psychologist's idea goes no further than this, he can obviously continue to attempt to find out what the situation is, from now on forever, since "The Situation" has no boundaries.

It might, for example, not only include the working circumstances of the clerks, but their home circumstances, their childhood histories, their dream life; and it is seen that the possibilities are unlimited. As then is obvious, the hypothesis has not been sufficiently explicitly formulated, nor the situation covered by it clearly enough delineated, for a decision to be able to be arrived at as to the correctness of the hypothesis.

But now, let the psychologist's statistical conscience awaken, and his ideas begin to crystallize out of their original diffuseness. "The Situation?—Well, to be more specific, let's just consider the office situation. And within the office situation, I'll pick three factors that I believe affect the performance of the clerks. The factors I'm selecting to study for their effects are: Temperature, Humidity, and Noise. And now, my explicit hypothesis: It makes a difference what the levels of temperature, humidity, and noise are with respect to the number of errors in addition made by the accounting clerks." The hypothesis could (and probably should) have been even more explicitly formulated (e.g., including as factors Illumination Level, Desk Space per employee, etc.) but the direction of the path to statistical virtue has been pointed out, and further travel along that path is left to the reader.

Now, assuming that the hypothesis has been sufficiently explicitly formulated, the scientist and statistician can together review the plan (or design) of the experiment, and assure themselves that such data will be obtained as will be sufficient to determine the correctness (or noncorrectness) of the scientist's idea.

That Portion of the World He Is Interested In

Again, the impertinent questioner must be careful in asking: "Just what are your ideas about?" Even though one may admit that his ideas are not as clearly and explicitly formulated as he would like, the question "Just what are your ideas about?" carries with it, to the person being asked, the implication that he isn't clear about the subject-matter of his ideas, surely not a flattering implication. The statistician has a reason for his implied aspersion on the basis of the scientist's self-esteem. The statistician's reason can be stated to the scientist thus: "It's for your own good. If I am to help you decide, on the basis of the experimental facts, whether your ideas are correct or not, I have to know, as explicitly as possible, not only what your ideas are, but *what they are about*. My name for this requirement is: MODEL FORMULATION." Technically, model formulation establishes the requirement that a clear differentiation be made as to whether the scientist's ideas are intended to be applicable only to the conditions of the experiment (the narrower range of application) or to conditions (i.e., levels of the factors) other than those specific ones under which the experiment is being conducted (the broader range of application). Why the necessity for this differentiation? Because, when the experimental data have been obtained, the analysis of the data is carried on in different ways, depending on whether the hypotheses are intended to have the broader or narrower range of application.

Let us again, for exemplification, return to our industrial psychologist. And, let us say, his experimental conditions are, for temperature, 40°, 55°, and 70°F.; for humidity, 40, 55, and 70 percent; and for noise level, 40, 55, and 70 decibels.

It may well make a difference in the way the experimental data are analyzed to arrive at conclusions (i.e., decisions as to correctness of ideas), and whether any conclusions can be arrived at, and, if so, what they are, depending on whether the scientist wants his conclusions to apply only to the three levels of temperature, humidity, and noise level that have been used in the experiment, or also to other (unspecified) temperature, humidity, and noise levels. Data that support narrow conclusions may not be sufficient to support broader conclusions. Therefore, the scientist must have clearly in mind what his hypotheses are about, and whether, consequently, his conclusions will be broad or narrow; and the statistician's effort to assure that the scientist does have this clearly in mind, may well, to the scientist, appear to be impertinent.

Whether His Idea Was Correct or Not

The statistician's third question—"How sure do you want to be of the correctness of your ideas?" is the least impertinent of the three. This question, unlike the other two, does not probe the foundations of the scientist's thinking, but rather requests him to quantify a previously unquantified aspect of it. (In fact, the request is in accordance with the scientist's own predilection for quantitative data.) This aspect is that dealing with levels of assurance, for which ordinary language supplies us with qualitatively descriptive terms (somewhat sure, rather sure, quite sure, extremely sure). But these terms are not sufficiently explicit for scientific use. Therefore, the statistician asks the scientist to decide upon and express his desired level of assurance in quantitative terms, so that it can be determined, by analysis of the quantitative data, whether the desired level of assurance of the conclusions has been achieved. The statistician's name for the choice and quantitative expression of the desired level of assurance is: SIGNIFICANCE LEVEL SELECTION. And how does the statistician help the scientist choose the desired level of assurance? By bringing to the forefront of the scientist's consciousness his already unconscious awareness of the inherent variability of events (i.e., that, because of chance alone, no repetition of an experiment will give exactly the same results); by helping the scientist decide what assurance is desired that the hypothesis has not been "confirmed" just by the operation of chance alone; and by furnishing the mathematical tools to decide, on the basis of the experimental data, whether the desired level of assurance has been attained. Say, for example, in the temperature-humidity-noise level experiment, when all the data have been accumulated, and the scientist is preparing them for analysis so that he may decide whether his hypotheses were correct or not, the statistician will then say to him: "You know, of course, that if you did the experiment over, under as near the same conditions as possible, you'd get slightly, or even somewhat different results. The results might even, just by chance, be different enough to lead you to believe that temperature does affect accuracy, even though it really doesn't. Or even if you didn't do the experiment over again, the particular experiment you've just done might be the one in which the data are such that you'd believe temperature has an effect though it really doesn't. *But I can test these data of yours.* I can assure you that when you state the conclusion, say, that temperature does affect accuracy, you'll have only a

5 percent, or 1 percent, or 1/10th of 1 percent chance of being wrong, as a result of that off chance I told you about. Now—what chance do you want to take? If you select a very small chance of being wrong in saying there is a temperature effect when there really isn't you're taking a bigger chance of saying there isn't a temperature effect when there really might be. I can figure this out for you also. So again, what chance do you want to take?"

When the scientist has selected the chance he is willing to take of being wrong (or what is equivalent, how sure he wants to be that he is correct) in his conclusions, the statistician can analyze the data and tell the scientist what conclusions he can validly draw (i.e., what decisions he can make about the correctness of his ideas).

Epilogue

One final word. *It is the statistician's responsibility to ask these questions, not to answer them.* It is the scientist's responsibility to decide exactly what his hypotheses are, what these hypotheses are about, and how sure he wants to be of their correctness.

The statistician, in asking his impertinent questions, is just explicitly bringing to the scientist's attention responsibilities that the scientist may not have been aware that he had. And the more the scientist becomes aware of his responsibilities, and takes them into account in his work, so much more accurate and valid will his conclusions be, and so much more properly related to the reality with which he deals.

A NOTE ON STATISTICAL ANALYSIS IN THE *AMERICAN SOCIOLOGICAL REVIEW*, THE *AMERICAN JOURNAL OF SOCIOLOGY*, AND *SOCIAL FORCES*

3.2

Instructions for Use of Guide 3.2

This analysis of statistics used by social scientists provides a basis for evaluating the kinds of statistics most commonly used in research. Note the continuing importance of nonstatistical reporting. However, Pollinger finds an increase in statistical analysis over the past twenty years. Only 23 percent of the earlier articles were statistical, while 57.5 percent of the recent ones are characterized by some type of statistical test.[1] Testing for association and significance lead in frequency. The use of partial correlation, multiple regression, and space analyses is probably an index of increasing application of the computer.

A content analysis was made on every article published in the *American Sociological Review* (*ASR*), the *American Journal of Sociology* (*AJS*), and *Social Forces* (*SF*) from June 1971 through May 1974. These three journals were selected because of their reputation for excellence. A study published in the *American Sociologist* revealed that the *ASR*, *AJS*, and *SF* occupy the three top positions of "prestigious and influential publications" in the field of sociology.[2] The *ASR* had the highest prestige rating, followed in order by the *AJS* and *SF*. The selection of the 1971 through 1974 volumes of the journals was made because of the desire to study the latest trends in sociology. Each of the 472 articles was analyzed for types of statistics employed.[3]

Notes

1. From 23 percent to 65.6 percent in the *ASR* alone.
2. Norval D. Glenn, "American Sociologists' Evaluations of Sixty-Three Journals," *American Sociologist* 6 (November 1971): 298–303.
3. The full article also reports on subject content of the 472 articles.

FROM "TEACHING STATISTICS IN SOCIOLOGY"[*]

Kenneth J. Pollinger

Content Analysis: Statistical Tests Used

In examining the articles for statistical analysis, an article that used no statistical analysis at all, or at the most, arranged the data into percentage tables, was categorized as "nonstatistical" while the "statistical" categories included tests of significance, association, partial correlation, path analysis, space analysis, and nonparametric tests. (Table 1 shows the results of the coding by journal; table 3 by subject area.)

Table 1. *Statistical Tests Used in Journal Articles in ASR, AJS, and SF, 1971–74*[a]

Category	Total		ASR		AJS		SF	
	N	%	*N*	%	*N*	%	*N*	%
No statistical tests	201	42.5	60	34.4	91	52.6	50	40.0
Testing for significance	121	25.6	44	25.2	35	20.2	42	33.6
Testing for association	173	36.6	67	38.5	53	30.6	53	42.4
Partial correlation	49	10.3	22	12.6	14	8.0	13	10.4
Multiple regression	113	23.9	46	26.4	39	22.5	28	22.6
Space analysis	39	6.3	19	10.9	9	5.2	11	8.8
Nonparametric tests	3	0.6	1	0.5	0	0.0	2	1.6
	699[b]		259[b]		241[b]		199[b]	

[a]Total Articles: *ASR*, 174; *AJS*, 173; *SF*, 125; a total of 472.
[b]Totals high because of multiple testing.

Of primary interest in table 1 is the fact that fully 42.5 percent of all the articles published in the three journals during 1971–74 did not employ statistical analysis. Included in this 42.5 percent are those articles that merely present the data in tables for percentage comparison.

In the past twenty years, however, there has been an understandable increase in the number of articles utilizing various forms of statistical analysis. (Methods and statistics is now the second highest ranking area of specialization of current professional Sociologists—Stehr and Larson 1972.) David Gold's analysis (1957) of all articles published in the *ASR* during 1944–53 found that only 170 out of a total of 743 articles used some form of statistical analysis beyond tabular presentation. The decline from 77.1 percent of the earlier articles being nonstatistical to 42.5 percent of the recent ones is significant; however, it still leaves us with a

[*]Reprinted by permission from Kenneth J. Pollinger, "Teaching Statistics in Sociology, a Content Analysis of Articles in the Top Three Sociological Journals." Manuscript.

notable amount of articles not taking advantage of methodological-statistical advances.

Obviously, it would not be appropriate for every published article to be concerned with statistical analysis. The question that comes to mind is whether or not more should. An important thing to remember about most statistical procedures is that basically they represent precautions:

> They are precautions we take before we risk generalizations from incomplete data. They are, moreover, precautions of a standardized nature. They enable us to better compare the results of one study with another. (Ray 1974:371)

Further examination can be made of the comparisons shown in table 2 with respect to the types of statistical tests used in the journal articles. The outstanding point is that the *AJS* consistently ranks lowest of all three journals in every category of statistical analysis. It is most noticeable when looking at an overall comparison of testing: for the *ASR*, 65.6 percent of the articles utilized at least one type of test; for *SF*, 60 percent; and for the *AJS*, just 47.4 percent.

Testing for significance is one of the more basic types of statistical analysis. Roughly 40 percent (121) of the articles that used statistical tests mentioned significance testing. (Table 2 shows the different types of tests of significance used.) At present, there is quite a controversy about the validity of significance tests—the major reasons against them seem to be that they are used for "substantive significance rather than statistical significance," and that they are used in place of other tests that might be more appropriate. As Morrison and Henkel remind us:

> At the risk of being too elementary, we must point out that the knowledge of only the level of significance of a sample statistic tells nothing about the magnitude of the relationship or the difference being studied, nor does it provide any clue as to its theoretical or other interpretation. (Morrison and Henkel 1969:132)

Table 2.   *Tests of Significance Used in Journal Articles in ASR, AJS, and SF, 1971–74*

	Total		ASR		AJS		SF	
	N	%	*N*	%	*N*	%	*N*	%
At least one test of significance used in the article	121	25.6	44	25.2	35	20.2	42	33.6
Chi-square	68	56.1	29	65.9	18	51.4	21	50.0
Analysis of variance	46	38.0	23	52.2	10	28.5	13	30.9
T-ratio	24	19.8	6	13.6	8	22.8	10	23.8
Z-score	10	8.2	2	4.5	3	8.5	5	11.9
Kruskall-Wallis (*H*)	3	2.4	3	6.8	0	—	0	—
Friedman—2-way w/ranks	1	0.8	1	2.2	0	—	0	—

In examining the data from table 1, however, it is encouraging to note that for the most part, the significance tests were used as complements to other tests, rather than as the base for final statements. Only 28 of the 472 articles (5.9 percent) used significance tests without also using another type of statistical test.

Another type of statistical test that requires special attention is the use (or nonuse) of nonparametric tests. These tests are usually used when the data examined violates one or more of the assumptions underlying the "usual" statistical tests. However, this freedom from restricting assumptions is also a drawback to test usage:

> Tests which make no assumptions about the distribution from which one is sampling will tend not to reject a null hypothesis when it is actually false as often as will those tests that do make assumptions. (Boneau 1960:49)

This lack of power of the nonparametric test is a definite handicap, since if it does not reject the null hypothesis, the research is usually not continued further.

With regard to the specific tests used, it is apparent that a few "favorites" are predominant. Tables 2, 3, and 4 itemize the tests used. Of those articles that utilize tests of significance, 56.1 percent mention the chi-square, 38 percent the analysis of variance, and 19.8 percent the t-ratio. Although there is a range of 23 tests of association mentioned, there are just three which occur with a constant amount of frequency. Pearson's product-moment correlation is used in 43.3 percent of the articles which test for association, a correlation matrix is shown in 25.4 percent, and gamma is used 19.6 percent of the time. Factor analysis is the only type of space analysis which occurs frequently (84.6 percent).

Although there has been much concentration on perfecting a variety of statistical methods, the articles studied here did not seem to take advantage of that variety. The tendency seems to be to stick with more established statistical tests.

Table 3. *Tests of Association Used in Journal Articles in ASR, AJS, and SF, 1971-74*

	Total		ASR		AJS		SF	
	N	%	*N*	%	*N*	%	*N*	%
At least one test of association used in article	173	36.6	67	38.5	53	30.6	53	42.4
Pearson's product-moment	75	43.3	22	32.8	31	58.4	22	41.5
Correlation matrix	44	25.4	16	23.8	16	30.1	12	22.6
Gamma	34	19.6	12	17.9	13	23.4	9	16.9
Spearman's rho	12	6.9	2	2.9	4	7.5	6	11.3
Lambda	8	4.6	4	5.9	3	5.6	1	1.8
Eta	7	4.0	4	5.9	1	1.8	2	3.7
Tau-b	7	4.0	0	0.0	2	3.7	5	9.4
Cramer's V	6	3.4	2	2.9	1	1.8	0	0
Phi-squared	5	2.8	4	5.9	1	1.8	0	0
Somer's d_{yx}	4	2.3	2	2.9	0	0	2	3.7
Fisher's Exact test	4	2.3	0	0	1	1.8	3	5.6
Cronbach's A	4	2.3	1	1.4	2	3.7	1	1.8
Tau c	3	1.7	2	2.9	0	0	1	1.8
Phi-coefficient	3	1.7	0	0	2	3.7	1	1.8
Pearson's C	2	1.1	0	0	1	1.8	1	1.8
Yule's Q	2	1.1	0	0	2	3.7	0	0
Koppa (Kruskall's q)	2	1.1	1	1.4	0	0	1	1.8
Goodman-Kruskall's tau-y	1	0.5	1	1.4	0	0	0	0
Tau-a	1	0.5	0	0	1	1.8	0	0
Omega-squared (w^2)	1	0.5	1	1.4	0	0	0	0
Kendall's Q	1	0.5	1	1.4	0	0	0	0
Goodman's Z_g	1	0.5	1	1.4	0	0	0	0
Kappa (K)	1	0.5	0	0	1	1.8	0	0

Table 4. *Tests of Space Analysis Used in Journal Articles in ASR, AJS, and SF, 1971-74*

	Total		ASR		AJS		SF	
	N	%	N	%	N	%	N	%
At least one test of space analysis used in article	39	8.2	19	10.9	9	5.2	11	8.8
Factor analysis	33	84.6	15	78.9	8	88	10	90.9
Smallest space analysis	5	12.8	4	21.0	1	11.1	0	—
Cluster analysis	1	2.5	0	—	0	—	1	9.1

References

BONNEAU, C. ALAN. "The Effects of Violations of Assumptions Underlying the T-test." *Psychological Bulletin* 57 (1960): 49–63.

BROWN, JULIA, and GILMARTIN, BRIAN. "Sociology Today: Lacunae, Emphasis, and Surfeits." *American Sociologist* 4 (November 1969): 283–90.

GOLD, DAVID. "A Note on Statistical Analysis in the American Sociological Review." *American Sociological Review* 22 (June 1957): 322–23.

MORRISON, DENTON, and HENKEL, RAMON. "Significance Tests Reconsidered." *American Sociologist* 4 (May 1969): 131–39.

RAY, JOHN. "Should Sociology Require Statistics?" *Pacific Sociological Review* (July 1974): 370–76.

SHIN, EUI HANG. "Statistics Requirements for Undergraduate Sociology Majors in Colleges and Universities in the United States." *American Sociologist* 10 (May 1975): 92–102.

STEHR, NICO, and LARSON, LYLE E. "Trends in the Ranking of Sociological Specialties." *American Sociologist* 7 (August 1972): 5–6.

3.2.a. ANALYSIS OF TYPES OF ARTICLES PUBLISHED IN THE *AMERICAN JOURNAL OF SOCIOLOGY*, 1965-70

The *American Journal of Sociology* is the oldest sociological journal extant. When the cumulative index for the *American Journal of Sociology* for the years 1965-70 was prepared, an analysis was made by Moshe Schwartz and Elizabeth S. Schmitt of the types of articles published for that period.*

The following list shows a breakdown corresponding to categories used in the Authors Index. The predominance of quantitative studies is clearly shown. The balance given to theoretical and methodological discussions is also to be noted. It will be recalled that Pollinger reported that his 1971–74 survey showed that *AJS* ranked *lowest* of all three major journals in every category of statistical analysis.

	N	%
Survey research and other quantitative studies using data collected for that purpose	94	38
Quantitative investigations based on precollected data, typically demographic studies, and secondary analysis	58	24

*The categories and frequencies reprinted from Supplementary Index to the Cumulative Index, *American Journal of Sociology* 71-75 (1971): v.

Nonquantitative empirical studies	11	5
Theoretical discussions	31	13
Methodological discussions	30	13
Cross-cultural comparisons	7	3
Experiments using controlled conditions	6	2
Case studies	5	2

3.3   THE IDEA OF PROPERTY-SPACE IN SOCIAL RESEARCH*

Allen H. Barton

Instructions for Use of Guide 3.3

This guide presents a technique of classifying qualitative data so that associations may be discovered. Arranging data in "property-space" is particularly useful in permitting the effects of various background variables to be compared, while other variables are held constant in each case. The concept of property-space is valuable because it becomes a way of thinking about qualitative data and the way in which relations may be ascertained. Hans Zeisel, *Say It With Figures* (5th ed. rev.; New York: Harper, 1968), presents a more elaborate description of causal analysis and the role of cross tabulation for the reader who wishes additional knowledge. The more advanced student should consult Herbert Hyman, *Survey Design and Analysis: Principles, Cases, and Procedures* (Glencoe, Ill.: Free Press, 1966). See also the selected readings on causal models and multivariate analysis in the bibliography at the end of part 3.

Everyone is familiar with the idea of indicating location in space by means of coordinates. Every point on this page can be described by two numbers: its distance from the left-hand side and its distance from the bottom (or from any other pair of axes we choose). The location of any point on the earth's surface can be indicated by giving its latitude and longitude, using as base lines the equator and the Greenwich meridian.

Other properties besides location in physical space can likewise be indicated by coordinates. A man can be characterized by his scores on tests of mathematical and linguistic ability, just as by his latitude and longitude. These two scores locate him in a "property-space" with the two dimensions of mathematical ability and linguistic ability. We can chart this property-space on paper by using mathematics score as one axis and linguistic score for the other, just as we can chart the earth's surface. Of course in the latter case we are making a spatial representation of actual spatial dimensions, only on a smaller scale. In the former our distances on paper represent the numbers of correct answers to questions given by people taking tests, or in a larger sense, the ability of their minds to perform certain tasks.

The dimensions on which we "locate" people in property-space can be of different kinds. Most psychological test scores are for all practical purposes *continuous variables*, but they usually do not have equal intervals or a meaningful zero point. They provide only a relative ordering of people. Once we have

*Reprinted by permission from Paul F. Lazarsfeld and Morris Rosenberg, eds., *The Language of Social Research* (Glencoe, Ill.: Free Press, 1955), pp. 40–44. Copyright 1955 by The Free Press, A Corporation.

located a representative sample of the United States population in our mathematical-linguistic property-space, we can say that a man is in the fifth percentile of the population in mathematical ability and in the fortieth in linguistic ability. Sometimes social scientists do work with continuous variables that do have a zero-point and equal intervals, at least formally; age, income, size of community, number of hours spent watching television.

More often, probably, the dimensions will be qualitative properties, which locate cases in one of a number of classes, like "state of birth," "military rank," or "occupation." State of birth locates everyone born in the continental U.S. in one of 51 *unordered classes* (counting District of Columbia). Military rank locates members of the armed forces in what is by definition a set of *rank-ordered classes*, ranging from buck private up to five-star general. Occupations in themselves do not necessarily form a set of ranked classes, although some of them are specifically defined in terms of degree of "skill." We might simply list them arbitrarily, as in alphabetical order. Or we might draw upon outside information about them—for example average income, as known from census data, or prestige status, as discovered through surveys—to arrange them in one or another rank-order.

The simplest type of property by which an object can be characterized is a *dichotomous attribute*, such as voter/nonvoter, white/nonwhite, male/female, or Democrat/Republican. It is always possible to simplify a more complex property by reducing the number of classes that are distinguished. A continuous variable can be cut up to form a set of ranked classes, like income brackets or age levels. A set of ranked classes, in turn, can be simplified by combining all those above a certain point into one class and all those below into a second class, forming a dichotomy. This is done when we reduce the military hierarchy to the distinction between officers and enlisted men, or the income brackets to above or below a certain amount. By picking out one aspect of a set of unordered classes we can sometimes order them into a dichotomy, as when we classify states as east or west of the Mississippi, or occupations as manual or nonmanual.

When we chart the property-space formed by two qualitative characteristics the result is not, of course, a continuous plane, but an array of cells each representing one combination of values on two properties. For example, a study of the 1952 election described people's "political position" in October 1952 in terms of the two dimensions of "usual party affiliations" and "degree of political interest." If one asks Americans what their usual party affiliation is almost everyone falls into three categories: Republicans, Democrats, and independents. These are natural divisions. Degree of interest on the other hand can be divided into any number of ranked categories we please, depending on the alternatives we offer the respondent. In the present case they could rate themselves as having high, medium, or low interest. These two trichotomous dimensions then define a ninefold property-space as shown in table 1.

We can locate a person within this property-space by giving as coordinates his usual party affiliation and his degree of political interest.

There is no reason why we cannot characterize objects by as many properties as we want. We can add a test in historical knowledge to tests in mathematics and language, and characterize our subjects by three coordinates. These can still be presented in the form of a physical model, by using a box in which everyone is located by distance from the left-hand side, from the front, and from the

Table 1. *A Qualitative Property-Space of Political Position*

USUAL PARTY AFFILIATION

		Republican	Democratic	Independent
Degree of Political Interest	High			
	Medium			
	Low			

bottom. If we add a fourth test, for instance, of reading speed, we can give our subjects four coordinates and locate them in a four-dimensional property-space. Thus we can say that someone is in the fifth percentile of the U.S. population in mathematics, the fortieth in language skill, the sixtieth in historical knowledge, and the twenty-ninth in reading speed. We can no longer represent this by a physical model, but we can perform mathematical operations on the four coordinates just as well as on two or three.

In dealing with qualitative property-spaces which have limited numbers of categories on each dimension, we can still chart the property-space on paper even though it is three-dimensional or even higher-dimensional. Let us take the two dimensions of occupation, dichotomized as manual/nonmanual, and political preference, dichotomized as Democratic/Republican. These give us a four-fold table. If we add the dimension of father's occupation, again dichotomized

Table 2. *A Three-Dimensional Attribute-Space Laid Out in Two Dimensions*

Father Manual Occupation

Son's Occupation

Son's Party		Manual	Nonmanual
	Democrat		
	Republican		

Father Nonmanual Occupation

Son's Occupation

Son's Party		Manual	Nonmanual
	Democrat		
	Republican		

as manual/nonmanual, we now have a "two-story" fourfold table: occupation and party of sons of manual workers and occupation and party of sons of non-manually employed people. This can be physically represented by a cube with eight cells, with the original fourfold table repeated on both the "first floor" and the "second floor." If we want to represent this cube on a flat piece of paper, all we have to do is to lay the two "stories" side by side, as an architect would two floor plans. (See table 2 on page 158.)

Now suppose that we ask a fourth question, for example, the father's usual party, again dichotomized as Democratic/Republican. Our property-space then becomes a four-dimensional "cube." But we can still lay out each level on this fourth dimension on paper as we did those on the third. (See table 3 reprinted below.)

The combination of dichotomous attributes produces a type of property-space that may be labeled "dichotomous attribute-space."[1] Position in a dichotomous attribute-space can be indicated as a response-pattern of plus and minus signs, where we have assigned these values (arbitrarily or otherwise) to the two sides of each dichotomy and arranged the dimensions in some order. Thus a Democratic manual worker, whose father was a Democratic manual worker, might be indicated by the coordinates (++++). A Republican nonmanually employed person, whose father was a Democratic manual worker, would have the coordinates (--++), and so on. (This system of notation is often used in "political score-sheets" that show how congressmen voted on a series of bills, a plus sign showing a "correct" vote and a minus sign a "wrong" vote, in terms of a given political viewpoint or economic interest.)

If we are particularly interested in one of the dimensions as a criterion or dependent variable, we may present a dichotomous attribute-space in abbreviated form by showing only the "background" factors as dimensions in the chart, and

Table 3. *A Four-Dimensional Attribute-Space Laid Out in Two Dimensions*

filling in each cell with a figure showing the percent who are "positive" on the criterion behavior. No information is lost since the attribute is a dichotomy, and all those not positive are classified as "negative" on the attribute. It is as if we had raised three-dimensional bars from the two-dimensional chart of background characteristics with a height proportional to the positive answers on the criterion behavior, and then replaced them with figures indicating their height just as altitudes are shown on a flat map. Thus table 3 could be presented as an eightfold table showing the dimensions of father's occupation, father's party, and son's occupation; the cells would be filled in with figures showing "percent Democrat" (or vice versa). (See table 4.)

Table 4. *Abbreviated Presentation of a Four-Dimensional Attribute-Space*

Father's Occupation

	Manual		Nonmanual	
	Son's Occupation		Son's Occupation	
	Manual	Nonmanual	Manual	Nonmanual
Democratic	____% Dem.	____% Dem.	____% Dem.	____% Dem.
Father's Party				
Republican	____% Dem.	____% Dem.	____% Dem.	____% Dem.

Such tables are particularly useful in permitting the effects of the various background variables to be compared, holding the others constant in each case.[2]

To suggest how far the use of very high-dimension property-spaces has actually developed in social research, we need only note that the results of each interview in a survey are normally punched on an IBM card containing 80 columns, each with twelve rows. Such a card provides for an 80-dimensional property-space, with each property having twelve classes. In practice one never uses all eighty dimensions simultaneously to characterize a respondent; however, they are all available to use in whatever smaller combinations we select. If we consider each position in the 80 by 12 matrix as representing a dichotomous attribute (each can either be punched or not punched), we have the possibility of locating each respondent in a dichotomous attribute-space of 960 dimensions.

Notes

1. This has special characteristics that are used in latent-structure analysis, but this will not be discussed here. A dichotomous system is also equivalent to a binary number system, or an "off/on" system of information, as used in computing machines and in communication theory.

2. Many concrete examples can be found in chap. 10 in Hans Zeisel, *Say It With Figures* (New York: Harper, 1968).

Instructions for Use of Guide 3.4

Statistical methods enable us to study and to describe precisely averages, differences, and relationships. The number of statistical tests has risen considerably in the last thirty years and has become so large that not even a professional statistician can keep all of them at his fingertips. As these tests have become more numerous so have the kinds of hypotheses that can be tested by statistical procedures.

Common questions that the researcher often asks are:

Is there a significant difference between these two (or more) groups on this variable? What confidence can I have that observed differences did not occur by chance?

Is there an association between these two (or more) variables? If so, how close is the association?

To ascertain the significance of differences between two or more groups on a given variable the most common statistics used include the t-test, χ^2, and F. A summary of the more common measures of association would include Pearson's product-moment r with its increasing display in correlation matrices, the correlation ratio eta, Gamma G, Spearman's rank difference coefficient rho, Lambda λ and the multiple correlation R.* Consult the bibliography Guide 3.9 for a statistical text describing these measures. Note that computation guides have been included in this handbook for the very useful statistics t, r, χ^2, and r_s.

Guide 3.4, which follows, summarizes common measures of association. Since a major object of scientific inquiry is to discover relationships, these measures become standard equipment in the training of the scientist who uses statistical tests to ascertain relationships.**

a. Pearson product-moment r: For measuring relationships between two variables when both are continuous and the relationship is rectilinear. The coefficient of correlation is most reliable when based upon a large number of pairs of observations.

b. The correlation ratio eta: For measuring relationships between two continuous variables that are related in a curvilinear fashion.

c. Spearman's rank difference coefficient rho r_s: For measuring the association between two rankings. The measure is based on the difference between ranks. It is primarily used where rankings of individual cases on two variables are available so that rankings range from 1 to N for each variable. Rho will have a value of $+1.0$ for a perfect match of ranks, to a value of -1.0 if the ranks are exactly opposite.

---

*Review Table 3: Tests of Association Used in Journal Articles in ASR, AJS, and SF, 1971–74 on page 154.

**See Herman J. Loether and Donald G. McTavish, *Descriptive Statistics for Sociologists* (Boston: Allyn and Bacon, 1974). Note especially pp. 256–57 for table listing current measures with formulae and guides to the selection of the measure appropriate to the dimensions of different problems.

d. Gamma G: For measuring the association between two ordinal variables, each of which is arranged in rank order. Gamma can always achieve the limiting values of -1.0 or +1.0 regardless of the number of ties between the pairs in the data.

e. Lambda λ: For measuring the association between two bivariate distributions where both variables are interpreted to be nominal variables. Lambda simply reverses the role of two variables predicting *x* from information about *y*.

f. Multiple correlation coefficient R: For measuring the maximum relationship that may be obtained between a combination of several continuous (independent) variables and some other continuous (dependent) variable.

g. Partial correlation coefficient $r_{12.3}$: For measuring the relationship between two continuous variables with the effects of a third continuous variable (or several others) held constant.

h. Biserial r: For measuring relationships when one variable is recorded in terms of a dichotomy and the other is continuous. Biserial *r* assumes that the individuals in each of the two categories represent a complete distribution (i.e., not just the two extremes), that the dichotomized variable is really continuous and normally distributed, and that the relationship between the two variables is rectilinear.

i. Point biserial r: For measuring the relationship between a truly dichotomous variable and a continuous variable.

j. Contingency coefficient c: For measuring the association between two variables that can be classified in two or more categories, but when the categories themselves are not quantitative.

k. Phi coefficient ϕ: For measuring the association between two variables that are truly dichotomous. Cf. with Yule's *Q* for appropriate use.

l. Kendall coefficient of concordance N: For measuring the degree of agreement among *m* sets of *n* ranks. If we have a group of *n* objects ranked by each of *m* judges, the coefficient of concordance tells us the degree of agreement among the *m* sets of ranks.*

3.5 FOUR LEVELS OF MEASUREMENT AND THE STATISTICS APPROPRIATE TO EACH LEVEL

Instructions for Use of Guide 3.5

In part 4 many sociometric scales have been included to measure social variables. These scales may be *nominal, ordinal, interval,* and *ratio* types.

A Nominal or Classificatory Scale refers to a level of measurement when numbers or other symbols are used simply to classify an object, person, or characteristic. *Example:* Folkways, Mores, Laws.

The Ordinal or Ranking Scale refers to a level of measurement when objects in various categories of a scale stand in some kind of *relation* to the categories.

*For a good treatment of this coefficient see Sidney Siegel, *Nonparametric Statistics for the Behavioral Sciences* (New York: McGraw-Hill Book Co., 1956), pp. 229–38.

Given a group of equivalence classes, if the relation greater than holds between some but not all pairs of classes we have a partially ordered scale. If the relation greater than holds for all pairs of classes so that a complete rank ordering of classes arises, we have an ordinal scale. *Example:* Socioeconomic status as conceived by Warner in his ranking from Lower Lower to Upper Upper.

The Interval Scale refers to a level of measurement when a scale has all the characteristics of an ordinal scale, and when in addition the distances between any two numbers on the scale are of known size. Then, measurement considerably stronger than ordinality has been achieved. *Example:* Thurstone's Equal-Appearing Interval Scale.

The Ratio Scale refers to a level of measurement when a scale has all the characteristics of an interval scale and in addition has a true zero point as its origin. The ratio of any two scale points is independent of the unit of measurement. *Example:* Centigrade temperature scale.

*Four Levels of Measurement and the Statistics Appropriate to Each Level**

Scale	Defining relations	Examples of appropriate statistics	Appropriate statistical tests
Nominal	1. Equivalence	Mode Frequency Contingency coefficient	Nonparametric test
Ordinal	1. Equivalence 2. Greater than	Median Percentile Spearman r_S Kendall T Kendall W	Nonparametric test
Interval	1. Equivalence 2. Greater than 3. Known ratio of any two intervals	Mean Standard deviation Pearson product- moment correlation Multiple product- moment correlation	Nonparametric and parametric tests
Ratio	1. Equivalence 2. Greater than 3. Known ratio of any two intervals 4. Known ratio of any two scale values	Geometric mean Coefficient of variation	Nonparametric and parametric tests

*By permission from Sidney Siegel, *Nonparametric Statistics for the Behavioral Sciences* (New York: McGraw-Hill, 1956). Copyright 1956 by McGraw-Hill Book Co., Inc.

Each of these scales has defining relations that make particular statistical tests appropriate. Nominal and ordinal scales require nonparametric tests; only interval and ratio scales may permit use of parametric tests. Since most indexes and scales are ordinal, the nonparametric test is of especial importance. It is necessary to match the appropriate statistic with the defining characteristics of the scale. The guide summarizes these relations between type of scale and appropriate statistic.

NONPARAMETRIC STATISTICAL TESTS APPROPRIATE TO VARIOUS TYPES OF SCALES

Instructions for Use of Guide 3.6

In the development of modern statistical methods, the first techniques of inference that appeared were those that made many assumptions about the nature of the population from which the scores were drawn. Since population values are "parameters" these statistical techniques are called *parametric*. For example, a technique of inference may be based on the assumption that the scores were drawn from a normally distributed population. Or the technique of inference may be based on the assumption that both sets of scores were drawn from populations having the same variance (σ^2) or spread of scores. Such techniques produce conclusions that contain qualifications, i.e., "If the assumptions regarding the shape of the population(s) are valid, then we may conclude that...."

More recently a large number of techniques of inference have been developed that do not make stringent assumptions about parameters. These newer nonparametric techniques are "distribution free," so that "Regardless of the shape of the population(s), we may conclude that...."

In the computation of parametric tests, we add, divide, and multiply the scores from samples. When these arithmetic processes are used on scores that are not truly numerical, they naturally introduce distortions in those data and thus throw doubt on conclusions from the test. Thus it is permissible to use the parametric techniques only with scores that are truly numerical. The mean and standard deviation are the central concepts of position and dispersion. Many nonparametric tests, on the other hand, focus on the order or ranking of the scores, not on their "numerical" values. The advantages of order statistics for data in the behavioral sciences are especially pronounced since so many "numerical" scores are numerical in appearance only.

Guide 3.6 presents a wide range of various nonparametric statistical tests. Note that each row divides the tests into those appropriate for nominal, ordinal, and interval scales. The first column contains those tests that may be used when one wishes to determine whether a single sample is from a specified sort of population. Columns 2 and 3 contain tests that may be used when one wishes to compare the scores obtained from two samples—one set considers tests for two related samples, while the other considers tests for two independent samples. Columns 4 and 5 are devoted to significance tests for k (3 or more) samples; one of these presents tests for k related samples and the other presents tests for k independent samples. Column 6 gives nonparametric measures of association and the tests of significance that are useful with some of these.

The field of statistics has developed to the extent that we now have, for almost all research designs, alternative statistical tests that might be used in order to come to a decision about a hypothesis. Having alternative tests, the researcher has two choices—read carefully about criteria to follow in choosing among various tests applicable to a given research design or get advice from a professional statistician. Preferably, he should do both. In order to use Guide 3.6 intelligently, the researcher should note where his problem falls within the table and then consult Sidney Siegel, *Nonparametric Statistics for the Behavioral Sciences* (New York: McGraw-Hill, 1956).

Guide 3.6. Nonparametric Statistical Test [ab]

LEVEL OF MEASURE-MENT	One-sample case	Two-sample case		k-sample case		NONPARAMETRIC MEASURE OF CORRELATION
	Col. 1 (Chap. 4)	Col. 2 Related samples (Chap. 5)	Col. 3 Independent samples (Chap. 6)	Col. 4 Related samples (Chap. 7)	Col. 5 Independent samples (Chap. 8)	Col. 6 (Chap. 9)
Nominal	Binomial test, pp. 36–42 χ^2 one-sample test, pp. 42–47	McNemar test for the significance of changes, pp. 63–67	Fisher exact probability test, pp. 96–104 χ^2 test for two independent samples, pp. 104–11	Cochran Q test, pp. 161–66	χ^2 test for k independent samples, pp. 175–79	Contingency coefficient: C, pp. 196–202
Ordinal	Kolmogorov-Smirnov one-sample test, pp. 47–52 One-sample runs test, pp. 52–58	Sign test, pp. 68–75 Wilcoxon matched-pairs signed-ranks test, pp. 75–83[c]	Median test, pp. 111–16 Mann-Whitney U test, pp. 116–27 Kolmogorov-Smirnov two-sample test, pp. 127–36 Wald-Wolfowitz runs test, pp. 136–45 Moses test of extreme reactions, pp. 145–52	Friedman two-way analysis of variance by ranks, pp. 166–72	Extension of the median test, pp. 179–84 Kruskal-Wallis one-way analysis of variance by ranks, pp. 184–93	Spearman rank correlation coefficient: r_s, pp. 202–13 Kendall rank correlation coefficient: r, pp. 213–23 Kendall partial rank correlation coefficient: $r_{xy.z}$, pp. 223–29 Kendall coefficient of concordance: W, pp. 229–38
Interval		Walsh test, pp. 83–87 Randomization test for matched pairs, pp. 88–92	Randomization test for two independent samples, pp. 152–56			

[a] Each column lists, cumulatively downward, the tests applicable to the given level of measurement. For example, in the case of k related samples, when ordinal measurement has been achieved both the Friedman two-way analysis of variance and the Cochran Q test are applicable.

[b] For use of this table, consult Sidney Siegel, Nonparametric Statistics for the Behavioral Sciences (New York: McGraw-Hill, 1956).

[c] The Wilcoxon test requires ordinal measurement not only within pairs, as is required for the sign test, but also of the differences between pairs. See the discussion on pp. 75–76 of Siegel.

Researchers at the Institute of Social Research, University of Michigan, have prepared a guide for selecting statistical techniques for both parametric and non-parametric statistics. The core of the guide—a "decision tree"—consists of sixteen pages of sequential questions and answers that lead the user to the appropriate technique. It presents a systematic but highly condensed overview of over one hundred currently used statistics and statistical techniques and their uses. These are indexed for the decision tree, which is built around two major questions:

How Many Variables Does the Problem Involve?

ONE VARIABLE_____   TWO VARIABLES_____
MORE THAN TWO VARIABLES_____

How Do You Want to Treat the Variables with Respect to Scale of Measurement?

NOMINAL_____   ORDINAL_____   INTERVAL_____
(Including all possible combinations for two and three variable measurements)

Appendices cite major references to each statistic, programs of the OSIRIS III computer software system that compute given statistics, and new or rarely used statistical techniques.[1]

Note

1. Frank M. Andrews, Laura Klem, Terrence N. Davidson, Patrick M. O'Malley, and Willard L. Rodgers, *A Guide for Selecting Statistical Techniques for Analyzing Social Science Data* (Ann Arbor, Mich.: Institute of Social Research, University of Michigan, 1974).

3.7   COMPUTATION GUIDES*

Instructions for Use of Guide 3.7

The computation guides that follow describe procedures for computing four statistics commonly needed by research workers in the behavioral sciences. Statistics t and r are parametric statistics, assuming randomness and normality of the populations; χ^2 *and* r_s are nonparametric or "distribution free," only randomness is generally assumed.

The computation design for the t test of the significance of the difference between two means is for the case of two independent samples. This is the test commonly used to test the difference between two means because we are often dealing with small samples, and we cannot assume that our data and values of t derived from them are normally distributed as are the parameters of large samples of 500 or more observations. However, it is assumed that the observations are drawn from normally distributed populations. The computation design for r, Pearson's product-moment coefficient of correlation, is useful when the number of cases is relatively large and the correlation chart is desired as a substitute for machine calculation. Pearson's r is for measuring relationships between two variables when both are continuous and the relationship is rectilinear. Both t and r may be used when the scores under analysis result from measurement in the strength of at least an *interval scale*.

*It should be understood that computer programs exist for all common statistical measures. These guides are used by researchers working with small samples or when a computer is not available.

The computation design for χ^2 is for testing significance of association between two attributes; for the general $r \times s$ case and for the special 2×2 table. This is the most widely used statistic for use with qualitative variables. The Spearman rank order coefficient r_s is the nonparametric statistic corresponding to the parametric Pearsonian r. This statistic is based on two sets of rankings of the same set of items. The Spearman rank order coefficient is not limited by the restrictions of normality and linearity imposed upon the Pearsonian product-moment r. While χ^2 is a test of the *existence* of a possible association, r_s provides a measure of the *degree of relationship* between two sets of rankings. Both χ^2 and r_s may be used when the scores under analysis result from measurements of *ordinal* or *nominal scales*.

3.7.a t TEST OF SIGNIFICANCE BETWEEN TWO MEANS OF INDEPENDENT SAMPLES

Computation Design for t Test of the Difference Between Two Means, for Two Independent Samples*

$$\text{from } S_1: \quad \overline{X}_1 = \Sigma X_{1i}/N_1$$

$$\Sigma x_1{}^2 = \Sigma X_{1i}{}^2 - (\Sigma X_{1i})^2/N_1$$

$$\text{from } S_2: \quad \overline{X}_2 = \Sigma X_{2i}/N_2$$

$$\Sigma x_2{}^2 = \Sigma X_{2i}{}^2 - (\Sigma X_{2i})^2/N_2$$

1. H_0: (See below for instructions.)

2. $s_{\overline{x}1-\overline{x}2} = \sqrt{\left(\dfrac{\Sigma x_1{}^2 + \Sigma x_2{}^2}{N_1 + N_2 - 2}\right) \left(\dfrac{1}{N_1} + \dfrac{1}{N_2}\right)}$

$$=$$

3. $t = \dfrac{\overline{X}_1 - \overline{X}_2}{s_{\overline{x}1-\overline{x}2}} =$

4. d.f. $= N_1 + N_2 - 2 =$

5. $P =$

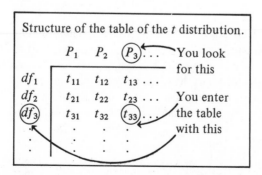

Structure of the table of the t distribution.

*From Morris Zelditch, Jr., *A Basic Course in Sociological Statistics* (New York: Holt, 1959), p. 245. See Theodore R. Anderson and Morris Zelditch, Jr., *A Basic Course in Statistics: With Sociological Applications* (3rd ed.; New York: Holt, 1975), pp. 272–77, for further discussion.

1. Formulate the null hypothesis you wish to test. This will determine whether you are to make a two-sided or one-sided test. The chief null hypotheses are $\mu_1 = \mu_2$ (two-sided), $\mu_1 \leqslant \mu_2$, or $\mu_1 \geqslant \mu_2$ (both one-sided). Write the hypothesis on line 1.

2. Compute the standard error of the difference by pooling estimates of the sums of squares. Enter on line 2.

3. Assume that both samples are normally and independently distributed; assume also that they have equal variances; then the distribution of t, which is the difference between the means divided by the estimated standard error of the difference, follows the t distribution with $N_1 + N_2 - 2$ degrees of freedom. Enter t on line 3 and d.f. on line 4.

4. With the value of t and d.f. you enter the table of t. You are looking for P, the probability that a value of t this large or larger would have been obtained by chance if the null hypothesis were true. P will be shown along the head of the table, d.f. down the side, and the values of t will be shown in the body of the table. The probability shown will be two-tailed (i.e., the *sum* of the probability to the right of t and to the left of $-t$); if the hypothesis is one-sided, use one-half the tabled probability.

5. If P is equal to, or less than, 0.05, reject the null hypothesis. (Set the level of significance at 0.01 if you prefer greater certainty.) If P is greater than 0.05, accept the null hypothesis.

3.7.b. PEARSONIAN r TO MEASURE LINEAR CORRELATION BETWEEN TWO VARIABLES

Instructions for Calculation of r from Coded Group Data by Means of a Correlation Chart*

After the scatter diagram has been completed, and the distribution has been judged to be rectilinear, the data are then transferred to some standard product-moment correlation chart. It is much cheaper, quicker, and more reliable to use a printed correlation chart than it is to lay one out by hand. The correlation chart that will be used in the present discussion was devised by Stuart Chapin.[1]

The following instructions summarize the various steps to be observed in computing a coefficient of correlation with this type of chart, which is shown on pages 169–70.

1. The class-intervals for both the X- and Y-variables should be written in the spaces at the top and left-hand side of the correlation chart and the number of cases recorded in the proper cells. The frequencies for the two variables should also be entered on the chart. This operation involves merely a transferral of the essential data from the scatter diagram to the correlation chart. In selecting the zero-intervals for the two variables, an attempt should be made to choose

*Calvin F. Schmid in Pauline V. Young, *Scientific Social Surveys and Research* (4th ed.; Englewood Cliffs, N.J.: Prentice-Hall, 1966), pp. 311–14. © 1966. By permission of Prentice-Hall, Inc.

Y \ X	-10	-9	-8 *61*	-7 *62*	-6 *63*	-5 *64*	-4 *65*	-3 *66*	-2 *67*	-1 *68*	0 *69*	+1 *70*	+2 *71*	+3 *72*	+4 *73*	+5 *74*	+6 *75*	+7 *76*	+8 *77*	+9	+10
+10	100	90	80	70	60	50	40	30	20	10	0	10	20	30	40	50	60	70	80	90	100
+9	90	81	72	63	54	45	36	27	18	9	0	9	18	27	36	45	54	63	72	81	90
+8	80	72	64	56	48	40	32	24	16	8	0	8	16	24	32	40	48	56	64	72	80
+7	70	63	56	49	42	35	28	21	14	7	0	7	14	21	28	35	42	49	56	63	70
+6 *200–209*	60	54	48	42	36	30	24	18	12	6	0 *1*	6	12 *1*	18	24	30 *1*	36	42	48	54	60
+5 *190–199*	50	45	40	35	30	25	20	15	10	5	0	5	10 *1*	15	20	25	30	35	40	45	50
+4 *180–189*	40	36	32	28	24	20	16	12	8	4	0 *1*	4 *2*	8	12 *1*	16 *4*	20 *3*	24	28	32	36	40
+3 *170–179*	30	27	24	21	18	15	12	9	6 *1*	3	0 *3*	3 *3*	6 *2*	9 *2*	12 *1*	15 *2*	18 *1*	21	24	27	30
+2 *160–169*	20	18	16	14	12	10	8	6	4	2 *4*	0 *5*	2 *7*	4 *8*	6 *9*	8 *3*	10 *2*	12	14	16 *1*	18	20
+1 *150–159*	10	9	8	7	6	5 *1*	4 *2*	3 *4*	2 *6*	1 *4*	0 *11*	1 *9*	2 *3*	3 *4*	4 *3*	5	6	7	8	9	10
0 *140–149*	0	0	0	0	0	0	0 *1*	0 *5*	0 *2*	0 *20*	-+*8*	0 *12*	0 *9*	0 *4*	0 *4*	0	0 *1*	0	0	0	0
-1 *130–139*	10	9	8	7	6	5	4 *2*	3 *5*	2 *12*	1 *7*	0 *7*	1 *5*	2 *3*	3 *1*	4	5	6	7	8	9	10
-2 *120–129*	20	18	16 *1*	14	12 *3*	10 *4*	8 *4*	6 *5*	4 *4*	2 *4*	0	2	4	6 *1*	8	10	12	14	16	18	20
-3 *110–119*	30	27	24	21	18 *1*	15 *1*	12 *1*	9	6 *2*	3 *3*	0 *1*	3	6	9	12	15	18	21	24	27	30
-4 *100–109*	40	36	32	28	24	20	16 *1*	12	8	4	0	4	8	12	16	20	24	28	32	36	40
-5 *90–99*	50	45	40 *1*	35	30	25	20	15	10	5	0	5	10	15	20	25	30	35	40	45	50
-6	60	54	48	42	36	30	24	18	12	6	0	6	12	18	24	30	36	42	48	54	60
-7	70	63	56	49	42	35	28	21	14	7	0	7	14	21	28	35	42	49	56	63	70
-8	80	72	64	56	48	40	32	24	16	8	0	8	16	24	32	40	48	56	64	72	80
-9	90	81	72	63	54	45	36	27	18	9	0	9	18	27	36	45	54	63	72	81	90
-10	100	90	80	70	60	50	40	30	20	10	0	10	20	30	40	50	60	70	80	90	100
f			*2*	*0*	*4*	*6*	*11*	*19*	*27*	*42*	*41*	*38*	*27*	*22*	*15*	*8*	*2*	*0*	*1*		
d_x	-10	-9	-8	-7	-6	-5	-4	-3	-2	-1	0	+1	+2	+3	+4	+5	+6	+7	+8	+9	+10
fd_x			*-16*	*0*	*-24*	*-30*	*-44*	*-57*	*-54*	*-42*		*38*	*54*	*66*	*60*	*40*	*12*	*0*	*8*	*+27*	
fd_x^2	100	81	64 *128*	49 *0*	36 *144*	25 *150*	16 *176*	9 *171*	4 *108*	1 *42*	0	1 *38*	4 *108*	9 *198*	16 *240*	25 *200*	36 *72*	49 *0*	64 *64*	81	100

Correlation Chart by F. Stuart Chapin

f	d_y	fd_y	fd_y^2	Σfd_{xy}^+	Σfd_{xy}^-
	+10		100		
	+9		81		
	+8		64		
	+7		49		
3	+6	18	36 108	42	
1	+5	5	25 25	10	
11	+4	44	16 176	144	
15	+3	45	9 135	99	6
39	+2	78	4 156	160	8
47	+1	47	1 47	39	41
66	0	Σ 237	0		
42	-1	-42	1 42	54	14
30	-2	-60	4 120	178	6
9	-3	-27	9 81	66	
1	-4	-4	16 16	16	
1	-5	-5	25 25	40	
	-6	Σ -138	36		
	-7		49		
	-8		64		
	-9		81		
	-10		100		

265 N $\Sigma fd_y = +99$ $\Sigma fd_y^2 = 931$

$\Sigma fd_{xy}^+ = 848$
$\Sigma fd_{xy}^- = 75$

$\Sigma fd_x = +11$
$\Sigma fd_x^2 = 1839$

$\Sigma fd_{xy} = +773$

X *Height*
Y *Weight*

r = +.59973

S.E.$_r$ = .039

$$r = \frac{N\Sigma fd_{xy} - [\Sigma fd_x][\Sigma fd_y]}{\sqrt{N\Sigma fd_x^2 - [\Sigma fd_x]^2} \cdot \sqrt{N\Sigma fd_y^2 - [\Sigma fd_y]^2}} = \frac{265[773] - [11][99]}{\sqrt{265[1839] - [11]^2} \sqrt{265[931] - [99]^2}}$$

$$= \frac{204,845 - 1089}{\sqrt{487,335 - 121} \sqrt{246,715 - 9801}}$$

$$= \frac{203,756}{\sqrt{487,214} \sqrt{236,914}}$$

$$= \frac{203,756}{339,746.53} = +.59973 \text{ or } .60$$

COMPUTED BY _____   DATE _____

intervals in which the means of the respective distributions are most likely to occur. In this problem, 69 was chosen to represent the zero-interval for the X-variable and 140 to 149 for the Y-variable.

2. For the X-variable determine the products of (f) (d_x) and record them in the fd_x row. Multiply (f) (d_y) for the Y-variable and enter in the fd_y column. Care should be taken to observe signs. Determine the algebraic sums of the fd_x row and the fd_y column. In the chart on pages 169–70 it will be observed that $\Sigma fd_x = +11$ and $\Sigma fd_y = +99$.

3. The respective values of fd_x^2 are next obtained, as are also the values of fd_y^2, and recorded on the chart. Add the fd_x^2 row and the fd_y^2 column. In the problem, $\Sigma fd_x^2 = 1,839$ and $\Sigma fd_y^2 = 931$. It will be recalled that the second and third steps are identical with those used in computing the standard deviation.

4. The fourth operation is different from anything that has thus far been discussed. First, note the small figures printed in the upper left-hand corner of each cell. Second, observe the signs for each of the quadrants indicated in the center of the field of the chart. The lower left-hand quadrant and the upper right-hand quadrant are plus (+) and the other two are minus (−). Multiply the number of cases in each cell by the corresponding printed figure in the cell, observing signs. The products are entered in either the $\Sigma fd_{xy}+$ or the $\Sigma fd_{xy}-$ column, depending on the sign. Let us illustrate this step by performing the computations in the row 130 to 139 in the chart on pages 169–70. Multiply each of the frequencies in the row designated by the class-interval 130 to 139 by the small printed figures in each of the corresponding cells. The products for the numbers located in the plus quadrant are as follows: $(4)(2) = 8$; $(3)(5) = 15$; $(2)(12) = 24$; and $(1)(7) = 7$. The sum of these products, which is 54, is entered in the $\Sigma fd_{xy}+$ column. The products of the numbers for this row that are located in the minus quadrant are: $(3)(1) = -3$; $(2)(3) = -6$; and $(1)(5) = -5$. By adding these products together we have −14, which is recorded in the $\Sigma fd_{xy}-$ column. The figures in each of the columns are added and entered on the chart. The next step is to determine the algebraic sum of $\Sigma fd_{xy}+$ and $\Sigma fd_{xy}-$. In the problem the figures are: $848 - 75 = 773$.

5. This completes all the preliminary computations on the chart. The final step is to substitute in the formula on the right side of the chart and proceed with the calculations. It will be observed from the chart that the proper substitutions have been made in the formula and the coefficient of correlation has been computed for the illustrative problem. The coefficient of correlation between height and weight for this sample of 265 men students is $r = +.60$. The standard error is $\pm.039$. S.E.$_r = (1 - r^2)/\sqrt{N}$.

Note

1. All of the printed forms for computing the coefficient of correlation are very similar. A few of the better known charts are: (1) Thurstone (published by C. H. Stoelting Company, Chicago); (2) Otis (World Book Company, New York); (3) Cureton and Dunlop (Psychological Corporation, New York); (4) Tryon (University of California); (5) Ruch-Stoddard (University of Iowa); (6) Holzinger (University of Chicago); (7) Kelley (World Book Company, New York); and (8) Durost-Walker (World Book Company).

3.7.c. χ^2 TEST OF ASSOCIATION

Computation Design for χ^2 for Testing Significance of Association Between Two Attributes; for the General $r_i \times s$ Case and for the Special 2×2*

n_{11}	n_{12}	n_{13}	$\cdots$	n_{1s}	$n_{1\cdot}$
n_{21}	n_{22}	n_{23}	$\cdots$	n_{2s}	$n_{2\cdot}$
n_{31}	n_{32}	n_{33}	$\cdots$	n_{3s}	$n_{3\cdot}$
$\cdot$	$\cdot$	$\cdot$		$\cdot$	$\cdot$
$\cdot$	$\cdot$	$\cdot$		$\cdot$	$\cdot$
n_{r1}	n_{r2}	n_{r3}	$\cdots$	n_{rs}	$n_{r\cdot}$
$n_{\cdot 1}$	$n_{\cdot 2}$	$n_{\cdot 3}$	$\cdots$	$n_{\cdot s}$	N

1	2	3	4	5
O	E	$O - E$	$(O - E)^2$	$(O - E)^2/E$
n_{11}	$n_1 . n_{\cdot 1}/N$			
n_{12}	$n_1 . n_{\cdot 2}/N$			
n_{13}	$n_1 . n_{\cdot 3}/N$			
$\cdot$	$\cdot$			
$\cdot$	$\cdot$			
n_{rs}	$n_r . n_{\cdot s}/N$			

$$\chi^2 = \Sigma [(O - E)^2/E]$$
$$d.f. = (r - 1)(s - 1)$$

1. Enter the observed frequencies in column 1.
2. Calculate the expected values, E, as follows: find the marginal in the row containing the cell ij and the marginal in the column containing the cell, and multiply them together, giving $n_i . n_{\cdot j}$; then divide by N, the total number of observations in the table, giving $n_i . n_{\cdot j}/N$, and enter in column 2.
3. Subtract the expected values from the observed, column 2 from 1, and enter the result in column 3.
4. Square the differences obtained and enter in column 4.
5. Divide each entry in column 4 by the expected values in column 2 and enter in column 5.
6. Add up column 5. This gives you χ^2.
7. To find the number of degrees of freedom with which you enter the table, take one less than the number of rows times one less than the number of columns $(r - 1)(s - 1)$.

Interpretation of χ^2 as a Test of Relationship Between Variables

As reported by David Gold in "A Note on Statistical Analysis in the *American Sociological Review*," "qualitative data are by far the most common data with

---

*From Zelditch, *Basic Course in Sociological Statistics*, p. 290. See also Theodore R. Anderson and Morris Zelditch, Jr., *A Basic Course in Statistics: With Sociological Applications* (3rd ed.; New York: Holt, Rinehart & Winston, 1975), pp. 256–64.

which the sociologist concerns himself.—It is evident that, on the most elementary descriptive level, there is markedly inadequate statistical analysis of qualitative data."

These statements should alert the social science researcher to the importance of the correct use and interpretation of χ^2. It is this coefficient which appears most frequently in social science research as a test of association and significance. The following article by Thomas J. Duggan and Charles W. Dean should be "must" reading for all social scientists.

3.7.d. COMMON MISINTERPRETATIONS OF SIGNIFICANCE LEVELS IN SOCIOLOGICAL JOURNALS*

Thomas J. Duggan and Charles W. Dean

Periodically, the uses and misuses of probability statistics in social and behavioral science research have been reviewed. For instance, in 1949 Lewis and Burke pointed to several misuses of the chi-square test[1] and in 1959 an article by Selvin stimulated discussion on the general question of using statistics in social surveys.[2] Most recently, Skipper, Guenther, and Nass reviewed the discussion of substantive interpretation associated with significant levels.[3] While such discussions have served to clarify some of the technical requirements and have corrected some of the misunderstandings often associated with the use of statistical tests, one crucial matter has received relatively little attention. This concerns the substantive interpretation of significance tests and the consequences of such interpretations.

The frequently used chi-square test, and the interpretations given to data analyzed by this statistic, will serve to illustrate the problem. This statistic can be used to test goodness of fit or independence although it is the latter which is more frequently used in reporting research. Since this is a test of the independence of variables, significant values of chi-square are often taken to indicate a dependence or relationship between variables. In interpreting such relationships, there are two serious problems which are often overlooked. The first concerns the strength of relationship and the second the form of relationship.

Strength of Relationship

As to the first problem, if the chi-square is significant at the chosen level, then the investigator routinely rejects the null hypothesis of independence and tentatively accepts the alternate hypothesis that the variables are dependent or are related. Regardless of how low the probability associated with the obtained value of chi-square, nothing can be inferred about the strength or degree of that relationship. However, in practice, this point is often overlooked.

Consider table 1 which was reported in a major sociological journal within the last year.[4] According to the author's interpretation, the significance level of the chi-square test was so high that if variables X and Y were not clearly separate measures, "We would suspect the relationship to be tautological." Since the authors failed to report the degree of association, Goodman and Kruskels' gamma was computed. In this instance, gamma equalled −.30 which suggests a

*Reprinted from *American Sociologist* 3 (February 1968): 45–46.

Table 1

Variable Y	Variable X			
	Very high	High	Low	Very low
High	5	24	17	9
Moderate	12	18	9	3
Low	19	22	16	2

$x^2 = 14.0, P < .05, G = -.30.$

Table 2

Variable Y	Variable X		
	High	Moderate	Low
High	24	18	10
Moderate	19	12	7
Low	19	18	21

$x^2 = 6.2, P < .20, G = .22.$

relationship which is far from tautological. The difference in the interpretation based on chi-square and gamma should be noted and emphasized. In contrast to the above data, consider table 2 which was presented in the same article.

In this case, the probability is such that the sociologist normally would accept the null hypothesis of independence. However, gamma was computed for these data and G equalled .22. Here, data non-significant according to chi-square has a relationship only slightly lower than that of the preceding example, where it was concluded that the variables were highly related. To further demonstrate the need for sensitivity to the difference between significance level and strength of association, table 3 was constructed.[5]

Table 3 clearly demonstrates that while chi-square, properly used, may be sensitive to the dependence of variables, after dependence is shown the usefulness of this statistic is exhausted. As the data of table 3 show, significance at the .001 level could mean that the relationship between the variables could be less than .09 or more than .80. At the .001 level, the distribution of the strength of

Table 3 *A Comparison of Level of Significance and Strength of Relationship (n = 45 articles)*

Level of significance	Strength of Relationship								
	.00 to .09	.10 to .19	.20 to .29	.30 to .39	.40 to .49	.50 to .59	.60 to .69	.70 to .79	.80 to .89
.001	3	2	2	8	..	1	..	2	3
.01	1	..	6	..	2	..	..	..	..
.05	4	3	..	..	..	..	..	..	..
.10	1	..	1	..	..	..	..	..	..
.20	1	1	1	..	..	..	..	..	..
.30+	..	3	..	..	..	..	..	..	..

association appears to approach randomness. While these data do show that non-significance, or significance at or about the arbitrary .05 level, will usually result in a relationship which is consistently weaker, the relationship is as likely to be above .10 at the .30 level as at the .05 level. Still, all three tables reporting significance above the .30 level had gammas ranging between .10 and .19. In contrast, of the seven tables reporting significance at .05, only three had gammas in the .10 to .19 range, while four tables had gammas below .10. If more non-significant tables were reported in the journals, the distribution of measures of association would probably be even broader. Generally, the lower the significance level, the greater the probability of a low relationship, but this cannot be assumed. These data emphatically demonstrate that a measure of strength of association is necessary before statements about strength of relationship can be made.

These data illustrate the serious problem in interpreting significance levels of the chi-square test of independence and indicate the need for a reminder that statistical significance is not equatable with practical significance. A significant chi-square value at best, permits one to say that *probably* there is some dependence between variables in the population, but the extent of dependence may be virtually zero *regardless of the significance level*. The consequences for understanding the phenomena under investigation and for the construction of theories require constant awareness of the limited interpretations which can be given to statistical significance.

Form of Relationship

The second problem refers to the form of relationship between variables. In using tables three by three or larger, users of the chi-square are often prone to think and interpret results in terms of linear relationships, but the contingency table and the chi-square statistic are not sensitive to and provide no basis for assuming the existence of this form of relationship.

The data of table 4, also presented in a major sociological journal within the last year, illustrate the error in interpreting the direction of the relationship in linear terms. The author stated that the data of this table confirmed the hypothesis that the greater the degree of variable X, the greater the degree of variable Y. An inspection of the table reveals that this is not the case. As table 4 indicates, the largest number of subjects ranking in the "frequent" category of variable X rank in the low category of variable Y. However, the largest number of subjects in the "occasional" and "infrequent" categories of variable X rank in the

Table 4

Variable Y	Variable X		
	Frequent	Occasional	Infrequent
High	3	9	6
Moderate	14	30	12
Low	17	12	6

x^2 (4df) = 8.51; $P < .05$.

"moderate" category of variable Y. Only those ranking "low" on variable Y are distributed in the expected pattern.

Another team of authors in a recent edition of another sociological journal presented data similar to that of table 4 to test the hypothesis that the greater the degree of variable A, the higher the degree of variable B. They computed chi-square values for their data table and stated, "The relationship shown is significant beyond the .001 level; therefore, the hypothesis is accepted." Throughout the article, the authors made similar statements from similar data about linear relationships.

While the above authors did not attempt to disguise their acceptance of linearity, frequently, other researchers state a linear hypothesis, present the data, table, accept the hypothesis on the basis of the chi-square probability and then discuss only those proportions of the table which fit the linear model. This more subtle but equally erroneous procedure appears frequently in the sociological literature.

A linear relationship exists only if the pattern of concentration of subjects lies along a diagonal of the table. If this is not the case, the relationship cannot be interpreted as a linear one. If the phenomenon of possible nonlinearity is not taken into account or if the implication of linearity is made in interpreting chi-square, serious consequences again arise in interpreting data and in developing explanatory theories. This problem can be averted by inspecting the data table, outlining the pattern of concentration and describing the pattern.

Conclusion

To avoid these errors of confusing significance with strength of association and of misinterpreting form of relationship, two elementary safeguards can be exercised in reporting results. One is routinely to compute and report a measure of degree of association in addition to the statistical test whenever this is possible. The second safeguard is the introduction of care and caution in the verbal interpretation of data tables and the inferred association of variables.

In this day when computer technology is so drastically improving the analytical tools of the sociologist, it seems paradoxical that there is a need to remind researchers of such basic rules of interpretation.

Notes

1. Don Lewis and C. J. Burke, "The Use and Misuse of The Chi-square Test," *Psychological Bulletin* 46 (1949): 433–89.

2. Hanan Selvin, "A Critique of Tests of Significance in Survey Research," *American Sociological Review* 22 (October 1957): 519–27.

3. James K. Skipper, Anthony L. Guenther, and Gilbert Nass, "The Sacredness of .05: A Note Concerning the Uses of Statistical Levels of Significance in Social Science," *American Sociologist* 2 (February 1967): 16–18.

4. Since the purpose of these tables is to illustrate peculiarities in the use of chi-square rather than to criticize individual research, no tables will identify either author, journal or original variables actually treated. However, all tables were reported in refereed sociological journals within a year prior to the writing of this piece.

5. These data were derived from major sociological journals published between 1955 and 1965 in a systematic search for three by three tables, both variables ordinal.

3.7.e. SPEARMAN'S RANK ORDER CORRELATION

Computation Design for Spearman Rank Order Correlation Coefficient, r_s*

K_i designates an ordered position. K_{xi} designates the position of the ith observation in an array of the X variable; K_{yi} designates the position of the *same* observation in the Y array. If, for example, the first observation, O_1, is first in the X array and fourth in the Y array, the first row of the layout form below should read

$$K_{x1} = 1, K_{y1} = 4, K_{x1} - K_{y1} = -3, (K_{x1} - K_{y1})^2 = 9$$

	(1) O_i	(2) K_{xi}	(3) K_{yi}	(4) d	(5) d^2
O_1	K_{x1}	K_{y1}	$K_{x1} - K_{y1}$	$(K_{x1} - K_{y1})^2$
O_2	K_{x2}	K_{y2}	$K_{x2} - K_{y2}$	$(K_{x2} - K_{y2})^2$
O_N	K_{xN}	K_{yN}	$K_{xN} - K_{yN}$	$(K_{xN} - K_{yN})$

$$\Sigma(K_{xi} - K_{yi})^2 = \Sigma d^2 =$$

$$r_s = 1 - \frac{6\Sigma d^2}{N(N^2 - 1)} =$$

$$t = r_s \sqrt{\frac{N - 2}{1 - r_s^2}} = \qquad , \text{d.f.} = N - 2.$$

1. Form an array of the observations on the X variable. (Start with the "best," "smallest," "highest." You may choose the starting point at will, but you must be consistent on both X and Y, or the sign of r_s will be meaningless.) Order the observations on the variable Y in the same manner.

2. Replace the X value of each observation by its rank in the X array and the Y value of each observation by its rank in the Y array. In column 2 at the right enter ranks of the observations on the X variable and in column 3 enter ranks of the observations on the Y variable. Ranks in the same row must be for the *same* observation.

3. Take the difference between ranks and enter in column 4.

4. Square these differences, enter in column 5, and sum column 5.

5. Compute r_s from the formula shown above.

6. For $N > 10$, to test $H_0: \rho_s = o$, use t, computed from the formula shown above with $(N - 2)$ d.f. (ρ_s [read "rho sub-s"] is the population parameter corresponding to r_s.)

*From Zelditch, *Basic Course in Sociological Statistics*, p. 326. See also Anderson and Zelditch, *Basic Course in Statistics: With Sociological Applications*, pp. 126–32.

From Univariate and Bivariate Problems to Multivariate Analysis of Social Behavior

It was once generally thought that for every effect there existed only one cause; if several causes were discovered, it was assumed the effect must really be more than one. The history of social theory is largely a series of statements asserting that one factor is the sole cause of social change. These notions have been called determinisms and include geographic, physical, racial, psychological, religious, political, economic, technological, and familial determinism. And there are many more.

It is characteristic of all these notions of determinism to assert that the sole factor operates according to its own inherent laws independently of all factors including human will and desires. These single-factor theories were relatively simple to understand and appealed to scholars and lay persons alike. They seemed to draw truth from the complex phenomena presented by social problems. But in their oversimplification the single-factor theories distorted reality and foisted a great amount of mischief and misery on people. For example, racial determinism bred prejudice and discrimination in every country of the world. In Hitler's Germany, it brought humankind's most cruel inhumanity.

Modern humans know better, although single-factor theories still abound. The contemporary approach involves allowing for and expecting a number of different causes for a single effect.

Four Manifestations of Causes

Causes may manifest themselves in a *sequence*, as a *convergence* or cluster, as producing *dispersion* effects, or as a *complex network.*

1. Causes may occur in a sequence, like the links on a chain. Some of these causes are direct and immediate, others are indirect and remote. Thus, a decline in worker motivation and sense of personal responsibility may be due to the direct fact that much labor is performed in the large corporation on highly repetitive jobs; the remote causes are the factory system and mass market, which in turn were brought about by the steam engine, the electric motor, and machine tools.
2. Several causes may converge to produce a change. Thus electric power and several transportation and communication inventions have converged to augment the decentralization of industry. These converging causes are often called a cluster.
3. The effects of a single cause may be dispersed outward into many different sectors of a society. Thus the average increase of formal education that is being acquired by Americans has many different effects on family, church, community, military organization, and labor relations.
4. The phenomena of convergence and of dispersion may be tied in with the phenomena of sequence to produce a complex network of causes. This is a very common manifestation, but the complexity can be simplified by recog-

nizing that causes vary in importance, and important causes may be identified that account for a large part of the effects observed.

Future Developments

New technology is ready to deal with these more complex notions of causation. Loether and McTavish have written about future developments in theory, research methods, and statistics stressing the importance of multivariage analysis.

Herman J. Loether and Donald G. McTavish *

The increasing availability of computers has shifted the emphasis in sociology from the study of univariate and bivariate problems to the study of multivariate problems. To be efficient predictors, sociological theories generally need to be stated in multivariate terms. Before computers, multivariate statistical techniques were so tedious that they were not commonly used. The computer has now made these techniques accessible and practical. In response to this breakthrough, sociological theories are increasingly becoming multivariate in form. It is becoming increasingly important for the sociologist to be a knowledgeable computer user. Computer technology is racing forward at a breathtaking pace, and the potential uses of computers for sociological analysis stagger the imagination.

Another very promising development in sociology is the gradual but dramatic disappearance of the chasm separating theory and research. Sociology appears to be moving forward by returning to the model which Durkheim set for us in the nineteenth century. The effect of this long overdue marriage of theory and research is the development of theory that is researchable and the appearance of more theory-oriented research. The advent of the computer in sociology and the increasing emphasis upon multivariate analysis have done much to facilitate this development.

There is a third important development that promises to have a significant impact on sociology and on the academic preparation of future sociologists. Traditionally, sociologists have used a structure rather than a process to theorizing and researching. Social behavior has been viewed in static terms, and much research has focused on single points in time, much like stopping a movie and studying a single frame. Sociologists are now beginning to realize that what is orderly about social behavior may be the way in which it changes rather than the way in which it resists change. This perspective focuses attention on time series and longitudinal analysis. The shift in statistics is toward the increasing use of stochastic processes and techniques of time series analysis. This emphasis will make the understanding of calculus an important requirement in the academic training of future sociologists. It seems inevitable that process models involving the use of calculus will appear with increasing frequency in the sociological literature.

Obviously sociology is coming of age. The public and our public leaders are beginning to realize that the pressing problems of today and the forseeable future are those for which solutions are encouched in a knowledge of social

*Herman J. Loether and Donald G. McTavish, *Inferential Statistics for Sociologists* (Boston: Allyn & Bacon, 1974), pp. 283–84.

behavior. Sociology is in a position to contribute that knowledge. This is an exciting time in which to be a part of it. We believe that those students of sociology who will make important contributions to that knowledge will be those who are well versed in theory, research methods, and statistics.

3.8.a. THE STATISTICAL WORLD OF MULTIVARIATE ANALYSIS

Multivariate analysis has now developed techniques for dealing with more than three variables or attributes at a time. The type of analysis to use in attempting to unravel a complex of variates in a real-life situation depends on what will best bring out the essential relationships under scrutiny. Multivariate analysis may give increased precision to prediction problems (the relation of a number of predictor variables to a criterion), offer greater control of interfering or confounding variables (holding more variables constant), and furnish guiding principles in the development of attitude scales, rating scales, psychological tests, and criterion measures (finding dimensions of behavior). Some of the most important multivariate techniques include:

Multiple Correlation and Classification Analysis
Path Analysis
Factor Analysis
Partial Correlation Analysis
Analysis of Variance and Covariance
Multiple Discriminant Analysis

The full description of these techniques is beyond the scope and purpose of the Handbook. Nevertheless, computer technology is advancing at a rapid rate and is an indispensable adjunct to multivariate analysis. An Introduction to the Computer is presented in 3.8.c for those who are seeking guidance in utilizing computer programs. Descriptions of Multiple Correlation and Classification Analysis (3.8.b), Path Analysis (3.8.d), and Factor Analysis (3.8.e) are also set out to provide an introduction to these forms of multivariate analysis now so common to sociological research.

3.8.b. MULTIPLE CORRELATION AND CLASSIFICATION ANALYSIS

R as a Coefficient

The multiple correlation ($R_{1.234}$) is simply the correlation between the actual scores on a single dependent variable and the scores derived from any linear combination of independent variables. The multiple correlation, like the simple product-moment correlation (r), varies on a scale from 0 to +1. The smaller the coefficient, the poorer the correlation; and the larger the coefficient, the stronger the correlation. The multiple correlation can be interpreted by squaring it. R^2 is called the coefficient of multiple determination and expresses the proportion of the variation in the dependent variable that is explained by the regression equation.

Scope of Application

The utility of R has been known for some time. But it was originally cumbersome to calculate when more than four or five independent variables (predictors) were introduced. The computer has erased that limitation, but a second limitation intervened. The coefficient was adaptable only when the variables were continuous. Modern methods of *multiple classification analysis* have removed this limitation. There are computer techniques that can handle predictors with no better than nominal measurement and interrelationships of any form among predictors or between predictors or between a predictor and the dependent variable. Many of the most interesting analysis problems involve the simultaneous consideration of several predictor variables (i.e., "independent" variables) and their relationships to a dependent variable. Sometimes one wants to know *how well* all the variables together explain variation in the dependent variable. Other times it is necessary to look at each predictor separately to see how it relates to the dependent variable, either considering or neglecting the effects of other predictors. A criterion generally used is its contribution to reduction in unexplained variance or "error." Another is the extent to which its class means differ from the grand mean.

A different but related concern is the matter of predicted relations. Instead of asking *how well* one can predict, one sometimes asks *what level* (i.e., what particular value or score) would one predict for a person or other unit having a certain combination of characteristics. This is the classic problem to which multiple regression has frequently been applied.

Finally, one sometimes wants to know whether one's ability to predict is significantly better than chance.

The Multiple Classification Analysis devised by Frank M. Andrews, James N. Morgan, John A. Sonquist, and Laura Klem (reported in section 3.8.c) implements a multivariate technique that is relevant for all the above problems and that may be applied to many kinds of data for which the simpler forms of the traditional techniques would be inappropriate. Its chief advantage over conventional dummy variable regression is a more convenient input arrangement and understandable output that focuses on sets of predictors, such as occupation groups, and on the extent and direction of adjustments made for intercorrelations among the sets of predictors.

Research Examples of Multivariate Analysis

DUNCAN, OTIS DUDLEY. "A Socioeconomic Index for All Occupations." In Albert J. Reiss, *Occupations and Social Status*. New York: Free Press of Glencoe, 1961. Pp. 109–38.

HODGE, ROBERT W.; SIEGEL, PAUL M.; and ROSSI, PETER H. "Occupational Prestige in the United States, 1925–1963." *American Journal of Sociology* 70 (November 1964): 286–302.

HOUSE, JAMES S., and MASON, WILLIAM M. "Political Alienation in America, 1952–68." *American Sociological Review* 40 (April 1975): 123–47.

LADINSKY, JACK L. "Occupational Determinants of Geographic Mobility Among Professional Workers." *American Sociological Review* 32 (April 1967): 253–64.

SCOTT, JOSEPH W., and EL-ASSAL, MOHAMED. "Multiversity, University Size, University Quality, and Student Protest: An Empirical Study." *American Sociological Review* 34 (October 1969): 702–9.

Brief Treatments of Multiple Correlation and Regression

LOETHER, HERMAN J., and McTAVISH, DONALD G. *Descriptive Statistics for Sociologists: An Introduction.* Boston: Allyn & Bacon, 1974. Pp. 306–40.
SCHUESSLER, KARL. *Analyzing Social Data.* Boston: Houghton Mifflin, 1971. Pp. 10–30.

General References

ANDERSON, T. W. *An Introduction to Multivariate Statistical Analysis.* New York: John Wiley, 1958.
BENNETT, S., and BOWERS, DONALD W. *An Introduction to Multi-Variable Techniques for the Social and Behavioral Sciences.* New York: Halsted, 1976.
BLALOCK, HUBERT M., JR. *Social Statistics.* 2nd ed. New York: McGraw-Hill, 1972.
COLEMAN, JAMES S. "Multivariate Analysis." In *Introduction to Mathematical Sociology.* New York: Free Press of Glencoe, 1964. Pp. 189–240.
COOLEY, WILLIAM W., and LOHNES, PAUL R. *Multivariate Procedures for the Behavioral Sciences.* New York: John Wiley, 1962. See chap. 3, "Multiple and Canonical Correlation."
COSTNER, HERBERT L., ed. *Sociological Methodology.* San Francisco: Jossey-Bass, 1971. See especially chap. 5 by George Bohrnstedt and T. Michael Carter, "Robustness in Regression Analysis"; also chap. 6 by Morgan Lyons, "Techniques for Using Ordinal Measures in Regression and Path Analysis."
DRAPER, NORMAN R., and SMITH, HARRY. *Applied Regression Analysis.* New York: John Wiley, 1966.
DUBOIS, PHILIP H. *Multivariate Correlation Analysis.* New York: Harper & Row, 1957.
EZEKIAL, MORDECAI, and FOX, KARL A. *Methods of Correlation Analysis.* 3rd ed. New York: John Wiley, 1959.
GORDON, ROBERT A. "Issues in Multiple Regression." *American Journal of Sociology* 73 (March 1968): 592–616.
KENDALL, M. G. *A Course in Multivariate Analysis.* London: Griffin, 1961.
JORESKOG, KARL G., and VAN THILLO, MARIELLE. *LISREL: A General Computer Program for Estimating a Linear Structural Equation System Involving Multiple Indicators of Unmeasured Variables.* Princeton, N.J.: Educational Testing Service, 1972.
LAZARSFELD, PAUL F.; PASANELLA, ANN K.; and ROSENBERG, MORRIS, eds. *Continuities in the Language of Social Research.* Rev. ed. of *Language of Social Research.* New York: Free Press of Macmillan, 1975. See section on Multivariate Analysis for articles and selected examples.

For additional references see section 3.10, Selected Readings on Causal Models and Multivariate Analysis for the Advanced Student.

3.8.c. AN INTRODUCTION TO THE COMPUTER

Purpose

The purpose of any process of data analysis is to condense information contained in a body of data into a form that can be easily comprehended and interpreted. Sometimes this process is used simply to describe a body of empirical data, but it is far more common for social science data analysis to involve a search for meaningful patterns of relationships among sets of variables, that is, a means to test empirical social theory. Computers are extremely useful for the routine processing of large quantities of data. Indeed, the need for large-scale processing led directly to the development of the computer. Such processing includes the classification, sorting, storing, and retrieval of data that have been presented to the computer in a suitable coded form. These routine tasks, termed *data processing*, constitute the most important use of computers at present.

Steps in the Use of the Computer

Generally, (1) data is gathered in the form of responses to items on a survey schedule or coded specifically in experimental situations. These responses are then usually (2) transferred to *80-column IBM computer cards*. These cards contain punches that are indicative of the original response code. There is always at least one card per case, but frequently more cards are necessary to complete the listing of all the information pertinent to that case. These cards are (3) punched upon a machine called a *keypunch*. This machine closely resembles a typewriter; however, it punches IBM cards instead of typing letters. Once the data has been recorded, it is often (4) reproduced on a machine called a *reproducer*. This permits the researcher to make a spare deck of data with a minimum amount of work in the event that his original deck is lost or damaged.

Once a deck of data cards has been made, other pieces of equipment can be utilized. For example, after the original deck has been reproduced on the reproducer, the new deck can be placed in a device called (5a) a *lister*. The lister prints in standard numerals and alphabetic letters the content of the punches on each particular card. This print appears at the top of every individual card. If a more easily read listing of the content of the cards is desired, the deck may be placed into a different machine, (5b) a *printer*, which will list the content on a computer sheet printout. This method of listing allows for the rapid scanning of the information by the researcher in order to check for typographical errors and punctuation that might lead to computer rejection of the data, or for the simple search for a particular case or variable.

The *card sorter*, another piece of unit record equipment, allows the researcher to separate his data deck into several categories. That is, the researcher may wish to (5c) separate several types of traits or subject responses from the others, and this is made possible through the employment of the card sorter. For example, it may be desirable to place all the subjects into categories based upon occupation. The card sorter can be adjusted to cause all cards with a specific number in a specific column—the code for a particular occupation—to fall into one bin, all cards with a different number in that same column to fall into another bin, and so forth.

Finally, once the data have been prepared accurately, they can either be (6) submitted to the computer in card form or transferred to a magnetic tape and then submitted. In addition, the data, however their initial form, cards or tape, can be (6a) retained by the computer for a specified period of time in the form of a storage file. This file is usually stored on a disc within the computer system. Once the data have been appropriately prepared and submitted and the computer has been programmed to handle the data, which is almost always done by computer specialists, (7) various data analytic procedures can be employed to obtain the desired statistics. These procedures are only restricted by the particular computer language used, the programming of the computer, and the scale level (nominal, ordinal, interval, ratio) of the data.

Computer languages vary widely in terms of their capabilities and structure. The appropriate language for data analysis depends to a great extent upon the kind of analysis to be done and the form of the data. For most social science data analysis, the fairly recent development and refinement of the SPSS (Statistical Package of the Social Sciences) packaged programs have been of great assistance.[1] However, other computer languages may frequently prove to be more appropriate. Computer consultants and operators, who are present at all computer facilities, are normally capable not only of assisting the researcher with the selection of the best language, but also of aiding him in any usage problems that may appear.

When trouble in running a program is incurred, however, the computer consultant is an invaluable aid to research. It must always be borne in mind that computer time is extremely valuable and, consequently, extremely expensive; thus errors must be eliminated before using the computer facility if possible. Careful preparation and intelligent use of consultants is essential to rapid and economical data analysis.[2]

Notes

1. Norman H. Nie, Dale H. Bent, C. Hadlei Hull, Jean G. Jenkins, and Karin Steinbrenner, *SPSS, Statistical Package for the Social Sciences* (2nd ed.; New York: McGraw-Hill, 1975).

2. For an excellent set of computer instructions for the beginning student, see Gerald S. Ferman and Jack Levin, *Social Science Research: A Handbook for Students* (Cambridge, Mass.: Schenkman, 1975), pp. 91–136.

Computer Programs

The Institute of Social Research at Indiana University has found the following program manuals useful:

Biomedical Computer Programs
Multiple Classification Analysis
Multivariate Model Building
Statistical Package for the Social Sciences

The Institute relies mainly on the SPSS computer program write-ups maintained in the University Computer Center. These include:

One-Way Frequency Distributions
Descriptive Statistics for Aggregated Data Files
Contingency Tables and Related Measures of Association
Description of Subpopulations and Mean Difference Testing: Subprograms, Breakdowns and *T*-test
Bivariate Correlation Analysis: Pearson Correlation, Rank-Order Correlation, and Scatter Diagrams

Partial Correlation
Multiple Regression Analysis
Path Analysis and Causal Interpretation
Analysis of Variance and Covariance
Discriminant Analysis
Factor Analysis
Canonical Correlation Analysis
Guttman Scalogram Analysis

OSIRIS is another widely used package of computer programs designed for the analysis of social science data. The statistical analysis capabilities include a variety of multivariate and nonparametric analysis programs.

The Institute itself maintains the computer write-ups listed below. All programs are currently running on the CDC 6600:

Instructions for use of RCC Library disk programs
Instructions for storing programs or data on a disk
YALE REVISED 1, 2, 3 and 4
BMB1D (Simple Data Description)
BMD1V (Analysis of Variance for One-Way Design)
BMD3R (Multiple Regression with Case Combinations)
BMD9S (Transgeneration)
MCA (Multiple Classification Analysis)
LISREL (General Covariance Structures)
ACOVS (Analysis of Covariance Structures)

Specialized Computer Programs

The Institute for Social Research at the University of Michigan is currently offering the following Computer Techniques in Social Science Research:

ANDREWS, FRANK M., and MESSENGER, ROBERT C. *Multivariate Nominal Scale Analysis: A Report on a New Analysis Technique and a Computer Program.* 1973.

This monograph describes a powerful new technique for conducting multivariate analysis of categorical dependent variables. It applies the most common analytic model—the additive one—to categorical dependent variables and arrives at answers to the usual questions addressed by multivariate analysis. It is uniquely useful in exploring the interrelationships of theoretical concepts involving categorical dependent variables and substantial numbers of independent variables at various levels of measurement.

ANDREWS, FRANK M.; MORGAN, JAMES N.; SONQUIST, JOHN A., and KLEM, LAURA. *Multiple Classification Analysis: A Report on a Computer Program for Multiple Regression Using Categorical Predictors.* 1967; rev. ed., 1974.

Multiple Classification Analysis is a technique for examining the interrelationship between several predictor variables and a dependent variable within the context of an additive model. The program will handle missing data on both the dependent and predictor variables.

MORGAN, JAMES N., and MESSENGER, ROBERT C. *THAID: A Sequential Analysis Program for the Analysis of Nominal Scale Dependent Variables.* 1973.

Like its companion volume, *Multivariate Nominal Scale Analysis*, this monograph describes a recently developed technique for conducting multivariate analyses of categorical dependent variables. Although common in social research, such variables have, until now, been difficult to handle with available statistical techniques. THAID describes a searching process that provides an efficient and effective means for sorting through a variety of analytic models to find the most able to produce useful predictions. The program searches for subgroups that differ maximally as to their distribution; it assumes neither additivity nor linearity, so requires substantial samples of 1000 or more cases.

RATTENBURY, JUDITH. *Introduction to the IBM 360 Computer and OS/JCL (Job Control Language)*. 1971; rev. 1974.

This monograph will be of value to both the complete novice and to those who have used other computers. It not only gives details of the most used subset of the IBM 360 job control language but also attempts to make it meaningful by describing the physical characteristics of tapes and disks and by explaining how the operating system works.

RATTENBURY, JUDITH, and VAN ECK, NEAL. *OSIRIS: Architecture and Design*. 1973.

This monograph provides technical documentation for the benefit of those involved with the writing and modification of the OSIRIS package of computer programs.

SONQUIST, JOHN A. *Multivariate Model Building: The Validation of a Search Strategy*. 1970; reprinted, 1971.

This book undertakes the validation of the Automatic Interaction Detection (AID) technique. It uses computer techniques for data-generation to produce models in which the actual structure of the relationship between variables is completely known. Then, applying both AID and Multiple Classification Analysis (MCA) techniques to the data, it explores the ability of each algorithm to lead the analyst to a correct assessment of the structure of the predictive model implicit in the data. The conclusion leads to further developments in a strategy for the back-to-back use of AID and MCA in the task of multivariate building.

SONQUIST, JOHN A.; LAUH BAKER, ELIZABETH; and MORGAN, JAMES N. *Searching for Structure*. 1971; rev. ed., 1974.

This report presents an approach to analysis of substantial bodies of micro-data and documentation for a computer program. The new computer program—AID 111— is a descendant of the original Automatic Interaction Detector program that started the application of search strategy; several new features have been added to the new program.

The Community and Family Study Center of the University of Chicago has the following computer techniques available:

Techniques for Making Population Projections: How To Make Age-Sex and Functional Projections by Electronic Computer, by DONALD J. BOGUE. Manual No. 12.

This manual presents the basic methodology of population forecasting and the techniques necessary for forecasting the future size of functional subgroupings of the population.

Mini-Regression: A Small Computer Program for Performing Multiple Regression Analysis, by MAURICE J. MOORE. Manual No. 14.

Basic principles of multiple regression analysis are presented. A computer program for calculating regression coefficients and related statistics is included.

Techniques of Pregnancy History Analysis, by DONALD J. BOGUE and ELIZABETH J. BOGUE.

This manual systematizes data collection, computerizes data processing, and codifies the steps involved in adjusting and interpreting the data of pregnancy histories. Computer programs for use on small computers are included.

The Fertility Components and Contraceptive History Techniques for Measuring Contraceptive Use-Effectiveness, by DONALD J. BOGUE and JAMES NELSON.

A contribution to the methodology for measuring and interpreting the implications of contraceptive use-effectiveness for fertility rates. The manual includes techniques for a new system of measurement, practicable procedures for data collection, and a "packaged" computer program for small computers.

An Empirical Model for Demographic Evaluation of the Impact of Contraception and Marital Status on Birth Rates with Computerized Applications to the Setting of Targets and Quotas for Family Planning Programs, by DONALD J. BOGUE, SCOTT EDMONDS, and ELIZABETH J. BOGUE.

This manual attempts to solve the practical problem of the valid projection of family-planning targets. It develops an empirical model which links birth rates to contraceptive behavior in a new form able to yield realistic results. A "packaged" computer program for small computers is included.

Mini-Tab Edit, Mini-Tab Frequencies and Mini-Tab Tables: A Set of Three Inter-related Statistical Programs for Small Computers, by HENRY G. ELKINS.

A set of simplified and versatile programs written in basic FORTRAN to tabulate social data where large computers and more elaborate programs are not readily available.

ADDLIB: A Computer Program for Addressing Mail and Indexing Libraries, by THOMAS MOSSBERG. Family Planning Research and Evaluation Manual No. 13.

ADDLIB is a computer program which performs two important functions: (1) It addresses labels for all mailings. Names and addresses written on ordinary punched cards can be selected, sorted, and printed on labels with respect to any desired combinations of up to five criteria of selection. (2) ADDLIB prints out bibliographies of items contained in a library, permitting selection by subject for any desired combinations of up to five subject matter classifications. Written for small (32K) computers, it eliminates costly addressing equipment and permits rapid information retrieval at many additional sites throughout the world.

Introductory References to the Role of the Computer

KEMENY, JOHN G. *Man and the Computer.* New York: Charles Scribner's Sons, 1972.

LATEL, PIERRE DE. *Thinking by Machine.* Boston: Houghton Mifflin, 1957.

MICALLEF, BENJAMIN A. *An Introduction to Data Processing.* Menlo Park, Calif.: Cummings, 1971.

PYLYSHYN, Z. W., ed. *Perspectives on the Computer Revolution.* Englewood Cliffs, N.J.: Prentice-Hall, 1970.

TAVISS, I., ed. *The Computer Impact.* Englewood Cliffs, N.J.: Prentice-Hall, 1970.

Technical Treatments of the Computer

DESMONDE, WILLIAM H. *Computers and Their Uses.* 2nd ed. Englewood Cliffs, N.J.: Prentice-Hall, 1971.

FAVRET, ANDREW G. *Digital Computer, Principles and Applications.* New York: Van Nostrand Reinhold, 1972.

Applications of the Computer to the Social Sciences

BRIER, ALAN, and ROBINSON, IAN. *Computers and the Social Sciences.* London: Hutchinson, 1974.

DUTTON, JOHN M., and STARBUCK, WILLIAM H. *Computer Simulation of Human Behavior.* New York: John Wiley & Sons, 1971.

GREENBERGER, MARTIN; CRENSON, MATTHEW A.; and CRISSEY, BRIAN L. *Models in the Policy Process.* New York: Russell Sage, 1976.

3.8.d. PATH ANALYSIS

Path Analysis as Causal Analysis

Path analysis has become a popular form of data analysis because it provides possibilities for causal determinations among sets of measured variables. A principal objective of science is to build theoretical explanations of social phenomena. Kaplan has said,

> Science is a search for constancies, for invariants. It is the enterprise of making those identifications in experience which prove to be most significant for the control or appreciation of the experience to come. The basic scientific question is "what the devil is going on around here?"[1]

When the underlying assumptions of path analysis are met, theory and data may be related in situations where many variables are to be handled simultaneously. Path analysis is essentially a data analytic technique using standardized multiple regression equations in examining theoretical models.

Extravagant hopes for causal explanations should not be entertained—at least not yet. The inability to deal with all variables in a social system, to measure and plot their exact interactions, makes the results in most problems only first approximations to causality. But the power of the technique continues to challenge researchers, and its use is proliferating.

A researcher commonly wishes to discover the relationship of independent factors to a dependent variable. Simple and multiple correlations are utilized and often yield important relationships, yet they never demonstrate causality. For example, if we wish to relate father's occupational status to son's occupational status, then, using correlational techniques, their correlational relationship can be determined, but causality can only be inferred. Using path analysis it is·possible to postulate that such independent factors as father's educational attainment and occupational status are causal factors in the son's subsequent educational attainment, the status of the first job achieved, and the status of the current job.

Six Steps in the Application of Path Analysis

1. Develop a causal scheme or model.
2. Establish a pattern of associations between the variables in the sequence.
3. Depict a path diagram.
4. Calculate path coefficients for the basic model.
5. Test for "goodness of fit" with the basic model.
6. Interpret the result.

Step 1: Develop a Causal Scheme. Path analysis allows the social theorist to state a theory in the form of a linear causal model. The crucial question has to do with the order of priority for the variables in the system in a causal or processual sequence. Causal models involve the construction of an oversimplified model of social reality in the sense that the model takes into account only a very limited number of variables that are of interest in the specific research area. The most important variables are sought; all others are regarded as "residual." The social scientist represents the process assumed to be in operation among the variables based upon the results of past research and current theory.

Let us suppose that we utilize stratification theory and research. We postulate that status changes in the life cycle of a cohort of males indicate that father's educational attainment (*A*) and father's occupational attainment (*B*) will determine the subsequent educational attainment of the son (*X*), his first job (*Y*), and his current job (*Z*). This is the linear statement or temporal order and may be written as follows:

$$(A \longrightarrow B) \longrightarrow X \longrightarrow Y \longrightarrow Z$$

The earlier variables may affect a later one not only through intervening variables but also directly.

Step 2: Establish a Pattern of Associations Between the Variables in the Sequence. The conceptual framework must be translated into quantitative estimates. This is done by establishing the pattern of association of the variables in the sequence. A correlation matrix is developed utilizing the simple correlations for the five status variables in the model. An adaptation of Blau and Duncan shows the matrix of their occupational mobility study (see table 1).[2] Simple correlation measures the gross magnitude of the effect of an antecedent variable upon the consequent variable. The current job status is the expected outcome of all the other four antecedent variables. Reading across the first row it is observed that all four antecedent variables show significant correlation to current job status, the highest being for the son's education (*r* = .596), and the next being his first job status (*r* = .541). As expected, father's occupational status and father's education are related in somewhat diminished magnitude (*r* = .405 and *r* = .322 respectively). The second row reports correlations with first-job status and again the same pattern of relationship with father's occupation and education appears. The third row repeats expected relationships of son's education to father's occupation and education. The fourth row demonstrates the high correlation of father's occupation and education (*r* = .516).[3]

Step 3: Depict a Path Diagram. Path diagrams are generally illustrated, as in figure 1, by means of one-headed arrows connecting some or all of the variables

Table 1. *Simple Correlations for Five Status Variables*

Variable	Z	Y	X	B	A
Z Son's current occupational status	—	.541	.596	.405	.322
Y Son's first-job status		—	.538	.417	.332
X Son's education			—	.438	.453
B Father's occupational status				—	.516
A Father's education					—

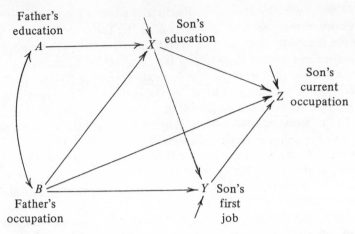

Figure 1. Basic Model of the Process of Stratification. The algebraic representation of the causal scheme now shown in the path model rests on a system of equations rather than the single equation more often employed in multiple regression analysis. This feature permits a flexible ordering of the inferred influences. Each line represents a search and a determination of direct (or net) influences. Note how much emphasis Blau and Duncan have given to the father's occupation as a causative factor as path coefficients are traced to son's education, first job, and current job. Father's education, on the other hand, is traced only through the son's education.

included in the basic model. Variables are distributed from left to right, depending upon their theoretical ordering. The first independent variables are placed at the extreme left. In this case, these are father's education and father's occupation, and the link is shown as an arrowhead at both ends to distinguish it from other paths of influence. Intercorrelations (zero-order) between variables not influenced by other variables in the model are called *exogenous* variables, which refer to all variables prior to and outside the model.

The remaining subset of variables (which may consist of only one variable) is taken as dependent, and these variables are called *endogenous* (X, Y, and Z). As contrasted with the exogenous variables, this subset is considered totally determined by some combination of the variables in the system. The straight lines above running from one measured variable to another represent the direct influences of one variable upon another. There are also indirect influences, as illustrated in the diagram under analysis. Variables recognized as effects of certain antecedent factors may, in turn, serve as causes for subsequent variables. For example, X is caused by A and B, which in turn influences Y and Z, thus Y and Z are affected indirectly by both A and B, in addition to any direct effects.

Finally, residual paths must be drawn. These are the lines with no source indicated carrying arrows to each of the endogenous or effect variables. Residuals are represented as the arrows coming from outside the system to X, Y, and Z, and are due to causes not recognized or measured, errors of measurement, and departures of the true relationships from additivity and linearity, properties that are assumed throughout the analysis.

Step 4: Calculate Path Coefficients. Path coefficients reflect the amount of direct contribution of a given variable on another variable when effects of other related variables are taken into account. Path coefficients are identical to partial regression coefficients (the betas) when the variables are measured in standard form. Two ways of computing path coefficients are frequently employed. The first uses regression programs that take raw data and compute partial coefficients from standardized input data. Both path coefficients and multiple correlation coefficients are generally provided by standard computer regression programs.[4] The second method uses only zero-order correlations among variables, a researcher can employ the "basic theorem" to compute the path coefficients.[5]

In figure 2 the path coefficients have been entered on the path diagram with the exception of antecedent variables *A* and *B*. The path basic model is now complete and awaits evaluation.

Step 5: Test for "Goodness of Fit" with Basic Model. The crux of the analysis is the test for "goodness of fit" between the observed data and the basic model. Three general approaches may be made:

1. Examining the amount of *variation* in dependent variables that is *explained* by variables linked as specified in the model
2. Examining the *size of path coefficients* to see whether they are large enough to warrant the inclusion of a variable or path in the model
3. Evaluating the ability of the model to *predict correlation coefficients* that were not used in computation of the path coefficients themselves[6]

An investigator usually contrasts the usefulness of the model in these three respects with alternative models. This is the heart of explanatory progress in any science.

The partial regression coefficients in standard form and the coefficients of determination for specified combinations of variables are essential for applying the first "goodness of fit" criterion. Table 2 is an adaption of the Blau and Duncan data. This table shows that the coefficient of determination for father's occupation, father's education, and son's education is .26, which is to say that

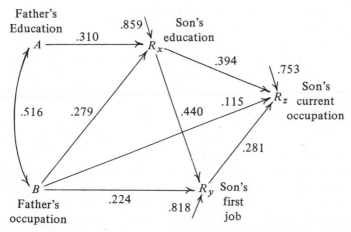

Figure 2. The Path Model for the Causal Scheme. Reprinted by permission and adapted from Blau and Duncan, *American Occupational Structure* (New York: Wiley, 1967), p. 170.

Table 2 *Partial Regression Coefficients in Standard Form (Beta Coefficients) and Coefficients of Determination, for Specified Combinations of Variables*

Dependent variable	First job	Son's education	Father's occupation	Father's education	Coefficient of determination (R^2)
Son's education			.279	.310	.26
First job		.433	.214	.026	.33
Current occupation	.282	.397	.120	−.014	.43

26 percent of the variation in son's education may be accounted for by the father's occupation and education.

Similarly, 33 percent of the variation in son's first job may be accounted for by father's occupation, father's education, and son's education. Finally, 43 percent of the variation in son's current occupation is due to father's occupation, father's education, son's education, and son's first job. Note that father's education is not helpful in explaining this variance. The unexplained variation $1 - R^2_{4.123} = .57$. The model leaves unexplained 57 percent of the variance in son's current job. This is not as satisfactory as might be hoped. The "unexplained" variation is due to variables or measurement error not included in the model and, for sake of completeness, the square root of these $1 - R^2$ values are ascribed to the residual variables, R_x, R_y and R_z as shown in figure 2. These "residual" paths are large and the investigator must reexamine his causal scheme. However, it must not be assumed that the size of the residual is necessarily a measure of success in explaining the phenomenon under study. "The relevant question about the residual is not really its size at all, but whether the unobserved factors it stands for are properly represented *as being uncorrelated* with the measured antecedent factors."[7]

In terms of the second criterion of goodness of fit, the model fares well. Most of the path coefficients are significant. It turned out that the net regressions of both father's occupation and son's first job on father's education were so small as to be negligible. Hence, father's education could be disregarded without loss of information.[8] One might consider eliminating father's education as a factor because of its low coefficients and recompute path coefficients.

Thirdly, one could examine the "fit" between observed correlations not previously used in formulas for calculating path coefficients and predictions of correlation coefficients which would be derived from the model. In this instance the correlation between father's education and son's first job (as well as between current job) was not used to estimate path coefficients.

The question of testing an alternative model involves a thorough reexamination of the basic mode. Two possibilities present themselves: (a) substituting factors in the basic model believed to be more important, (b) adding new factors to the basic model. Whether a path diagram or the causal scheme it represents is adequate depends on both theoretical and empirical considerations. The causal scheme must be complete in the sense that all causes are accounted for. Unmeasured causes presumed to be uncorrelated with the dependent variable must be represented.

Step 6: Interpret the Result. The variables in the causal scheme may be studied for their direct and indirect effects. The direct effect of father's occupation on son's education, first job, and current occupation is shown by path coefficients of .279, .224, and .115, none of which are particularly large. Nevertheless, the cumulative indirect effects are significant. Father's occupation and education do influence son's education, and this in turn influences the son's first job, which in turn influences the son's current occupation. At the same time, many other factors of even greater influence are clearly operating to determine this last dependent variable of interest.

The technique of path analysis is not a method of discovering causal laws but a procedure for giving a quantitative interpretation of an assumed causal system as it operates within a given population.

Nygreen has reported a program called the Interactive Path Analyzer to increase the practical power of path analyses. He describes on-line path analysis for those who have access to computer facilities. He writes:

> In many locations, social science researchers are beginning to gain access to computer facilities via remote typewriter-like "time-sharing" terminals. The increasing ubiquity of such "on-line" computer resources has given many social scientists access to the computational power of digital computers in a much more convenient form than has been the case in the past. Time-sharing computers are becoming increasingly commonplace on college campuses either in addition to or in lieu of the more conventional "batch" processing techniques.
>
> In a time-sharing environment, the analyst can "talk" with the computer by specifying different input criteria to his problem and observing the results immediately. These characteristics of the "conversational" environment provide an advantageous setting in which path analyses can be performed. Specifically, the researcher can think through and then specify his causal model, but the computer can do the numerical calculations, displaying the coefficients for inspection almost immediately. The sociologist is able to postulate alternative theoretical causal formulations, modify his current model[9] and again have the lengthy computations performed in milliseconds, with the results arrayed on the typewriter before him. Properly utilized, the time-sharing computer environment increases the practical power of path analyses, reducing turn-around time literally to seconds.

A program called the Interactive Path Analyzer (IPA) has been written and tested in this on-line environment with very favorable results.[10] The availability of the time-shared computer and the Interactive Path Analyzer lend flexibility and convenience to an otherwise tedious procedure in calculating path coefficients.

Notes

1. Abraham Kaplan, *The Conduct of Inquiry* (San Francisco: Chandler, 1964), p. 85.

2. Peter M. Blau and Otis Dudley Duncan, *The American Occupational Structure* (New York: John Wiley, 1967), p. 169.

3. Ibid.

4. For explanations of this procedure in the most understandable terms, see one of the following: Blau and Duncan, *American Occupational Structure*, pp. 171–77; Herman J. Loether and Donald C. McTavish, *Descriptive Statistics for Sociologists* (Boston: Allyn & Bacon, 1974), pp. 321–28. Other references are appended.

5. G. T. Nygreen, "Interactive Path Analysis," *American Sociologist* 6 (February 1971): 37–43.

6. Kenneth C. Land, "Principles of Path Analysis," in *Sociological Methodology, 1969*, ed. Edgar F. Borgatta (San Francisco: Jossey-Bass, 1969).

7. Blau and Duncan, *American Occupational Structure*, p. 175.

8. Ibid., p. 173.

9. Evaluation procedures that require reformulation of the causal model and recomputation of the path coefficients will not be dealt with in this paper.

10. Nygreen, "Interactive Path Analysis," p. 41; requests for copies of this program should be directed to Ms. Judith Rowe, Office for Survey Research and Statistical Studies, O-S-17 Green Hall, Princeton University, Princeton, N.J. Source decks and listings with documentation are available for $10.

Brief Treatment of Path Analysis

BOYLE, RICHARD P. "Path Analysis and Ordinal Data." *American Journal of Sociology* 75 (January 1970): 461–80.

DUNCAN, OTIS D. "Path Analysis: Sociological Examples." *American Journal of Sociology* 72 (July 1966): 1–16. Traces history of path analysis and provides many examples.

LOETHER, HERMAN J., and MCTAVISH, DONALD G. *Descriptive Statistics for Sociologists.* Boston: Allyn & Bacon, 1974. Pp. 321–28.

Research Examples of Path Analysis

BLAU, PETER M., and DUNCAN, OTIS DUDLEY. *The American Occupational Structure.* New York: John Wiley, 1967. Pp. 163–205.

FEATHERMAN, DAVID L. "Achievement Orientations and Socioeconomic Career Attainments." *American Sociological Review* 37 (April 1972): 131–43.

KELLEY, JONATHAN. "Causal Chain Models for the Socioeconomic Career." *American Sociological Review* 38 (August 1973): 481–93.

LAND, KENNETH C. "Path Models of Functional Theories of Social Stratification as Representations of Cultural Beliefs on Stratification." *Sociological Quarterly* 11 (Fall 1970): 474–84.

SEWELL, WILLIAM H.; HALLER, ACHIBALD O.; and OHLENDORF, GEORGE W. "The Educational and Early Occupational Status Attainment Process: Replication and Revision." *American Sociological Review* 35 (December 1970): 1014–27.

General References for Path Analysis

BLALOCK, HUBERT M., JR. *Causal Inferences in Nonexperimental Research.* Chapel Hill, N.C.: University of North Carolina Press, 1964.

BOUDON, RAYMOND. "A Method of Linear Causal Analysis: Dependence Analysis." *American Sociological Review* 30 (June 1965): 365–74.

COSTNER, HERBERT L., and LEIK, ROBERT K. "Deductions from 'Axiomatic Theory.'" *American Sociological Review* 29 (December 1964): 819–35.

FORBES, H. D., and TUFTE, E. R. "A Note of Caution in Causal Modelling." *American Political Science Review* 62 (December 1968): 1258–64.

HEISE, D. R. "Problems in Path Analysis and Causal Inference." In *Sociological Methodology*, edited by Edgar Borgatta. San Francisco: Jossey-Bass, 1969. Pp. 38–71.

LI, C. C. *Population Genetics.* Chicago: University of Chicago Press, 1955.

SIMON, HERBERT A. *Models of Man.* New York: John Wiley & Sons, 1957.

STINCHCOMBE, ARTHUR. *Construction of Social Theories.* New York: Harcourt, Brace & World, 1968. See chap. 3 and Appendix for application of path analysis to tests of sociological theories.

WRIGHT, SEWELL. "The Method of Path Coefficients." *Annals of Mathematical Statistics* 5 (1934): 161–215.

——. "Path Coefficients and Path Regressions: Alternative or Complementary Concepts?" *Biometrics* 16 (June 1960): 189–202.

——. "The Treatment of Reciprocal Interaction, with or without Lag in Path Analysis." *Biometrics* 16 (September 1960): 423–45.

For additional references see section 3.10, Selected Readings on Causal Models and Multivariate Analysis.

3.8.e. FACTOR ANALYSIS

Explaining Relations among Numerous Variables in Simpler Terms

The purpose of this introduction is to provide the sociological researcher with a working knowledge of the basic concepts of factor analysis without burdening him with statistical details. It will be assumed in the following discussion, however, that the user has some grasp of the meaning of correlation and regression coefficients. Factor analysis is a procedure for investigating the possibility that a large number of variables have a small number of factors in common which account for their intercorrelations. As Schuessler explains, "We observe that pupils who score high in reading tend to score high in spelling and arithmetic. We ascribe this consistency, or correlation, in pupils' marks to the general factor of intelligence."[1] Thus, it can be seen in brief that this principle holds that a circumstance common to a succession of categorically identical events, which otherwise have nothing in common, may be regarded as a cause of that event. Therefore, to discover the cause of an event, we search for the lone circumstance that is always present when the event occurs. In a similar manner, by means of factor analysis, we seek to isolate those common elements that are present in two or more variables and to which the intercorrelations among these variables may be attributed. It can be seen then that factor analysis is an arithmetical procedure for determining whether the intercorrelations among many variables could be due to a few common factors.

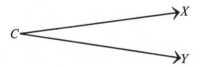

C may be considered as either a cause of both X and Y or simply an element present in both variables. Factor analysis considers the possibility that X and Y are indicators of the same thing. From the observed correlation between X and Y, the inference can be drawn that they were produced by the same cause or that they are, in varying degrees, different aspects of the same thing.

Finding Underlying Factors

To distinguish the observed variables, which are manipulated, from the common variables, which are hidden components in them, it is customary to speak of the latter as factors rather than variables. Thus, for the simplest case of two variables, Z_1 and Z_2, where each is the sum of the two parts, one part common (A)

and one part distinct to each variable (B_i), where

$$Z_1 = A + B_1$$
$$Z_2 = A + B_2$$

Z is conventionally spoken of as a variable and A and B_i as factors. Before proceeding any further, it should be emphasized that factors are statistical variables in the usual sense in all respects: factors posess both a mean and a variance, they may be symmetrically distributed, and they may also be correlated with other factors. The special term "factor" serves to maintain the distinction between the composite variable, which is observed, and its component parts, which are hypothetical.

Data Reduction Capability of Factor Analysis

The single most distinctive characteristic of factor analysis is its data-reduction capability. This means that given an array of correlation coefficients for a set of variables, factor-analytic techniques enable the researcher to see whether some underlying pattern of relationships exist such that the data may be "rearranged" or reduced to a smaller set of factors that may be considered source variables accounting for the observed interrelations in the data. There are multiple uses for this statistical capability, but the most frequent applications of the method fall into one of the following three categories: (1) exploratory uses, the exploration and detection of patterning of variables with a view to the discovery of new concepts and a possible reduction of data; (2) confirmatory uses, the testing of hypotheses about the structuring of variables in terms of the expected number of significant factors and factor loadings; and (3) uses as a measuring device, the construction of indices to be used as new variables in later analysis.[2]

Factor Analysis as Research Design

Factor analysis presents one of the few methods capable of teasing out what *would* happen through manipulation where manipulation is impossible. It seeks conclusions by statistical techniques rather than the more traditional experimental route of manipulative control.

Three Major Steps in Factor Analysis Procedure

Factor analysis includes a fairly large variety of statistical techniques, but there are basically three steps in a factor analysis procedure. The three usual steps are: (1) the preparation of a correlation matrix; (2) the extraction of the initial factors—the exploration of possible data reduction; and (3) the rotation to a terminal solution—the search for simple and interpretable factors. Major options at each of these three stages may be summed up by three dichotomies: R-type versus Q-type factor analysis in step 1, defined versus inferred factors in step 2, and orthogonal versus oblique in step 3. These are defined in detail in the treatments of factor analysis listed in the following bibliography.

Notes

1. Karl Schuessler, *Analyzing Social Data* (Boston: Houghton Mifflin, 1971), p. 44.
2. N. H. Nie et al., *Statistical Package for the Social Sciences* (New York: McGraw-Hill, 1970).

Research Examples of Factor Analysis

BALES, ROBERT F., and COUCH, ARTHUR S. "The Value Profile: A Factor Analytic Study of Value Statements." *Sociological Inquiry* 39 (Winter 1969): 3–17.

CREW, ROBERT E. "Dimensions of Public Policy: A Factor Analysis of State Expenditures." *Social Science Quarterly* 50 (September 1969): 381–88.

McRAE, DUNCAN, JR. *Issues and Parties in Legislative Voting.* New York: Harper & Row, 1970.

NEAL, ARTHUR, and RETTIG, SOLOMON. "On the Multidimensionality of Alienation." *American Sociological Review* 32 (February 1967): 54–63.

Brief Treatment of Factor Analysis

COTTRELL, RAYMOND F. "Factor Analysis: An Introduction to Essentials. I. The Purpose and Underlying Models." *Biometrics* 21 (March 1965): 190–215. II. "The Role of Factor Analysis in Research." *Biometrics* 21 (June 1965): 405–35.

RUMMEL, RUDOLPH J. "Understanding Factor Analysis." *Journal of Conflict Resolution* 11 (December 1967): 444–80.

SCHUESSLER, KARL. *Analyzing Social Data.* Boston: Houghton Mifflin, 1971. Pp. 44–84.

General References for Factor Analysis

FRUCHTER, BENJAMIN. *Introduction to Factor Analysis.* Princeton, N.J.: D. Van Nostrand, 1954.

CATTELL, RAYMOND B. *Factor Analysis: An Introduction and Manual for the Psychologist and Social Scientist.* New York: Harper & Row, 1952.

HARMAN, HARRY H. *Modern Factor Analysis.* 2nd ed. Chicago: University of Chicago Press, 1967.

HORST, PAUL. *Factor Analysis of Data Matrices.* New York: Holt, Rinehart & Winston, 1965.

NIE, N. H.; BENT, D. H.; and HULL, C. H. *Statistical Package for the Social Sciences.* New York: McGraw-Hill, 1970.

RUMMEL, RUDOLPH J. *Applied Factor Analysis.* Evanston, Ill.: Northwestern University Press, 1970. Recent applications of factor analysis in political and social research are listed in a special chapter.

THURSTONE, LOUIS L. *Multiple Factor Analysis.* Chicago: University of Chicago Press, 1947.

A BIBLIOGRAPHY OF STATISTICAL METHODS

3.9

The following books are especially valuable as reference books when the researcher is seeking a readable step-by-step explanation or procedure. The selections are based on the simplicity of the description and the inclusion of illustrative examples.

ANDERSON, THEODORE R., and ZELDITCH, MORRIS, JR. *A Basic Course in Statistics: With Sociological Applications.* 3rd ed. New York: Holt, Rinehart & Winston, 1975.

Step-by-step computation guides for all basic statistics; well illustrated.

ARKIN, HERBERT, and COLTON, RAYMOND R. *An Outline of Statistical Methods.* 5th ed. New York: Barnes & Noble, 1968.

A guide to elementary statistics.

BERNSTEIN, ALLEN L. *A Handbook of Statistical Solutions for the Behavioral Sciences.* New York: Holt, Rinehart & Winston, 1964.

Presents solutions to typical problems.

BLALOCK, HUBERT M., JR. *Social Statistics.* 2nd ed. New York: McGraw-Hill, 1972.

Well-written book introducing the student to modern developments.

CHILD, DENNIS. *The Essentials of Factor Analysis.* New York: Holt, Rinehart & Winston, 1973.

Elementary treatment with examples and application to psychology, sociology, and the medical sciences.

CONWAY, FREDA. *Sampling: An Introduction for Social Scientists.* New York: Humanities Press, 1967.

Lucid, neatly organized book on statistics using large-sample theory.

COOMBS, CLYDE H.; DAWES, ROBYN M.; and TVERSKY, AMOS. *Mathematical Psychology: An Elementary Introduction.* Englewood Cliffs, N.J.: Prentice-Hall, 1970.

An elementary treatment with applications to psychology.

CROWLEY, FRANCIS J., and COHEN, MARTIN. *Basic Facts of Statistics.* New York: Collier Books, 1963.

Digests elementary statistics in a very brief and comprehensive manner within 62 pages.

EDWARDS, ALLEN. *Statistical Methods.* 2nd ed. New York: Holt, Rinehart & Winston, 1967.

Statistical techniques and methods presented for the student with a minimum amount of mathematical knowledge. Parametric and nonparametric methods are integrated into the text.

FREUND, JOHN E.; LIVERMORE, PAUL E.; and MILLER, IRVIN. *Manual of Experimental Statistics.* Englewood Cliffs, N.J.: Prentice-Hall, 1960.

Presents in outline form the most frequently used statistical techniques, including appropriate computing formulas and completely worked out examples of each method.

HAUSER, PHILIP M. *Social Statistics in Use.* New York: Russell Sage Foundation, 1975.

Stresses importance of and shows how social statistics are put to public use.

HOLLANDER, MYLES, and WOLFE, DOUGLAS A. *Nonparametric Statistical Methods.* New York: John Wiley, 1973.

An updated description of nonparametric statistics.

LOETHER, HERMAN J., and MCTAVISH, DONALD G. *Descriptive Statistics for Sociologists.* Boston: Allyn & Bacon, 1974.

Careful treatment of statistical techniques that sociologists commonly use and illustrations showing how sociologists make use of them. A companion volume, *Inferential Statistics for Sociologists*, is available by these same writers and focuses attention on statistical techniques that make inferences possible from samples.

MAXWELL, ALBERT E. *Analyzing Qualitative Data*. New York: John Wiley & Sons, 1961.

The book, which might have been given the title χ^2 tests, aims at providing the research worker with a simple but up-to-date account of statistical techniques available for the analysis of qualitative data.

MORONEY, M. J. *Facts from Figures*. Baltimore: Penguin Books, 1956.

Lucid explanation of the background of statistics; well illustrated.

MUELLER, JOHN H.; SCHUESSLER, KARL F.; and COSTNER, HERBERT. *Statistical Reasoning in Sociology*. 3rd ed. Boston: Houghton Mifflin, 1976.

Emphasizes reasons for each statistical procedure.

SCHMID, CALVIN F. *Handbook of Graphic Presentation*. New York: Ronald Press, 1954.

Methods for presenting social statistics in a visual manner.

SMITH, G. MILTON. *A Simplified Guide to Statistics for Psychology and Education*. 3rd ed. New York: Holt, Rinehart & Winston, 1962.

Integrates most commonly used tools.

WALKER, HELEN M. *Mathematics Essential for Elementary Statistics: A Self-Teaching Manual*. Rev. ed. New York: Henry Holt, 1951.

Material permits student to proceed with mathematical training by self-instruction.

TANUS, JUDITH M.; MOSTELLER, FREDERICK; KRUSKUL, WILLIAM H.; LINK, RICHARD F.; PIETERS, RICHARD S.; and RISING, GERALD R. *Statistics: A Guide to the Unknown*. San Francisco: Holden-Day, 1972.

Everyday use of statistics.

WEISS, ROBERT S. *Statistics in Social Research*. New York: John Wiley & Sons, 1968.

The traditional topics are treated from the point of view of someone guiding a student through the research process.

WIKE, EDWARD L. *Data Analysis: A Statistical Primer for Psychology Students*. Chicago: Aldine-Atherton, 1971.

A "how to do it" text that illustrates the use of statistics in data obtained from small samples. Intended for students who are conducting experiments for the first time. Organized around types of experimental designs.

ZEISEL, HANS. *Say It with Figures*. 5th ed. New York: Harper & Row, 1968.

A guide to the assembly and interpretation of social statistics.

A SPECIALIZED BIBLIOGRAPHIC SECTION FOR THE ADVANCED STUDENT

3.10

Selected Readings on Causal Models and Multivariate Analysis

BLALOCK, HUBERT M., JR., ed. *Measurement in the Social Sciences: Theories, and Strategies*. Chicago: Aldine, 1974.

——. *Causal Inferences in Non-Experimental Research.* Chapel Hill: University of North Carolina Press, 1964.

——, and BLALOCK, ANN B., eds. *Methodology in Social Research.* New York: McGraw-Hill, 1968.

——; AGANBEGIAN, A.; BORODKIN, F. M.; BOUDON, RAYMOND; and CAPECCHI, VITTORIO, eds. *Quantitative Sociology, International Perspectives on Mathematical and Statistical Modelling.* New York: Academic Press, 1975.

COOLEY, WILLIAM W., and LOHNES, PAUL R. *Multivariate Data Analysis.* New York: John Wiley & Sons, 1971.

COOMBS, CLYDE H. *A Theory of Data.* New York: John Wiley & Sons, 1964.

COSTNER, HERBERT L., ed. *Sociological Methodology.* San Francisco: Jossey-Bass, 1974.

DUNCAN, OTIS D. *Introduction to Structural Equation Models.* New York: Academic Press, 1975.

GRAWOIG, DENNIS E. *Decision Mathematics.* New York: McGraw-Hill, 1967.

HEISE, DAVID R. *Causal Analysis.* New York: John Wiley & Sons, 1975.

KERLINGER, FRED N., and PEDHAZUR, ELAZAR J. *Multiple Regression in Behavioral Research.* New York: Holt, Rinehart, & Winston, 1973.

LEIK, ROBERT K., and MEEKER, BARBARA F. *Mathematical Sociology.* Englewood Cliffs, N.J.: Prentice-Hall, 1975.

LIEBERMAN, BERNHARDT. *Contemporary Problems in Statistics: A Book of Readings for the Behavioral Sciences.* New York: Oxford University Press, 1971.

MORRISON, DONALD F. *Multivariate Statistical Methods.* New York: McGraw-Hill, 1967.

NOWAK, S. "Some Problems of Causal Interpretation of Statistical Relationships." *Philosophy of Science* 27 (January 1960): 23–38.

POLK, KENNETH. "A Note on Asymmetric Causal Models." *American Sociological Review* 27 (August 1962): 539–42.

ROBINSON, W. S. "Asymmetric Causal Models: Comments on Polk and Blalock," *American Sociological Review* 27 (August 1962): 545–48.

SCHUESSLER, KARL. *Analyzing Social Data.* Boston: Houghton Mifflin, 1971.

SIMON, HERBERT A. "Causal Ordering and Identifiability." In *Studies in Econometric Methods*, edited by W. C. Hood and T. C. Koopmans. New York: John Wiley & Sons, 1953. Pp. 49–74.

——. "Spurious Correlation: A Causal Interpretation." *Journal of the American Statistical Association* 49 (September 1954): 467–79.

——. *Models of Man: Social and Rational.* New York: John Wiley & Sons, 1957. Pp. 37–49.

TUFTE, EDWARD R. *Data Analysis for Politics and Policy.* Englewood Cliffs, N.J.: Prentice-Hall, 1974.

WOLD, HERMAN. "Causal Inference from Observational Data." *Journal of the Royal Statistical Society* 119, ser. A, pt. 1 (1956): 28–60.

——, and JUREEN, L. *Demand Analysis: A Study in Econometrics.* New York: John Wiley & Sons, 1953.

Contents of Sociological Methodology *1969–76*

Sociological Methodology is an official publication of the American Sociological Association. It is an annual series that began in 1969 and was designed to keep social scientists abreast of methodological changes and innovations in all areas of sociological inquiry. Because of its importance in defining the cutting edge of the discipline, the contents are reproduced to provide a ready reference for the researcher. All volumes are published by Jossey-Bass, Inc., 615 Montgomery Street, San Francisco, Calif. 94111.

1969: Edgar F. Borgatta and George W. Bohrnstedt, eds.
  Part One: Path Analysis, Causal Inferences, and the Measurements of Change
  1. "Principles of Path Analysis," Kenneth C. Land
  2. "Problems in Path Analysis and Causal Inference," David R. Heise
  3. "Contingencies in Constructing Causal Models," Otis Dudley Duncan
  4. "Observations on the Measurement of Change," George W. Bohrnstedt

  Part Two: General Papers
  5. "Logic and Levels of Scientific Explanation," John T. Doby
  6. "Ecological Variables," Desmond S. Cartwright
  7. "Covariance Analysis in Sociological Research," Karl Schuessler
  8. "Stochastic Processes," Thomas J. Fararo

  Part Three: Shorter Papers and Notes
  9. "Testing a Measurement Model," Richard Ofshe and Ronald E. Anderson
  10. "Use of Ad Hoc Definitions," Jeffrey K. Hadden
  11. "Probabilities from Longitudinal Records," Peter A. Morrison

1970: Edgar F. Borgatta and George W. Bohrnstedt, eds.
  Part One: Theory Building and Causal Models
  1. "Causal Inference from Panel Data," David R. Heise
  2. "Heise's Causal Model Applied," Donald C. Pelz and Robert A. Lew
  3. "Partials, Partitions, and Paths," Otis Dudley Duncan
  4. "Evaluating Axiomatic Theories," Kenneth D. Bailey

  Part Two: Measurement, Reliability, and Validity
  5. "Statistical Estimation with Random Measurement Error," H. M. Blalock, Caryll S. Wells, and Lewis F. Carter
  6. "Validity, Invalidity, and Reliability," David R. Heise and George Bohrnstedt
  7. "Effect of Reliability and Validity on Power of Statistical Tests," T. Anne Cleary, Robert L. Linn, and G. William Walster
  8. "Bivariate Agreement Coefficients for Reliability of Data," Klaus Krippendorff
  9. "Validity and the Multitrait-Multimethod Matrix," Robert P. Althauser and Thomas A. Heberlein
  10. "Validation of Reputational Leadership by the Multitrait-Multimethod Matrix," Gene F. Summers, Lauren H. Seiler, and Glenn Wiley

  Part Three: Statistical Techniques
  11. "Statistics According to Bayes," Gudmund R. Iversen
  12. "Uncertainty Analysis Applied to Sociological Data," Doris R. Entwisle and Dennis Knepp
  13. "Multivariate Analysis for Attribute Data," James S. Coleman
  14. "Statistical Significance as a Decision Rule," G. William Walster and T. Anne Cleary

  Part Four: Mathematical Sociology
  15. "Mathematical Formalization of Durkheim's Theory of Division of Labor," Kenneth C. Land

16. "Status Dynamics," Thomas J. Fararo

17. "Structure of Semantic Space," Andy B. Anderson

1971: Herbert L. Costner, ed.

Part One: Strategies of Data Production

1. "Systematic Observation of Natural Social Phenomena," Albert J. Reiss, Jr.

2. "Detection Theory and Problems of Psychosocial Discrimination," Darrell K. Adams and Z. Joseph Ulehla

3. "Coding Responses to Open-Ended Questions," Kenneth C. W. Kammeyer and Julius Roth

Part Two: Measurement Error in Regression and Path Analysis

4. "The Treatment of Unobservable Variables in Path Analysis," Robert M. Hauser and Arthur S. Goldberger

5. "Robustness in Regression Analysis," George W. Bohrnstedt and T. Michael Carter

6. "Techniques for Using Ordinal Measures in Regression and Path Analysis," Morgan Lyons

Part Three: Path and Process Models

7. "Formal Theory," Kenneth C. Land

8. "Key Variables," Phillip Bonacich and Kenneth D. Bailey

9. "Coleman's Process Approach," Martin Jaeckel

Part Four: Association and Prediction of Variables

10. "Integrated Approach to Measuring Association," Robert K. Leik and Walter R. Grove

11. "Continuities in Social Prediction," Karl Schuessler

1972: Herbert L. Costner, ed.

1. "Strategies for Meaningful Comparison," Ronald Schoenberg

2. "Unmeasured Variables in Linear Models for Panel Analysis," Otis Dudley Duncan

3. "Polythetic Reduction of Monothetic Property Space," Kenneth Bailey

4. "The Generation of Confidence: Evaluating Research Findings by Random Subsample Replication," Bernard M. Finifter

5. "Technique for Analyzing Overlapping Memberships," Phillip Bonacich

6. "Retest of a Measurement Model," Cynthia J. Flynn and Lewis F. Carter

7. "Using Monotone Regression to Estimate a Correlation Coefficient," Lawrence S. Mayer

1973–74: Herbert L. Costner, ed.

Prologue, Herbert L. Costner

1. "Some Issues in Sociological Measurement," David R. Heise

2. "Theta Reliability and Factor Scaling," David J. Armor

3. "Construction of Composite Measures by the Canonical-Factor-Regression Method," Michael Patrick Allen

4. "Approaches to the Interpretation of Relationships in the Multitrait-Multimethod Matrix," Duane F. Alwin

5. "Inferring Validity from the Multitrait-Multimethod Matrix: Another Assessment," Robert P. Althauser

6. "Correlation of Ratios or Difference Scores Having Common Terms," Glenn V. Fuguitt and Stanley Lieberson
7. "Alternative Approaches to Analysis-of-Variance Tables," Peter J. Burke and Karl Schuessler
8. "Hierarchical Models for Significance Tests in Multivariate Contingency Tables: An Exegesis of Goodman's Recent Papers," James A. Davis
9. "Questions About Attitude Survey Questions," Howard Schuman and Otis Dudley Duncan
10. "Problems of Statistical Estimation and Causal Inference in Time-Series Regression Models," Douglas A. Hibbs, Jr.
11. "Spectral Analysis and the Study of Social Change," Thomas F. Mayer and William Ray Arney
12. "Social Mobility Models for Heterogeneous Populations," Burton Singer and Seymour Spilerman

1975: David R. Heise, ed.
1. "Toward the Integration of Content Analysis and General Methodology," John Markoff, Gilbert Shapiro, and Sasha R. Weitman
2. "Cluster Analysis," Kenneth D. Bailey
3. "Scaling Replicated Conditional Rank-Order Data," Forrest W. Young
4. "Method for Classifying Interval-Scale and Ordinal-Scale Data," Kenneth R. Bryson and David P. Phillips
5. "Multiple Indicators and the Relationship Between Abstract Variables," Lawrence S. Mayer and Mary Sue Younger

1976: David R. Heise, ed.
1. "Local Structure in Social Networks," Paul W. Holland and Samuel Leinhardt
2. "Comparing Causal Models," David A. Specht and Richard D. Warren
3. "The Relationship Between Modified and Usual Multiple-Regression Approaches to the Analysis of Dichotomous Variables," Leo A. Goodman
4. "Analyzing Contingency Tables with Linear Flow Graphs," D. Systems and James A. Davis
5. "Predictive-Logic Approach to Causal Models of Qualitative Variates," David K. Hildebrand, James D. Laing, and Howard Rosenthal
6. "Effects of Grouping on Measures of Ordinal Association," Roland K. Hawkes
7. "Can We Find a Genuine Ordinal Slope Analogue?," H. M. Blalock, Jr.
8. "Using Assumptions of Linearity to Establish a Metric," Phillip Bonacich and Douglas Kirby
9. "Monotonic Regression Analysis for Ordinal Variables," Richard K. Leik
10. "Causal Models with Nominal and Ordinal Data," Richard K. Leik
11. "Rank-Sum Comparisons Between Groups," Stanley Lieberson

Selected Bibliography for the Application of Mathematics to Social Analysis and Special Problems

BIJNEN, E. *Cluster Analysis*. Netherlands: Tilburg University Press, 1973.

A sociologist describes cluster analysis and its social applications.

COLEMAN, JAMES S. *Introduction to Mathematical Sociology*. Glencoe, Ill.: Free Press, 1964.

The emphasis in this book is on mathematics as a tool for the elaboration of sociological theory.

——. *The Mathematics of Collective Action*. Chicago: Aldine, 1973.

A theory relating the decisions and actions of social groups with instrumental powers to the specific interests and resources of group members.

DODD, STUART C., and CHRISTOPHER, STEFAN C. "The Reactants Models." In *Essays in Honor of George Lundberg*. Great Barrington, Mass.: Behavioral Research Council, 1968. Pp. 143–79.

A search for laws of communicative behavior by fitting curves to diffusion data as item moves through a population.

DOREIAN, PATRICK. *Mathematics and the Study of Social Relations*. New York: Schocken, 1971.

GOLDBERG, SAMUEL. *Introduction to Difference Equations*. New York: John Wiley & Sons, 1958.

Revised edition of monograph on difference equations written in 1954 at the invitation of SSRC Committee on the Mathematical Training of Social Scientists.

HAMLIN, ROBERT L.; JACOBSEN, R. BROOKE; and MILLER, JERRY L. *A Mathematical Theory of Social Change*. New York: John Wiley & Sons, 1973.

HAYES, PATRICK. *Mathematical Methods in Social and Managerial Sciences*. New York: Wiley Interscience, 1975.

HARMAN, HARRY H. *Modern Factor Analysis*. 2nd ed. Chicago: University of Chicago Press, 1967.

HORST, PAUL. *Factor Analysis of Data Matrices*. New York: Holt, Rinehart, & Winston, 1967.

KEMENY, JOHN G., and SNELL, LAURIE J. *Mathematical Models in the Social Sciences*. Boston: Blaisdell, 1962.

This book is for a mathematics course, not a social science course; the problems in the social sciences are introduced only as an incentive to learn mathematics.

LAZARSFELD, PAUL F. "Notes on the History of Quantification in Sociology— Trends, Sources, and Problems." In *Quantification*, edited by Harry Woolf. Indianapolis: Bobbs-Merrill, 1961.

——, ed. *Mathematical Thinking in the Social Sciences*. Glencoe, Ill.: Free Press, 1954.

LUNDBERG, GEORGE A. "Statistics in Modern Social Thought." In *Contemporary Social Theory*, edited by Harry Elmer Barnes, Howard Becker, and Francis Bennett Becker. New York: Appleton Century, 1940. Pp. 110–40.

Historical account of the rise of social statistics.

MARTINDALE, DON. "Limits to the Uses of Mathematics in the Study of Sociology." In *Mathematics and the Social Sciences*, edited by James C. Charlesworth. Philadelphia: American Academy of Political and Social Science, June 1963. Pp. 95–121.

McGINNIS, ROBERT. *Mathematical Foundations for Social Analysis*. Indianapolis: Bobbs-Merrill, 1965.

Provides an introduction to mathematical procedures which are being increasingly employed in sociology: sets, relations, real numbers, matrices, and limits.

MOKKEN, R. J. *A Theory and Procedure of Scale Analysis*. The Hague, Paris: Mouton, 1971.

Theoretical and practical issues of Guttman Scale techniques.

MORRISON, DENTON E., and HENCKEL, RAMON E., eds. *The Significance Test Controversy: A Reader*. Chicago: Aldine, 1970.

RASHEVSKY, NICHOLAS. *Mathematical Biology of Social Behavior*. Chicago: University of Chicago Press, 1950.

Application of mathematical methods to study of social stratification.

SOLOMON, HERBERT, ed. *Mathematical Thinking in the Measurement of Behavior*. Glencoe, Ill.: Free Press, 1960.

Includes contributions by James S. Coleman on mathematics and small-group research; Ernest W. Adams on utility theory; and Herbert Solomon on factor analysis.

STONE, RICHARD. "Mathematics in the Social Sciences." *Scientific American* 211, no. 3 (September 1964): 168–86.

STOUFFER, SAMUEL A.; GUTTMAN, LOUIS; SUCHMAN, EDWARD A.; LAZARSFELD, PAUL F.; STAR, SHIRLEY A.; and CLAUSEN, JOHN A. *Measurement and Prediction*. Princeton, N.J.: Princeton University Press, 1950.

Theoretical and empirical analysis of scales and problems of prediction.

WHITE, HARRISON. "Uses of Mathematics in Sociology." In *Mathematics and the Social Sciences*, edited by James C. Charlesworth. Philadelphia: American Adademy of Political and Social Science, June 1963. Pp. 77–94.
———. *An Anatomy of Kinship*. Englewood Cliffs, N.J.: Prentice-Hall, 1963.

Attempt to analyze logic underlying kinship systems by mathematical methods.

ZIPF, GEORGE KINGSLEY. *Human Behavior and the Principle of Least Effort*. Cambridge, Mass.: Addison-Wesley, 1949.

Selected References to Multiple Discriminant Analysis

HOEL, P. G. *Introduction to Mathematical Statistics*. 3rd ed. New York: John Wiley & Sons, 1962.
LOY, JOHN W., JR. "Social Psychological Characteristics of Innovators." *American Sociological Review* (February 1969): 73–82.
RAO, C. R. *Advanced Statistical Methods in Biometric Research*. New York: John Wiley & Sons, 1952.
RETTIG, SOLOMON. "Multiple Discriminant Analysis: An Illustration." *American Sociological Review* 29 (June 1964): 398–402.
RULON, PHILLIP J. "Distinctions Between Discriminant and Regression Analysis and a Geometric Interpretation of the Discriminant Function." *Harvard Educational Review* 21 (Spring 1951): 80–90.
TIEDEMAN, DAVID V. "The Utility of the Discriminant Function in Psychological and Guidance Investigations." *Harvard Educational Review* 21 (Spring 1951): 71–80.

part 4

Selected Sociometric Scales and Indexes

THERE are literally thousands of scales and indexes to measure social variables. Social scientists have often elected to construct new measures even when scales of high reliability and validity have been available. This practice is wasteful of time, energy, and money. In addition, it makes replication and accumulation of research findings difficult if not impossible. The selection of scales to be found in this handbook was based on such criteria as validity, reliability, and utility. The variables most commonly used in social measurement were studied and measures for them were sought. Those with the highest reliability and validity were selected. It is hoped that this handbook will encourage greater use of these scales or stimulate the search for better ones.

In general, three groups of variable factors need to be observed and measured in any research design that seeks to test a basic hypothesis or social relationship.

First, there is the dependent variable, the effect we wish to observe and describe.

Second, there is the independent variable (or variables) that has been designated as the causal factor. Sometimes this factor must be broken down into the component parts that operate more or less as a unit pattern.

Third, there are intervening or other independent variables that must be controlled lest they obscure the relationship we wish to measure by use of experimental design.

Sociometric scales have been constructed in substantial numbers to permit quantitative description of these factors in human relations.

Three areas of social measurement can be identified. These are:

1. Psychometric and social psychological scales: psychological measurements including intelligence scales, personality tests and scales, attitude tests and scales.

Examples of these scales that are included in this part are the Minnesota Multiphasic Personality Inventory, the Authoritarian Personality (F) Scale, Morale and Job Satisfaction Scales, as well as attitude scales to measure leisure satisfactions; community attitudes, achievement orientation, and alienation.

2. Demographic Scales: measurements of the forms or results of social behavior in large units such as the community, state, or nation.

Examples in this part include community rating scales, community services activity, citizen political activity, and a community solidarity index.

3. Sociometric Scales: measurements of the social structure and process.

Examples in this part include sociometric tests to measure informal friendship constellations, measurements of social participation, of social distance, and of group cohesiveness. Other scales are provided to assess marital adjustment and group dimensions. The measurement of social status is of such crucial importance that a number of scales are included, such as *Duncan's Socioeconomic Index, U.S. Census Socioeconomic Status Scores, Hollingshead's Two Factor Index of Social Position, Alba Edwards' Socioeconomic Scale, Warner's Revised Occupational Scale for Social Class.*

If you do not find a scale that fits your particular research interest, consult the inventory of measures used by researchers represented in the *American Sociological Review* during 1965-74. This inventory has been placed at the end of part 4. Introducing this inventory is a listing of major sources for scale information and appraisal. One very important source are the occupational, political, and social psychological scales carefully selected and appraised by John P. Robinson and his co-workers at the Institute of Social Research of the University of Michigan. A complete listing is shown on pages 446-55.

Also presented at the end of part 4 is the list of attitude scales from Marvin E. Shaw and Jack M. Wright, *Scales for the Measurement of Attitudes* (New York: McGraw-Hill, 1967). The complete scale can be found in their book.

Scale construction yields four types of scales: the *nominal* scale, consisting simply of distinguishable categories with no implication of "more" or "less"; the *ordinal* scale, on which positions can be identified in a rank order with no implication as to the distance between positions; the *interval* scale, which has equal distance between any two adjacent positions on the continuum; and the *ratio* scale, which has not only equal intervals but an absolute zero.

The ideal scale is a ratio scale, but with the possible exception of the procedures for measuring certain psychophysical phenomena, none of the measurement techniques currently used fits the requirements for a ratio scale. The nominal scale permits neither rank ordering nor a metric scale. It is so elemental as a classification scheme that such scales are generally regarded as first approximations toward the quantification of a social variable. The result is that ordinal and interval scales are the most frequent types in use. There is considerable disagreement over whether an ordinal or interval scale provides the most appropriate model for social data. Some writers have taken the view that few, if any, of the techniques now in use provide data that can be considered appropriate to more than ordinal scales. Others believe that various types of scales may properly be treated as conforming to interval scales. Still others have taken the position that, although most of the measurements used do not go beyond ordinal scales, little harm is done in applying statistics to them that are appropriate to interval scales.

The result is that statistics appropriate to interval scales continue to be widely used in the analysis of social data whether the assumptions are met or not. However, there is also an increasing use of statistics that are specifically appropriate to ordinal scales. The statistical tools included in part 3 of the handbook are for the use of the ordinal and interval scales included in this section.

The selection of a good scale involves weighing a number of criteria. Frequency of use is one useful criterion for choice of a scale, because of the possibility of maximizing accumulated research in the test of hypotheses. In the selection of scales for the revised edition this frequency criterion has been utilized. However, it is not the only determinant. Frequency can be misleading. New and better scales are constantly appearing. Moreover, use of a scale by others does not guarantee that they have chosen the "best" scale as described by rigorous criteria. For this reason some of the scales selected for this section may not be high on frequency count, but it is believed that they are the scales the researcher should use *now*. The most important single consideration is validity. Does the scale measure what it purports to measure? How much and what kind of evidence is available? Does the scale fit the problem selected for study?

Other considerations include its reliability, its precision, its simplicity and ease of administration. In recent years there has been considerable emphasis on unidimensionality. The Guttman technique enables the researcher to identify and construct scales of a single dimension. This may be very important in increasing the precision and predictability of a given variable. However, two qualifications must be kept in mind. Such a scale may not be the most effective either for measuring attitudes toward complex objects or for making predictions about behavior in relation to such objects. It must also be remembered that a given scale may be unidimensional for one group of individuals but not for another.

The scales assembled in this part include those constructed by arbitrary or judgmental ranking, by item analysis techniques, by Thurstone's equal-appearing interval method, by Guttman's technique of scale analysis, and by factor analysis. Regardless of the method used in construction, what the researcher seeks is the scale that best fits his problem, has the highest reliability and validity, is precise, and is relatively easy to apply.[1] When he has made his selection he must be aware of the statistical techniques he may subsequently apply. Generally, he will be using nonparametric statistics for ordinal scales and parametric statistics for interval scales and for those ordinal scales that do not deviate too far from the assumptions of randomness and normal distribution.

Note

1. For an excellent discussion of these criteria, see Paul F. Lazarsfeld and Morris Rosenberg, *The Language of Social Research* (Glencoe, Ill.: Free Press, 1955); Hans Zeisel, *Say It With Figures* (5th ed., rev.; New York: Harper, 1968), pp. 76–102. Cf. George W. Bohrnstedt, "A Quick Method for Determining the Reliability and Validity of Multiple-Item Scales," *American Sociological Review* 34 (August 1969): 542–48.

Social Status

Social class or status is one of the most important variables in social research. The socioeconomic position of a person affects his or her chances for education, income, occupation, marriage, health, friends, and even life expectancy. The variable has proved difficult to measure in a pluralistic, equalitarian, and fluid society such as exists in the United States. However, many researchers have tried to identify the social strata and to measure associated variables. Nearly 30 percent of all research articles in the major sociological journals are devoted to social stratification. The best research bibliography is that of Norval D. Glenn, Jon P. Alston, and David Weiner, *Social Stratification: A Research Bibliography* (Berkeley: Glendessary Press, 1970). Occupation has been shown to be the best single predictor of social status, and overall occupational prestige ratings have been found to be highly stable. A number of factors act in close relationship between occupation and social status. Both individual income and educational attainment are known to be correlated with occupational ranks. Education is a basis for entry into many occupations, and for most persons income is derived from the occupation. House type and dwelling area constitute other highly correlated factors.

Five scales are presented here for the researcher's choice. They vary in length and the number of factors included in the scale.

1. O. D. Duncan's Socioeconomic Index
2. U.S. Census Socioeconomic Status Scores
3. August B. Hollingshead's Two Factor Index of Social Position
4. The Revised Occupational Rating Scale from Warner, Meeker, and Eell's Index of Status Characteristics
5. Alba M. Edwards' Social-Economic Grouping of Occupations

Of the five, the standard Duncan Socioeconomic Index is being most widely used and is generally considered to be superior for most survey and large-sample situations. It takes into account income, education, and occupational prestige.

The Bureau of the Census has devised socioeconomic status scores for all occupations listed in the Census. The scores are based on average levels of education and income for U.S. males in 1960. Researchers have the option of choosing

the Census Socioeconomic Scores if they wish to employ a measurement without prestige weights. A correlation of .97 is reported between the Duncan Socioeconomic Index and Census Socioeconomic Status scores.

Hollingshead's Two Factor Index of Social Position is based on occupation and
education. The occupation scale differentiates among kinds of professionals and
the size and economic strength of business. The seven-point educational scale is
premised upon the assumption that men and women who possess similar educations will tend to have similar tastes and similar attitudes and will exhibit similar
behavior patterns. The Hollingshead and Duncan indices have been shown to be
moderately correlated. When they differ it is usually because Duncan has had to
use one of the grosser census categories. Researchers concerned especially about
the professional and business personnel in their sample may elect Hollingshead's
index.

Choose the Warner, Meeker, and Eell's Occupational Rating Scale if a short
scale is desired. This seven-point occupation scale is probably the most sophisticated short classification available. Occupation is one measure in the Index of
Status Characteristics. Other measures include source of income, house type, and
dwelling area. If these data are available, somewhat greater precision can be obtained. The scale provides scores ranging from 12 to 84, but occupations are
grouped into 7 classifications. The scale is comparable to Edwards' socioeconomic
groupings, but the Warner scale obtained greater rigor by increased homogeneity
of its classifications.

Choose Edwards' socioeconomic grouping if a relatively broad classification is
satisfactory for your problem. This grouping makes it possible to use the U.S.
Census for many kinds of comparative purposes. This nominal scale has been
used widely in research on occupational mobility and occupational trends
generally. The most often cited criticisms of the Edwards' classifications concern
the lack of homogeneity of the categories and the weak scale properties of
hierarchical grouping.

Two questions concern the researcher: What is the relative validity of the
available social status scales? Can social status be regarded as unidimensional and
measurable by a single socioeconomic index? Some tentative answers are possible.

THE RELATIVE VALIDITY OF SOCIAL-STATUS SCALES

The concern here tends to narrow down to the two most widely used measures
in current research: Duncan's Socioeconomic Index and Hollingshead's Two
Factor Index of Social Position. Meager research exists on the comparative
analysis of the two indices. Haug and Sussman have made a comparison based on
data they gathered and conclude that the Duncan index suffers from weaknesses
that undermine its usefulness, while the Hollingshead index requires updating.
They mention the need for a valid index based on the theoretical distinction
between class (economic position) and social status (prestige) and adapted to
current structural realities.[1] They express concern over the changes in income
and education in various age cohorts since the construction of the scales. However, remarkable stability in occupational stratification has been reported by
Robert W. Hodge, Paul M. Siegel, and Peter H. Rossi, who found only small
changes in prestige ratings and conclude that "there have been no substantial
changes in occupational prestige in the United States since 1925."[2]

Another attempt to measure changes in occupational status was made by Charles B. Nam and Mary G. Powers, who compared the 1960 and 1950 status scores of nearly 500 occupations using the Census index for 1950 and a similar scoring scheme for 1960.[3] They found small changes in ninety-two occupations; only four had higher scores, while the remainder had lower scores. The overall correlation was .96 indicating a very close association between the 1950 and 1960 scores. A review of the changes makes it clear that the conclusion of Hodge, Siegel, and Rossi that there have not been any *substantial* recent changes in occupational *prestige* can also be extended to other aspects of occupational *status*.

These reassuring facts about stability do not resolve some difficulties that are inherent in the differing social repute assigned to education and income. Because status variables are only loosely intertwined, the vast majority of individuals in modern societies are able to advance some legitimate claims to recognition and the other rewards of society. Those with little education may still achieve ample income, and those with modest incomes may land a prestigious job. At the moment the only way to weigh the merits of a scale is for the researcher to examine the data on occupations among his or her respondents and to compare the categories incorporated in the scales. The researcher should be urged to consider the second question.

Can socioeconomic status be considered unidimensional? Caplow and Hatt say no;[4] Hodge goes still further and urges a multidimensional approach claiming that different indicators of social participation and psychological well-being are in fact associated with different indicators of socioeconomic status. "Any attempt to combine these indicators—educational attainment, occupational pursuit, family income or occupational origins into a single index of socioeconomic status will prove unsatisfactory because its component parts have different consequences for the same variable."[5]

Researchers have options. Regression, factor, and path analysis all offer the opportunity to use socioeconomic characteristics as independent variables when seeking correlations with a dependent variable. When appropriate, the "best" indices of social status should be utilized. There is good evidence, with all their shortcomings, that the socioeconomic indices described in this section are among the most valid and useful scales among sociological instruments. If your problem indicates use, employ them; they will permit your research findings to be cumulative and hence valuable to the advance of social knowledge.

Notes

1. Marie R. Haug and Marvin B. Sussman, "The Indiscriminate State of Social Class Measurement," *Social Forces* 49 (June 1971): 549–63. See the commentary by Hollingshead on pp. 563–67 defending his index.

2. Robert W. Hodge, Paul M. Siegel, and Peter H. Rossi, "Occupational Prestige in the United States, 1925–1963," *American Journal of Sociology* 70 (November 1964): 296.

3. Charles B. Nam and Mary G. Powers, "Changes in the Relative Status Levels of Workers in the United States, 1950–60." *Social Forces* 47 (December 1968): 167–70.

4. Theodore Caplow, *Sociology of Work* (Minneapolis: University of Minnesota Press, 1954), pp. 33–57; Paul K. Hatt, "Occupation and Social Stratification," *American Journal of Sociology* 55 (May 1950): 538–43.

5. Robert W. Hodge, "Social Integration, Psychological Well-Being, and their SES Corre-lates," in E. O. Laumann, ed., *Social Stratification: Research and Theory for the 1970's* (Indianapolis: Bobbs-Merrill Co., 1970), pp. 182-206.

4.A.1 DUNCAN'S SOCIOECONOMIC INDEX

VARIABLE MEASURED: A socioeconomic index relating such character-istics as occupational prestige, education, and income.

DESCRIPTION: This measure was developed to secure two objectives: (1) to extend the North-Hatt (NORC) occupational prestige scores from 90 to 446 occupations in the detailed classification of the 1950 Census of Population; and (2) to obtain a socioeconomic index in terms of the relationship between the NORC prestige ratings and socioeconomic characteristics of the population. This index has been developed and has face validity, in terms of its constituent vari-ables, and sufficient predictive efficiency with respect to the NORC occupa-tional prestige ratings.

The Duncan index differs from NORC prestige scores in that NORC scores rely solely on subjective occupational ratings of representative samples of respon-dents. Duncan constructed the occupational socioeconomic index in terms of the relationship between the NORC prestige ratings X_1 and socioeconomic char-acteristics of the occupations, such as education X_2 and income X_3 with a multi-ple correlation of $R_{123} = 0.91$. Each occupation was given an education weight (X_2) based on the percentage of those in the occupation who were high school graduates. Income weights (X_3) were determined by those in each occupation reporting $3500 or more in 1949. Occupational scores on each of these indi-cators were compared with NORC prestige scores (X_1) for the 45 occupations on the NORC list that were reasonably equivalent to U.S. Census titles. In addi-tion to specific socioeconomic scores, a population decile scale was constructed permitting the researcher the option of arranging his data in a ten-point ranking order. For more information on the construction of the index, the researcher is referred to Albert J. Reiss, with Otis D. Duncan, Paul K. Hatt, and C. C. North, *Occupations and Social Status* (Glencoe, Ill.: Free Press, 1961), pp. 109-61 and Appendix B.

A researcher interested in a prestige measure is urged to use the Hatt-North ratings or Duncan's transformed NORC scores. See Paul K. Hatt and C. C. North, "Jobs and Occupations: A Popular Evaluation," *Opinion News* 9 (September 1947), University of Chicago: National Opinion Research Center, 3-13; or see Robert W. Hodge, Paul M. Siegel, and Peter Rossi, "Occupational Prestige in the United States, 1925-63," *American Journal of Sociology* 70 (November 1964): 286-302. This is reprinted in R. Bendix and S. Lipset, eds., *Class, Status and Power* (New York: Free Press, 1965). Numerous prestige studies exist, and corre-spondence between independent samples of respondents is quite high. For an excellent comparative analysis, see Lawrence Thomas, *The Occupational Struc-ture and Education* (Englewood Cliffs, N.J.: Prentice-Hall, 1956), pp. 181-82.

WHERE PUBLISHED: Albert J. Reiss, with O. D. Duncan, Paul K. Hatt, and C. C. North, *Occupations and Social Status* (Glencoe, Ill.: Free Press, 1961).

RELIABILITY: Reliability problems emerge as respondent's description of his occupation is translated into an occupational code number using the U.S. Census *Index of Occupations and Industries* or the *Dictionary of Occupational Titles* published by the U.S. Department of Labor. For increasing reliability or expediting of clerical labor, see Donald G. McTavish, "A Method for More Reliable Coding Detailed Occupations into Duncan's Socio-Economic Categories," *American Sociological Review* 29 (June 1964): 402–6; Robert F. Winch, Samuel A. Mueller, and Lois Godiksen, "The Reliability of Respondent-Coded Occupational Prestige," *American Sociological Review* 34 (April 1969): 245–51.

VALIDITY: The prestige variable is rather highly related to each predictor: with education, $r = 0.84$; with income, 0.85. The multiple correlation between the three variables $R_{1(23)} = 0.91$. Overall occupational ratings have been found to be highly stable over time ($r = .99$ from 1947 to 1963) and across social systems. See Hodge, Siegel, and Rossi, "Occupational Prestige in the United States."

A moderate correlation ($r = .74$) has been found between the Hollingshead and Duncan indices. However, these scales are constructed differently, and the correlation can be explained. See August B. Hollingshead, "Commentary on 'The Indiscriminate State of Social Class Measurement'," *Social Forces* 49 (June 1971): 567. It is of consequence, however, that the two "leading" measures of social status express such a variance.

Certain anomalies appear. For example, since clergymen typically earn small salaries, their Duncan score is considerably below that found by more subjective procedures. In the blue-collar world, large differences are found among semi-skilled workers in various industries. Important regional differences are not expressed. For these reasons Duncan does not recommend that the scale be used for comparisons within certain regions of the country or within certain segments of the status hierarchy, such as skilled workers. The researcher concerned with these discrepancies should consult Haug and Sussman, "The Indiscriminate State of Social Class Measurement," *Social Forces* 49 (June 1971): 549–63.

UTILITY: The basic data required are the subject's description of his or her occupation. This description must then be translated into an occupational code by the researcher, and the occupational title is then converted into a preexisting Duncan SEI score (or NORC transformed prestige score if desired). There are many subtleties in the art of occupation coding, especially for blue-collar occupations. One should reserve adequate time for training and cross-checking. Anyone planning detailed occupation coding should heed the sound recommendations of McTavish, "Method for More Reliable Coding," and Winch, Mueller, and Godiksen, "Reliability of Respondent-Coded Occupational Prestige." For codes and decile scores, see John B. Robinson et al., *Measures of Occupational Attitudes and Occupational Characteristics* (Ann Arbor: Survey Research Center, University of Michigan, 1969), pp. 342–58.

RESEARCH APPLICATIONS:

BLAU, PETER M. "The Flow of Occupational Supply and Recruitment." *American Sociological Review* 30 (August 1965): 475–90. See p. 476.

CLARK, JOHN P., and WENNINGER, EUGENE P. "Socioeconomic Class and

Areas as Correlates of Illegal Behavior among Juveniles." *American Sociological Review* 27 (December 1962): 826–34. See p. 828.

———. "Goal Orientations and Illegal Behavior among Juveniles." *Social Forces* 42 (October 1963): 49–59. See p. 51.

ECKLAND, BRUCE K. "Academic Ability, Higher Education, and Occupational Mobility." *American Sociological Review* 30 (October 1965): 735–46. See p. 739.

———. "Social Class and College Graduation: Some Misconceptions Corrected." *American Journal of Sociology* 70 (July 1964): 36–50. See p. 43.

ERBE, WILLIAM. "Social Involvement and Political Activity: A Replication and Elaboration." *American Sociological Review* 29 (April 1964): 198–215. See p. 203.

REISS, IRA L. "Social Class and Premarital Sexual Permissiveness: A Reexamination." *American Sociological Review* 30 (October 1965): 747–56. See p. 749.

For more recent research use, see all references in the period 1965-74 in the *American Sociological Review Inventory* under Duncan's Socioeconomic Index Section 4.M.1, p. 418 and pp. 426–27.

4.A.2   U.S. CENSUS SOCIOECONOMIC STATUS SCORES

VARIABLE MEASURED: The socioeconomic status score is a multiple-item measure derived by averaging scores for the component items of occupation, education, and family income. A companion measure of status consistency is also available.

The Bureau of the Census has devised Socioeconomic Status Scores for occupations based on 1960 Census data for income and education without use of prestige ratings. The procedure employed to compute the scores is quite similar to that used by Duncan with these differences: (1) median education and income were used rather than percentages of specified education and income levels; (2) Duncan indirectly standardized the scores by age; and (3) Duncan used the 1947 NORC prestige ratings in deriving weights for Census characteristics. The similarity of the Census and Duncan's index is attested to, however, by the Pearsonian coefficient of .97 as previously reported.

WHERE PUBLISHED: U.S. Bureau of the Census, *Methodology and Scores of Socioeconomic Status*, Working Paper No. 15 (Washington, D.C.: U.S. Government Printing Office, 1963); U.S. Bureau of the Census, U.S. Census of Population, 1960, *Socioeconomic Status*, Final Rept. PC(2)-5C (Washington, D.C.: U.S. Government Printing Office, 1967).

RESEARCH APPLICATIONS:

NAM, CHARLES B., and POWERS, MARY G. "Variations in Socioeconomic Structure by Race, Residence, and the Life Cycle." *American Sociological Review* 30 (February 1965): 97–103.

———. "Changes in the Relative Status Level of Workers in the United States, 1950-1960." *Social Forces* 47 (December 1968): 167–70.

Both Duncan and U.S. Census scores are shown for all occupations listed in the 1960 U.S. Census of Population. The scores can take values approximately between 0 and 100 on both indexes, but since they are constructed somewhat differently it is not appropriate to make direct comparisons. Wide variations indicate that caution should be used in interpreting the status of individual occupations.

Socioeconomic Index Scores for Major Occupation Groups by Duncan's SEI (Weighted Prestige, Education, Income) and by U.S. Census (Based on Simple Average of Scores for Occupation, Education, and Income for Males)

Duncan's SEI Score	Census SEI Score	Category
75	90	Professional, technical, and kindred workers
57	81	Managers, officials, and proprietors, except farm
47	71	Clerical, sales, and kindred workers
31	58	Craftsmen, foremen, and kindred workers
18	45	Operatives and kindred workers
17	34	Service workers, including private household
7	20	Laborers, except farm and mine

Socioeconomic Index Scores for Occupations by Duncan's SEI (Weighted Prestige, Education, Income)* and by U.S. Census (Based on Simple Average Scores for Occupation, Education, and Income for Males)**

Duncan's SEI Score	Census SEI Score	Category
		Professional, technical and kindred workers
78	92	Accountants and auditors
60	84	Actors
79	96	Airplane pilots and navigators
90	98	Architects
67	88	Artists and art teachers
52	60	Athletes
76	93	Authors
75	89	Chiropractors
52	67	Clergymen
84	96	College presidents, professors, and instructors (n.e.c.)
45	61	Dancers and dancing teachers
96	99	Dentists
73	91	Designers
39	65	Dietitians and nutritionists

*O. D. Duncan, in Albert J. Reiss, Jr., *Occupations and Social Status* (New York: Free Press, 1961), pp. 263–75.

**Revised scores based on 1970 census data are now available. See Charles B. Nam, John LaRocque, Mary G. Powers, and John Holmberg, "Occupational Status Scores: Stability and Change," *Proceedings of the American Statistical Association*, 1975, pp. 570–75.

Duncan's SEI Score	Census SEI Score	Category
		Professional, technical and kindred workers
67	87	Draftsmen
82	95	Editors and reporters
85		Engineers, technical
87	97	Aeronautical
90	98	Chemical
84	96	Civil
84	97	Electrical
86	95	Industrial
82	96	Mechanical
82	97	Metallurgical, and metallurgists
85	97	Mining
87	96	Not elsewhere classified
31	48	Entertainers (n.e.c.)
83	94	Farm and home management advisors
48	78	Foresters and conservationists
59	83	Funeral directors and embalmers
93	98	Lawyers and judges
60	64	Librarians
52	72	Musicians and music teachers
		Natural scientists
79	94	Chemists
80	95	Other natural scientists
46	71	Nurses, professional
51	50	Nurses, student professional
79	96	Optometrists
96	99	Osteopaths
84	96	Personnel and labor relations workers
82	95	Pharmacists
50	73	Photographers
92	99	Physicians and surgeons
82	95	Public relations men and publicity writers
69	90	Radio operators
67	84	Recreation and group workers
56	63	Religious workers
64	85	Social and welfare workers, except group
81	96	Social scientists
64	87	Sports instructors and officials
48	71	Surveyors
72	89	Teachers (n.e.c.)
48	73	Technicians, medical and dental
62	80	Technicians, electrical and electronic
62	80	Technicians, other engineering and physical sciences
62	85	Technicians (n.e.c.)
58	81	Therapists and healers (n.e.c.)

Duncan's SEI Score	Census SEI Score	Category
		Professional, technical and kindred workers
78	95	Veterinarians
65	86	Professional, technical, and kindred workers (n.e.c.)
		Managers, officials, and proprietors, except farm
72	92	Buyers and department heads, store
33	51	Buyers and shippers, farm products
58	73	Conductors, railroad
74	92	Credit men
50	79	Floormen and floor managers, store
63	—	Inspectors, public administration
72	89	Federal public administration and postal service
54	81	State public administration
56	82	Local public administration
32	41	Managers and superintendents, building
54	79	Officers, pilots, pursers, and engineers, ship
66	—	Officials & administrators (n.e.c.), public administration
84	94	Federal public administration
66	90	State public administration
54	79	Local public administration
58	82	Officials, lodge, society, union, etc.
60	82	Postmasters
77	92	Purchasing agents and buyers (n.e.c.)
68		Managers, officials, and proprietors (n.e.c.)–Salaried
60	84	Construction
79	95	Manufacturing
71	87	Transportation
76	93	Communications, and utilities and sanitary services
70	90	Wholesale trade
56	—	Retail trade
50	78	Food and dairy products stores
39	70	Eating and drinking places
68	90	General merchandise and limited price variety stores
69	89	Apparel and accessories stores
68	89	Furniture, housefurnishings, and equipment stores
64	88	Motor vehicles and accessories retailing
31	63	Gasoline service stations
64	87	Hardware, farm implement, & building material retailing
59	84	Other retail trade
85	96	Banking and other finance
84	96	Insurance and real estate
80	96	Business services
47	76	Automobile repair services and garages
53	81	Miscellaneous repair services

Duncan's SEI Score	Census SEI Score	Category
		Managers, officials, and proprietors, except farm
50	78	Personal services
62	89	All other industries (incl. not reported)
48		Managers, officials, & proprietors (n.e.c.)–Self-employed
51	79	Construction
61	88	Manufacturing
43	73	Transportation
44	72	Communications, and utilities and sanitary services
59	85	Wholesale trade
43	—	Retail trade
33	54	Food and dairy products stores
37	71	Eating and drinking places
47	72	General merchandise and limited price variety stores
65	88	Apparel and accessories stores
59	86	Furniture, housefurnishings, and equipment stores
70	89	Motor vehicles and accessories retailing
33	63	Gasoline service stations
61	90	Hardware, farm implement, & building material retailing
49	75	Other retail trade
85	97	Banking and other finance
76	95	Insurance and real estate
67	91	Business services
36	68	Automobile repair services and garages
34	60	Miscellaneous repair services
41	68	Personal services
49	76	All other industries (incl. not reported)
		Clerical and kindred workers
68	90	Agents (n.e.c.)
44	50	Attendants and assistants, library
38	56	Attendants, physician's and dentist's office
25	54	Baggagemen, transportation
52	75	Bank tellers
51	73	Bookkeepers
44	69	Cashiers
39	66	Collectors, bill and account
40	73	Dispatchers and starters, vehicle
67	85	Express messengers and railway mail clerks
44	73	File clerks
62	89	Insurance adjusters, examiners, and investigators
53	80	Mail carriers
28	43	Messengers and office boys
45	69	Office machine operators
44	73	Payroll and timekeeping clerks

Duncan's SEI Score	Census SEI Score	Category
		Clerical and kindred workers
44	73	Postal clerks
44	73	Receptionists
61	82	Secretaries
22	58	Shipping and receiving clerks
61	82	Stenographers
44	73	Stock clerks and storekeepers
22	33	Telegraph messengers
47	75	Telegraph operators
45	72	Telephone operators
60	82	Ticket, station, and express agents
61	82	Typists
44	73	Clerical and kindred workers (n.e.c.)
		Sales workers
66	90	Advertising agents and salesmen
40	67	Auctioneers
35	62	Demonstrators
08	08	Hucksters and peddlers
66	89	Insurance agents, brokers, and underwriters
27	20	Newsboys
62	86	Real estate agents and brokers
73	94	Stock and bond salesmen
47		Salesmen and sales clerks (n.e.c.)
65	88	Manufacturing
61	85	Wholesale trade
39	61	Retail trade
50	77	Other industries (incl. not reported)
		Craftsmen, foremen, and kindred workers
22	50	Bakers
16	31	Blacksmiths
33	59	Boilermakers
39	69	Bookbinders
27	50	Brickmasons, stonemasons, and tile setters
23	48	Cabinet makers
19	35	Carpenters
19	34	Cement and concrete finishers
52	79	Compositors and typesetters
21	52	Cranemen, derrickmen, and hoistmen
40	67	Decorators and window dressers
44	74	Electricians
55	81	Electrotypers and stereotypers
47	75	Engravers, except photoengravers
24	57	Excavating, grading, and road machinery operators

Duncan's SEI Score	Census SEI Score	Category
		Craftsmen, foremen, and kindred workers
49	–	Foremen (n.e.c.)
40	65	Construction
53	–	Manufacturing
54	76	Metal industries
60	82	Machinery, except electrical
60	82	Electrical machinery, equipment, and supplies
66	84	Transportation equipment
41	71	Other durable goods
39	66	Textiles, textile products, and apparel
53	79	Other nondurable goods (incl. not specified mfg.)
36	61	Railroads and railway express service
45	74	Transportation, except railroad
56	79	Communications, and utilities and sanitary services
44	73	Other industries (incl. not reported)
23	51	Forgemen and hammermen
39	66	Furriers
26	57	Glaziers
22	58	Heat treaters, annealers, and temperers
23	48	Inspectors, scalers, and graders, log and lumber
41		Inspectors (n.e.c.)
46	76	Construction
41	65	Railroads and railway express service
45	74	Transportation, etc. R.R., commun. & other public util.
38	71	Other industries (incl. not reported)
36	63	Jewelers, watchmakers, goldsmiths, and silversmiths
28	64	Job setters, metal
49	76	Linemen and servicemen, telegraph, telephone, and power
58	68	Locomotive engineers
45	76	Locomotive firemen
10	32	Loom fixers
33	68	Machinists
25		Mechanics and repairmen
–	61	Air conditioning, heating, and refrigeration
48	79	Airplane
19	52	Automobile
36	66	Office machine
36	62	Radio and television
23	52	Railroad and car shop
27	61	Not elsewhere classified
19	39	Millers, grain, flour, feed, etc.
31	62	Millwrights
12	41	Molders, metal
43	73	Motion picture projectionists

Duncan's SEI Score	Census SEI Score	Category
		Craftsmen, foremen, and kindred workers
39	72	Opticians, and lens grinders and polishers
16	37	Painters, construction and maintenance
10	22	Paperhangers
44	74	Pattern and model makers, except paper
64	84	Photoengravers and lithographers
38	54	Piano and organ tuners and repairmen
25	46	Plasterers
34	64	Plumbers and pipe fitters
49	77	Pressmen and plate printers, printing
22	54	Rollers and roll hands, metal
15	34	Roofers and slaters
12	22	Shoemakers and repairers, except factory
47	72	Stationary engineers
25	44	Stone cutters and stone carvers
34	66	Structural metal workers
23	40	Tailors
33	68	Tinsmiths, coppersmiths, and sheet metal workers
50	77	Toolmakers, and die makers and setters
22	53	Upholsterers
32	62	Craftsmen and kindred workers (n.e.c.)
18	36	Former members of the Armed Forces
		Operatives and kindred workers
35		Apprentices
25	46	Auto mechanics
32	57	Bricklayers and masons
31	50	Carpenters
37	61	Electricians
41	59	Machinists and toolmakers
34	60	Mechanics, except auto
33	60	Plumbers and pipe fitters
29	49	Building trades (n.e.c.)
33	55	Metalworking trades (n.e.c.)
40	57	Printing trades
31	51	Other specified trades
39	55	Trade not specified
32	63	Asbestos and insulation workers
17	61	Assemblers
19	44	Attendants, auto service and parking
11	33	Blasters and powdermen
24	50	Boatmen, canalmen, and lock keepers
42	71	Brakemen, railroad
24	65	Bus drivers
25	47	Chainmen, rodmen, and axmen, surveying

Duncan's SEI Score	Census SEI Score	Category
		Operatives and kindred workers
17	61	Checkers, examiners, and inspectors, mfg.
30	61	Conductors, bus and street railway
32	59	Deliverymen and routemen
23	35	Dressmakers and seamstresses, except factory
12	36	Dyers
22	57	Filers, grinders, and polishers, metal
10	19	Fruit, nut, and vegetable graders and packers, exc. factory
18	45	Furnacemen, smeltermen, and pourers
17	14	Graders and sorters, mfg.
29	56	Heaters, metal
21	47	Knitters, loopers, and toppers, textile
15	37	Laundry and dry cleaning operatives
29	60	Meat cutters, except slaughter and packing house
46	73	Milliners
10	–	Mine operatives and laborers (n.e.c.)
02	18	Coal mining
38	70	Crude petroleum and natural gas extraction
12	36	Mining and quarrying, except fuel
03	28	Motormen, mine, factory, logging camp, etc.
34	64	Motormen, street, subway, and elevated railway
15	44	Oilers and greasers, except auto
18	38	Packers and wrappers (n.e.c.)
18	47	Painters, except construction and maintenance
42	65	Photographic process workers
50	78	Power station operators
16	40	Sailors and deck hands
05	10	Sawyers
17	39	Sewers and stichers, mfg.
05	20	Spinners, textile
17	40	Stationary firemen
44	72	Switchmen, railroad
10	37	Taxicab drivers and chauffeurs
15	40	Truck and tractor drivers
06	27	Weavers, textile
24	62	Welders and flame—cutters
18	–	Operatives and kindred workers (n.e.c.)
17	–	Manufacturing
–	–	Durable goods
07	–	Sawmills, planing mills, and misc. wood products
07	12	Sawmills, planing mills, and mill work
09	25	Miscellaneous wood products
09	27	Furniture and fixtures
17	–	Stone, clay, and glass products
23	50	Glass and glass products

Duncan's SEI Score	Census SEI Score	Category
		Operatives and kindred workers
10	29	Cement, and concrete, gypsum, and plaster products
10	31	Structural clay products
21	49	Pottery and related products
15	41	Misc. nonmetallic mineral and stone products
		Metal industries
15	—	Primary metal industries
17	49	Blast furnaces, steel works, and rolling and finishing mills
12	39	Other primary iron and steel industries
15	47	Primary nonferrous industries
16		Fabricated metal industries (incl. not spec. metal)
16	48	Cutlery, handtools, and other hardware
16	48	Fabricated structural metal products
15	48	Miscellaneous fabricated metal products
14	47	Not specified metal industries
22	—	Machinery, except electrical
21	59	Farm machinery and equipment
31	67	Office, computing, and accounting machines
22	57	Miscellaneous machinery
26	62	Electrical machinery, equipment, and supplies
23		Transportation equipment
21	61	Motor vehicles and motor vehicle equipment
34	71	Aircraft and parts
16	41	Ship and boat building and repairing
23	56	Railroad and misc. transportation equipment
29	—	Professional and photographic equipment, and watches
23	57	Professional equipment and supplies
40	73	Photographic equipment and supplies
28	62	Watches, clocks, and clockwork-operated devices
16	42	Miscellaneous manufacturing industries
		Nondurable goods
16	—	Food and kindred products
16	43	Meat products
22	53	Dairy products
09	26	Canning and preserving fruits, vegetables, and sea foods
14	36	Grain-mill products
15	38	Bakery products
12	34	Confectionery and related products
19	48	Beverage industries
11	32	Misc. food preparations and kindred products
19	46	Not specified food industries
02	13	Tobacco manufacturers

Duncan's SEI Score	Census SEI Score	Category
		Operatives and kindred workers
06	—	Textile mill products
21	47	Knitting mills
08	38	Dyeing & finishing textiles, exc. wool & knit goods
14	44	Floor coverings, except hard surface
02	14	Yarn, thread, and fabric mills
10	33	Miscellaneous textile mill products
21		Apparel and other fabricated textile products
22	39	Apparel and accessories
17	36	Miscellaneous fabricated textile products
19		Paper and allied products
19	51	Pulp, paper, and paperboard mills
17	37	Paperboard containers and boxes
19	52	Miscellaneous paper and pulp products
19	60	Printing, publishing, and allied industries
20	—	Chemicals and allied products
09	51	Synthetic fibers
26	57	Drugs and medicines
15	51	Paints, varnishes, and related products
23	55	Miscellaneous chemicals and allied products
51	—	Petroleum and coal products
56	79	Petroleum refining
14	44	Miscellaneous petroleum and coal products
22	—	Rubber and misc. plastic products
12	59	Rubber products
—	42	Miscellaneous plastic products
16	—	Leather and leather products
10	37	Leather: tanned, curried, and finished
09	31	Footwear, except rubber
14	36	Leather products, except footwear
16	44	Not specified manufacturing industries
18	—	Nonmanufacturing industries (incl. not reported)
18	38	Construction
15	42	Railroads and railway express service
23	53	Transportation, except railroad
21	52	Communications, and utilities and sanitary services
17	38	Wholesale and retail trade
19	45	Business and repair services
11	29	Personal services
17	50	Public administration
20	36	All other industries (incl. not reported)
		Private household workers
07	07	Baby sitters, private household
19	—	Housekeepers, private household

Duncan's SEI Score	Census SEI Score	Category
		Private household workers
10	25	Living in
21	32	Living out
12	–	Laundresses, private household
–	09	Living in
12	09	Living out
7	–	Private household workers (n.e.c.)
12	26	Living in
6	07	Living out
		Service workers, except private household
13	38	Attendants, hospital and other institution
26	46	Attendants, professional and personal service (n.e.c.)
19	26	Attendants, recreation and amusement
17	37	Barbers
19	46	Bartenders
30	35	Boarding and lodging house keepers
08	02	Bootblacks
11	18	Chambermaids and maids, except private household
10	15	Charwomen and cleaners
15	31	Cooks, except private household
17	41	Counter and fountain workers
10	28	Elevator operators
17	37	Hairdressers and cosmetologists
31	61	Housekeepers and stewards, except private household
9	18	Janitors and sextons
11	18	Kitchen workers (n.e.c.), except private household
37	51	Midwives
4	16	Porters
22	32	Practical nurses
		Protective service workers
37	73	Firemen, fire protection
18	38	Guards, watchmen, and doorkeepers
21	44	Marshals and constables
39	–	Policemen and detectives
40	74	Public
36	67	Private
34	66	Sheriffs and bailiffs
17	39	Watchmen (crossing) and bridge tenders
25	34	Ushers, recreation and amusement
16	39	Waiters
11	18	Service workers, except private household (n.e.c.)
		Laborers, except farm and mine
07	16	Carpenters' helpers, except logging and mining
10	11	Fishermen and oystermen

Duncan's SEI Score	Census SEI Score	Category
		Laborers, except farm and mine
8	24	Garage laborers, and car washers and greasers
11	19	Gardeners, except farm, and groundskeepers
11	25	Longshoremen and stevedores
04	04	Lumbermen, raftsmen, and wood choppers
08	13	Teamsters
09	28	Truck drivers' helpers
08	28	Warehousemen (n.e.c.)
		Laborers (n.e.c.)
08	—	Manufacturing
		Durable goods
03	—	Sawmills, planing mills, and misc. wood products
03	04	Sawmills, planing mills, and mill work
02	09	Miscellaneous wood products
05	19	Furniture and fixtures
07	—	Stone, clay, and glass products
14	31	Glass and glass products
05	22	Cement, and concrete, gypsum, and plaster products
05	19	Structural clay products
07	30	Pottery and related products
05	23	Misc. nonmetallic mineral and stone products
07	—	Metal industries
07	—	Primary metal industries
09	35	Blast furnaces, steel works, and rolling and finishing mills
04	18	Other primary iron and steel industries
06	34	Primary nonferrous industries
07	—	Fabricated metal industries (incl. not spec. metal)
07	27	Cutlery, hand tools, and other hardware
07	27	Fabricated structural metal products
10	27	Misc. fabricated metal products
09	28	Not specified metal industries
11	—	Machinery, except electrical
14	38	Farm machinery and equipment
17	45	Office, computing, and accounting machines
10	32	Miscellaneous machinery
14	45	Electrical machinery, equipment and supplies
11	—	Transportation equipment
13	42	Motor vehicles and motor vehicle equipment
15	51	Aircraft and parts
02	19	Ship and boat building and repairing
08	31	Railroad and misc. transportation equipment
11	—	Professional and photographic equipment, and watches

Duncan's SEI Score	Census SEI Score	Category
		Laborers, except farm and mine
10	37	Professional equipment and supplies
16	41	Photographic equipment and supplies
11	29	Watches, clocks, and clockwork-operated devices
12	28	Miscellaneous manufacturing industries
	—	Nondurable goods
09	—	Food and kindred products
08	32	Meat products
13	34	Dairy products
06	15	Canning and preserving fruits, vegetables, and sea foods
06	23	Grain-mill products
10	30	Bakery products
10	33	Confectionery and related products
16	34	Beverage industries
05	17	Misc. food preparations and kindred products
14	40	Not specified food industries
00	10	Tobacco manufactures
03	—	Textile mill products
01	12	Yarn, thread, and fabric mills
06	14	Other textile mill products
09	21	Apparel and other fabricated textile products
07	—	Paper and allied products
06	27	Pulp, paper, and paperboard mills
10	31	Paperboard containers and boxes
08	30	Miscellaneous paper and pulp products
23	50	Printing, publishing, and allied industries
08	—	Chemical and allied products
04	30	Synthetic fibers
22	48	Drugs and medicines
08	42	Paints, varnishes, and related products
08	18	Miscellaneous chemicals and allied products
22	—	Petroleum and coal products
26	59	Petroleum refining
03	26	Miscellaneous petroleum and coal products
12	41	Rubber and miscellaneous plastic products
06	27	Leather and leather products
02	26	Not specified manufacturing industries
07	—	Nonmanufacturing industries (incl. not reported)
07	16	Construction
03	20	Railroads and railway express service
09	28	Transportation, except railroad
06	18	Communications, and utilities and sanitary services
12	28	Wholesale and retail trade

Duncan's SEI Score	Census SEI Score	Category
		Laborers, except farm and mine
09	26	Business and repair services
05	01	Personal services
07	29	Public administration
06	07	All other industries (incl. not reported)
19	33	Occupation not reported
—	63	Present members of the Armed Forces

4.A.3 HOLLINGSHEAD'S TWO FACTOR INDEX OF SOCIAL POSITION

VARIABLE MEASURED: Positions individuals occupy in the status structure.

DESCRIPTION: There are two- and three-factor forms of the index that have been used extensively. The two-factor index is composed of an occupational scale and an educational scale. The three-factor index includes a residential scale. Since the residential scale was based on sociological analysis previously made by Davis and Myers in New Haven, many communities would not be amenable until residential areas were mapped into a six-position scale. The two-factor index requires only knowledge of occupation and education.

The occupational scale is a seven-point scale representing a modification of the Edwards' system of classifying occupations into socioeconomic groups. The Edwards' system does not differentiate among kinds of professionals or the size and economic strength of businesses. The Hollingshead index of social position ranks professions into different groups and business by their size and value.

The educational scale is also divided into seven positions. In the two-factor index, occupation is given a weight of 7 and education is given a weight of 4. If one were to compute a score for the manager of a Kroger store who had completed high school and one year of business college, the procedure would be as follows:

Factor	Scale Score	X	Factor Weight	=	Partial Score
Occupation	3		7		21
Education	3		4		12
Index of Social Position Score					33

The range of scores in each of five social classes (of New Haven, Connecticut) are:

Class	Range of Scores
I	11–17
II	18–31
III	32–47
IV	48–63
V	64–77

WHERE PUBLISHED: August B. Hollingshead, *Two Factor Index of Social Position* (copyright 1957), privately printed 1965, Yale Station, New Haven, Connecticut. August B. Hollingshead and Frederick C. Redlich, *Social Class and Mental Illness* (New York: John Wiley, 1958), pp. 387-97.

RELIABILITY AND VALIDITY OF INDEX OF SOCIAL POSITIONS: High correlation is reported between the Hollingshead and Redlich measure and the index of class position devised by R. Ellis, W. Lane, and V. Olesen, "The Index of Class Position: An Improved Intercommunity Measure of Stratification," *American Sociological Review* 28 (April 1963): 271-77.

Various combinations of the scale score for occupation and education are reproducible in the Guttman sense, for there is no overlap between education-occupation combinations. If an individual's education and occupation are known, one can calculate his or her score; if one knows an individual's score, one can calculate both occupational position and educational level.

Hollingshead and Redlich report a correlation between judged class with education and occupation as $R_{1(23)} = .906$. Judged class with residence, education, and occupation $R_{.(234)} = .942$.

Hollingshead and others have made extensive studies of the reliability of scoring, and validity of the index on over one hundred variables. *See* Research Applications.

The researcher will find Hollingshead's account of the background and rationale for the two factor scale in August B. Hollingshead, "Commentary on 'The Indiscriminate State of Social Class Measurement,'" *Social Forces* 49 (June 1971): 563-67.

UTILITY: Because of the difficulty in obtaining residential information where adequate ecological maps do not exist, the two factor variation of the Index of Social Position has been used widely. Only occupation and education is needed and these data are relatively easy to obtain. The scale score can be quickly computed and individual social position established.

RESEARCH APPLICATIONS:

BELL, GERALD D. "Processes in the Formation of Adolescents' Aspirations." *Social Forces* 42 (December 1963): 179-86. See p. 182.

ELLIS, ROBERT A. "Social Stratification and Social Relations: An Empirical Test of the Disjunctiveness of Social Classes." *American Sociological Review* 22 (October 1957): 570-78. See p. 571.

HOLLINGSHEAD, AUGUST B., and REDLICH, FREDERICK C. "Social Stratification and Psychiatric Disorders." *American Sociological Review* 18 (April 1953): 163-69. See p. 165.

——. "Social Stratification and Schizophrenia." *American Sociological Review* 19 (June 1954): 302-6. See p. 302.

——. "Social Mobility and Mental Illness." *American Journal of Psychiatry* 112 (September 1955): 179-85. See pp. 180-82.

——. *Social Class and Mental Illness: A Community Study.* New York: John Wiley & Sons, 1958. Pp. 390-91.

——; ELLIS, ROBERT; and KIRBY, E. "Social Mobility and Mental Illness." *American Sociological Review* 19 (October 1954): 577-84. See p. 579.

——, and FREEMAN, L. Z. "Social Class and the Treatment of Neurotics." In

The Social Welfare Forum. New York: Columbia University Press, 1955. Pp. 194–205. See p. 195.

HUNT, RAYMOND G.; GURSSLIN, ORVILLE; and ROACH, JACK L. "Social Status and Psychiatric Science in a Child Guidance Clinic." *American Sociological Review* 23 (February 1958): 81–83. See p. 81.

KOHN, MELVIN L. "Social Class and Parental Values." *American Journal of Soeiology* 64 (January 1959): 337–51. See p. 338.

———, and CARROLL, ELEANOR E. "Social Class and the Allocation of Parental Responsibilities." *Sociometry* 23 (December 1960): 372–92. See p. 374.

LAWSON, EDWIN D., and BOCK, WALTER E. "Correlations of Indexes of Families' Socio-economic Status." *Social Forces* 39 (December 1960): 149–52. See p. 150.

LEFTON, MARK; ANGRIST, SHIRLEY; DINITZ, SIMON; and PASAMANICK, BENJAMIN. "Social Class, Expectations, and Performance of Mental Patients." *American Journal of Sociology* 68 (July 1962): 79–87. See p. 82.

LESLIE, GERALD R., and JOHNSEN, KATHRYN P. "Changed Perceptions of the Maternal Role." *American Sociological Review* 28 (December 1963): 919–28. See p. 923.

LEVINGER, GEORGE. "Task and Social Behavior in Marriage." *Sociometry* 27 (December 1964): 433–48. See pp. 442 and 446.

LEWIS, LIONEL S. "Knowledge, Danger, Certainty, and the Theory of Magic." *American Journal of Sociology* 69 (July 1963): 7–12. See p. 9.

———, and LOPREATO, JOSEPH. "Arationality, Ignorance, and Perceived Danger in Medical Practices." *American Sociological Review* 27 (August 1962): 508–14. See p. 508.

MIZRUCHI, EPHRAIM H. "Social Structure and Anomia in a Small City." *American Sociological Review* 25 (October 1960): 645–54. See p. 647.

PSATHAS, GEORGE. "Ethnicity, Social Class and Adolescent Independence from Parental Control." *American Sociological Review* 22 (August 1957): 415–23. See p. 417.

ROSEN, BERNARD C. "The Achievement Syndrome: A Psychocultural Dimension of Social Stratification." *American Sociological Review* 21 (April 1956): 203–11. See p. 204.

———. "Race, Ethnicity, and the Achievement Syndrome." *American Sociological Review* 24 (February 1959): 47–60. See p. 48.

———. "Family Structure and Achievement Motivation." *American Sociological Review* 26 (August 1961): 574–85. See p. 576.

———. "Socialization and Achievement Motivation in Brazil." *American Sociological Review* 27 (October 1962): 612–24. See p. 613.

———. "The Achievement Syndrome and Economic Growth in Brazil." *Social Forces* 42 (March 1964): 341–54. See p. 345.

———, and D'ANDRADE, ROY. "The Psychosocial Origins of Achievement Motivation." *Sociometry* 22 (September 1959): 185–218. See p. 189.

SMITH, BULKELEY, JR. "The Differential Residential Segregation of Working Class Negroes in New Haven." *American Sociological Review* 24 (August 1959): 529–33. See p. 530.

STRODTBECK, FRED L.; MCDONALD, MARGARET R.; and ROSEN, BERNARD C. "Evaluation of Occupations: A Reflection of Jewish and Italian Mobility Differences." *American Sociological Review* 22 (October 1957): 546–53. See p. 547.

WECHSLER, HENRY. "Community Growth, Depressive Disorders, and Suicide." *American Journal of Sociology* 67 (July 1961): 9–16. See p. 15.

YARROW, MARIAN R.; SCOTT, PHYLLIS; DELEEUW, LOUISE; and HEINIG, CHRISTINE. "Child-Rearing in Families of Working and Nonworking Mothers." *Sociometry* 25 (June 1962): 122–40. See p. 124.

For more recent use see all references in the period 1965–74 in the *American Sociological Review Inventory* under Hollingshead Two Factor Index of Social Position in Section 4.M.1, p. 418 and p. 427.

HOLLINGSHEAD'S TWO FACTOR INDEX OF SOCIAL POSITION

1. The Occupational Scale*

1. *Higher Executives of Large Concerns, Proprietors, and Major Professionals*

A. *Higher Executives* (Value of corporation $500,000 and above as rated by Dun and Bradstreet)

Bank
  Presidents
  Vice-Presidents
  Assistant vice-presidents
Business
  Directors
  Presidents

Business
  Vice-Presidents
  Assistant vice-presidents
  Executive secretaries
  Research directors
  Treasurers

B. *Proprietors* (Value over $100,000 by Dun and Bradstreet)

Brokers
Contractors
Dairy owners

Farmers
Lumber dealers

C. *Major Professionals*

Accountants (CPA)
Actuaries
Agronomists
Architects
Artists, portrait
Astronomers
Auditors
Bacteriologists
Chemical engineers
Chemists
Clergymen (professional trained)
Dentists
Economists
Engineers (college graduates)
Foresters
Geologists

Judges (superior courts)
Lawyers
Metallurgists
Military: commissioned officers, major and above
Officials of the executive branch of government, federal, state, local: e.g., Mayor, City manager, City plan director, Internal Revenue director
Physicians
Physicists, research
Psychologists, practicing
Symphony conductor
Teachers, university, college
Veterinarians (veterinary surgeons)

2. *Business Managers, Proprietors of Medium-Sized Businesses, and Lesser Professionals*

A. *Business Managers in Large Concerns* (Value $500,000)

Advertising directors
Branch managers
Brokerage salesmen
Directors of purchasing
District managers
Executive assistants

Manufacturer's representatives
Office managers
Personnel managers
Police chief; Sheriff
Postmaster
Production managers

*This scale and The Educational Scale (p. 238) reprinted with permission from Hollingshead and Redlich, *Social Class and Mental Illness* (New York: Wiley, 1958). © 1958 by John Wiley & Sons, Inc.

Export managers, international
 concerns
Farm managers
Government officials, minor, e.g.,
 Internal Revenue agents

Sales engineers
Sales managers, national concerns
Store managers

B. *Proprietors of Medium Businesses* (Value $35,000-$100,000)

Advertising
Clothing store
Contractors
Express company
Farm owners
Fruits, wholesale
Furniture business

Jewelers
Poultry business
Real estate brokers
Rug business
Store
Theater

C. *Lesser Professionals*

Accountants (not CPA)
Chiropodists
Chiropractors
Correction officers
Director of Community House
Engineers (not college graduate)
Finance writers
Health educators
Labor relations consultants
Librarians

Military: commissioned officers,
 lieutenant, captain
Musicians (symphony orchestra)
Nurses
Opticians
Optometrists, D.O.
Pharmacists
Public health officers (MPH)
Research assistants, university
 (full-time)
Social workers

3. *Administrative Personnel, Owners of Small Businesses, and Minor Professionals*

A. *Administrative Personnel*

Advertising agents
Chief clerks
Credit managers
Insurance agents
Managers, departments
Passenger agents, railroad
Private secretaries
Purchasing agents
Sales representatives

Section heads, federal, state and local
 governmental offices
Section heads, large businesses and
 industries
Service managers
Shop managers
Store managers (chain)
Traffic managers

B. *Small Business Owners* ($6,000-$35,000)

Art gallery
Auto accessories
Awnings
Bakery
Beauty shop
Boatyard
Brokerage, insurance
Car dealers
Cattle dealers
Cigarette machines

Furniture
Garage
Gas station
Glassware
Grocery, general
Hotel proprietors
Jewelry
Machinery brokers
Manufacturing
Monuments

Cleaning shops
Clothing
Coal businesses
Contracting businesses
Convalescent homes
Decorating
Dog supplies
Dry goods
Engraving business
Feed
Finance companies, local
Fire extinguishers
Five and dime
Florist
Food equipment
Food products
Foundry
Funeral directors

Music
Package stores (liquor)
Paint contracting
Poultry
Real estate
Records and radios
Restaurant
Roofing contractor
Shoe
Signs
Tavern
Taxi company
Tire shop
Trucking
Trucks and tractors
Upholstery
Wholesale outlets
Window shades

C. *Semiprofessionals*

Actors and showmen
Army, master sergeant
Artists, commercial
Appraisers (estimators)
Clergymen (not professionally
   trained)
Concern managers
Deputy sheriffs
Dispatchers, railroad
Interior decorators
Interpreters, courts
Laboratory assistants
Landscape planners
Morticians

Navy, chief petty officer
Oral hygienists
Physiotherapists
Piano teachers
Publicity and public relations
Radio, TV announcers
Reporters, court
Reporters, newspapers
Surveyors
Title searchers
Tool designers
Travel agents
Yard masters, railroad

D. *Farmers*
Farm owners ($20,000–$35,000)

4. *Clerical and Sales Workers, Technicians, and Owners of Little Businesses*
(Value under $6,000)

A. *Clerical and Sales Workers*

Bank clerks and tellers
Bill collectors
Bookkeepers
Business machine operators,
   offices
Claims examiners
Clerical or stenographic
Conductors, railroad
Factory storekeepers

Factory supervisors
Post Office clerks
Route managers
Sales clerks
Sergeants and petty officers, military
   services
Shipping clerks
Supervisors, utilities, factories
Supervisors, toll stations

B. *Technicians*

Dental technicians	Locomotive engineers
Draftsmen	Operators, PBX
Driving teachers	Proofreaders
Expeditor, factory	Safety supervisors
Experimental tester	Supervisors of maintenance
Instructors, telephone company, factory	Technical assistants
	Telephone company supervisors
Inspectors, weights, sanitary, railroad, factory	Timekeepers
	Tower operators, railroad
Investigators	Truck dispatchers
Laboratory technicians	Window trimmers (stores)

C. *Owners of Little Businesses* ($3,000–$6,000)

Flower shop	Newsstand
Grocery	Tailor shop

D. *Farmers*

Owners (Value $10,000–$20,000)

5. *Skilled Manual Employees*

Auto body repairers	Locksmiths
Bakers	Loom fixers
Barbers	Machinists (trained)
Blacksmiths	Maintenance foremen
Bookbinders	Linoleum layers (trained)
Boilermakers	Masons
Brakemen, railroad	Masseurs
Brewers	Mechanics (trained)
Bulldozer operators	Millwrights
Butchers	Moulders (trained)
Cabinet makers	Painters
Cable splicers	Paperhangers
Carpenters	Patrolmen, railroad
Casters (founders)	Pattern and model makers
Cement finishers	Piano builders
Cheese makers	Piano tuners
Chefs	Plumbers
Compositors	Policemen, city
Diemakers	Postmen
Diesel engine repair and maintenance (trained)	Printers
	Radio, television maintenance
Diesel shovel operators	Repairmen, home appliances
Electricians	Rope splicers
Engravers	Sheetmetal workers (trained)
Exterminators	Shipsmiths
Firemen, city	Shoe repairmen (trained)
Firemen, railroad	Stationary engineers (licensed)
Fitters, gas, steam	Stewards, club
Foremen, construction, dairy	Switchmen, railroad
Gardeners, landscape (trained)	Tailors (trained)

Glass blowers
Glaziers
Gunsmiths
Gauge makers
Hair stylists
Heat treaters
Horticulturists
Linemen, utility
Linotype operators
Lithographers
Small Farmers
Owners (Value under $10,000)

Teletype operators
Tool makers
Track supervisors, railroad
Tractor-trailer trans.
Typographers
Upholsters (trained)
Watchmakers
Weavers
Welders
Yard supervisors, railroad

Tenants who own farm equipment

6. *Machine Operators and Semiskilled Employees*

Aides, hospital
Apprentices, electricians, printers,
  steam fitters, toolmakers
Assembly line workers
Bartenders
Bingo tenders
Bridge tenders
Building superintendents
  (construction)
Bus drivers
Checkers
Coin machine fillers
Cooks, short order
Deliverymen
Dressmakers, machine
Elevator operators
Enlisted men, military services
Filers, sanders, buffers
Foundry workers
Garage and gas station attendants
Greenhouse workers
Guards, doorkeepers, watchmen
Hairdressers
Housekeepers
Meat cutters and packers
Meter readers
Operators, factory machines
Oilers, railroad

Practical nurses
Pressers, clothing
Pump operators
Receivers and checkers
Roofers
Setup men, factories
Shapers
Signalmen, railroad
Solderers, factory
Sprayers, paint
Steelworkers (not skilled)
Standers, wire machines
Strippers, rubber factory
Taxi drivers
Testers
Timers
Tire moulders
Trainmen, railroad
Truck drivers, general
Waiters-waitresses ("better places")
Weighers
Welders, spot
Winders, machine
Wiredrawers, machine
Wine bottlers
Wood workers, machine
Wrappers, stores and factories

Farmers
Smaller tenants who own little equipment

7. *Unskilled Employees*

Amusement park workers
  (bowling alleys, pool rooms)
Ash removers

Laborers, unspecified
Laundry workers
Messengers

Attendants, parking lots
Cafeteria workers
Car cleaners, railroad
Carriers, coal
Countermen
Dairy workers
Deck hands
Domestics
Farm helpers
Fishermen (clam diggers)
Freight handlers
Garbage collectors
Gravediggers
Hod carriers
Hog killers
Hospital workers, unspecified
Hostlers, railroad
Janitors (sweepers)
Laborers, construction

Platform men, railroad
Peddlers
Porters
Relief, public, private
Roofer's helpers
Shirt folders
Shoe shiners
Sorters, rag and salvage
Stage hands
Stevedores
Stock handlers
Street cleaners
Struckmen, railroad
Unemployed (no occupation)
Unskilled factory workers
Waitresses ("Hash Houses")
Washers, cars
Window cleaners
Woodchoppers

Farmers
Sharecroppers

2. The Educational Scale

The educational scale is premised upon the assumption that men and women who possess similar educations will tend to have similar tastes and similar attitudes, and they will also tend to exhibit similar behavior patterns.

The educational scale is divided into seven positions:

1. Graduate professional training: Persons who completed a recognized professional course that led to the receipt of a graduate degree were given scores of 1.
2. Standard college or university graduation: All individuals who had completed a four-year college or university course leading to a recognized college degree were assigned the same scores. No differentiation was made between state universities or private colleges.
3. Partial college training: Individuals who had completed at least one year but not a full college course were assigned this position.
4. High school graduation: All secondary school graduates whether from a private preparatory school, public high school, trade school, or parochial school were given this score.
5. Partial high school: Individuals who had completed the tenth or eleventh grades, but had not completed high school were given this score.
6. Junior high school: Individuals who had completed the seventh grade through the ninth grade were given this position.
7. Less than seven years of school: Individuals who had not completed the seventh grade were given the same scores irrespective of the amount of education they had received.

VARIABLE MEASURED: Social class position according to a seven-point rating.

DESCRIPTION: The rating of occupations is one measure included in the Index of Status Characteristics. The index is composed of four status characteristics: Occupation, Source of Income, House Type, and Dwelling Area. Each of these is rated on a seven-point scale, and this rating is then weighted according to its separate contributions to the total index. The weighted ratings are totaled to yield the scores that are appropriate to the various classes. The scores on the Index of Status Characteristics range from 12 to 84. The ranges are calculated by validating preliminary scores using the Evaluated Participation method of determining social class position. Occupation is the single measure most highly correlated with class position.

WHERE PUBLISHED: W. Lloyd Warner, Marcia Meeker, and Kenneth Eells, *Social Class in America* (Chicago: Science Research Associates, 1949), pp. 121–59. The occupational rating scale is shown on pp. 140–41.

VALIDITY OF INDEX OF STATUS CHARACTERISTICS:

1. Accuracy in prediction: 85 percent of the Old Americans in *Yankee City* were placed correctly or within one point. Not as valid for ethnics.
2. Correlation with the Evaluative Participation Method as reported by Warner et al., on p. 168.

Occupation	$r = .91$
Source of Income	$r = .85$
House Type	$r = .85$
Dwelling Area	$r = .82$
I.S.C. (all four measures)	$r = .97$

3. Comparative Study by John L. Haer.

   Five indexes of social stratification were compared and evaluated by examining their capacities for predicting variables that have been shown in previous studies to be related to measures of stratification. These five indexes include Centers' class identification question, an open-end question, occupation, education, and Warner's Index of Status Characteristics. An overall comparison reveals that coefficients are higher for the Index of Status Characteristics than for other indexes in 18 out of 22 comparisons. Its greater efficiency may be due to the fact that it is a composite index that provides a continuous series of ranks. These features make it possible to discern minute variations in relation to other variables. John L. Haer, "Predictive Utility of Five Indices of Social Stratification," *American Sociological Review* 22 (October 1957): 541–46.

Warner, Meeker, Eells' Revised Scale for Rating Occupation

Rating assigned to occupation	Professionals	Proprietors and managers	Businessmen	Clerks and kindred workers, etc.	Manual workers	Protective and service workers	Farmers
1	Lawyers, doctors, dentists, engineers, judges, high-school superintendents, veterinarians, ministers (graduated from divinity school), chemists, etc., with postgraduate training, architects	Businesses valued at $75,000 and over	Regional and divisional managers of large financial and industrial enterprises	Certified Public Accountants			Gentlemen farmers
2	High-school teachers, trained nurses, chiropractors, undertakers, ministers (some training), newspaper editors, librarians (graduate)	Businesses valued at $20,000 to $75,000	Assistant managers and office and department managers of large businesses, assistants to executives, etc.	Accountants, salesmen of real estate and insurance, postmasters			Large farm owners, farm owners
3	Social workers, grade-school teachers, optometrists, librarians (not graduate), undertaker's assistants, ministers (no training)	Businesses valued at $5,000 to $20,000	All minor officials of businesses	Auto salesmen, bank clerks and cashiers, postal clerks, secretaries to executives, supervisors of railroad, telephone, etc., justices of the peace	Contractors		

4	Businesses valued at $2,000 to $5,000	Stenographers, bookkeepers, rural mail clerks, railroad ticket agents, sales people in dry goods stores, etc.	Factory foreman, electricians, plumbers, carpenters, watchmakers (own business)	Dry cleaners, butchers, sheriffs, railroad engineers and conductors	Tenant farmers
5	Businesses valued at $500 to $2,000	Dime store clerks, hardware salesmen, beauty operators, telephone operators	Carpenters, plumbers, electricians (apprentice), timekeepers, linemen, telephone or telegraph, radio rapairmen, medium skilled workers	Barbers, firemen, butcher's apprentices, practical nurses, policemen, seamstresses, cooks in restaurant, bartenders	
6	Businesses valued at less than $500		Moulders, semi-skilled workers, assistants to carpenter, etc.	Baggage men, night policemen and watchmen, taxi and truck drivers, gas station attendants, waitresses in restaurants	Small tenant farmers, laborers
7			Heavy labor, migrant work, odd-job men, miners	Janitors, scrubwomen, newsboys	Migrant farm laborers

VALIDITY OF THE OCCUPATION SCALE: Joseph A. Kahl and James A. Davis selected 19 single measures of socioeconomic status and measured their intercorrelations. They report a product moment correlation of .74 between occupation (Warner) and status of friends, and a multiple correlation of .80 between occupation plus education and status of friends—". . . our data agree with Warner's that occupation (as he measures it) is the best predictor of either social participation or the whole socioeconomic cluster represented by the general factor identified by factor analysis." "A Comparison of Indexes of Socio-Economic Status," *American Sociological Review* 20 (June 1955): 317-25.

Stanley A. Hetzler reports the following coefficients between seven rating scales and ratings of social class and social position.

Rating Scales	Social Class	Social Position
Occupational prestige	.69	.57
Residential area	.54	.46
Family background	.53	.48
Personal influence	.49	.52
Dwelling unit	.47	.39
Family wealth	.45	.45
Personal income	.34	.44

The four rating scales showing the highest coefficients were occupational prestige, family background, residential area, and personal influence. The multiple correlation of these four scales with social class is .75; with social position it is .68. "An Investigation of the Distinctiveness of Social Classes," *American Sociological Review* 18 (October 1953): 493-97. See also J. L. Haer, "A Test of the Unidimensionality of the Index of Status Characteristics," *Social Forces* 34 (1955): 56-58.

UTILITY: The Index of Status Characteristics presents a comparatively objective means of determining social-class position. The limits defined for the various seven-point ratings are sufficiently precise to eliminate to a great degree any subjective judgment. All one needs to know is a person's name, occupation, and address; the source of income can generally be derived from the occupation, and the house type and dwelling area can be evaluated through the address. This eliminates extensive, time-consuming interviewing.

The Occupation Scale is the best single predictor of social-class position within a seven-point range. The high correlation it exhibits with the evaluative participative method of social-class position ($r = .91$) commends occupation as a single dimension. Researchers will achieve a high degree of predictive efficiency by use of the one scale. Robinson and his co-workers call Warner's Index "the most sophisticated short classification of occupational status available." See John B. Robinson, Robert Athanasiou, and Kendra B. Head, *Measures of Occupational Attitudes and Occupational Characteristics*, Institute of Social Research, University of Michigan, Ann Arbor, 1969, p. 338 and pp. 362-66.

RESEARCH APPLICATIONS:

FREEMAN, HOWARD E., and SIMMONS, OZZIE G. "Social Class and Post-Hospital Performance Levels." *American Sociological Review* 24 (1959): 345-51.

GOFFMAN, IRWIN W. "Status Consistency and Preference for Change in Power Distribution." *American Sociological Review* 22 (June 1957): 275–81. See p. 277.

KANIN, EUGENE, JR., and HOWARD, DAVID H. "Postmarital Consequences of Premarital Sex Adjustments." *American Sociological Review* 23 (October 1958): 556–62. See p. 557.

HAVIGHURST, ROBERT J., and DAVIS, ALLISON. "A Comparison of the Chicago and Harvard Studies of Social Class Differences in Child Rearing." *American Sociological Review* 20 (August 1955): 438–42. See p. 439.

LAWSON, EDWIN D., and BOCK, WALTER E. "Correlations of Indexes of Families' Socioeconomic Status." *Social Forces* 39 (December 1960): 149–52.

LITTMAN, RICHARD A.; MOORE, ROBERT C. A.; and PIERCE-JONES, JOHN. "Social Class Differences in Child-Rearing: A Third Community for Comparison with Chicago and Newton." *American Sociological Review* 22 (December 1957): 694–704. See p. 695.

MORLAND, J. KENNETH. "Racial Recognition by Nursery School Children in Lynchburg, Virginia." *Social Forces* 37 (December 1958): 132–41. See p. 132.

——. "Educational and Occupational Aspirations of Mill and Town School Children in a Southern Community." *Social Forces* 39 (December 1960): 169–75.

SALISBURY, W. SEWARD. "Religion and Secularization." *Social Forces* 36 (March 1958): 197–205. See p. 198.

SCUDDER, RICHARD, and ANDERSON, C. ARNOLD. "Range of Acquaintance and of Repute as Factors in Prestige Rating Methods of Studying Social Status." *Social Forces* 32 (March 1954): 248–53. See p. 252.

——. "Migration and Vertical Occupational Mobility." *American Sociological Review* 19 (June 1954): 329–34. See p. 330.

STONE, GREGORY P., and FORM, WILLIAM H. "Instabilities in Status: The Problem of Hierarchy in the Community Study of Status Arrangements." *American Sociological Review* 18 (April 1953): 149–62.

——. "The Local Community Clothing Market: A Study of the Social and Social Psychological Contexts of Shipping." Technical Bulletin No. 247. East Lansing, Mich.: Michigan State University, June 1955.

SWINEHART, JAMES W. "Socioeconomic Level, Status Aspiration, and Maternal Role." *American Sociological Review* 28 (June 1963): 391–99.

WARNER, W. LLOYD, et al. *Democracy in Jonesville.* New York: Harper & Brothers, 1949.

WESTIE, FRANK R., and HOWARD, DAVID H. "Social Status Differentials and the Race Attitudes of Negroes." *American Sociological Review* 19 (October 1954): 584–91. See p. 587.

WHITE, MARTHA STURM. "Social Class, Child Rearing Practices and Child Behavior." *American Sociological Review* 22 (December 1957): 704–712.

ALBA M. EDWARDS' SOCIAL-ECONOMIC GROUPING OF OCCUPATIONS

4.A.5

VARIABLE MEASURED: Socioeconomic position.

DESCRIPTION: Occupations are classified into six major groups with each group purported to have a somewhat distinct economic standard of life and to exhibit intellectual and social similarities. The two major dimensions for the ranking order are income and education.

WHERE PUBLISHED: Alba M. Edwards, *Comparative Occupation Statistics for the United States* (Washington, D.C.: U.S. Government Printing Office, 1934), pp. 164-69; U.S. Bureau of the Census, 1960 Census of Population, *Classified Index of Occupations and Industries* (Washington, D.C.: U.S. Government Printing Office, 1960).

RELIABILITY: Occupational grouping shows high comparability with similar occupational ranking systems such as Barr-Taussig, Beckman Goodenough and Anderson, Centers, etc.

VALIDITY: Major occupational groups can be ranked on the two dimensions of income and education with realtively high correspondence as shown for the following occupational groups.

	Men		Women	
Occupational Group	Mean School Years Completed 25 years & Over (1970)[a]	Mean Earnings 25–64 years (1969)[b]	Mean School Years Completed 25 years & Over 1970[a]	Mean Earnings 25–64 years 1969[b]
Professional, technical, and kindred workers	16.5	$16,007	16.1	$6,366
Managers and administrative workers, except farm	12.9	13,733	12.5	6,430
Sales workers	12.8	11,537	12.2	3,290
Clerical and kindred workers	12.5	8,461	12.5	4,605
Craftsman, foremen, and kindred workers	11.8	8,749	11.8	5,048
Operatives and kindred workers	10.7	7,376	10.3	3,810
Laborers, except farm and mine	9.3	6,089	10.6	3,466

[a] 1970 U.S. Census of Population, *Educational Attainment*, PC (2)-5B (Washington, D.C.: U.S. Government Printing Office, March 1973), table 11, pp. 213-14.
[b] 1970 U.S. Census of Population, *Earnings by Occupation and Education*, PC (2)-8B (Washington, D.C.: U.S. Government Printing Office, January 1973), tables 1 and 7.

UTILITY: This has been a widely used scale of social-economic groupings of gainful workers in the United States. It is the basis on which the U.S. Census has grouped workers since 1930 in the decennial census.

The universe of gainful workers is fully enumerated every ten years. Any research worker can check his sample against enumeration parameters and can draw generalizations with high confidence.

RESEARCH APPLICATIONS:
ANDERSON, H. DEWEY, and DAVIDSON, PERCY E. *Occupational Trends in the United States.* Stanford: Stanford University Press, 1940.
——. *Occupational Mobility in an American Community.* Stanford: Stanford University Press, 1937.

BLAU, PETER M., and DUNCAN, OTIS D. *The American Occupational Structure in the United States.* New York: John Wiley & Sons, 1967.

DAVIDSON, PERCY E., and ANDERSON, DEWEY. *Ballots and the Democratic Class Struggle.* Stanford: Stanford University Press, 1943.

GLENN, NORVAL D., and ALSTON, JOHN P. "Cultural Distances Among Occupational Categories." *American Sociological Review* 33 (June 1968): 365–82.

JAFFE, A. J., and CARLETON, R. O. *Occupational Mobility in the United States, 1930–1960.* New York: Columbia University Press, 1954.

LIPSET, SEYMOUR MARTIN, and BENDIX, REINHARD. *Social Mobility and Industrial Society.* Berkeley: University of California Press, 1959.

TAUSSIG, F. W., and JOSLYN, C. S. *American Business Leaders.* New York: Macmillan, 1932.

WARNER, W. LLOYD, and ABEGGLEN, JAMES C. *Occupational Mobility in American Business and Industry, 1928–1952.* Minneapolis: University of Minnesota Press, 1955.

For an extensive list of applications, see Charles M. Bonjean, Richard J. Hill, and S. Dale McLemore, *Sociological Measurement* (San Francisco: Chandler, 1967), pp. 423–37.

Social-Economic Grouping of Occupations (After Alba M. Edwards)

Present U.S. Census Classification of Occupational Groups.

1. Professional, technical, and kindred workers
2. Business managers, officials, and proprietors
    a. Nonfarm managers, officials, and proprietors
    b. Farm owners and managers
3. Clerical sales workers
    a. Clerical and kindred workers
    b. Sales workers
4. Craftsmen, foremen, and kindred workers
5. Operatives and kindred workers
6. Unskilled, service, and domestic workers
    a. Private household workers
    b. Service workers, except private household
    c. Farm laborers, unpaid family workers
    d. Laborers, except farm and mine

Group Structure and Dynamics

This section contains five scales, each of which measures a different variable relating to group structure and dynamics. Hemphill's Index of Group Dimensions, which ascertains thirteen dimensions of a group, is the most ambitious attempt to measure the structural properties of groups. Bales's Interactional Process Analysis is a nominal scale, widely used to assess the characteristics of personal interaction in problem-solving groups. Seashore's Group Cohesiveness Index provides a measure of the strength of a group to maintain its identity and to persist. The Sociometry Scales of Sociometric Choice and Sociometric Preference reveal the interpersonal attractions of members in groups. These scales may be widely adapted to suit many different kinds of situations. They are useful not only to a researcher seeking basic relationships, but also to the action researcher or social worker. New groupings of individuals can be quickly arranged and new measurements of morale or productivity can be made. The Bogardus Social Distance Scale may also be adapted to many different purposes. The social distance between two persons, person and group, or between groups can be measured in such diverse situations as that involving an outgroup member and a country, a community, or an organization.

4.B.1   HEMPHILL'S INDEX OF GROUP DIMENSIONS

VARIABLE MEASURED: The index is designed to measure group dimensions or characteristics.

DESCRIPTION: The index is built upon thirteen comparatively independent group dimensions: autonomy, control, flexibility, hedonic tone, homogeneity, intimacy, participation, permeability, polarization, potency, stability, stratification, and viscidity. The 150 items are answered on a five-point scale. The dimensions were selected from a list of group adjectives used by authorities. Items were suggested from a free-response type questionnaire administered to 500 individuals, and 5 judges then put the items into the dimensional categories.

WHERE PUBLISHED: John K. Hemphill, *Group Dimensions: A Manual for Their Measurement*, Research Monograph No. 87 (Columbus, Ohio: Bureau of Business Research, Ohio State University, 1956).

RELIABILITY: Split-half reliabilities range from .59 to .87. The relationship between an item and high-low categories ranges from .03 to .78 with a median of .36 on the keyed items and from .01 to .36 with a median of .12 on the randomly selected items. Intercorrelation of dimension scores ranges from −.54 to .81, with most within +.29 (which has a .01 significance level). Agreement between different reporters of the same group ranges from .53 to .74.

VALIDITY: The dimension scores describing the characteristics of two quite different groups vary accordingly, while those describing the characteristics of two similar groups are quite similar. A careful critique of reliability and validity is available in Dale G. Lake, Mathew B. Miles, and Ralph B. Earle, Jr., *Measuring Human Behavior* (New York: Teachers College Press, 1973), p. 91.

UTILITY: The index can be useful in studying the relationships between the behavior of leaders and characteristics of groups in which they function. Although fairly long, it is comparatively easy to administer and score.

RESEARCH APPLICATIONS: Validation and reliability studies on 200 descriptions of 35 groups.

BENTZ, V. J. "Leadership: A Study of Social Interaction." Unpublished report, Bureau of Business Research, Ohio State University.

HEMPHILL, JOHN K., and WESTIE, CHARLES M. "The Measurement of Group Dimensions." *Journal of Psychology* 29 (April 1950): 325–42.

SEEMAN, M. "A Sociological Approach to Leadership: The Case of the School Executive." Unpublished report, Bureau of Business Research, Ohio State University.

GROUP DIMENSIONS DESCRIPTIONS QUESTIONNAIRE

Directions:

Record your answer to each of the items on the answer sheet for the group you are describing. Make no marks on the question booklet itself.

In considering each item go through the following steps:

1. Read the item carefully.
2. Think about how well the item tells something about the group you are describing.
3. Find the number on the answer sheet that corresponds with the number of the item you are considering.
4. After each number on the answer sheet you will find five pairs of dotted lines lettered A, B, C, D, or E.

   If the item you are considering tells something about the group that is definitely true, blacken the space between the pair of dotted lines headed by A.

If the item you are considering tells something that is mostly true, blacken the space between the pair of lines headed by B.

If the item tells something that is to an equal degree both true and false, or you are undecided about whether it is true or false, blacken the space between the pair of lines headed by C.

If the item you are considering tells something that is mostly false, blacken the space between the pair of lines headed by D.

If the item you are considering tells something about the group that is definitely false, blacken the space between the pair of dotted lines headed by E.

5. When blackening the space between a pair of lines, fill in all the space with a heavy black line. If you should make an error in marking your answer, erase thoroughly the mark you made and then indicate the correct answer.

6. In rare cases where you believe that an item does not apply at all to the group or you feel that you do not have sufficient information to make any judgment concerning what the item tells about the group, leave that item blank.

7. After you have completed one item, proceed to the next one in order. You may have as long as you need to complete your description. Be sure the number on the answer sheet corresponds with the number of the item being answered in the booklet.

Questions:

The questions that follow make it possible to describe objectively certain characteristics of social groups. The items simply describe characteristics of groups; they do not judge whether the characteristic is desirable or undesirable. Therefore, in no way are the questions to be considered a "test" either of the groups or of the person answering the questions. We simply want an objective description of what the group is like.

1. The group has well understood but unwritten rules concerning member conduct.
2. Members fear to express their real opinions.
3. The only way a member may leave the group is to be expelled.
4. No explanation need be given by a member wishing to be absent from the group.
5. An individual's membership can be dropped should he fail to live up to the standards of the group.
6. Members of the group work under close supervision.
7. Only certain kinds of ideas may be expressed freely within the group.
8. A member may leave the group by resigning at any time he wishes.
9. A request made by a member to leave the group can be refused.
10. A member has to think twice before speaking in the group's meetings.
11. Members are occasionally forced to resign.
12. The members of the group are subject to strict discipline.
13. The group is rapidly increasing in size.
14. Members are constantly leaving the group.
15. There is a large turnover of members within the group.
16. Members are constantly dropping out of the group but new members replace them.
17. During the entire time of the group's existence no member has left.

18. Each member's personal life is known to other members of the group.

19. Members of the group lend each other money.

20. A member has the chance to get to know all other members of the group.

21. Members are not in close enough contact to develop likes or dislikes for one another.

22. Members of the group do small favors for one another.

23. All members know each other very well.

24. Each member of the group knows all other members by their first names.

25. Members are in daily contact either outside or within the group.

26. Members of the group are personal friends.

27. Certain members discuss personal affairs among themselves.

28. Members of the group know the family backgrounds of other members of the group.

29. Members address each other by their first names.

30. The group is made up of individuals who do not know each other well.

31. The opinions of all members are considered as equal.

32. The group's officers hold a higher status in the group than other members.

33. The older members of the group are granted special privileges.

34. The group is controlled by the actions of a few members.

35. Every member of the group enjoys the same group privileges.

36. Experienced members are in charge of the group.

37. Certain problems are discussed only among the group's officers.

38. Certain members have more influence on the group than others.

39. Each member of the group has as much power as any other member.

40. An individual's standing in the group is determined only by how much he gets done.

41. Certain members of the group hold definite office in the group.

42. The original members of the group are given special privileges.

43. Personal dissatisfaction with the group is too small to be brought up.

44. Members continually grumble about the work they do for the group.

45. The group does its work with no great vim, vigor, or pleasure.

46. A feeling of failure prevails in the group.

47. There are frequent intervals of laughter during group meetings.

48. The group works independently of other groups.

49. The group has support from outside.

50. The group is an active representative of a larger group.

51. The group's activities are influenced by a larger group of which it is a part.

52. People outside the group decide on what work the group is to do.

53. The group follows the examples set by other groups.

54. The group is one of many similar groups that form one large organization.

55. The things the group does are approved by a group higher up.

56. The group joins with other groups in carrying out its activities.

57. The group is a small part of a larger group.

58. The group is under outside pressure.

59. Members are disciplined by an outside group.

60. Plans of the group are made by other groups above it.

61. The members allow nothing to interfere with the progress of the group.

62. Members gain a feeling of being honored by being recognized as one of the group.

63. Membership in the group is a way of acquiring general social status.
64. Failure of the group would mean little to individual members.
65. The activities of the group take up less than ten percent of each member's waking time.
66. Members gain in prestige among outsiders by joining the group.
67. A mistake by one member of the group might result in hardship for all.
68. The activities of the group take up over ninety percent of each member's waking time.
69. Membership in the group serves as an aid to vocational advancement.
70. Failure of the group would mean nothing to most members.
71. Each member would lose his self-respect if the group should fail.
72. Membership in the group gives members a feeling of superiority.
73. The activities of the group take up over half the time each member is awake.
74. Failure of the group would lead to embarrassment for members.
75. Members are not rewarded for effort put out for the group.
76. There are two or three members of the group who generally take the same side on any group issue.
77. Certain members are hostile to other members.
78. There is constant bickering among members of the group.
79. Members know that each one looks out for the other one as well as for himself.
80. Certain members of the group have no respect for other members.
81. Certain members of the group are considered uncooperative.
82. There is a constant tendency toward conniving against one another among parts of the group.
83. Members of the group work together as a team.
84. Certain members of the group are responsible for petty quarrels and some animosity among other members.
85. There are tensions among subgroups that tend to interfere with the group's activities.
86. Certain members appear to be incapable of working as part of the group.
87. There is an undercurrent of feeling among members that tends to pull the group apart.
88. Anyone who has sufficient interest in the group to attend its meetings is considered a member.
89. The group engages in membership drives.
90. New members are welcomed to the group on the basis "the more the merrier."
91. A new member may join only after an old member resigns.
92. A college degree is required for membership in the group.
93. A person may enter the group by expressing a desire to join.
94. Anyone desiring to enter the group is welcome.
95. Membership is open to anyone willing to further the purpose of the group.
96. Prospective members are carefully examined before they enter the group.
97. No applicants for membership in the group are turned down.
98. No special training is required for membership in the group.
99. Membership depends upon the amount of education an individual has.
100. People interested in joining the group are asked to submit references which are checked.

101. There is a high degree of participation on the part of members.

102. If a member of the group is not productive he is not encouraged to remain.

103. Work of the group is left to those who are considered most capable for the job.

104. Members are interested in the group but not all of them want to work.

105. The group has a reputation for not getting much done.

106. Each member of the group is on one or more active committees.

107. The work of the group is well divided among members.

108. Every member of the group does not have a job to do.

109. The work of the group is frequently interrupted by having nothing to do.

110. There are long periods during which the group does nothing.

111. The group is directed toward one particular goal.

112. The group divides its efforts among several purposes.

113. The group operates with sets of conflicting plans.

114. The group has only one main purpose.

115. The group knows exactly what it has to get done.

116. The group is working toward many different goals.

117. The group does many things that are not directly related to its main purpose.

118. Each member of the group has a clear idea of the group's goals.

119. The objective of the group is specific.

120. Certain members meet for one thing and others for a different thing.

121. The group has major purposes which to some degree are in conflict.

122. The objectives of the group have never been clearly recognized.

123. The group is very informal.

124. A list of rules and regulations is given to each member.

125. The group has meetings at regularly scheduled times.

126. The group is organized along semimilitary lines.

127. The group's meetings are not planned or organized.

128. The group has an organization chart.

129. The group has rules to guide its activities.

130. The group is staffed according to a table of organization.

131. The group keeps a list of names of members.

132. Group meetings are conducted according to "Robert's Rules of Order."

133. There is a recognized right and wrong way of going about group activities.

134. Most matters that come up before the group are voted upon.

135. The group meets at any place that happens to be handy.

136. The members of the group vary in amount of ambition.

137. Members of the group are from the same social class.

138. Some members are interested in altogether different things than other members.

139. The group contains members with widely varying backgrounds.

140. The group contains whites and Negroes.

141. Members of the group are all about the same ages.

142. A few members of the group have greater ability than others.

143. A number of religious beliefs are represented by members of the group.

144. Members of the group vary greatly in social background.

145. All members of the group are of the same sex.

146. The ages of members range over a period of at least 20 years.

147. Members come into the group with quite different family backgrounds.

148. Members of the group vary widely in amount of experience.

149. Members vary in the number of years they have been in the group.

150. The group includes members of different races.

Scoring Key and Directions for Scoring

A subject's score for a particular dimension is the sum of the item scores for that dimension. For example, the raw score for the dimension "Control" is the sum of the scores for items 1 to 12 inclusive. The total (raw) score for this dimension can range from 12 to 60.

Occasionally a respondent may fail to indicate his answer. Such omissions are scored as C responses (neither true nor false). However, if the number of omitted items exceeds half the total number of items assigned to a given dimension, no score for that dimension is assigned. In general, experience has shown that few respondents deliberately omit items.

The answers are marked on a separate answer sheet (IBM Answer Sheet No. 1100 A 3870). A separate blank answer sheet may be used for preparing a scoring key for each dimension.

SCORING KEYS

Control	A	B	C	D	E
1	5	4	3	2	1
2	5	4	3	2	1
3	5	4	3	2	1
4	1	2	3	4	5
5	5	4	3	2	1
6	5	4	3	2	1
7	5	4	3	2	1
8	1	2	3	4	5
9	5	4	3	2	1
10	5	4	3	2	1
11	5	4	3	2	1
12	5	4	3	2	1

Stability	A	B	C	D	E
13	1	2	3	4	5
14	1	2	3	4	5
15	1	2	3	4	5
16	1	2	3	4	5
17	5	4	3	2	1

Intimacy	A	B	C	D	E
18	5	4	3	2	1
19	5	4	3	2	1
20	5	4	3	2	1
21	1	2	3	4	5
22	5	4	3	2	1
23	5	4	3	2	1
24	5	4	3	2	1
25	5	4	3	2	1
26	5	4	3	2	1
27	5	4	3	2	1
28	5	4	3	2	1
29	5	4	3	2	1
30	1	2	3	4	5

Stratification	A	B	C	D	E
31	1	2	3	4	5
32	5	4	3	2	1
33	5	4	3	2	1
34	5	4	3	2	1
35	1	2	3	4	5
36	5	4	3	2	1
37	5	4	3	2	1
38	5	4	3	2	1

Stratification	A	B	C	D	E
39	1	2	3	4	5
40	5	4	3	2	1
41	5	4	3	2	1
42	5	4	3	2	1

Hedonic Tone	A	B	C	D	E
43	5	4	3	2	1
44	1	2	3	4	5
45	1	2	3	4	5
46	1	2	3	4	5
47	5	4	3	2	1

Autonomy	A	B	C	D	E
48	5	4	3	2	1
49	1	2	3	4	5
50	1	2	3	4	5
51	1	2	3	4	5
52	1	2	3	4	5
53	1	2	3	4	5
54	1	2	3	4	5
55	1	2	3	4	5
56	1	2	3	4	5
57	1	2	3	4	5
58	1	2	3	4	5
59	1	2	3	4	5
60	1	2	3	4	5

Potency	A	B	C	D	E
61	5	4	3	2	1
62	5	4	3	2	1
63	5	4	3	2	1
64	1	2	3	4	5
65	1	2	3	4	5
66	5	4	3	2	1
67	5	4	3	2	1
68	5	4	3	2	1
69	5	4	3	2	1
70	1	2	3	4	5
71	5	4	3	2	1
72	5	4	3	2	1
73	5	4	3	2	1
74	5	4	3	2	1
75	1	2	3	4	5

SCORING KEYS

Viscidity	A	B	C	D	E		Polarization	A	B	C	D	E
76	1	2	3	4	5		111	5	4	3	2	1
77	1	2	3	4	5		112	1	2	3	4	5
78	1	2	3	4	5		113	1	2	3	4	5
79	5	4	3	2	1		114	5	4	3	2	1
80	1	2	3	4	5		115	5	4	3	2	1
81	1	2	3	4	5		116	1	2	3	4	5
82	1	2	3	4	5		117	1	2	3	4	5
83	5	4	3	2	1		118	5	4	3	2	1
84	1	2	3	4	5		119	5	4	3	2	1
85	1	2	3	4	5		120	1	2	3	4	5
86	1	2	3	4	5		121	1	2	3	4	5
87	1	2	3	4	5		122	1	2	3	4	5

Permeability	A	B	C	D	E		Flexibility	A	B	C	D	E
88	5	4	3	2	1		123	5	4	3	2	1
89	5	4	3	2	1		124	1	2	3	4	5
90	5	4	3	2	1		125	1	2	3	4	5
91	1	2	3	4	5		126	1	2	3	4	5
92	1	2	3	4	5		127	5	4	3	2	1
93	5	4	3	2	1		128	1	2	3	4	5
94	5	4	3	2	1		129	1	2	3	4	5
95	5	4	3	2	1		130	1	2	3	4	5
96	1	2	3	4	5		131	1	2	3	4	5
97	5	4	3	2	1		132	1	2	3	4	5
98	5	4	3	2	1		133	1	2	3	4	5
99	1	2	3	4	5		134	1	2	3	4	5
100	1	2	3	4	5		135	5	4	3	2	1

Participation	A	B	C	D	E		Homogeneity	A	B	C	D	E
101	5	4	3	2	1		136	5	4	3	2	1
102	5	4	3	2	1		137	1	2	3	4	5
103	1	2	3	4	5		138	1	2	3	4	5
104	1	2	3	4	5		139	1	2	3	4	5
105	1	2	3	4	5		140	1	2	3	4	5
106	5	4	3	2	1		141	5	4	3	2	1
107	5	4	3	2	1		142	1	2	3	4	5
108	1	2	3	4	5		143	1	2	3	4	5
109	1	2	3	4	5		144	1	2	3	4	5
110	1	2	3	4	5		145	5	4	3	2	1
							146	1	2	3	4	5
							147	1	2	3	4	5
							148	1	2	3	4	5
							149	1	2	3	4	5
							150	1	2	3	4	5

GROUP DIMENSIONS PROFILE AND FACE SHEET

Name _____ Age _____ Date _____

Name of group _____

Length of your membership _____ No. of group members _____

General purpose of the group _____

	Dimension		*Stanine Score*
			1 2 3 4 5 6 7 8 9
A	Autonomy		. . . .
B	Control		. . . .
C	Flexibility		. . . .
D	Hedonic Tone		. . . .
E	Homogeneity		. . . .
F	Intimacy		. . . .
G	Participation		. . . .
H	Permeability		. . . .
I	Polarization		. . . .
J	Potency		. . . .
K	Stability		. . . .
L	Stratification		. . . .
M	Viscidity		. . . .

BALES'S INTERACTION PROCESS ANALYSIS   *4.B.2*

VARIABLE MEASURED: Group interaction.

DESCRIPTION: This index consists of twelve categories—shows solidarity, shows tension release, agrees, gives suggestion, gives opinion, gives orientation, asks for orientation, asks for opinion, asks for suggestion, disagrees, shows tension, shows antagonism. Scoring is made by designating each person in the group with a number. All interaction is analyzed according to the category and marked in the fashion of 1–5 or 1–0 as the interaction takes place. After observation, a summary or profile can be constructed and inferences made to describe the underlying workings of the group.

A slightly revised version of the categories has been developed by Bales and is presented in R. F. Bales, *Personality and Interpersonal Behavior* (New York: Holt, Rinehart & Winston, 1970). See Appendix 4 for description of the changes. A new interpersonal behavior rating system is organized around the dimensions of "up/down," "forward/back," and "positive/negative."

Category 1 is now labeled "Seems Friendly" and category 12 "Seems Unfriendly"; category 2 is now "Dramatizes," and categories 6 and 7 are "Gives Information" and "Asks for Information." Content of other categories (except 3, 8, and 10) have also been changed.

While the Bales' scheme is not widely used today in its original form, it remains the model in its field. It did much to aid early development of small-group analysis. The new form is somewhat simpler and easier to use. New norms are not available, but Bales provides estimates of how the changes may influence percentage distributions.

WHERE PUBLISHED: R. F. Bales, *Interaction Process Analysis: A Method for the Study of Small Groups* (Cambridge, Mass.: Addison-Wesley, 1950). Cf. John Madge, *The Origins of Scientific Sociology* (New York: Free Press, 1967), pp. 424-77.

RELIABILITY: With competent and trained observers an inter-observer correlation of between .75 and .95 can be obtained.

VALIDITY: Face validity. Consult critique of Dale G. Lake, Mathew B. Miles, and Ralph B. Earle, *Measuring Human Behavior* (New York: Teachers College Press, 1973).

UTILITY: A general purpose, standard set of categories well suited for the observation and analysis of small groups. The chief disadvantage is that the training of observers requires long practice. Frequent retraining is also necessary.

RESEARCH APPLICATIONS:

BALES, ROBERT F. *Personality and Interpersonal Behavior.* New York: Holt, Rinehart, & Winston, 1970. See Bibliography, pp. 532-42.

BURKE, PETER J. "Participation and Leadership in Small Groups." *American Sociological Review* 39 (December 1974): 832-43.

HARE, PAUL A. *Handbook of Small Group Research.* Second ed. Glencoe, Ill.: Free Press, 1975.

HARE, PAUL A.; BORGATTA, EDGAR F.; and BALES, ROBERT F., eds. *Small Groups: Studies in Social Interaction.* Rev. ed. New York: Alfred A. Knopf, 1965. See the bibliography of small-group research.

SMITH, H. W. "Some Developmental Interpersonal Dynamics Through Childhood." *American Sociological Review* 38 (October 1973): 543-52.

1 SHOWS SOLIDARITY, raises others' status, gives help, reward:					
2 SHOWS TENSION RELEASE, jokes, laughs, shows satisfaction:					
3 AGREES, shows passive acceptance, understands, concurs, complies:					
4 GIVES SUGGESTION, direction, implying autonomy for other:					
5 GIVES OPINION, evaluation, analysis, expresses feeling, wish:					
6 GIVES ORIENTATION, information, repeats, clarifies, confirms:					

7 ASKS FOR ORIENTATION, information, repetition, confirmation:						
8 ASKS FOR OPINION, evaluation, analysis, expression of feeling:						
9 ASKS FOR SUGGESTION, direction, possible ways of action:						
10 DISAGREES, shows passive rejection, formality, withholds help:						
11 SHOWS TENSION, asks for help, withdraws "Out of Field":						
12 SHOWS ANTAGONISM, deflates other's status, defends or asserts self:						

PERCENT: 0

Prepared for use with Interaction Process Analysis by Robert F. Bales. Printed in U.S.A. INTERACTION SCORING FORM Published by Addison-Wesley Publishing Co., Reading, Mass. 01867.

SEASHORE'S GROUP COHESIVENESS INDEX   *4.B.3*

VARIABLE MEASURED: The index measures group cohesiveness, defined as attraction to the group or resistance to leaving.

DESCRIPTION: The test consists of three questions: "Do you feel that you are really a part of your work group?" "If you had a chance to do the same kind of work for the same pay, in another work group, how would you feel about moving?" and "How does your work group compare with other work groups at Midwest on each of the following points?"–The way people get along together, the way people stick together, and the way people help each other on the job. The first two questions can be answered by five degrees, while the three items of the third question are answered by four degrees.

WHERE PUBLISHED: Stanley E. Seashore, *Group Cohesiveness in the Industrial Work Group* (Ann Arbor: Survey Research Center, Institute for Social Research, University of Michigan, 1954).

RELIABILITY: Intercorrelations among mean scale values for the groups on scales comprising the index of cohesiveness ranged from .15 to .70.

VALIDITY: The variance found between groups on this scale was significant beyond the .001 level.

UTILITY: As the questions are phrased, the index is especially set up for an industrial situation. It can probably, with a few changes, be adapted to almost any situation where an index of group cohesiveness is required. The test takes very little time to administer. The subject should be assured that his replies will be kept confidential.

RESEARCH APPLICATIONS: The study of 228 section-shift groups in a company manufacturing heavy machinery, described in the aforementioned Seashore article.

Index of Group Cohesiveness

"Do you feel that you are really a part of your work group?"

- ☐ Really a part of my work group
- ☐ Included in most ways
- ☐ Included in some ways, but not in others
- ☐ Don't feel I really belong
- ☐ Don't work with any one group of people
  - ☐ Not ascertained

"If you had a chance to do the same kind of work for the same pay, in another work group, how would you feel about moving?"

- ☐ Would want very much to move
- ☐ Would rather move than stay where I am
- ☐ Would make no difference to me
- ☐ Would rather stay where I am than move
- ☐ Would want very much to stay where I am
  - ☐ Not ascertained

"How does your work group compare with other work groups at Midwest on each of the following points?"

	Better than most	About the same as most	Not as good as most	Not ascertained
The way people get along together	☐	☐	☐	☐
The way people stick together	☐	☐	☐	☐
The way people help one another on the job	☐	☐	☐	☐

4.B.4   SOCIOMETRY SCALES OF SPONTANEOUS CHOICE AND SOCIOMETRIC PREFERENCE

VARIABLE MEASURED: The degree to which individuals are accepted in a group, interpersonal relationships that exist among individuals, and structure of the group.

DESCRIPTION: Results are most satisfactory for small cohesive groups. The sociometric technique consists of asking each individual in a group to state with whom among the members of the group he would prefer to associate for specific activities or in particular situations. Criteria (selected areas that should include different aspects of possible association: work, play, visiting) range in number from 1 to 8 or more; and choices, from 1 to as many as desired by the researcher.

WHERE PUBLISHED: J. L. Moreno, *Who Shall Survive?* (Beacon, N.Y.: Beacon House, 1934).

RELIABILITY:

Loeb's correlation between odd-even items	r = .65 to .85
Loeb's correlation between split-halves	r = .53 to .85
Mary L. Northway between general criteria	r = .64 to .84
Mary L. Northway between skill criteria	r = .37 to .50

Correlations between scores on tests given at different times	r = .74
Constancy of choice (actual preference on 1st test repeated later on)	r = .69

VALIDITY: Eugene Byrd comparison of sociometric choice with actual choice and then an 8-week interval retest shows r = .76, .80, .89. See Eugene Byrd, "A Study of Validity and Constancy of Choices in a Sociometric Test," *Sociometry* 9 (1946): 21.

N. Gronlund comparison of judgment of teachers vs. testing shows r = .59. See N. Gronlund, *Accuracies of Teachers' Judgments Concerning the Sociometric Status of Sixth Grade Pupils*, Sociometry Monograph No. 25 (Beacon, N.Y.: Beacon House, 1951).

For discussion of reliability and validity, see Mary L. Northway, *A Primer of Sociometry* (Toronto: University of Toronto, 1952), pp. 16–20. Also cf. Merl E. Bonney, "A Study of Constancy of Sociometric Ranks Among College Students Over a Two-Year Period," *Sociometry* 18 (December 1955): 531–42.

STANDARD SCORES: None.

RESEARCH APPLICATIONS:

BRONFENBRENNER, URIE. *The Measurement of Sociometric Status, Structure and Development*. Sociometry Monograph No. 6. Beacon, N.Y.: Beacon House, 1945.

HOLLAND, PAUL W., and LEINHARDT, SAMUEL. "A Method of Detecting Structure in Sociometric Data." *American Journal of Sociology* 76, no. 3 (November 1970): 492–513.

JACOBS, JOHN H. "The Application of Sociometry to Industry." *Sociometry* 8 (May 1945): 181–98.

JENNINGS, HELEN H. *Leadership and Isolation: A Study of Personality in Interpersonal Relations*. 2nd ed. New York: David McKay, 1950.

LEINHARDT, SAMUEL. "Developmental Change in the Sentiment Structure of Children's Groups." *American Sociological Review* 37 (April 1972): 202–12.

LUNDBERG, GEORGE A., and DICKSON, LENORE. "Inter-Ethnic Relations in a High School Population." *American Journal of Sociology* 57 (July 1952): 1–10.

MASSARIK, FRED; TANNENBAUM, ROBERT; RAHANE, MURRAY; and WESCHLER, IRVING. "Sociometric Choice and Organizational Effectiveness: A Multi-Relational Approach." *Sociometry* (August 1953): 211–38. Or see MASSARIK, FRED, et al. *Leadership and Organization*. New York: McGraw-Hill, 1961. Pp. 346–70.

MORENO, J. L. *Who Shall Survive? A New Approach to the Problem of Human Relationships*. Beacon, N.Y.: Beacon House, 1934. See also MORENO, J. L. *Sociometry and the Science of Man*. Beacon, N.Y.: Beacon House, 1956.

WHITE, HARRISON. "Management Conflict and Sociometric Structure." *American Journal of Sociology* 67 (September 1961): 185–99.

ZELENY, LESLIE D. "Selection of Compatible Flying Partners." *American Journal of Sociology* 52 (March 1947): 424–31.

For an excellent review of the literature on "Measures of Sociometric Structure" see M. Glanzer and R. Glaser, "Techniques for the Study of Group Structure and Behavior: I. Analysis of Structure," *Psychological Bulletin* 56 (September 1959): 317-32. Cf. J. L. Moreno, "Contributions of Sociometry to Research Methodology in Sociology," *American Sociological Review* 12 (June 1947): 287-92; Jacob L. Moreno et al., *The Sociometry Reader* (Glencoe, Ill.: Free Press, 1959).

Spontaneous Choice Test

Opposite each name check how you feel about persons in your group.

	Like	Dislike	Indifferent
Mary J.			
James F.			
John J.			
Etc.			

Sociometric Preference Test

Choose five persons you would most like to work with.* Mark 1st, 2nd, 3rd, 4th, 5th choice.

Mary J.	
James F.	
John J.	
Sam E.	
Etc.	

*Many criteria may be employed. For example, to have in a discussion group, to have in your neighborhood, to play bridge with, to work on a project with, etc.

4.B.5   BOGARDUS' SOCIAL-DISTANCE SCALE

VARIABLE MEASURED: The social distance or degree of social acceptance that exists between given persons and certain social groups. The scale may be adapted to measure the social distance between two persons or between two or more social groups. The method has been applied to racial distance, regional distance, sex distance, age distance, parent-child distance, educational distance, class distance, occupational distance, religious distance, international distance.

DESCRIPTION: Typically, a group of persons is asked to rank a series of social types with respect to the degrees of social distance on seven attributes starting with *acceptance to close kinship by marriage* and concluding with *would exclude from my country*. One hundred persons acting as judges have identified these seven attributes among 60 as those ordered on a continuant of social distance.

WHERE PUBLISHED: Best source is Emory S. Bogardus, *Social Distance* (Yellow Springs, Ohio: Antioch Press, 1959); Emory S. Bogardus, *Immigration and Race Attitudes* (Boston: Heath, 1928); E. S. Bogardus, "A Social Distance Scale," *Sociology and Social Research* 17 (January-February 1933): 265-71. Excellent instructions may be found in William J. Goode and Paul K. Hatt, *Methods in Social Research* (New York: McGraw-Hill, 1952), pp. 26, 245-49.

RELIABILITY: Split-half reliability coefficient reported at .90 or higher in repeated tests by Eugene L. Hartley and Ruth E. Hartley.

VALIDITY: Theodore Newcomb reports high validity if we use "agreement with other scales that in certain particulars are more exact." Application of the known-group method is advocated in determination of validity. This involves finding groups known to be favorable toward some of the ethnic types and unfavorable toward others. If the responses of these groups fit the requisite pattern, evidence for validity may be accepted. For full discussion see E. S. Bogardus, *Social Distance* (Yellow Springs, Ohio: Antioch Press, 1959), pp. 92-95.

SCORING: A variety of scoring methods has been used. A simple method that has been found to be as reliable as the more complex ones is that of counting the numbers of the "nearest column" that is checked. That is, if the racial distance quotient, *RDQ*, of a number of persons is desired, then the arithmetic mean of the total number of the "nearest columns" that are checked by all the subjects for each race is obtained. If the *RDQ* of a person is sought, then the arithmetic mean of the total numbers of the "nearest column" for each race is obtained.

STANDARD SCORES: Racial Distance Quotients Given Racial Groups in 1956 by 2053 selected persons throughout the United States.

1.	Americans (U.S. White)	1.08
2.	Canadians	1.16
3.	English	1.23
4.	French	1.47
5.	Irish	1.56
6.	Swedish	1.57
7.	Scots	1.60
8.	Germans	1.61
9.	Hollanders	1.63
10.	Norwegians	1.56
11.	Finns	1.80
12.	Italians	1.89
13.	Poles	2.07

14. Spanish	2.08
15. Greeks	2.09
16. Jews	2.15
17. Czechs	2.22
18. Armenians	2.33
19. Japanese Americans	2.34
20. Indians (American)	2.35
21. Filipinos	2.46
22. Mexican Americans	2.51
23. Turks	2.52
24. Russians	2.56
25. Chinese	2.68
26. Japanese	2.70
27. Negroes	2.74
28. Mexicans	2.79
29. Indians (from India)	2.80
30. Koreans	2.83

Arithmetic Mean of 61,590 Racial Reactions: 2.08.

UTILITY: The Bogardus Scale may be used to estimate the amount of potential and real conflict existing between any cultural groups, anywhere in the industrial, political, racial, religious, and other phases of life. It also helps to determine the extent of the trend toward conflict or toward cooperation between groups. The test is easy to administer and to score. It can be adapted easily to other problems of social distance.

A good illustration of such an adaptation is to be found in the Mock Table for a Scale to Measure the Attractiveness of Different Communities. See William J. Goode and Paul K. Hatt, *Methods in Social Research* (New York: McGraw-Hill, 1952), p. 248. The fullest description of applications is to be found in Emory S. Bogardus, *Social Distance* (Yellow Springs, Ohio: Antioch Press, 1959).

RESEARCH APPLICATIONS:

BARBER, BERNARD. *Social Stratification.* New York: Harcourt, Brace, 1957.
BARDIS, PANOS D. "Social Distance among Foreign Students." *Sociology and Social Research* 41: 112–15.
——. "Social Distance in a Greek Metropolitan City." *Social Science* 37 (April 1962): 108–11.
BEST, W. H., and SOHNER, C. P. "Social Distance Methodology in the Measurement of Political Attitudes." *Sociology and Social Research* 40: 266–70.
——. "Social Distance and Politics," *Sociology and Social Research* 40: 339–42.
BIESANZ, J., and BIESANZ, M. "Social Distance in the Youth Hostel Movement." *Sociology and Social Research* 25: 237–45.
BINNEWIES, W. G. "A Method of Studying Rural Social Distance." *Sociology and Social Research* 10: 239–42.
BOGARDUS, EMORY S. *Sociometry* 10: 306–11; *International Journal of Opinion and Attitude Research* 1: 55–62; *American Sociological Review* 16: 48–53; *Journal of Educational Sociology* 3: 497–502; *Survey Graphic* 9: 169–70, 206, 208; *Journal of Applied Sociology* 9: 216–26; *Sociology and Social Research* 12: 173–78; 13: 73–81; 13: 171–75; 14: 174–80; 17: 167–73; 17: 265–71; 18: 67–73; 20: 473–77; 22: 462–76; 24: 69–75; 32: 723–27; 32: 798–802;

32: 882-87; 33: 291-95; 36: 40-47; 43: 439-41; *The Urban Community*, edited by E. W. Burgess. Chicago: University of Chicago Press, 1927. Pp. 48-54.

BRADWAY, JOHN S. "Social Distance Between Lawyers and Social Workers." *Sociology and Social Research* 14: 516-24.

BRIGGS, ARTHUR E. "Social Distance Between Lawyers and Doctors." *Sociology and Social Research*, 13: 156-63.

BROOKS, LEE M. "Racial Distance as Affected by Education." *Sociology and Social Research* 21: 128-33.

CAMPBELL, DONALD T. "The Bogardus Social Distance Scale." *Sociology and Social Research* 36: 322-25.

CATAPUSAN, BENICIO T. "Social Distance in the Philippines." *Sociology and Social Research* 38: 309-12.

DODD, STUART C. "A Social Distance Test in the Near East." *American Journal of Sociology* 41 (September 1935): 194-204.

———, and NEHNEVAJSA, J. "Physical Dimensions of Social Distance," *Sociology and Social Research* 38: 287-92.

DUNCAN, W. L. "Parent-Child Isolations." *The Family* 10: 115-18.

DUVALL, EVERETT W. "Child-Parent Social Distance." *Sociology and Social Research* 21: 458-63.

EISENSTADT, S. N. *From Generation to Generation: Age Groups and the Social Structure.* Glencoe, Ill.: Free Press, 1956.

ELLEFSEN, J. B. "Social Distance Attitudes of Negro College Students." *Phylon* 17: 79-83.

ELLIS, ROBERT A. "Social Status and Social Distance." *Sociology and Social Research* 40: 240-46.

FRANKLIN, CLAY. "The Effect of the Format Upon the Scale Values of the Bogardus Social Distance Scale." *Research Studies of the State College of Washington* 18: 117-20.

GLEASON, GEORGE. "Social Distance in Russia," *Sociology and Social Research* 17: 37-43.

GRACE, H. A., and NEUHAUS, J. O. "Information and Social Distance as Predictors of Hostility Toward Nations." *Journal of Abnormal and Social Psychology* 47 (1952): 540-45.

GREIFER, JULIAN L. "Attitudes to the Stranger." *American Sociological Review* 10 (December 1945): 739-45.

GURNEE, H., and BAKER, E. "Social Distances of Some Common Social Relationships." *Journal of Abnormal and Social Psychology* 33 (1938): 265-69.

HALBWACHS, M. *The Psychology of Social Classes.* Glencoe, Ill.: Free Press, 1958.

HAMREN, VANDYCE. "Social Farness Between the A.F. of L. and the C.I.O." *Sociology and Social Research* 24: 442-52.

———. "Social Nearness Between the A.F. of L. and the C.I.O." *Sociology and Social Research* 26: 232-40.

HARTLEY, EUGENE L. *Problems in Prejudice.* New York: Columbia University Press, 1946.

———, and HARTLEY, RUTH E. *Fundamentals of Social Psychology.* New York: Alfred A. Knopf, 1952. Pp. 431-43.

HUNT, CHESTER L. "Social Distance in the Philippines." *Sociology and Social Research* 40: 253-60.

HYPES, E. L. "The Social Distance Score Card as a Teaching Device." *Social Forces* 7 (December 1928): 234-37.

JAMESON, S. H. "Social Distance between Welfare Organizations." *Sociology and Social Research* 5: 230-43.

———. "Social Nearness among Welfare Organizations." *Sociology and Social Research* 15: 322–33.

KAHL, JOSEPH A. *The American Class Structure*. New York: Rinehart, 1957.

KOCH, H. L. "Study of Some Factors Conditioning the Social Distance between the Sexes." *Journal of Social Psychology* 20: 79–107.

KROUT, M. H. "Periodic Change in Social Distance; A Study in the Shifting Bases of Perception." *Sociology and Social Research* 27: 339–51.

LAMBERT, W. E. "Comparison of French and American Modes of Response to the Bogardus Social Distance Scale." *Social Forces* 31: 155–60.

McDONAGH, EDWARD C. "Social Distance between China and Japan." *Sociology and Social Research* 22: 131–36.

———. "Asiatic Stereotypes and National Distance." *Sociology and Social Research* 22: 474–78.

———. "Military Social Distance." *Sociology and Social Research* 29: 289–96.

McKENZIE, R. D. "Spatial Distance and Community Organization Pattern." *Social Forces* 5: 623–27.

———. "Spatial Distance," *Sociology and Social Research* 13: 536–44.

McMATH, ELLA M. "A Girl without a Country." *Journal of Applied Sociology* 11: 65–71.

MARTIN, R. R. "Sudden Change in Social Distance." *Sociology and Social Research* 22: 53–56.

MITCHELL, ROY. "An Ethnic Distance Study in Buffalo." *Sociology and Social Research* 40: 35–40.

MOWRER, E. R. *Domestic Discord*. Chicago: University of Chicago Press, 1928. Chap. 3.

NEPRASH, J. A. "Minority Group Contacts and Social Distance." *Phylon* 14: 207–12.

NEWCOMB, THEODORE M. *Social Psychology*. Rev. ed. New York: Holt, Rinehart & Winston, 1955. Pp. 154–75.

NIMKOFF, M. F. "Parent-Child Conflict." *Sociology and Social Research* 12: 446–58.

———. "Parent-Child Conflict." *Sociology and Social Research* 14: 135–50.

NORTH, C. C. *Social Differentiation*. Chapel Hill: University of North Carolina Press, 1926.

OWEN, JOHN E. "Social Distance in England." *Sociology and Social Research* 30: 460–65.

PARISH, HELEN R. "Social Nearness between Latin America and the United States." *Sociology and Social Research* 19: 253–58.

PARK, R. E. "The Concept of Social Distance." *Journal of Applied Sociology* 8: 339–44.

PETTIGREW, THOMAS F. "Social Distance Attitudes of South African Students." *Social Forces* 38 (March 1960): 246–53.

POOLE, W. C., JR. "Distance in Sociology." *American Journal of Sociology* 33: 99–104.

———. "Social Distance and Social Pathology." *Sociology and Social Research* 12: 268–72.

———. "Social Distance and Personal Distance." *Journal of Applied Sociology* 11: 114–20.

———. "The Social Distance Margin Reviewed." *Sociology and Social Research* 13: 49–54.

———, and POOLE, HARRIET K. "Laws of Social Distance." *Journal of Applied Sociology* 11: 365–69.

PROTHRO, E. T., and MILES, O. K. "Social Distance in the Deep South as Measured by a Revised Bogardus Scale." *Journal of Social Psychology* 37: 171–74.

RUNNER, JESSIE R. "Social Distance in Adolescent Relationships." *American Journal of Sociology* 43: 428-39.

SARTAIN, A. I., and BELL, HAROLD V., JR. "An Evaluation of the Bogardus Scale of Social Distance by the Method of Equal-Appearing Intervals." *Journal of Social Psychology* 29: 85-91.

SARVIS, GUY W. "Social Distance in Religion." *Christian Century* 49: 1331-33.

SCHENK, Q. F., and ROMNEY, A. K. "Some Differential Attitudes among Adolescent Groups as Revealed by Bogardus' Social Distance Scale." *Sociology and Social Research* 35: 38-45.

SCHNETZ, ALFRED. "The Stranger." *American Journal of Sociology* 49: 499-508.

SCHROFF, RUTH. "Charting Social Distance." *Sociology and Social Research* 14: 567-70.

SEYMOUR, J. G. "Rural Social Distance of Normal School Students." *Sociology and Social Research* 14: 238-48.

SHERIF, MUZAFER, and SHERIF, CAROLYN W. *An Outline of Social Psychology.* New York: Harper & Brothers, 1956. Pp. 659-78.

SHIDELER, ERNEST. "The Social Distance Margin." *Sociology and Social Research* 12: 243-52.

SOROKIN, P. *Social Mobility.* New York: Harper & Brothers, 1927. Chap. 6, "Occupational Stratification."

STEPHENSON, C. M., and WILCOX, CAROL G. "Social Distance Variations of College Students." *Sociology and Social Research* 39: 240-41.

TURBEVILLE, GUS. "A Social Distance Study of Duluth, Minnesota." *Sociology and Social Research* 18: 420-30.

VAN DER BERGHE, PIERRE L. "Distance Mechanisms of Stratification." *Sociology and Social Research* 44 (January-February 1960): 155-64.

WESTIE, F. R. "Negro-White Status Differentials and Social Distance," *American Sociological Review* 17 (October 1952): 550-58.

WESTIE, FRANK R., and WESTIE, MARGARET L. "The Social Distance Pyramid: Relationships between Caste and Class." *American Journal of Sociology* 63 (September 1957): 190-96.

——. "Social Distance Scales, a Tool for the Study of Stratification." *Sociology and Social Research* 43: 251-58.

WOOD, MARGARET MARY. *Paths of Loneliness.* New York: Columbia University Press, 1953.

ZELIGS, ROSE, and HENDRICKSON, G. "Checking the Social Distance Technique through Personal Interviews." *Sociology and Social Research* 18: 420-30.

ZIEGLER, GEORGE H. "Social Farness between Hindus and Moslems." *Sociology and Social Research* 33: 188-95.

Interesting adaptations of the social distance scale are found in:

DEFLEUR, M. L., and WESTIE, FRANK R. "Verbal Attitudes and Overt Acts: An Experiment on the Salience of Attitudes." *American Sociological Review* 23 (December 1958): 667-73.

JACKSON, ELTON F. "Status Consistency and Symptoms of Stress." *American Sociological Review* 27 (August 1962): 469-80.

LONGWORTHY, RUSSELL L. "Community Status and Influence in a High School." *American Sociological Review* 24 (August 1959): 537-39.

MARTIN, JAMES G., and WESTIE, FRANK R. "The Tolerant Personality." *American Sociological Review* 24 (August 1959): 521-28.

PHOTIADIS, JOHN D., and BIGGAR, JEANNE. "Religiosity, Education, and Ethnic Distance." *American Journal of Sociology* 67 (May 1962): 666-73.

PHOTIADIS, JOHN D., and JOHNSON, ARTHUR L. "Orthodoxy, Church Participation, and Authoritarianism." *American Journal of Sociology* 69 (November
1963): 244–48.

WESTIE, FRANK R. "A Technique for the Measurement of Race Attitudes."
American Sociological Review 18 (February 1953): 73–78.

See his "Note to Prospective Users of the Summated Differences Technique," in *Sociological Measurement*, ed. Charles M. Bonjean, Richard J. Hill, and Dale McLemore (San
Francisco: Chandler, 1976), p. 158.

BOGARDUS' RACIAL-DISTANCE SCALE

(Race is defined here largely as a cultural group.)

1. Remember to give your *first feeling reactions* in every case.

2. Give your reactions to each race as a *group*. Do not give your reactions to the
best or to the worst members that you have known, but think of the picture
or stereotype that you have of the whole race.

3. Put a cross after each race in as many of the seven rows as your feeling
dictate.

Category	English	Swedes	Poles	Koreans	Etc.
1. To close kinship by marriage					
2. To my club as personal chums					
3. To my street as neighbors					
4. To employment in my occupation					
5. To citizenship in my country					
6. As visitors only to my country					
7. Would exclude from my country					

Social Indicators

The role of social indicators known as Social Reporting, Social Systems Accounting, and Social Intelligence is set forth in the following definition:

Social indicators—statistics, statistical series, and all other forms of evidence—are summary measures that enable policy and decision makers to assess various social aspects of an ongoing society and to evaluate specific programs and determine their impact. Social indicators help experts and lay persons alike to better understand their own and other societies with respect to values and goals and the nature of social change. Stuart Rice has provided a most compact statement:

> Social Indicators, the tools, are needed to find pathways through the maze of society's interconnections. They delineate *social states*, define *social problems* and trace *social trends*, which by *social engineering* may hopefully be guided toward *social goals* formulated by *social planning*.[1]

The potential scope of social indicators is very broad. The question of goals must be resolved before the appropriate scope can be determined. The final answer may best be given by the needs of a society and the requests of policy makers for information about problems they must meet and solve. On February 17, 1974, the Office of Management and Budget released a pioneering study in the field of social reporting, *Social Indicators, 1973*. This study began by identifying widely held basic social objectives: good health and long life, freedom from crime and the fear of crime, sufficient education to take part in society and make the most of one's abilities, the opportunity to work at a job that is satisfying and rewarding, income sufficient to cover the necessities of life with opportunities for improving one's income, housing that is comfortable within a congenial environment, and time and opportunity for discretionary activities. For each identified social concern, one or more indicators—statistical measures of important aspects of the concerns—has been identified. *Social Indicators, 1973*, is restricted almost entirely to data about objective conditions. The indicators are primarily time series showing national totals. The list of the indicators is reproduced on the following pages and may be compared with "Economic Indicators," which follow.[2] Social indicators have not yet been institutionalized as have economic indicators, which were mandated by the Employment Act of 1946. The legislation necessary to enact the development of a social report was first presented in 1967 calling for a Council of Social

Advisers and the publication of an annual social report. Senator Walter Mondale of Minnesota was not able to muster sufficient votes for its enactment, but support has been growing.

Notes

1. Stuart A. Rice, "Social Accounting and Statistics for the Great Society," *Public Administration Review* 27 (June 1967): 173.

2. *Social Indicators, 1976,* is scheduled; plans call for three new areas: family, social welfare and security, social mobility and stratification.

4.C.1   **NATIONAL SOCIAL INDICATORS, 1973***

1. Health
  Long life
  1/1   Life Expectancy at Birth: 1901–1971 By Sex
  1/2   Life Expectancy at Birth, By Sex and Race: 1901–1971
  1/3   Life Remaining at Ages 30 and 50: 1901–1971 By Sex and Race
  1/4   Death Rates: 1940–1971 By Race and Sex
  1/5   Death Rates, By Age and Sex: 1971
  1/6   Death Rates, for Selected Causes: 1940–1971
  1/7   Death Rates Ranked for Four Leading Causes: 1969 By Age and Sex
  1/8   Infant Mortality Rates: 1940–1971 By Race

  Disability
  1/9   Days of Disability, By Type of Disability: 1969 Per Person, Per Year
  1/10 Days of Disability, By Type of Disability and Age: 1969 Per Person, Per Year
  1/11 Persons with Long-term Disability, By Type of Disability and Age: 1969

  Long-term disability—institutional
  1/12 Patients in Health-related Institutions: 1950, 1960, and 1970 By Type of Disability and Age
  1/13 Patients in Mental Hospitals: 1950–1972 Resident Patients, Admissions, Releases, and Deaths
  1/14 Mental Retardation Rates: 1940–1971 Residents of Public Mental Retardation Facilities
  1/15 Admission Rates to Mental Hospitals, By Age, Race, and Sex: 1970
  1/16 Persons in Nursing and Personal Care Homes, By Age, Race, and Sex: 1969
  1/17 Persons in Nursing and Personal Care Homes, By Mobility Status and Age, 1969

  Long-term disability—noninstitutional
  1/18 Persons Limited in Major Activity Due to Chronic Conditions: 1960–1971 By Age and Degree of Limitation
  1/19 Persons Limited in Activity Due to Chronic Conditions, By Sex, Race, and Degree of Limitation: 1971

*Document available from the U.S. Government Printing Office, Washington, D.C. 20402. $7.80 per copy.

Freedom from fear of crime

2/20 Persons Afraid to Walk Alone at Night: 1965–1972 By Sex and Community Size

2/21 Persons Afraid to Walk Alone at Night, By Race, Age, Education, and Income: 1972

3. Education

Basic Skills—attainment

3/1   High School Graduation Rate: 1946–1972

3/2   The High School Education Population: 1940–1972 By Age and Race

3/3   School Retention Rates: 1924–1970 From Fifth Grade to High School Graduation

3/4   School Enrollment: 1953–1971 By Level of Instruction and Type of School

3/5   Prekindergarten Enrollment, By Race: 1964–1972

3/6   Prekindergarten Enrollment, By Family Income and Race: 3-Year Average, 1970–1972

3/7   Modal Grade Enrollment, By Race, Sex, and Age: 1972

Basis skills—achievement

3/8   Reading Achievement: 1971

3/9   Science Achievement: 1970

3/10   Reading Achievement, By Selected Theme: 1971

3/11   Science Achievement, By Objective: 1970

Higher and continuing education

3/13   Educational Participation of Adult Population: 1969

3/13   Undergraduate Enrollment, 18- To 24-Year Olds: 1940–1972 By Sex and Race

3/14   College Entrance Rates, By Student Ability and Socioeconomic Status of Parents: 1967

3/15   Enrollment in Institutions of Higher Education: 1957–1971 By Level and Degree-Credit Status

3/16   The College-Educated Population: 1940–1972 By Age, Sex and Race

3/17   Bachelor's, Master's, and Doctor's Degrees Earned: 1940–1972 By Sex

3/18   Associate and First-Professional Degrees Earned: 1950–1972 By Sex

3/19   Degrees Earned: 1952, 1962, 1972 By Level and Subject Area

3/20   Participation in Adult Education, By Sex, Race, Age, and Instructional Source: 1969

4. Employment

Employment opportunities

4/1   Unemployment Rates: 1947–1972 By Duration

4/2   Unemployment Rates, By Race: 1948–1972

4/3   Unemployment Rates, By Age, Sex, and Race: 1954–1972

4/4   Unemployment Rates, By Educational Attainment: 1964–1972 By Age and Race

4/5   Unemployment Rates, By Occupation: 1972

4/6   Persons with Unemployment, By Number of Spells of Unemployment: 1971

5/11 Family Income, By Race, Sex, and Age of Family Head: 1971

Expenditure of income

5/12 Personal Consumption Expenditures, By Type of Product and Service: 1940–1972

5/13 Consumer Unit Expenditures, By Type of Product and Service: 1960 for Selected Income Groups

5/14 Personal Debt of Consumer Units, By Selected Income Groups: 1962

5/15 Distribution of Wealth: 1962 Fifths of Consumer Units Ranked By Wealth, Income, and Age

5/16 Wealth of Consumer Units, By Amount of Wealth: 1962

The low-income population

5/17 Persons Below the Low-Income Level: 1959–1971

5/18 Persons Below the Low-Income Level, By Age: 1959–1971

5/19 Persons Below the Low-Income Level, By Race: 1959–1971

5/20 Persons Below the Low-Income Level, By Residence: 1959–1971

5/21 Persons Below the Low-Income Level, By Region and Race: 1959–1971

5/22 Persons Below the Low-Income Level, By Race and Sex of Family Head: 1959–1971

5/23 Mean Income Deficit for Families and for Unrelated Individuals By Race: 1959–1971

5/24 Profile of the Low-Income Population: 1971

6. Housing

Housing quality

The housing unit

6/1   Households Living in Substandard Units: 1940–1970

6/2   Households Living in Substandard Units, By Size of Household: 1950–1970

6/3   Households Living in Substandard Units, By Race: 1950–1970

6/4   Households Living in Substandard Units, By Tenure: 1940–1970

6/5   Households Living in Substandard Units, By Location: 1970

6/6   Households Living in Substandard Units, By Income and Race: 1970

6/7   Households Living in Substandard Units, By Tenure and Year Structure Built: 1970

Living space

6/8   Households Living in Crowded Conditions: 1940–1970

6/9   Households Living in Crowded Conditions, By Size of Household: 1950–1970

6/10 Households Living in Crowded Conditions, By Race: 1940, 1960, 1970

6/11 Households Living in Crowded Conditions, By Tenure: 1940–1970

6/12 Households Living in Crowded Conditions, By Location: 1970

6/13 Households Living in Crowded Conditions, By Income and Race: 1970

6/14 Households Living in Crowded Conditions, By Quality of Housing Unit: 1950–1970

6/15 Married Couples Without Their Own Households: 1940–1972

The neighborhood

6/16 Satisfaction with Neighborhood: 1971 By Age, Race, Income, and Education

6/17 Personal Assessment of Specific Neighborhood Attributes: 1971

7. Leisure and Recreation

Leisure time
7/1   Daily Use of Time: 1966 By Sex and Occupation
7/2   Daily Use of Leisure Time: 1966 By Sex and Occupation

Outdoor recreation
7/3   Participation in Outdoor Recreation, By Sex: 1970 By Type of Activity
7/4   Participation in Outdoor Recreation, By Sex and Age: 1970
7/5   Participation in Outdoor Recreation, By Region: 1970 By Type of Activity
7/6   Participation in Outdoor Recreation, By Activity: 1970
7/7   Participation in Outdoor Recreation, By Activity and Household Income: 1970

Television viewing
7/8   Television viewing by Households: 1954–1972
7/9   Households with Television Sets: 1950–1972
7/10 Television Viewing, By Sex and Age: November 1970
7/11 Television Viewing, By Household Income and Sex: November 1970

8. Population

Population growth
8/1   Rate of Population Growth: 1910–1972
8/2   Actual and Projected Population: 1900–2020
8/3   Birth and Death Rates: 1900–1972
8/4   Immigration Rate: 1900–1972
8/5   Fertility Rate: 1909–1972 By Race
8/6   Birth Rate, By Age of Mother: 1940–1968
8/7   Average Number of Children Expected: 1955–1972 By Age and Race of Married Women
8/8   Population, By Age and Sex: 1900–1970
8/9   Population, By Age and Race: 1960 and 1970
8/10 Actual and Projected Population, By Age: 1950–2000
8/11 Actual and Projected Population for Selected Ages: 1950–2000

Population distribution
8/12 Population in Urban and Rural Areas: 1900–1970 By Size of Place
8/13 Population in Metropolitan Areas: 1900–1970 By Race
8/14 Population Density By Counties: 1970
8/15 Change in Total Population by Counties: 1960–1970

NATIONAL ECONOMIC INDICATORS   *4.C.2*

Monthly Report Prepared for the Joint Economic Committee by the Council of Economic Advisers

Contents

Total Output, Income, and Spending
  The Nation's Income, Expenditure, and Saving
  Gross National Product or Expenditure
  National Income

Sources of Personal Income
Disposition of Personal Income
Farm Income
Corporate Profits
Gross Private Domestic Investment
Expenditures for New Plant and Equipment
Employment, Unemployment, and Wages
Status of the Labor Force
Selected Measures of Unemployment and Part-Time Employment
Unemployment Insurance Programs
Nonagricultural Employment
Weekly Hours of Work—Selected Industries
Average Hourly and Weekly Earnings—Selected Industries
Production and Business Activity
Industrial Production
Production of Selected Manufactures
Weekly Indicators of Production
New Construction
New Housing Starts and Applications for Financing
Business Sales and Inventories—Total and Trade
Manufacturers' Shipments, Inventories, and New Orders
Merchandise Exports and Imports
U.S. Balances on Goods, Services, and Transfers
U.S. Overall Balances on International Transactions
Prices
Consumer Prices
Wholesale Prices
Prices Received and Paid by Farmers
Money, Credit, and Security Markets
Money Stock
Private Liquid Asset Holdings—Nonfinancial Investors
Bank Loans, Investments, Debits, and Reserves
Consumer and Real Estate Credit
Bond Yields and Interest Rates
Common Stock Prices, Yield, and Earnings
Federal Finance
Federal Budget Receipts and Outlays and Debt
Federal Budget Receipts by Source and Outlays by Function
Federal Sector, National Income Accounts Basis

4.C.3   SOCIAL INDICATORS AT THE STATE LEVEL

The social-indicator movement has not neglected the state level. The U.S. Department of Labor has developed state economic and social indicators. The public welfare load, infant mortality, crime, and educational deficiency are cited as problem areas to provide the clues to social problems requiring social action to resolve. Indicators are presented under education, aid to families with dependent children, infant mortality rates under one year, and crime rates.

The Midwest Research Institute has devised a Social-Economics-Political Scale which measures "the good life" of a state. The S-E-P index is designed to reflect both a state's general economic health and its willingness to provide services essential to continual well-being. The study uses nine areas for measurement.

1. Status of the individual: enhancing personal dignity and widening areas of choice
2. Equality: efforts to end discrimination
3. Democratic process: informed and involved citizenry, good public administration
4. Education: improving quantity and quality of education at all levels
5. Economic growth: public capital investment, improved standard of living, education for a better-trained work force
6. Technological change: research and availability of manpower and facilities for economic growth
7. Agriculture: seeking efficient-size farm sector and helping excess farm workers relocate
8. Living conditions: alleviation of poverty and improvement of decayed urban areas
9. Health and welfare: improving level of welfare assistance, vocational rehabilitation, and provision of good public and private medical services.[1]

California ranks first and Mississippi fiftieth on the S-E-P index.[2]

Notes

1. U.S. Department of Labor, *State Economic and Social Indicators*, Bulletin No. 328 (Washington, D.C.: U.S. Government Printing Office, 1973). $1 per copy.
2. John O. Wilson, *Quality of Life in the United States: An Excursion into the New Frontier of Socio-Economic Indicators* (Kansas City, Mo.: Midwest Research Institute, 1969). An updated and more detailed quality of life study rating the states by Ben-chieh Liu, March 1973, is available from the institute.

SOCIAL INDICATORS AT THE COMMUNITY LEVEL   *4.C.4*

Community social indicators should meet the same criteria as do national and state indicators. They should demonstrate *measureability, tap social importance and shared goals*, have *policy importance*, and *fit into a model* that explicates the most important relationships between the indicator and empirically associated variables.[1]

Clark suggests a focus on policy outputs and policy impact as the two types of phenomena important for an understanding of community dynamics. He indicates that development of community indicators is at an early stage but suggests that policy outputs may be measured by fiscal indicators such as "funds spent for given activities" and by performance indicators such as "tons of refuse collected."

A comparative measure of policy outputs in various communities would allow a community on a relative basis to evaluate the services it is getting.

Policy outputs can be contrasted with *policy impacts*. Policy impacts are "changes resulting in a social system as a consequence of policy outputs." Policy impacts can be considered in terms of these criteria on: (1) citizen preferences, (2) community leader preferences, (3) extra-community actor preferences, (4) professional criteria, and (5) social scientific criteria. Suggestions for indicators are developed in the cited article.

Clark and his co-workers have completed a study of 54 American cities ranking them on 29 fiscal strain indicators. Factors associated with fiscal strain have been identified and policy recommendations have been set forth.[2]

A tested community indicator is an index called Social Vulnerability developed by John C. Maloney, Community Service Council of Metropolitan Indianapolis, Inc. (July 1973).[3] This index was constructed "to measure the relative extent to which persons residing in specified geographic areas of the community were vulnerable to experiencing adverse social and physical strains beyond their ability to cope without help." It consists of eight sufficient but not exhaustive variables determined by factor analysis: (1) median family income, (2) percent of families below poverty level, (3) percent of families with both husband and wife, (4) percent of housing without some or all plumbing facilities, (5) percent of the civilian labor force unemployed, (6) percent of households lacking an available automobile, (7) rate of ambulance runs per 1000 population, and (8) rate of tuberculosis per 1000 population.

This index has identified areas in Marion County "most urgently requiring the investment of both human and capital social resources" in order to mitigate adverse conditions. Scores are available for all census tracts of Marion County. Listing of the scores for each census tract are shown on each of the eight variables listed above.

Notes

1. Terry N. Clark, "Community Social Indicators: From Analytical Models and Policy Applications," *Urban Affairs Quarterly*, September 1973, pp. 5-7. Cf. Peter H. Rossi, "Community Social Indicators," in *The Human Meaning of Social Change*, ed. A. Campbell and P.E.Converse (New York: Russell Sage, 1972), pp. 87-126.

2. Terry N. Clark, Irene S. Rubin, Lynne C. Pettler, and Erwin Zimmerman, "How Many New Yorks? The New York Fiscal Crisis in Comparative Perspective" (Research report No. 72 of the Comparative Study of Community Decision Making, Sociology Department, University of Chicago, Chicago, Ill., 1976).

3. For further information write Research Department, Community Service Council of Metropolitan Indianapolis, Inc., 615 N. Alabama Street, Indianapolis, Ind. 46204.

4.C.5   RANGE OF SOCIAL INDICATORS AND CURRENT DEVELOPMENTS

The number of social indicators that are currently available to measure social trends is large. The potential is huge. Scholars and decision makers vary in the choice of the social areas or facets of society that they believe are important. In the comparative table below, three writers exhibit the social areas in which they suggest a broad range of indicators.

Comparative List of Social Areas with Compilation of Indicators

O. D. Duncan[a]	U.S. Department of Health Education, & Welfare[b]	Raymond A. Bauer[c]
1. Occupational changes	1. Health and illness	1. Population
2. Conditional probabilities for attending college (SES and mental ability)	2. Social mobility	2. Technological advances
	3. Physical environment	3. Education
	4. Income and property	4. Military appropriations
	5. Public order and safety	5. Utilities and transportation
3. Air-pollution index	6. Learning, science and art	6. Governmental growth
4. Incidence of victimization by criminal acts	7. Participation and alienation	7. Natural resources
5. Educational opportunity		8. Welfare
6. Political participation		
7. Voluntary association membership		
8. Tolerance of political dissent		
9. Mental health		
10. Alienation		
11. Time budgets		
12. Income and assets		
13. Value change		
14. Religious affiliation and belief		

[a]Otis Dudley Duncan, *Toward Social Reporting: Next Steps* (New York: Russell Sage Foundation, 1969).
[b]U.S. Department of Health, Education, and Welfare, *Toward a Social Report* (Ann Arbor: University of Michigan Press, 1970).
[c]Raymond A. Bauer, ed., *Social Indicators* (Cambridge, Mass.: MIT Press, 1969).

Current Developments in Social-Indicator Research

IN THE UNITED STATES:

Russell Sage Foundation. This foundation has had a long interest in social indicators as a part of its study on social change. It has supported research on indicators of social trends by developing a general orientation as shown by *Indicators of Social Change: Concepts and Measurements*, edited by Eleanor B. Sheldon and Wilbert E. Moore (1968). A number of specific research volumes published by Russell Sage are listed in the bibliography on social indicators (p. 280).

Social Science Research Council. This is an interdisciplinary organization that maintains several research committees. One of these is the Social Indicators, Advisory and Planning Committee formed in 1972. Under the guidance of this committee is the Center for Coordination of Research on Social Indicators, which has the basic purpose of enhancing social science research in the development of indicators of social change in order to fulfill "current and anticipated demands from both research and policy communities." The major role of the Center is "to identify the best sources for social indicators data and the best work under way, and to direct researchers to those sources." The Center issues a Social Indicators Newsletter on research in the field and is assisting via its library, newsletter, and mailing list in the preparation of a new journal called *Social*

Indicator Research. Communications may be sent to the Center at 1785 Massachusetts Avenue N.W., Washington, D.C. 20036.

The Center has published *Survey Data for Trend Analysis: An Index to Repeated Questions in U. S. National Surveys Held by the Roper Public Opinion Research Center.* The index covers repeated questions in over 4000 U.S. national surveys between 1936 and October 1973 that are archived at the Roper Center. Funded research projects are under way to make use of time-series data for studies of social change. Three projects in progress include Religious Indicators, Public Opinion and Taxes, and Environmental Concern.

National Science Foundation (NSF). The NSF's major role in current activities is the funding of research projects in various social-indicator-oriented areas, such as in developing goals accounting systems, trend analysis of political opinions, and measurement of social and urban indicators. The increased interest in social indicators resulted in the NSF's awarding twenty-two grants in 1971. In 1974 the NSF awarded grants for such things as developing a goals accounting system, comparative study of societal stability, and the funding of a Center for the Coordination of Research on Social Indicators (SSRC).

U.S. Department of Labor. In 1974 the U.S. Department of Labor organized a Working Group on Indicators of the Quality of Employment. This group intends to clarify conceptual issues involved in developing measures of the quality of employment to be used in an accounting system of national social indicators. See the bibliography (p. 279) for published work.

Office of President of the U.S.: Office of Management and Budget. The Office of Management and Budget has issued a publication (1974) called "Social Indicators." A list of indicators was reproduced in this section.

Institute for Social Research, University of Michigan. On a general level, this institute is continuing its interest in social indicators. It has done several studies to measure change including studies of attitudes and values, regarding violence, radical attitudes and behavior, regarding reactions to stress, quality of cities, and changes in people's goals and economic well-being. Note the work of Angus Campbell and associates in bibliography.

Survey Research Center, University of California (Berkeley). This research center, under the direction of J. Merrill Shanks, received an NSF grant in 1971 to do a study called "Toward the Development of Model Social Indicators." The two objectives of this study include: (1) the preparation of a social-indicator model and then research in areas of racial prejudice, political alienation, and the changing role of women in society; and (2) the clarification of common methodological and theoretical problems encountered in social-indicator research. This project is designed to be a five-year program.

Bank of America. In early 1970, this company's Committee on Social Performance Priorities selected minority upgrading, housing, social unrest, and environment as general areas to concentrate its resources for the development of possible future action programs.

General Motors. This corporation has involved itself in societal analysis by organizing a new activity in its Research Laboratories called Societal Analysis Activity. This activity finds its importance in the assessment of the impact of a corporation on society and as a resource base for a number of research topics dealing with society and its analysis.

ON THE INTERNATIONAL LEVEL:

Organization for Economic Cooperation and Development. This is an international program consisting of fifteen member states concerned with developing measurement instruments related to the quality of living across several countries. The program is designed to last several years, looking at such "agreed-upon" primary goal areas as personal health and safety, time and leisure, the physical environment, the social environment, and the political environment.

United Nations Research Institute for Social Development. This institute has been established as a result of government grants from both the United States and the Netherlands. This agency is concerned with studying problems from an international viewpoint not often examined by national universities and institutes. Some of its activity areas are the "quantitative analysis of socio-economic development, methods of decision-making, preparation of the child for economic and technological modernization and measurement of real progress at the local level" (UNRISD, 1971).

SELECTED BIBLIOGRAPHY STRESSING HISTORY, THEORY, AND ROLE OF SOCIAL INDICATORS

4.C.6

BAUER, RAYMOND A., ed. *Social Indicators*. Cambridge, Mass: MIT Press, 1966.
DUNCAN, OTIS DUDLEY. *Toward Social Reporting: Next Steps*. New York: Russell Sage Foundation, 1969.
FOX, KARL A. *Social Indicators and Social Theory, Elements of an Operational System*. New York: John Wiley & Sons, 1974.
LAND, KENNETH C., and SPILERMAN, SEYMOUR, eds. *Social Indicator Models*. New York: Russell Sage Foundation, 1975.
NEUFVILLE, JUDITH INNES DE. *Social Indicators and Public Policy*. New York: Elsevier, 1975.

Bibliography of Special Indicators

BIDERMAN, ALBERT D., and DRURY, THOMAS F., eds. "The Quality of Employment Indicators." *American Behavioral Scientist* 17 (January–February 1975): 299–432.

The volume includes the following papers: "Introduction," Albert D. Biderman; "The Role of Quality Employment Indicators in General Social Reporting Systems," Kenneth C. Land; "Job Satisfaction Indicators and Their Correlates," Stanley E. Seashore and Thomas D. Taber; "Going Beyond Current Income: A Preliminary Appraisal," E. Thomas Juster and Greg Duncan; "Equity Concepts and the World of Work," Lester Thurow; "Evaluating Changes in the Occupational Distribution and the Occupational System," Arthur L. Stinchcombe.

——. *Measuring Work Quality for Social Reporting*. New York: John Wiley & Sons, 1976.

A collection of papers dealing with problems of matching concepts and indicators of work in relation to: health criteria, psychic values, general well-being, life careers, positive and negative aspects of job mobility, social and moral qualities of jobs, responsiveness to workers of employment systems, and the dynamics of the occupational system.

CAMPBELL, ANGUS; CONVERSE, PHILIP E.; and RODGERS, WILLARD L. *The Quality of American Life: Perceptions, Evaluations, and Satisfactions.* New York: Russell Sage Foundation, 1976.

DAVIS, LOUISE E., and CHERNS, ALBERT B. *The Quality of Working Life.* Vol. 1. New York: Free Press, 1975. See especially chapter 2, Defining and Measuring the Overall Quality of Working Life.

FERRISS, ABBOTT L. *Indicators of Trends in American Education; Indicators of Change in the American Family; Indicators of Trends in the Status of American Women.* 3 vols. New York: Russell Sage Foundation, 1970, 1971.

United Nations, *Social Indicators for Housing and Urban Development.* New York: UNIPUB, Box 433, Murray Hill Station. 1973.

A Comprehensive Annotated Bibliography

WILCOX, LESLIE D., et al. *Social Indicators and Societal Monitoring: An Annotated Bibliography.* New York: Elsevier, 1974.

A Specialized Research Journal

Social Indicators Research: An International and Interdisciplinary Journal for Quality of Life Measurement. Established 1974. Editor: Alex C. Michalos. University of Guelph, Department of Philosophy, Guelph, Ontario, Canada. Publisher: D. Reidel Publishing Co., Dordrecht, The Netherlands.

section **D**

Measures of Organizational Structure

There are a number of basic facts about organizational measurement:

1. A very large number of structural attributes and interpersonal relationships exist within the same and different organizations.
2. The development of organizational measurement has come a long way in recent years, but serious shortcomings remain.
3. There is little standardization of the measures used in studying organizations. The lack of standardization hinders the development of organizational theory; it forces the researcher to use a high degree of judgment in selecting an organizational measure.
4. While the measurement and description of structure is an interesting process and exercise in its own right, important research problems are centered about the correlation of various structural arrangements in organizations.
5. Correlates will range from such internal factors as morale and decision making to the impact of structure on external relationships such as cooperative, defensive, and competitive postures vis-à-vis other organizations. Interrelationships of structural relationships themselves reveal a great deal about the character of the organization as a collective unit.
6. Some consensus about the most important structural variables is emerging. These include: Size, Formalization, and Centralization. Whatever else may be of interest, these variables usually cannot be ignored in research designs.
7. There is high interest in many other variables including Absenteeism, Administrative Staff, Alienation, Autonomy, Communication, Complexity, Consensus, Coordination, Dispersion, Distributive Justice, Effectiveness, Innovation, Mechanization, Motivation, Bases of Power, Routinization, Satisfaction, Span of Control, Specialization, and Succession.
8. Two different sets of measures exist to assess many of these variables. One set represents the institutional approach, which relies on documents and informants; the other set relies on the survey approach, which is characterized by the use of questionnaire and interview schedules.
9. The best available guide for the selection of an organizational measure is James L. Price, *Handbook of Organizational Measurement* (Lexington, Mass.:

281

D. C. Heath, 1972). The researcher will save time by using it for immediate reference. For research design, see Victor H. Vroom, ed., *Methods of Organizational Research* (Pittsburgh: University of Pittsburgh Press, 1967), and James D. Thompson, ed., *Approaches to Organizational Design* (Pittsburgh: University of Pittsburgh Press, 1966).

Measures for the three variables believed most important in analyzing correlates between themselves and other variables—*Size, Formalization*, and *Centralization*—are selected and reproduced.

4.D.1   SIZE

DEFINITION: Size is the scale of operations of an organization. A measure of size might be the number of personnel, the amount of assets, and the degree of expenditures. In organizational research, size is generally expressed as the number of employees even though the number of employees is not necessarily the best way to measure the scale of operations. A firm may be quite large, but because of a very high degree of mechanization it may have relatively few personnel. Still, as an operating index the number of employees remains the most common measure.

MEASUREMENT: Advice to a researcher about the measurement of size would be conditioned by the design of the research. Will it involve few or many organizations? Will these organizations be small, intermediate, or large in size? What breakdowns will you need? by department, division, by total organization? What sensitivity about the data may be involved by the nature of the organizations to be studied—health, governmental, industrial, etc. What resources do you have? Only funds to write? or telephone? Funds to make a personal interview?

Organizations do not usually give out information casually. They make some information public as a matter of custom or of law. It is suggested that the data may be available from the last annual report of the organization. Try this first if you need only total employment.

The number of employees for industrial and commercial organizations is found in the following volumes: *Standard and Poor's Register of Corporations, Directors, and Executives* (Dun and Bradstreet): vol. 1, *Million Dollar Directory*, vol. 2, *Middle Market Directory*, and *Moody's Industrial Manuals*.

If not available publicly, a letter, telephone call, or visit should be directed to the industrial relations director or personnel director stating the needs, reasons, and sponsorship of the research. The officials may be able to provide what you need as expressed in department and division breakdown. (Be sure to indicate what you can do with their data that may be useful to them.)

You will probably find that the employment department stores personal records and the payroll department has an official payroll printout. The latter record may be the most accurate. Of course, payrolls (and employment) often fluctuate greatly during the course of the year. It is important to indicate how your computations take this fact into account.

Validity of Size as an Independent Factor in Organization Structuring and Dynamics

A summary of research on size and its correlates is provided by Richard H. Hall in his *Organizations: Structures and Process* (Englewood Cliffs, N.J.: Prentice-Hall, 1972), pp. 112–39. This summary points out that the size factor has led to rather contradictory conclusions in the determination of the form of the organization. There is, however, growing consensus that larger organizations tend to have more specialization, more standardization, and more formalization than smaller organizations. But a lack of relationship between size and the remaining structural dimensions, i.e., concentration of authority and line control of work flows is equally striking. Hall, Haas, and Johnson, using data on seventy-five North American organizations, report on the conclusions of their findings:

> The most immediate implication of these findings is that neither complexity nor formalization can be implied from organizational size. A social scientist conducting research in a large organization would do well to question the frequent assumption that the organization under study is necessarily highly complex and formalized.... He will need to examine empirically, for each organization, the level of complexity and formalization extant at that time.[1]

Pugh and his associates used size as a "contextual variable" relating it to various aspects of organizational structure in forty-six English organizations. Their conclusions are generally supportive of the consensus reported above.[2]

In Hall's review of research on size, conclusions are drawn about correlates with technology, professionalization, work flow, administrative components, the individual, organization, and society. The most important conclusions may be stated:[3]

1. The size factor is greatly modified by the technology or technologies employed by the organization.
2. The administrative component in relation to overall size of the organization displays a curvilinear relationship: the administrative component tends to decrease in size as organizational size increases; however, in very large organizations the relative size of the administrative component again increases with overall size.
3. Large size has an impact on the individuals in the organization. There is more stress, and the depersonalization process can lead to a great deal of discomfort for many members. Negative consequences are partially alleviated by the presence of informal friendship groups found in all organizations.
4. Large size creates difficulties in organizational control, coordination, and communications; at the same time it gives the organization more power over its environment, more resources for planning, and less dependence on particular individuals.
5. The concentration of power in large organizations may concentrate power in the society with threats to democratic processes.

Notes

1. Richard H. Hall, J. Eugene Haas, and Norman J. Johnson, "Organizational Size, Complexity, and Formalization," *American Sociological Review* 32, no. 6 (December 1967): 111.

2. D. S. Pugh, D. J. Hickson, C. R. Hinings, and C. Turner, "The Context of Organizational Structures," *Administrative Science Quarterly* 14, no. 1 (March 1969): 98.

3. Hall et al., "Organizational Size," p. 138.

4.D.2   FORMALIZATION

DEFINITION: Formalization represents the use of rules in an organization. Some organizations carefully describe the specific authority, responsibility, duties, and procedures to be followed in every job and then supervise job occupants to ensure conformity to the job definitions. A penalty system may be spelled out in writing for impartial monitoring of discipline for infractions. Other organizations have loosely defined jobs and do not carefully control work behavior.

The two dimensions of formalization may be specified as job codification, the degree of work standardization; and rule leniency, the measure of the latitude of behavior that is tolerated from standards.

MEASUREMENT: Extensive research on formalization has been done by Aiken and Hage, Richard Hall and his associates, and by Pugh-Hickson and their colleagues. Aiken and Hage have relied on the traditional type of survey. Both Hall and Pugh have relied more on documentary data. Both approaches are recommended, but for economy the Aiken-Hage measure is reproduced.

*Hage and Aiken Formalization Inventory**

The data are collected by means of interviews. Fifteen questions are used.

"I'm going to read a series of statements that may or may not be true for your job in [name of organization]. For each item I read, please answer as it applies to you and your organization; using the answer categories on this card.

1. Definitely true
2. More true than false
3. More false than true
4. Definitely false"

	Definitely true	More true than false	More false than true	Definitely false
1. First, I feel that I am my own boss in most matters.	____	____	____	____
2. A person can make his own decisions here without checking with anybody else.	____	____	____	____
3. How things are done around here is left pretty much up to the person doing the work.	____	____	____	____
4. People here are allowed to do almost as they please.	____	____	____	____

*A minor adaptation has been made by James L. Price. Used with permission.

	Definitely true	More true than false	More false than true	Definitely false
5. Most people here make their own rules on the job.	___	___	___	___
6. The employees are constantly being checked on for rule violations.	___	___	___	___
7. People here feel as though they are constantly being watched to see that they obey all the rules.	___	___	___	___
8. There is no rules manual.	___	___	___	___
9. There is a complete written job description for my job.	___	___	___	___
10. Whatever situation arises, we have procedures to follow in dealing with it.	___	___	___	___
11. Everyone has a specific job to do.	___	___	___	___
12. Going through the proper channels is constantly stressed.	___	___	___	___
13. The organization keeps a written record of everyone's job performance.	___	___	___	___
14. We are to follow strict operating procedures at all times.	___	___	___	___
15. Whenever we have a problem we are supposed to go to the same person for an answer.	___	___	___	___

Computation. The five following measures are constructed from the 15 questions: job codification (questions 1–5), rule observation (questions 6–7), rule manual (question 8), job descriptions (question 9), specificity of job descriptions (questions 10–15). Replies to these 15 questions are scored from 1 (definitely true) to 4 (definitely false). A mean is constructed for each respondent for each of the five measures of formalization. The higher the mean (4 is the highest mean), the higher the formalization. The researchers report no ranges for the means of the five measures. Each respondent is then classified by "social position," and based on the first mean, a second mean is computed for each social position in the organization for each of the five measures. A social position is defined by the level or stratum in the organization, and the department or type of professional activity. For example, if an agency's professional staff consists of psychiatrists and social workers, each divided into the hierarchical levels, the agency has four social positions: supervisory psychiatrists, psychiatrists, supervisory social workers, and social workers. The organizational scores for each of the five measures are determined by computing an average of all social position means in the organization.

WHERE PUBLISHED: Michael Aiken and Jerald Hage, "Organizational Alienation," *American Sociological Review* 31 (August 1966): 497–507. Scale and data on reliability and validity reproduced in James L. Price, *Handbook of Organizational Measurement* (Lexington, Mass.: D.C. Heath, 1972) pp. 108–11.

RELIABILITY: The study contains no data relevant to reliability.

VALIDITY: Formalization is positively related to alienation. The greater the degree of formalization in the organization, the greater the likelihood of alienation from work. There is great dissatisfaction with work in those organizations in which jobs are rigidly structured. Strict enforcement of rules was strongly related to work dissatisfaction; social relations are also disturbed when rules are strictly enforced. Significant positive relationships are found between routine work and rule manual, job description, and specificity of job descriptions.

UTILITY: The interview can be conducted in less than five minutes in most cases.

RESEARCH APPLICATIONS:
AIKEN, MICHAEL, and HAGE, JERALD. "Organizational Alienation." *American Sociological Review* 31 (August 1966): 497–507.
HAGE, JERALD, and AIKEN, MICHAEL. "Program Change and Organizational Properties." *American Journal of Sociology* 72 (March 1967): 503–19.
———. "Relationship of Centralization to Other Structural Properties." *Administrative Science Quarterly* 12 (June 1967): 72–92.
———. *Social Change in Complex Organizations.* New York: Random House, 1970.

DOCUMENTARY MEASURES OF FORMALIZATION:
The measures developed by Hall and his associates may be found in Richard H. Hall, J. Eugene Haas, and Norman J. Johnson, "Organizational Size, Complexity, and Formalization," *American Sociological Review* 32, no. 6 (December 1967).

The measures developed by Inkson, Pugh, and Hickson may be found in J. H. K. Inkson, D. S. Pugh, and D. J. Hickson, "Organization Context and Structure: An Abbreviated Replication," *Administrative Science Quarterly* 15 (September 1970): 318–29. The measure and data on reliability and validity are reproduced in James L. Price, *Handbook of Organizational Measurement* (Lexington, Mass.: D. C. Heath, 1972), pp. 111–15.

The serious researcher will examine each of these excellent measures and choose the one that best fits his research design.

4.D.3   CENTRALIZATION

DEFINITION: Centralization is the degree to which power is concentrated in an organization.

Power is an important component in every type of organization. The distribution of power has major consequences for the performance of an organization and the behavior of its members.

An important consideration in dealing with power is the manner in which it is distributed. The maximum degree of centralization would exist if all power were exercised by a single individual; the minimum degree of centralization would exist if all power were exercised equally by all members of the organization. Most organizations fall between these two extremes.

Various problems are generated by the degree of centralized power and the manner in which actors wield their power and influence over superordinate, coordinate, and subordinate members of the organization. The following topics are commonly generated by problems of power stratification: participation-management, industrial democracy, group decision making, employee representation, collective bargaining, alienation, and organizational conflict.

MEASUREMENT: As with most measures, centralization may be assessed by the institutional approach using documents and informants or by the use of the survey approach with questionnaires and interview schedules as the principal instruments.

Pugh and his associates rely on data that are obtained by interviewing one or a few top executives and from documents which organizations (24 manufacturing and 16 services) made available to the researchers. Aiken and Hage collected all their data on centralization by interviewing executive directors, department heads, and staff members in 16 social welfare and health organizations.

Johannes Pennings has submitted the measures used by these researchers to validity tests. He contrasts the two research approaches as shown below:

Institutional approach

A_1. Centralization

    Autonomy: This scale consists of 23 issues to measure whether decisions on these issues are made inside or outside the organization (Pugh et al. 1968, pp. 102–4).

    Chief executive span of control: This indicates the number of subordinates who report directly to the chief executive, regardless of the hierarchical position of the subordinates (Pugh et al. 1968, p. 104).

    Worker/supervisory ratio: This value indicates the number of subordinates in production departments per first-line supervisor (Pugh et al. 1968, p. 104).

    Number of direct supervisors (%): This indicates the number of first-line supervisors in production departments, including the assistants and deputies (Pugh et al. 1968, p. 104).

Questionnaire approach

A_2. Centralization

    Personal participation in decision making: This is a Likert scale measuring how much the individual participates in decisions about the allocation of resources and the determination of organizational policies (Hage and Aiken 1967, p. 78).

    Hierarchy of authority: This scale measures the degree to which the organization member participates in decisions involving the tasks associated with his position (Hage and Aiken 1967, pp. 78–79).

    Departmental participation in decision making: This Likert scale measures how much an individual "and his colleagues" participate in decisions involving their work and work environment (personal communication).[1]

The organizational researcher should examine these measures carefully in choosing those most suitable to his design. Again for economy, only Aiken and Hage's scales of *personal participation in decision making and hierarchy of authority* are reproduced.

Aiken and Hage Scale of Personal Participation in Decision Making and Hierarchy of Authority*

The questions for the index of actual participation are as follows:

1. How frequently do you usually participate in the decision to hire new staff?

        ____ Never   ____ Often
        ____ Seldom   ____ Always
        ____ Sometimes

2. How frequently do you usually participate in the decisions on the promotion of any of the professional staff?
3. How frequently do you participate in decisions on the adoptions of new policies?
4. How frequently do you participate in the decisions on the adoptions of new programs?

The questions for the scale of hierarchy of authority are as follows:

1. There can be little action taken here until a supervisor approves a decision.

        ____ Definitely false   ____ True
        ____ False   ____ Definitely true

2. A person who wants to make his or her own decisions would be quickly discouraged here.
3. Even small matters have to be referred to someone higher up for a final decision.
4. I have to ask my boss before I do almost anything.
5. Any decision I make has to have my boss' approval.

COMPUTATION: The computations differ for the two types of decisions. For the index of actual participation, the five responses are assigned numbers from 1 (low participation) to 5 (high participation). A "Never" response receives 1; at the other extreme, an "Always" response receives 5. An average score on these five questions is computed for each respondent. Each respondent is then classified by "social position" and a second mean computed for each social position in the organization. "A social position," according to Aiken and Hage, "is defined by the level or stratum in the organization and the department or type of professional activity. For example, if an agency's professional staff consists of psychiatrists and social workers, each divided into two hierarchical levels, the agency has four social positions: supervisory psychiatrists, psychiatrists, supervisory social workers, and social workers." The organizational score is determined by computing the average of all social position means in the organization.

Computations for the hierarchy of authority scale are similar to those for the index of actual participation. The responses are assigned numbers from 1 (definitely false) to 4 (definitely true). As with the index of actual participation, the organizational score for the hierarchy of authority scale is based on social position means which in turn are based on the means for each respondent.

*Used with permission.

WHERE PUBLISHED: M. Aiken and J. Hage, "Organizational Interdependence and Intraorganizational Structure," *American Sociological Review* 33, no. 6 (1968): 912-30. Scales are described in footnotes 6 and 7, p. 924. For measures used by Pugh and associates, see D. S. Pugh, D. J. Hickson, C. R. Hinings, and C Turner, "Dimensions of Organization Structure," *Administrative Science Quarterly* 13, no. 1 (1968): 65-105; J. H. K. Inkson, D. S. Pugh, and D. J. Hickson, "Organization Context and Structure: A Replication Study," *Administrative Science Quarterly* 15, no. 3 (1970): 318-29.

RELIABILITY: No relevant data provided by Aiken and Hage.

VALIDITY: Organizations in which the decisions were made by only a few people at the top relied on rules and close supervision as a means of ensuring consistent performance by the workers. These organizations were also characterized by a less professional staff. The presence of a well-trained staff is related to a reduced need for extensive rules. Penning reports that organizations that are highly autonomous tend to have a nonparticipative internal decision structure. The greater the autonomy, the larger the executive's span of control.

RESEARCH APPLICATIONS:

AIKEN, MICHAEL, and HAGE, JERALD. "Organizational Alienation." *American Sociological Review* 31 (August 1966): 497-507.

HAGE, JERALD, and AIKEN, MICHAEL. "Program Change and Organizational Properties." *American Journal of Sociology* 72 (March 1967): 503-19.

———. "Relationship of Centralization to Other Structural Properties." *Administrative Science Quarterly* 12 (June 1967): 72-92.

———. *Social Change in Complex Organization.* New York: Random House, 1970.

HALL, RICHARD H. "An Empirical Study of Bureaucratic Dimensions and Their Relation to Other Organizational Characteristics." Ph.D. dissertation, Columbus, The Ohio State University, 1961.

———. "The Concept of Bureaucracy: An Empirical Assessment." *American Journal of Sociology* 69 (July 1963): 32-40.

SMITH, CLAGETT G., and TANNENBAUM, ARNOLD S. "Organization Control Structure: A Comparative Analysis." *Human Relations* 16 (1963): 299-316. For a critique of the Tannenbaum Organizational Control Questionnaire see Lake, Miles, and Earle, Jr., *Measuring Human Behavior.* New York: Teachers College Press, 1973. Pp. 214-19.

Notes

1. Johannes Pennings, "Measures of Organizational Structures: A Methodological Note," *American Journal of Sociology* 79, no. 3 (November 1973): 688-89.

Evaluation Research and Organizational Effectiveness

EVALUATION RESEARCH AS A PROCESS

Every attempt to reduce or eliminate a social problem involves a theory, a program, and usually a large amount of money. The effectiveness of programs to reduce crime and delinquency, combat drug addiction, conquer health problems, improve neighborhoods and communities and the quality of life generally—all pose problems of evaluation. Because these problems are so important to national and community life and are so costly, evaluation has been given a high priority and evaluation research is increasing.

Edward Suchman wrote:

> It may be helpful to visualize the evaluation process as a circular one, stemming from and returning to the formation of values, as shown in figure 1.*

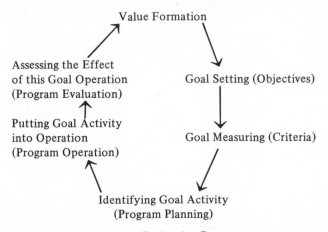

Figure 1. Evaluation Process

Evaluation always starts with some value, either explicit or implicit—for example, it is good to live a long time; then a goal is formulated derived from this value. The selection of goals is usually preceded by or concurrent with *"value formation."* An example of *"goal-setting"* would be the statement that fewer people should develop coronary disease, or that not so many people should die from cancer. Goal-setting forces are always in competition with each other for money, resources, and effort.

There next has to be some way of *"measuring goal attainment."* If we set as our goal that fewer people should die from cancer, then we need some means of discovering how many are presently dying from cancer (for example, vital statistics). The nature of the evaluation will depend largely on the type of measure we have available to determine the attainment of our objective.

The next step in the process is the identification of some kind of *"goal-attaining activity."* In the case of cancer, for example, a program of cancer-detecting activities aimed at early detection and treatment might be considered. Then the goal-attaining activity is put into operation. Diagnostic centers are set up and people urged to come in for check-ups.

Then, at some point, we have the *assessment* of this goal-directed operation. This stage includes the evaluation of the degree to which the operating program has achieved the predetermined objectives. As stated previously, this assessment may be scientifically done or it may not.

Finally, on the basis of the assessment, a *judgment* is made as to whether the goal-directed activity was worthwhile. This brings us back to value formation. Someone now may say that it is "good" to have cancer diagnostic centers. At the end of the evaluation process, we may get a new value, or we may reaffirm, reassess, or redefine an old value. For example, if the old value was "It is good to live a long time," the new value might be, "It is good to live until 100 if you remain healthy; but if you can't remain healthy it's better not to live past eighty."

In actuality, when the evaluation process begins, activities may be, and usually are, already going on. The evaluator may come in at any point. A crucial question in evaluative research is, "What do we mean by a successful result?" All programs will have some effects, but how do we measure these effects and how do we determine whether they are the particular effects we are interested in producing? As in the case of the independent program variables, we note a multiplicity and interdependence of effect variables. Again, our main problem is one of selecting from among the myriad of possible effects, those most relevant to our objectives.

We have already noted five major criteria for determining relevance: (1) effort or activity; (2) performance or accomplishment; (3) adequacy or impact; (4) efficiency or output relative to input; and (5) process or specification of conditions of effectiveness. In a sense we may classify the first two criteria as *evaluative*, that is, concerned with the determination of the relationship between activities and effects; the second two as *administrative*, dealing with a judgment about the size and cost of the effort relative to the effects; while the last one is really a *research* criterion, concerned with increased knowledge or understanding irrespective of effect.

Indices for the first two, effort and performance, are likely to be defined by the public service worker in terms of professional standards; the next two, adequacy and efficiency, are more likely to be determined by the administrator in terms of basic knowledge. To a large extent, the formulation of the objectives and design of an evaluative research project will depend upon who is conducting the project and what use will be made of the results.

EFFECTIVENESS INDICES AS EVALUATIVE RESEARCH CRITERIA

Effectiveness may be defined as the degree to which a social system achieves its goals. For example, a drug addiction center that has a therapeutic goal that successfully reduces addiction in a high proportion of its treatment population would be considered an effective center.

Effectiveness must be distinguished from efficiency. Efficiency is mainly concerned with cost relative to output. Effectiveness is directly concerned with goal attainments. The social researcher may be asked to make a cost/benefit analysis but such a request would be supplementary to any effectiveness assessment.

Organizational effectiveness is the task best performed by sociological or social-psychological researchers. Economists are best prepared to provide cost/benefit analyses.

The organizational goals most commonly set by their leaders are high productivity and employee will to work. How these goals are translated within different organizations varies greatly. Organizations functioning in the market sector must achieve a level of productivity sufficient to maintain profitability. Those private and public organizations that dispense services must maintain a level of efficiency that continues to attract funds from their contributors (donors or taxpayers). In all cases the quality of the good or service must satisfy the needs of the consumer.

A general appraisal of an organization is based on some concept of the interaction of employees with the organization. The most commonly accepted assumption is that effective teamwork is related to productivity and morale and that both goals should be appraised. Two superior efforts are represented in Rensis Likert, *The Human Organization* (New York: McGraw-Hill, 1967) and E. Wight Bakke, *Bonds of Organization* (New York: Harper & Row, 1950).

Likert describes many years of research conducted at the Institute of Social Research of the University of Michigan on the effect of performance of four management systems. He calls these (1) exploitive-authoritative, (2) benevolent-authoritative, (3) consultative, and (4) participative group. Each refers to a cluster of motivating and decision-making beliefs and behaviors. He demonstrates that as management systems move from (1) to (4), they demonstrate higher productivity, lower costs, more favorable attitudes, and excellent labor relations.

Bakke, in his appraisal of effective teamwork, assesses the adequacy of five elements that he regards as most important in achieving high productivity and will to work. They are *functional specifications*, which weld men together as partners in production; *the status system*, as directors and directed employees; *the communication system*, as givers and receivers of information; *the reward and penalty system*, as agents of reward and penalty; *the organizational charter*, as sharers of a conception of the organization as a whole.

The researcher seeking general criteria for assessment of organizational effectiveness will find yardsticks in both these books that may be applied to almost any organization, private or public. Likert's Profile of Organizational Characteristics is reproduced in section 4.E.1. It is a well-tested set of rating scales that may be applied to probe the motivating facets of the relevant organizational variables. Productivity measures themselves must usually be devised by operating officials in the given organization. Appraisals have been conducted in many different kinds of organizations: hospitals, schools, government agencies, banks, voluntary organizations, and the like. Special criteria have been formulated to deal with the different qualities of these organizations. A selected bibliography is appended to provide suggestions to the researcher.

Researchers may wish to compare the Profile of Organizational Characteristics with the *Survey of Organizations* by James C. Taylor and David G. Bowers (Ann Arbor: Institute of Social Research, University of Michigan, 1974). This is a machine-scored questionnaire that taps certain critical dimensions of organizational climate, managerial leadership, peer behavior, group processes, and satisfaction. The manual traces the origin, concepts, development, methodology, and administrative procedure of the survey. The 1970 questionnaire is composed of 92 items, about half of which probe attitudes using the Likert scale response set. The items are drawn from numerous studies made at the Institute including many from the Profile of Organizational Characteristics. The survey has been administered to more than 20,000 respondents in many different organizations. It takes from 30 to 45 minutes to complete. Numerous tests of reliability and validity are reported. For further information, write Organizational Development Research Program, Institute for Social Research, P.O. Box 1248, Ann Arbor, Mich. 48106.

The Profile of Organizational Characteristics on pages 293-301 is a set of rating scales used in interviewing managers in the organization. They are applicable for any group of supervisory heads in any organization. The form can be used to measure the management system of any unit within an organization, as well as that of the total organization.

Data gathered by the researcher through observation and records may be assembled, if desired, to validate further the dominant system of the organization as exploitive-authoritative, benevolent-authoritative, consultative, or participative group. Likert has prepared a chart of the Organizational and Performance Characteristics of Different Management Systems Based on a Comparative Analysis (see *The Human Organization*, pp. 14-24; or see Rensis Likert, *New Patterns of Management* [New York: McGraw-Hill, 1961]). Responses to the profile indicate that leadership styles and related organizational characteristics display a remarkably consistent set of interrelationships. In Appendix I of *The Human Organization*, Pearsonian coefficients of correlation are shown that measure the extent to which answers to one item are consistent with answers to the other. Apart from the performance items, all correlations between an item and the total score are greater than +.73. (For the validation of the high relationship between productivity and the consultative and participative group systems, see the results reported on the Weldon Plant, Plant L, and Company H. For an excellent critique, see Dale G. Lake et al., *Measuring Human Behavior* (New York: Teachers College Press, 1973), pp. 262-64.

PROFILE OF ORGANIZATIONAL CHARACTERISTICS*   *4.E.1*

Instructions (for managers to be interviewed)

1. On the lines below each organizational variable (item), please place an *n* at the point which, *in your experience*, describes your organization at the present time (*n* = now). Treat each item as a continuous variable from the extreme at one end to that at the other.

2. In addition, if you have been in your organization one or more years, please also place a *p* on each line at the point which, *in your experience*, describes your organization as it was one to two years ago (*p* = previously).
3. If you were not in your organization one or more years ago, please check here _____ and answer as of the present time, i.e., answer only with an *n*.

Organizational variable					Item no.
1. Leadership processes used					
a. Extent to which superiors have confidence and trust in *subordinates*	Have no confidence and trust in subordinates	Have condescending confidence and trust, such as master has in servant	Substantial but not complete confidence and trust; still wishes to keep control of decisions	Complete confidence and trust in all matters	
	├──┴──┴──┴──┼──┴──┴──┴──┼──┴──┴──┴──┼──┴──┴──┴──┤				1
b. Extent to which subordinates, in turn, have confidence and trust in *superiors*	Have no confidence and trust in superiors	Have subservient confidence and trust, such as servant has to master	Substantial but not complete confidence and trust	Complete confidence and trust	
	├──┴──┴──┴──┼──┴──┴──┴──┼──┴──┴──┴──┼──┴──┴──┴──┤				2
c. Extent to which superiors display supportive behavior toward others	Display no supportive behavior or virtually none	Display supportive behavior in condescending manner and situations only	Display supportive behavior quite generally	Display supportive behavior fully and in all situations	
	├──┴──┴──┴──┼──┴──┴──┴──┼──┴──┴──┴──┼──┴──┴──┴──┤				3
d. Extent to which superiors behave so that subordinates feel free to discuss important things about their jobs with their immediate superior	Subordinates feel completely free to discuss things about the job with their superior	Subordinates feel rather free to discuss things about the job with their superior	Subordinates do not feel very free to discuss things about the job with their superior	Subordinates do not feel at all free to discuss things about the job with their superior	
	├──┴──┴──┴──┼──┴──┴──┴──┼──┴──┴──┴──┼──┴──┴──┴──┤				4
e. Extent to which immediate superior in solving job problems generally tries to get subordinates' ideas and opinions and makes constructive use of them	Always gets ideas and opinions and always tries to make constructive use of them	Usually gets ideas and opinions and usually tries to make constructive use of them	Sometimes gets ideas and opinions of subordinates in solving job problems	Seldom gets ideas and opinions of subordinates in solving job problems	
	├──┴──┴──┴──┼──┴──┴──┴──┼──┴──┴──┴──┼──┴──┴──┴──┤				5
2. Character of motivational forces					
a. Underlying motives tapped	Physical security, economic needs, and some use of the desire for status	Economic needs and moderate use of ego motives, e.g., desire for status, affiliation, and achievement	Economic needs and considerable use of ego and other major motives, e.g., desire for new experiences	Full use of economic, ego, and other major motives, as, for example, motivational forces arising from group goals	
	├──┴──┴──┴──┼──┴──┴──┴──┼──┴──┴──┴──┼──┴──┴──┴──┤				6
b. Manner in which motives are used	Fear, threats, punishment, and occasional rewards	Rewards and some actual or potential punishment	Rewards, occasional punishment, and some involvement	Economic rewards based on compensation system developed through participation; group participation and involvement in setting goals, improving methods,	

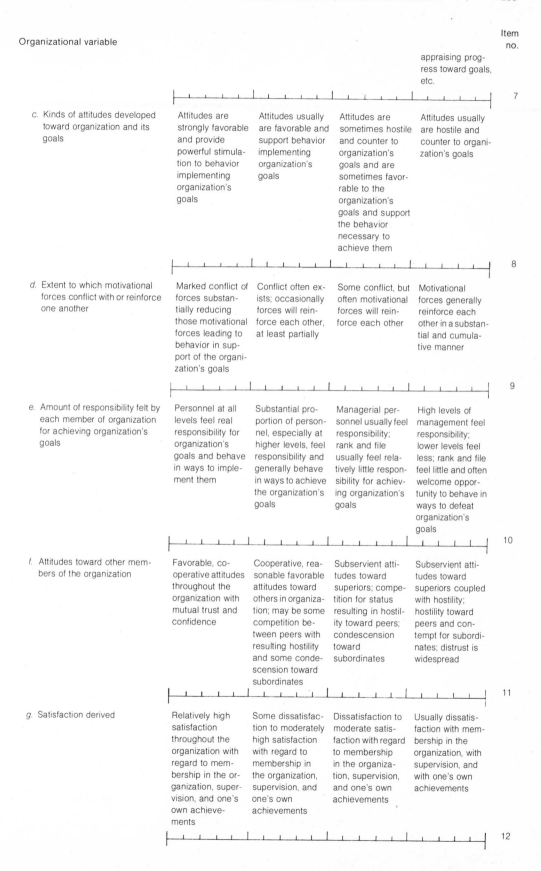

Organizational variable					Item no.
				appraising progress toward goals, etc.	7
c. Kinds of attitudes developed toward organization and its goals	Attitudes are strongly favorable and provide powerful stimulation to behavior implementing organization's goals	Attitudes usually are favorable and support behavior implementing organization's goals	Attitudes are sometimes hostile and counter to organization's goals and are sometimes favorable to the organization's goals and support the behavior necessary to achieve them	Attitudes usually are hostile and counter to organization's goals	8
d. Extent to which motivational forces conflict with or reinforce one another	Marked conflict of forces substantially reducing those motivational forces leading to behavior in support of the organization's goals	Conflict often exists; occasionally forces will reinforce each other, at least partially	Some conflict, but often motivational forces will reinforce each other	Motivational forces generally reinforce each other in a substantial and cumulative manner	9
e. Amount of responsibility felt by each member of organization for achieving organization's goals	Personnel at all levels feel real responsibility for organization's goals and behave in ways to implement them	Substantial proportion of personnel, especially at higher levels, feel responsibility and generally behave in ways to achieve the organization's goals	Managerial personnel usually feel responsibility; rank and file usually feel relatively little responsibility for achieving organization's goals	High levels of management feel responsibility; lower levels feel less; rank and file feel little and often welcome opportunity to behave in ways to defeat organization's goals	10
f. Attitudes toward other members of the organization	Favorable, cooperative attitudes throughout the organization with mutual trust and confidence	Cooperative, reasonable favorable attitudes toward others in organization; may be some competition between peers with resulting hostility and some condescension toward subordinates	Subservient attitudes toward superiors; competition for status resulting in hostility toward peers; condescension toward subordinates	Subservient attitudes toward superiors coupled with hostility; hostility toward peers and contempt for subordinates; distrust is widespread	11
g. Satisfaction derived	Relatively high satisfaction throughout the organization with regard to membership in the organization, supervision, and one's own achievements	Some dissatisfaction to moderately high satisfaction with regard to membership in the organization, supervision, and one's own achievements	Dissatisfaction to moderate satisfaction with regard to membership in the organization, supervision, and one's own achievements	Usually dissatisfaction with membership in the organization, with supervision, and with one's own achievements	12

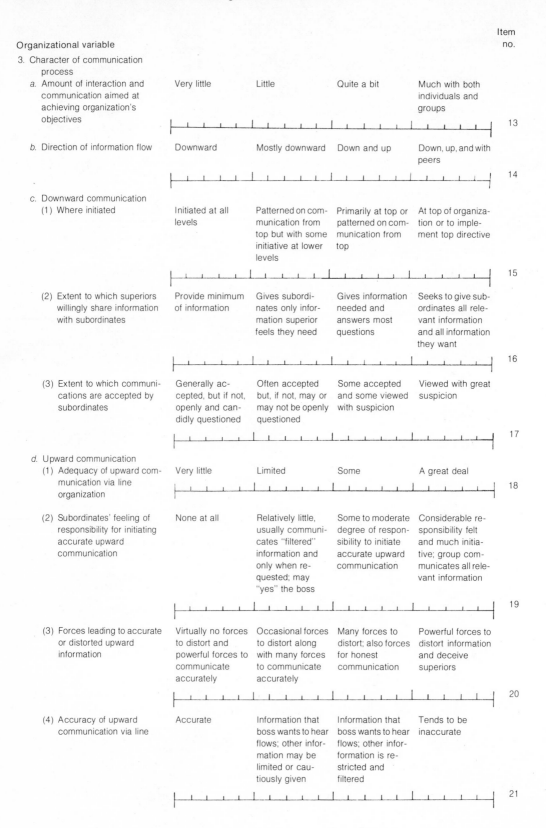

Organizational variable

Item no.

3. Character of communication process

a. Amount of interaction and communication aimed at achieving organization's objectives

Very little · Little · Quite a bit · Much with both individuals and groups

13

b. Direction of information flow

Downward · Mostly downward · Down and up · Down, up, and with peers

14

c. Downward communication

(1) Where initiated

Initiated at all levels · Patterned on communication from top but with some initiative at lower levels · Primarily at top or patterned on communication from top · At top of organization or to implement top directive

15

(2) Extent to which superiors willingly share information with subordinates

Provide minimum of information · Gives subordinates only information superior feels they need · Gives information needed and answers most questions · Seeks to give subordinates all relevant information and all information they want

16

(3) Extent to which communications are accepted by subordinates

Generally accepted, but if not, openly and candidly questioned · Often accepted but, if not, may or may not be openly questioned · Some accepted and some viewed with suspicion · Viewed with great suspicion

17

d. Upward communication

(1) Adequacy of upward communication via line organization

Very little · Limited · Some · A great deal

18

(2) Subordinates' feeling of responsibility for initiating accurate upward communication

None at all · Relatively little, usually communicates "filtered" information and only when requested; may "yes" the boss · Some to moderate degree of responsibility to initiate accurate upward communication · Considerable responsibility felt and much initiative; group communicates all relevant information

19

(3) Forces leading to accurate or distorted upward information

Virtually no forces to distort and powerful forces to communicate accurately · Occasional forces to distort along with many forces to communicate accurately · Many forces to distort; also forces for honest communication · Powerful forces to distort information and deceive superiors

20

(4) Accuracy of upward communication via line

Accurate · Information that boss wants to hear flows; other information may be limited or cautiously given · Information that boss wants to hear flows; other information is restricted and filtered · Tends to be inaccurate

21

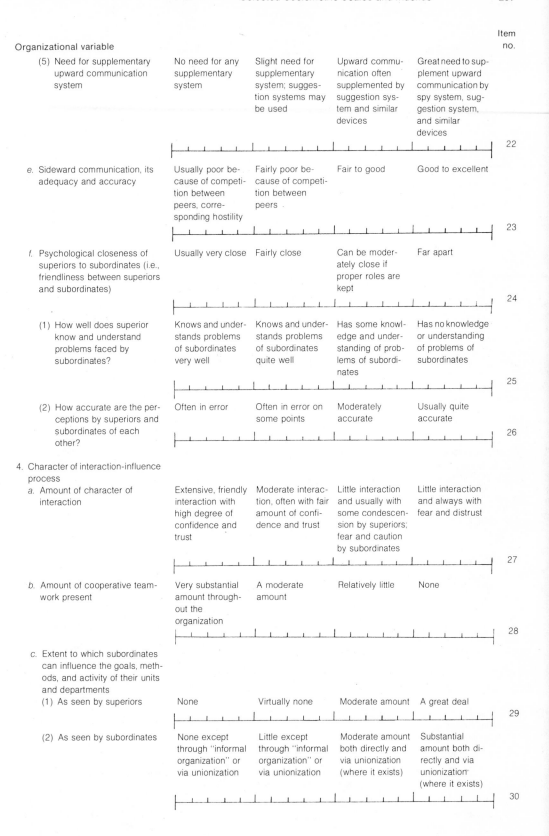

Organizational variable					Item no.
(5) Need for supplementary upward communication system	No need for any supplementary system	Slight need for supplementary system; suggestion systems may be used	Upward communication often supplemented by suggestion system and similar devices	Great need to supplement upward communication by spy system, suggestion system, and similar devices	22
e. Sideward communication, its adequacy and accuracy	Usually poor because of competition between peers, corresponding hostility	Fairly poor because of competition between peers	Fair to good	Good to excellent	23
f. Psychological closeness of superiors to subordinates (i.e., friendliness between superiors and subordinates)	Usually very close	Fairly close	Can be moderately close if proper roles are kept	Far apart	24
(1) How well does superior know and understand problems faced by subordinates?	Knows and understands problems of subordinates very well	Knows and understands problems of subordinates quite well	Has some knowledge and understanding of problems of subordinates	Has no knowledge or understanding of problems of subordinates	25
(2) How accurate are the perceptions by superiors and subordinates of each other?	Often in error	Often in error on some points	Moderately accurate	Usually quite accurate	26
4. Character of interaction-influence process					
a. Amount of character of interaction	Extensive, friendly interaction with high degree of confidence and trust	Moderate interaction, often with fair amount of confidence and trust	Little interaction and usually with some condescension by superiors; fear and caution by subordinates	Little interaction and always with fear and distrust	27
b. Amount of cooperative teamwork present	Very substantial amount throughout the organization	A moderate amount	Relatively little	None	28
c. Extent to which subordinates can influence the goals, methods, and activity of their units and departments					
(1) As seen by superiors	None	Virtually none	Moderate amount	A great deal	29
(2) As seen by subordinates	None except through "informal organization" or via unionization	Little except through "informal organization" or via unionization	Moderate amount both directly and via unionization (where it exists)	Substantial amount both directly and via unionization (where it exists)	30

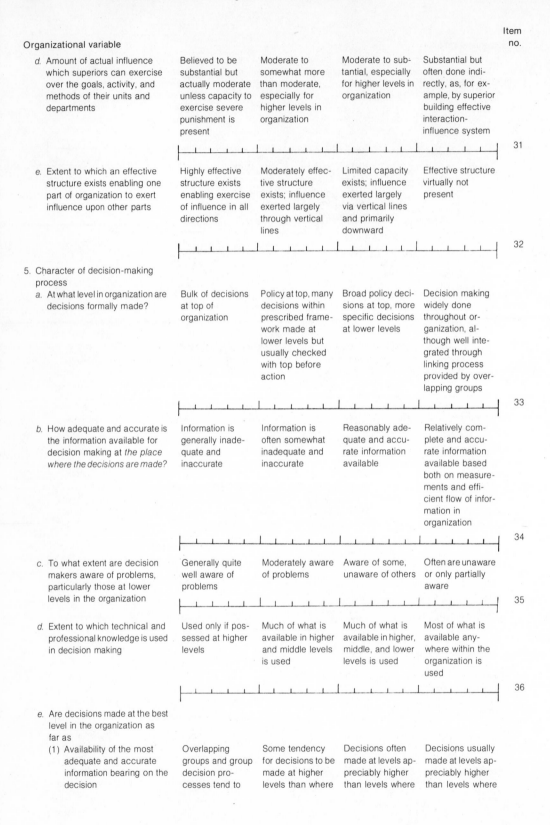

Item no.

Organizational variable

d. Amount of actual influence which superiors can exercise over the goals, activity, and methods of their units and departments

Believed to be substantial but actually moderate unless capacity to exercise severe punishment is present

Moderate to somewhat more than moderate, especially for higher levels in organization

Moderate to sub- tantial, especially for higher levels in organization

Substantial but often done indi- rectly, as, for ex- ample, by superior building effective interaction- influence system

31

e. Extent to which an effective structure exists enabling one part of organization to exert influence upon other parts

Highly effective structure exists enabling exercise of influence in all directions

Moderately effec- tive structure exists; influence exerted largely through vertical lines

Limited capacity exists; influence exerted largely via vertical lines and primarily downward

Effective structure virtually not present

32

5. Character of decision-making process

a. At what level in organization are decisions formally made?

Bulk of decisions at top of organization

Policy at top, many decisions within prescribed frame- work made at lower levels but usually checked with top before action

Broad policy deci- sions at top, more specific decisions at lower levels

Decision making widely done throughout or- ganization, al- though well inte- grated through linking process provided by over- lapping groups

33

b. How adequate and accurate is the information available for decision making at *the place where the decisions are made?*

Information is generally inade- quate and inaccurate

Information is often somewhat inadequate and inaccurate

Reasonably ade- quate and accu- rate information available

Relatively com- plete and accu- rate information available based both on measure- ments and effi- cient flow of infor- mation in organization

34

c. To what extent are decision makers aware of problems, particularly those at lower levels in the organization

Generally quite well aware of problems

Moderately aware of problems

Aware of some, unaware of others

Often are unaware or only partially aware

35

d. Extent to which technical and professional knowledge is used in decision making

Used only if pos- sessed at higher levels

Much of what is available in higher and middle levels is used

Much of what is available in higher, middle, and lower levels is used

Most of what is available any- where within the organization is used

36

e. Are decisions made at the best level in the organization as far as
   (1) Availability of the most adequate and accurate information bearing on the decision

Overlapping groups and group decision pro- cesses tend to

Some tendency for decisions to be made at higher levels than where

Decisions often made at levels ap- preciably higher than levels where

Decisions usually made at levels ap- preciably higher than levels where

Organizational variable					Item no.
	push decisions to point where information is most adequate or to pass the relevant information to the decision-making point	most adequate and accurate information exists	most adequate and accurate information exists	most adequate and accurate information exists	
					37
(2) The motivational consequences (i.e., does the decision-making process help to create the necessary motivations in those persons who have to carry out the decision?)	Substantial contribution by decision-making processes to motivation to implement	Some contribution by decision making to motivation to implement	Decision making contributes relatively little motivation	Decision making contributes little or nothing to the motivation to implement the decision, usually yields adverse motivation	
					38
f. To what extent are subordinates involved in decisions related to their work?	Not at all	Never involved in decisions; occasionally consulted	Usually are consulted but ordinarily not involved in the decision making	Are involved fully in all decisions related to their work	
					39
g. Is decision making based on man-to-man or group pattern of operation? Does it encourage or discourage teamwork?	Man-to-man only, discourages teamwork	Man-to-man almost entirely, discourages teamwork	Both man-to-man and group, partially encourages teamwork	Largely based on group pattern, encourages teamwork	
					40
6. Character of goal setting or ordering a. Manner in which usually done	Except in emergencies, goals are usually established by means of group participation	Goals are set or orders issued after discussion with subordinates of problems and planned action	Orders issued, opportunity to comment may or may not exist	Orders issued	
					41
b. To what extent do the different hierarchial levels tend to strive for high performance goals?	High goals sought by all levels, with lower levels sometimes pressing for higher goals than top levels	High goals sought by higher levels but with occasional resistance by lower levels	High goals sought by top and often resisted moderately by subordinates	High goals pressed by top, generally resisted by subordinates	
					42
c. Are there forces to accept, resist, or reject goals?	Goals are overtly accepted but are covertly resisted strongly	Goals are overtly accepted but often covertly resisted to at least a moderate degree	Goals are overtly accepted but at times with some covert resistance	Goals are fully accepted both overtly and covertly	
					43

Organizational variable					Item no.
7. Character of control processes					
a. At what hierarchial levels in organization does major or primary concern exist with regard to the performance of the control function?	At the very top only	Primarily or largely at the top	Primarily at the top but some shared feeling of responsibility felt at middle and to a lesser extent at lower levels	Concern for performance of control functions likely to be felt throughout organization	
					44
b. How accurate are the measurements and information used to guide and perform the control function, and to what extent do forces exist in the organization to distort and falsify this information?	Strong pressures to obtain complete and accurate information to guide own behavior and behavior of own and related work groups; hence information and measurements tend to be complete and accurate	Some pressure to protect self and colleagues and hence some pressures to distort; information is only moderately complete and contains some inaccuracies	Fairly strong forces exist to distort and falsify; hence measurements and information are often incomplete and inaccurate	Very strong forces exist to distort and falsify; as a consequence, measurements and information are usually incomplete and often inaccurate	
					45
c. Extent to which the review and control functions are concentrated	Highly concentrated in top management	Relatively highly concentrated, with some delegated control to middle and lower levels	Moderate downward delegation of review and control processes; lower as well as higher levels perform these tasks	Review and control done at all levels with lower units at times imposing more vigorous reviews and tighter controls than top management	
					46
d. Extent to which there is an informal organization present and supporting or opposing goals of formal organization	Informal organization present and opposing goals of formal organization	Informal organization usually present and partially resisting goals	Informal organization may be present and may either support or partially resist goals of formal organization	Informal and formal organization are one and the same; hence all social forces support efforts to achieve organization's goals	
					47
e. Extent to which control data (e.g., accounting, productivity, cost, etc.) are used for self-guidance or group problem solving by managers and nonsupervisory employees, or used by superiors in a punitive, policing manner	Used for policing and in punitive manner	Used for policing coupled with reward and punishment, sometimes punitively; used somewhat for guidance but in accord with orders	Used for policing with emphasis usually on reward but with some punishment; used for guidance in accord with orders; some use also for self-guidance	Used for self-guidance and for coordinated problem solving and guidance; not used punitively	
					48
8. Performance goals and training					
a. Level of performance goals which superiors seek to have organization achieve	Seek to achieve extremely high goals	Seek very high goals	Seek high goals	Seek average goals	
					49

Item
no.

Organizational variable

b. Extent to which you have been given the kind of management training you desire	Have received no management training of kind I desire	Have received some management training of kind I desire	Have received quite a bit of management training of kind I desire	Have received a great deal of management training of kind I desire	

|—————————————————————————| 50

c. Adequacy of training resources provided to assist you in training your subordinates	Training resources provided are excellent	Training resources provided are very good	Training resources provided are good	Training resources provided are only fairly good	

|—————————————————————————| 51

The table above can be used for other purposes by appropriate modifications in the instructions. The table was used to obtain from managers their descriptions of particularly high- and low-producing organizations. The directions below indicate other uses:

Form S Instructions

On the line below each organizational variable (item), please indicate the kind of organization you are trying to create by the management you are providing. Treat each item as a continuous variable from the extreme at one end to that at the other. Place a check mark on each line to show the kind of management you are using and the kind of organization you are creating.

Form D Instructions

On the line below each organizational variable (item), please indicate by a check mark where you would *like* to, have your organization fall with regard to that item. Treat each item as a continuous variable from the extreme at one end to that at the other.

SELECTED REFERENCES TO ASSESSMENT OF ORGANIZATIONAL EFFECTIVENESS

4.E.2

ARGYRIS, CHRIS. *Organization of a Bank.* New Haven: Labor and Management Center, Yale University, 1954.

BAKKE, E. WIGHT. *Bonds of Organization.* New York: Harper & Row, 1950.

BECKER, SELWYN W., and NEUHAUSER, DUNCAN. *The Efficient Organization.* New York: Elsevier, 1975.

CUMMINGS, LARRY L., and SCHWAB, DONALD P. *Performance in Organizations: Determinants and Appraisal.* Glenview, Ill.: Scott, Foresman, 1973.

GEORGOPOULOS, BASIL S., and MANN, FLOYD C. *The Community General Hospital.* New York: Macmillan, 1962.

GHORPADE, JAISINGH, ed. *Assessment of Organizational Effectiveness: Issue, Analysis, and Readings.* Pacific Palisades, Calif.: Goodyear, 1971. Articles by A. W. Gouldner, A. Etzioni, D. Katz and R. L. Kahn, B. S. Georgopoulos, and A. S. Tannenbaum, et al.

LIKERT, RENSIS. *The Human Organization: Its Management and Value.* New York: McGraw-Hill, 1967.

LUCK, THOMAS J. *Personnel Audit and Appraisal.* New York: McGraw-Hill, 1955.

PRICE, JAMES L. *Organizational Effectiveness; An Inventory of Propositions.* Homewood, Ill.: R. D. Irwin, 1968.

WICKERT, FREDERICK R., and MCFARLAND, DALTON E., eds. *Measuring Executive Effectiveness.* New York: Appleton-Century-Crofts, 1967.

An Annotated Bibliography

FRANKLIN, JEROME L. *Organization Development: An Annotated Bibliography.* Ann Arbor: Institute of Social Research, University of Michigan, 1974.

Abstracts of books and articles that focus on the improvement of organizational performance. Each abstract contains summary description of the major ideas, a listing of major topics, a table of contents, and a list of contributing authors.

4.E.3 **SELECTED REFERENCES TO EVALUATION RESEARCH**

ABERT, JAMES G., and KAMRASS, MURRAY, eds. *Social Experiments and Social Program Evaluation.* Cambridge, Mass.: Ballinger, 1974.

BERNSTEIN, ILENE N., and FREEMAN, HOWARD E. *Academic and Entrepreneurial Research: The Consequences of Diversity in Federal Evaluation Studies.* New York: Russell Sage Foundation, 1975.

Provides data about "high" and "low" quality evaluation research and contains recommendations for restructuring the entire evaluation research enterprise.

BERNSTEIN, ILENE N., ed. *Validity Issues in Evaluative Research.* Sage Contemporary Social Science Issues, No. 23. Beverly Hills, Calif.: Sage Publications, August 1975.

DOLBEARE, KENNETH M., ed. *Public Policy Evaluation.* Beverly Hills, Calif.: Sage Publications, 1975.

See especially chapter 1 by James S. Coleman on "Problems of Studying Policy Impacts."

FRANKLIN, JACK L., and THRASHER, JEAN H. *Introduction to Program Evaluation.* New York: Wiley Interscience, John Wiley, 1976.

LIVINGSTONE, JOHN LESLIE, and GUNN, SANFORD. C. *Accounting for Social Goals: Budgeting and Analysis of Non-market Projects.* New York: Harper & Row, 1974.

MOREHOUSE, THOMAS A. *The Problem of Measuring the Impacts of Social-Action Programs.* Fairbanks, Alaska: Institute of Social Economic and Government Research, 1972.

MOOS, RUDOLF H. *Evaluating Treatment Environments: A Social Ecological Approach.* New York: Wiley-Interscience, 1974.

Compares and evaluates treatment milieus in hospital-based and community-based programs.

MOURSUND, JANET. *Evaluation: An Introduction to Research Design.* Monterey, Calif.: Brooks/Cole, 1973.

National Research Council. *Policy and Program Research in a University Setting: A Case Study Report.* Washington, D.C.: National Academy of Sciences, 1971.

RIECKEN, HENRY W., and BORUCH, ROBERT F. *Social Experimentation: A Method For Planning and Evaluating Social Intervention.* New York: Academic Press, 1974.

RIVLIN, ALICE M. *Systematic Thinking for Social Action.* Washington, D.C.: Brookings Institution, 1971.

STRUENING, ELMER L., and GUTTENTAG, MARCIA, eds. *Handbook of Evaluation Research.* 2 vols. Beverly Hills, Calif.: Sage Publications, 1975.

Symposium Proceedings at Fordham University. *Evaluation of Social Intervention.* San Francisco, Jossey-Bass, 1972.

The most comprehensive survey available for the entire evaluation process. A panel of fifty expert consultants offer guidance on program types and content, strategies and methods of evaluation, reviews of relevant literature, data aggregation across program parameters, determination of program effects, obstacles, and errors.

WEISS, CAROL H. *Evaluation Research: Methods for Assessing Program Effectiveness.* Englewood Cliffs, N.J.: Prentice-Hall, 1972.

——, comp. *Evaluating Action Programs: Readings in Social Action and Education.* Boston: Allyn & Bacon, 1972.

WILLIAMS, WALTER. *The Capacity of Social Science Organizations to Perform Large Scale Evaluative Research.* Seattle: Institute of Governmental Research, 1971.

——. *Social Policy Research and Analysis: The Experience in the Federal Agencies.* New York: Elesevier, 1971.

Analyzes use of policy research to improve anti-poverty and equal-opportunity programs.

Selected Examples of Evaluation Research

ARGYRIS, CHRIS. *Diagnosing Human Relations in Organizations: A Case Study of a Hospital.* New Haven: Yale University Press, 1956.

COMREY, A. L.; PFIFNER, J. M.; and BEEM, H. P. *Studies in Organizational Effectiveness I.* Los Angeles: U.S. Forest Survey, University of Southern California, 1951.

KATZ, DANIEL; GUTEK, BARBARA A.; KAHN, ROBERT L.; and BARTON, EUGENIA. *Bureaucratic Encounters, A Pilot Study in the Evaluation of Government Services.* Ann Arbor: Institute for Social Research, 1975.

LIPTON, DOUGLAS; MARTINSON, ROBERT; and WILKS, JUDITH. *The Effectiveness of Correctional Treatment: A Survey of Evaluation Treatment Studies.* 2 vols. New York: Praeger, 1975.

MEYER, HENRY J., and BORGATTA, EDGAR F. *An Experiment in Mental Patient Rehabilitation.* New York: Russell Sage Foundation, 1959.

WILLIAMS, WALTER, and ELMORE, RICHARD F., eds. *Social Programs Implementation.* New York: Academic, 1976.

WILNER, DANIEL M.; WALKLEY, ROSABELLE P.; PINKERTON, THOMAS C.; and TAYBACK, MATTHEW. *The Housing Environment and Family Life.* Baltimore: Johns Hopkins Press, 1962.

A Specialized Research Journal

Evaluation Quarterly: A Journal of Applied Social Research. 1977. Editors: Richard A. Berk, Department of Sociology, University of California at Santa Barbara; Howard E. Freeman, Institute for Social Research, University of California, Los Angeles.

Community

Measures of community variables are scarce. One of the first attempts to secure measures of the "goodness" of a city was made by E. L. Thorndike. His research monograph, *Our City* (New York: Harcourt, Brace, 1939), provided the first careful attempt to evaluate the quality of American cities. Ratings of 310 American cities over 30,000 population were made. In his *144 Smaller Cities*, Thorndike applied his "goodness" rating to cities between 20,000 and 30,000 population. The method requires the gathering of statistics on factors not too easily obtained. Paul B. Gillen in his *The Distribution of Occupations as a City Yardstick* (New York: Columbia University Press, 1951) presents a shorter technique based on the occupational distribution of the city. These indexes are recommended if a comparative rating of cities is desired.

The scales chosen for this section are chosen for more diagnostic research within a given community. Bosworth's Community Attitude Scale is designed to assess the degree of progressive attitude evidenced by members of a community. Fessler's Community Solidarity Index purports to measure community member solidarity. This scale is useful in determining relationships between community progress and solidarity. The Community Rating Schedule is a useful rating device in ascertaining the different views of such groups as businessmen, labor leaders, ministers, teachers, welfare workers, and so on. The Scorecard for Community Services Activity can be used to assess participation in the community services activity of the community. The relationship of community member progressiveness and community service activity might be fruitfully explored. Each scale opens possibilities of studying the relation of such background factors as occupation, social class, education, age, sex, and marital status upon community participation and progress.

4.F.1 COMMUNITY ATTITUDE SCALE

VARIABLE MEASURED: The degree of progressive attitude evidenced on such areas of community life as (1) general community improvement, (2) living conditions, (3) business and industry, (4) health and recreation, (5) education, (6) religion, (7) youth programs, (8) utilities, and (9) communications.

DESCRIPTION: A cross section of a wide range of groups in various communities defined the meaning of progress by submitting a number of statements that they designated as progressive and unprogressive. These statements provided 364 items that were placed in a five point Likert-type format. A representative panel of leaders independently designated each item as progressive or unprogressive. Various tests showed that 60 items were most discriminating. These 60 items were compiled into three subscales with 20 items each. These scales are identified as Community Integration, Community Services, and Civic Responsibilities.

WHERE PUBLISHED: A Ph.D. dissertation by Claud A. Bosworth, submitted to the University of Michigan, 1954.

RELIABILITY: 60 item scale, $r = .56$.

VALIDITY: Total mean scores discriminated significantly between a progressive and an unprogressive group at the .025 level. It was also found that those citizens who positively endorsed the scale items designed to measure attitudes toward other phases of community progress also voted for the sewer extension plan.

UTILITY: The scale is easily administered either in an interview or by questionnaire. Approximate time required is 20 minutes.

COMMUNITY ATTITUDE SCALE

Claud A. Bosworth

(Community Services Subscale)	St. Agree	Agree	?	Dis- agree	St. Dis.
	—	—	—	—	—
1. The school should stick to the 3 R's and forget about most of the other courses being offered today.	—	—	—	—	—
2. Most communities are good enough as they are without starting any new community improvement programs.	—	—	—	—	—
3. Every community should encourage more music and lecture programs.	—	—	—	—	—
4. This used to be a better community to live in.	—	—	—	—	—
5. Long term progress is more important than immediate benefits.	—	—	—	—	—
6. We have too many organizations for doing good in the community.	—	—	—	—	—

(Community Services Subscale)	St. Agree	Agree	?	Dis- agree	St. Dis.
7. The home and the church should have all the responsibility for preparing young people for marriage and parenthood.	—	—	—	—	—
8. The responsibility for older people should be confined to themselves and their families instead of the community.	—	—	—	—	—
9. Communities have too many youth programs.	—	—	—	—	—
10. Schools are good enough as they are in most communities.	—	—	—	—	—
11. Too much time is usually spent on the planning phases of community projects.	—	—	—	—	—
12. Adult education should be an essential part of the local school program.	—	—	—	—	—
13. Only the doctors should have the responsibility for the health program in the community.	—	—	—	—	—
14. Mental illness is not a responsibility of the whole community.	—	—	—	—	—
15. A modern community should have the services of social agencies.	—	—	—	—	—
16. The spiritual needs of the citizens are adequately met by the churches.	—	—	—	—	—
17. In order to grow, a community must provide additional recreation facilities.	—	—	—	—	—
18. In general, church members are better citizens.	—	—	—	—	—
19. The social needs of the citizens are the responsibility of themselves and their families and not of the community.	—	—	—	—	—
20. Churches should be expanded and located in accordance with population growth.	—	—	—	—	—

(Community Integration Subscale)

	St. Agree	Agree	?	Dis- agree	St. Dis.
21. No community improvement program should be carried on that is injurious to a business.	—	—	—	—	—
22. Industrial development should include the interest in assisting local industry.	—	—	—	—	—

(Community Integration Subscale)	St. Agree	Agree	?	Dis- agree	St. Dis.
	—	—	—	—	—
23. The first and major responsibility of each citizen should be to earn dollars for his own pocket.	—	—	—	—	—
24. More industry in town lowers the living standards.	—	—	—	—	—
25. The responsibility of citizens who are not actively participating in a community improvement program is to criticize those who are active.	—	—	—	—	—
26. What is good for the community is good for me.	—	—	—	—	—
27. Each one should handle his own business as he pleases and let the other business-men handle theirs as they please.	—	—	—	—	—
28. A strong Chamber of Commerce is bene-ficial to any community.	—	—	—	—	—
29. Leaders of the Chamber of Commerce are against the welfare of the majority of the citizens in the community.	—	—	—	—	—
30. A community would get along better if each one would mind his own business and others take care of theirs.	—	—	—	—	—
31. Members of any community organization should be expected to attend only those meetings that affect him personally.	—	—	—	—	—
32. Each of us can make real progress only when the group as a whole makes prog-ress.	—	—	—	—	—
33. The person who pays no attention to the complaints of the persons working for him is a poor citizen.	—	—	—	—	—
34. It would be better if we would have the farmer look after his own business and we look after ours.	—	—	—	—	—
35. All unions are full of Communists.	—	—	—	—	—
36. The good citizens encourage the wide-spread circulation of all news including that which may be unfavorable to them and their organizations.	—	—	—	—	—

	St. Agree	Agree	?	Dis- agree	St. Dis.
(Community Integration Subscale)					

37. The good citizen should help minority groups with their problems.	—	—	—	—	—
38. The farmer has too prominent a place in our society.	—	—	—	—	—
39. A citizen should join only those organizations that will promote his own interests.	—	—	—	—	—
40. Everyone is out for himself at the expense of everyone else.	—	—	—	—	—

(Civic Responsibilities Subscale)

41. Busy people should not have the responsibility for civic programs.	—	—	—	—	—
42. The main responsibility for keeping the community clean is up to the city officials.	—	—	—	—	—
43. Community improvements are fine if they don't increase taxes.	—	—	—	—	—
44. The younger element have too much to say about our community affairs.	—	—	—	—	—
45. A progressive community must provide adequate parking facilities.	—	—	—	—	—
46. Government officials should get public sentiment before acting on major municipal projects.	—	—	—	—	—
47. A good citizen should be willing to assume leadership in a civic improvement organization.	—	—	—	—	—
48. Progress can best be accomplished by having only a few people involved.	—	—	—	—	—
49. Community improvement should be the concern of only a few leaders in the community.	—	—	—	—	—
50. A community would be better if less people would spend time on community improvement projects.	—	—	—	—	—
51. Only those who have the most time should assume the responsibility for civic programs.	—	—	—	—	—

(Civic Responsibilities Subscale)	St. Agree	Agree	?	Dis- agree	St. Dis.
52. Living conditions in a community should be improved.	—	—	—	—	—
53. A good citizen should sign petitions for community improvement.	—	—	—	—	—
54. Improving slum areas is a waste of money.	—	—	—	—	—
55. The police force should be especially strict with outsiders.	—	—	—	—	—
56. The paved streets and roads in most communities are good enough.	—	—	—	—	—
57. The sewage system of a community must be expanded as it grows even though it is necessary to increase taxes.	—	—	—	—	—
58. Some people just want to live in slum areas.	—	—	—	—	—
59. The main problem we face is high taxes.	—	—	—	—	—
60. Modern methods and equipment should be provided for all phases of city government.	—	—	—	—	—

COMMUNITY SOLIDARITY INDEX

4.F.2

VARIABLE MEASURED: Amount of consensus among members of primary rural communities (250–2000 pop.).

DESCRIPTION: Eight major areas of community behavior are examined:

1. community spirit
2. interpersonal relations
3. family responsibility toward the community
4. schools
5. churches
6. economic behavior
7. local government
8. tension areas

These eight areas are covered in a series of 40 statements that are rated by the respondent on a five-item scale according to his judgment of how the statements apply to his community. The items range from "very true" to "definitely untrue" with scores ranging from 5 for the "very true" response to 1 for the "definitely untrue" response. The standard deviation of the scores of all the schedules for the community is taken as a measure of the degree of consensus and, there-fore, of solidarity in the community. The smaller the S, the greater the solidarity is assumed to be. The mean of the total score is considered to be an index of the members' opinion of the quality of the community. For comparison with other communities an octagonal profile may be used.

WHERE PUBLISHED: Donald R. Fessler, "The Development of a Scale for Measuring Community Solidarity," *Rural Sociology* 17 (1952): 144-52.

RELIABILITY: Split-half r was described as being high but not given.

VALIDITY: Face validity.

UTILITY: This index measures an important community variable. When rela-tionships are examined between community action programs and community solidarity, this measure may be highly predictive of the success or failure of com-munity efforts.

RESEARCH APPLICATIONS: Other scales and efforts to measure community attachment and identification include:

ANDERSON, C. ARNOLD. "Community Chest Campaigns as an Index of Com-munity Integration." *Social Forces* 33 (October 1954): 76–81.

FANELLI, A. ALEXANDER. "Extensiveness of Communication Contacts and Per-ceptions of the Community." *American Sociological Review* 21 (August 1956): 439–45.

KASARDA, JOHN D., and JANOWITZ, M. "Community Attachment in Mass Society." *American Sociological Review* 39 (June 1974): 328–39.

WILENSKY, HAROLD L. "Mass Society and Mass Culture: Interdependence or Independence?" *American Sociological Review* 29 (April 1964): 173–97.

COMMUNITY SOLIDARITY INDEX SCHEDULE

Name _____ Community _____

Occupation _____ Married _____ Single _____

If married, number of children in school, if any _____

boys _____ girls _____, number of children out of school _____

Number of years resident in community _____. Location of residence:

in town _____ outside of town _____ how far _____ miles?

Think of each of the statements below as relating to the people of this entire community both in town and on neighboring farms. If you think the statement fits this community very well, after the statement circle *vt* (for very true); if it applies only partially, circle *t* (for true); if you cannot see how it relates one way or another to this particular community, circle *nd* (for not decided); if you think it is not true, circle *u* (for untrue); and if it definitely is not true, circle *du* (for definitely untrue). PLEASE RECORD THE IMPRESSION THAT FIRST OCCURS TO YOU. Do not go back and change your answers.

1. Real friends are hard to find in this community. *vt t nd u du* (2)*
2. Our schools do a poor job of preparing young people for life. *vt t nd u du* (4)
3. Local concerns deal fairly and squarely with everyone. *vt t nd u du* (6)
4. The community is very peaceful and orderly. *vt t nd u du* (8)
5. A lot of people here think they are too nice for you. *vt t nd u du* (1)
6. Families in this community keep their children under control. *vt t nd u du* (3)
7. The different churches here cooperate well with one another. *vt t nd u du* (5)
8. Some people here "get by with murder" while others take the rap for any little misdeed. *vt t nd u du* (7)
9. Almost everyone is polite and courteous to you. *vt t nd u du* (2)
10. Our schools do a good job of preparing students for college. *vt t nd u du* (4)
11. Everyone here tries to take advantage of you. *vt t nd u du* (6)
12. People around here show good judgment. *vt t nd u du* (8)
13. People won't work together to get things done for the community. *vt t nd u du* (1)
14. Parents teach their children to respect other people's rights and property. *vt t nd u du* (3)
15. Most of our church people forget the meaning of the word brotherhood when they get out of church. *vt t nd u du* (5)
16. This community lacks real leaders. *vt t nd u du* (7)
17. People give you a bad name if you insist on being different. *vt t nd u du* (2)
18. Our high-school graduates take an active interest in making their community a better place in which to live. *vt t nd u du* (4)
19. A few people here make all the dough. *vt t nd u du* (6)
20. Too many young people get into sex difficulties. *vt t nd u du* (8)
21. The community tries hard to help its young people along. *vt t nd u du* (1)
22. Folks are unconcerned about what their kids do so long as they keep out of trouble. *vt t nd u du* (3)
23. The churches are a constructive factor for better community life. *vt t nd u du* (5)
24. The mayor and councilmen run the town to suit themselves. *vt t nd u du* (7)
25. I feel very much that I belong here. *vt t nd u du* (2)
26. Many young people in the community do not finish high school. *vt t nd u du* (4)
27. The people here are all penny pinchers. *vt t nd u du* (6)
28. You must spend lots of money to be accepted here. *vt t nd u du* (8)
29. The people as a whole mind their own business. *vt t nd u du* (1)
30. Most people get their families to Sunday School or church on Sunday. *vt t nd u du* (3)
31. Every church wants to be the biggest and the most impressive. *vt t nd u du* (5)

*The number in parentheses indicates the area to which the statement belongs.

32. A few have the town politics well sewed up. *vt t nd u du* (7)
33. Most of the students here learn to read and write well. *vt t nd u du* (4)
34. People are generally critical of others. *vt t nd u du* (2)
35. Local concerns expect their help to live on low wages. *vt t nd u du* (6)
36. You are out of luck here if you happen to be of the wrong nationality. *vt t nd u du* (8)
37. No one seems to care much how the community looks. *vt t nd u du* (1)
38. If their children keep out of the way, parents are satisfied to let them do whatever they want to do. *vt t nd u du* (3)
39. Most of our churchgoers do not practice what they preach. *vt t nd u du* (5)
40. The town council gets very little done. *vt t nd u du* (7)

4.F.3   COMMUNITY RATING SCHEDULE

VARIABLE MEASURED: The quality of community life, of "goodness" of the community, is assessed.

DESCRIPTION: Ten institutional areas of community life are rated as good, fair, or poor. The areas selected include education, housing and planning. religion, equality of opportunity, economic development, cultural opportunities, recreation, health and welfare, government, and community organization. Scores range from 0–100.

WHERE PUBLISHED: New York State Citizen's Council, *Adult Leadership* 1, No. 5 (October 1952): 19.

RELIABILITY: Not known.

VALIDITY: Rests upon face validity.

STANDARD SCORES:

> Good communities = 90–100
> Fair communities = 70–89
> Poor communities = 0–69

UTILITY: The schedule is easy to administer; the time required is about 10 minutes. Raters often have difficulty in making a general judgment and express qualifications. These should be expected. The special advantage of this index is that it permits analysis of individual raters. Individual raters from business, labor, welfare, education, and religion often differ widely in their assessments of the same community.

RESEARCH APPLICATIONS: No reported studies. However, the index opens possibilities of examining the patterns of new industrial locations with quality of the community. The relationship of leadership to community quality is an important area that should be explored.

COMMUNITY RATING SCHEDULE*

Ask respondent to rate community as good, fair, or poor as judged by similar communities in the United States.

	Good	Fair	Poor

Standard No. 1 Education
Modern education available for every child, youth and adult. Uncrowded, properly equipped schools in good physical conditions. Highly qualified, well paid teachers.

Standard No. 2 Housing and Planning
Every family decently housed. Continuous planning for improvement of residential areas, parks, highways, and other community essentials. Parking, traffic, and transportation problems under control.

Standard No. 3 Religion
Full opportunity for religious expression accorded to every individual—churches strong and well supported.

Standard No. 4 Equality of Opportunity
People of different races, religions, and nationalities have full chance for employment and for taking part in community life. Dangerous tensions kept at minimum by avoidance of discrimination and injustices.

Standard No. 5 Economic Development
Good jobs available. Labor, industry, agriculture, and government work together to insure sound economic growth.

Standard No. 6 Cultural Opportunities
Citizens' lives strengthened by ample occasion to enjoy music, art, and dramatics. A professionally administered library service benefits people of all ages. Newspapers and radio carefully review community affairs.

Standard No. 7 Recreation
Enough supervised playgrounds and facilities for outdoor activities. Full opportunity to take part in arts and crafts, photography, and other hobbies.

Standard No. 8 Health and Welfare
Positive approach to improving health of entire community. Medical care and hospitalization readily available. Provision made for underprivileged children, the aged, and the handicapped. Families in trouble can secure needed assistance.

*Prepared by New York State Citizen's Council; Reprinted in *Adult Leadership* 1, no. 5 (October 1952): 19.

	Good	Fair	Poor

Standard No. 9 Government
Capable citizens seek public office. Officials concerned above all with community betterment. Controversy stems from honest differences of opinion, not from squabbles over privilege.

Standard No. 10 Community Organization
An organization-community forum, citizen's council, or community federation-representative of entire town is working for advancement of the whole community. Citizens have opportunity to learn about and take part in local affairs. There is an organized, community-wide discussion program. Specialized organizations give vigorous attention to each important civic need.

Total Score for your Town   Good _____ 10 points for each item _____

Fair _____   5 points for each item _____

Poor _____ no points

Total   _____

4.F.4   SCORECARD FOR COMMUNITY SERVICES ACTIVITY

VARIABLE MEASURED: Individual participation in community services.

DESCRIPTION: The scorecard is an arbitrary index to assess individual participation in community services. Fifteen possible behavioral items are presented as those that compose bulk of community service activity. Scores of 0–15 may be recorded as each item participation is given a weight of one.

WHERE PUBLISHED: Unpublished.

RELIABILITY: No tests have been made.

VALIDITY: Rests on face validity.

STANDARD SCORES:

>   10–15 outstanding community member
>   6–9   an average member
>   0–5   low participating member

Cutting points were based upon a random sample of 100 adults in a middle-class community.

UTILITY: Administration of the scorecard takes less than four minutes. It provides for both individual and group assessment.

RESEARCH APPLICATIONS: None reported. However, the index opens possibilities of exploring important facets of citizenship including the importance of background factors such as age, sex, education, race, and social class. The relation between community service activity, community solidarity, and community rating is a challenging research endeavor.

SCORECARD FOR COMMUNITY SERVICES ACTIVITY

Constructed by Delbert C. Miller

(*Score one point for each "yes")

FINANCIAL SUPPORT—Did you, in the past year,

_____ Contribute money to a community chest campaign?

_____ Contribute money to a church?

_____ Contribute money for other charitable purposes?

GENERAL ACTIVITY—Did you, in the past year,

_____ Serve on any board responsible for civic programs?

_____ Serve on any committee working to improve civic life?

_____ Assume leadership of any civic action program?

COMMUNITY ISSUES AND PROBLEMS—Did you, in the past year,

_____ Inform yourself about civic issues and problems?

_____ Discuss civic problems frequently with more than one person?

_____ Persuade others to take a particular position?

_____ Get advice from others?

_____ Speak to key leaders about problems?

_____ Visit community organizations or board meetings to inform yourself?

_____ Write letters, or circulate literature, or hold home meetings?

GROUP ACTION—Did you, in the past year,

_____ Belong to one or more organizations that takes stands on community issues and problems?

_____ Make group visits or invite visits of community officials to your organization?

_____ Total Score

*10–15 points—An outstanding community member
  6–9   points—An average member
  0–5   points—A low participating member

4.F.5 SELECTED REFERENCES FOR THE ADVANCED STUDENT

1. GIBBS, JACK P., ed. *Urban Research Methods*. Princeton, N.J.: Van Nostrand, 1961.
2. ANGELL, ROBERT C. "Moral Integration of Cities." *American Journal of Sociology* 57, pt. 2 (July 1951).
3. SHEVKY, ESHREF, and BELL, WENDELL. *Social Area Analysis*. Stanford: Stanford University, 1955.

   Contains indexes of social rank, urbanization, and segregation. Cf. Robert C. Tryon, *Identification of Social Areas by Cluster Analysis* (Berkeley: University of California, 1955).

4. JONASSEN, CHRISTIAN T. *The Measurement of Community Dimensions and Elements*. Columbus: Center for Educational Administration, Ohio State University, 1959.

   Cf. his "Functional Unities in Eighty-eight Community Systems," *American Sociological Review* 26 (June 1961): 399–407.

5. LEVY, FRANK S.; MELTSNER, ARNOLD J.; and WILDAVSKY, AARON. *Urban Outcomes: Schools, Streets, and Libraries*. Berkeley: University of California Press, 1974.

   Provides analysis and measurement of outcomes in Oakland, California, as basis for policy analysis and new ways of understanding decisions that affect cities.

6. For measurement of occupational, ethnic, and social-class segregation, see the work of TAEUBER, KARL E., and TAEUBER, ALMA F. *Negroes in Cities*. Chicago: Aldine, 1965. Pp. 195–245.

   Cf. also Donald O. Cowgill, "Segregation Scores for Metropolitan Areas," *American Sociological Review* 27 (June 1962): 400–402; Otis D. Duncan and Beverly Duncan, "Measuring Segregation," *American Sociological Review* 28 (February 1963): 133; Julius Jahn and Calvin F. Schmid, "The Measurement of Ecological Segregation," *American Sociological Review* 12 (June 1947): 293–303; Theodore R. Anderson and Lee L. Bean, "The Shevky-Bell Social Areas: Confirmation of Results and a Reinterpretation," *Social Forces* 40 (December 1961): 119–24; Gerald T. Slatin, "Ecological Analysis of Delinquency: Aggregation Effects" 34 (December 1969): 894–907.

7. For comprehensive research information on urban problems, see *Index to Current Urban Documents*.

   A quarterly index to documents from over 200 American and Canadian cities. Greenwood Press, 51 Riverside Avenue, Westport, Conn. 06880.

8. FORM, WILLIAM H., and MILLER, DELBERT C. *Industry, Labor, and Community*. New York: Harper & Bros., 1960.

   Provides field study guides for assessing industry-community relations, community power structure, and community leadership. Discusses research problems of industry-community relations.

Social Participation

This section includes Chapin's Social Participation Scale. It is a general scale of participation in voluntary organizations of all kinds—professional, civic, and social. It is used when the total participation pattern is an important variable. The Leisure Participation and Enjoyment Scale enables the researcher to get a detailed picture of leisure patterns and also to get a score for each respondent on both participation and enjoyment.

A measure of neighborhood participation is included. Wallin Women's Neighborliness Scale is a Guttman-type scale that has exhibited unidimensionality on the samples of respondents that have been tested. It is designed to be answered by women respondents only.

The Citizen Political Action Schedule is a scorecard for political behavior reported by a community resident. If the respondent reports accurately, the scale can reveal the behavioral acts in the political sphere.

CHAPIN'S SOCIAL PARTICIPATION SCALE, 1952 EDITION   *4.G.1*

VARIABLE MEASURED: Degree of a person's or family's participation in community groups and institutions.

DESCRIPTION: This is a Guttman-type scale with reproducibility coefficients of .92 to .97 for groups of leaders. High scores of 18 and over represent titular leader achievement. The five components are (1) member, (2) attendance, (3) financial contributions, (4) member of committees, (5) offices held. These components measure different dimensions: intensity of participation by 2, 3, 4, and 5; extensity by 1. Also, rejection-acceptance in formal groups is measured by 1, 4, and 5, for which the intercorrelations are found to be of the order of $r_{14} = .53$ to $.58$; $r_{15} = .36$ to $.40$; $r_{45} = .36$ to $.40$. Social participation is measured by 2 and 3 with intercorrelations of $r_{23} = .80$ to $.89$. Other intercorrelations among the components have been found to be of the order of $r_{12} = .88$; $r_{13} = .89$; $r_{24} = .60$; $r_{34} = .40$; $r_{35} = .35$; and $r_{45} = .50$ to .58.

WHERE PUBLISHED: F. Stuart Chapin, *Experimental Designs in Sociological Research* (New York: Harper, 1955), Appendix B, pp. 275-78.

RELIABILITY: $r = .89$ to .95.

VALIDITY:

With Chapin's social status scale scores	$r = .62$ to .66
With income class	$r = .52$
With occupational groups	$r = .63$
With years of formal education	$r = .54$
Between husband and wife	$r = .76$

STANDARD SCORES: Mean scores for occupational groups are as follows:

I. Professional, 20.
II. Managerial and Proprietary, 20.
III. Clerical, 16.
IV. Skilled, 12.
V. Semiskilled, 8.
VI. Unskilled, 4.

UTILITY: One sheet is used for entries on each group affiliation of subject recorded in five entries under five columns by the visitor in reply to questions answered by the subject. It takes 10 to 15 minutes to fill in the subject's answers. The scale may also be self-administered.

RESEARCH APPLICATIONS:

CHAPIN, F. S. "The Effects of Slum Clearance on Family and Community Relationships in Minneapolis in 1935-1936." *American Journal of Sociology* 43 (March 1938): 744-63.

———. "Social Participation and Social Intelligence." *American Sociological Review* 4 (April 1939): 157-66.

ERBE, WILLIAM M. "Social Involvement and Political Activity: A Replication and Elaboration." *American Sociological Review* 29 (April 1964): 198-215.

EVAN, WILLIAM M. "Dimensions of Participation on Voluntary Associations." *Social Forces* 35 (December 1957): 148-53.

LUNDBERG, G. A., and LANSING, MARGARET. "The Sociography of Some Community Relations." *American Sociological Review* 2 (June 1937): 318-28.

MARTIN, WALTER T. "A Consideration of Differences in the Extent and Location of the Formal Associational Activities of Rural-Urban Fringe Residents." *American Sociological Review* 17 (December 1952): 687-94.

NELSON, JOEL I. "Participation and Integration: The Case of the Small Businessman." *American Sociological Review* 33 (June 1968): 427-38.

SOCIAL PARTICIPATION SCALE, 1952 EDITION*

F. Stuart Chapin

Directions

1. List by name the organizations with which the husband and wife are affiliated (at the present time) as indicated by the five types of participation
   No. 1 to No. 5 across the top of the schedule.

   It is not necessary to enter the date at which the person became a member
   of the organization. It is important to enter L if the membership is in a
   purely local group, and to enter N if the membership is in a local unit of
   some state or national organization.

2. An organization means some active and organized grouping, usually but not
   necessarily in the community or neighborhood of residence, such as club,
   lodge, business or political or professional or religious organization, labor
   union, etc.; subgroups of a church or other institution are to be included
   separately *provided they are organized* as more or less independent entities.

3. Record under attendance the mere fact of attendance or nonattendance
   without regard to the number of meetings attended (corrections for the number attended *have not* been found to influence the final score sufficiently
   to justify such labor).

4. Record under contributions the mere fact of financial contributions or
   absence of contributions, and *not the amount* (corrections for amount of
   contributions *have not* been found to influence the final score sufficiently
   to justify such labor).

5. Previous memberships, committee work, offices held, etc., should *not be*
   counted or recorded or used in computing the final score.

6. Final score is computed by counting each membership as 1, each attended as
   2, each contributed to as 3, each committee membership as 4, and each office
   held as 5. If both parents are living regularly in the home, add their total
   scores and divide the sum by two. The result is the mean social participation
   score of the family. In case only one parent lives in the home, as widow,
   widower, etc., the sum of that one person's participations is the score for the
   family (unless it is desired to obtain scores on children also).

*University of Minnesota Press, Minneapolis. Copyright 1938 by the University of
Minnesota.

Social Participation Scale

Address _____

Husband _____

Age _____ Education _____ Race or Nationality _____

Occupation _____ Income _____

Case No. _____

Name of organization	1. Member[a]	2. Attendance	3. Financial contributions	4. Member of committees (not name)	5. Offices held
1.					
2.					
3.					
4.					
5.					
6.					
7.					
8.					
9.					
10.					
Totals					

Wife _____

Age _____ Education _____

Occupation _____

Race or Nationality _____

Income _____

Name of organization	1. Member[a]	2. Attendance	3. Financial contributions	4. Member of committees (not name)	5. Offices held
1.					
2.					
3.					
4.					
5.					
6.					
7.					
8.					
9.					
10.					
Totals					

Date _____　　Investigator _____

[a]Enter L if purely local group; enter N if a local unit of a state or national organization.

Distribution of total scores from a representative sample of an urban population, a J-curve; skewed to higher scores of 100 and over; mode at 0 to 11 points.

4.G.2 LEISURE PARTICIPATION AND ENJOYMENT

VARIABLE MEASURED: The customary use of and degree of enjoyment of leisure time.

DESCRIPTION: The scale includes 47 items that are activities in which one might be expected to participate. Each item is ranked on two five-point scales. Leisure participation is scaled according to frequency of participation (1. Never, 2. Rarely, 3. Occasionally, 4. Fairly Often, 5. Frequently), and leisure enjoyment is scaled according to likes (1. Dislike very much, 2. Dislike, 3. Indifferent, 4. Like, 5. Like very much). The appropriate degree on each scale is circled for each item. No ranking on the like-dislike scale is given for those items in which the individual never participates.

WHERE PUBLISHED: C. R. Pace, *They Went to College* (Minneapolis: University of Minnesota, 1941). Copyright 1941 by the University of Minnesota.

RELIABILITY: Not known.

VALIDITY: Leisure participation

With income	$r = .019$
With sociocivic activities scale	$r = .40$
With cultural status	$r = .039$

STANDARD SCORES: A summary of responses to the questionnaire on the Minnesota study is included on pages 142–45 of the Pace Book.

	1924–25		1928–29	
	Grads.	Nongrads.	Grads.	Nongrads.
Median leisure participation for men	125.00	123.24	132.29	131.72
Median leisure enjoyment for men	169.83	167.53	171.67	170.65
Median leisure participation for women	139.80	137.90	137.50	133.97
Median leisure enjoyment for women	177.73	178.75	180.38	176.87

UTILITY: This scale is easily administered and may be self-administered. It is equally easy to score. It takes little time to administer. Both leisure participation and leisure enjoyment scores are derived and can be compared.

RESEARCH APPLICATIONS: Comparative study of 951 graduates and non-graduates of the University of Minnesota (C. R. Pace, *They Went to College*).

YOUR LEISURE-TIME ACTIVITIES

The use of leisure time is supposed to be an increasingly important social problem. We want to know how people usually spend their leisure time. Here is a list of activities. On the left side of the page put a circle around the number that tells how often you do these things now, using the key at the top of the column. On the right side of the page put a circle around the number that tells how well you like these things, using the key at the top of the column. If you never do the activity mentioned, circle number one in the left column to indicate no participation, and circle no number on the right side of the page. Try not to skip any item.

How Often Do You Do These Things		*How Well Do You Like These Things*
1. Never		1. Dislike very much
2. Rarely		2. Dislike
3. Occasionally		3. Indifferent
4. Fairly often		4. Like
5. Frequently		5. Like very much

1 2 3 4 5	1. Amateur dramatics	1 2 3 4 5
1 2 3 4 5	2. Amusement parks and halls	1 2 3 4 5
1 2 3 4 5	3. Art work (individual)	1 2 3 4 5
1 2 3 4 5	4. Attending large social functions (balls, benefit bridge, etc.)	1 2 3 4 5
1 2 3 4 5	5. Attending small social entertainments (dinner parties, etc.)	1 2 3 4 5
1 2 3 4 5	6. Book reading for pleasure	1 2 3 4 5
1 2 3 4 5	7. Conventions	1 2 3 4 5
1 2 3 4 5	8. Conversation with family	1 2 3 4 5
1 2 3 4 5	9. Card playing	1 2 3 4 5
1 2 3 4 5	10. Church and related organizations	1 2 3 4 5
1 2 3 4 5	11. Dancing	1 2 3 4 5
1 2 3 4 5	12. Dates	1 2 3 4 5
1 2 3 4 5	13. Entertaining at home	1 2 3 4 5
1 2 3 4 5	14. Fairs, exhibitions, etc.	1 2 3 4 5
1 2 3 4 5	15. Informal contacts with friends	1 2 3 4 5
1 2 3 4 5	16. Informal discussions, e.g., "bull sessions"	1 2 3 4 5
1 2 3 4 5	17. Indoor team recreation or sports—basketball, volleyball	1 2 3 4 5
1 2 3 4 5	18. Indoor individual recreation or sports—bowling, gym, pool, billiards, handball	1 2 3 4 5
1 2 3 4 5	19. Knitting, sewing, crocheting, etc.	1 2 3 4 5
1 2 3 4 5	20. Lectures (not class)	1 2 3 4 5
1 2 3 4 5	21. Listening to radio or TV	1 2 3 4 5
1 2 3 4 5	22. Literary writing—poetry, essays, stories, etc.	1 2 3 4 5
1 2 3 4 5	23. Magazine reading (for pleasure)	1 2 3 4 5
1 2 3 4 5	24. Movies	1 2 3 4 5
1 2 3 4 5	25. Newspaper reading	1 2 3 4 5
1 2 3 4 5	26. Odd jobs at home	1 2 3 4 5

1 2 3 4 5	27. Organizations or club meetings as a member	1 2 3 4 5
1 2 3 4 5	28. Organizations or club meetings as a leader (as for younger groups)	1 2 3 4 5
1 2 3 4 5	29. Outdoor individual sports—golf, riding, skating, hiking, tennis	1 2 3 4 5
1 2 3 4 5	30. Outdoor team sports—hockey, baseball, etc.	1 2 3 4 5
1 2 3 4 5	31. Picnics	1 2 3 4 5
1 2 3 4 5	32. Playing musical instrument or singing	1 2 3 4 5
1 2 3 4 5	33. Shopping	1 2 3 4 5
1 2 3 4 5	34. Sitting and thinking	1 2 3 4 5
1 2 3 4 5	35. Spectator of sports	1 2 3 4 5
1 2 3 4 5	36. Symphony or concerts	1 2 3 4 5
1 2 3 4 5	37. Telephone visiting	1 2 3 4 5
1 2 3 4 5	38. Theater attendance	1 2 3 4 5
1 2 3 4 5	39. Traveling or touring	1 2 3 4 5
1 2 3 4 5	40. Using public library	1 2 3 4 5
1 2 3 4 5	41. Visiting museums, art galleries, etc.	1 2 3 4 5
1 2 3 4 5	42. Volunteer work—social service, etc.	1 2 3 4 5
1 2 3 4 5	43. Writing personal letters	1 2 3 4 5
1 2 3 4 5	44. Special hobbies—stamps, photography, shop work, gardening, and others not included above	1 2 3 4 5
1 2 3 4 5	45. Fishing or hunting	1 2 3 4 5
1 2 3 4 5	46. Camping	1 2 3 4 5
1 2 3 4 5	47. Developing and printing pictures	1 2 3 4 5

4.G.3   A GUTTMAN SCALE FOR MEASURING WOMEN'S NEIGHBORLINESS

VARIABLE MEASURED: The neighborliness of women under sixty years of age.

DESCRIPTION: This instrument is a unidimensional Guttman scale consisting of twelve items. The scale items can be simply scored for any sample by counting each *GN* (greater neighborliness) answer as 1 and each *LN* (lesser neighborliness) as 0. The possible range of scores is 12 to 0.

WHERE PUBLISHED: Paul Wallin, "A Guttman Scale for Measuring Women's Neighborliness," *The American Journal of Sociology* 59 (1953): 243-46. Copyright 1953 by the University of Chicago.

RELIABILITY: The coefficient of reproducibility of the scale from two samples of women was .920 and .924.

VALIDITY: Face validity.

UTILITY: A short, easy-to-administer scale that may be used for investigating factors accounting for individual differences in neighborliness. The scale also can be used for testing hypotheses as to intracommunity and intercommunity difference in neighborliness.

RESEARCH APPLICATIONS:

EDELSTEIN, ALEX S., and LARSEN, OTTO N. "The Weekly Press's Contribution to a Sense of Urban Community." *Journalism Quarterly* (Autumn 1960): 489-98.

FAVA, SYLVA F. "Suburbanism as a Way of Life." *American Sociological Review* 21 (1956): 34-37.

GREER, SCOTT. "Urbanism Reconsidered: A Comparative Study of Local Areas in a Metropolis." *American Sociological Review* 21 (1956): 19-25.

LARSEN, OTTO N., and EDELSTEIN, ALEX S. "Communication, Consensus and the Community Involvement of Urban Husbands and Wives." *Acta Sociologia* (Copenhagen) 5 (1960): 15-30.

For some related research on neighborhood satisfaction and integration see:

FELLIN, PHILLIP, and LITWAK, EUGENE. "Neighborhood Cohesion under Conditions of Mobility." *American Sociological Review* 28 (June 1963): 364-76.

FISHMAN, JOSHUA. "A Sociolinguistic Census of a Bilingual Neighborhood." *American Journal of Sociology* 75 (November 1969): 323-39.

LITWAK, EUGENE. "Voluntary Associations and Neighborhood Cohesion." *American Sociological Review* 26 (April 1961): 258-71.

OLSEN, MARVIN E. "Social Participation and Voting Turnout." *American Sociological Review* 37 (June 1972): 317-33.

SEWELL, WILLIAM H. and ARMER, J. MICHAEL. "Neighborhood Context and College Plans." *American Sociological Review* 31 (April 1966): 159-68.

STUCKERT, ROBERT P. "Occupational Mobility and Family Relationships." *Social Forces* 41 (March 1963): 301-7.

SWINEHART, JAMES W. "Socio-Economic Level, Status Aspiration, and Maternal Role." *American Sociological Review* 28 (June 1963): 391-99.

A GUTTMAN SCALE FOR MEASURING WOMEN'S NEIGHBORLINESS

Paul Wallin

1. How many of your best friends who live in your neighborhood did you get to know since you or they moved into the neighborhood? Two or more (*GN*); one or none (*LN*).
2. Do you and any of your neighbors go to movies, picnics, or other things like that together? Often or sometimes (*GN*); rarely or never (*LN*).
3. Do you and your neighbors entertain one another? Often or sometimes (*GN*); rarely or never (*LN*).
4. If you were holding a party or tea for an out-of-town visitor, how many of your neighbors would you invite? Two or more (*GN*); one or none (*LN*).
5. How many of your neighbors have ever talked to you about their problems when they were worried or asked you for advice or help? One or more (*GN*); none (*LN*).

6. How many of your neighbors' homes have you ever been in? Four or more (*GN*); three or less (*LN*).
7. Do you and your neighbors exchange or borrow things from one another such as books, magazines, dishes, tools, recipes, preserves, or garden vegetables? Often, sometimes, or rarely (*GN*); none (*LN*).
8. About how many of the people in your neighborhood would you recognize by sight if you saw them in a large crowd? About half or more (*GN*); a few or none (*LN*).
9. With how many of your neighbors do you have a friendly talk fairly frequently? Two or more (*GN*); one or none (*LN*).
10. About how many of the people in your neighborhood do you say "Hello" or "Good morning" to when you meet on the street? Six or more (*GN*); five or less (*LN*).
11. How many of the names of the families in your neighborhood do you know? Four or more (2); one to three (1); none (0).
12. How often do you have a talk with any of your neighbors? Often or sometimes (*GN*); rarely or never (*LN*).

4.G.4   CITIZEN POLITICAL ACTION SCHEDULE

VARIABLE MEASURED: Individual participation in citizen political action.

DESCRIPTION: This is an arbitrary index to assess individual participation in community services. Twelve possible behavioral items are presented as those that compose bulk of citizen political activity. Scores of 0–12 may be recorded as each item participation is given a weight of one.

WHERE PUBLISHED: League of Women Voters of Pennsylvania, Publication No. 101, Philadelphia, Pa.

RELIABILITY: No tests have been made.

VALIDITY: Face validity.

STANDARD SCORES:

> 10–12 an outstanding citizen!
> 6–9   an average citizen.
> 0–5   a citizen?

UTILITY: May be administered in less than four minutes. It provides a measure suitable for both individual and group assessment.

RESEARCH APPLICATION: None reported. However, index opens possibilities of exploring important facets of political behavior including the importance of background factors of age, sex, education, race, and social class. For selection of alternate scales and related research, see John P. Robinson et al., *Measures of Political Attitudes* (Ann Arbor, Mich.: Institute of Social Research, University of Michigan, 1968), pp. 427-35.

SCORECARD FOR CITIZEN POLITICAL ACTION

Published by the League of Women Voters of Pennsylvania, Publication No. 101

(*Score one point for each "yes")

VOTING—Did you vote

—Once in the last four years? _____

—Two to five time? _____

—Six or more times? _____

PUBLIC ISSUES—Do you

—Inform yourself from more than one source on public issues? _____

—Discuss public issues frequently with more than one person? _____

INDIVIDUAL ACTION ON PUBLIC ISSUES— Did you

—Write or talk to your Congressman or any other public official—local, state or national—to express your views once in the past year? _____

—Two or more times? _____

GROUP ACTION ON PUBLIC ISSUES—Do you

—Belong to one or more organizations that take stands on public issues? _____

PRIMARY ELECTION ACTIVITY—Did you

—Discuss the qualifications needed for the offices on the ballot? _____

—Work for the nomination of a candidate before the primary election once in the last four years? _____

GENERAL OR MUNICIPAL ELECTION ACTIVITY—Did you

—Work for the election of a candidate once in the last four years? _____

FINANCIAL SUPPORT—Did you

—Contribute money to a party or candidate once in the last four years? _____

TOTAL SCORE _____

*10-12 points—An outstanding citizen!
6-9 points—An average citizen.
5-0 points—a citizen?

Leadership in the Work Organization

This section contains two leadership scales that may be widely used in work organizations. The first scale, the Leadership Opinion Questionnaire, is designed to find answers to the question, "What *should you* as a supervisor do?" The second scale, the Supervisory Behavior Description, is designed to find answers to the question, "What does *your own supervisor* actually do?" Note that these two scales make it possible to get measures of two levels of leadership in an organization. The relation of a supervisor to his immediate superior has been shown to be a very important one. The use of both questionnaires makes it possible to secure a comparison between the two levels. However, each scale may be used for the specific purpose for which it was designed. Use the Leadership Opinion Questionnaire whenever a measure of a leader's personal orientation is desired. Use the Supervisory Behavior Description when it is desirable to get the perceptions of a supervisor by those who report to him. This scale can be given to employees or any group of supervisors or managers. These two scales have been subjected to repeated refinement and may be considered highly reliable and valid in terms of present progress in scale construction.

The Work Patterns Profile is an analysis form, which permits a description of work activity patterns. This schedule has its greatest worth as a diagnostic instrument. The relation of the work patterns profile to the leadership orientation of initiation and consideration offer interesting research problems.

Many measures of organizational performance might be included. Space prevents their addition, but the following measures are annotated for the consideration of the organizational researcher:

Executive Position Description. This description contains 191 items to determine the basic characteristics of executive positions in business and industry. Part 1 covers Position Activities; part 2, Position Responsibilities; part 3, Position Demands and Restrictions; part 4, Position Characteristics. See John K. Hemphill, *Dimensions of Executive Positions* (Columbus: Ohio State University Bureau of Business Research, 1960).

Responsibility, Authority, and Delegation Scales. These scales were designed to measure different degrees of perceived responsibility, authority, and delegation as exhibited by individuals who occupy administrative or supervisory positions. See Ralph M. Stogdill and Carroll L. Shartle, *Methods in the Study of Administrative Leadership* (Columbus: Ohio State University Bureau of Business Research, 1955), pp. 33–43.

Multirelational Sociometric Survey. This survey measures interpersonal variables surrounding work activities. Five dimensions are included: the prescribed, the perceived, the actual, the desired, and the rejected. See Robert Tannenbaum, Irving W. Weschler, and Fred Massarik, *Leadership and Organization: A Behavioral Science Approach* (New York: McGraw-Hill, 1961), pp. 346–70.

A Method for the Analysis of the Structure of Complex Organizations. This is an application of sociometric analysis based on work contacts. The method enables the researcher to depict the organization coordination structure as established through the activities of liaison persons and the existence of the contacts between groups. See Robert S. Weiss and Eugene Jacobson, "A Method for the Analysis of the Structure of Complex Organizations," *American Sociological Review* 20 (December 1955): 661–68. Cf. with Ralph M. Stogdill and Carroll L. Shartle, *Methods in the Study of Administrative Leadership* (Columbus: Ohio State University Bureau of Business Research, 1955), pp. 18–32.

LEADERSHIP OPINION QUESTIONNAIRE

4.H.1

VARIABLE MEASURED: The questionnaire measures leader's orientation around two major factors, *Structure* and *Consideration.*

Structure (*S*): Reflects the extent to which an individual is likely to define and structure his own role and those of his subordinates toward goal attainment. A high score on this dimension characterizes individuals who play a more active role in directing group activities through planning, communicating information, scheduling, trying out new ideas, etc.

Consideration (*C*): Reflects the extent to which an individual is likely to have job relationships characterized by mutual trust, respect for subordinate's ideas, and consideration of their feelings. A high score is indicative of a climate of good rapport and two-way communication. A low score indicates the superior is likely to be more impersonal in his relations with group members.

DESCRIPTION: This is a forty-item questionnaire divided into the two factors, *Structure* and *Consideration.* Each factor is tested by 20 items. The items are presented with a five-point continuum with scoring weights of zero to four depending on item's orientation to total dimension.

WHERE PUBLISHED: Copyright © 1960, Science Research Associates, Inc., Chicago, Illinois. Scale is sold as Leadership Opinion Questionnaire by Edwin A. Fleishman. It was first presented to social scientists in Ralph M. Stogdill and Alvin E. Coons, eds., *Leader Behavior: Its Description and Measurement* (Columbus: Ohio State University Bureau of Business Research, 1957), pp. 120–33.

RELIABILITY: Test-retest coefficients *for 31 foremen* after a 3-month interval show

$r = .80$ on Consideration,
$r = .74$ on Initiating Structure;

for 24 Air Force NCO's

$r = .77$ on Consideration,

$r = .67$ on Initiating Structure.

Split-half reliability estimates for the Consideration and Initiating Structure were found to be .69 and .73, respectively.

VALIDITY: Validity was evaluated through correlations with independent leadership measures, such as merit rating by supervisors, peer ratings, forced choice performance reports by management, and leaderless group situation tests. Relatively low validities were found for the particular criteria employed, although a few statistically significant correlations were found. Correlations with other measures revealed that scores on the Leadership Opinion Questionnaire were independent of the "intelligence" of the supervisor, an advantage not achieved by other available leadership attitude questionnaires.

The questionnaire scores have been found to be sensitive for discriminating reliably between leadership attitudes in different situations as well as for evaluating the effects of leadership training.

Science Research Associates has compiled evidence for validity from recent studies in many different organizational settings. It has been used in a test battery to ascertain effectiveness of sales supervisors. It has been administered to foremen in a large wholesale pharmaceutical company, to first line supervisors in a large petrochemical refinery, to department managers in a large shoe manufacturing company, and to bank managers. In all instances, significant correlations between the questionnaire and proficiency have been shown. The Leadership Opinion Questionnaire has also shown that leadership patterns are directly related to organizational stress and effectiveness in three hospitals.

STANDARDIZED SCORES: Published in Edwin A. Fleishman, "The Measurement of Leadership Attitudes in Industry," *Journal of Applied Psychology* (June 1953): 156.

Dimension	Level in Organization	Mean	S.D.
Consideration	Superintendents (N = 13)	52.6	8.1
	General Foremen (N = 30)	53.2	7.1
	Foremen (N = 122)	53.9	7.2
	Workers (N = 394)		
Structure	Superintendents (N = 13)	55.5	5.7
	General Foremen (N = 30)	53.6	6.9
	Foremen (N = 122)	53.3	7.8
	Workers (N = 394)	44.2	3.9

UTILITY: Easily administered and scored. Time of administration, 10-15 minutes. See Edwin A. Fleishman, *A Manual for Administering the Leadership Opinion Questionnaire* (Chicago: Science Research Associates, 1960).

RESEARCH APPLICATIONS:

BASS, B. M. "Leadership Opinions as Forecasters of Supervisory Success," *Journal of Applied Psychology* (1956): 345–46.

FLEISHMAN, E. A. *Leadership Climate and Supervisory Behavior*. Columbus: Ohio State University Personnel Research Board, 1951.

———. "The Measurement of Leadership Attitudes in Industry." *Journal of Applied Psychology* (June 1953): 153–58.

———. "Leadership Climate, Human Relations Training, and Supervisory Behavior." *Personnel Psychology* 6 (1953): 205–22.

———, HARRIS, E. F., and BURTT, H. E. *Leadership and Supervision in Industry*. Columbus: Ohio State University, Bureau of Educational Research.

HEMPHILL, J. K. *Leader Behavior Description*. Columbus: Personnel Research Board, Ohio State University, 1950.

SEEMAN, MELVIN. "Social Mobility and Administrative Behavior." *American Sociological Review* 23 (December 1958): 633–42.

LEADERSHIP OPINION QUESTIONNAIRE*

This questionnaire contains 40 items when presented as a complete scale. The items that follow exemplify the type found in the longer questionnaire. They are presented here so that the researcher may evaluate them for his possible use of the complete scale.

Structure

ASSIGN PEOPLE IN THE WORK GROUP TO PARTICULAR TASKS.

  1. Always   2. Often   3. Occasionally   4. Seldom   5. Never

STRESS BEING AHEAD OF COMPETING WORK GROUPS.

  1. A great deal   2. Fairly much   3. To some degree
  4. Comparatively little   5. Not at all

CRITICIZE POOR WORK.

  1. Always   2. Often   3. Occasionally   4. Seldom   5. Never

EMPHASIZE MEETING OF DEADLINES.

  1. A great deal   2. Fairly much   3. To some degree
  4. Comparatively little   5. Not at all

Consideration

PUT SUGGESTIONS MADE BY PEOPLE IN THE WORK GROUP INTO OPERATION.

  1. Always   2. Often   3. Occasionally   4. Seldom   5. Never

HELP PEOPLE IN THE WORK GROUP WITH THEIR PERSONAL PROB-
LEMS.

    1. Often   2. Fairly often   3. Occasionally   4. Once in a while
    5. Seldom

GET THE APPROVAL OF THE WORK GROUP ON IMPORTANT MATTERS
BEFORE GOING AHEAD.

    1. Always   2. Often   3. Occasionally   4. Seldom   5. Never

---

4.H.2 SUPERVISORY BEHAVIOR DESCRIPTION

VARIABLE MEASURED: Perceptions of subordinates of the leadership behavior
demonstrated by their immediate superior. Factor analysis revealed that "Initiating Structure" and "Consideration" items are the most significant factors in
distinguishing leadership performance. "Initiating Structure" reflects the extent
to which the supervisor facilitates group interaction toward goal attainment;
"Consideration" reflects the extent to which the supervisor is considerate of the
feelings of those under him. All questions are worded in terms of "What does
your own supervisor actually do?"

DESCRIPTION: This is a 48-item questionnaire divided into two independent
areas of leadership called "Initiating Structure" and "Consideration." The first
area includes 20 items and the second is made up of 28 items. The items were
presented with a five-point continuum answer scale that has scoring weights of
zero to four depending on the item orientation to the total dimension. Highest
possible score was 112 on "Consideration" and 80 for "Initiation."

WHERE PUBLISHED: Edwin A. Fleishman, "A Leader Behavior Description for
Industry," in *Leader Behavior: Its Description and Measurement*, ed. Ralph M.
Stogdill and Alvin E. Coons (Columbus: Ohio State University Bureau of Busi-
ness Research, 1957), pp. 103–19.

RELIABILITY: Test-retest reliability coefficients based on numerous samples
range from .46 to .87.

		Dimension	
	Time Between		Initiating
Sample	Administration	Consideration	Structure
		r	r
Workers describing 18 foremen	11 months	.87	.75
Workers describing 59 foremen	11 months	.58	.46
Workers describing 31 foremen	3 weeks	.56	.53

Split-half reliabilities are reported for samples as between .68 to .98.

VALIDITY: The correlation between "Consideration" and "Initiating Structure" was found to be −.02 when based on replies of 122 foremen. The intercorrelation was shown to be −.33 when administered to 394 workers who

described the 122 foremen. The correlation between the two scales was shown to be −.05 when administered to 176 Air Force and Army ROTC students who described their superior officers. The independence of the two factors appears to be confirmed.

Correlations have been obtained between descriptions of foremen behavior and independent indexes of accident rates, absenteeism, grievances, and turnover among the foreman's own work groups. In production departments, high scores on the "Consideration" scale were predictive of low ratings of proficiency by the foreman's supervisor, but low absenteeism among the workers. A high score on "Initiating Structure" was predictive of a high proficiency rating, but high absenteeism and labor grievances as well.

STANDARD SCORES:

Means and Standard Deviations of Supervisory Behavior Description Scores

	Dimension			
	Consideration		Initiating Structure	
Sample	M	SD	M	SD
Descriptions of 122 foremen	79.8	14.5	41.5	7.6
Descriptions of 31 foremen	71.5	13.2	37.5	6.3
Descriptions of 31 foremen	73.0	12.7	40.7	7.3
Descriptions of 8 civil service supervisors	75.1	17.6	37.3	9.6
Descriptions of 60 general foremen	82.3	15.5	51.5	8.8

UTILITY: The questionnaire may be administered in a 10-15 minute period. When used in group applications, it is very efficient. By using this questionnaire in conjunction with the Leader Behavior Description, it is possible to get a view of how a supervisor thinks he should lead and compare this view with an assessment by his subordinates of his actual leadership performance.

RESEARCH APPLICATIONS: The best summary of research is found in the monograph cited in the aforementioned. Other references may be found in the publications cited under the Leadership Opinion Questionnaire. Most of the research has been done by E. A. Fleishman in the plants of the International Harvester Company.

Revised Form of the Supervisory Behavior Description

Item Number	Item*

Consideration: revised key

1. He refuses to give in when people disagree with him.
2. He does personal favors for the foremen under him.
3. He expresses appreciation when one of us does a good job.
4. He is easy to understand.
5. He demands more than we can do.

*Most items were answered as: 1. always; 2. often; 3. occasionally; 4. seldom; 5. never.

Item Number	Item*

6. He helps his foremen with their personal problems.
7. He criticizes his foremen in front of others.
8. He stands up for his foremen even though it makes him unpopular.
9. He insists that everything be done his way.
10. He sees that a foreman is rewarded for a job well done.
11. He rejects suggestions for changes.
12. He changes the duties of people under him without first talking it over with them.
13. He treats people under him without considering their feelings.
14. He tries to keep the foremen under him in good standing with those in higher authority.
15. He resists changes in ways of doing things.
16. He "rides" the foreman who makes a mistake.
17. He refuses to explain his actions.
18. He acts without consulting his foreman first.
19. He stresses the importance of high morale among those under him.
20. He backs up his foremen in their actions.
21. He is slow to accept new ideas.
22. He treats all his foremen as his equal.
23. He criticizes a specific act rather than a particular individual.
24. He is willing to make changes.
25. He makes those under him feel at ease when talking with him.
26. He is friendly and can be easily approached.
27. He puts suggestions that are made by foremen under him into operation.
28. He gets the approval of his foremen on important matters before going ahead.

Initiating structure: revised key

1. He encourages overtime work.
2. He tries out his new ideas.
3. He rules with an iron hand.
4. He criticizes poor work.
5. He talks about how much should be done.
6. He encourages slow-working foremen to greater effort.
7. He waits for his foremen to push new ideas before he does.
8. He assigns people under him to particular tasks.
9. He asks for sacrifices from his foremen for the good of the entire department.
10. He insists that his foremen follow standard ways of doing things in every detail.
11. He sees to it that people under him are working up to their limits.
12. He offers new approaches to problems.
13. He insists that he be informed on decisions made by foremen under him.
14. He lets others do their work the way they think best.
15. He stresses being ahead of competing work groups.
16. He "needles" foremen under him for greater effort.
17. He decides in detail what shall be done and how it shall be done.
18. He emphasizes meeting of deadlines.
19. He asks foremen who have slow groups to get more out of their groups.
20. He emphasizes the quantity of work.

4.H.3   WORK PATTERNS PROFILE

VARIABLE MEASURED: The roles in the organization as composed of certain activities.

DESCRIPTION: The profile includes fourteen descriptions of leadership functions that have been found within leadership jobs. These include inspection of the organization; investigation and research; planning; preparation of procedures and methods; coordination; evaluation; interpretation of plans and procedures; supervision of technical operations; personnel activities; public relations; professional consultation; negotiations; scheduling, routing, and dispatching; technical and professional operations. By using questionnaire and interview methods, each person studied in the organization indicates the proportion of time spent on each activity.

WHERE PUBLISHED: Ralph M. Stogdill and Carroll L. Shartle, *Methods in the Study of Administrative Leadership* (Columbus: Ohio State University Bureau of Business Research, 1955), pp. 44–53; also Carroll L. Shartle, *Executive Performance and Leadership* (Englewood Cliffs, N.J.: Prentice-Hall, 1956), pp. 81–93.

RELIABILITY: Forms were administered to 32 officers in a Naval District Command Staff. One month later, the forms were administered again to the same officers. Test-retest coefficients are shown for the fourteen major responsibilities.

Inspection	.51
Research	.59
Planning	.49
Preparing procedures	.55
Coordination	.60
Evaluation	.58
Interpretation	.18
Supervision	.03
Personal functions	.46
Professional consultation	.61
Public relations	.83
Negotiations	.83
Scheduling	.38
Technical and professional performance	.59

VALIDITY: In a study of a Naval Air Station, 34 officers kept a log of work performance for a period of three days. Results suggest that there is a fairly high degree of correspondence between logged time and estimated time for objectively observable performances. More subjective, less observable performances, such as planning and reflection, are not estimated in terms that correspond highly with time recorded on the log. A number of officers expressed the feeling that their estimates of time spent in planning were more accurate than the log, for the reason that they were not always aware at the moment that what they were doing constituted planning.

STANDARD SCORES: The fourteen activities are plotted in percent of time spent in the activities. No standard scores have been developed since many roles must first be analyzed.

UTILITY: This instrument will make it possible to compare patterns of performance. Therefore, executive selection may be made more appropriately in relation to the role as defined in the organization.

RESEARCH APPLICATIONS:
STOGDILL, RALPH M.; SHARTLE, CARROLL L.; COONS, ALVIN E.; and JANES, WILLIAM E. *A Predictive Study of Administrative Work Patterns.* Columbus: Ohio State University Bureau of Business Research, 1956.
——, and others. *Patterns of Administrative Performance.* Columbus: Ohio State University Bureau of Business Research, 1956. Chap. 4.

WORK PATTERNS PROFILE

The Ohio State University Personnel Research Board

The purpose of this analysis is to determine the relative proportion of your time devoted to major administrative and operative responsibilities, disregarding the methods of accomplishment.

Please consider your entire range of responsibilities from day to day. Attempt to account as accurately as possible for the relative percentage of time devoted to various administrative and technical functions.

Before each item below, please write the approximate percentage of time spent in the responsibility described.

(%) 1. *Inspection of the Organization*—Direct observation and personal inspection of installations, buildings, equipment, facilities, operations, services or personnel—for the purpose of determining conditions and keeping informed.

(%) 2. *Investigation and Research*—Acts involving the accumulation and preparation of information and data. (Usually prepared and presented in the form of written reports.)

(%) 3. *Planning*—Preparing for and making decisions that will affect the aims or future activities of the organization as to volume or quality of business or service. (Including thinking, reflection, and reading, as well as consultations and conferences with persons relative to short-term and long-range plans.)

(%) 4. *Preparation of Procedures and Methods*—Acts involving the mapping of procedures and methods for putting new plans into effect, as well as devising new methods for the performance of operations under existing plans.

(%) 5. *Coordination*—Acts and decisions designed to integrate and coordinate the activities of units within the organization or of persons within units, so as to achieve the maximal overall efficiency, economy, and control of operations.

(%) 6. *Evaluation*—Acts involving the consideration and evaluation of reports, correspondence, data, plans, divisions, or performances in relation to the aims, policies, and standards of the organization.

(%) 7. *Interpretation of Plans and Procedures*—Acts involving the interpretation and clarification for assistants and other personnel of directives, regulations, practices, and procedures.

(%)   8. *Supervision of Technical Operations*—Acts involving the direct supervision of personnel in the performance of duties.

(%)   9. *Personnel Activities*—Acts involving the selection, training, evaluation, motivation or disciplining of individuals, as well as acts designed to affect the morale, motivation, loyalty, or harmonious cooperation of personnel.

(%) 10. *Public Relations*—Acts designed to inform outside persons, regarding the program and functions of the organization, to obtain information regarding public sentiment, or to create a favorable attitude toward the organization.

(%) 11. *Professional Consultation*—Giving professional advice and specialized assistance on problems of a specific or technical nature to persons within or outside the organization. (Other than technical supervision and guidance of own staff personnel.)

(%) 12. *Negotiations*—Purchasing, selling, negotiating contracts or agreements, settling claims, etc.

(%) 13. *Scheduling, Routing, and Dispatching*—Initiating action and determining the time, place, and sequence of operations.

(%) 14. *Technical and Professional Operations*—The performance of duties specific to a specialized profession (e.g., practice of medicine, conducting religious services, classroom teaching, auditing records, operating machines, or equipment).

_____
(100%)   Total time spent in major responsibilities.

Morale and Job Satisfaction

Morale has been viewed as a global concept and also as a set of specific dimensions. The Minnesota (Rundquist-Sletto) Survey of Opinions (General Adjustment and Morale Scales) is a Likert-type scale that was carefully constructed to tap a general variable. Use the Short Form of the Minnesota Scale of General Adjustment and Morale when the problem calls for an overall assessment of morale. Use the Long Form to assess specific attitudes toward personal inferiority, family, law, conservatism, and education, in addition to morale and general adjustment.

Many social scientists believe that morale is a meaningful concept only when the separate dimensions of morale have been identified. Scale analysis has shown repeatedly that morale is composed of many dimensions. The SRA Employee Morale Inventory is a diagnostic tool that was constructed by including dimensions of job morale. This is the most widely used instrument for diagnosis of employee morale problems. Item analysis was used in its construction. Use the SRA Employee Morale Inventory if you are seeking to diagnose morale problems in work organizations. Norms are available that make possible departmental and interorganizational comparisons. This is probably the best standardized of all sociometric scales.

Nancy Morse and associates have constructed a set of subscales to measure intrinsic job satisfaction, pride in performance, company involvement, and financial and job status. Use the Morse Scales if short scales are needed to tap these dimensions. For a critical review of general job satisfaction scales see John P. Robinson & Associates, *Measures of Occupational Attitudes and Occupational Characteristics*. Ann Arbor: Institute of Social Research 1969, pp. 99–103.

Guttman-type scales insure that the factor in the scale has been demonstrated to be of one dimension only in the respondent population. The military morale scales are of this type, the reproducibility coefficients providing evidence for the response pattern. Use these scales for military or organizational research of any kind by substituting appropriate units in place of Air Force, Air Site, and Air Craft and Warning Stations (AC&W). Check scalability by Guttman methods for your respondents. The probability is high that these items will scale for any respondent sample to which they would logically apply.

The Brayfield and Rothe Index of Job Satisfaction has been constructed by applying Thurstone's Method of Equal-Appearing Intervals and combining Likert's scoring system that gives an intensity measure. This scale fits two important criteria: a continuum of interval measures and an intensity measure. Use the Brayfield and Rothe Index when a precise general measure of job satisfaction is desired.

SHORT FORM OF THE MINNESOTA SURVEY OF OPINIONS (GENERAL ADJUSTMENT AND MORALE SCALES)

4.I.1

VARIABLE MEASURED: Individual morale and general adjustment.

DESCRIPTION: This short form is taken from the Minnesota Scale for the Survey of Opinions that consists of 132 items. The short form consists of only 31 of the most discriminating items. These items are taken from seven scales that make up the Minnesota Scale for the Survey of Opinions. These scales are the morale scale, the general adjustment scale, inferiority scale, family scale, law scale, conservatism, and education scale.

WHERE PUBLISHED: Edward A. Rundquist and Raymond F. Sletto, *Personality in the Depression*, Child Welfare Monograph Series No. 12 (Minneapolis: University of Minnesota). Copyright 1936 by the University of Minnesota.

RELIABILITY: Split-half reliability in the .80s may be expected for the adjustment *score* and the total morale *score*. Split-half reliability coefficients for the general adjustment *scale* range from .686 to .821 with high school seniors as the lowest correlation and an all male group as the highest correlation. The females on the same basis range from .686 to .836. Reliability of actual scores from test to retest was measured over a sixty-day period. The average changes were 4.03 for 68 General College men and 5.03 for 68 General College women. Test-retest *r*'s are .793 for men and .668 for women.

VALIDITY: Validity for the general adjustment scale was determined by two general methods: (1) relating it to those outside variables that imply maladjustment and (2) relating it to scores on the other six scales. An extensive report of validity is included in Rundquist and Sletto, *Personality in the Depression*, pp. 226–41.

Karl Schuessler and Larry Freshnock have analyzed 31 separate tests of morale and similar concepts (e.g., anomie, alienation, life satisfaction, social isolation, etc.). Their factor analysis reveals seven different factors operating within their universe of selected items. They call these factors pessimism, depression, cynicism, anxiety, passivism, job satisfaction, general life satisfaction, and zest for living. A relatively high correlation ($r = .682$) was found between the factor score on "pessimism" or "anomie" and the test scores shown for selected items of the Rundquist-Sletto morale scale. It can be said that the Rundquist-Sletto morale scale compares favorably with such scales as Srole's

Anomia and the Struening-Richardson measure of Alienation via Rejection. Karl Schuessler and Larry Freshnock, "Dimensionality of Tests of Morale and Related Concepts" (forthcoming).

UTILITY: This short form is presented to assist those who may wish to obtain a measure of general adjustment and morale without administering the entire survey. It consists of only 31 items in the questionnaire and can be administered in 15 to 20 minutes. There are 16 items in the general adjustment scale and 22 items in the morale scale, both scales included in the 31 item survey. The Long Form of the Survey takes 30 to 40 minutes.

RESEARCH APPLICATIONS:

CHAPIN, F. STUART. "The Effects of Slum Clearance and Rehousing on Family and Community Relationships in Minneapolis." *American Journal of Sociology* 43 (March 1938): 744–63.

――――, and JAHN, JULIUS. "The Advantages of Work Relief over Direct Relief in Maintaining Morale in St. Paul in 1939." *American Journal of Sociology* 46 (July 1940): 13–22.

MILLER, D. C. "Morale of College Trained Adults." *American Sociological Review* 5 (December 1940): 880–89.

――――. "Economic Factors in the Morale of College Trained Adults." *American Journal of Sociology* 47 (September 1941): 139–57.

SCORING INSTRUCTIONS FOR THE SHORT FORM MINNESOTA SCALE FOR THE SURVEY OF OPINIONS

Administration

The survey requires between 15 and 20 minutes for all to complete it. Although the printed directions on the survey are self-explanatory, it is advisable to read the directions aloud while the subjects are reading them silently. To secure frankness and cooperation, it is well to assure the group that their opinions are valued, will be held in complete confidence, and will not affect their grades in any course or their standing with their employers or other persons of responsibility. They may be directed to fill in all the information items (name, age, sex, etc.) or to omit those that the examiner does not require for research or counseling purposes.

Scoring

The five alternative responses to each item are weighted from 1 to 5 in scoring. The sum of the scores in the extreme lefthand column is the adjustment score; the sum of the next column is the score on the acceptable morale items; the sum of the next is the score on the unacceptable morale items. To obtain the total morale score, add the total scores on acceptable and unacceptable items.

Norms

The scoring norms in the table permit conversion of raw scores into standard scores. These norms are based on the scores of 1000 young people, 500 of each sex. The standardization group included 400 college students, 200 high school seniors, and 400 youth employed and unemployed persons in continuation classes at high school level. The distribution of paternal occupation for the standardization group approximates the census distribution of occupations and indicates that it is composed of a fairly representative sample of young persons between the ages of sixteen and twenty-five years. No significant differences between the scores of high school and college students were found, and the norms are adequate for both groups.

The standard scores given in the table were obtained by the McCall T-Score technique, which expresses scores in tenths of standard deviation units from the mean score for the standardization group. *The mean raw score of the standardization group becomes the standard score of 50.* A standard score of 60 is one standard deviation higher than the mean; a standard score of 40 is one standard deviation below the mean. Response weights to items have been so assigned that a high standard score is unfavorable.

To illustrate the use of the table, suppose an individual makes the same raw scores—say 57—on the morale, economic conservatism, and education scales. We find 57 in the raw score column. Reading to the right, we observe that the individual's standard scores are 50 on the morale scale, 40 on the economic conservatism scale, and 60 on the education scale. These scores indicate that the individual is average, that he is conservative in his economic views (one standard deviation below the mean), and that his estimate of the value of education is relatively unfavorable (one standard deviation above the mean).

Standard Score Equivalents for Raw Scores
(Based on Standardization Group of 1000)

Raw Score	Standard Score Equivalents*							Raw Score	Standard Score Equivalents						
	M	I	F	L	EC	E	GA		M	I	F	L	EC	E	GA
110								62	55	46	55	53	45	65	78
109					91			61	54	45	54	52	44	64	77
108					90			60	53	44	53	51	43	63	76
107					89										
106					88			59	52	43	52	50	42	62	74
105					87			58	51	42	51	49	41	61	73
104					86			57	50	41	51	48	40	60	72
103					85			56	49	40	50	47	39	59	70
102			92		84			55	48	39	49	46	38	58	69
101		86	91		83			54	47	37	48	45	37	57	68
100		85	90		82			53	46	36	47	44	36	56	66
								52	45	35	46	43	35	55	65
99		84	89		81			51	43	34	45	42	34	54	64
98		83	88		80			50	42	33	44	41	33	53	62
97		82	87		79										
96		81	86		78			49	41	32	43	39	32	52	61
95	90	80	85		77			48	40	31	42	38	31	51	60
94	89	79	84		76			47	39	30	41	37	30	49	58
93	88	78	84		75			46	38	29	40	36	29	48	57
92	87	77	83		74			45	37	28	40	35	28	47	56
91	86	76	82		73		96	44	36	27	39	34	27	46	54
90	85	75	81	84	72		95	43	35	26	38	33	26	45	53
								42	34	25	37	32	25	44	52

Standard Score Equivalents for Raw Scores (Continued)
(Based on Standardization Group of 1000)

Raw Score	Standard Score Equivalents*							Raw Score	Standard Score Equivalents						
	M	I	F	L	EC	E	GA		M	I	F	L	EC	E	GA
89	83	74	80	82	71	94		41	33	24	36	31	24	43	50
88	82	73	79	81	70	93		40	32	23	35	30	23	42	49
87	81	72	78	80	69	92									
86	80	71	77	79	68	90		39	31	22	34	29	22	41	48
85	79	70	76	78	67	89		38	30	21	33	28	21	40	47
84	78	68	75	77	66	88		37	29	20	32	27	20	39	45
83	77	67	74	76	65	87		36	28	19	31	26	19	38	44
82	76	66	73	75	64	86		35	27	18	30	24	18	37	43
81	75	65	73	74	63	85		34	26	17	29	23	17	36	41
80	74	64	72	73	62	84		33	25	16	29	22	16	35	40
								32	23	15	28	21	15	34	39
79	73	63	71	72	61	83		31	22	14	27	20	14	33	37
78	72	62	70	71	60	82		30	21	13	26	19	13	32	36
77	71	61	69	70	59	81									
76	70	60	68	69	58	80		29	20	12	25	18	12	31	35
75	69	59	67	67	57	79		28	19	11	24	17	11	30	33
74	68	58	66	66	56	78		27	18	10	23	16	10	28	32
73	67	57	65	65	56	77		26	17	9	22	15	9	27	31
72	66	56	64	64	55	76		25						26	29
71	65	55	63	63	54	75		24						25	28
70	63	54	62	62	53	74	89	23						24	27
								22						23	25
69	62	53	62	61	52	73	87	21							24
68	61	52	61	60	51	72	86	20							23
67	60	51	60	59	50	71	85								
66	59	50	59	58	49	69	83	19							21
65	58	49	58	57	48	68	82	18							20
64	57	48	57	56	47	67	81	17							19
63	56	47	56	55	46	66	79	16							17

*M—Morale; I—Inferiority; F—Family; L—Law; EC—Economic Conservatism; GA—General Adjustment.

4.I.1.a. MINNESOTA SURVEY OF OPINION (SHORT FORM)

E. A. Rundquist and R. F. Sletto

Name _____ Age _____ Sex _____ Date _____
        (Last)   (First)

The following pages contain a number of statements about which there is no general agreement. People differ widely in the way they feel about each item. There are no right answers. The purpose of the survey is to see how different groups feel about each item. We should like your honest opinion on each of these statements.

READ EACH ITEM CAREFULLY AND UNDERLINE QUICKLY THE PHRASE THAT BEST EXPRESSES YOUR FEELING ABOUT THE STATE-MENT. Wherever possible, let your own personal experience determine your answer. Do not spend much time on any item. If in doubt, underline the phrase that seems most nearly to express your present feeling about the statement. WORK RAPIDLY. Be sure to answer every item.

1. TIMES ARE GETTING BETTER.
   Strongly agree[1] Agree[2] Undecided[3]
   Disagree[4] Strongly disagree[5]

_____ _____

2. ANY MAN WITH ABILITY AND WILLING-NESS TO WORK HARD HAS A GOOD CHANCE OF BEING SUCCESSFUL.
   Strongly agree[1] Agree[2] Undecided[3]
   Disagree[4] Strongly disagree[5]

_____

3. IT IS DIFFICULT TO SAY THE RIGHT THING AT THE RIGHT TIME.
   Strongly agree[5] Agree[4] Undecided[3]
   Disagree[2] Strongly disagree[1]

_____

4. MOST PEOPLE CAN BE TRUSTED.
   Strongly agree[1] Agree[2] Undecided[3]
   Disagree[4] Strongly disagree[5]

_____

5. HIGH SCHOOLS ARE TOO IMPRACTICAL.
   Strongly agree[5] Agree[4] Undecided[3]
   Disagree[2] Strongly disagree[1]

_____

6. A PERSON CAN PLAN HIS FUTURE SO THAT EVERYTHING WILL COME OUT ALL RIGHT IN THE LONG RUN.
   Strongly agree[1] Agree[2] Undecided[3]
   Disagree[4] Strongly disagree[5]

_____

7. NO ONE CARES MUCH WHAT HAPPENS TO YOU.
   Strongly agree[5] Agree[4] Undecided[3]
   Disagree[2] Strongly disagree[1]

_____ _____

8. SUCCESS IS MORE DEPENDENT ON LUCK THAN ON REAL ABILITY.
   Strongly agree[5] Agree[4] Undecided[3]
   Disagree[2] Strongly disagree[1]

_____

9. IF OUR ECONOMIC SYSTEM WERE JUST, THERE WOULD BE MUCH LESS CRIME.
   Strongly agree[5] Agree[4] Undecided[3]
   Disagree[2] Strongly disagree[1]

_____

10. A MAN DOES NOT HAVE TO PRETEND HE IS SMARTER THAN HE REALLY IS TO "GET BY."
   Strongly agree[1] Agree[2] Undecided[3]
   Disagree[4] Strongly disagree[5]

_____

11. LAWS ARE SO OFTEN MADE FOR THE BENEFIT OF SMALL SELFISH GROUPS THAT A MAN CANNOT RESPECT THE LAW.
Strongly agree[5] Agree[4] Undecided[3]
Disagree[2] Strongly disagree[1]
_____

12. ONE SELDOM WORRIES SO MUCH AS TO BECOME VERY MISERABLE.
Strongly agree[1] Agree[2] Undecided[3]
Disagree[4] Strongly disagree[5]
_____

13. THE FUTURE LOOKS VERY BLACK.
Strongly agree[5] Agree[4] Undecided[3]
Disagree[2] Strongly disagree[1]
_____   _____

14. REAL FRIENDS ARE AS EASY TO FIND AS EVER.
Strongly agree[1] Agree[2] Undecided[3]
Disagree[4] Strongly disagree[5]
_____

15. POVERTY IS CHIEFLY A RESULT OF IN-JUSTICE IN THE DISTRIBUTION OF WEALTH.
Strongly agree[5] Agree[4] Undecided[3]
Disagree[2] Strongly disagree[1]
_____

16. IT IS DIFFICULT TO THINK CLEARLY THESE DAYS.
Strongly agree[5] Agree[4] Undecided[3]
Disagree[2] Strongly disagree[1]
_____

17. THERE IS LITTLE CHANCE FOR ADVANCE-MENT IN INDUSTRY AND BUSINESS UN-LESS A MAN HAS UNFAIR PULL.
Strongly agree[5] Agree[4] Undecided[3]
Disagree[2] Strongly disagree[1]
_____   _____

18. IT DOES NOT TAKE LONG TO GET OVER FEELING GLOOMY.
Strongly agree[1] Agree[2] Undecided[3]
Disagree[4] Strongly disagree[5]
_____

19. THE YOUNG MAN OF TODAY CAN EXPECT MUCH OF THE FUTURE.
Strongly agree[1] Agree[2] Undecided[3]
Disagree[4] Strongly disagree[5]
_____ _____

20. IT IS GREAT TO BE LIVING IN THESE EX-CITING TIMES.
Strongly agree[1] Agree[2] Undecided[3]
Disagree[4] Strongly disagree[5]
_____

21. LIFE IS JUST ONE WORRY AFTER AN-
    OTHER.
    Strongly agree⁵   Agree⁴   Undecided³
    Disagree²   Strongly disagree¹

    _____   _____

22. THE DAY IS NOT LONG ENOUGH TO DO
    ONE'S WORK WELL AND HAVE ANY TIME
    FOR FUN.
    Strongly agree⁵   Agree⁴   Undecided³
    Disagree²   Strongly disagree¹

                 _____

23. A MAN CAN LEARN MORE BY WORKING
    FOUR YEARS THAN BY GOING TO HIGH
    SCHOOL.
    Strongly agree⁵   Agree⁴   Undecided³
    Disagree²   Strongly disagree¹

    _____

24. THIS   GENERATION   WILL   PROBABLY
    NEVER SEE SUCH HARD TIMES AGAIN.
    Strongly agree¹   Agree²   Undecided³
    Disagree⁴   Strongly disagree⁵

          _____

25. ONE CANNOT FIND AS MUCH UNDER-
    STANDING AT HOME AS ELSEWHERE.
    Strongly agree⁵   Agree⁴   Undecided³
    Disagree²   Strongly disagree¹

    _____

26. THESE DAYS ONE IS INCLINED TO GIVE
    UP HOPE OF AMOUNTING TO SOMETHING.
    Strongly agree⁵   Agree⁴   Undecided³
    Disagree²   Strongly disagree¹

          _____

27. EDUCATION IS OF NO HELP IN GETTING
    A JOB TODAY.
    Strongly agree⁵   Agree⁴   Undecided³
    Disagree²   Strongly disagree¹

    _____

28. THERE IS REALLY NO POINT IN LIVING.
    Strongly agree⁵   Agree⁴   Undecided³
    Disagree²   Strongly disagree¹

          _____

29. MOST PEOPLE JUST PRETEND THAT THEY
    LIKE YOU.
    Strongly agree⁵   Agree⁴   Undecided³
    Disagree²   Strongly disagree¹

    _____

30. THE FUTURE IS TOO UNCERTAIN FOR A
    PERSON TO PLAN ON MARRYING.
    Strongly agree⁵   Agree⁴   Undecided³
    Disagree²   Strongly disagree¹

          _____

31. LIFE IS JUST A SERIES OF DISAPPOINT-
    MENTS.
    Strongly agree⁵   Agree⁴   Undecided³
    Disagree²   Strongly disagree¹

_____   _____   _____
 GA   Ma   Mu   Ma + Mu = Total Morale Score

4.I.1.b. LONG FORM OF THE MINNESOTA SURVEY OF OPINIONS*

Directions

READ EACH ITEM CAREFULLY AND UNDERLINE QUICKLY THE PHRASE THAT BEST EXPRESSES YOUR FEELING ABOUT THE STATEMENT. WORK RAPIDLY. BE SURE TO ANSWER EVERY ITEM.

1. THE FUTURE IS TOO UNCERTAIN FOR A PERSON TO PLAN ON MARRYING.
Strongly agree^5 Agree^4 Undecided^3 Disagree^2
Strongly disagree^1 (M)

2. AFTER BEING CAUGHT IN A MISTAKE, IT IS HARD TO DO GOOD WORK FOR A WHILE.
Strongly agree^5 Agree^4 Undecided^3 Disagree^2
Strongly disagree^1 (I)

3. HOME IS THE MOST PLEASANT PLACE IN THE WORLD.
Strongly agree^1 Agree^2 Undecided^3 Disagree^4
Strongly disagree^5 (F)

4. THE LAW PROTECTS PROPERTY RIGHTS AT THE EXPENSE OF HUMAN RIGHTS.
Strongly agree^5 Agree^4 Undecided^3 Disagree^2
Strongly disagree^1 (L)

5. THE GOVERNMENT SHOULD TAKE OVER ALL LARGE INDUSTRIES.
Strongly agree^5 Agree^4 Undecided^3 Disagree^2
Strongly disagree^1 (EC)

6. A MAN CAN LEARN MORE BY WORKING FOUR YEARS THAN BY GOING TO HIGH SCHOOL.
Strongly agree^5 Agree^4 Undecided^3 Disagree^2
Strongly disagree^1 (E)

7. IT IS DIFFICULT TO THINK CLEARLY THESE DAYS.
Strongly agree^5 Agree^4 Undecided^3 Disagree^2
Strongly disagree^1 (M)

8. IT IS EASY TO EXPRESS ONE'S IDEAS.
Strongly agree^1 Agree^2 Undecided^3 Disagree^4
Strongly disagree^5 (I)

9. PARENTS EXPECT TOO MUCH FROM THEIR CHILDREN.
Strongly agree^5 Agree^4 Undecided^3 Disagree^2
Strongly disagree^1 (F)

---

*Containing the Scales of General Adjustment, Morale, Inferiority, Family, Law, Conservatism, and Education. For scoring, see Rundquist and Sletto, *Personality in the Depression*, p. 385. Add numbers given by response. Norms are shown above. Items marked *M* are in Morale Scale; *I* items are in Inferiority Scale; *F* items, Family Scale; *L* items, Law Scale; *EC*, Economic Conservatism Scale; *E*, Education Scale.

10. A PERSON SHOULD OBEY ONLY THOSE LAWS THAT SEEM REASONABLE.
Strongly agree^5 Agree^4 Undecided^3 Disagree^2
Strongly disagree^1 (L)

11. LABOR SHOULD OBEY ONLY THOSE LAWS THAT SEEM REASON-ABLE.
Strongly agree^5 Agree^4 Undecided^3 Disagree^2
Strongly disagree^1 (EC)

12. THE MORE EDUCATION A MAN HAS THE BETTER HE IS ABLE TO ENJOY LIFE.
Strongly agree^1 Agree^2 Undecided^3 Disagree^4
Strongly disagree^5 (E)

13. THE FUTURE LOOKS VERY BLACK.
Strongly agree^5 Agree^4 Undecided^3 Disagree^2
Strongly disagree^1 (M)

14. IT IS DIFFICULT TO SAY THE RIGHT THING AT THE RIGHT TIME.
Strongly agree^5 Agree^4 Undecided^3 Disagree^2
Strongly disagree^1 (I)

15. ONE OUGHT TO DISCUSS IMPORTANT PLANS WITH MEMBERS OF HIS FAMILY.
Strongly agree^1 Agree^2 Undecided^3 Disagree^4
Strongly disagree^5 (F)

16. IT IS ALL RIGHT TO EVADE THE LAW IF YOU DO NOT ACTUALLY VIOLATE IT.
Strongly agree^5 Agree^4 Undecided^3 Disagree^2
Strongly disagree^1 (L)

17. LEGISLATURES ARE TOO READY TO PASS LAWS TO CURB BUSI-NESS FREEDOM.
Strongly agree^1 Agree^2 Undecided^3 Disagree^4
Strongly disagree^5 (EC)

18. EDUCATION HELPS A PERSON TO USE HIS LEISURE TIME TO BETTER ADVANTAGE.
Strongly agree^1 Agree^2 Undecided^3 Disagree^4
Strongly disagree^5 (E)

19. LIFE IS JUST ONE WORRY AFTER ANOTHER.
Strongly agree^5 Agree^4 Undecided^3 Disagree^2
Strongly disagree^1 (M)

20. ONE CAN USUALLY KEEP COOL IN IMPORTANT SITUATIONS.
Strongly agree^1 Agree^2 Undecided^3 Disagree^4
Strongly disagree^5 (I)

21. IN PLANS FOR THE FUTURE, PARENTS SHOULD BE GIVEN FIRST CONSIDERATION.
Strongly agree^1 Agree^2 Undecided^3 Disagree^4
Strongly disagree^5 (F)

22. THE SENTENCES OF JUDGES IN COURTS ARE DETERMINED BY THEIR PREJUDICES.
Strongly agree[5] Agree[4] Undecided[3] Disagree[2]
Strongly disagree[1]   (L)

23. FOR MEN TO DO THEIR BEST, THERE MUST BE THE POSSIBILITY OF UNLIMITED PROFIT.
Strongly agree[1] Agree[2] Undecided[3] Disagree[4]
Strongly disagree[5]   (EC)

24. A GOOD EDUCATION IS A GREAT COMFORT TO A MAN OUT OF WORK.
Strongly agree[1] Agree[2] Undecided[3] Disagree[4]
Strongly disagree[5]   (E)

25. MOST PEOPLE CAN BE TRUSTED.
Strongly agree[1] Agree[2] Undecided[3] Disagree[4]
Strongly disagree[5]   (M)

26. IT IS EASY TO GET ONE'S OWN WAY IN MOST SITUATIONS.
Strongly agree[1] Agree[2] Undecided[3] Disagree[4]
Strongly disagree[5]   (I)

27. A MAN SHOULD BE WILLING TO SACRIFICE EVERYTHING FOR HIS FAMILY.
Strongly agree[1] Agree[2] Undecided[3] Disagree[4]
Strongly disagree[5]   (F)

28. ON THE WHOLE, JUDGES ARE HONEST.
Strongly agree[1] Agree[2] Undecided[3] Disagree[4]
Strongly disagree[5]   (L)

29. POVERTY IS CHIEFLY A RESULT OF INJUSTICE IN THE DISTRI-BUTION OF WEALTH.
Strongly agree[5] Agree[4] Undecided[3] Disagree[2]
Strongly disagree[1]   (EC)

30. ONLY SUBJECTS LIKE READING, WRITING, AND ARITHMETIC SHOULD BE TAUGHT AT PUBLIC EXPENSE.
Strongly agree[5] Agree[4] Undecided[3] Disagree[2]
Strongly disagree[1]   (E)

31. TIMES ARE GETTING BETTER.
Strongly agree[1] Agree[2] Undecided[3] Disagree[4]
Strongly disagree[5]   (M)

32. IT IS EASY TO HAVE A GOOD TIME AT A PARTY.
Strongly agree[1] Agree[2] Undecided[3] Disagree[4]
Strongly disagree[5]   (I)

33. PARENTS TOO OFTEN EXPECT THEIR GROWN-UP CHILDREN TO OBEY THEM.
Strongly agree[5] Agree[4] Undecided[3] Disagree[2]
Strongly disagree[1]   (F)

34. JURIES SELDOM UNDERSTAND A CASE WELL ENOUGH TO MAKE A REALLY JUST DECISION.
Strongly agree[5] Agree[4] Undecided[3] Disagree[2]
Strongly disagree[1]   (L)

35. THE GOVERNMENT SHOULD NOT ATTEMPT TO LIMIT PROFITS.
Strongly agree[1] Agree[2] Undecided[3] Disagree[4]
Strongly disagree[5]   (EC)

36. EDUCATION IS OF NO HELP IN GETTING A JOB TODAY.
Strongly agree[5] Agree[4] Undecided[3] Disagree[2]
Strongly disagree[1]   (E)

37. IT DOES NOT TAKE LONG TO GET OVER FEELING GLOOMY.
Strongly agree[1] Agree[2] Undecided[3] Disagree[4]
Strongly disagree[5]   (M)

38. MEETING NEW PEOPLE IS USUALLY EMBARRASSING.
Strongly agree[5] Agree[4] Undecided[3] Disagree[2]
Strongly disagree[1]   (I)

39. ONE CANNOT FIND AS MUCH UNDERSTANDING AT HOME AS ELSEWHERE.
Strongly agree[5] Agree[4] Undecided[3] Disagree[2]
Strongly disagree[1]   (F)

40. ON THE WHOLE, POLICEMEN ARE HONEST.
Strongly agree[1] Agree[2] Undecided[3] Disagree[4]
Strongly disagree[5]   (L)

41. THE MORE A MAN LEARNS ABOUT OUR ECONOMIC SYSTEM, THE LESS WILLING HE IS TO SEE CHANGES MADE.
Strongly agree[1] Agree[2] Undecided[3] Disagree[4]
Strongly disagree[5]   (EC)

42. MOST YOUNG PEOPLE ARE GETTING TOO MUCH EDUCATION.
Strongly agree[5] Agree[4] Undecided[3] Disagree[2]
Strongly disagree[1]   (E)

43. THE DAY IS NOT LONG ENOUGH TO DO ONE'S WORK WELL AND HAVE ANY TIME FOR FUN.
Strongly agree[5] Agree[4] Undecided[3] Disagree[2]
Strongly disagree[1]   (M)

44. IT IS EASY TO KEEP UP ONE'S COURAGE.
Strongly agree[1] Agree[2] Undecided[3] Disagree[4]
Strongly disagree[5]   (I)

45. ONE OWES HIS GREATEST OBLIGATION TO HIS FAMILY.
Strongly agree[1] Agree[2] Undecided[3] Disagree[4]
Strongly disagree[5]   (F)

46. A MAN SHOULD OBEY THE LAWS NO MATTER HOW MUCH THEY INTERFERE WITH HIS PERSONAL AMBITIONS.
Strongly agree[1] Agree[2] Undecided[3] Disagree[4]
Strongly disagree[5]   (L)

47. THE GOVERNMENT OUGHT TO GUARANTEE A LIVING TO THOSE
WHO CANNOT FIND WORK.
Strongly agree[5] Agree[4] Undecided[3] Disagree[2]
Strongly disagree[1]   (EC)

48. A HIGH SCHOOL EDUCATION IS WORTH ALL THE TIME AND
EFFORT IT REQUIRES.
Strongly agree[1] Agree[2] Undecided[3] Disagree[4]
Strongly disagree[5]   (E)

49. NO ONE CARES MUCH WHAT HAPPENS TO YOU.
Strongly agree[5] Agree[4] Undecided[3] Disagree[2]
Strongly disagree[1]   (M)

50. IT IS EASY TO IGNORE CRITICISM.
Strongly agree[1] Agree[2] Undecided[3] Disagree[4]
Strongly disagree[5]   (I)

51. IT IS HARD TO KEEP A PLEASANT DISPOSITION AT HOME.
Strongly agree[5] Agree[4] Undecided[3] Disagree[2]
Strongly disagree[1]   (F)

52. COURT DECISIONS ARE ALMOST ALWAYS JUST.
Strongly agree[1] Agree[2] Undecided[3] Disagree[4]
Strongly disagree[5]   (L)

53. LARGE INCOMES SHOULD BE TAXED MUCH MORE THAN THEY
ARE NOW.
Strongly agree[5] Agree[4] Undecided[3] Disagree[2]
Strongly disagree[1]   (EC)

54. OUR SCHOOLS ENCOURAGE AN INDIVIDUAL TO THINK FOR
HIMSELF.
Strongly agree[1] Agree[2] Undecided[3] Disagree[4]
Strongly disagree[5]   (E)

55. ANY MAN WITH ABILITY AND WILLINGNESS TO WORK HARD
HAS A GOOD CHANCE OF BEING SUCCESSFUL.
Strongly agree[1] Agree[2] Undecided[3] Disagree[4]
Strongly disagree[5]   (M)

56. IT IS EASY TO ACT NATURALLY IN A GROUP.
Strongly agree[1] Agree[2] Undecided[3] Disagree[4]
Strongly disagree[5]   (I)

57. PEOPLE IN THE FAMILY CAN BE TRUSTED COMPLETELY.
Strongly agree[1] Agree[2] Undecided[3] Disagree[4]
Strongly disagree[5]   (F)

58. IN THE COURTS A POOR MAN WILL RECEIVE AS FAIR TREAT-
MENT AS A MILLIONAIRE.
Strongly agree[1] Agree[2] Undecided[3] Disagree[4]
Strongly disagree[5]   (L)

59. MEN WOULD NOT DO THEIR BEST, IF GOVERNMENT OWNED ALL INDUSTRY.
Strongly agree[1]   Agree[2]   Undecided[3]   Disagree[4]
Strongly disagree[5]   (EC)

60. THERE ARE TOO MANY FADS AND FRILLS IN MODERN EDUCA-TION.
Strongly agree[5]   Agree[4]   Undecided[3]   Disagree[2]
Strongly disagree[1]   (E)

61. IT IS GREAT TO BE LIVING IN THESE EXCITING TIMES.
Strongly agree[1]   Agree[2]   Undecided[3]   Disagree[4]
Strongly disagree[5]   (M)

62. IT IS HARD TO BRING ONESELF TO CONFIDE IN OTHERS.
Strongly agree[1]   Agree[2]   Undecided[3]   Disagree[4]
Strongly disagree[5]   (I)

63. ONE BECOMES NERVOUS AT HOME.
Strongly agree[5]   Agree[4]   Undecided[3]   Disagree[2]
Strongly disagree[1]   (F)

64. PERSONAL CIRCUMSTANCES SHOULD NEVER BE CONSIDERED AN EXCUSE FOR LAWBREAKING.
Strongly agree[1]   Agree[2]   Undecided[3]   Disagree[4]
Strongly disagree[5]   (L)

65. MOST GREAT FORTUNES ARE MADE HONESTLY.
Strongly agree[1]   Agree[2]   Undecided[3]   Disagree[4]
Strongly disagree[5]   (EC)

66. EDUCATION ONLY MAKES A PERSON DISCONTENTED.
Strongly agree[5]   Agree[4]   Undecided[3]   Disagree[2]
Strongly disagree[1]   (E)

67. THESE DAYS ONE IS INCLINED TO GIVE UP HOPE OF AMOUNT-ING TO SOMETHING.
Strongly agree[5]   Agree[4]   Undecided[3]   Disagree[2]
Strongly disagree[1]   (M)

68. IT IS HARD TO DO YOUR BEST WHEN PEOPLE ARE WATCHING YOU.
Strongly agree[5]   Agree[4]   Undecided[3]   Disagree[2]
Strongly disagree[1]   (I)

69. THE JOYS OF FAMILY LIFE ARE MUCH OVERRATED.
Strongly agree[5]   Agree[4]   Undecided[3]   Disagree[2]
Strongly disagree[1]   (F)

70. A MAN SHOULD TELL THE TRUTH IN COURT, REGARDLESS OF CONSEQUENCES.
Strongly agree[1]   Agree[2]   Undecided[3]   Disagree[4]
Strongly disagree[5]   (L)

71. PRIVATE OWNERSHIP OF PROPERTY IS NECESSARY FOR ECONOMIC PROGRESS.
Strongly agree[1] Agree[2] Undecided[3] Disagree[4]
Strongly disagree[5]   (EC)

72. SCHOOL TRAINING IS OF LITTLE HELP IN MEETING THE PROBLEMS OF REAL LIFE.
Strongly agree[5] Agree[4] Undecided[3] Disagree[2]
Strongly disagree[1]   (E)

73. THERE IS LITTLE CHANCE FOR ADVANCEMENT IN INDUSTRY AND BUSINESS UNLESS A MAN HAS UNFAIR PULL.
Strongly agree[5] Agree[4] Undecided[3] Disagree[2]
Strongly disagree[1]   (M)

74. IT IS EASY TO GET ALONG WITH PEOPLE.
Strongly agree[1] Agree[2] Undecided[3] Disagree[4]
Strongly disagree[5]   (I)

75. ONE'S PARENTS USUALLY TREAT HIM FAIRLY AND SENSIBLY.
Strongly agree[1] Agree[2] Undecided[3] Disagree[4]
Strongly disagree[5]   (F)

76. A PERSON WHO REPORTS MINOW LAW VIOLATIONS IS ONLY A TROUBLEMAKER.
Strongly agree[5] Agree[4] Undecided[3] Disagree[2]
Strongly disagree[1]   (L)

77. WITHOUT SWEEPING CHANGES IN OUR ECONOMIC SYSTEM, LITTLE PROGRESS CAN BE MADE IN THE SOLUTION OF SOCIAL PROBLEMS.
Strongly agree[5] Agree[4] Undecided[3] Disagree[2]
Strongly disagree[1]   (EC)

78. EDUCATION TENDS TO MAKE AN INDIVIDUAL LESS CONCEITED.
Strongly agree[1] Agree[2] Undecided[3] Disagree[4]
Strongly disagree[5]   (E)

79. THE YOUNG MAN OF TODAY CAN EXPECT MUCH OF THE FUTURE.
Strongly agree[1] Agree[2] Undecided[3] Disagree[4]
Strongly disagree[5]   (M)

80. IT IS EASY TO FEEL AS THOUGH YOU HAD A WORLD OF SELF-CONFIDENCE.
Strongly agree[1] Agree[2] Undecided[3] Disagree[4]
Strongly disagree[5]   (I)

81. ONE SHOULD CONFIDE MORE FULLY IN MEMBERS OF HIS FAMILY.
Strongly agree[1] Agree[2] Undecided[3] Disagree[4]
Strongly disagree[5]   (F)

82. A PERSON IS JUSTIFIED IN GIVING FALSE TESTIMONY TO PROTECT A FRIEND ON TRIAL.
Strongly agree[5]   Agree[4]   Undecided[3]   Disagree[2]
Strongly disagree[1]   (L)

83. ON THE WHOLE, OUR ECONOMIC SYSTEM IS JUST AND WISE.
Strongly agree[1]   Agree[2]   Undecided[3]   Disagree[4]
Strongly disagree[5]   (EC)

84. SOLUTION OF THE WORLD'S PROBLEMS WILL COME THROUGH EDUCATION.
Strongly agree[1]   Agree[2]   Undecided[3]   Disagree[4]
Strongly disagree[5]   (E)

85. THIS GENERATION WILL PROBABLY NEVER SEE SUCH HARD TIMES AGAIN.
Strongly agree[1]   Agree[2]   Undecided[3]   Disagree[4]
Strongly disagree[5]   (M)

86. MOST PEOPLE JUST PRETEND THAT THEY LIKE YOU.
Strongly agree[5]   Agree[4]   Undecided[3]   Disagree[2]
Strongly disagree[1]   (I)

87. ONE FEELS MOST CONTENTED AT HOME.
Strongly agree[1]   Agree[2]   Undecided[3]   Disagree[4]
Strongly disagree[5]   (F)

88. A HUNGRY MAN HAS A RIGHT TO STEAL.
Strongly agree[5]   Agree[4]   Undecided[3]   Disagree[2]
Strongly disagree[1]   (L)

89. LABOR DOES NOT GET ITS FAIR SHARE OF WHAT IT PRODUCES.
Strongly agree[5]   Agree[4]   Undecided[3]   Disagree[2]
Strongly disagree[1]   (EC)

90. HIGH SCHOOL COURSES ARE TOO IMPRACTICAL.
Strongly agree[5]   Agree[4]   Undecided[3]   Disagree[2]
Strongly disagree[1]   (E)

91. REAL FRIENDS ARE AS EASY TO FIND AS EVER.
Strongly agree[1]   Agree[2]   Undecided[3]   Disagree[4]
Strongly disagree[5]   (M)

92. SO MANY PEOPLE DO THINGS WELL THAT IT IS EASY TO BECOME DISCOURAGED.
Strongly agree[5]   Agree[4]   Undecided[3]   Disagree[2]
Strongly disagree[1]   (I)

93. FAMILY TIES ARE STRENGTHENED WHEN TIMES ARE HARD.
Strongly agree[1]   Agree[2]   Undecided[3]   Disagree[4]
Strongly disagree[5]   (F)

94. ALL LAWS SHOULD BE STRICTLY OBEYED BECAUSE THEY *ARE* LAWS.
Strongly agree[1] Agree[2] Undecided[3] Disagree[4]
Strongly disagree[5]   (L)

95. WHEN A RICH MAN DIES, MOST OF HIS PROPERTY SHOULD GO TO THE STATE.
Strongly agree[5] Agree[4] Undecided[3] Disagree[2]
Strongly disagree[1]   (EC)

96. A MAN IS FOOLISH TO KEEP ON GOING TO SCHOOL IF HE CAN GET A JOB.
Strongly agree[5] Agree[4] Undecided[3] Disagree[2]
Strongly disagree[1]   (E)

97. LIFE IS JUST A SERIES OF DISAPPOINTMENTS.
Strongly agree[5] Agree[4] Undecided[3] Disagree[2]
Strongly disagree[1]   (M)

98. IT IS HARD NOT TO BE SELF-CONSCIOUS.
Strongly agree[5] Agree[4] Undecided[3] Disagree[2]
Strongly disagree[1]   (I)

99. PARENTS ARE INCLINED TO BE TOO OLD-FASHIONED IN THEIR IDEAS.
Strongly agree[5] Agree[4] Undecided[3] Disagree[2]
Strongly disagree[1]   (F)

100. LAWS ARE SO OFTEN MADE FOR THE BENEFIT OF SMALL SELF-ISH GROUPS THAT A MAN CANNOT RESPECT THE LAW.
Strongly agree[5] Agree[4] Undecided[3] Disagree[2]
Strongly disagree[1]   (L)

101. IF OUR ECONOMIC SYSTEM WERE JUST, THERE WOULD BE MUCH LESS CRIME.
Strongly agree[5] Agree[4] Undecided[3] Disagree[2]
Strongly disagree[1]   (EC)

102. SAVINGS SPENT ON EDUCATION ARE WISELY INVESTED.
Strongly agree[1] Agree[2] Undecided[3] Disagree[4]
Strongly disagree[5]   (E)

103. ONE SELDOM WORRIES SO MUCH AS TO BECOME VERY MISER-ABLE.
Strongly agree[1] Agree[2] Undecided[3] Disagree[4]
Strongly disagree[5]   (M)

104. IT IS NO TRICK TO BE THE LIFE OF THE PARTY.
Strongly agree[1] Agree[2] Undecided[3] Disagree[4]
Strongly disagree[5]   (I)

105. MEMBERS OF THE FAMILY ARE TOO CURIOUS ABOUT ONE'S PERSONAL AFFAIRS.
Strongly agree[5] Agree[4] Undecided[3] Disagree[2]
Strongly disagree[1]   (F)

106. ALMOST ANYTHING CAN BE FIXED UP IN THE COURTS IF YOU HAVE ENOUGH MONEY.
Strongly agree[5] Agree[4] Undecided[3] Disagree[2]
Strongly disagree[1]   (L)

107. THE INCOMES OF MOST PEOPLE ARE A FAIR MEASURE OF THEIR CONTRIBUTION TO HUMAN WELFARE.
Strongly agree[1] Agree[2] Undecided[3] Disagree[4]
Strongly disagree[5]   (EC)

108. AN EDUCATED MAN CAN ADVANCE MORE RAPIDLY IN BUSINESS AND INDUSTRY.
Strongly agree[1] Agree[2] Undecided[3] Disagree[4]
Strongly disagree[5]   (E)

109. A MAN DOES NOT HAVE TO PRETEND HE IS SMARTER THAN HE REALLY IS TO "GET BY."
Strongly agree[1] Agree[2] Undecided[3] Disagree[4]
Strongly disagree[5]   (M)

110. IT IS EASY TO KEEP PEOPLE FROM TAKING ADVANTAGE OF YOU.
Strongly agree[1] Agree[2] Undecided[3] Disagree[4]
Strongly disagree[5]   (I)

111. PARENTS KEEP FAITH IN THEIR CHILDREN EVEN THOUGH THEY CANNOT FIND WORK.
Strongly agree[1] Agree[2] Undecided[3] Disagree[4]
Strongly disagree[5]   (F)

112. IT IS DIFFICULT TO BREAK THE LAW AND KEEP ONE'S SELF-RESPECT.
Strongly agree[1] Agree[2] Undecided[3] Disagree[4]
Strongly disagree[5]   (L)

113. A MAN SHOULD STRIKE IN ORDER TO SECURE GREATER RETURNS TO LABOR.
Strongly agree[5] Agree[4] Undecided[3] Disagree[2]
Strongly disagree[1]   (EC)

114. PARENTS SHOULD NOT BE COMPELLED TO SEND THEIR CHILDREN TO SCHOOL.
Strongly agree[5] Agree[4] Undecided[3] Disagree[2]
Strongly disagree[1]   (E)

115. SUCCESS IS MORE DEPENDENT ON LUCK THAN ON REAL ABILITY.
Strongly agree[5] Agree[4] Undecided[3] Disagree[2]
Strongly disagree[1]   (M)

116. MOST PEOPLE ARE TOO CRITICAL OF ONE'S BEHAVIOR.
Strongly agree[5] Agree[4] Undecided[3] Disagree[2]
Strongly disagree[1]   (I)

117. PARENTS ARE TOO PARTICULAR ABOUT THE KIND OF COMPANY ONE KEEPS.
Strongly agree[5]   Agree[4]   Undecided[3]   Disagree[2]
Strongly disagree[1]   (F)

118. ON THE WHOLE, LAWYERS ARE HONEST.
Strongly agree[1]   Agree[2]   Undecided[3]   Disagree[4]
Strongly disagree[5]   (L)

119. A MAN SHOULD BE ALLOWED TO KEEP AS LARGE AN INCOME AS HE CAN GET.
Strongly agree[1]   Agree[2]   Undecided[3]   Disagree[4]
Strongly disagree[5]   (EC)

120. EDUCATION IS MORE VALUABLE THAN MOST PEOPLE THINK.
Strongly agree[1]   Agree[2]   Undecided[3]   Disagree[4]
Strongly disagree[5]   (E)

121. A PERSON CAN PLAN HIS FUTURE SO THAT EVERYTHING WILL COME OUT ALL RIGHT IN THE LONG RUN.
Strongly agree[1]   Agree[2]   Undecided[3]   Disagree[4]
Strongly disagree[5]   (M)

122. FEAR OF SOCIAL BLUNDERS KEEPS ONE FROM HAVING A GOOD TIME AT A PARTY.
Strongly agree[5]   Agree[4]   Undecided[3]   Disagree[2]
Strongly disagree[1]   (I)

123. OBLIGATIONS TO ONE'S FAMILY ARE A GREAT HANDICAP TO A YOUNG MAN TODAY.
Strongly agree[5]   Agree[4]   Undecided[3]   Disagree[2]
Strongly disagree[1]   (F)

124. VIOLATORS OF THE LAW ARE NEARLY ALWAYS DETECTED AND PUNISHED.
Strongly agree[1]   Agree[2]   Undecided[3]   Disagree[4]
Strongly disagree[5]   (L)

125. MONEY SHOULD BE TAKEN FROM THE RICH AND GIVEN TO THE POOR DURING HARD TIMES.
Strongly agree[5]   Agree[4]   Undecided[3]   Disagree[2]
Strongly disagree[1]   (EC)

126. A HIGH SCHOOL EDUCATION MAKES A MAN A BETTER CITIZEN.
Strongly agree[1]   Agree[2]   Undecided[3]   Disagree[4]
Strongly disagree[5]   (E)

127. THERE IS REALLY NO POINT IN LIVING.
Strongly agree[5]   Agree[4]   Undecided[3]   Disagree[2]
Strongly disagree[1]   (M)

128. IT IS EASY TO LOSE CONFIDENCE IN ONESELF.
Strongly agree[5]   Agree[4]   Undecided[3]   Disagree[2]
Strongly disagree[1]   (I)

129. SO FAR AS IDEAS ARE CONCERNED, PARENTS AND CHILDREN
LIVE IN DIFFERENT WORLDS.
Strongly agree[5] Agree[4] Undecided[3] Disagree[2]
Strongly disagree[1]   (F)

130. IT IS ALL RIGHT FOR A PERSON TO BREAK THE LAW IF HE
DOESN'T GET CAUGHT.
Strongly agree[5] Agree[4] Undecided[3] Disagree[2]
Strongly disagree[1]   (L)

131. OUR ECONOMIC SYSTEM IS CRITICIZED TOO MUCH.
Strongly agree[1] Agree[2] Undecided[3] Disagree[4]
Strongly disagree[5]   (EC)

132. PUBLIC MONEY SPENT ON EDUCATION FOR THE PAST FEW
YEARS COULD HAVE BEEN USED MORE WISELY FOR OTHER
PURPOSES.
Strongly agree[5] Agree[4] Undecided[3] Disagree[2]
Strongly disagree[1]   (E)

THE SCIENCE RESEARCH ASSOCIATES ATTITUDE SURVEY   *4.1.2*

VARIABLE MEASURED: The SRA Attitude Survey provides a measure of
employee attitudes toward the work environment. It is a diagnostic instrument
identifying attitudinal levels for individuals and groups in such areas as job
demands, working conditions, pay, employee benefits, friendliness and cooperation of fellow employees, supervisor-employee interpersonal relations, confidence in management, technical competence of supervision, effectiveness of administration, adequacy of communication, security of job and work relations,
status and recognition, identification with the company, opportunity for growth
and advancement, and finally reactions to the inventory itself. See Zile S. Dabas,
"The Dimensions of Morale: An Item Factorization of the SRA Inventory,"
Personnel Psychology 11 (Summer 1958): 217–34.

DESCRIPTION: The inventory is not just an opinion survey. It is a kind of
"morale audit" for work organizations that provides standard scores in each
category based upon more than one million employees in a wide variety of
business firms. Practical uses include assessing the general level of morale in
an organization, locating the problem departments in the organization, determining satisfactions and dissatisfactions among employees, evaluating supervisory and executive training needs, and providing material for supervisory
training programs.

WHERE PUBLISHED: Science Research Associates, Inc., 259 East Erie Street,
Chicago, Ill. 60611. Copyright, 1952, by the Industrial Relations Center of the
University of Chicago. All rights reserved. Authors of the survey include Robert
K. Burns, L. L. Thurstone, David G. Moore, and Melony E. Baehr.

RELIABILITY: Both individual and group reliability have been determined by the test-retest method with an interval of one week between the test administrations. A sample of 134 employees shows a product moment correlation of .89. Group reliabilities range from .96 to .99 with reliability greater for groups of 50 or more employees.

VALIDITY: Good correspondence was found to exist between the inventory results and the considered judgments of experienced observers. In three of the companies surveyed, validity was established by conducting nondirective interviews among a cross section of the employees. Cf. Robert J. Wherry, "Factor Analysis of Morale Data: Reliability and Validity," *Personnel Psychology* 11 (Spring 1958): 78-89.

STANDARD SCORES: Well standardized scores are available for comparative analysis of attitude levels in similar business firms and within similar departments. National, industrial, and occupational norms were checked and revised in 1970.

Science Research Associates

SRA Attitude Survey   *Instructions*   *Form A*

Purpose of the Survey

Your company would like to know what you think about your job, your pay, your boss, and the community in general. This Inventory is designed to help you tell us your ideas and opinions quickly and easily without signing your name. This booklet contains a number of statements. All you have to do is to mark a cross by each statement to show how you feel. It is easy to do and you can be completely frank in your answers.

How to fill in the Survey

Read each statement carefully and decide how you feel about it. You will agree with some statements, and you will disagree with others. You may be undecided about some. To help you express your opinion, three possible answers have been placed beside each statement:

AGREE ? DISAGREE

I would rather work in a large city than in a small town . . . . □ □ □
Choose the answer most like your own opinion and mark a cross in the box under it.

For example:
This person feels he wants to work in a large city: AGREE ? DISAGREE
I would rather work in a large city than in a small town . . . . ☒ □ □

This person wants to work in a small town: AGREE ? DISAGREE
I would rather work in a large city than in a small town . . . . □ □ ☒

This person can't decide between a large city and a small town: AGREE ? DISAGREE
I would rather work in a large city than in a small town . . . . □ ☒ □

This is not a test

There are no "right" answers and no "wrong" answers. It is your own, honest opinion that we want.

Work rapidly but answer all statements

Do *not* spend too much time on any one statement. If you cannot decide about a statement, mark the "?" box, and go on to the next statement. If you make a mistake, erase your mark, or fill in the box completely. Then mark a cross in the correct box.

General information

Do *not* sign your name on the booklet. Be *sure* to fill in the blanks for general information such as age, sex, department, etc., that will be asked of you. This information will be used only to make the results more meaningful. It will not be used to identify you in any way.

When you have finished

When you have finished filling out the questionnaire, check to see that you have marked every statement. Then turn to last page where you will find the space to write your comments. In this space we would like you to write anything about your job or the company that is important to you. If something is irritating or trying for you, please comment on it. If something is pleasing or satisfying, please comment on that also. Or if you have a suggestion to help your job or the company, write that also.

PART I. THE CORE SURVEY

	AGREE	?	DISAGREE
1. The hours of work here are O.K..	☐	☐	☐
2. Management does everything possible to prevent accidents in our work	☐	☐	☐
3. Management is doing its best to give us good working conditions .	☐	☐	☐
4. In my opinion, the pay here is lower than in other companies . . .	☐	☐	☐
5. They should do a better job of handling pay matters here	☐	☐	☐
6. I understand what the company benefit program provides for employees	☐	☐	☐
7. The people I work with help each other out when someone falls behind or gets in a tight spot	☐	☐	☐
8. My boss is too interested in his own success to care about the needs of employees	☐	☐	☐
9. My boss is always breathing down our necks; he watches us to closely	☐	☐	☐
10. My boss gives us credit and praise for work well done.	☐	☐	☐
11. Management here does everything it can to see that employees get a fair break on the job	☐	☐	☐
12. If I have a complaint to make, I feel free to talk to someone up-the-line	☐	☐	☐
13. My boss sees that employees are properly trained for their jobs	☐	☐	☐
14. My boss sees that we have the things we need to do our jobs	☐	☐	☐
15. Management here is really trying to build the organization and make it successful	☐	☐	☐
16. Management here sees to it that there is cooperation between departments	☐	☐	☐
17. Management tells employees about company plans and developments.	☐	☐	☐
18. They encourage us to make suggestions for improvements here	☐	☐	☐

19. I am often bothered by sudden speedups or unexpected slack periods in my work . . . .
AGREE ☐ ? ☐ DISAGREE ☐

20. Changes are made here with little regard for the welfare of employees . . . .
AGREE ☐ ? ☐ DISAGREE ☐

21. Compared with other employees, we get very little attention from management . . . .
AGREE ☐ ? ☐ DISAGREE ☐

22. Sometimes I feel that my job counts for very little in this organization . . . .
AGREE ☐ ? ☐ DISAGREE ☐

23. The longer you work for this company the more you feel you belong. . . . .
AGREE ☐ ? ☐ DISAGREE ☐

24. I have a great deal of interest in this company and its future . . . .
AGREE ☐ ? ☐ DISAGREE ☐

25. I have little opportunity to use my abilities in this organization . . . .
AGREE ☐ ? ☐ DISAGREE ☐

26. There are plenty of good jobs here for those who want to get ahead . . . .
AGREE ☐ ? ☐ DISAGREE ☐

27. I often feel worn out and tired on my job . . . .
AGREE ☐ ? ☐ DISAGREE ☐

28. They expect too much work from us around here. . . . .
AGREE ☐ ? ☐ DISAGREE ☐

29. Poor working conditions keep me from doing my best in my work . . . .
AGREE ☐ ? ☐ DISAGREE ☐

30. For my kind of job, the working conditions are O.K. . . . .
AGREE ☐ ? ☐ DISAGREE ☐

31. I'm paid fairly compared with other employees . . . .
AGREE ☐ ? ☐ DISAGREE ☐

32. Compared with other companies, employee benefits here are good. . . . .
AGREE ☐ ? ☐ DISAGREE ☐

33. A few of the people I work with think they run the place . . . . .
AGREE ☐ ? ☐ DISAGREE ☐

34. The people I work with get along well together . . . .
AGREE ☐ ? ☐ DISAGREE ☐

35. My boss has always been fair in his dealings with me . . . .
AGREE ☐ ? ☐ DISAGREE ☐

36. My boss gets employees to work together as a team. . . . .
AGREE ☐ ? ☐ DISAGREE ☐

37. I have confidence in the fairness and honesty of management . . . .
AGREE ☐ ? ☐ DISAGREE ☐

38. Management here is really interested in the welfare of employees . . . .
AGREE ☐ ? ☐ DISAGREE ☐

39. Most of the higher-ups are friendly toward employees . . . .
AGREE ☐ ? ☐ DISAGREE ☐

40. My boss keeps putting things off; he just lets things ride . . . . . .
AGREE ☐ ? ☐ DISAGREE ☐

41. My boss lets us know exactly what is expected of us . . . .
AGREE ☐ ? ☐ DISAGREE ☐

42. Management fails to give clear-cut orders and instructions. . . . .
AGREE ☐ ? ☐ DISAGREE ☐

	AGREE	?	DISAGREE
43. I know how my job fits in with other work in this organization	☐	☐	☐
44. Management keeps us in the dark about things we ought to know.	☐	☐	☐
45. Long service means something in this organization	☐	☐	☐
46. You can get fired around here without much cause	☐	☐	☐
47. I can be sure of my job as long as I do good work	☐	☐	☐
48. I have plenty of freedom on the job to use my own judgment	☐	☐	☐
49. Everybody in this organization tries to boss us around	☐	☐	☐
50. I really feel part of this organization	☐	☐	☐
51. The people who get promotions around here usually deserve them.	☐	☐	☐
52. I can learn a great deal on my present job	☐	☐	☐
53. My job is often dull and monotonous.	☐	☐	☐
54. There is too much pressure on my job	☐	☐	☐
55. Some of the working conditions here are annoying	☐	☐	☐
56. I have the right equipment to do my work	☐	☐	☐
57. My pay is enough to live on comfortably	☐	☐	☐
58. I'm satisfied with the way employee benefits are handled here	☐	☐	☐
59. The company's employee benefit program is O.K.	☐	☐	☐
60. The people I work with are very friendly	☐	☐	☐
61. My boss really tries to get our ideas about things	☐	☐	☐
62. My boss ought to be friendlier toward employees	☐	☐	☐
63. My boss lives up to his promises	☐	☐	☐
64. Management here has a very good personnel policy	☐	☐	☐
65. Management ignores our suggestions and complaints	☐	☐	☐
66. My boss knows very little about his job.	☐	☐	☐

	AGREE	?	DISAGREE
67. My boss has the work well organized.	☐	☐	☐
68. This company operates efficiently and smoothly	☐	☐	☐
69. Management really knows its job	☐	☐	☐
70. They have a poor way of handling employee complaints here	☐	☐	☐
71. You can say what you think around here.	☐	☐	☐
72. You always know where you stand with this company	☐	☐	☐
73. When layoffs are necessary, they are handled fairly	☐	☐	☐
74. I am very much underpaid for the work that I do	☐	☐	☐
75. I'm really doing something worthwhile in my job	☐	☐	☐
76. I'm proud to work for this company	☐	☐	☐
77. Filling in this Inventory is a good way to let management know what employees think.	☐	☐	☐
78. I think some good may come out of filling in an Inventory like this one	☐	☐	☐

PART II. CUSTOM-BUILT SURVEY

This survey consists of up to 21 items designed especially for the client with the advice and assistance of SRA professionals. Responses to these items enable management to learn what needs to be known about situations specific to that company alone. SRA reproduces and collates this set of questions along with the other survey parts to be administered. A few sample items might be:

	STRONGLY AGREE	AGREE	?	DISAGREE	STRONGLY AGREE
79. Our hospital-surgical-medical plan provides good protection	☐	☐	☐	☐	☐
80. My best source of information concerning company plans is through the "grapevine."	☐	☐	☐	☐	☐

General information

1	2	3
4	5	6

PART III. ANONYMOUS COMMENTS

Employees are urged to express feelings on subjects they find most important to them.

Please write your comments here

UTILITY: Inexpensive, easily interpreted, quickly scored, and permits use in all kinds of work organizations. Comparative analysis is facilitated by available standard scores. There are two different supplemental surveys available, one for supervisors and one for salesmen.

RESEARCH APPLICATIONS:

ASH, PHILIP. "The SRA Employee Inventory—A Statistical Analysis." *Personnel Psychology* 7 (Autumn 1954): 337–63.

MOORE, DAVID G., and BURNS, ROBERT K. "How Good Is Good Morale?" *Factory* (February 1956): 130–36.

The *SRA Attitude Survey* (originally called *Employee Inventory*) was prepared by the Employee Attitude Research Group of the Industrial Relations Center, University of Chicago. This group has members from both the University and industry. Thus, both the theoretical and practical aspects are well represented in all development work. Further details are given in the *Manual.*

The researcher may wish to compare the *SRA Attitude Survey* with the newer *Survey of Organizations* by James C. Taylor and David G. Bowers (Ann Arbor: Institute of Social Research, University of Michigan, 1974). The Survey is described on page 293 of the Handbook.

MORSE INDEXES OF EMPLOYEE SATISFACTION

4.I.3

VARIABLE MEASURED: The degree of satisfaction that individuals obtain from the various roles they play in an organization; specifically (1) satisfaction with doing the actual content of the work, (2) satisfaction with being in the work group, (3) satisfaction with working in the company, (4) satisfaction with pay and job status.

DESCRIPTION: These are indexes of employee satisfaction, each of which contains four items developed through a combined logical and empirical method. The items were initially selected from an employee interview on the basis of the definitions of each area of employee satisfaction. Intercorrelations were then computed among all items that logically appeared to belong in each area. Items that showed very low correlations were removed. The items making up each index were not differentially weighed, but were added with unit weights to give a single measure of each type of employee satisfaction. The four indexes are called *intrinsic job satisfaction, company involvement, financial and job status satisfaction*, and *pride in group performance.* Each index has four items that are answered on a five-point scale ranging from strong like to strong dislike. This gives a range of scores from 4–20 on each index.

WHERE PUBLISHED: Nancy C. Morse, *Satisfactions in the While Collar Job* (Ann Arbor: University of Michigan, Institute for Social Research, 1953).

RELIABILITY: No split half or test-retest reliabilities are reported. Internal consistency of the scales is attested by the average intercorrelations of items:

Intrinsic job satisfaction	$r = .50$
Company involvement	$r = .45$
Financial and job status satisfaction	$r = .52$
Pride in group performance	$r = .39$

VALIDITY: The intrinsic job satisfaction, company involvement, and financial job status indexes, both from the intercorrelations of the total index scores and from the item analysis, appear to be significantly interrelated (intercorrelations ranging from $r = .35$ to $r = .43$). These three areas can be used to represent a general morale factor. This factor predicts the individual's desire to stay in the company rather than his productivity.

Pride in group performance (and its subitems) is, with few exceptions, not significantly related to the items of the other indexes or to the indexes themselves. It must be treated as an independent factor. This index was related to the amount of voluntary help given by members to one another, friendliness in interpersonal relations, and the absence of antiproductivity group norms. It was also correlated with supervisor's identification with employees.

STANDARD SCORES:

		Range	N
Intrinsic Job Satisfaction	High Group	04–07	(717)
	Medium Group	08–11	(222)
	Low Group	12–20	(181)
Financial and Job Status Satisfaction	High Group	04–08	(160)
	Medium Group	09–12	(227)
	Low Group	13–20	(248)
Company Involvement	High Group	04–08	(250)
	Medium Group	09–12	(255)
	Low Group	13–20	(165)
Pride in Group Performance	High Group	04–08	(227)
	Medium Group	09–10	(264)
	Low Group	11–20	(251)

UTILITY: The indexes consist of easily administered questionnaire items. The time required is about 10 minutes for the administration of all four indexes.

RESEARCH APPLICATIONS: Morse reports relationships between the indexes and various supervisory practices, working conditions, and various background factors such as sex, age, length of service, and education. See Morse, *Satisfactions in the White Collar Job*.

Company Involvement Index

1. "How do you like working here?"
   code: Five-point scale ranging from strong like, complete satisfaction to strong dislike.
2. "Would you advise a friend to come to work for the Company?"
   code: Three-point scale including: yes, pro-con, and no.
3. An overall coder rating of the employee's feelings about the fairness of the company, based on answers to questions throughout the interview.
   code: Three-point scale including: feels company fair and generous, feels company fair but very exacting, feels company unfair.
4. An overall coder rating of the employee's degree of identification with the company based on answers to questions throughout the interview.
   code: Three-point scale including: strong identification, some identification, and no identification.

Financial and Job Status Index

1. "How well satisfied are you with your salary?"
   code: Five-point scale ranging from very well satisfied to very dissatisfied.
2. "How satisfied are you with your chances of getting more pay?"
   code: Five-point scale ranging from very satisfied to very dissatisfied.
3. "How about your own case, how satisfied are you with the way things have been working out for you?" (This question was preceded by two questions on "getting ahead here at the Company" and was answered in that context.)
   code: Five-point scale ranging from very satisfied to very dissatisfied.
4. Coder overall rating of degree of frustration evidenced by respondent in advancing in his job or in his main vocational objectives. Answers to questions throughout the interview were used to measure the degree to which employee felt his vocational desires were blocked.
   code: Five-point scale ranging from strong frustration to high adjustment, no frustration.

Intrinsic Job Satisfaction Index

1. "How well do you like the sort of work you are doing?"
   code: Five-point scale varying from strong like to strong dislike.
2. "Does your job give you a chance to do the things you feel you do best?"
   code: Five-point scale varying from yes (strong) to no (strong).
3. "Do you get any feeling of accomplishment from the work you are doing?"
   code: Five-point scale varying from strong sense of task completion to no sense of task completion.
4. "How do you feel about your work, does it rate as an important job with you?"
   code: Five-point scale varying from very important to of no importance.

Pride-in-Group-Performance Index

1. "How well do you think your section compares with other sections in the Company in getting a job done?"
code: Five-point scale ranging from very good, one of best in company, to very poor, one of worst in company.

2. Answers to the section comparison question were also coded on the degree of emotional identification with the section that employee showed. (The use of "we" as opposed to "it" or "they" was one of the indications to the coder of identification.)
code: Three-point scale: strong identification, mild identification, indifference or lack of identification.

3. "How well do you think your division compares with other divisions in the Company in getting a job done?"
code: Five-point scale ranging from very good, one of best in company, to very poor, one of worst in company.

4. Answers to the division comparison question were also coded on degree of emotional identification with the division the employee showed.
code: Three-point scale: strong identification, mild identification, indifference or lack of identification.

4.1.4 GUTTMAN SCALES OF MILITARY BASE MORALE

VARIABLE MEASURED: Satisfaction with Air Force, satisfaction with Air Site, satisfaction with the job, personal commitment to Aircraft Control and Warning Mission.

WHERE PUBLISHED: Delbert C. Miller and Nahum Z. Medalia, "Efficiency, Leadership, and Morale in Small Military Organizations," *Sociological Review* 3 (July 1955): 93–107.

RELIABILITY: Scalability shown by reproducibility coefficients.

Satisfaction with Air Force	$R = .93$
Satisfaction with the Air Site	$R = .90$
Satisfaction with the job	$R = .90$
Personal commitment to AC&W Mission	$R = .94$

VALIDITY: Correlation between ratings made by outside military inspectors of site morale and satisfaction with Air Site scale in 50 squadrons show Spearman Rank Correlation of $r_s = .52$.

UTILITY: Scales are short and unidimensional. They may be easily converted for use in other organizations by substituting appropriate unit names. However, as in all Guttman Scales reproducibility varies with respondent samples and must be recomputed.

RESEARCH APPLICATIONS:
GROSS, EDWARD, and MILLER, DELBERT C. "The Impact of Isolation on Worker Adjustment in Military Installations of the United States and Japan." *Estudios de Sociologia* (Buenos Aires) 1 (Fall 1961): 70–86.

MCCANN, GLENN C. *Morale and Human Relations Problems in A C & W Sites.* Air Force Personnel and Training Research Center Technical Memorandum CRL-TM-56-5, April 1956.

MEDALIA, NAHUM Z. "Unit Size and Leadership Perception." *Sociometry* 17 (February 1954): 64–67.

——. "Authoritarianism, Leader Acceptance, and Group Cohesion." *Journal of Abnormal and Social Psychology* 51 (September 1955): 207–13.

——, and MILLER, DELBERT C. "Human Relations Leadership and the Association of Morale and the Effectiveness of Work Groups." *Social Forces* 33 (May 1955): 348–52.

MILLER, DELBERT C., and MEDALIA, N. Z. "Efficiency, Leadership, and Morale in Small Military Organizations." *Sociological Review* 3, no. 1 (July 1955): 93–107.

——; MEDALIA, NAHUM Z.; MCCANN, GLENN C.; and others. "Morale and Human Relations Leadership as Factors in Organizational Effectiveness." In *Studies in Organizational Effectiveness*, edited by R. V. Bowers. Washington, D.C.: Air Force Office of Scientific Research, 1962.

MORALE SCALES FOR MILITARY ORGANIZATIONS

Satisfaction with Air Force (All items answered by Strongly agree, Agree, Undecided, Disagree, Strongly disagree.)

1. I have a poor opinion of the Air Force most of the time.
2. Most of the time the Air Force is not run very well.
3. I am usually dissatisfied with the Air Force.
4. The Air Force is better than any of the other Services.
5. If I remain in military service I would prefer to stay in the Air Force.

Satisfaction with the Air Site

1. In general this Air Site is run very well.
2. This Air Site is the best in the whole Division.
3. I am usually dissatisfied with this Air Site.
4. I would rather be stationed at this Air Site than any I know about.
5. I would like to stay at this Air Site.

Satisfaction with the Job

1. I would be more satisfied with some other job in AC&W than I am with my usual job.
2. My Air Force job is usually interesting to me.
3. I believe the Air Force has placed me in a job that suits me very well.
4. I believe my Air Force job is usually worthwhile.
5. If I have a chance, I will change to some other job at this Site.

Personal Commitment to Aircraft Control and Warning Mission

1. Under present world conditions, I would advise many of my civilian friends to get into AC&W if they should ask my advice on joining the service. (*a*) No, I would advise them to stay out of AC&W. (*b*) I would tell them it makes no difference what you join. (*c*) Yes, I would advise them to join AC&W.

2. Under present world conditions, I feel that I can do more for my country as a member of AC&W than as a civilian. (*a*) No, I would be more valuable as a civilian. (*b*) I am undecided about this. (*c*) Yes, I am more valuable in AC&W.
3. Under present world conditions I feel that I can do more for my country as a member of some other part of the armed services, rather than as a member of AC&W. (*a*) Yes, I could be of more value elsewhere in the armed services. (*b*) It is a toss-up where I could contribute the most. (*c*) No, I am of more value in AC&W.
4. Under present world conditions I feel I can do more for my country as a member of AC&W than some other part of the Air Force. (*a*) No, I would be of more value elsewhere in the Air Force. (*b*) I am about of equal value any place in the Air Force. (*c*) Yes, I am definitely more valuable in AC&W.
5. If present world conditions continue to be about the same, I would want to continue to be a member of AC&W as long as I remain in military service. (*a*) No, I would want to transfer from AC&W. (*b*) It doesn't matter whether I am in AC&W or not. (*c*) Yes, I would definitely want to remain in AC&W.
6. If the U.S. should enter a third world war and if I should remain in military service, I would want to stay in AC&W. (*a*) No, I prefer to be in some other part of the service. (*b*) I wouldn't make much difference where I serve. (*c*) Yes, I would prefer to remain in AC&W. (All of the aforementioned items are interspersed when they are administered.)

4.1.5 **BRAYFIELD AND ROTHE'S INDEX OF JOB SATISFACTION**

VARIABLE MEASURED: General measure of job satisfaction.

WHERE PUBLISHED: Arthur H. Brayfield and Harold F. Rothe, "An Index of Job Satisfaction." *Journal of Applied Psychology* 35 (October 1951): 307–11.

CONSTRUCTION: As a working approach for this study it was assumed that job satisfaction could be inferred from the individual's attitude toward his work. This approach dictated the methodology of attitude scaling. The following requirements were formulated as desirable attributes of an attitude scale designed to provide a useful index of job satisfaction: (1) it should give an index of "overall" job satisfaction rather than specific aspects of job satisfaction; (2) it should be applicable to a wide variety of jobs; (3) it should be sensitive to variations in attitude; (4) the items should be of such a nature (interesting, realistic, and varied) that the scale would evoke cooperation from both management and employees; (5) it should yield a reliable index; (6) it should yield a valid index; (7) it should be brief and easily scored.

The construction of this scale was made a class project in Personnel Psychology for members of an Army Specialized Training Program in personnel psychology at the University of Minnesota in the summer and fall of 1943. Seventy-seven men cooperated. Items referring to specific aspects of a job were eliminated since an "overall" attitudinal factor was desired.

The present index contains 18 items with Thurstone scale values ranging from 1.2 to 10.0 with approximately .5 step intervals. The items are not arranged in the order of magnitude of scale values. The Likert scoring system consisting of five categories of agreement-disagreement was applied to each item, and the Thurstone scoring system of five categories is applied to the items. The Thurstone scale value gives the direction of scoring method so that a low total score would represent the dissatisfied end of the scale and a high total score the satisfied end. The items are selected so that the satisfied end of the scale was indicated by *Strongly agree* and *Agree*, and *Disagree* and *Strongly disagree* for the other half. The neutral response is *Undecided*. The Likert scoring weights for each item range from 1 to 5, and the range of possible total scores is 18 to 90 with 54 (Undecided) the neutral point.

RELIABILITY: The revised scale (which is the present one) was administered as part of a study of 231 female office employees. The blanks were signed along with other tests. One of the investigators personally administered the tests to employees in small groups. The range of job satisfaction scores for this sample was 35–87. The mean score was 63.8 with an S. D. of 9.4. The odd-even product moment reliability coefficient computed for this sample was .77, which was corrected by the Spearman-Brown formula to a reliability coefficient of .87.

VALIDITY: Evidence for the high validity of the blank rests upon the nature of the items, the method of construction, and its differentiating power when applied to two groups that could reasonably be assumed to differ in job satisfaction. The nature of the individual items is partial, although not crucial, evidence for the validity of the scale. This is an appeal to "face" validity. Additional evidence is furnished by the method of construction. The attitude variable of job satisfaction is inferred from verbal reactions to a job expressed along a favorable-unfavorable continuum.

The job satisfaction blank was administered to 91 adult night school students in classes in Personnel Psychology at the University of Minnesota during 1945 and 1946. The range of job satisfaction scores for this sample was 29–89. The mean score was 70.4 with an S. D. of 13.2. The assumption was made that those persons employed in occupations appropriate to their expressed interest should, on the average, be more satisfied with their jobs than those members of the class employed in occupations inappropriate to their expressed interest in personnel work. The 91 persons accordingly were divided into two groups (personnel and nonpersonnel) with respect to their employment in a position identified by payroll title as a personnel function. The mean of the personnel group was 76.9 with an S.D. of 8.6 as compared to a mean of 65.4 with an S. D. of 14.02 for the nonpersonnel group. This difference of 11.5 points is significant at the 1 per cent level; the difference between the variances also is significant at the 1 per cent level. It might also be mentioned that scores on this index correlated .92 with scores on the Hoppock job satisfaction scale. See review of James L. Price, *Handbook of Organizational Measurement* (New York: Heath, 1972), pp. 156–73.

RESEARCH APPLICATIONS:

BRAYFIELD, ARTHUR H.; WELLS, RICHARD V.; and STRATE, MARVIN W. "Interrelationships Among Measures of Job Satisfaction and General Satisfaction." *Journal of Applied Psychology* 41 (August 1957): 201–5.

EWEN, ROBERT B. "Weighting Components of Job Satisfaction." *Journal of Applied Psychology* 51 (February 1967): 68–73.

AN INDEX OF JOB SATISFACTION* †

Some jobs are more interesting and satisfying than others. We want to know how people feel about different jobs. This blank contains 18 statements about jobs. You are to cross out the phrase below each statement that has best described how you feel about your present job. There are no right or wrong answers. We should like your honest opinion on each one of the statements. Work out the sample item numbered (0).

0. There are some conditions concerning my job that could be improved.
   Strongly agree, agree, undecided, disagree, strongly disagree.
1. My job is like a hobby to me.
   Strongly agree, agree, undecided, disagree, strongly disagree.
2. My job is usually interesting enough to keep me from getting bored.
   Strongly agree, agree, undecided, disagree, strongly disagree.
3. It seems that my friends are more interested in their jobs.
   Strongly agree, agree, undecided, disagree, strongly disagree.
4. I consider my job rather unpleasant.
   Strongly agree, agree, undecided, disagree, strongly disagree.
5. I enjoy my work more than my leisure time.
   Strongly agree, agree, undecided, disagree, strongly disagree.
6. I am often bored with my job.
   Strongly agree, agree, undecided, disagree, strongly disagree.
7. I feel fairly well satisfied with my job.
   Strongly agree, agree, undecided, disagree, strongly disagree.
8. Most of the time I have to force myself to go to work.
   Strongly agree, agree, undecided, disagree, strongly disagree.
9. I am satisfied with my job for the time being.
   Strongly agree, agree, undecided, disagree, strongly disagree.
10. I feel that my job is no more interesting than others I could get.
    Strongly agree, agree, undecided, disagree, strongly disagree.
11. I definitely dislike my work.
    Strongly agree, agree, undecided, disagree, strongly disagree.
12. I feel that I am happier in my work than most other people.
    Strongly agree, agree, undecided, disagree, strongly disagree.
13. Most days I am enthusiastic about my work.
    Strongly agree, agree, undecided, disagree, strongly disagree.
14. Each day of work seems like it will never end.
    Strongly agree, agree, undecided, disagree, strongly disagree.
15. I like my job better than the average worker does.
    Strongly agree, agree, undecided, disagree, strongly disagree.
16. My job is pretty uninteresting.
    Strongly agree, agree, undecided, disagree, strongly disagree.
17. I find real enjoyment in my work.
    Strongly agree, agree, undecided, disagree, strongly disagree.
18. I am disappointed that I ever took this job.
    Strongly agree, agree, undecided, disagree, strongly disagree.

*Arthur H. Brayfield and Harold F. Rothe, *Journal of Applied Psychology* 35, no. 5 (October 1951): 307-11.

†This blank containing 18 items with Thurstone scale values ranging from 1.2 to 10.0 with approximately .5 step intervals is not arranged in order of magnitude of scale values. The Likert scoring system of five categories is applied to each item. Thurstone scale values give the direction of scoring method. Likert scoring weights range for each item 1 to 5. The range of possible total scores became 18 to 90 with the undecided or neutral point at 54.

section **J**

Scales of Attitudes, Values, and Norms

This section includes some attitude scales that revolve around problems of current interest and concern. The most common is concern with alienation and three scales are included which assess various dimensions. These are the Neal and Seeman Powerlessness Scale, the Srole Anomia Scale, and the Dean Alienation Scale.

Achievement orientation has commanded considerable attention and Kahl's scale is shown.

The measurement of international patterns and norms relates to the growing interest in comparative study. Miller's Battery of Rating Scales are included for such measurements.

Innumerable attitude scales are in existence. Some important sources of other scales are to be found in Section 4M., Inventories of Sociometric and Attitude Scales.

Interest in the measurement of *values* is growing. Some important sources of information on this topic are:

ALLPORT, GORDON W.; VERNON, PHILLIP E.; and LINDZEY, GARDNER. *Study of Values.* Boston: Houghton Mifflin Co., 1950.

ALMOND, GABRIEL A., and VERBA, SIDNEY. *The Civic Culture.* Boston: Little, Brown, 1963.

CANTRIL, HADLEY. *The Pattern of Human Concerns.* New Brunswick, N.J.: Rutgers University Press, 1965.

CARTER, ROY E. "An Experiment in Value Measurement." *American Sociological Review* 21 (April 1956): 156–63.

DODD, STUART C. "Ascertaining National Goals: Project Aimscales." *American Behavioral Scientist* 4 (March 1961): 11–15.

FALLDING, HAROLD. "A Proposal for the Empirical Study of Values." *American Sociological Review* 30 (April 1965): 223–33.

HALLER, ARCHIBALD O., and MILLER, IRWIN W. *The Occupational Aspiration Scale: Theory, Structure, and Correlates.* 2nd ed. Cambridge, Mass.: Schenkman Publishing Co., 1971.

NEAL, SISTER MARIE AUGUSTA. *Values and Interest in Social Change.* Englewood Cliffs, N.J.: Prentice-Hall, 1965.

SCOTT, WILLIAM A. "Empirical Assessment of Values and Ideologies." *American Sociological Review* 24 (June 1959): 299–310.

THURSTONE, L. L. *The Measurement of Values.* Chicago: University of Chicago Press, 1959.

WILSON, WILLIAM J., and NYE, F. IVAN. *Some Methodological Problems in the Empirical Study of Values.* Washington Agricultural Experiment Station Bulletin No. 672. Pullman: Washington State University, July 1966.

THE MEASUREMENT OF ALIENATION AND ANOMIE

The concepts of alienation and anomie have enjoyed a new popularity as social events have demonstrated a weakening of personal and social identities to traditional groups and institutions. The "rediscovery of alienation," as Daniel Bell puts it, has only recently encouraged scientists to develop scales to measure these phenomena.[1] The research has been demonstrating that a number of independent factors may be identified. In 1959 Melvin Seeman set forth a fivefold classification: powerlessness, meaninglessness, normlessness, isolation, and self-estrangement.[2] The scales which have been produced have sought to isolate such factors and measure them. The first element, powerlessness, was suggested by Hegel, Marx, and Weber in their discussions of the workers' "separation" from effective control over their economic destiny; of their helplessness; of their being used for purposes other than their own. Weber argued that in the industrial society, the scientist, the civil servant, the professor is likewise "separated from control over his work."

The first scale presented is the Neal and Seeman Powerlessness Scale. It is especially useful for the measurement of worker alienation.[3] Other applications in the hospital, reformatory, and ghetto are cited in Research Applications of the scale.

The second scale taps anomie or normlessness, a concept attributed to Durkheim. The loss or absence of social norms is seen to bring personal insecurity, the loss of intrinsic values that might give purpose or direction to life. Leo Srole has sought to isolate this variable by measuring self-to-others sense of belonging. Note the extensive applications shown in the cited research.

Dwight Dean has developed three subscales to measure powerlessness, normlessness, and social isolation. He combined the three subscales to make up an alienation scale. He believes that the pattern of intercorrelations demonstrates that alienation may be treated as a composite concept but "there appears to be enough independence among the subscales to warrant treating them as independent variables." Neal and Rettig using factor analysis have found empirical evidence for the structural independence of powerlessness, normlessness, and Srole's Anomia Scale. At this time, the subscales should be utilized when the greatest precision is desired. There is great variety in the scales being used and consensus is low. The scales presented are those most widely used.[4]

However, the researcher may wish to examine other scales not exhibited in this handbook:

MCCLOSKY, HERBERT, and SCHAAR, JOHN H. "Psychological Dimensions of Anomy." *American Sociological Review* 30 (February 1965): 14–40.

MIDDLETON, RUSSELL. "Alienation, Race, and Education." *American Sociological Review* 28 (December 1963): 973–77.

NETTLER, GWYNN. "A Measure of Alienation." *American Sociological Review* 22 (December 1957): 670–77.

For a more thorough listing and appraisal, see John P. Robinson and Phillip R. Shaver, *Measures of Social Psychological Attitudes* (rev. ed.; Ann Arbor: Institute of Social Research, University of Michigan, 1973), pp. 254–94.

Notes

1. See, for example, Allan H. Roberts and Milton Rokeach, "Anomie, Authoritarianism, and Prejudice: A Replication," *American Journal of Sociology* 61 (January 1956): 355–58; Gwynn Nettler, "A Measure of Alienation," *American Sociological Review* 22 (December 1957): 670–77; and Leo Srole, "Social Integration and Certain Corollaries: An Exploratory Study," *American Sociological Review* 21 (December 1956): 709–16. The concepts of alienation and anomie have not only become widely used but also misused terms of our times. Researchers need to be especially cautious in estimating the size of the alienated segment of the population when using the scales.
2. Melvin Seeman, "On the Meaning of Alienation," *American Sociological Review* 24 (December 1959): 783–91.
3. Arthur G. Neal and Solomon Rettig, "Dimensions of Alienation among Manual and Non-Manual Workers," *American Sociological Review* 26 (August 1963): 599–608.
4. Cf. J. L. Simmons, "Some Inter-correlations Among 'Alienation' Measures," *Social Forces* 44 (March 1966): 370–72.

NEAL AND SEEMAN'S POWERLESSNESS SCALE

4.J.1

VARIABLE MEASURED: The authors define powerlessness as "low expectancies for control of events" as lack of control over the political system, the industrial economy, and international affairs. Basically measures the subjectively held probabilities that the outcome of political and economic events cannot be adequately controlled by oneself or collectively by persons like oneself.

DESCRIPTION: This instrument is a unidimensional 7-item scale that presents a choice between mastery and powerlessness.

The scale, as most of the powerlessness scales, is an adaptation of the forced-choice instrument developed by the late Professor Shephard Liverant and his colleagues at the Ohio State University. For further description of this method see Julian B. Rotter, Melvin Seeman, and Shephard Liverant, "Internal vs. External Control of Reinforcements: A Major Variable in Behavior Theory," in *Decisions, Values and Groups*, ed. Norman E. Washburne, vol. 2 (London: Pergamon, 1962), pp. 473–516.

WHERE PUBLISHED: Arthur G. Neal and Melvin Seeman, "Organizations and Powerlessness: A Test of the Mediation Hypothesis," *American Sociological Review* 29 (April 1964): 216–26.

RELIABILITY: The seven items yielded a reproducibility coefficient of .87 on the sample used by Neal and Seeman. An early version of the scale shows that the split-half reliability coefficient was .70. See Melvin Seeman and John Evans, "Alienation in a Hospital Setting," *American Sociological Review* 27 (December 1962): 772–82.

VALIDITY: The mean difference of alienation scores of organized and un-organized workers is significant at the .01 level. The difference of means for mobility-oriented and nonmobility-oriented nonmanual workers is significant at the .001 level. Correlation between anomie and powerlessness $r = .33$. M. Seeman and J. Evans found a negative relation between powerlessness and objective information concerning nature of illness among patients in hospital settings.

M. Seeman and J. Evans, "On the Personal Consequences of Alienation in Work," *American Sociological Review* 32 (April 1967): 273–85, report the following correlation between powerlessness and anomie for nonmanual workers and manual workers in Sweden:

	Manual workers	Nonmanual workers
Anomie	$.37 P < .01$	$.39 P < .01$
Expert Orientation	$.13 P < .05$	$.29 P < .01$
Mobility Attitude	$.15 P < .05$	$.14$
Prejudice	$.24 P < .01$	$.29 P < .01$

Each of the seven items is scored dichotomously and the scores are summed. The powerlessness response is scored as "1" and the alternate response is scored as "0." A reproducibility coefficient of .87 (Guttman Scalogram Technique) was obtained for a community-wide sample (Columbus, Ohio) of 604 respondents.

RESEARCH APPLICATIONS:

BULLOUGH, BONNIE. "Alienation in the Ghetto." *American Journal of Sociology* 72 (March 1967): 469.

GROAT, THEODORE, and NEAL, ARTHUR G. "Social Psychological Correlates of Urban Fertility." *American Sociological Review* 32 (December 1967): 945–49.

NEAL, ARTHUR G. "Stratification Concomitants of Powerlessness and Normlessness: A Study of Political and Economic Alienation." Ph.D. dissertation, Ohio State University, Columbus, 1959.

——, and RETTIG, SOLOMON. "Dimensions of Alienation Among Manual and Non-Manual Workers." *American Sociological Review* 28 (August 1963): 599–608.

——. "On the MultiDimensionality of Alienation." *American Sociological Review* 32 (February 1967): 54–63.

SEEMAN, MELVIN. "On the Personal Consequences of Alienation in Work." *American Sociological Review* 32 (April 1967): 273–85.

——. "Alienation and Social Learning in a Reformatory." *American Journal of Sociology* 69 (November 1963): 270–84.

——, and EVANS, JOHN. "Alienation and Learning in a Hospital Setting." *American Sociological Review* 27 (December 1962): 772–82.

THE POWERLESSNESS SCALE*

(Respondent chooses between the 7 pairs of statements)

1. _____ I think we have adequate means for preventing runaway inflation.
_____ There's very little we can do to keep prices from going higher.

*These seven items were derived from a larger "internal-external control" scale by Neal and Seeman; cf. J. B. Rotter, "Generalized Expectancies for Internal vs. External Control of Reinforcements," *Psychological Monographs* 80, no. 1 (Whole #609, 1966): 1–28.

2. _____ Persons like myself have little chance of protecting our personal interests when they conflict with those of strong pressure groups.

_____ I feel that we have adequate ways of coping with pressure groups.

3. _____ A lasting world peace can be achieved by those of us who work toward it.

_____ There's very little we can do to bring about a permanent world peace.

4. _____ There's very little persons like myself can do to improve world opinion of the United States.

_____ I think each of us can do a great deal to improve world opinion of the United States.

5. _____ This world is run by the few people in power, and there is not much the little guy can do about it.

_____ The average citizen can have an influence on government decisions.

6. _____ It is only wishful thinking to believe that one can really influence what happens to society at large.

_____ People like me can change the course of world events if we make ourselves heard.

7. _____ More and more, I feel helpless in the face of what's happening in the world today.

_____ I sometimes feel personally to blame for the sad state of affairs in our government.

SROLE'S ANOMIA SCALE

4.J.2

VARIABLE MEASURED: According to Srole, this scale refers to the individual eunomia-anomia continuum representing "the individual's generalized pervasive sense of self-to-others belongingness at one extreme compared with self-to-others distance and self-to-others alienation at the other pole of the continuum."

DESCRIPTION: Srole's Anomia Scale contains five items with which the respondent may either agree or disagree. Each item was scored 0 to 1 according to whether the subject disagrees or agrees. Thus, respondent scores fall in a range from 0 to 5; the higher the score, the greater anomie manifested by the respondent.

WHERE PUBLISHED: Leo Srole, "Social Integration and Certain Corollaries: An Exploratory Study," *American Sociological Review* 21 (December 1956): 709–16. See p. 713.

RELIABILITY: The coefficient of reproducibility when used as a Guttman scale = .90 in L. Killian and C. Grigg, "Urbanism, Race, and Anomia," *American Journal of Sociology* 67 (May 1962): 661–65; and .90 in Dorothy L. Meier and Wendell Bell, "Anomia and Differential Access to the Achievement of Life Goals," *American Sociological Review* 24 (April 1959): 189–202. See correction, 24: 566. Cf. C. Miller and E. Butler, "Anomia and Eunomia: A Methodological Evaluation of Srole's Anomia Scale," *American Sociological Review* 31 (June 1966): 400–406.

VALIDITY: Relationships with Anomia.

Authoritarianism F $r = .47$
Attitudes toward minorities $r = .43$
Socioeconomic status $r = .30$

in Srole, "Social Integration."

SROLE'S ANOMIA SCALE

(5-item scale)

1. In spite of what some people say, the lot of the average man is getting worse.
2. It's hardly fair to bring children into the world with the way things look for the future.
3. Nowadays a person has to live pretty much for today and let tomorrow take care of itself.
4. These days a person doesn't really know who he can count on.
5. There's little use writing to public officials because often they aren't really interested in the problems of the average man.

RESEARCH APPLICATIONS:

ANGELL, ROBERT C. "Preferences for Moral Norms in Three Problem Areas." *American Journal of Sociology* 67 (May 1962): 650–60. See pp. 650–51.

BELL, WENDELL. "Anomie, Social Isolation, and the Class Structure." *Sociometry* 20 (June 1957): 105–16. See pp. 106–7.

BLALOCK, H. M., JR. "Making Causal Inferences for Unmeasured Variables from Correlations among Indicators." *American Journal of Sociology* 69 (July 1963): 53–62. See p. 56.

CARR, LESLIE G. "The Srole Items and Acquiescence." *American Sociological Review* 36 (April 1971): 287–92.

CARTER, ROY E., JR., and CLARKE, PETER. "Public Affairs Opinion Leadership among Educational Television Viewers." *American Sociological Review* 27 (December 1962): 792–99. See p. 795.

EHRLICH, HOWARD J. "Instrument Error and the Study of Prejudice." *Social Forces* 43 (December 1964): 197–206. See p. 200.

FREEMAN, HOWARD E., and SIMMONS, OZZIE G. "Wives, Mothers, and the Posthospital Performance of Mental Patients." *Social Forces* 37 (December 1958): 153–59. See p. 156.

KILLIAN, LEWIS M., and GRIGG, CHARLES M. "Urbanism, Race, and Anomia." *American Journal of Sociology* 67 (May 1962): 661–65. See p. 661.

LENSKI, GERHARD E., and LEGGETT, JOHN C. "Caste, Class, and Deference in the Research Interview." *American Journal of Sociology* 65 (March 1960): 463–67. See pp. 464–65.

LIPMAN, AARON, and HAVENS, A. EUGENE. "The Columbia Violence: An Ex Post Facto Experiment." *Social Forces* 44 (December 1965): 238–45. See p. 240.

LOWENTHAL, MARJORIE FISKE. "Social Integration and Mental Illness in Old Age." *American Sociological Review* 29 (February 1964): 54–70. See p. 63.

MCDILL, EDWARD L. "Anomie, Authoritarianism, Prejudice, and Socio Economic Status: An Attempt at Clarification." *Social Forces* 39 (March 1961): 239–45. See pp. 239–40.

———, and RIDLEY, JEANNE CLARE. "Status, Anomia, Political Alienation, and Political Participation." *American Journal of Sociology* 67 (September 1962): 205–13. See p. 208.

MEIER, DOROTHY L., and BELL, WENDELL. "Anomia and Differential Access to the Achievement of Life Goals." *American Sociological Review* 24 (April 1959): 189–202. See p. 190.

MIZRUCHI, EPHRAIM H. "Social Structure and Anomia in a Small City." *American Sociological Review* 25 (October 1960): 645–54. See p. 647.

PHOTIADIS, JOHN D., and BIGGAR, JEANNE. "Religiosity, Education, and Ethnic Distance." *American Journal of Sociology* 67 (May 1962): 666–72. See p. 669.

———, and JOHNSON, ARTHUR L. "Orthodoxy, Church Participation, and Authoritarianism." *American Journal of Sociology* 69 (November 1963): 244–48. See p. 244.

RHODES, LEWIS. "Anomia, Aspiration, and Status." *Social Forces* 42 (May 1964): 433–40. See p. 436.

ROBERTS, A. H., and ROKEACH, MILTON. "Anomie, Authoritarianism, and Prejudice: A Replication." *American Journal of Sociology* 61 (January 1956): 355–58. See p. 357.

ROSE, ARNOLD M. "Alienation and Participation: A Comparison of Group Leaders and the 'Mass.'" *American Sociological Review* 27 (December 1962): 834–38. See p. 836.

———. "Attitudinal Correlates of Social Participation." *Social Forces* 37 (March 1959): 202–6. See pp. 203–4.

SEEMAN, MELVIN. "On the Personal Consequences of Alienation in Work." *American Sociological Review* 32 (April 1967): 273–85.

WEINSTEIN, EUGENE A., and GEISEL, PAUL N. "Family Decision Making over Desegregation." *Sociometry* 25 (March 1962): 21–29. See p. 25.

DEAN'S ALIENATION SCALE

4.J.3

VARIABLE MEASURED: The variable measured is considered as having three major components: powerlessness, normlessness, and social isolation.

DESCRIPTION: The scale consists of nine powerlessness items, six normlessness items, and nine social isolation items. The three subscales are combined to make up the alienation scale, which thus consists of 24 items.

WHERE PUBLISHED: Dwight G. Dean, "Alienation: Its Meaning and Measurement," *American Sociological Review* 26 (October 1961): 753–58.

RELIABILITY: The powerlessness scale, tested by the "split-half" technique, was .78 ($N = 378$). When corrected by the Spearman-Brown prophecy formula, the normlessness reliability was .73. The social isolation reliability when corrected for attenuation was .84. The total alienation scale had a reliability of .78 when corrected.

VALIDITY: Correlation coefficients between alienation and five background factor ($N = 384$).

Components:	Education	Occupation	Income	Age	Community
Powerlessness	-.20[b]	-.22[b]	-.26[b]	.14[b]	-.10[a]
Normlessness	-.21[b]	-.18[b]	-.14[b]	.13[b]	-.10[a]
Social isolation	-.07	-.11[a]	-.13[b]	-.03	-.06
Alienation	-.19[b]	-.21[b]	-.23[b]	.12[b]	-.10[a]

[a]Significant at the .05 level of confidence.
[b]Significant at the 0.1 level of confidence.

The correlation coefficients between the various components of alienation and Adorno "F" scale (for a college sample pretest of 73 respondents) were as follows:

$$
\begin{array}{ll}
\text{Powerlessness} & r = .37 \\
\text{Normlessness} & r = .33 \\
\text{Social isolation} & r = .23 \\
\text{Total alienation} & r = .26
\end{array}
$$

STANDARD SCORES (Alienation Scores on Dean Scale for Six Samples):

	(1)[a]	(2)[b]	(3)[c]	(4)[d]	(5)[e]	(6)[f]
Powerlessness:						
Mean	13.65			12.73	10.90	
Standard deviation	6.1					
Normlessness:						
Mean	7.62	8.63	3.77	7.63	3.55	see
Standard deviation	4.7	3.26	3.50			below
Social Isolation:						
Mean	11.76			14.85	15.16	
Standard deviation	4.6					
(Total) Alienation:						
Mean	36.64			36.25	30.16	
Standard deviation	13.5					

[a]Columbus, Ohio, N = 384 (men), stratified sample, 1955 (See Dean, "Alienation: Its Meaning and Measurement.")

[b]Protestant liberal arts college, N = 135 (women), random sample, 1960.

[c]Catholic women's college, N = 121 (women), random sample, 1960.

[d]Protestant liberal arts college, N = 75 (women), random sample, 1955.

[e]Catholic women's college, N = 65 (women), random sample, 1955. This and sample number three are identical except for date. (Samples 4 and 5 are described in Dwight G. Dean and Jon A. Reeves, "Anomie: A Comparison of a Catholic and a Protestant Sample," *Sociometry* 25 [June 1962]: 209-12.)

[f]A state university, Midwest, normlessness scores were: Catholic 12.84, S.D. 3.51; Protestant 14.40, S.D. 3.13. Questionnaires sent to a sample of 245, about 55 percent return.

RESEARCH APPLICATIONS: Alienation (Dean) (Subscales: powerlessness, normlessness, social isolation)

BONJEAN, CHARLES M. "Mass, Class, and the Industrial Community: A Comparative Analysis of Managers, Businessmen, and Workers." *American Journal of Sociology* 71 (September 1966): 149-62.

DEAN, DWIGHT G. "Alienation and Political Apathy." *Social Forces* 38 (March 1960): 185-89. See p. 188.

———. "Alienation: Its Meaning and Measurement." *American Sociological Review* 26 (October 1961): 753-58. See p. 757.

————, and REEVES, JON A. "Anomie: A Comparison of a Catholic and Protestant Sample." *Sociometry* 25 (June 1962): 209–12. See p. 210 (only the normlessness subscale is used here).

ERBE, WILLIAM. "Social Involvement and Political Activity: A Replication and Elaboration." *American Sociological Review* 29 (April 1964): 198–215. See pp. 205–6.

DEAN SCALE FOR MEASURING ALIENATION

Below is a keyed copy of the alienation scale. The letter to the left of each item indicates whether it belongs to the powerlessness, normlessness, or isolation subscale. When scoring, it is helpful to cut a "stencil" from a manila folder for each subscale.

PUBLIC OPINION QUESTIONNAIRE*

Below are some statements regarding public issues, with which some people agree and others disagree. Please give us your opinion about these items, i.e., whether you agree or disagree with the items as they stand.

Please check in the appropriate blank, as follows:

——————A (Strongly agree)
——————a (Agree)
——————U (Uncertain)
——————d (Disagree)
——————D (Strongly disagree)

I   1. Sometimes I feel all alone in the world.

    4 A   3 a   2 U   1 d   0 D

P   2. I worry about the future facing today's children.

    4 A   a   U   d   D

I   3. I don't get invited out by friends as often as I'd really like.

    4 A   a   U   d   D

N   4. The end often justifies the means.

    4 A   a   U   d   D

I   5. Most people today seldom feel lonely.

    0 A   1 a   2 U   3 d   4 D

P   6. Sometimes I have the feeling that other people are using me.

    4 A   a   U   d   D

N   7. People's ideas change so much that I wonder if we'll ever have anything to depend on.

    4 A   a   U   d   D

I   8. Real friends are as easy as ever to find.

    0 A   a   U   d   D

P   9. It is frightening to be responsible for the development of a little child.

    4 A   a   U   d   D

N 10. Everything is relative, and there just aren't any definite rules to live by.

    4 A   a   U   d   D

*Obviously, scores would be omitted when administered.

I   *11.* One can always find friends if he shows himself friendly.

_0_ A   ___ a   ___ U   ___ d   ___ D

N   *12.* I often wonder what the meaning of life really is.

_4_ A   ___ a   ___ U   ___ d   ___ D

P   *13.* There is little or nothing I can do towards preventing a major "shooting" war.

_4_ A   ___ a   ___ U   ___ d   ___ D

I   *14.* The world in which we live is basically a friendly place.

_0_ A   ___ a   ___ U   ___ d   ___ D

P   *15.* There are so many decisions that have to be made today that sometimes I could just "blow up."

_4_ A   ___ a   ___ U   ___ d   ___ D

N   *16.* The only thing one can be sure of today is that he can be sure of nothing.

_4_ A   ___ a   ___ U   ___ d   ___ D

I   *17.* There are few dependable ties between people any more.

_4_ A   ___ a   ___ U   ___ d   ___ D

P   *18.* There is little chance for promotion on the job unless a man gets a break.

_4_ A   ___ a   ___ U   ___ d   ___ D

N   *19.* With so many religions abroad, one doesn't really know which to believe.

_4_ A   ___ a   ___ U   ___ d   ___ D

P   *20.* We're so regimented today that there's not much room for choice even in personal matters.

_4_ A   ___ a   ___ U   ___ d   ___ D

P   *21.* We are just so many cogs in the machinery of life.

_4_ A   ___ a   ___ U   ___ d   ___ D

I   *22.* People are just naturally friendly and helpful.

_0_ A   ___ a   ___ U   ___ d   ___ D

P   *23.* The future looks very dismal.

_4_ A   ___ a   ___ U   ___ d   ___ D

I   *24.* I don't get to visit friends as often as I'd really like.

_4_ A   ___ a   ___ U   ___ d   ___ D

4.J.4   **KAHL'S ACHIEVEMENT ORIENTATION SCALE**

VARIABLE MEASURED: "It is an index of a generalized motivation to do well, to excel in a variety of tasks."

DESCRIPTION: It is composed of four scales derived through the use of factor analysis from a series of studies in the United States, Mexico, and Brazil. The four scales were: (1) Occupational primacy, "occupational success [is placed] ahead of alternative possibilities." In Mexico and Brazil this scale was used with three items. (2) Trust, "belief in the stability of life and the trustworthiness of people." Composed of six items. (3) Activism, "emphasizes planning for a controllable future." Composed of seven items. (4) Integration with relatives, "loyalty to parents instead of to self or to career." Composed of three items.

WHERE PUBLISHED: Joseph A. Kahl, "Some Measurements of Achievement Orientation," *American Journal of Sociology* 70 (May 1965): 669–81; and his book, *The Measurement of Modernism: A Study of Values in Brazil and Mexico* (Austin, Texas: University of Texas Press, 1968).

RELIABILITY: Not known from the original study, but inferred from Michael A. LaSorte's Ph.D. dissertation, which used similar scales. Applying the Spearman-Brown prophecy formula for correction, the reliability coefficients were occupational primacy, .81, trust, .94, mastery (activism), .94, and familism (which departs significantly from the integration with relatives), .86.

VALIDITY: Trust, activism, and independence from family scales are positively correlated with an index of socioeconomic status (based on occupation, education, and self-identification); occupational primacy is negatively correlated with the others and with status:

	Brazil	Mexico
Trust	.30	.26
Activism	.42	.49
Occupational (primacy)	−.20	−.09
Integration with relatives	−.30	−.46

RESEARCH APPLICATIONS:

COX, HENRIETTA. "Study of Social Class Variations in Value Orientations in Selected Areas of Mother-Child Behavior." Ph.D. dissertation, Washington University, St. Louis, 1964.

KAHL, JOSEPH A. "Urbanizacão e Mudancas Occupacionais no Brasil." *America Latina* 5 (October 1962): 21–30.

———. "Some Measurements of Achievement Orientation." *American Journal of Sociology* 70 (May 1965): 669–81.

LaSORTE, MICHAEL ANTONIO. "Achievement Orientation and Community of Orientation." Ph.D. dissertation, Indiana University, Bloomington, 1967.

SCANZONI, JOHN. "Socialization, Achievement, and Achievement Values." *American Sociological Review* 32 (June 1967): 449–56.

SEWELL, WILLIAM H.; HAUSER, ROBERT M.; FEATHERMAN, DAVID L., eds. *Schooling and Achievement in American Society.* New York: Academic Press. 1976.

The serious student should read the communication between Wallace D. Loh, Harry J. Crockett, Jr., Clyde Z. Nunn, and John Scanzoni over the relation of socialization practices and occupational achievement values. See *American Sociological Review* 33 (April 1968): 284–91.

For another important scale that incorporates occupational aspiration, see David Horton Smith and Alex Inkeles, "The OM Scale: A Comparative Socio-Psychological Measure of Individual Modernity," *Sociometry* 29 (December 1966): 353–77. Cf. A. O. Haller and I. W. Miller, *The Occupational Aspiration Scale: Theory, Structure, and Correlates* (2nd ed.; Cambridge, Mass.: Schenkman, 1971).

KAHL'S INDEX OF ACHIEVEMENT ORIENTATION

(Scale Items Show Factor Loadings)

TRUST

Mexico	Brazil	
−.66	−.78	It is not good to let your relatives know everything about your life, for they might take advantage of you.
−.71	−.74	It is not good to let your friends know everything about your life, for they might take advantage of you.
−.67	−.55	Most people will repay your kindness with ingratitude.
+.38		Most people are fair and do not try to get away with something.
−.62		People help persons who have helped them not so much because it is right but because it is good business.
−.40		You can only trust people whom you know well.

ACTIVISM

Mexico	Brazil	
−.63	−.74	Making plans only brings unhappiness because the plans are hard to fulfil.
−.58	−.65	It doesn't make much difference if the people elect one or another candidate for nothing will change.
−.67	−.63	With things as they are today an intelligent person ought to think only about the present, without worrying about what is going to happen tomorrow.
−.54	−.57	We Brazilians (Mexicans) dream big dreams, but in reality we are inefficient with modern industry.
−.61	−.47	The secret of happiness is not expecting too much out of life, and being content with what comes your way.
+.46		It is important to make plans for one's life and not just accept what comes.
+.41		How important is it to know clearly in advance your plans for the future? (*Very important* is coded positively.)

OCCUPATIONAL PRIMACY

Mexico	Brazil	
+.59	+.69	The job should come first, even if it means sacrificing time from recreation.
+.64	+.59	The best way to judge a man is by his success in his occupation.
+.80	+.62	The most important qualities of a real man are determination and driving ambition.
	+.46	The most important thing for a parent to do is to help his children get further ahead in the world than he did.

INTEGRATION WITH RELATIVES

Mexico	Brazil	
+.73	+.76	When looking for a job, a person ought to find a position in a place located near his parents, even if that means losing a good opportunity elsewhere.
+.78	+.75	When you are in trouble, only a relative can be depended upon to help you out.
+.65	+.64	If you have the chance to hire an assistant in your work, it is always better to hire a relative than a stranger.

4.J.5   MILLER'S SCALE BATTERY OF INTERNATIONAL PATTERNS AND NORMS

VARIABLE MEASURED: Norms and patterns of national cultures.

DESCRIPTION: It consists of a scale battery of twenty rating scales to ascertain important norms and patterns within national cultures: (1) social acceptance; (2) standards of personal and community health; (3) concern for and trust of others; (4) confidence in personal security and protection of property; (5) family solidarity; (6) independence of the child; (7) moral code and role definitions of men and women; (8) definition of religion and moral conduct; (9) class structure and class consciousness; (10) consensus on general philosophy and objectives of the society; (11) labor's orientation to the prevailing economic and social system; (12) belief in democratic political system; (13) definition of work and individual achievement; (14) civic participation and voluntary activity; (15) definition of the role of private and public ownership of property. Five more scales are under development with tests in United States, England, and Spain already completed. All rating scales have six positions ranging between two contrasting poles.

WHERE PUBLISHED: Delbert C. Miller, "The Measurement of International Patterns and Norms: A Tool for Comparative Research," *Southwestern Social Science Quarterly* 48 (March 1968): 531–47; Delbert C. Miller, "Measuring Cross National Norms: Methodological Problems in Identifying Patterns in Latin American and Anglo-Saxon Cultures," *International Journal of Comparative Sociology* 13, nos. 3-4 (September–December 1972): 201–16. See also D. C. Miller, *International Community Power Structures, Comparative Studies of Four World Cities* (Bloomington: Indiana University, 1970).

RELIABILITY: Test-retest correlations for the fifteen scales range from .74 to .97 as tested in the United States and Peru. Most scales have reliabilities of .90 and above.

VALIDITY: Three criteria for validity have been met. These are: (1) the mean difference on each rating scale is 2.00 or more when the United States and Peru are rated and compared; (2) average deviation of each scale shows a dispersion less than 1.00 when United States and Peru are rated; (3) judges' rankings permit a structuring of significant variations in the social patterning of the United States and Peru. Extended research in Argentina, Spain, England, and the United States reinforces these tests of validity.

UTILITY: Scales are rated by qualified judges who have experience in two or more national cultures. The rating requires approximately 30 minutes. The scales may be applied to numerous problems of cross-cultural research including the impact of a foreign culture on the stranger. The use of foreign and native judges rating the same two national cultures in which they have both had extensive experience reveals the significance of cross-cultural differences. Ratings can be made of national cultures by raters who have had no previous experience to examine stereotyping. The relation of the class position of the respondent offers the possibility of revealing international differences when viewed from varying class or racial positions occupied by the respondent in the national society.

COMPARATIVE SCORES: The mean scores shown for the rating scales on the seven samples may be used for comparative study.

RESEARCH APPLICATIONS: Delbert C. Miller, *International Community Power Structures, Comparative Studies of Four World Cities* (Bloomington: Indiana University Press, 1970), pp. 228–56. Chapter 14, "The Role of Values in International Decision Making: Anglo-American vs. Latin American Differences," reports on a test of the hypothesis that respondent exposure to any two countries in Latin America are more alike in cultural patterning than any Latin American country compared with the United States. Comparisons with samples in Spain and England are also reported to establish identity of Anglo-Saxon and Ibero-Latin American cultures. Ratings were made using panels of judges, both foreign and native, in Peru, Argentina, United States, Spain, and England. Studies have been made also with American university students who go abroad to study. Before-and-after ratings of their own country and the host country have been secured.

Teresa Camacho de Pinto has completed research on Colombia; her report of respondent ratings is shown in table 1. Paul D. Starr has completed a study in Lebanon to provide a valuable Middle East comparison and perspective. See "Social Patterns and Norms in Lebanon and the United States," *Human Relations* 26, no. 4 (1976): 357–66.

New scales have been added to the original fifteen to include: (1) degree of honesty and integrity in government; (2) degree of nepotism in business, govern-

Table 1

Scale of International Patterns and Norms	U.S.[a] (1966) N = 21	U.S.[b] (1968) N = 32	Spain[c] (1968) N = 17	Argen- tina[d] (1967) N = 15	Peru[e] (1966) N = 21	England[f] (1968) N = 15	Colom- bia[g] (1969) N = 10
1. Social Acceptance	1.7	1.6	3.1	3.2	4.5	4.0	4.2
2. Personal and Community Health	1.4	1.9	3.2	2.9	4.7	3.1	4.4
3. Concern and Trust of Others	1.8	2.7	4.1	3.3	4.9	2.0	4.3
4. Personal Security and Protection of Property	2.3	3.7	2.2	3.5	5.0	2.1	5.7
5. Family Solidarity	5.4	4.0	2.3	2.7	1.9	2.9	1.8
6. Independence of the Child	1.3	2.1	4.5	2.8	4.4	2.1	4.4
7. Moral Code and Role Definition	2.0	2.3	4.6	2.8	4.9	3.4	4.9
8. Religion and Moral Conduct	4.6	4.3	2.6	3.7	2.1	4.6	2.6
9. Class Structure and Consciousness	5.0	4.9	2.1	3.1	1.4	3.1	1.8
10. Societal Consensus	1.6	2.1	5.0	3.9	4.6	2.1	3.9
11. Labor's Orientation	5.3	5.4	2.3	2.7	3.1	4.0	2.7
12. Democratic Belief	1.4	1.8	4.6	2.8	3.7	2.1	3.8
13. Work and Achievement	1.5	2.1	4.0	3.1	4.8	3.1	4.2
14. Civic Participation	1.2	1.9	4.8	3.6	4.8	3.1	4.2
15. Role of Property	1.2	1.7	3.1	3.6	3.3	3.3	2.7
16. Honesty of Government Officials		1.8	3.5			1.3	
17. Political Influence of Foreign Enterprise		5.2	3.8			5.3	
18. Encouragement of Foreign Enterprise		2.2	2.5			2.3	
19. Nepotism in Organizations		4.8	1.5			4.0	
20. Reciprocity of Favors		3.9	1.5			5.0	

[a] American raters.
[b] American raters.
[c] Spanish raters in Madrid, Barcelona, and Seville.
[d] Argentine raters. (Data gathered by Judson Yearwood.)
[e] American raters living in Peru.
[f] Englishmen living in London, Liverpool, and Bristol, England.
[g] Colombian raters. (Data gathered by Dr. Teresa Camacho de Pinto.)

mental and organizational life generally; (3) degree of expected reciprocity in favors and rewards; (4) encouragement of foreign enterprise; (5) degree to which foreign enterprise is believed to influence the host government. The scales and scores are shown for the United States and Spain in the following test battery.

Applying Scales: Instructions to the Judge

(A qualified judge is a college graduate, especially trained to appraise his own country and with six months or more consecutive experience with the host country. He must be able to read and speak the language of the host country.)

Each characteristic has been placed on a scale of six points. The descriptions defining the scale are shown at 1 and 2, 3 and 4, and 5 and 6. Thus, the first characteristic, social acceptance, attributes highest social acceptance to number 1 position and lowest social acceptance to the number 6 position. The range between represents a continuum of different degrees of the characteristic.

Task 1. Establish anchor points for each scale by selecting countries from anywhere in the world that reflect the extreme positions of the scale for social acceptance. These countries may or may not be known to you personally. In making a selection *think of the way the pattern appears on the average throughout the country and as it is experienced by a person in the middle sector of society*—i.e., omitting the very rich and the very poor. When the selection has been made, write the names of the countries in the answer sheets. Proceed to select countries representing the extremes of all 19 remaining characteristics— i.e., standards of health, standards of personal and community health, etc. Write the names on the answer sheets.

Task 2. Now place the two countries in their proper positions on all 20 characteristics. Again, think of the pattern as it appears on the average throughout the country and as it is experienced by a person in the middle sector of society— i.e., omitting the very rich and the very poor. Write answers on answer sheet.

Task 3. Place a third country on the scale if you have lived six months or more within it. Write answers on answer sheet.

MILLER'S SCALE BATTERY OF INTERNATIONAL PATTERNS AND NORMS

Delbert C. Miller

Respondent: Kindly check if you are male or female and indicate years lived in native country and in other countries. Sign your name and give your address if you wish a final report. Read the accompanying directions carefully before you begin. Thank you.

Check: Male___Female___
Years lived in:
Native Country _____
Other Countries _____
_____
_____

(Optional)
Name: _____
Address: _____
_____
_____

1. Social acceptance

1	2	3	4	5	6

High social acceptance. Social contacts open and non-restric-   Medium social acceptance. Ready acceptance in neigh-   Low social acceptance. Acceptance in specifically

1. Social acceptance

1	2	3	4	5	6
tive. Introductions not needed for social contacts. Short acquaintance provides entry into the home and social organizations.		borhood and in community organizations but not in family and social life. Friendly in business and other public contacts.		designated groups in which membership has been validated. Sponsored introduction is needed for social contacts in all parts of community life.	

2. Standards of personal and community health

1	2	3	4	5	6
High standards of personal and community hygiene. Hygienic habits valued in all parts of society.		Varied. High community standards for water and sewage. Personal habits and community standards for cleanliness and hygiene vary widely across the community.		Personal and community standards of hygiene are not valued highly.	

3. Concern for and trust of others

1	2	3	4	5	6
High concern for others. Respect for the motives and integrity of others. Mutual trust prevails.		Moderate or uneven pattern of concern for and trust of others.		Lack of concern for others and lack of trust.	

4. Confidence in personal security and protection of property

1	2	3	4	5	6
High confidence in personal security. Free movement, night and day, for both sexes. High sense of security of property. Locking of homes is optional.		Moderate confidence in personal security. Confidence of men is high in personal security but women are warned to take precautions. Movements of women restricted to daytime. Simple property precautions essential.		Low confidence in both personal security and protection of property. Men and women restrict all movement at night to predetermined precautions. Many property precautions obligatory. Extensive use of locks, dogs, and guards.	

5. Family solidarity

1	2	3	4	5	6
High solidarity with many obligations of kinship relations within large, extended family system.		Relations of solidarity within a limited kinship circle with specified obligations only.		Small, loosely integrated, independent family with highly specific individual relations.	

6. Independence of the child

1	2	3	4	5	6
Child is raised to be self-reliant and independent in both thought and action.		Child is given specified areas of independence only.		Child is raised to be highly dependent and docile.	

7. *Moral code and role definitions of men and women*

1	2	3	4	5	6

Single code of morality prevails for men and women. Separate occupational and social roles are not defined for men and women. Similar amounts and standards of education prevail.	Variations between moral definitions for men and women exist for certain specified behaviors. Occupational and social role definitions vary in degree. Varying educational provisions for the sexes.	Double code of morality prevails. Separate occupational and social roles for men and women exist and are sharply defined. Amount and standards of education vary widely between the sexes.

8. *Definition of religion and moral conduct*

1	2	3	4	5	6

Belief in the sacred interpretation of life as primary explanation of purpose of life and role of death. Emphasis is placed on importance of worshiper role in fulfilling spiritual obligations and duties.	Belief in supreme being a sacred purpose for life. Emphasis is placed on secular interpretation of moral values and importance of applying them to daily conduct.	Belief in secular interpretation of life. Emphasis on importance of achieving the good society for achieving the good life. Moral values prescribed by social and scientific definitions of human well being in the society. Emphasis on social conduct as moral conduct.

9. *Class structure and class consciousness*

1	2	3	4	5	6

Highly conscious of class differences. Extensive use of status symbols. Social classes and social circles rigidly defined. Very small upward class movement. Contacts between classes limited by social distinctions. Private schools predominate for upper social groups.	Class consciousness prevails moderately. Upward class movement occurs but definite characteristics mark off and limit contact between classes.	Class consciousness low. Class differences devalued. Minimal use of status symbols. Considerable upward class movement. Relatively free social contacts between social classes. Public schools dominate for all social classes.

10. *Consensus over general philosophy and objectives of the society*

1	2	3	4	5	6

High consensus over philosophy and objectives of the society as achieved either through evolution or revolution. Competition and conflict between parties takes place within generally accepted goals of the society. Stable governments usually prevail.	Consensus is partial. Differing ideological systems conflict. Stable government may be maintained but under threat of overthrow.	Absence of consensus (or very low) over philosophy and objectives of the society. Conflicting and splinter parties may represent the divergent ideologies and cleavages. Unstable governments prevail.

11. Labor's orientation to the prevailing economic and social system

1	2	3	4	5	6
Highly alienated. Ideologically opposed to the prevailing economic and social system. Revolutionary in orientation.		Antagonistic. Partly alienated with some unions ideologically in support and some in opposition to prevailing economic and social system.		Highly assimilated. Ideologically in agreement with prevailing economic and social system. Labor disputes over distribution shares of goods and services to working people but accepts on-going system.	

12. Belief in democratic political system

1	2	3	4	5	6
Strongly committed. Deep and persistent belief in the democratic processes regardless of problems or crisis.		Reserved commitment. Belief in democracy as process requiring careful control against mass abuse. Accepts necessity of dictatorial intervention in crisis situations or special safeguard such as one-party systems, relinquishing freedoms in internal crises, etc.		Lack of belief in democracy as political system. Regarded as weak and ineffectual in the solving of problems and improving the lot of the average man. Generally regarded as dangerous because it exposes government to mob psychology.	

13. Definition of work and individual achievement

1	2	3	4	5	6
A belief in hard work as obligation to self, employer, and God. Efficiency values accepted. Individual is expected to progress in his work life.		Work is important to the advancement of self and family. Efficiency values accepted. Achievement expectations vary.		Lack of belief in hard work. Work is regarded as necessary, but involves no obligation beyond delivery of minimum services. Efficiency values rejected. Individual is expected only to maintain family status at his inherited level.	

14. Civic participation and voluntary activity

1	2	3	4	5	6
High civic activity. People work together to get things done for the community. High identity with volunteer groups. Civic participation and volunteer activity in groups is an important source of social prestige. Moral and altruistic motives are important sources of motivation.		Moderate activity in special areas. Organized participation exists for economic or political self-interest but often is lacking for a general community need.		Low civic activity, often deliberately avoided with no social sanctions. Low identity with volunteer groups. Civic participation is not an important source of prestige. Mistrust of motives is common since self-interest is generally assumed as the principle motivation for all persons.	

15. *Definition of the role of private and public ownership of property*

1	2	3	4	5	6

Strong belief in the right of private property for all persons in all types of goods. Private ownership and control of means of production is accepted for all industries and services except for a few natural monopolies (i.e., water, post office, etc.)

Belief in the wide mixture of private ownership and public ownership in all industries and services. Public ownership of large basic industries (steel, coal, electricity, etc.) and services (transport and communication) is especially common.

Strong belief in the public ownership and governmental controls of all industries and services except for small enterprises. Private ownership accepted in the ownership of personal goods.

16. *Standards of honesty and integrity of government officials*

1	2	3	4	5	6

Government officials at all levels have a high standard of honesty and integrity. Violations are prosecuted vigorously and punished with appropriate penalties.

Government officials are generally honest but there are differences in the honesty of officials at different levels. Violations do occur and are prosecuted. The certainty of detection and the severity of penalty varies according to differing practices.

Government officials at all levels commonly engage in various kinds of corrupt practices. Most violations are seldom prosecuted. Occasionally token prosecutions are made when abuse becomes excessive.

17. *Political influence of foreign enterprise on host government*

1	2	3	4	5	6

Foreign enterprise has marked political influence on major economic and political policies of the nation. It can resist attempted nationalization of its own enterprises and enforce favorable trade and political relations.

Foreign enterprise does have significant political influence over certain economic conditions of its special concern, but it has no real influence over political policy and process within the host country.

Foreign enterprise has no real influence over national policies—economic or political. Host government may enforce strict control over all foreign enterprise but often permits foreign enterprise to operate within same set of guidelines as domestic firms.

18. *Encouragement of foreign enterprise*

1	2	3	4	5	6

All foreign enterprise is strongly encouraged to invest and operate businesses of all kinds throughout the country.

Selected forms of foreign investment are encouraged. Use of foreign management personnel may be discouraged.

Foreign investment and operation of enterprise is discouraged by official and unofficial means.

19. *Degree of nepotism in organizational life*

1	2	3	4	5	6

Family members of owners, managers, clerical, and manual workers are given preferential and sometimes priviledged opportunities for employment in all types of organizations.	Family members of owners, managers, and professionals are given priority within organizations owned or managed by their relatives.	Merit and training is the sole basis for selection of all persons in all types of organizations.

20. *Degree of expected reciprocity in favors and rewards*

1	2	3	4	5	6

Pattern of expected reciprocity in favors prevails in regard to economic or political support given to individual or group. Personal basis of contact is encouraged and reciprocity is expected by a returned favor (or gift) in near future.	Reciprocity is expected only in specific situations when both parties have a written or oral agreement to exchange political and social support for services rendered.	No pattern of expected reciprocity prevails in economic or political life. Favors or special gifts for service and business rendered is regarded as self-serving and "wrong."

Family and Marriage

The Marriage-Prediction Schedule and the Marriage-Adjustment Schedule are products of intensive research efforts led by Ernest W. Burgess and his associates and aided by many social researchers who have been seeking factors associated with success or failure in marriage.

The Marriage-Prediction Schedule is used in assessing the probabilities of engaged couples to be able to establish happy marital adjustment if they should marry.

The Marriage-Adjustment Schedule is for married couples. It can be used as a diagnostic instrument to help the marriage counselor detect the social areas where difficulties exist. The researcher may use it to assess new relationships such as the role of parent-child relations and marital adjustment.

MARRIAGE-PREDICTION SCHEDULE AND
MARRIAGE-ADJUSTMENT SCHEDULE

4.K.1

VARIABLE MEASURED: The marital prediction schedule predicts the statistical probabilities of success in marriage; the marriage adjustment schedule is predictive of adjustment in marriage.

DESCRIPTION: The marital adjustment schedule was the first schedule developed. Five hundred twenty-six Illinois couples who had been married one to six years were studied. Marital adjustment was defined as (1) agreement between husband and wife upon matters that might be made critical issues; (2) common interests and joint activities; (3) frequent overt demonstrations of affection and mutual confidence; (4) few complaints; (5) few reports of feeling lonely, miserable, irritable, and so on. Items classified under these five headings serve as indicators of marital adjustment. Each of the items shows a measurable relationship to the ratings given by the couples to their expressed happiness rating of their marriage. For the development of the marital adjustment schedule see E. W. Burgess and Leonard S. Cottrell, *Predicting Success or Failure in Marriage* (Englewood Cliffs, N.J.: Prentice-Hall, 1939). Cf. Nathan Hurvitz, "The Measurement of Marital Strain," *American Journal of Sociology* 65 (May 1960): 610–15.

The marital prediction schedule was developed by seeking items predictive of marriage adjustment among 1000 engaged couples. Selected background items significantly associated with marital adjustment were combined into an expectancy table for premarital prediction of success in marriage. For the development of the marital prediction schedule see Ernest W. Burgess and Paul Wallin, *Engagement and Marriage* (Philadelphia: Lippincott, 1953).

WHERE PUBLISHED: Ernest W. Burgess and Harvey J. Locke, *The Family* (2nd ed.; New York: American Book, 1960), pp. 693–716. (Contains the refined version of the schedules based upon approximately 25 years of research.)

RELIABILITY: Husband-wife adjustment scores correlated with $r = .88$. ($N = 526$ couples.)

VALIDITY:

Happiness ratings and adjustment scores correlated .92. ($N = 526$ couples.)

Second sample of 63 cases showed correlation between happiness ratings and adjustment scores of .95.

Correlation between happiness ratings and absence of marital disorganization, divorce, separation, and contemplation of divorce or separation. $r = .89$.

Harvey Locke computed Burgess-Cottrell Adjustment scores for divorced men, divorced women, happily married men, and happily married women. Correlations between scores attained in this way and scores from the 29 questions in his test were respectively, .83, .87, .85, and .88.

Burgess and Wallin gave an adjustment test to 1000 engaged couples, and then, three years after marriage, gave a marital adjustment test to as many couples as could be contacted. Correlation between adjustment scores of engaged couples was .57; three years after marriage, marital adjustment scores of 505 husbands and wives correlated .41. See Lewis M. Terman and Paul Wallin, "The Validity of Marriage Prediction and Marital Adjustment Tests," *American Sociological Review* 14 (August 1949): 497–504; Harvey J. Locke and Robert G. Williamson, "Marriage Adjustment: A Factor Analysis Study," *American Sociological Review* 23 (October 1958): 562–69.

Scoring the Marriage-Prediction and Marriage-Adjustment Schedules

The narrow columns at the right side of each page of the Marriage-Prediction Schedule and the Marriage-Adjustment Schedule are provided for scoring the replies to the questions. The score values assigned are arbitrary in the sense that usually each gradation in reply differs by one point. Although arbitrary, the score values are in general conformity with the findings of the studies in this field, particularly those of E. W. Burgess and L. S. Cottrell, *Predicting Success or Failure in Marriage;* L. M. Terman and Others, *Psychological Factors in Marital Happiness;* E. W. Burgess and Paul Wallin, *Engagement and Marriage;* and Harvey J. Locke, *Predicting Adjustment in Marriage: A Comparison of a Divorced and a Happily Married Group.*

The two-digit numbers after each subdivision of the questions provide the code for scoring the replies. The score value of each response is obtained simply by adding together the two digits in the number that is a subscript under the last letter of the final word of the response that has been checked. For example, if you have checked a response numbered 42, your score for that item is $4 + 2 = 6$. To obtain your total score, follow these steps:

1. For each item, enter in Column 1 at the right-hand side of each page the two-digit number that appears as a subscript under the last letter of the final word of the answers to each question. An example is: What is your present state of health? chronic ill-health (13)_____; temporary ill-health (23)_____; average health (15)_____; healthy (25)_____; very healthy (17)_____. If your answer to this question is "average health," then write 15 in Column 1.

   In Part Two of the Marriage-Prediction Schedule, put only the score of your fiancé(e) in the blank on the right-hand margin.
2. Enter in Column 2 the sum of the two digits appearing in Column 1 for each item. For each part of the questionnaire, compute the total of the values appearing in Column 2, and enter that figure in the space provided at the end of that section.
3. In scoring Part Two of the Marriage-Adjustment Schedule, multiply the total number of check marks in each of the four columns as follows:

Column A by 6	Column C by 4
Column B by 5	Column D by 6

   Add together the four figures obtained in the four columns. This sum equals your total score for Part Two.
4. Enter the total score for each part in the spaces provided at the end of the questionnaire. Your total score on the inventory equals the sum of the total scores of the separate parts and is your marriage-adjustment score.

Standard Scores

A. Marriage-Prediction Schedule

High scores on the Marriage-Prediction Schedule, those above 630, are favorable for marital adjustment, as indicated by research findings that approximately 75 percent of persons with these scores in the engagement period are well adjusted in their marriages. Low scores, or those below 567, are much less favorable for happiness in marriage, as shown by the probability that only 25 percent of persons with these scores will be well adjusted in married life. Scores between 567 and 630 indicate that there is about a 50 percent chance for marital success and about a 50 percent chance for marital failure.

The prediction score of a person and his corresponding matrimonial-risk-group assignment should be interpreted with extreme caution. The following points should be kept in mind:

1. The prediction does not apply directly to the individual. It states the statistical probabilities of marital success for a group of persons of which the individual is one. If he belongs to the lower risk group, in which 75 percent of the marriages turn out unhappily, there is no way of telling by this statistical prediction whether he falls in the 25 percent of the marriages with varying degrees of happiness or in the 75 percent of unhappy unions.
2. The prediction is for an individual's general matrimonial risk irrespective of

the particular person to whom he is engaged. The individual's specific matrimonial risk for marriage to a given person is much more valuable but also more complicated, and therefore not suited for self-scoring.

3. In the majority of cases the specific matrimonial risk of a couple may be roughly estimated from the two general matrimonial-risk groups to which the two persons are assigned. An average of the two scores will generally be close to what may be expected from a specific matrimonial-risk-group assignment.

4. With the aforementioned reservations in mind, a low prediction score should not be taken as indicating lack of suitability for marriage. It should, however, be helpful to the person in stimulating him to secure adequate preparation for marriage, to be more careful in the selection of a marriage partner, and to give attention to the solving of any difficulties in the relation before, rather than after, the marriage.

B. Marriage-Adjustment Schedule

In evaluating the total score secured on the Marriage-Adjustment Schedule, see the following table:

Marriage-Adjustment Scores as Indicative of Adjustment in Marriage

Marital-adjustment scores	Adjustment in marriage
720 and over	Extremely well adjusted
700 to 719	Decidedly well adjusted
680 to 699	Fairly adjusted
660 to 679	Somewhat adjusted
640 to 659	Indifferently adjusted
620 to 639	Somewhat unadjusted
600 to 619	Unadjusted
580 to 599	Decidedly unadjusted
579 and under	Extremely unadjusted

UTILITY: Each form may be filled out in approximately 30 minutes. The measure may be used for both research and counseling purposes. Short marital-adjustment and prediction tests are now available. It is claimed that "with the short tests, measurement or prediction can be accomplished with approximately the same accuracy in a few minutes as ordinarily would require an hour or more with the longer ones." Harvey J. Locke and Karl M. Wallace, "Short Marital-Adjustment and Prediction Tests: Their Reliability and Validity," *Marriage and Family Living* 21 (August 1959): 251–55.

RESEARCH APPLICATIONS:

BOWERMAN, CHARLES. "Adjustment in Marriage, Overall and in Specific Areas." *Sociology and Social Research* 41 (March-April 1957): 257–63.

BURGESS, E. W., and WALLIN, PAUL. "Predicting Adjustment in Marriage from Adjustment in Engagement." *American Journal of Sociology* 49 (1944): 324–30.

HURVITZ, NATHAN. "The Measurement of Marital Strain." *American Journal of Sociology* 65 (May 1960): 610–15.

KARLSSON, GEORG. *Adaptability and Communication in Marriage: A Swedish Predictive Study of Marital Satisfaction.* Uppsala, Sweden: Almquist & Wiksell, 1951.

KING, CHARLES. "The Burgess-Cottrell Method of Measuring Marital Adjustment Applied to a Non-White Southern Urban Population." *Marriage and Family Living* 14 (November 1952): 280–85.

LOCKE, HARVEY J. *Predicting Adjustment in Marriage: A Comparison of a Divorced and a Happily Married Group.* New York: Henry Holt, 1951

——, and KARLSSON, GEORG. "Marital Adjustment and Prediction in Sweden and the United States." *American Sociological Review* 17 (February 1952): 10–17.

——, and KLAUSNER, WILLIAM J. "Marital Adjustment of Divorced Persons in Subsequent Marriages." *Sociology and Social Research* 33 (1948): 97–101.

——, and MACKEPRANG, MURIEL. "Marital Ajustment and the Employed Wife." *American Journal of Sociology* 54 (1949): 536–38.

——, and SNOWBARGER, VERNON A. "Marital Adjustment and Predictors in Sweden." *American Journal of Sociology* 60 (July 1954): 51–53.

——, and WILLIAMSON, ROBERT C. "Marital Adjustment: A Factor Analysis Study." *American Sociological Review* 23 (October 1958): 562–69.

LUCKEY, ELEANORE BRAUN. "Marital Satisfaction and Congruent Self-Spouse Concepts." *Social Forces* 39 (December 1960): 153–57.

NIMKOFF, MEYER F., and GRIGG, C. M. "Values and Marital Adjustment of Nurses." *Social Forces* 37 (October 1958): 67–70.

SCHNEPP, GERALD J. "Do Religious Factors Have Predictive Value?" *Marriage and Family Living* 14 (1952): 301–4.

WILLIAMSON, ROBERT C. "Socio-Economic Factors and Marital Adjustment in an Urban Setting." *American Sociological Review* 19 (April 1954): 213–16.

WINCH, ROBERT F. "Personality Characteristics of Engaged and Married Couples." *American Journal of Sociology* 46 (1941): 686–97.

SCHEDULES FOR THE PREDICTION AND MEASUREMENT OF MARRIAGE ADJUSTMENT

1. Marriage-Prediction Schedule *

Please Read Carefully Before and After Filling Out Schedule.

This schedule is prepared for persons who are seriously considering marriage. Although designed for couples who are engaged or who have a private understanding to be married, it can also be filled out by other persons who would like to know their probability of success in marriage. The value of the findings of the schedule depends upon your frankness in answering the questions.

The following points should be kept in mind in filling out the schedule:

1. Be sure to answer every question.
2. Do not leave a blank to mean a "no" answer.
3. The word "fiancé(e)" will be used to refer to the person to whom you are engaged or are considering as a possible marriage partner.
4. Do not confer with your fiancé(e) on any of these questions.

*Reproduced by permission of Ernest W. Burgess, Leonard S. Cottrell, Paul Wallin, and Harvey J. Locke.

	1	2

Part One

1. What is your present state of health? chronic ill-health (13)____;
temporary ill-health (23)____; average health (15)____; healthy
(25)____; very healthy (17)____

2. Give your present marital status: single (35)____; widowed (43)____;
separated (41)____; divorced (31)____

3. Total number of years of schooling completed at present time:

        Grades (22)   High School (32)   College (15)

    1_2_3_4_5_6_7_8_; 1_2_3_4_; 1_2_3_4_;

graduate of college (25); number of years beyond college in graduate
work or professional training (35)____

4. Work record: regularly employed (17)____; worked only during vaca-
tions and/or only part time while in school (34)____; none because in
school or at home (24)____; always employed but continually changing
jobs (32)____; irregularly employed (13)____

5. Are you a church member? yes (16)____; no (23)____

Your activity in church: never attend (40)____; attend less than once a
month (23)____; once or twice a month (33)____; three times a month
(16)____; four times a month (26)____

6. At what age did you stop attending Sunday school or other religious
school for children and young people? never attended (31)____; before
10 years old (23)____; 11–18 years (42)____; 19 and over (16)____;
still attending (35)____

7. How many organizations do you belong to or attend regularly, such as
church club, athletic club, social club, luncheon club (like the Rotary,
Kiwanis, Lions), fraternal order, college fraternity, college sorority, civic
organization, music society, patriotic organization, Y.W.C.A., Y.M.C.A.,
C.Y.O., Y.M.H.A.? none (22)____; one (32)____; two (15)____; three
or more (25)____

8. What do you consider to have been the economic status of your parents
during your adolescence? well-to-do (34)____; wealthy (43)____;
comfortable (15)____; meager (32)____; poor (40)____

9. What do you consider to be the social status of your parents in their
own community? one of the leading families (26)____; upper class
(16)____; upper-middle class (42)____; middle class (32)____; lower-
middle class (40)____; lower class (21)____; no status as they are
dead (33)____

10. Marital status of your parents: married (both living) (24)____; separated (41)____; divorced (31)____; both dead (15)____; one dead
(specifiy which one) (33)____

11. Your appraisal of the happiness of your parents' marriage; very happy
(36)____; happy (16)____; average (24)____; unhappy (41)____; very
unhappy (31)____

12. Indicate your attitudes toward your parents on the following scales:

    (1) Your attitude toward your father when you were a child; very
strong attachment (35)____; considerable attachment (25)____;
mild attachment (41)____; mild hostility (13)____; considerable
hostility (30)____; very strong hostility (21)____

    (2) Your present attitude toward your father: very strong attachment
(44)____; considerable attachment (16)____; mild attachment
(23)____; mild hostility (22)____; considerable hostility (12)____;
very strong hostility (21)____; no attitude as he is dead (24)____

	1	2

(3) Your attitude toward your mother when you were a child: very strong attachment (26)____; considerable attachment (34)____; mild attachment (14)____; mild hostility (31)____; considerable hostility (30)____; very strong hostility (12)____

(4) Your present attitude toward your mother: very strong attachment (17)____; considerable attachment (43)____; mild attachment (32)____; mild hostility (13)____; considerable hostility (21)____; very strong hostility (30)____; no attitude as she is dead (15)____

13. Rate your parents' appraisal of the happiness of their marriage. Write **M** for mother's rating; **F** for father's rating; extraordinarily happy (27)____; decidedly happy (25)____; happy (41)____; somewhat happy (30)____; average (30)____; somewhat unhappy (12)____; unhappy (21)____; decidedly unhappy (30)____; extremely unhappy (12)____

14. Outside your family and kin, how many separated and divorced people do you know personally? none (26)____; one (43)____; two (23)____; three (40)____; four (30)____; five (12)____; six or more (21)____

15. How do you rate your first information about sex? wholesome (16) ____; unwholesome (23)____
Where did you get your first information about sex? from parent (35)____; from wholesome reading (16)____; brother (41)____; sister (41)____; other relative (41)____; other adult or teacher (24) ____; other children (31)____; from pernicious reading (12)____; other (specify) (15)____
Do you consider your present knowledge of sex adequate for marriage? yes (34)____; no (14)____; doubtful (42)____

16. Do you smoke? not at all (26)____; rarely (15)____; occasionally (32)____; often (22)____

17. Do you drink? not at all (35)____; rarely (42)____; occasionally (33)____; often (31)____

Part Two

Rate the following personality traits of yourself, your fiancé(e), your father, your mother. Write *F* for father, *M* for mother, *S* for fiancé(e), and *Y* for yourself. If either of your parents is dead, rate as remembered. Be sure to rate your father, your mother, your fiancé(e), and yourself on each trait.

						1	2
Trait	Very much so	Con-siderably	Some-what	A little	Not at all		
Willingly takes responsibility	26	16	6	23	13		
Dominating	13	23	33	16	44		
Irritable	40	14	24	25	17		
Punctual	35	25	15	14	13		
Moody	22	41	51	43	35		
Angers easily	40	50	60	34	26		
Ambitious	13	23	33	25	44		

					1	2

Trait	Very much so	Con- siderably	Some- what	A little	Not at all	1	2
Jealous	31	41	15	16	26		
Sympathetic	17	16	24	32	4		
Easygoing	44	43	42	14	22		
Stubborn	22	14	24	25	17		
Sense of duty	26	25	15	41	31		
Sense of humor	35	34	24	23	22		
Easily hurt	31	23	51	52	35		
Self-confident	44	16	15	14	13		
Selfish	22	23	33	43	44		
Nervous	22	23	24	25	35		
Likes belonging to organizations	26	16	33	41	13		
Impractical	40	14	6	34	17		
Easily depressed	13	5	42	16	26		
Easily excited	31	32	24	7	44		

T

Part Three

	1	2

1. What is the attitude of your closest friend or friends to your fiancé(e)? approve highly (25)_____; approve with qualification (15)_____; are resigned (32)_____; disapprove mildly (13)_____; disapprove seriously (31)_____

2. How many of your present men and women friends are also friends of your fiancé(e)? all (17)_____; most of them (25)_____; a few (23)_____; none (13)_____

3. How would you rate the physical appearance of your fiancé(e)? very good looking (35)_____; good looking (25)_____; fairly good looking (41)_____; plain looking (22)_____; very plain looking (31)_____

4. Do you think your fiancé(e) is spending a disproportionate amount of present income on any of the following (check only one)? clothes (or other personal ornamentation) (13)_____; recreation (41)_____; hobbies (22)_____; food (24)_____; rent (33)_____; education (16)_____; do not think so (35)_____

5. With how many of the opposite sex, other than your fiancé(e), have you gone steadily? none (25)_____; one (42)_____; two (24)_____; three or more (15)_____

6. Defining friends as something more than mere acquaintances but not necessarily as always having been boon companions, give an estimate of the number of your men friends before going steadily with your fiancé(e): none (31)_____; few (14)_____; several (24)_____; many (34)_____; (in round numbers, how many? _____)

7. Estimate the number of your women friends before going steadily with your fiancé(e): none (4)_____; few (32)_____; several (33)_____; many (16)_____; (in round numbers, how many? _____)

	1	2

8. Have you ever been engaged before (or had any previous informal under-standing that you were to be married)? never (35)_____; once (42)_____; twice (14)_____; three or more times (31)_____

9. Give the attitude of your father and mother toward your marriage: both approve (26)_____; both disapprove (31)_____; one disapproves: (your father (22)_____, your mother (31)_____)

10. What is your attitude toward your future father-in-law? like him very much (25)_____; like him considerably (15)_____; like him mildly (32)_____; mild dislike (40)_____; considerable dislike (12)_____; very strong dislike (30)_____; no attitude, as he is dead (42)_____
mother-in-law: like her very much (34)_____; like her considerably (24)_____; like her mildly (41)_____; mild dislike (22)_____; consider-able dislike (21)_____; very strong dislike (12)_____; no attitude, as she is dead (24)_____

11. How long have you been keeping company with your fiancé(e)? less than 3 months (13)_____; 3 to 5 months (32)_____; 6 to 11 months (24)_____; 12 to 17 months (25)_____; 18 to 23 months (35)_____; 24 to 35 months (17)_____; 36 months or more (44)_____

12. How many months will elapse between your engagement (or time at which you both had a definite understanding that you were to be married) and the date selected for your marriage? less than 3 months (40)_____; 3 to 5 months (14)_____; 6 to 11 months (33)_____; 12 to 17 months (25)_____; 18 to 23 months (35)_____; 24 or more months (44)_____

T

Part Four

1. Do you and your fiancé(e) engage in interests and activities together? all of them (43)_____; most of them (15)_____; some of them (23)_____; a few of them (31)_____; none of them (22)_____

2. Is there any interest vital to you in which your fiancé(e) does not engage? yes (31)_____; no (43)_____

3. Do you confide in your fiancé(e)? about everything (36)_____; about most things (16)_____; about some things (23)_____; about a few things (22)_____; about nothing (30)_____

4. Does your fiancé(e) confide in you? about everything (27)_____; about most things (25)_____; about some things (41)_____; about a few things (31)_____; about nothing (12)_____

5. What is the frequency of demonstrations of affection you show your fiancé(e) (kissing, embracing, etc.)? occupies practically all of the time you are alone together (18)_____; very frequent (26)_____; occasional (14)_____; rare (31)_____; almost never (12)_____

6. Who generally takes the initiative in the demonstration of affection? mutual (26)_____; you (23)_____; your fiancé(e) (41)_____

7. Are you satisfied with the amount of demonstration of affection? yes (35)_____; (no: desire less (30)_____; desire more (12)_____)

8. Is your fiancé(e) satisfied with the amount of demonstration of affec-tion? yes (44)_____; (no : desires less (3)_____; desires more (30)_____)

9. In leisure-time activities: we both prefer to stay at home (26)_____; we both prefer to be "on the go" (14)_____; one prefers to stay at home and the other to be "on the go" (40)_____

10. State the present approximate agreement or disagreement with your fiancé(e) on the following items. Please place a check in the proper column opposite every item.

			Occa-	Fre-	Almost			1	2
Check one column for each item below	Always agree (35)	Almost always agree (16)	sionally dis- agree (42)	quently dis- agree (14)	always dis- agree (22)	Always dis- agree (30)	Never dis- cussed (15)		
Money matters									
Matters of recreation									
Religious matters									
Demonstrations of affection									
Friends									
Table manners									
Matters of conventionality									
Philosophy of life									
Ways of dealing with your families									
Arrangements for your marriage									
Dates with one another									

11. When disagreements arise between you and your fiancé(e) they usually result in: agreement by mutual give and take (53)____; your giving in (16)____; your fiancé(e) giving in (30)____; neither giving in (21)____

12. Do you ever wish you had not become engaged? never (44)____; once (14)____; occasionally (13)____; frequently (40)____

13. Have you ever contemplated breaking your engagement? never (35) ____; once (41)____; occasionally (31)____; frequently (40)____

14. Has your steady relationship with your fiancé(e) ever been broken off temporarily? never (61)____; once (23)____; twice (40)____; three or more times (13)____

15. How confident are you that your marriage will be a happy one? very confident (25)____; confident (33)____; a little uncertain (14)____; very uncertain (40)____

T

Part Five | 1 | 2 |

1. Where do you plan to be married? at church (35)____; at home (16) ____; elsewhere (32)____

2. By whom do you plan to be married? minister, priest, or rabbi (16) ____; other person (14)____

3. Where do you plan to live after marriage? private house (26)____; small apartment building (52)____; large apartment building (15)____; apartment hotel (41)____; hotel (22)____; rooming house (30)____

	1	2
4. Have bought a home (44)____; plan to buy a home (25)____; plan to rent a home (14)____		
5. Population of city or town where you plan to live: open country (27) ____; 2,500 or under (35)____; 2,500 to 10,000 (16)____; 10,000 to 50,000 (42)____; 50,000 to 100,000 (32)____; 100,000 to 500,000 (4)____; over 500,000 (30)____; suburb (17)____		
6. After marriage where do you plan to live? in own home (53)____; with your parents (13)____; with parents-in-law (30)____; with other relatives (21)____; with relatives-in-law (3)____; with other persons (12) ____		
7. What is your attitude toward having children? desire children very much (25)____; mildly desire them (41)____; mild objection to them (31) ____; object very much to having them (13)____		
8. How many children would you like to have? four or more (17)____; three (52)____; two (33)____; one (41)____; none (13)____		
9. What is your fiancé(e)'s attitude toward having children? desires children very much (43)____; mildly desires them (14)____; mild objection to them (40)____; objects very much to having them (31)____		
T		

Part I____, Part II____, Part III____, Part IV____, Part V____, Total____

II. Marriage-Adjustment Schedule*

To Be Filled Out by Married Persons

This schedule may be filled out by either the husband or the wife. Frank and sincere replies are of the highest importance if the findings are to be of value to the person filling it out or for research purposes. There are no right or wrong answers.

The following points are to be kept in mind in filling out the schedule:

1. Be sure to answer all questions.
2. Do not leave any blanks, as is sometimes done, to signify a "no" reply.
3. The word spouse is used to refer to your husband or wife.
4. Do not confer with your spouse in answering these questions or show your answers to your spouse.

Your Present Marital Status

1. Are your now (check): married____? divorced____? separated____? widowed____?
2. If divorced or separated, how long have you been separated? months____
(If you are divorced or separated, answers the questions as of the time of your separation.)

*Reproduced by permission of Ernest W. Burgess, Leonard S. Cottrell, Paul Wallin, and Harvey J. Locke.

Part One

	1	2

1. Present occupation of husband (be as specific as possible) _____
    _____ If unemployed, check here _____
    How satisfied are you, on the whole, with present occupation of hus-
    band? If unemployed, answer this question about his usual occupation:
    extremely satisfied (26)_____; very much satisfied (34)_____; satisfied
    (14)_____; somewhat satisfied (40)_____; somewhat dissatisfied (3)_____;
    dissatisfied (21)_____; very much dissatisfied (30)_____; extremely
    dissatisfied (12)_____

2. To what extent were you in love with your spouse before marriage?
    "head over heels" (17)_____; very much (25)_____; somewhat (32)
    _____; a little (22)_____; not at all (13)_____

3. To what extent was your spouse in love with you before your marriage?
    "head over heels" (26)_____; very much (43)_____; somewhat (23)
    _____; a little (40)_____; not at all (22)_____

4. How much conflict (arguments, etc.) was there between you before
    your marriage? none at all (35)_____; a little (43)_____; some (5)_____;
    considerable (31)_____; very much (13)_____

5. To what extent do you think you knew your spouse's faults and weak
    points before your marriage? not at all (44)_____; a little (52)_____;
    somewhat (32)_____; considerably (40)_____; very much (4)_____

6. To what extent do you think your spouse knew your faults and weak-
    nesses before your marriage? not at all (17)_____; a little (43)_____;
    somewhat (41)_____; considerably (22)_____; very much (13)_____

7. What is your attitude toward your father-in-law? like him very much
    (61)_____; considerably (15)_____; somewhat (50)_____; a little (4)_____;
    dislike him a little (30)_____; dislike him somewhat (12)_____; dislike
    him considerably (3)_____; dislike him very much (21)_____; no atti-
    tude, as he is dead (24)_____

8. What is your attitude toward your mother-in-law? like her very much
    (25)_____; like her considerably (42)_____; like her somewhat (32)_____;
    like her a little (22)_____; dislike her a little (12)_____; dislike her some-
    what (30)_____; dislike her considerably (3)_____; dislike her very much
    (21)_____; no attitude, as she is dead (51)_____

9. What is your attitude to having children? desire children very much
    (16)_____; desire children a good deal (62)_____; desire children some-
    what (33)_____; desire children a little (5)_____; desire no children
    (31)_____

10. If children have been born to you, what effect have they had on your
    happiness? added to it very much (27)_____; added to it considerably
    (61)_____; added to it somewhat (14)_____; added to it a little (40)
    _____; have had no effect (30)_____; have decreased it a little (12)_____;
    have decreased it somewhat (21)_____; have decreased it considerably
    (3)_____; have decreased it very much (30)_____; no children (24)_____

11. In leisure-time activities: we both prefer to stay at home (26)_____;
    we both prefer to be "on the go" (41)_____; one prefers to be "on the
    go" and the other to stay at home (22)_____

12. Do you and your spouse engage in outside interests together? all of
    them (44)_____; most of them (51)_____; some of them (14)_____; a
    few of them (40)_____; none of them (22)_____

13. Do you kiss your spouse? every day (62)_____; almost every day (70)
    _____; quite frequently (24)_____; occasionally (32)_____; rarely (13)
    _____; almost never (40)_____

	1	2

14. Do you confide in your spouse? about everything (17)_____; about most things (52)_____; about some things (5)_____; about a few things (13) _____; about nothing (40)_____

15. Does your spouse confide in you? about everything (26)_____; about most things (52)_____; about some things (41)_____; about a few things (4)_____; about nothing (31)_____

16. Are you satisfied with the amount of demonstration of affection in your marriage? yes (25)_____; no: (desire less (22)_____; desire more (13) _____)

17. Is your spouse satisfied with the amount of demonstration of affection? yes (16)_____; no: (desires less (40)_____; desires more (31)_____)

18. How frequently do you "humor" your spouse? frequently (4)_____; occasionally (32)_____; rarely (51)_____; never (16)_____

19. Has your spouse ever failed to tell you the truth? often (22)_____; a few times (14)_____; once (33)_____; never (25)_____

20. If until now your marriage has been at all unhappy, how confident are you that it will work out all right in the future? very confident (32) _____; confident (13)_____; somewhat uncertain (21)_____; very uncertain (30)_____; marriage has not been at all unhappy (15)_____

21. Everything considered, how happy has your marriage been for you? extraordinarily happy (45)_____; decidedly happy (16)_____; happy (50)_____; somewhat happy (13)_____; average (31)_____; somewhat unhappy (3)_____; unhappy (12)_____; decidedly unhappy (30)_____; extremely unhappy (21)_____

22. If your marriage is now at all unhappy, how long has it been so (in months)? less than 3 (23)_____; 3 to 11 (31)_____; 12 or more (12)_____; marriage has not been at all unhappy (33)_____

23. Everything considered, how happy has your marriage been for your spouse? extraordinarily happy (36)_____; decidedly happy (43)_____; happy (32)_____; somewhat happy (4)_____; average (21)_____; somewhat unhappy (30)_____; unhappy (12)_____; decidedly unhappy (3)_____; extremely unhappy (21)_____

24. Indicate your approximate agreement or disagreement with your spouse on the following things. Do this for each item by putting a check in the column that shows extent of your agreement or disagreement.

Check one column for each item below	Always agree (35)	Almost always agree (16)	Occasionally disagree (42)	Frequently disagree (23)	Almost always disagree (22)	Always disagree (12)		
Handling family finances								
Matters of recreation								
Religious matters								
Demonstration of affection								
Friends								
Table manners								

Check one column for each item below	Always agree (35)	Almost always agree (16)	Occasionally disagree (42)	Frequently disagree (23)	Almost always disagree 22)	Always disagree (12)		
Matters of conventionality								
Philosophy of life								
Ways of dealing with your families								
Wife's working								
Intimate relations								
Caring for the baby								
Sharing of household tasks								
Politics								

25. When disagreements arise between you and your spouse they usually result in: agreement by mutual give and take (44)_____; your giving in (52)_____; your spouse giving in (33)_____; neither giving in (40)_____

26. Have you ever considered either separating from or divorcing your spouse? have never consider it (26)_____; not seriously (61)_____; somewhat seriously (40)_____; seriously (22)_____

27. How many serious quarrels or arguments have you had with your spouse in the past twelve months? none (27)_____; one (42)_____; two (32) _____; three (13)_____; four or more (30)_____

28. Indicate to what extent you are in love with your spouse by placing a check in one square on the boxed line below, which ranges from extraordinarily in love to somewhat in love:

Extraordinarily in love	A B C D E F G H I J 36 17 25 43 15 33 23 41 40 13	Somewhat in love

Indicate by a cross in the above scale the extent to which you think your spouse is in love with you.

29. How does your present love for your spouse compare with your love before marriage? very much stronger (27)_____; considerably stronger (52)_____; somewhat stronger (24)_____; a little stronger (14)_____; a little weaker (30)_____; somewhat weaker (12)_____; considerably weaker (3)_____; very much weaker (21)_____

30. If you had your life to live over, what do you think you would do? marry the same person: (certainly (35)_____; possibly (41)_____;) marry a different person (22)_____; not marry at all (31)_____

31. If your spouse could do it over again, do you think your spouse would marry you? (certainly (44)_____; possibly (50)_____); marry a different person (13)_____; not marry at all (40)_____

32. How satisfied, on the whole, are you with your marriage? entirely satisfied (18)_____; very much satisfied (52)_____; satisfied (23)_____; somewhat satisfied (31)_____; somewhat dissatisfied (3)_____; dissatisfied (12)_____; very much dissatisfied (30)_____; entirely dissatisfied (21) _____

	1	2
T		

33. How satisfied, on the whole, is your spouse with your marriage? entirely satisfied (45)____; very much satisfied (34)____; satisfied (41)____; somewhat satisfied (22)____; somewhat dissatisfied (21)____; dissatisfied (30)____; very much dissatisfied (12)____; entirely dissatisfied (3)____

34. Have you ever been ashamed of your spouse? never (44)____; once (14)____; a few times (31)____; often (40)____

35. Even if satisfied with your spouse, have you ever felt that you might have been at all happier if married to another type of person? never (26)____; rarely (41)____; occasionally (22)____; frequently (13)____

36. Do you ever regret your marriage? never (17)____; rarely (50)____; occasionally (13)____; frequently (40)____

Part Two

In responding to the following items, place a check in the appropriate column to the right of each item below.

Check Column A to indicate the things that have occurred in your marriage but have not interfered with your happiness.

Check Column B to indicate those things that have made your marriage less happy than it should have been.

Check Column C to indicate those things that have done most to make your marriage unhappy.

Check Column D if the item was not present in your marriage.

For the husband or wife to fill out	A	B	C	D
	24	32	13	33
Insufficient income				
Poor management of income				
Lack of freedom due to marriage				
Spouse considerably older than I				
Spouse considerably younger than I				
Matters relating to in-laws				
My spouse and I differ in:				
Education				
Intellectual interests				
Religious beliefs				
Choice of friends				
Preferences for amusements and recreation				
Attitude toward drinking				
Tastes in food				
Respect for conventions				
My spouse:				
is argumentative				

For the husband or wife to fill out	A	B	C	D
	24	32	13	33
My spouse:				
is not affectionate				
is narrow-minded				
is not faithful to me				
complains too much				
is lazy				
is quick-tempered				
criticizes me				
spoils the children				
is untruthful				
is conceited				
is easily influenced by others				
is jealous				
is selfish and inconsiderate				
is too talkative				
smokes				
drinks				
swears				

For the husband to fill out (cont.)	A 24	B 32	C 13	D 33
For the husband to fill out				
My wife:				
is slovenly in appearance				
has had much poor health				
is interested in other men				
is nervous or emotional				
neglects the children				
My wife:				
is a poor housekeeper				
is not interested in my business				
is extravagant				
lets her feelings be hurt too easily				
is too interested in social affairs				
has annoying habits and mannerisms				
is a poor cook				
interferes with my business				
For the wife to fill out				
My husband:				
pays attention to other women				
is nervous or impatient				
takes no interest in the children				
is untidy				
is always wrapped up in his business				
gambles				
is touchy				
is not interested in the home				
has vulgar habits				
dislikes to go out with me evenings				
is late to meals				
is harsh with the children				
has poor table manners				

For the husband to fill out (cont.)	A 24	B 32	C 13	D 33
For the husband to fill out				
My wife:				
wants to visit or entertain a lot				
does not have meals ready on time				
interferes if I discipline the children				
tries to improve me				
My wife:				
is a social climber				
is too interested in clothes				
is insincere				
gossips indiscreetly				
nags me				
interferes with my hobbies				
works outside the home				
is fussy about keeping the house neat				
For the wife to fill out				
My husband:				
is tight with money				
has no backbone				
does not talk things over freely				
is rude				
is bored if I tell him of the things that happen in my everyday life				
is unsuccessful in his business				
does not show his affection for me				
gets angry easily				
drinks too much				
has friends I do not approve of				
is constantly nagging and bickering				
lacks ambition				
T				

Part I _____, Part II _____, Total _____

section L

Personality Measurements

Of the hundreds of personality inventories, only two are selected for presentation. These two measures are probably the most widely used personality measures in research today. The Minnesota Multiphasic Personality Inventory is described but not reproduced. It is a battery of scales containing 550 statements. It is thorough and so well constructed that it has generally won the confidence of researchers as the best scale to probe the personality. The research applications included in the description of the instrument attest to its use.

The California F-Scale to measure the authoritarian personality has won high acceptance and has stimulated wide research application.

Of all the personality measures, it was believed the social researcher might find these two scales to be the most useful for his purpose. For a compilation of other measures of personality the following might be consulted:

ANDERSON, HAROLD H., and ANDERSON, GLADYS L. *An Introduction to Projective Techniques and Other Devices for Understanding the Dynamics of Human Behavior.* Englewood Cliffs, N.J.: Prentice-Hall, 1951.

CATTELL, R. B. *Personality and Motivation Structure and Measurement.* New York: World Book, 1957.

GREENE, EDWARD B. *Measurements of Human Behavior.* Rev. ed. New York: Odyssey Press, 1952.

KRECH, DAVID; CRUTCHFIELD, RICHARD S.; and BALACHEY, EGERTON L. *Individual in Society.* New York: McGraw-Hill, 1962.

MEGAREE, E. I. *The California Psychological Inventory Handbook.* San Francisco: Jossey-Bass, 1972.

The Psychological Corporation has a catalog of personality and other psychological tests. This organization distributes such widely used tests as the Minnesota Multiphasic Personality Inventory, California Psychological Inventory, Edward's Personal Preference Schedule; Bernreuter Personality Inventory; Allport, Vernon, and Lindzey's Study of Values; Rorschach Technique; and Murray's Thematic Apperception Test. For a catalog of the Test Division, write The Psychological Corporation, 304 East 45 Street, New York, N.Y. 10017.

Also consult Section 4M.2 for encyclopedic sources of psychological tests.

VARIABLE MEASURED: Measures twenty-six areas of personality traits and attitudes.

DESCRIPTION: The MMPI is primarily designed to provide, in a single test, scores on all the more clinically important phases of personality. The instrument itself comprises 550 statements covering a wide range of subject matter, from the physical condition of the individual being tested to his morale and social attitude. For administration of the inventory the subject is asked to respond to all statements, which are in the first person, as True, False, or Cannot Say. The MMPI yields scores on nine scales of personality characteristics indicative of clinical syndromes.

WHERE PUBLISHED: Starke R. Hathaway, *The Minnesota Multiphasic Personality Inventory* (Minneapolis: University of Minnesota, 1942); Starke R. Hathaway and J. Charnley McKinley, *Manual for the Minnesota Multiphasic Personality Inventory* (rev. ed.; New York: Psychological Corporation, 1951); W. Grant Dahlstrom and George Schlager Welsh, *An MMPI Handbook: A Guide to Use in Clinical Practice and Research* (Minneapolis: University of Minnesota, 1960).

RELIABILITY: $r = .71$ to .83. See Starke R. Hathaway and J. Charnley McKinley, *Manual for the Minnesota Multiphasic Personality Inventory* (rev. ed.; New York: The Psychological Corporation, 1951).

See also Harrison G. Gough, "Simulated Patterns on the Minnesota Multiphasic Personality Inventory," *Journal of Abnormal and Social Psychology* 42 (April 1947): 215–25; Charles A. Weisgerber, "The Predictive Value of the Minnesota Multiphasic Personality Inventory with Student Nurses," *Journal of Social Psychology* 33 (February 1951): 3–11.

VALIDITY: Hathaway and McKinley maintain, ". . . the chief criterion of excellence has been the valid prediction of clinical cases against the neuropsychiatric staff diagnosis, rather than statistical measures of reliability and validity." Hathaway and McKinley, *Manual for the Minnesota Multiphasic Personality Inventory*.

See also:

ALTUS, W. D., and TAFEJIAN, T. T. "MMPI Correlates of the California E-F Scale." *Journal of Social Psychology* 38 (August 1953): 145–49.

BENTON, A. L., and PROBST, K. A. "A Comparison of Psychiatric Ratings with Minnesota Multiphasic Personality Inventory Scores." *Journal of Abnormal and Social Psychology* 41 (January 1946): 75–78.

ELLIS, A. "The Validity of Personality Questionnaires." *Psychological Bulletin* 43 (September 1946): 385–440.

LOUGH, ORPHA M., and GREEN, MARY E. "Comparison of the Minnesota Multiphasic Personality Inventory and the Washburne S-A Inventory as Measures of Personality of College Women." *Journal of Social Psychology* 32 (August 1950): 23–30.

MEEHL, PAUL E., and HATHAWAY, STARKE R. "The K Factor as a Suppressor Variable in the Minnesota Multiphasic Personality Inventory." *Journal of Applied Psychology* 30 (1946): 525–64.

UTILITY: The inventory is easily administered. The time required varies from 30 to 90 minutes. No supervision is needed beyond that required for the subject to understand clearly the nature of his task and to assure his optimal cooperation.

RESEARCH APPLICATIONS:

ALTUS, WILLIAM D. "A College Achiever and Non-Achiever Scale for the Minnesota Multiphasic Personality Inventory." *Journal of Applied Psychology* 32 (August 1948): 385–97.

——, and TAFEJIAN, T. T. "MMPI Correlates of the California E-F Scale." *Journal of Social Psychology* 38 (August 1953): 145–49.

BENTON, ARTHUR L., and PROBST, KATHRYN A. "A Comparison of Psychiatric Ratings with Minnesota Multiphasic Personality Inventory Scores." *Journal of Abnormal and Social Psychology* 41 (January 1946): 75–78.

BROWER, DANIEL. "The Relation Between Intelligence and Minnesota Multiphasic Personality Inventory Scores." *Journal of Social Psychology* 25 (May 1947): 243–45.

——. "The Relations Between Minnesota Multiphasic Personality Inventory Scores and Cardio-Vascular Measures Before and After Experimentally Induced Visuo-Motor Conflict." *Journal of Social Psychology* 26 (August 1947): 55–60.

BURTON, ARTHUR. "The Use of the Masculinity-Femininity Scale of the Minnesota Multiphasic Personality Inventory as an Aid in the Diagnosis of Sexual Inversion." *Journal of Psychology* 24 (July 1947): 161–64.

CARP, ABRAHAM. "MMPI Performance and Insulin Shock Therapy." *Journal of Abnormal and Social Psychology* 45 (October 1950): 721–26.

CARPENTER, LEWIS G., JR. "An Experimental Test of an Hypothesis for Predicting Outcome with Electroshock Therapy." *Journal of Psychology* 36 (July 1953): 131–35.

CLARK, JERRY H. "Application of the *MMPI* in Differentiating A.W.O.L. Recidivists from Non-Recidivists." *Journal of Psychology* 26 (July 1948): 229–34.

CLARK, J. H. "Grade Achievement of Female College Students in Relation to Non-Intellective Factors: MMPI Items." *Journal of Social Psychology* 37 (May 1953): 275–81.

COFER, C. N.; CHANCE, JUNE; and JUDSON, A. J. "A Study of Malingering on the Minnesota Multiphasic Personality Inventory." *Journal of Psychology* 27 (April 1949): 491–99.

COOK, ELLSWORTH B., and WHERRY, ROBERT J. "A Factor Analysis of MMPI and Aptitude Test Data." *Journal of Applied Psychology* 34 (August 1950): 260–66.

COTTLE, WILLIAM C. "Card Versus Booklet Forms of the MMPI." *Journal of Applied Psychology* 34 (August 1950): 255–59.

DANIELS, E. E., and HUNTER, W. A. "MMPI Personality Patterns for Various Occupations." *Journal of Applied Psychology* 33 (December 1949): 559–65.

DRAKE, LEWIS E. "A Social *I.E.* Scale for the Minnesota Multiphasic Personality Inventory." *Journal of Applied Psychology* 30 (1946): 51–54.

——. "Differential Sex Responses to Items of the MMPI." *Journal of Applied Psychology* 37 (February 1953): 46.

ENGELHARDT, OLGA E. DE C., and ORBISON, WILLIAM D. "Comparison of the Terman-Miles M-F Test and the Mf Scale of the MMPI." *Journal of Applied Psychology* 34 (October 1950): 338–42.

FRY, FRANKLIN D. "A Normative Study of the Reactions Manifested by College Students and by State Prison Inmates in Response to the Minnesota Multiphasic Personality Inventory, the Rozenweig Picture-Frustration Study, and the Thematic Apperception Test." *Journal of Psychology* 34 (July 1952): 27–30.

———. "A Study of the Personality Traits of College Students and of State Prison Inmates as Measured by the Minnesota Multiphasic Personality Inventory." *Journal of Psychology* 28 (October 1949): 439–49.

GOUGH, HARRISON. "A New Dimension of Status: I. The Development of a Personality Scale." *American Sociological Review* 13 (August 1948): 401–9.

———. "A New Dimension of Status: II. Relationship of the *St* Scale to Other Variables." *American Sociological Review* 13 (October 1948): 534–37.

———. "A New Dimension of Status: III. Discrepancies Between the *St* Scale and 'Objective' Status." *American Sociological Review* 14 (April 1949): 275–81.

———. "Simulated Patterns on the Minnesota Multiphasic Personality Inventory." *Journal of Abnormal and Social Psychology* 42 (April 1947): 215–25.

GREENBERG, PAUL, and GILLILAND, A. R. "The Relationship Between Basal Metabolism and Personality." *Journal of Social Psychology* 35 (February 1952): 3–7.

GUTHRIE, GEORGE M. "Six MMPI Diagnostic Profile Patterns." *Journal of Psychology* 30 (October 1950): 317–23.

HAMPTON, PETER J. "The Minnesota Multiphasic Personality Inventory as a Psychometric Tool for Diagnosing Personality Disorders among College Students." *Journal of Social Psychology* 26 (August 1947): 99–108.

HARMON, LINDSEY R., and WIENER, DANIEL N. "Use of the Minnesota Multiphasic Personality Inventory in Vocational Advisement." *Journal of Applied Psychology* 29 (April 1945): 132–41.

HATHAWAY, STARKE R., and MONACHESI, ELIO D. *Analyzing and Predicting Juvenile Delinquency with the MMPI.* Minneapolis: University of Minnesota Press, 1953.

———. "The Minnesota Multiphasic Personality Inventory in the Study of Juvenile Delinquents." *American Sociological Review* 17 (December 1952): 704–10.

LOUGH, ORPHA M. "Teachers College Students and the Minnesota Multiphasic Personality Inventory." *Journal of Applied Psychology* 30 (June 1946): 241–47.

———. "Women Students in Liberal Arts, Nursing, and Teacher Training Curricula and the Minnesota Multiphasic Personality Inventory." *Journal of Applied Psychology* 31 (August 1947): 437–45.

———, and GREEN, MARY E. "Comparison of the Minnesota Multiphasic Personality Inventory and the Washburne S-A Inventory as Measures of Personality of College Women." *Journal of Social Psychology* 32 (August 1950): 23–30.

MAC LEAN, A. G., et al. "F Minus K Index on the MMPI." *Journal of Applied Psychology* 37 (August 1953): 315–16.

MASLOW, A. H., et al. "A Clinically Derived Test for Measuring Psychological Security-Insecurity." *Journal of General Psychology* 33 (1945): 21–41.

MEEHL, PAUL E., and HATHAWAY, STARKE R. "The *K* Factor as a Suppressor Variable in the Minnesota Multiphasic Personality Inventory." *Journal of Applied Psychology* 30 (1946): 525–64.

MICHAELIS, JOHN U., and TYLER, FRED T. "MMPI and Student Teaching." *Journal of Applied Psychology* 35 (April 1951): 122–24.

MONACHESI, ELIO D. "Some Personality Characteristics of Delinquents and Non-Delinquents." *Journal of Criminal Law and Criminology* 37 (January–February 1948): 487–500.

NORMAN, RALPH D., and REDLO, MIRIAM. "MMPI Personality Patterns for Various College Major Groups." *Journal of Applied Psychology* 36 (December 1952): 404–9.

SCHMIDT, HERMANN O. "Test Profiles as a Diagnostic Aid: The Minnesota Multiphasic Inventory." *Journal of Applied Psychology* 29 (April 1945): 115–31.

SCHOFIELD, WILLIAM. "A Further Study of the Effects of Therapies on MMPI Responses." *Journal of Abnormal and Social Psychology* 48 (January 1953): 67–77.

——. "A Study of Medical Students with the MMPI: I. Scale Norms and Profile Patterns." *Journal of Psychology* 36 (July 1953): 59–65.

——. "A Study of Medical Students with the MMPI: II. Group and Individual Changes after Two Years." *Journal of Psychology* 36 (July 1953): 137–41.

——. "A Study of Medical Students with the MMPI: III. Personality and Academic Success." *Journal of Applied Psychology* 37 (February 1953): 47–52.

SOPCHACK, ANDREW L. "Parental 'Identification' and 'Tendency Toward Disorders' as Measured by the Minnesota Multiphasic Personality Inventory." *Journal of Abnormal and Social Psychology* 47 (April 1952): 159–65.

TYDLASKA, M., and MENGEL, R. "Scale for Measuring Work Attitude for the MMPI." *Journal of Applied Psychology* 37 (December 1953): 474–77.

TYLER, FRED T., and MICHAELIS, JOHN U. "Comparison of Manual and College Norms for the MMPI." *Journal of Applied Psychology* 37 (August 1953): 273–75.

VERNIAUD, WILLIE MAUDE. "Occupational Differences in the Minnesota Multiphasic Personality Inventory." *Journal of Applied Psychology* 30 (December 1946): 604–13.

WEISGERBER, CHARLES A. "The Predictive Value of the Minnesota Multiphasic Personality Inventory with Student Nurses." *Journal of Social Psychology* 33 (February 1951): 3–11.

WINFIELD, DON L. "The Relationship Between IQ Scores and Minnesota Multiphasic Personality Inventory Scores." *Journal of Social Psychology* 38 (November 1953): 299–300.

For a few more recent applications, see section 4M.1.

Contents of Minnesota Multiphasic Personality Invenstory (MMPI)*

1. General health (9 items)
2. General neurologic (19 items)
3. Cranial nerves (11 items)
4. Motility and coordination (6 items)
5. Sensibility (5 items)
6. Vasomotor, trophic, speech, secretory (10 items)
7. Cardio-respiratory system (5 items)
8. Gastro-intestinal system (11 items)
9. Genito-urinary system (5 items)
10. Habits (19 items)
11. Family and marital (26 items)
12. Occupational (18 items)
13. Educational (12 items)
14. Sexual attitudes (16 items)
15. Religious attitudes (19 items)
16. Political attitudes—law and order (46 items)

*By permission of Hathaway and McKinley and the University of Minnesota Press.

17. Social attitudes (72 items)
18. Affect, depressive (32 items)
19. Affect, manic (24 items)
20. Obsessive and compulsive states (15 items)
21. Delusions, hallucinations, illusions, ideas of reference (31 items)
22. Phobias (29 items)
23. Sadistic, masochistic trends (7 items)
24. Morale (33 items)
25. Item primarily related to masculinity-femininity (55 items)
26. Items to indicate whether the individual is trying to place himself in an acceptable light (15 items)

4.L.2 AUTHORITARIAN PERSONALITY (*F*) SCALE, FORMS 45 AND 40

VARIABLE MEASURED: "Authoritarianism" or antidemocratic potential.

DESCRIPTION: The scale consists of thirty items grouped into nine attitudinal categories considered as variables in a personality syndrome. The items are rated on a seven-point scale, from +3 to -3, according to the subjects' agreement or disagreement with the statement.

WHERE PUBLISHED: T. W. Adorno, Else Frenkel-Brunswik, D. J. Levinson, and R. N. Sanford, *The Authoritarian Personality* (New York: Harper, 1950).

RELIABILITY: Authors' report on studies—mean $r = .90$, range .81 to .97.
Correlation with Ethnocentrism Scale—mean $r = .75$ with a range from $r = .59$ to $r = .87$.
Using Fisher's Z_r, each item was correlated with every other item—mean $r = .13$ and the range was from $r = -.05$ to $r = .44$.
In addition, each item was correlated with the remainder of the scale, the mean r being .33, the range .15 to .52.
See also:
CHRISTIE, RICHARD; HAVEL, JOAN; SEIDENBERG, BERNARD. "Is the *F* Scale Irreversible?" *Journal of Abnormal and Social Psychology* 56 (1958): 143–59.
———, and JAHODA, MARIE, eds. *Studies in the Scope and Method of "The Authoritarian Personality."* Glencoe, Ill.: Free Press, 1954.

VALIDITY: The authors used the case study method to validate the scale. The scale has been correlated with the Campbell Xenophobia: $r = .60$.
See also:
BASS, BERNARD M. "Authoritarianism or Acquiescence?" *Journal of Abnormal and Social Psychology* 51 (November 1955): 616–23.
CAMILLERI, SANTO F. "A Factor Analysis of the *F*-Scale." *Social Forces* 37 (May 1959): 316–23.
CHRISTIE, RICHARD, and JAHODA, MARIE, eds. *Studies in the Scope and Method of "The Authoritarian Personality."* Glencoe, Ill.: Free Press, 1954.
HIMMELHOCH, JEROME. "Tolerance and Personality Needs: A Study of the Liberalization of Ethnic Attitudes among Minority Group College Students." *American Sociological Review* 15 (February 1950): 79–88.

KIRSCHT, J. P., and DILLEHAY, R. C. *Dimensions of Authoritarianism: A Review of Research and Theory.* Lexington: University of Kentucky Press, 1967.

PROTHRO, E. TERRY, and MELIKIAN, LEVON. "The California Public Opinion Scale in an Authoritarian Culture." *Public Opinion Quarterly* 17 (1953): 115–35.

UTILITY: The test may be administered either in interviews or by questionnaire.

RESEARCH APPLICATIONS:

ADELSON, JOSEPH. "A Study of Minority Group Authoritarianism." *Journal of Abnormal and Social Psychology* 48 (October 1953): 477–85.

BASS, BERNARD M. "Authoritarianism or Acquiescence?" *Journal of Abnormal and Social Psychology* 51 (November 1955): 616–23.

BROWN, ROGER W. "A Determinant of the Relationship Between Rigidity and Authoritarianism." *Journal of Abnormal and Social Psychology* 48 (October 1953): 469–76.

CAMILLERI, SANTO F. "A Factor Analysis of the *F*-Scale." *Social Forces* 37 (May 1959): 316–23.

CAMPBELL, DONALD T., and McCORMACK, THELMA H. "Military Experience and Attitudes Toward Authority." *American Journal of Sociology* 62 (March 1957): 482–90.

CHRISTIE, RICHARD. "Changes in Authoritarianism as Related to Situational Factors." *American Psychologist* 8 (1952): 307–8.

——, and COOK, PEGGY. "Guide to Published Literature Relating to the Authoritarian Personality." *Journal of Psychology* 45 (1958): 171–99 (bibliography).

——, and GARCIA, JOHN. "Subcultural Variation in Authoritarian Personality." *Journal of Abnormal and Social Psychology* 46 (October 1951): 457–69.

——; HAVEL, JOAN; and SEIDENBERG, BERNARD. "Is the *F*-Scale Irreversible?" *Journal of Abnormal and Social Psychology* 56 (1958): 143–59.

——, and JAHODA, MARIE, eds. *Studies in the Scope and Method of "The Authoritarian Personality."* Glencoe, Ill.: Free Press, 1954.

DAVIDS, ANTHONY. "Some Personality and Intellectual Correlates of Intolerance of Ambiguity." *Journal of Abnormal and Social Psychology* 51 (November 1955): 415–20.

GELBMANN, FREDERICK JOHN. *Authoritarianism and Temperament.* Washington, D.C.: Catholic University of America Press, 1958.

GOUGH, HARRISON G. "Studies of Social Intolerance: I. Some Psychological and Sociological Correlates of Anti-Semitism." *Journal of Social Psychology* 33 (May 1951): 237–46.

——. "Studies of Social Intolerance: II. A Personality Scale for Anti-Semitism." *Journal of Social Psychology* 33 (May 1951): 247–55.

——. "Studies of Social Intolerance: III. Relationship of the *Pr* Scale to Other Variables." *Journal of Social Psychology* 33 (May 1951): 257–62.

GREENBERG, HERBERT, and HUTTO, DOLORES. "The Attitudes of West Texas College Students Toward School Integration." *Journal of Applied Psychology* 42 (October 1958): 301–4.

HAYTHORN, WILLIAM; COUCH, ARTHUR; FAEFNER, DONALD; LANGHAM, PETER; and CARTER, LAUNOR F. "The Behavior of Authoritarian and Equalitarian Personalities in Groups." *Human Relations* 9 (February 1956): 57–73.

HIMMELHOCH, JEROME. "Tolerance and Personality Needs: A Study of the Liberalization of Ethnic Attitudes among Minority Group College Students." *American Sociological Review* 15 (February 1950): 79–88.

JONES, EDWARD E. "Authoritarianism as a Determinant of First-Impression Formation." *Journal of Personality* 23 (September 1954): 107–27.

KATES, SOLIS L. "First-Impression Formation and Authoritarianism." *Human Relations* 12 (August 1959): 277–85.

———, and DIAB, LUFTY N. "Authoritarian Ideology and Attitudes on Parent-Child Relationships." *Journal of Abnormal and Social Psychology* 51 (July 1955): 13–16.

KAUFMAN, WALTER C. "Status, Authoritarianism, and Anti-Semitism." *American Journal of Sociology* 62 (January 1957): 379–82.

MACKINNON, WILLIAM J., and CENTERS, RICHARD. "Authoritarianism and Urban Stratification." *American Journal of Sociology* 61 (May 1956): 610–20.

MARTIN, JAMES G., and WESTIE, FRANK R. "The Tolerant Personality." *American Sociological Review* 24 (August 1959): 521–28.

MEER, SAMUEL J. "Authoritarianism Attitudes and Dreams." *Journal of Abnormal and Social Psychology* 51 (July 1955): 74–78.

MISHLER, ELLIOT G. "Personality Characteristics and the Resolution of Role Conflicts." *Public Opinion Quarterly* 17, no. 1 (1953): 115–35.

O'NEIL, WILLIAM M., and LEVINSON, DANIEL J. "A Factorial Exploration of Authoritarianism and Some of Its Ideological Concomitants." *Journal of Personality* 22 (June 1954): 449–63.

PROTHRO, E. TERRY, and MELIKIAN, LEVON. "The California Public Opinion Scale in an Authoritarian Culture." *Public Opinion Quarterly* 17, no. 3 (1953): 353–62.

ROBERTS, ALAN H., and ROKEACH, MILTON. "Anomie, Authoritarianism, and Prejudice: A Replication." *American Journal of Sociology* 61 (January 1956): 355–58.

SANFORD, NEVITT. "Recent Developments in Connection with the Investigation of the Authoritarian Personality." *Sociological Review* 2 (July 1954): 11–33.

SCODEL, ALVIN, and MUSSEN, PAUL. "Social Perceptions of Authoritarians and Nonauthoritarians." *Journal of Abnormal and Social Psychology* 48 (April 1953): 181–84.

SMITH, CHARLES U., and PROTHRO, JAMES W. "Ethnic Differences in Authoritarian Personality." *Social Forces* 35 (May 1957): 334–38.

SROLE, LEO. "Social Integration and Certain Corollaries: An Exploratory Study." *American Sociological Review* 21 (December 1956): 709–16.

THIBAUT, JOHN W., and RIECKEN, HENRY W. "Authoritarianism, Status, and the Communication of Aggression." *Human Relations* 8 (May 1955): 95–120.

For a few more recent applications, see section 4M.1.

F-SCALE CLUSTERS: FORMS 45 AND 40*

A. Conventionalism: Rigid adherence to conventional, middle-class values.

    1. Obedience and respect for authority are the most important virtues children should learn.

    12. A person who has bad manners, habits, and breeding can hardly expect to get along with decent people.

    37. If people would talk less and work more, everybody would be better off.

*From T. W. Adorno et al., "F-Scale Clusters: Forms 45 and 40," *The Authoritarian Personality* (New York: Harper, 1950).

41. The businessman and the manufacturer are much more important to society than the artist and the professor.

B. Authoritarian Submission: Submissive, uncritical attitude toward idealized moral authorities of the ingroup.
  1. Obedience and respect for authority are the most important virtues children should learn.
  4. Science has its place, but there are many important things that can never possibly be understood by the human mind.
  8. Every person should have complete faith in some supernatural power whose decisions he obeys without question.
  21. Young people sometimes get rebellious ideas, but as they grow up they ought to get over them and settle down.
  23. What this country needs most, more than laws and political programs, is a few courageous, tireless, devoted leaders in whom the people can put their faith.
  42. No sane, normal, decent person could ever think of hurting a close friend or relative.
  44. Nobody ever learned anything really important except through suffering.

C. Authoritarian Aggression: Tendency to be on the lookout for, and to condemn, reject, and punish, people who violate conventional values.
  12. A person who has bad manners, habits, and breeding can hardly expect to get along with decent people.
  13. What youth needs most is strict discipline, rugged determination, and the will to work and fight for family and country.
  19. An insult to our honor should always be punished.
  25. Sex crimes, such as rape and attacks on children, deserve more than mere imprisonment; such criminals ought to be publicly whipped, or worse.
  27. There is hardly anything lower than a person who does not feel a great love, gratitude, and respect for his parents.
  34. Most of our social problems would be solved if we could somehow get rid of the immoral, crooked, and feebleminded people.
  37. If people would talk less and work more, everybody would be better off.
  39. Homosexuals are hardly better than criminals and ought to be severely punished.

D. Anti-intraception: Opposition to the subjective, the imaginative, and tender-minded.
  9. When a person has a problem or worry, it is best for him not to think about it, but to keep busy with more cheerful things.
  31. Nowadays more and more people are prying into matters that should remain personal and private.
  37. If people would talk less and work more, everybody would be better off.
  41. The businessman and the manufacturer are much more important to society than the artist and the professor.

E. Superstition and Stereotypy: The belief in mystical determinants of the individual's fate; the disposition to think in rigid categories.
  4. Science has its place, but there are many important things that can never possibly be understood by the human mind.

   8. Every person should have complete faith in some supernatural power whose decisions he obeys without question.

  16. Some people are born with an urge to jump from high places.

  26. People can be divided into two distinct classes: the weak and the strong.

  29. Some day it will probably be shown that astrology can explain a lot of things.

  33. Wars and social troubles may someday be ended by an earthquake or flood that will destroy the whole world.

F. Power and "Toughness": Preoccupation with the dominance-submission, strong-weak, leader-follower dimension; identification with power figures; overemphasis upon the conventionalized attributes of the ego; exaggerated assertion of strength and toughness.

  2. No weakness or difficulty can hold us back if we have enough willpower.

  13. What youth needs most is strict discipline, rugged determination, and the will to work and fight for family and country.

  19. An insult to our honor should always be punished.

  22. It is best to use some prewar authorities in Germany to keep order and prevent chaos.

  23. What this country needs most, more than laws and political programs, is a few courageous, tireless, devoted leaders in whom the people can put their faith.

  26. People can be divided into two distinct classes: the weak and the strong.

  38. Most people don't realize how much our lives are controlled by the plots hatched in secret places.

G. Destructiveness and Cynicism: Generalized hostility, vilification of the human.

  6. Human nature being what it is, there will always be war and conflict.

  43. Familiarity breeds contempt.

H. Projectivity: The deposition to believe that wild and dangerous things go on in the world; the projection outwards of unconscious emotional impulses.

  18. Nowadays when so many different kinds of people move around and mix together so much, a person has to protect himself especially carefully against catching an infection or disease from them.

  31. Nowadays more and more people are prying into matters that should remain personal and private.

  33. Wars and social troubles may someday be ended by an earthquake or flood that will destroy the whole world.

  35. The wild sex life of the old Greeks and Romans was tame compared to some of the goings-on in this country, even in places where people might least expect it.

  38. Most people don't realize how much our lives are controlled by plots hatched in secret places.

I. Sex: Exaggerated concern with sexual "goings-on."

  25. Sex crimes, such as rape and attacks on children, deserve more than mere imprisonment; such criminals ought to be publicly whipped, or worse.

  35. The wild sex life of the old Greeks and Romans was tame compared to some of the goings-on in this country, even in places where people might least expect it.

  39. Homosexuals are hardly better than criminals and ought to be severely punished.

Inventories of Sociometric and Attitude Scales

AN INVENTORY OF MEASURES UTILIZED IN THE
AMERICAN SOCIOLOGICAL REVIEW, 1965-1974

4.M

Instructions for Use of 4.M

A researcher who has not found scales in the Handbook to fit his particular problem should carry out the following search:

First, review the inventory of the *American Sociological Review* 1965-68, 1969-74, to check on scales and related research. This journal is widely believed to set the highest standards for sociological research. The inventory has been deliberately broken into two parts so that the researcher can examine any trend patterns of scale use. He should evaluate carefully because instrument development and standardization are relatively rare; simple indices are being constructed de novo for the problem, while scales with far more validity and stability languish unused. The disappointing fact is that few researchers are willing to search for and to examine measuring instruments that are essential for scientific cumulation of knowledge. It is apparent that editors everywhere are failing to establish these requirements for acceptance of research. This does not relieve the researcher of the responsibility to use standardized instruments with demonstrated reliability and validity if he wishes his work to establish a place in cumulative knowledge. He now has a wealth of information on scales if he will only *search*. The researcher who does not find a scale suitable in the ASR Inventory should continue to examine the various compilations which follow. They report on a great number of scales and, in most instances, offer evaluations to aid in selection.

INVENTORY FOR 1965–68

Scales for Measuring Social Status

Duncan's Index of Socioeconomic Status	Bruce K. Eckland, "Academic Ability, Higher Education and Occupational Mobility," 30 (October 1965): 735–46.
	Ira. L. Reiss, "Social Class and Premarital Sexual Permissiveness: A Reconsideration," 30 (October 1965): 747–56.
	Edward O. Laumann and Louis Guttman, "The Relative Associational Contiguity of Occupations in an Urban Setting," 31 (April 1966): 169–78.
	Peter M. Blau, "The Flow of Occupational Supply and Recruitment," 30 (August 1965): 475–90.
	Carolyn Cummings Perrucci, "Social Origins, Mobility Patterns and Fertility," 32 (August 1967): 615–25.
	Margaret A. Parman and Jack Sawyer, "Dimensions of Ethnic Intermarriage in Hawaii," 32 (August 1967): 593–607.
Occupational Prestige Scores; 1964 Study by National Opinion Research Center	Robert Hodge and Donald J. Treiman, "Social Participation and Social Status," 33 (October 1968): 722–40.
Ellis and Lane Index of Class Position for College Populations	Robert Ellis and W. Clayton Lane, "Social Mobility and Social Isolation: A Test of Sorokin's Dissociate Hypotheses," 32 (April 1967): 237–53.
Hollingshead Two-Factor Index of Social Position	R. Jay Turner and Morton O. Wagenfeld, "Occupational Mobility and Schizophrenia: An Assessment of the Social Causation and Social Selection Hypothesis," 32 (February 1967): 104–12.
Author Constructed Index, Which Includes Measure of Father's Educational Level, Mother's Educational Level, an Estimate of the Funds the	William H. Sewell and Michel Armer, "Neighborhood Context and College Plans," 31 (April 1966): 159–68.

Family Could Provide if the Student Were to Attend College, the Degree of Sacrifice This Would Entail for the Family, and the Approximate Wealth and Income Status of Student's Family

Census "Index of Socioeconomic Status"

Charles B. Nam and Mary G. Powers, "Variations in Socioeconomic Structure By Race, Residence, and the Life Cycle," 30 (February 1965): 81-96.

Scales for Measuring Group Structures and Dynamics

Intergroup Hostility Scale for Measuring Hostility Toward Negroes, Americans, Estonians, Jews, and Gypsies. Based on Bogardus-Type Social Distance Scale

Melvin Seeman, "On the Personal Consequences of Alienation in Work," 32 (April 1967): 273-85.

Social Distance Scale for Measuring the Willingness to Accept Ex-Mental-Hospital-Patient; Author Constructed

Bruce P. Dohrenwend and Edwin Chin-Song, "Social Status and Attitudes Toward Psychological Disorder: The Problem of Tolerance of Deviance," (June 1967): 417-33.

Degree of Bureaucratization Scale Measuring Six Dimensions: Hierarchy of Authority, Division of Labor, Rules, Procedures, Impersonality, Technical Competence; Author Constructed Scale, Likert-Type

Richard Hall, "Professionalization and Bureaucratization," 33 (February 1968): 92-104.

Social Distance Scale for Measuring Reactions to Physical Handicaps; Author Constructed

Victor Matthews and Charles Westie, "A Preferred Method for Obtaining Rankings Reactions to Physical Handicaps," 31 (December 1966): 851-54.

Scales for Measuring Community Factors

Rancorous Conflict Index

William Gamson, "Rancorous Conflict in Community Politics," 31 (February 1966): 71-81.

Index of Occupational Community Involvement of Professional Workers; Author Constructed Index

Harold Wilensky and Jack Ladinsky, "From Religious Community to Occupational Group: Structural Assimilation Among Professors, Lawyers, and Engineers," 32 (August 1967): 541.

Scales for Measuring Social Participation and Alienation

Kuznets Index of Inequality for Measuring the Distribution of Material Rewards Within Nations

Phillips Cutright, "Inequality: A Cross-National Analysis," 32 (August 1967): 562.

Index of Religious Community Involvement of Professional Worker; Author Constructed Index	Harold Wilensky and Jack Ladinsky, "From Religious Community to Occupational Group: Structural Assimilation Among Professors, Lawyers, and Engineers," 32 (August 1967): 451.
Glock's Index of Religiosity Which Measures Several Dimensions of Religious Involvement	Gary T. Marx, "Religion: Opiate or Inspiration of Civil Rights Militancy Among Negores," 37 (February 1967): 64-72.
Powerlessness Scale, Based on Arthur G. Neal and Salomon Rettig Scale	Theordore Groat and Arthur G. Neal, "Social Psychological Correlates of Urban Fertility," 32 (December 1967): 945-59.
Social Isolation Scale; Modified Version of Dwight Dean Scale	Theodore Groat and Arthur G. Neal, "Social Psychological Correlates of Urban Fertility," 32 (December 1967): 945-59.
Anomie Scale to Measure Feelings of Normlessness, Author Constructed	Herbert McClosky and John H. Scharr, "Psychological Dimensions of Anomy," 30 (February 1965): 14-40. See application of Robert C. Atchley and M. Patrick McCabe, "Socialization in Correctional Communities: A Replication," 35 (October 1968): 784.
Work Alienation Scale (Guttman-Type) of Five Items; Three Were Developed by the Author and Two by N. Morse	George Miller, "Professionals in Bureaucracy: Alienation Among Industrial Scientists and Engineers," 32 (October 1967): 755-68.
Author Constructed Index of Alienation from Work and from Expressive Relations; Based on a Selection from Thirteen Items of the Neal Gross, M. Mason, and H. McEachern Scales	Michael Aiken and Jerald Hage, "Organizational Alienation: A Comparative Analysis," 31 (August 1966): 497-507.
L. Pearlin's Alienation from Work Scale, Guttman-Type	Louis A. Zurcher, Jr., Arnold Meadow, and Susan Lee Zurcher, "Value Orientation, Role Conflict and Alienation From Work: A Cross-Cultural Study," 30 (August 1965): 539-48.
Marcus R-Scale for Measurement of Union Homogeneity (Guttman-Type)	Philip M. Marcus, "Union Conventions and Executive Boards: A Formal Analysis of Organizational Structure," 31 (February 1966): 61-70.
Author Constructed Index of Hierarchy of Authority and of Participation in Decision Making as Measure of Organizational Centralization	Michael Aiken and Jerald Hage, "Organizational Alienation: A Comparative Analysis," 31 (August 1966): 497-507.

Strole's Anomia Scale; Swedish Translated

Melvin Seeman, "On the Personal Consequences of Alienation in Work," 32 (April 1967): 273-85.

Neal and Seeman Powerlessness Scale

Melvin Seeman, "On the Personal Consequences of Alienation in Work," 32 (April 1967): 273-85.

Meaninglessness Scale, Author Constructed

Theodore Groat and Arthur G. Neal, "Social Psychological Correlates of Urban Fertility," 32 (December 1967): 945-59.

Normlessness Scale, Author Constructed

Theodore Groat and Arthur G. Neal, "Social Psychological Correlates of Urban Fertility," 32 (December 1967): 945-59.

Index of Work Alienation, Based on Blauner's Index

Melvin Seeman, "On The Personal Consequences of Alienation in Work," 32 (April 1967): 273-85.

Scales to Measure Leadership

Scale of Supervisory Responsibility, Author Constructed

Carolyn Cummings Perrucci, "Social Origins, Mobility Patterns and Fertility," 32 (August 1967): 615-25.

Measure of Political Involvement and Political Cleavages

Robert R. Alford and Harry M. Scoble, "Community Leadership, Education, and Political Behavior," 33 (April 1968): 259-71.

Technical Responsibility Scale, Author Constructed

Carolyn Cummings Perrucci, "Social Origins, Mobility Patterns and Fertility," 32 (August 1967): 615-25.

Scales to Measure Attitudes and Values

Racial Attitude Scale, Author Constructed

James M. Fendrich, "Perceived Reference Group Support: Racial Attitudes and Overt Behavior," 32 (December 1967): 960-70.

Degree of Professionalization Scale Measuring Four Additional Dimensions: Belief in Self-Regulation, Belief in Service to Public, Sense of Calling to Field and Reference; Author Constructed Scale; Likert-Type

Richard Hall, "Professionalization and Bureaucratization," 33 (February 1968): 92-104.

Mobility Orientation Scale for Measuring the Degree to Which the Respondent Placed the Value of Occupational Mobility Above Other Values in His Hierarchy of Goals

Melvin Seeman, "On the Personal Consequences of Alienation in Work," 32 (April 1967): 273-85.

University Student Political Attitudes and Behavior, Student Voice Factor Score

David Nasatir, "A Note on Contextual Effects and the Political Orientations of University Students," 33 (April 1968): 210-19.

Peer Value Teen-Age Index, Author Constructed

Paul Lerman, "Individual Values, Peer Values, and Sub-Cultural Delinquency," 33 (April 1968): 219-35.

Four Teen-Age Non-Conformity Scales: Ratfink, Ace-in-the-Hole, Sociability, and Deviance

LaMar T. Empey and Steven G. Lubeck, "Conformity and Deviance in the 'Situation of Company,'" 33 (October 1968): 760-74.

Measure of Political Attitude Toward the Cuban Revolution

Maurice Zeitlin, "Economic Insecurity and the Political Attitudes of Cuban Workers," 31 (February 1966): 35-51.

Rosenberg Attitudes Toward Work Scale for Measuring the Degree of Orientation Toward "Professional" or "Acquisitive" Values

John F. Marsh, Jr., and Frank P. Stafford, "The Effects of Values on Pecuniary Behavior: The Case of Academicians," 32 (October 1967): 740-54.

Orientation Toward Feminine Role Behavior, Author Constructed Scale, Guttman-Type

Kenneth C. Kammeyer, "Birth Order and the Feminine Sex Role Among College Women," 31 (August 1966): 508-15.

Measure of Political Liberalism: This Scale Includes Four Dimensions: Civil Rights, Civil Liberties, Internationalism, and Welfare, Each of Which Was Measured by a Guttman Scale Constructed by the Authors

K. Dennis Kelly and William J. Chambliss, "Status Consistency and Political Attitudes," 31 (June 1966): 375-82.

Pro-Integration Sentiments Scale Based on Favorable (Pro-Negro) Responses to Items Referring Largely to Interracial Contact, Author Constructed, Guttman-Type

Robert W. Hodge and Donald J. Treiman, "Occupational Mobility and Attitudes Toward Negroes," 31 (February 1966): 93-102.

Conformity Scale to Measure Attitudes Toward Conforming Behavior; the Scale Items Are from Four Sources: F. Baron, R. S. Crutchfield, M. L. Hoffman and T. F. Pettigrew

Howard E. Freeman, J. Michael Ross, David J. Armor and Thomas F. Pettigrew, "Color Gradation and Attitudes Among Middle Income Negroes," 31 (June 1966): 365-74.

Right-Wing Extremism Scale, Likert-Type, Author Constructed

Gary B. Rush, "Status Consistency and Right-Wing Extremism," 32 (February 1967): 86-92.

Anti-White Scale to Measure Resentment Against Caucasians; A Combination of Items From R. Johnson and G. A. Stedeler Scales

Howard Freeman, J. Michael Ross, David Armor and Thomas F. Pettigrew, "Color Gradation and Attitudes Among Middle Income Negroes," 31 (June 1966): 365-74.

Career Orientation Anchorage Scale, Author Constructed

Curt Tausky and Robert Dubin, "Career Anchorage: Managerial Mobility Motivations," 30 (October 1965): 725-35.

Male and Female Premarital Sexual Permissiveness Scales, Author Constructed

Ira. L. Reiss, "Social Class and Premarital Sexual Permissiveness: A Re-Examination," 30 (October 1965): 747-56.

Mysticism Scale for Measuring Belief in Such Things as Spiritualism, Necromancy, and Astrology, Author Constructed

Herbert McClosky and John H. Scharr, "Psychological Dimensions of Anomy," 30 (February 1965): 14-40.

Scales Measuring Family and Marriage Factors

Index of Extended Familism Which Measures Four Dimensions: Intensity, Extensity, Interaction, and Verba Cross-Cultural Study

Robert F. Winch, Scott Greer, and Rae L. Blumberg, "Ethnicity Familism in an Upper-Middle-Class Suburb," 32 (April 1967): 265-72.

Index of Parent-Youth Relations, Author Constructed Index Based on Items of Almond and Verba Cross-Cultural Study

Glen H. Elder, Jr., "Family Structure and Educational Attainment: A Cross-National Analysis," 30 (February 1965): 81-96.

Developmental Scale of Wife Independence, Author Constructed

Robert K. Leik and Merlyn Matthews, "A Scale for Developmental Processes," 33 (February 1968): 62-75.

Student Perception of Parental Encouragement Toward Attending College, Author Constructed Scale

William H. Sewell and Vimal P. Shah, "Parents, Education, and Children's Educational Aspirations and Achievements," 33 (April 1968): 191-209.

Index of Intermarriage Distance, Author Constructed

Margaret A. Parkman and Jack Sawyer, "Dimensions of Ethnic Intermarriage in Hawaii," 32 (August 1967): 593-607.

Measures of Personality Factors

Minnesota Multiphasic Personality Inventory

Bernard E. Segal, Robert J. Weiss, and Robert Sokol, "Emotional Adjustment, Social Organization and Psychiatric Treatment Rates," 30 (August 1965): 548-56.

Minnesota Multiphasic Personality Inventory Reports

Omer R. Galle and Karl E. Taeuber, "Metropolitan Migration and Intervening Opportunities," 31 (February 1966): 5-34.

United States Army Neuropsychiatric Screening Adjunct

Omer R. Galle and Karl E. Taeuber, "Metropolitan Migration and Intervening Opportunities," 31 (February 1966): 5-34.

Beliefs About Female Personality Traits, Author Constructed Scale; Likert-Type

Kenneth Kammeyer, "Birth Order and the Feminine Sex Role Among College Women," 31 (August 1966): 508–15.

Inflexibility Index, Author Constructed

Herbert McClosky and John H. Scharr, "Psychological Dimensions of Anomy," 30 (February 1965): 14–40.

Subjective Victimization Scale, Perceived Effects on Self of Racial Restrictions, A Reformulation of G. W. Allport and B. M. Kramer Scale

Howard Freeman, J. Michael Ross, David Armor, and Thomas F. Pettigrew, "Color Gradation and Attitudes Among Middle Income Negroes," 31 (June 1966): 365–74.

Authoritarianism Scale, The Authoritarian Personality Syndrome

Howard Freeman, J. Michael Ross, David Armor, and Thomas F. Pettigrew, "Color Gradations and Attitudes Amond Middle Income Negroes," 31 (June 1966): 365–74.

Measures of Intelligence and Achievement

American Council on Education Psychological Examination

Bruce K. Eckland, "Academic Ability, Higher Education, and Occupational Mobility, 30 (October 1965): 735–46.

Hennon-Nelson Test of Mental Ability

William H. Sewell and Michael Armor, "Neighborhood Context and College Plans," 31 (April 1966): 159–68.

Measures of Identification

Peer-Value Index for Measuring Identification With Peer Groups, Author Constructed

Paul Lerman, "Argot, Symbolic Deviance and Subcultural Delinquency," 32 (April, 1967): 209–24.

Index of Religious Identification of Professional Workers, Author Constructed

Harold Wilensky and Jack Ladinsky, "From Religious Community To Occupational Group: Structural Assimilation Among Professors, Lawyers and Engineers," 32 (August 1967): 541–61.

Wilensky Index of Professional Identification

Harold Wilensky and Jack Ladinsky, "From Religious Community To Occupational Group: Structural Assimilation Among Professors, Lawyers and Engineers," 32 (August 1967): 541–61.

Miscellaneous Scales

Index of Professional Incentives, Author Constructed

George Miller, "Professionals in Bureaucracy: Alienation Among Industrial Scientists and Engineers," 32 (October 1967): 755–68.

Acquiescence Scale for Measuring the Consistency-Logicality Dimension of Cognitive Function, Author Constructed

Herbert McClosky and John H. Scharr, "Psychological Dimensions of Anomy," 30 (February, 1965): 14-40.

Reference Group Support Scale, Author Constructed

James M. Fendrich, "Perceived Reference Group Support: Racial Attitudes and Overt Behavior," 32 (December 1967): 960-70.

Index of Militancy, Measuring Several Dimensions of Racial Protest, Author Constructed

Gary T. Marx, "Religion: Opiate or Inspiration of Civil Rights Militancy Among Negroes," 32 (February 1967): 64-72.

Index of Perceived Legitimate Educational and Occupational Opportunities, Author Constructed

James F. Short, Jr., Ramon Rivera, and Ray A. Tennyson, "Perceived Opportunities, Gang Membership and Delinquency," 30 (February 1965): 56-67.

Stouffer-Toby Conflict Scale

Louis A. Zurcher, Jr., Arnold Meadow, and Susan Lee Zurcher, "Value Orientation, Role Conflict, and Alienation from Work: A Cross-Cultural Study," 30 (August 1965): 539-48.

Political Awareness Test for Measuring Degree of Information on Political Affairs, Author Constructed

Melvin Seeman, "On the Personal Consequences of Alienation in Work." 32 (April 1967): 273-85.

Social Indicators

Index of Political Representativeness for Measuring Degree of Political Organization and Constitutionalization, Author Constructed

Phillips Cutright, "Inequality: A Cross-National Analysis," 32 (August 1967): 562-78.

Index of Argot for Measuring Symbolic Deviance, Author Constructed

Paul Lerman, "Argot, Symbolic Deviance and Subcultural Delinquency," 32 (April 1967): 209-24.

Author Constructed Scale to Measure the Degree of Coercive vs. Persuasive Sanctions Toward Hospital Patients

Joseph Julian, "Compliance Patterns and Communication Blocks in Complex Organizations," 31 (June 1966): 382-89.

Index of Economic Development Based on Data From B. Russett et al., *World Handbook of Political and Social Indicators*

Phillips Cutright, "Inequality: A Cross-National Analysis," 32 (August 1967): 562-78.

Index of Democratic Political Enlightenment (Use of Moscos' items)

Arvin W. Murch, "Political Integration as an Alternative to Independence in the French Antilles," 33 (August 1968): 544-61.

Index of Governmental Reformism,
  Author Constructed

Terry N. Clark, "Community Structure, Decision Making, Budget Expenditures, and Urban Renewal in 51 American Communities," 33 (August 1968): 576-93.

INVENTORY FOR 1969-74

Scales for Measuring Social Status

Duncan's Index of Socioeconomic Status

Edward O. Laumann, "The Social Structure of Religious and Ethnoreligious Groups in a Metropolitan Community," 34 (April 1969): 186.

William A. Rushing, "Two Patterns in the Relationship Between Social Class and Mental Hospitalization," 34 (August 1969): 535.

Carolyn Cummings Perrucci and Robert Perrucci, "Social Origins, Educational Contexts, and Career Mobility," 35 (June 1970): 453.

William H. Sewell et al., "The Educational and Early Occupational Status Attainment Process: Replication and Revision," 35 (December 1970): 1017.

Reta D. Artz, Dianne Timbers Fairbank, Richard F. Curtis, and Elton F. Jackson, "Community Rank Stratification: A Factor Analysis," 36 (December 1971): 987.

Elton F. Jackson and Richard F. Curtis, "Effects of Vertical Mobility and Status Inconsistency: A Body of Negative Evidence," 37 (December 1972): 702.

Norvall D. Glenn, Adreain A. Ross, Judy Corder Tully, "Patterns of Intergenerational Mobility of Females Through Marriage," 39 (August 1974): 688.

Archibald O. Haller, Luther B. Otto, Robert F. Meir, and George W. Ohlendorf, "Level of Occupational Aspiration: An Empirical Analysis," 39 (February 1974): 116.

Duane F. Alwin, "College Effects on Occupational Attainments," 39 (April 1974): 212-13.

Duncan SEI Used to Classify Head of Household, and to Derive Measures of Occupational Aspiration, Expectation, and Occupational Attainment

James N. Porter, "Race, Socialization and Mobility in Educational and Early Occupational Attainment," 39 (June 1974): 306-8.

Three Measures of Socioeconomic Status: Duncan SEI Scale, Education, and Subjective Social Class

David Knoke and Michael Hout, "Social and Demographic Factors in American Political Party Affiliations, 1952-72," 39 (August 1974): 702.

Charles W. Mueller, "City Effects on Socioeconomic Achievements: The Case of Large Cities," 39 (August 1974): 655-56.

Author Constructed Eight-Category SES Index Including Occupation of Head of Household (Coded by Duncan SES Index), Education of the Respondent, and Total Family Income

Marvin E. Olsen, "Social and Political Participation of Blacks," 35 (August 1970): 685.

Hollingshead's Two-Factor Index of Social Position

Melvin L. Kohn and Carmi Schooler, "Class, Occupation, and Orientation," 34 (October 1969): 660.

Gerald T. Slatin, "Ecological Analysis of Delinquency: Aggregation Effects," 34 (December 1969): 896.

Glen H. Elder, Jr., "Appearance and Education in Marriage Mobility," 34 (August 1969): 523.

Richard A. Rehberg, Walter E. Schafer and Judie Sinclair, "Toward A Temporal Sequence of Adolescent Achievement Variables," 35 (February 1970): 34-37.

Roberta G. Simmons and Morris Rosenberg, "Functions of Children's Perceptions of the Stratification System," 30 (April 1971): 241.

Melvin L. Kohn, "Bureaucratic Man: A Portrait and an Interpretation," 36 (June 1971): 468.

Lloyd H. Rogler, "The Changing Role of a Political Boss in a Puerto Rican Migrant Community," 39 (February 1974): 63.

Hollingshead Index of Social Position, Use of Educational Seven Category Scale Only

Thomas Ewin Smith, "Foundations of Parental Influence upon Adolescents: An Application of Social Power Theory," 35 (October 1970): 864.

North-Hatt Scale of Occupational Prestige (NORC)

Roberta G. Simmons and Morris Rosenberg, "Functions of Children's Perceptions of the Stratification System," 30 (April 1971): 237.

Sanford Labovitz, "The Assignment of Numbers to Rank Order Categories," 35 (June 1970): 516–17.

C. Norman Alexander, Jr., "Status Perceptions," 37 (December 1972): 769.

Edwards Socio-Economic Grouping (U.S. Census)

Samuel H. Preston, "Differential Fertility, Unwanted Fertility, and Racial Trends in Occupational Achievement," 39 (August 1974): 498.

Classification of Occupations, London: Her Majesty's Stationery Office, 1966; for Study in England as Cited

John W. Loy, Jr., "Social Psychological Characteristics of Innovators," 34 (February 1969): 75.

Socioeconomic Status: Factor Weighted Combination of Education of Respondent's Father and Mother, Respondent's Perception of Economic Status of the Family, Respondent's Perception of Possible Parental Support Should He Go to College and Amount of Support, and Occupation of His Father; Author Constructed

William H. Sewell, Archibald O. Haller, and Alejandro Portes, "The Educational and Early Occupational Attainment Process," 34 (February 1969): 87.

Family Background Status: Mother's Education, Father's Education, Father's Occupational Status, and Acquisition Index; Author Constructed

Karl L. Alexander and Bruce K. Eckland, "Sex Differences in the Educational Attainment Process," 39 (August 1974): 672.

Status of High School: Author Constructed; Educational Status Index: Author Constructed

Joel I. Nelson, "High School Context and College Plans: The Impact of Social Structure on Aspirations," 37 (April 1972): 144.

Significance of External Status Characteristic in Small-Group Decision-Making

Joseph Berger, Bernard P. Cohen, and Morris Zelditch, Jr., "Status Conceptions and Social Interaction," 37 (June 1972): 249.

Socioeconomic Status Using Bogue Scale

H. Edward Ransford, "Blue Collar Anger: Reactions to Student and Black Protest," 37 (June 1972): 337–38.

Achieved Socioeconomic Status Index; Author Constructed

Ascribed Status; Author Constructed

Marvin E. Olsen and Judy Corder Tully, "Socioeconomic-Ethnic Status Inconsistency and Preference for Political Change," 37 (October 1972): 565.

Scales for Measuring Group Structures and Dynamics

Indicators of Organizational Interdependence, Complexity, Innovation, Internal Communication, Centralization, and Formalization; Author Constructed

Michael Aiken and Jerald Hage, "Organizational Interdependence and Intra-Organizational Structure," 33 (December 1968): 919, 921, 926.

Indices of Social Power: Coercive, Reward, Expert, Legitimate, and Referent

Donald I. Warren, "Power, Visibility, and Conformity in Formal Organizations," 33 (December 1968): 957.

Subscription to an Inmate Code, Inmate Cohesion, Criminal Subcultural Orientation, Disorganization of Social Background, Indicators of Contact; Author Constructed

Charles R. Little, "Inmate Organization: Sex Differentiation and the Influences of Criminal Subcultures," 34 (August 1969): 495-97.

Origin of Status Persistence; Author Constructed Index

Leo A. Goodman, "On the Measurement of Social Mobility: An Index of Status Persistence," 34 (December 1969): 938.

Indices of the Diversity of Institutions for Measurement of Social System Differentiation

Frank W. Young, "Reactive Subsystems," 35 (April 1970): 300.

Degrees of Status Crystallization; Author Constructed Index

Thomas S. Smith, "Structural Crystallization, Status Inconsistency, and Political Partisanship," 34 (December 1969): 915.

Indices of Organizational Size Consisting of Total Number of Employees in Organization Where Respondent Works and Size of Respondent's Immediate Work Group; Author Constructed

Carolyn Cummings Perrucci and Robert Perrucci, "Social Origins, Educational Contexts, and Career Mobility," 35 (June 1970): 453-54.

Index of Job Specificity in an Organization

Jerald Hage, Michael Aiken, and Cora Bagley Marrett, "Organization Structure and Communications," 36 (October 1971): 870.

Index of Participation in Organizational Decision-Making

Index of Regeneration for Social Organizations; Author Constructed	Kenneth McNeil and James D. Thompson, "The Regeneration of Social Organizations," 36 (August 1971): 625–26.
Index of Bureaucracy (Hierarchical Organization of Authority Dimension	Melvin L. Kohn, "Bureaucratic Man: A Portrait and an Interpretation," 36 (June 1971): 462.
Index of Protest Definition; Author Constructed	Vincent Jeffries, Ralph H. Turner, and Richard T. Morris, "The Public Perception of the Watts Riot as Social Protest," 36 (June 1971): 443–45.
Industrial Conflict; Author Constructed	David Britt and Omer R. Gallo, "Industrial Conflict and Unionization," 37 (February 1972): 48.
Public Awareness of a Social Protest Incident; Author Constructed	David L. Altheide and Robert P. Gilmore, "The Credibility of Protest," 37 (February 1972): 102–3.
Sociomatrices of Children's Classroom Groups	Samuel Leinhardt, "Developmental Change in the Sentiment Structure of Children's Groups," 37 (April 1972): 203–5.
Index of Occupational Dispersion	David F. Sly, "Migration and the Ecological Complex," 37 (October 1972): 621.
Power and Prestige Order in Small Groups; Author Constructed	Elizabeth G. Cohen and Susan S. Roper, "Modification of Intersocial Interaction Disability: An Application of Status Characteristic Theory," 37 (December 1972): 647.
Organization Locus; Ownership, Bureaucratization, and Position in Supervisory Hierarchy; Author Constructed	Melvin L. Kohn and Carmi Schooler, "Occupational Experience and Psychological Functioning: An Assessment of Reciprocal Effects," 38 (February 1973): 103–4.
Visible and Legitimate Leadership in the Community	James M. Williams, "The Ecological Approach in Measuring Community Power Concentration: An Analysis of Hawley's MPO Ratio," 38 (April 1973): 235.
Bales' Interactional Process Analysis-Borgatta's Revision)	H. W. Smith, "Some Developmental Interpersonal Dynamics through Childhood," 38 (October 1973): 544.
Occupational Mobility; 12 Categories of Skill Histories; Author Constructed	Barbara Jackson and John M. Kendrick, "Education and Mobility: From Achievement to Ascription," 38 (August 1973): 446–47.

Measure of Managerial Component of Communal Units; Measure of Communicative Component of Communal Units; Measure of Professional and Technical Component of Communal units; All Scales Author Constructed

John D. Kasarda, "The Structural Implications of Social System Size: A Three Level Analysis," 39 (February 1974): 22.

Revivalism Measure; Author Constructed

John L. Hammond, "Revival Religion and Antislavery Politics," 39 (April 1974): 179.

Scales for Measuring Community Factors

National Headquarters Index of Extralocal Integration for 1960, Provided by National Headquarters of Voluntary Associations Found in *Encyclopedia of Associations* (1961)

Herman Turk, "Interorganizational Networks in Urban Society: Initial Perspectives and Comparative Research," 35 (February 1970): 1-5, 9-10, 10.

Community-Wide Association Index of Local Integration "taken to signify the presence of mechanisms for concerned action as well as the absence of highly organized cleavages within the city"

Municipal Revenue Index of Local Integration, Measuring Integration in Terms of Control Exercised by the City's Government over the Communities' Affairs

Index of Interorganizational Activity Level Based on Per Capita Number of Poverty Dollars Flowing into a Particular City

Measures of Community Structure Compiled from *Municipal Year Books* ('63, '64), 1950 Census of Housing, and 1960 Census of Population

Michael Aiken and Robert R. Alford, "Community Structure and Innovation: The Case of Urban Renewal," 35 (August 1970): 652.

Measure of Community Innovation, i.e., Participation in Urban Renewal Program, compiled from *Urban Renewal Directory* (June 30, 1966, Department of Housing and Urban Development, U.S. Government, Washington, D.C.

The Speed of Community Innovation Is Measured by Number of Years City Took to Enter Urban Renewal

Program Either After 1944 or After State Enabling Legislation Was Enacted

Level of Community Output Measured by Number of Urban Renewal Dollars Reserved Per Capita as of June 30, 1966

Patterns of Vandalism; Author Constructed	Richard A. Berk and Howard E. Aldrich, "Patterns of Vandalism During Civil Disorders as an Indicator of Selection of Targets," 37 (October 1972): 538.
Reward Distribution in Kibbutz; Author Constructed	Ephraim Yuchtman, "Reward Distribution and Work-Role Attractiveness in the Kibbutz—Reflections on Equity Theory," 37 (October 1972): 584.
Community Elite Influence and Relationship of Pairs of Elite Members	Edward O. Laumann, Lois M. Verbrugge, and Franz U. Pappi, "A Causal Modeling Approach to the Study of a Community Elite's Influence Structure," 39 (April 1974): 163–66.
Community Attitudes and Sentiments; Friendship and Kinship Bonds in Local Community; Respondent's Participation in Formal Associations within the Local Community; Author Constructed	John D. Kasarda and Morris Janowitz, "Community Attachment in Mass Society," 39 (June 1974): 331.

Scales for Measuring Social Participation and Alienation

Index of Esteem (Evaluation of Others); Author Constructed	Rodolfo Alvarez, "Informal Reactions to Deviance in Simulated Work Organizations: A Laboratory Experiment," 33 (December 1968): 906.
Index of Relative Centrality in Group Association Based on Peer Nomination, Author Constructed	"Location and Innovativeness: Reformulation and Extension of the Diffusion Model," 35 (April 1970): 270.
Voluntary Association Participation Index; Political Organization Participation Index; Mass Media Exposure Index; Political News Exposure Index; Community Activities Index; Cultural Events Index; Church Participation Index; Friends Interaction Index; Relatives Interaction Index; Political Discussion Index; Registration and Voting	Marvin E. Olsen, "Social and Political Participation of Blacks," 35 (August 1970): 685, 686.

Index; Partisan Political Activities Index; Partisan Political Involvement Index (All 12 Above Scales Author Constructed); Governmental Contacts Index

Index of Company Evaluation (5 Items) as Measure of Worker Integration; Author Constructed

Michael Fullan, "Industrial Technology and Worker Integration in the Organization," 35 (December 1970): 1035-36.

Integration Policy Strength Scale (10 Items), Guttman type; Author Constructed

James R. Wood, "Authority and Controversial Policy: The Churches and Civil Rights," 35 (December 1970): 1059-60.

Social Isolation Index (Geschwender et al.)

Clark McPhail, "Civil Disorder Participation: A Critical Examination of Recent Research," 36 (December 1971): 1069.

Index of Professional Activity

Jerald Hage, Michael Aiken, and Cora Bagley Marrett, "Organization Structure and Communications," 36 (October 1971): 870.

Index of Dissimilarity (ID) (Duncan and Duncan, 1955); Measure of Ghettoization (Taeuber and Taeuber, 1965)

Robert M. Jiobu and Harvey H. Marshall, Jr., "Urban Structure and the Differentiation Between Blacks and Whites," 36 (August 1971): 642, 643.

Strole Anomie Scale

Leslie G. Carr, "The Strole Items and Acquiescence," 36 (April 1971): 287-92.

Nominal Scale of Voluntary Associations; Author Constructed

Alan Booth, "Sex and Social Participation," 37 (April 1972): 188-89.

Social Participation; Author Constructed: (1) Voluntary Association Participation Index (2) Church Participation Index (3) Community Participation Index (4) Friends Interaction Index (5) Neighbors

Marvin E. Olsen, "Social Participation and Voting Turnout: A Multivariate Analysis," 37 (June 1972): 320-21.

Middleton Alienation Scale (1963), Internal-External Control (Powerlessness) Scale (Rotler 1966), Index of Work Alienation (Seeman 1967), Anomia Scale (Srole 1956)

Melvin Seeman, "The Signals of '68: Alienation in Pre-Crisis France," 37 (August 1972): 387, 391.

Formal Social Participation, Informal Social Participation, Anomia; Author Constructed

Elton F. Jackson and Richard F. Curtis, "Effects of Vertical Mobility and Status Inconsistency: A Body of Negative Evidence," 37 (December 1972): 707.

Orientation to Self and Society; Based on Factor Analysis of Fifty-Seven Questions; Author Constructed	Melvin L. Kohn and Carmi Schooler, "Occupational Experience and Psychological Functioning: An Assessment of Reciprocal Effects," 38 (February 1973): 100.
Rosenberg "Misanthropy" Scale (Variations of)	Claude S. Fisher, "On Urban Alienations and Anomie: Powerlessness and Social Isolation," 38 (June 1973): 311-26.
Membership and Participation in Voluntary Associations (Author definition: average number of organizations belonged to by a particular population.)	J. Allen Williams, Jr., and Nicholas Babchuk, "Voluntary Associations and Minority Status: A Comparative Analysis of Anglo, Black, and Mexican Americans," 38 (October 1973): 637-46.
Political Knowledge, Political Awareness, and Political Participation; Author Constructed	Anthony M. Orum and Roberta S. Cohen, "The Development of Political Orientations among Black and White Children," 38 (February 1973): 66.
Participation in Interpersonal Violence; Author Constructed	Sandra J. Ball-Rokeach, "Values and Violence: A Test of the Subculture of Violence Thesis," 38 (December 1973): 737-38.
Powerlessness Measured by Institute for Social Research: Personal Competency Scale of Robinson and Shaver	Claude S. Fisher, "On Urban Alienations and Anomie: Powerlessness and Social Isolation," 38 (June 1973): 313.
Occupational Self-Direction, Job Pressures and Uncertainties; Author Constructed	Melvin L. Kohn and Carmi Schooler, "Occupational Experience and Psychological Functioning: An Assessment of Reciprocal Effects," 38 (February 1973): 104-5.
Career Orientation Anchorage Scale (COAS) by Tausky and Dubin; Central Life Interest Instrument (CLI)	Daniel R. Goldman, "Managerial Mobility Motivations and Central Life Interests," 38 (February 1973): 120-21.
Measure of Professional Orientation Among Bureaucratic Managers; Author Constructed	William J. Haga, George Graen, and Fred Dansereau, Jr., "Professional and Role Making In a Service Organization: A Longitudinal Investigation," 39 (February 1974): 127.
Political Participation Scale; Political Discussion Scale (Designed for Children in Fourth Through Twelfth Grades)	Anthony M. Orum, Roberta S. Cohen, Sherri Grasmuck, and Amy W. Orum, "Sex, Socialization, and Politics," 39 (April 1974): 203.
Bales Interaction Process Analysis	Peter J. Burke, "Participation and Leadership in Small Groups," 39 (December 1974): 833.

Scales to Measure Leadership

Closeness of Supervision Index, Guttman Type (Kohn 1969)

Melvin L. Kohn, "Bureaucratic Man: A Portrait and an Interpretation," 36 (June 1971): 469.

Index of Relative Centrality in Group Association Based on Peer Nomination; Author Constructed

Marshall H. Becker, "Sociometric Location and Innovativeness: Reformulation and Extension of the Diffusion Model," 35 (April 1970): 270.

Scales to Measure Attitudes and Values

Index of Significant Other's Influence: Summated Score of Three Variables; Author Constructed

William H. Sewell, Archibald O. Haller, and Alejandro Portes, "The Educational and Early Occupational Attainment Process" (February 1969): 87.

Verbal Attitude Scale to Measure Prejudice toward Negroes; Author Constructed

Lyle G. Warner and Melvin L. DeFleur, "Attitude as an Interactional Concept: Social Constraint and Social Distance as Interviewing Variables between Attitudes and Action," 34 (April 1969): 156-57.

Commitment to Values Index: 20 Item Likert-Scale to Measure Commitment to a Specific Organization; Author Constructed

George Brager, "Commitment and Conflict in a Normative Organization," 34 (August 1969): 486.

Attractiveness: Scores on Selected Scales; Status Aspirations: Author Constructed; Aspiration for High Status: 101 Item California Q Set (Block 1961)

Glen H. Elder, Jr., "Appearance and Education in Marriage Mobility," 34 (August 1969): 522.

Indices of Parental Values, Values for Self, Social Orientation, Self-Conception; Author Constructed

Melvin L. Kohn and Carmi Schooler, "Class, Occupation, and Orientation," 34 (October 1969): 622-67.

Adolescent's Socio-Economic Level of Wish, Adolescent's Socioeconomic Level of Expectation; Author Constructed

Wan Sang Han, "Two Conflicting Themes: Common Values Versus Class Differential Values," 34 (October 1969): 681.

Author Constructed Index of Mobility Attitudes Including Six Factors: Educational Orientation, Person Orientation, Master Orientation, Occupational Primacy, Time Orientation, and Fatalism

Richard A. Rehberg, Walter E. Schafer and Judie Sinclair, "Toward A Temporal Sequence of Adolescent Achievement Variables," 35 (February 1970): 36-37.

Scale of Occupational Values, Based on Six Characteristics Associated with Work Roles; Author Constructed

Carolyn Cummings Perrucci and Robert Perrucci, "Social Origins, Educational Contexts, and Career Mobility," 35 (June 1970): 453.

Level of Occupational Aspiration Determined by Assigning Duncan SES Index Scores to the Occupation Respondent Previously Indicated He Hoped to Enter in Future; Index of Significant Others Influence, Including Perceived Parental Encouragement to Attend College, Perceived Teacher Encouragement for College, and Friends' College Plans; Author Constructed	William H. Sewell et al., "The Educational and Early Occupational Status Attainment Process: Replication and Revision," 35 (December 1970): 1017.
Indices of Attitudes toward Negroes; Author Constructed	Vincent Jeffries, Ralph H. Turner, and Richard T. Morris, "The Public Perception of the Watts Riot as Social Protest," 36 (June 1971): 445–46.
Index of Values or Standards of Desirability (Kohn 1969); Indices of Social Orientation Including Authoritarian Conservatism, Criteria of Morality, and Stance toward Change (Kohn 1969).	Melvin L. Kohn, "Bureaucratic Man: A Portrait and an Interpretation," 36 (June 1971): 463, 464.
Lenski's Index of Work Values	Howard Schuman, "The Religious Factor in Detroit: Review, Replication, and Reanalysis," 36 (February 1971): 33.
Occupational Aspiration Scale (Haller and Miller 1963); Occupational and Aspiration Scale (Haller and Woelfel 1969)	Joseph Woeffel and Archibald O. Haller, "Significant Others, The Self-Reflexive Act and the Attitude Formation Process," 36 (February 1971): 77.
Adolescent Conformity; Author Constructed	Darwin L. Thomas and Andrew J. Weigert, "Socialization and Adolescent Conformity to Significant Others: A Cross-National Analysis," 36 (October 1971): 839–40.
Indices of Leftist Radicalism; Author Constructed	Alejandro Portes, "Political Primitivism, Differential Socialization, and Lower-Class Leftist Radicalism," 36 (October 1971): 823.
Hall's Professionalism Scale (Attitude Scale)	William E. Snizek, "Hall's Professionalism Scale: An Empirical Reassessment," 37 (February 1972): 110.
Attitude Toward Work, Personal Satisfaction with Socioeconomic Attainment; Author Constructed	David L. Featherman, "Achievement Orientations and Socioeconomic Career Attainments," 37 (April 1972): 123, 133.

Individual Modernity: Compiled from Smith and Inkeles' 0-M6 Modernity Scale, Kahl's Modernity I and II Scales, Schnaiberg's Emancipation Scale, Armer's Individual Modernity Scale

Michael Armer and Allan Schnaiberg, "Measuring Individual Modernity: A Near Myth," 37 (June 1972): 304.

Hostility Demonstrated by Blue Collar Political and Social Attitudes and Values; Author Constructed

E. Edward Ransford, "Blue Collar Anger: Reactions to Student and Black Protest," 37 (June 1972): 338.

Preference for Political Change; Modified Likert Scale Items from Kelly and Chamblis

Marvin E. Olsen and Judy Corder Tully, "Socioeconomic-Ethnic Status Inconsistency and Preference for Political Change," 37 (October 1972): 563.

Work-Role Attractiveness (Thibant and Kelly 1959)

Ephraim Yuchtman, "Reward Distribution and Work-Role Attractiveness in the Kibbutz—Reflections on Equity Theory," 37 (October 1972): 585.

Five Scales of Race and Class Consciousness of Blacks; Author Constructed

Charles E. Hurst, "Race, Class and Consciousness," 37 (December 1972): 660-61.

Political Liberalism, Satisfaction and Symptoms of Stress, Intolerance, Aspirations for Son

Elton F. Jackson and Richard F. Curtis, "Effects of Vertical Mobility and Status Inconsistency: A Body of Negative Evidence," 37 (December 1972): 707.

Anti-Semitism Scale (Selznick and Steinberg)

Russell Middleton, "Do Christian Beliefs Cause Anti-Semitism?" 38 (February 1973): 39.

Political Cynicism, Government Benevolence, Favorable Image of the President; All Scales Author Constructed

Anthony M. Orum and Roberta S. Cohen, "The Development of Political Orientations Among Black and White Children," 38 (February 1973): 64, 65.

Occupational Commitment, Job Satisfaction, Valuation of Self-Direction or Conformity to External Authority

Melvin L. Kohn and Carmi Schooler, "Occupational Experience and Psychological Functioning: An Assessment of Reciprocal Effects," 38 (February 1973): 99-100.

Receptivity toward Protest; Author Constructed

Hart M. Nelson, Raytha L. Yokley, and Thomas W. Madron, "Ministerial Roles and Social Actionist Stance: Protestant Clergy and Protest in the Sixties," 38 (June 1973): 377.

Self Image Based on Four Guttman-Type Scales; Author Constructed

Roberta G. Simmons and Florence Rosenberg, "Disturbance in the Self-Image of Adolescence," 38 (October 1973): 566-67.

Attitude toward Violence, Author Constructed; Rokeach Value Survey

Sandra J. Ball-Rokeach, "Values and Violence: A Test of the Subculture of Violence Thesis," 31 (December 1973): 736–49.

Occupational Aspiration Scale (Haller and Miller 1971)

Archibald O. Haller, Luther B. Otto, Robert F. Meir, and George W. Ohlendorf, "Level of Occupational Aspiration: An Empirical Analysis," 39 (February 1974): 116.

Image of the President Scale, Government Benevolence Scale, Political Cynicism Scale (Designed for Children in Fourth through Twelfth Grades); Author Constructed

Anthony M. Orum, Roberta S. Cohen, Sherri Grasmuck, and Amy W. Orum, "Sex, Socialization, and Politics," 39 (April 1974): 202-3.

Scales to Measure Inner-Directedness, Religious Experience, Modern Values, Loneliness, Work Satisfaction, Decision to Stay in the Public Ministry; Author Constructed

Richard A. Schoenherr and Andrew M. Greeley, "Role Commitment Processes and the American Catholic Priesthood," 39 (June 1974): 413.

Scales to Measure Academic Self-Concept, Educational Expectations, and Adult Influences; Author Constructed

Karl L. Alexander and Bruce K. Eckland, "Sex Differences in the Educational Attainment Process," 39 (October 1974): 673.

Scales Measuring Family and Marriage Factors

Index of Decision-Making in Marriages; Blood and Wolfe's Index of Most Valued Part of Marriage

Richard Centers, Bertram H. Raven, and Aroldo Rodrigues, "Conjugal Power Structure: A Re-examination," 36 (April 1971): 266, 267.

Cornell Parent Behavior Description Scale, Short Form

Darwin L. Thomas and Andrew J. Weigert, "Socialization and Adolescent Conformity to Significant Others: A Cross-National Analysis," 36 (October 1971): 839.

Indices of Family Stability Based on Current Marital Status, Family Types and Family Headship, Illegitimacy, and Changes in Living Arrangements of Young Children

Reynolds Farley and Albert I. Hermalin, "Family Stability: A Comparison of Trends Between Blacks and Whites," 36 (February 1971): 1-14.

Index of Marital Tension, Author Constructed; Index of Husband-Wife Communication, Author Constructed

Robert Edward Mitchell, "Some Social Implications of High Density Housing," 36 (February 1971): 25.

Verbal and Nonverbal Family Interactional Analysis; Author Constructed

Bernard C. Rosen, "Social Change, Migration, and Family Interaction in Brazil," 38 (April 1973): 203.

Maternal Restrictions Scale, Guttman Type, White and Saltz; Husband Involvement Scale; Intramarital (Bargaining) Transactions

Karen E. Paige and Jeffrey M. Paige, "The Politics of Birth Practices: A Strategic Analysis," 38 (December 1973): 671.

Indices of the Approval of Spanking Children; Author Constructed

Howard S. Erlanger, "Social Class and Corporal Punishment in Childrearing: A Reassessment," 39 (February 1974): 73.

Family Tension (Scale Range 1.0-5.0 Based on Items in NORC 1972 Report)

Richard A. Schoenherr and Andrew M. Greeley, "Role Commitment Processes and the American Catholic Priesthood," 39 (June 1974): 412.

Measures of Personality Factors

Minnesota Multiphasic Personality Inventory, IPAT Anxiety Scale (Cattell and Scheier 1963), Faith in People and Self-Esteem (Rosenberg Guttman-Type Scales)

Raymond J. Adamek and Edward Z. Dager, "Social Structure Identification and Change in a Treatment-Oriented Institution," 33 (December 1968): 935, 936.

Form A, Cattell's Sixteen Personality Factor Questionnaire

John W. Loy, Jr., "Social Psychological Characteristics of Innovators," 34 (February 1969): 75.

Mental Health Index Consisting of a 22-Item Screening Inventory by Thomas S. Langner

Derek L. Phillips and Kevin J. Clancy, "Response Biases in Field Studies of Mental Illness," 35 (June 1970): 504. See also D. L. Phillips and Bernard E. Segal, "Sexual Status and Psychiatric Symptoms," 34 (February 1969): 60.

California F-Scale Measuring Authoritarianism (Adorno et al. 1950); Rokeach's Dogmatism Scale

Walter Korpi, "Working Class Communism in Western Europe: Rational or Nonrational," 36 (December 1971): 975, 976.

Sanford and Older's 7-Item Scale of Authoritarianism Derived from Adorno's F-Scale; Douvan and Walker's Personal Competence Scale; Guttman Type

Richard Centers, Bertram H. Raven, and Aroldo Rodrigues, "Conjugal Power Structure: A Re-examination," 36 (April 1971): 266-67.

Srole Anomie Scale; Social Acquiescence Scale (Bass)

Leslie G. Carr, "The Srole Items and Acquiescences," 36 (April 1971): 288-90.

Indices of Emotional Strain Including Index of Superficial Levels of Strain, Index of Emotional Illness, Index of Hostility, Index of Behavioral Impairment, Index of Behavioral Withdrawal; Author Constructed

Robert Edward Mitchell, "Some Social Implications of High Density Housing," 36 (February 1971): 21-22.

Survey Research Center Index of Personal Effectiveness, Conceptualized as a Measure Tapping Seeman's Concept of Powerlessness	Bill Tudor, "A Specification of Relationships Between Job Complexity and Powerlessness," 37 (October 1972): 598.

Measures of Intelligence and Achievement

Henmon-Nelson Test of Mental Ability	William H. Sewell, Archibald O. Haller, and Alejandro Portes, "The Educational and Early Occupational Attainment Process," 34 (February 1969): 87.
Henmon-Nelson Test of Mental Ability	William H. Sewell et al., "The Educational and Early Occupational Status Attainment Process: Replication and Revision," 35 (December 1970): 1017.
California Test of Mental Maturity and Otis Quick Scoring Mental Ability, Beta Form	Richard A. Rehberg, Walter E. Schafer, and Judie Sinclair, "Toward a Temporal Sequence of Adolescent Achievement Variables," 35 (February 1970): 36-37.
Indices of Academic Achievement, Author Constructed; Indices of Career Success, Author Constructed	Carolyn Cummings Perrucci and Robert Perrucci, "Social Origins, Educational Contexts, and Career Mobility," 35 (June 1970): 453, 454.
Indices of Intelligence; Author Constructed	Melvin L. Kohn, "Bureaucratic Man: A Portrait and an Interpretation," 36 (June 1971): 464-65.
Minnesota Scholastic Aptitude Test	Joel I. Nelson, "High School Context and College Plans: The Impact of Social Structure on Aspirations," 37 (April 1972): 145.
Measure of Intellectual Flexibility and Demands (Self-Imposed) on Intellectual Resources; Author Constructed	Melvin L. Kohn and Carmi Schooler, "Occupational Experience and Psychological Functioning: An Assessment of Reciprocal Effects," 38 (February 1973): 101.
Measure of Parents' Emphasis on Son's Achievement	Bernard C. Rosen, "Social Change, Migration, and Family Interaction in Brazil," 38 (April 1973): 198-212.
Science Citation Index	Paul D. Allison and John A. Stewart, "Productivity Differences Among Scientists: Evidence for Accumulative Advantage," 39 (August, 1974): 599.
Science Citation Index	Warren O. Hagstrom, "Competition in Science," 39 (February 1974): 2, 5.

Measures of Identification

Indentification with the Institution (for Delinquent Girls), 35-item Likert Scale

Raymond J. Adamek and Edward Z. Dager, "Social Structure Identification and Change in a Treatment-Oriented Institution," 33 (December 68): 934.

Personal Integration into U.S. Culture, Six Indicators; Author Constructed

Alejandro Portes, "Dilemmas of a Golden Exile: Integration of Cuban Refugee Families in Milwaukee," 34 (August 1969): 508-9.

Gough's Masculinity-Femininity Scale of Sex Identity; Franck Drawing Completion Test of Sex Identity

William Bezdek and Fred L. Strodtbeck, "Sex-Role Identity and Pragmatic Action," 35 (June 1970): 494, 496.

Role-Taking; Author Constructed

Darwin L. Thomas, David D. Franks, and James M. Calonico, "Role-Taking and Power in Social Psychology," 37 (October 1972): 608.

Political Party Identification: Party Differences; Author Constructed

Anthony M. Orum and Roberta S. Cohen, "The Development of Political Orientations Among Black and White Children," 38 (February 1973): 68, 69.

Miscellaneous Scales

Author Constructed Measure of Educational Expectations—Considering Your Abilities, Grades, Financial Resources, etc., How Far Do You Actually Expect to Go in School?

Richard A. Rehberg, Walter E. Schafer and Judie Sinclair, "Toward A Temporal Sequence of Adolescent Achievement Variables," 35 (February 1970): 36-37.

Mueller and Schuessler's Index of Qualitative Variation

Kathleen S. Crittenden and Richard J. Hill, "Coding Reliability and Validity of Interview Data," 36 (December 1971): 1075.

Featherman's Religio-Ethnic Categories Based on Nationality Background and Religious Affiliation

David L. Featherman, "The Socioeconomic Achievement of White Religio-Ethnic Subgroups: Social and Psychological Explanations," 36 (April 1971): 209.

Scientists' Analysis of Scientific Content of Various Fields, Behaviors and Attitudes; Author Constructed

Janice Beyer Lodahl and Gerald Gordon, "The Structure of Scientific Fields and the Functioning of University Graduate Departments," 37 (February 1972): 66-67.

Thirty-Seven Indicators of Institutional (High School and University) Innovations; Author Constructed

Ronald G. Corwin, "Strategies for Organizational Innovation: An Empirical Comparison," 37 (August 1972): 444.

Indices of Dissimilarity of Origins and of Occupational Destinations of Men and Women in Occupational Mobility	Andrea Tyree and Judith Treas, "The Occupational and Marital Mobility of Women," 39 (June 1974): 297.
Honoring of Accounts, Account Adequacy, Account Credibility, Demand Appropriateness, Demand Legitimacy, Offensiveness of Violation; Author Constructed	Philip W. Blumstein et al., "The Honoring of Accounts," 39 (August 1974): 555.

Social Indicators

Political Complexity Index, Social Differentiation Index; Author Constructed	Mark Abrahamson, "Correlates of Political Complexity," 34 (October 1969): 695.
"Multiversity" Index; Author Constructed	Joseph W. Scott and Mohamed El-Assal, "Multiversity Quality and Student Protest: An Empirical Study," 34 (October 1969): 704.
Index of Crime of Federal Bureau of Investigation	Edward Green, "Race, Social Status, and Criminal Arrest," 35 (June 1970): 476.
Indicators of Regional Integration Based on Urbanization, Industrialization, Occupational Redistribution, Income, and Education	John C. McKinney and Linda Brookover Bourque, "The Changing South: National Incorporation of a Region," 36 (June 1971): 400-407.
Index of Southerness; Author Constructed	Raymond D. Gastil, "Homicide and a Regional Culture of Violence," 36 (June 1971): 425-26.
Two Indices of National Economic Development; Author Constructed	Marion Blute, "The Growth of Science and Economic Development," 37 (August 1972): 457.
Social Insurance Program Experience (SIPE) Index, Author Adapted from Cutright	Robert W. Jackman, "Political Democracy and Social Equality: A Comparative Analysis," 39 (February 1974): 32-33, 33, 34.
Measurement of Income Inequality, Kuznets	
Social Welfare Index, Author Adapted from Hibbs	
Serious Ratings of 140 Criminal Offenses	Peter A. Rossi, Emily Waite, Christine E. Bose, and Richard E. Berk, "The Seriousness of Crimes: Normative Structure and Individual Differences," 39 (April 1974): 228-29.

Measure of "Best" Colleges	Duane F. Alwin, "College Effects on Educational and Occupational Attainments," 39 (April 1974): 213.
Index of Unionization	Richard Child Hill, "Unionization and Racial Income Inequality in the Metropolis," 39 (August 1974): 514.
Degree of Unionization, Index of Industrial Conflict	David W. Britt and Omer Galle, "Structural Antecedents of the Shape of Strikes: A Comparative Analysis," 39 (August 1974): 645.
Structural Poverty Index, Gini Index of Income Inequality	Colin Loftin and Robert H. Hill, "Regional Subculture and Homicide: An Examination of the Gastil-Hackney Thesis," 39 (October 1974): 719-20.
Sellin-Wolfgang Seriousness of Crime Index	Alfred Blumstein, "Seriousness Weights in an Index of Crime," 39 (December 1974): 854.

ALL-INCLUSIVE AND SPECIAL COMPILATIONS OF SOURCES *4.M.2*

A listing of major sources for scale information and appraisal are shown:

ALL-INCLUSIVE COMPILATIONS

BONJEAN, CHARLES M.; HILL, RICHARD J.; and MCLEMORE, S. DALE. *Sociological Measurement: An Inventory of Scales and Indices*. San Francisco: Chandler, 1967.

This book is essentially an extensive bibliography that references 3609 uses of citations of 2080 separate scales or indexes. Scales are not generally analyzed for reliability and validity. Although limited to research up to 1965, this is still the most comprehensive bibliography. Use this book to locate various scales and research in which the scale was used.

LAKE, DALE G.; MILES, MATTHEW B.; and EARLE, RALPH B., JR. *Measuring Human Behavior*. New York: Teachers College Press, 1973.

A selection of 84 different instruments meeting stringent criteria including reasonably current information on reliability and validity. Included are 38 measures of personal variables, 24 interpersonal, 10 group, and 12 organizational. Information is provided for availability, variables measured, description of the instrument, administration and scoring, development, critique, and general comment. Truly a model for scale evaluation!

SPECIAL COMPILATIONS

SHAW, MARVIN E., and WRIGHT, JACK W. *Scales for the Measurement of Attitudes*. New York: McGraw-Hill, 1967.

Thorough information on 176 attitude measures. Entries are reasonably complete with criticism of the adequacy of the scales. A bibliography of more than 600 attitude scales is appended. The list of attitude scales is appended in the latter part of this section for the researcher seeking a particular attitude scale in which he may be interested.

Occupational Attitudes and Characteristics

ROBINSON, JOHN P.; ATHANASIOU, ROBERT; and HEAD, KENDRA B. *Measures of Occupational Attitudes and Occupational Characteristics*. Ann Arbor: Institute for Social Research, University of Michigan, 1969.

Reviews a total of 77 test instruments and provides accurate assessments of the form and scope. The author's criteria include sample adequacy, norms, reliability, homogeneity, discrimination of known groups. Typical items and ease of administration and scoring are indicated. (Contents reproduced in section 4.M.3.a.)

Political Attitudes

ROBINSON, JOHN P.; RUSK, JERROLD G.; and HEAD, KENDRA B. *Measures of Political Attitudes*. Ann Arbor: Institute of Social Research, University of Michigan, 1969.

Ninety-five measures of political attitudes are reviewed with similar criteria to that of the companion volume cited above. Accurate assessments of the form and scope of each study are made. (Contents reproduced in section 4.M.3.b.)

Social-Psychological Attitudes

ROBINSON, JOHN P., and SHAVER, PHILLIP R. *Measures of Social Psychological Attitudes*. Ann Arbor: Institute of Social Research, University of Michigan, 1969. Revised 1973, with expanded sections on internality-externality and self-esteem.

One hundred six measures of social-psychological attitudes are reviewed. There is a long review of the major attempts to measure "life satisfaction" and "happiness" over the past 15 years. As with its companion volumes, accurate assessments are made using the criteria cited. (Contents reproduced in section 4.M.3.c.)

Family Measurement

STRAUS, MURRAY A. *Family Measurement Techniques*. Minneapolis: University of Minnesota Press, 1969.

Abstracts of 319 instruments focusing on one or more of the following domains: adolescent, 20; child, 75; family, 63; parent, 129; premarital, 20; and spousal, 81. Criteria used include validity evidence, reliability, norms, availability, and references. Well-organized collection of measures. Discusses problems of scales with lack of reliability and validity—roughly 56 percent of measures abstracted.

Organizational Measurement

PRICE, JAMES L. *Handbook of Organizational Measurement*. Lexington, Mass.: D. C. Heath, 1972.

Describes measures for 22 concepts about which there is the greatest agreement among organizational researchers. Selection of the measures was derived from seven criteria that include reliability, validity, ease of administration. Each measure is discussed under such headings as description, definition, data collection, computation, validity, reliability, comments, source, and further sources. Additional readings are appended. This is the book that organizational researchers should consult first in designing their research.

KEGAN, DANIEL L. *Scales/RIQS: An Inventory of Research Instruments*. Evanston, Ill.: Technological Institute, Northwestern University, 1970.

This inventory contains 360 instruments measuring variables relevant to organizational theory. For each instrument the information is fully computer stored and retrievable. Requests from users can be handled without charge or at minimum cost. The following information is stored: author, reference, date, where instrument was used, reliability and validity, variables measured, comments by author or person depositing the item in *SCALES/RIQS*. Total length of entries is usually 100 to 150 words. A useful working tool for researchers prepared to make their own judgments of adequacy.

INDIK, B. P.; HOCKMEYER, M.; and CASTORE, C. *A Compendium of Measures of Individuals, Groups, and Organizations Relevant to the Study of Organizational Behavior.* Technical Report No. 16, Nour-404. New Brunswick, N.J.: Rutgers, The State University, 1968.

A file of several hundred measures can be assessed by writing Dr. Bernard P. Indik, Graduate School of Social Work, Rutgers University, New Brunswick, N.J. 08903. A nominal fee is charged to cover xeroxing and other costs. The variables covered are reviewed in B. P. Indik and F. K. Berrien, *People, Groups, and Organizations* (New York: Teachers College Press, 1968).

Personality and Motivation

BUROS, OSCAR KRISEN. *The Seventh Mental Measurements Yearbook.* Highland Park, N.J.: Gryphon Press, 1971.

The Buros Series of Mental Measurements Yearbooks dates from 1938 and has become the reference work in the field. The reader with particular interest in personality measures should consult *Personality Tests and Review* (Highland Park, N.J.: Gryphon Press, 1970). It includes 513 personality measures. Each test is briefly described with a complete bibliography. A variety of supporting indexes makes the user's task easy. Historical trend data are provided showing numbers of published references for each test over the past thirty years.

Numerous other compendia of special instruments are described and analyzed by Dale G. Lake, Matthew B. Miles, and Ralph B. Earle, Jr., in *Measuring Human Behavior.* See pp. 341–87. These should be consulted especially by researchers in education and personality.

CHUN, KI-TAEK; COBB, SYDNEY; and FRENCH, JOHN R. P., JR. *Measures for Psychological Assessment: A Guide to 3000 Original Sources and Their Applications.* Ann Arbor: Institute of Social Research, University of Michigan, 1975.

Compilation of annotated references to social science measures. Work grew out of an effort to build a comprehensive, computerized national repository of social science measures. The first of the volume's two major sections lists the original sources for each of 3000 instruments of attitude measurement. The Applications section cites and annotates all studies in which each measure was subsequently used. The entries were obtained through a search of 26 measurement-related journals in psychology and sociology from the period 1960–70. Author and descriptor indices are included to facilitate the use of these major sections.

WEBB, EUGENE J.; CAMPBELL, DONALD T.; SCHWARTZ, RICHARD D.; and SECHREST, LEE. *Unobtrusive Measures: Nonreactive Research in the Social Sciences.* Chicago: Rand McNally and Company, 1966.

Discusses measures not obtained by interview or questionnaire. The measures are observational in nature which do not require the cooperation of a respondent and that do not themselves contaminate the response.

4.M.3.a CONTENTS OF JOHN P. ROBINSON, ROBERT ATHANASIOU, AND KENDRA HEAD, *MEASURES OF OCCUPATIONAL ATTITUDES AND OCCUPATIONAL CHARACTERISTICS**

CHAPTER

*Published by Institute for Social Research, University of Michigan, Ann Arbor, 1969.

4.M.3.b CONTENTS OF JOHN P. ROBINSON, JERROLD G. RUSK, AND KENDRA P. HEAD, *MEASURES OF POLITICAL ATTITUDES**

*Published by Institute for Social Research, University of Michigan, Ann Arbor, 1968.

4.M.3.C CONTENTS OF JOHN P. ROBINSON AND PHILLIP P. SHAVER, *MEASURES OF SOCIAL PSYCHOLOGICAL ATTITUDES**

*Published by Institute of Social Research, University of Michigan, Ann Arbor. Revised edition 1973.

SHAW AND WRIGHT COMPILATION OF SCALES FOR THE MEASUREMENT OF ATTITUDES

4.M.4

The following list of 175 attitude inventories and scales have been classified so that the researcher may examine such common areas of interest as: Family and Child, Education, Work and Occupations, Economics, Religion, Welfare, Politics and Law, Nationalism and Internationalism, War, Mass Media, Race and Ethnicity, Health and Medicine, and Personal Interaction and Customary Behavior. All scales may be examined in Marvin E. Shaw and Jack M. Wright, *Scales for the Measurement of Attitudes* (New York: McGraw-Hill, 1967).

Family and Child

A Survey of Opinions Regarding the Bringing Up of Children (Itkin 1952)
A Survey of Opinions Regarding the Discipline of Children (Itkin 1952)
Attitude Toward Discipline Exercised by Parents (Itkin 1952)
Attitude Toward the Freedom of Children (Koch, Dentler, Dysart, and Streit 1934)
Attitude Toward Parental Control of Children's Activities (Stott 1940)
Attitude Toward Self-Reliance (Ojemann 1934)
Attitude Toward the Use of Fear as a Means of Controlling the Behavior of Children (Ackerley 1934)
Attitude Toward Parents Giving Sex Information to Children Between the Ages of Six and Twelve (Ackerley 1934)
Attitude Toward Older Children Telling Lies (Ackerley 1934)
The Traditional Family Ideology (TFI) Scale (Levinson and Huffman 1955)
Familism Scale (Bardis 1959)
The Family Scale (Rundquist and Sletto 1936)
Attitudes Toward Parents (Form F) (Itkin 1952)
Parents' Judgment Regarding a Particular Child (Itkin 1952)
Attitudes Toward Feminism Belief Patterns Scale (Kirkpatrick 1936)
The Open Subordination of Women (OSW) Scale (Nadler and Morrow 1959)
Attitude Toward Divorce (Thurstone 1929–34)
A Divorce Opinionnaire (Hardy 1957)
Attitude Toward Birth Control (Wang and Thurstone 1931)
Birth Control (Scale BC) Scale (Wilke 1934)
[Panos D. Bardis has constructed "A Pill Scale: A Technique for the Measurement of Attitudes Toward Oral Contraception," *Social Science* (January 1969): 35–42.]

Education

Attitude Toward Teaching (F. D. Miller 1934)
Attitude Toward Teaching as a Career (Merwin and DiVesta 1960)
Attitude Toward Physical Education as a Career for Women (Drinkwater 1960)
Attitude Toward Education (Mitchell 1941)
Opinionnaire on Attitudes Toward Education (Lindgren and Patton 1958)
Education Scale (Kerlinger and Kaya 1959)
Attitude Toward Intensive Competition in Team Games (McCue 1953)
Attitude Toward Intensive Competition for High School Girls (McGee 1956)
The Education Scale (Rundquist and Sletto 1936)
Attitude Toward Education (Glassey 1945)
Attitudes Toward Mathematics (Gladstone, Deal, and Drevdahl 1960)
Revised Math Attitude Scale (Aiken and Dreger 1961)
Physical Education Attitude Scale (Wear 1955)
Counseling Attitude Scale (Form 1955)
Problem-Solving Attitude Scale (Carey 1958)
High School Attitude Scale (Remmers 1960)
Knowledge About Psychology (KAP) Test (Costin 1963)
An Attitude Scale for Measuring Attitude Toward Any Teacher (Hoshaw 1935)
Attitude Toward Any School Subject (Silance and Temmers 1934)
A Scale to Study Attitudes Toward College Courses (Hand 1953)
Attitudes Toward School Integration (IA) Scale Form I (Greenberg, Chase, and Cannon 1957)
Faculty Morale Scale for Institutional Improvement (AAUP 1963)
Attitude Toward College Fraternities (Banta 1961)

Work and Occupation

Attitude Toward Labor Scale (Newcomb 1939)
IRC (Industrial Relations Center) Union Attitude Questionnaire (Uphoff and Dunnette 1956)
Scale for Management Attitude Toward Union (Stagner, Chalmers, and Derber 1958)
About Your Company (Storey 1955)
Scales to Measure Attitudes Toward the Company, Its Policies, and Its Community Contributions (Riland 1959)
Attitude Toward Earning a Living (Hinckley and Hinckley 1939)
Attitude Toward Work Relief as a Solution to the Financial Depression (Hinckley and Hinckley 1939)
Attitude Toward Farming (Myster 1944)
Attitude Toward Any Practice (Bues 1934)
Attitude Toward Any Home-Making Activity (Kellar 1934)
Attitude Toward Any Occupation (H. E. Miller 1934)
Attitude Toward the Supervisor (AS) Scale (Schmid, Morsh, and Detter 1956)
The Superior-Subordinate (SS) Scale (Chapman and Campbell 1957)
Attitude Toward the Supervisor (Nagle 1953)
Attitude Toward Employment of Older People (Kirchner, Lindbom, and Patterson 1952)
The (Work Related) Change Scale (Trumbo 1961)

Attitudes Toward Dependability: Attitude Scale for Clerical Workers (Dudycha 1941)
Attitudes Toward Legal Agencies (Chapman 1953)
Older Workers Questionnaire (Tuckman and Lorge, 1952)

Economic

Attitude Toward the Tariff (Thurstone 1929-34)
Distribution of the Wealth (DW) Scale (Wilke 1934)

Religion

Religionism Scale: Scale I (Ferguson 1944)
Belief Pattern Scale; Attitude of Religiosity (Kirkpatrick 1949)
Religious Ideology Scale (Putney and Middleton 1961)
The Religious Attitude Inventory (Ausubel and Schpoont 1957)
The Religion Scale (Bardis 1961)
Religious Belief Scale (Martin and Nichols 1962)
A Survey of Attitudes Toward Religion and Philosophy of Life (Funk 1958)
The Existence of God Scale (Scale G) (Wilke 1934)
Attitude Toward God: The Reality of God (Chave and Thurstone 1931)
Attitude Toward God: Influence on Conduct (Chave and Thurstone 1931)
Attitude Toward the Church (Thurstone 1931)
Attitudes and Beliefs of LDS Church Members Toward Their Church and Religion (Hardy 1940)
Attitude Toward Sunday Observance (Thurstone 1929-34)
An Attitude Scale Toward Church and Religious Practices (Dynes 1955)
Relation Between Religion and Psychiatry Scale (Webb and Kobler 1961)
Attitudes Toward Evolution (Thurstone 1931)
Death Attitudes Scale (Kalish 1963)

Welfare

Attitude Toward Receiving Relief (Hinckley and Hinckley 1939)
Humanitarianism Scale: Scale II (Ferguson 1944)
Belief Pattern Scale; Attitude of Humanitarianism (Kirkpatrick 1949)
Attitudes Toward Any Proposed Social Action (Remmers 1934)

Politics and Law

The Conservatism-Radicalism (C-R) Opinionnaire (Lentz 1935)
The Florida Scale of Civic Beliefs (Kimbrough and Hines 1963)
The Economic Conservatism Scale (Rundquist and Sletto 1936)
Questionnaire on Politico-Economic Attitudes (Sanai 1950)
Conservatism-Radicalism (C-R) Battery (Centers 1949, Case 1963)
Tulane Factors of Liberalism-Conservatism Attitude Value Profile (Kerr 1936)
The Social Attitudes Scale (Kerlinger 1965)
Political and Economic Progressivism (PAP) Scale (Newcomb 1943)
Public Opinion Questionnaire (Edwards 1941)
Attitude Toward the Law (Katz and Thurstone 1931)
The Law Scale (Rundquist and Sletto 1936)

The Ideological and Law-Abidingness Scales (Gregory 1939)
Attitudes Toward Law and Justice (Watt and Maher 1958)
Attitude Toward the Constitution of the United States (Rosander and Thurstone 1931)
Attitude Toward Capital Punishment (Balogh and Mueller 1960)
Attitude Toward Capital Punishment (Thurstone 1932)
Attitude Toward Punishment of Criminals (Wang and Thurstone 1931)
Attitude Toward the Police (Chapman 1953)
Attitude Toward Probation Officers (Chapman 1953)
Juvenile Deliquency Attitude (JDA) Scale (Alberts 1962)
The Academic Freedom Survey (Academic Freedom Committee, American Civil Liberties Union 1954)

Nationalism and Internationalism

Internationalism Scale (Likert 1932)
Nationalism Scale: Scale III (Ferguson 1942)
A Survey of Opinions and Beliefs about International Relations (Helfant 1952)
The Internationalism-Nationalism (IN) Scale (Levinson 1957)
The Worldmindedness Scale (Sampson and Smith, 1957)
The Patriotism (NP) Scale (Christiansen 1959)
Attitude Toward Patriotism Scale (Thurstone 1929-34)
Attitude Toward Communism Scale (Thurstone 1929-34)

War

The Peterson War Scale (Thurstone 1929-34)
A Scale of Militarism-Pacifism (Droba 1931)
Attitude Toward Defensive, Cooperative, and Aggressive War (Day and Quackenbush 1942)
Attitude Toward War (Scale W) (Wilke 1934)
A Scale for Measuring Attitude Toward War (Stagner 1942)
The M-P Opinion Scale (Gristle 1940)

Mass Media

Attitude Toward Newspapers (Rogers 1955)
Attitude Toward Freedom of Information (Rogers 1955)
Attitude Toward Movies (Thurstone 1930)
Semantic Distance Questionnaire (Weaver 1959)

Race and Ethnicity

Attitude Toward the Negro (Hinckley 1932)
Attitude Toward Segregation Scale (Rosenbaum and Zimmerman 1959)
The Segregation Scale (Peak, Morrison, Spivak, and Zinnes 1956)
The Desegregation Scale (Kelly, Ferson, and Holtzman 1958)
Attitude Toward Accepting Negro Students in College (Grafton 1964)
Attitude Toward Negroes (Thurstone 1931)
Attitude Toward the Negro Scale (Likert 1932)
The Anti-Negro Scale (Steckler 1957)
Negro Behavior Attitude Scale (Rosander 1937)

Experiences with Negroes (Ford 1941)
The Social Situations Questionnaire (Kogan and Downey 1956)
The Anti-Semitism (A-S) Scale (Levinson and Sanford 1944)
Attitude Toward Jews Scale (Harlan 1942)
Opinions on the Jews (Eysenck and Crown 1949)
The Anti-White Scale (Steckler 1957)
Attitude Toward the German People (Thurstone 1931)
Attitude Toward the Chinese (Thurstone 1931)
A Survey of Opinions and Beliefs about Russia: The Soviet Union (Smith 1946)
Ethnocentrism Scale (Levinson 1949)
Intolerant-Tolerant (IT) Scale (Prentice 1956)
The Social Distance Scale (Bogardus 1925)
Scale to Measure Attitudes Toward Defined Groups (Grice 1935)

Health and Medicine

Attitudes Toward Physical Fitness and Exercise (Richardson 1960)
Opinions About Mental Illness (Cohen and Struening 1959)
The Socialized Medicine Attitude Scale (Mahler 1953)
Attitude Toward Censorship Scale (Rosander and Thurstone 1931)
Attitudes Toward Mentally Retarded People (Bartlett, Quay, and Wrightsman 1960)
The Custodial Mental Illness Ideology (CMI) Scale (Gilbert and Levinson 1956)
The Psychotherapy-Sociotherapy Ideology (PSI) Scale (Sharaf and Levinson 1957)
Medication Attitudes (Gorham and Sherman 1961)
Attitude to Blindness Scale (Cowen, Underberg, and Verrillo 1958)
Attitude Toward Disabled People (ATDP) Scale (Yuker, Block, and Campbell 1960)
Medical Information Test (Perricone 1964)
Attitude Toward Menstruation (McHugh and Wasser 1959)
The Vivisection Questionnaire (Molnar 1955)
Attitudes Toward Mental Hospitals (Souelem 1955)
Attitudes Relating to the State Hospital (Pratt, Giannitrapani, and Khanna 1960)

Personal Interaction and Customary Behavior

The Self-Others Questionnaire (Phillips 1951)
Acceptance of Self and Others (Berger 1952)
People in General (Banta 1961)
An Intimacy Permissiveness Scale (Christensen and Carpenter 1962)
Old People (OP) Scale (Kogan 1961)
The "CI" Attitude Scale (Khanna, Pratt, and Gardiner 1962)
The Chivalry (C) Scale (Nadler and Morrow 1959)
Attitudes Toward Old People (Tuckman and Lorge 1953)
Attitude Toward Any Institution (Kelley 1934)
Attitude Toward the Aesthetic Value (Cohen 1941)
The Competitive Attitude (CA) Scale (Lakie 1964)
The "Value Inventory" (Jarrett and Sherriffs 1953)
Attitude Toward Safe Driving: Siebrecht Attitude Scale (Siebrecht 1941)

part 5

Research Funding, Costing, and Reporting

THE end product of research designing is a proposal. The student setting forth on his or her first independent research or the professional with a lifetime of research achievement both face the same requirement. They must produce an acceptable proposal. Other professionals will critically examine the proposal and decide if it is acceptable. The planning and submission of proposals may take up to a year or more—always longer than expected. The competition for funds is often intense. More proposals are generally rejected than accepted because of the quality of the proposal or the limitation of funds. The researcher must know where the money is and develop the skill of research negotiation.

Section A, *Research Funding*, lists various guides to research agencies. A.1 is a list of major financing agencies of social science research and information providing guides to a search for research funding. A.2 is a selected list of federal government and private organizations offering fellowships and grants, with sources of more comprehensive listings. A.3 describes programs of particular relevance including predoctoral and postdoctoral fellowships offered by the National Science Foundation, National Institute of Mental Health, Social Security Administration, and the U.S. Office of Education. The National Science Foundation and the U.S. Department of Health, Education, and Welfare provide the major source of competitive fellowships in the social sciences outside of the universities themselves.

Section B, *Research Costing*, is introduced because this task is difficult. Most researchers have never had training in this aspect of research and they acquire their knowledge by trial and error. Most researchers drastically underestimate the time and effort that will be required to complete their own proposal. There are many unforeseen handicaps and delays.

The Guide to Research Costing, B.1, requires detailed cost data before it can be used. The researcher must secure the going wage rate for interviewers, the cost of transportation, the rate for machine calculation, and so forth. These can not be provided here since they vary by time and place. However, the guide will alert the social scientist to the factors that must be taken into account in planning the cost of the research. It should be remembered that overhead costs are not shown. Universities usually demand substantial overhead costs ranging from 30 to 50 percent of the total contract.

The Guide to Research Budgeting, B.2, is the form used by the National Science Foundation. This guide provides all items in the budget that may be required in a research project. If the college or university has a contract research officer, seek his help. The researcher can easily overlook some important items or misjudge the expenditures required. Most universities have strict regulations governing all expenditures, and the researcher must learn of these and follow them.

Section C, *Research Reporting.* Finally, plans for the report must be made. This is the "payoff" for the researcher. Specifications for Sociological Report Rating, C.1, indicates the criteria that judges will commonly use in appraising the publishing possibilities of the report. The Form for Sociological Report Rating, C.2, will provide a final check on the research design at the point where it counts—transmission to the profession.

Generally, two or three professional examiners will be using similar criteria in determining upon their recommendation for acceptance or rejection of the research report. Recently the editors of the five journals sponsored by the American Sociological Association reported an average acceptance of fifteen percent. Learning how to handle rejection, the most common experience, is never taught to researchers. It is probably one of the most significant adjustments they must make. They must learn to utilize the criticism of their work and try to meet objections if possible. Often what is needed is better writing. The best advice for all researchers is to rewrite and resubmit. There are scores of journals. Try to get in the best, but above all, try to get published.

John Pease and Joan (Rytina) Huber began a compilation of world sociological journals in 1967. Since then, Lawrence Rhoades has compiled an author's guide to selected sociological and related journals. This is Guide to Sociological Journals and Related Journals, C.3.

C.4 is devoted to publishing in books and journals. Norval Glenn lists the prestige accorded sixty-three journals used frequently by sociologists. C.5 describes how sociologists get published.

A professional research life includes professional communication and reporting to professional meetings. C.6, Professional Communication and Reporting, describes the leading sociological associations and the role they play in professional socialization.

C.7 is a calendar of annual meetings of various sociological societies and some related societies in the social sciences. Although these meetings change officers and meeting places each year, the national offices can supply current information. Common patterns of topical sections for sociology, psychology, and anthropology are shown.

C.8 and C.9 list journals sponsored by the American Sociological Association and the American Psychological Association respectively.

C.10 through C.13 are Guides to Major Journals in Political Science and Public Administration, Anthropology, Education, and Business respectively.

section **A**

Research Funding

MAJOR FINANCING AGENCIES OF SOCIAL SCIENCE RESEARCH   *5.A.1*

1. U.S. Department of Health, Education, and Welfare

National Institute of Mental Health
5454 Wisconsin Avenue
Chevy Chase, Md. 20203

U.S. Office of Education
Bureau of Research
Washington, D.C. 20201

Social Security Administration
Office of Research and Statistics
330 Independence Avenue
Washington, D.C. 20201

2. National Science Foundation
The Fellowship Office
National Research Council
2101 Constitution Avenue, N.W.
Washington, D.C. 20418

3. U.S. Department of Labor
Office of Manpower Policy, Education, and Research
Washington, D.C. 20201

4. Social Science Research Council
230 Park Avenue
New York, N.Y. 10017

5. Ford Foundation
320 East 43 Street
New York, N.Y. 10017

6. Rockefeller Foundation
111 West 50 Street
New York, N.Y. 10020

7. Carnegie Foundation
   589 Fifth Avenue
   New York, N.Y. 10017

8. Russell Sage Foundation
   230 Park Avenue
   New York, N.Y. 10017

9. National Endowment for the Humanities
   806 15 Street, N.W.
   Washington, D.C. 20506
   (Grants for humanistically oriented sociology projects)

For further information see *Annual Register of Grant Support* (current edition) Marquis Academic Media, subsidiary of Marquis Who's Who, Inc., which lists more than 1700 sources of nonrepayable funds.

Another way of conducting a research for research funding is to consult the information compiled by The Foundation Center on about 26,000 American foundations.

Information compiled by The Foundation Center is available to the public through national collections in three cities, regional collections in 39 states, publications and services, and membership in an associates program.

The national collections of source materials on the foundations and their grant-making activities includes the basic records filed by every private foundation with the Internal Revenue Service, annual reports, and the Center's standard reference works. Also available are books, reports, and guides relating to the foundation field.

The New York collection also includes reference materials on foundations in other countries, as well as information on the international activities of American foundations.

The national collections are located at the following addresses:

The Foundation Center, 888 Seventh Avenue, New York, N.Y. 10019.

The Foundation Center, 1001 Connecticut Avenue, N.W., Washington, D.C. 20036.

Donors' Forum, 208 South LaSalle Street, Chicago, Ill. 60604.

In addition, 49 regional collections are located in 39 states. These collections contain the Center's standard reference works, some recent books and reports on foundations, foundation annual reports on film, and a smaller collection of foundation information returns limited usually to the state in which the collection is located. Selected computer listings of grants data on topics of broad general interest are available for consultation. A listing of the regional collections is available from the New York office.

Anyone who visits the national or regional collections may consult all of the published sources and film records, including subject lists of recent foundation grants, without charge. Reference staff is available to assist visitors.

In addition to the collections, The Foundation Center produces some publications which are most likely available in the reference section of a nearby college, university or public library. They may also be purchased from the Columbia University Press.

The publications are:

The Foundation Directory and *Supplements* which contain information on the 2533 largest foundations in the country. These foundations account for about 90 percent of all foundation assets and 80 percent of all grants given in this country.

The Center also plans to publish regional directories in order to provide information on the smaller foundations.

The Foundation Grants Index which is published bimonthly in *Foundation News*. The *Index* report grants by state in which foundation is located, by recipient and by subject matter.

Foundation News is published by the Council on Foundations, Inc., 888 Seventh Ave., New York, N.Y. 10019.

Several leaflets dealing with information sources to foundation facts, proposal writing, and evaluation of proposal are available for free from the Center.

Selected listings of grants made by the foundations in 1972 and 1973 may be purchased on microfiche for a nominal charge from the Center. The grants are grouped into 31 broad subject areas including psychology/sociology. Request order forms from the New York office.

Finally, the Center's Associates Program provides individuals and nonprofit organizations with telephone reference services, mail service, copying services, custom searches, library research service and custom computer searches. A membership fee is charged.

The Center is an educational corporation chartered in 1956 by the Board of Regents of the University of the State of New York and is governed by its own Board of Trustees. It has been supported principally by foundation grants.

Federal Government Contract Research

Any academic institution seriously interested in contract research should have somebody who reads *Commerce Business Daily* and refers relevant announcements to interested faculty immediately. Subscriptions to the *Commerce Business Daily* may be obtained from the Superintendent of Documents, U.S. Government Printing Office, Washington, D.C. 20402.

The Art and Science of Grantsmanship

The procurement of grants and contracts is a game that many universities and research institutes play. For many of these organizations, research funding is big business amounting to millions of dollars yearly.[1] A large part of the funding of graduate students rests upon a steady flow of federal research grants.

"Grantsmanship" sometimes refers to a personality attribute (like showmanship): The ability to persuade and influence others to trade their research dollars for a promised performance. At other times, it refers to an elaborate institutional mechanism (Division of Research and Development) erected solely to influence the flow of research dollars to a given institution. Prestige and power are thrown into the operation in a competitive game to get more and more. Individual researchers who stay outside these contests often pay the price: underfunding. Those who get in pay another kind of price: large amounts of time and energy expended in cultivating contacts and writing proposals. It is also not commonly understood that the recipient of a large research grant is almost automatically converted from a research investigator to a research administrator. He or she gives up field research for the recruiting of personnel, drafting of reports, supervision of professional and staff members, and the endless flow of paper between the financial offices of the university and the granting agency. (Of course, well-funded researchers get the right people to assume much of the administrative responsibility.)

Since grantsmanship is part art and part management, no one can teach it with high efficiency. Experience is the best teacher. And it is necessary to have experience in both grants and contracts. Clive Veri provides experienced guidance for successful pursuance of grants.[2] Keith Baker describes how to get a contract that he calls "the new grantsmanship" and by which he means "contractmanship."[3] Dave Krathwohl and George R. Allen have detailed advice for proposal writing in general.[4]

Notes

1. According to the National Science Foundation, federal spending in 1971 for applied research totaled $89,099,000 for Sociology, $49,855,000 for Economics, and $66,833,000 for Psychology.

2. Clive C. Veri, "How to Write a Proposal and Get It Funded," *Adult Leadership* 16, no. 9 (March 1968): 318–20; 343–44.

3. Keith Baker, "A New Grantsmanship," *American Sociologist* 10, no. 4 (November 1975): 206–18.

4. David R. Krathwohl, *How to Prepare a Research Proposal* (Syracuse, N.Y.: Syracuse University Bookstore, 1965); George R. Allen, *The Graduate Student's Guide to Theses and Dissertations: A Political Manual for Writing and Research* (San Francisco: Jossey-Bass, 1973).

5.A.2 **SELECT LIST OF FEDERAL GOVERNMENT AGENCIES AND PRIVATE ORGANIZATIONS OFFERING FELLOWSHIPS AND GRANTS**

American Council of Learned Societies, 345 East 46 Street, New York, N.Y. 10017. Several categories of fellowships and grants for which scholars in various fields whose research programs have predominantly humanistic emphasis may apply.

American Philosophical Society, 104 South Fifth Street, Philadelphia, Pa. 19106. Grants averaging $800 and not exceeding $2000 to individuals for expenses of research in all fields, including the social sciences. Awards made on the first Fridays of October, December, February, April, and June; applications due 8 weeks in advance; the Society does not offer fellowships or predoctoral grants.

Danforth Foundation, 222 South Central Avenue, St. Louis, Mo. 63105. Several fellowship programs for men and women at various stages of graduate study. Applicants must be planning for careers in college teaching or administration; fields of study common to the undergraduate liberal arts curriculum in the United States.

Henry L. and Grace Doherty Foundation, Doherty Fellowship Committee, Program in Latin American Studies, 240 East Pyne, Princeton University, Princeton, N.J. 08540. Fellowships for advanced study in Latin America.

The Ford Foundation. 1. Postdoctoral grants for research in Southeast Asia in the social sciences and humanities: address inquiries to Southeast Asia Regional Council, Box 17, 5828 South University Avenue, Chicago, Ill. 60637.

2. Graduate Fellowship Program for black Americans, Mexican-Americans, Native Americans (American Indians), and Puerto Ricans planning a career in higher education and enrolled in or planning to enter an accredited U.S. graduate school in the social sciences, natural sciences, or humanities: black American students address inquiries to Graduate Fellowships for Black Americans, National Fellowships Fund, 795 Peachtree Street, N.E., Suite 484, Atlanta, Ga. 30308; Mexican-American and Native American students address inquiries to Educational Testing Service, Box 200, Berkeley, Calif. 94704; Puerto Rican students address inquiries to Graduate Fellowships for Puerto Ricans, Educational Testing Service, Box 2822, Princeton, N.J. 08540.

Japan Foundation, Suite 430, Watergate Office Building, 600 New Hampshire Avenue, N.W., Washington, D.C. 20037. Postdoctoral grants and dissertation fellowships for research conducted in Japan in the social sciences, the humanities, and professional fields.

Fulbright-Hays and other U.S. Government awards for predoctoral study and postdoctoral research in certain foreign countries: address inquiries concerning predoctoral applications to Institute of International Education, 809 United Nations Plaza, New York, N.Y. 10017; postdoctoral applications to Council for International Exchange of Scholars, 2101 Constitution Avenue, N.W., Washington, D.C. 20418.

John Simon Guggenheim Memorial Foundation, 90 Park Avenue, New York, N.Y. 10016. Postdoctoral fellowships in social sciences and other fields.

National Endowment for the Humanities, 806 15 Street, N.W., Washington, D.C. 20506. Research grants and fellowships for humanists and certain social scientists whose projects will strengthen the humanistic aspects of a social science.

The National Institutes of Health offer research and research-training grants and awards in the biomedical and health-related sciences. For information, write Division of Research Grants, National Institutes of Health, Bethesda, Md. 20014.

The National Institute of Mental Health. For information on research grants, address Social Sciences Section, Behavioral Sciences Research Branch, Division of Extramural Research Programs, NIMH, Parklawn Bldg., 5600 Fishers Lane, Rockville, Md. 20852.

Other Agencies of the U.S. Department of Health, Education, and Welfare (Washington, D.C. 20201) that offer grants for research relevant to their respective responsibilities are the following: Office of Education, Social Security Administration, Vocational Rehabilitation Administration, Welfare Administration.

National Science Foundation, Washington, D.C. 20550. Research grants and fellowships in anthropology, economics, geography, history and philosophy of science, linguistics, political science, psychology, and sociology. Also included are interdisciplinary areas composed of two or more overlapping fields, and work in the field of law which employs the methodology of the social sciences or which interrelates with research in the natural or social sciences and research on science policy. Not supported is research or study in business administration, clinical psychology, or social work. Predoctoral fellowships are open only to students who have completed not more than one year of graduate study. The NSF also administers NATO Postdoctoral and Senior Fellowships, in cooperation with the Department of State. Research grants are intended primarily for established scholars. A special program of doctoral dissertation research grants provides assistance toward the expenses of research but does not include a stipend.

Population Council, 245 Park Avenue, New York, N.Y. 10017. Fellowships and grants for training and research in demography and in family planning.

The Rockefeller Foundation, 1133 Avenue of the Americas, New York, N.Y. 10036. Several categories of research fellowships and grants including a fellowship program in environmental affairs, fellowships in conflict in international relations, and the Rockefeller Foundation and Ford Foundation program in support of population policy research in the social sciences.

Social Science Research Council, 605 Third Avenue, New York, N.Y. 10016. Several categories of research fellowships and grants including (1) postdoctoral research training fellowships, (2) grants to minority scholars for research on racism and other social factors in mental health, (3) postdoctoral fellowships in criminal justice indicators, (4) fellowships for international doctoral research, (5) postdoctoral grants for research on foreign areas, (6) grant programs for training and travel in foreign countries. Programs 4, 5, 6 sponsored jointed with American Council of Learned Societies.

More comprehensive listings of other fellowship and grant opportunities may be found in:

A Selected List of Major Fellowship Opportunities and Aids to Advanced Education for United States Citizens. National Research Council, 2101 Constitution Avenue, N.W., Washington, D.C. 20418.

Handbook on International Study for U.S. Nationals. Institute of International Education, 809 United Nations Plaza, New York, N.Y. 10017.

Study Abroad. UNESCO, 75 Place de Fontenoy, Paris VII, France.

A Guide to Selected Fellowships and Grants for Research on Latin America and the Caribbean, by Michael Potashnik. Social Science Research Council, 605 Third Avenue, New York, N.Y. 10016.

5.A.3. PROGRAMS OF PARTICULAR RELEVANCE INCLUDING PREDOCTORAL AND POSTDOCTORAL FELLOWSHIPS

National Science Foundation
Washington, D.C. 20550

Information may be obtained by writing to the foundation, and informal communication with the foundation's staff is encouraged prior to formal submission of a proposal. Among a variety of forms of foundation support, the activities of greatest interest to sociologists are:

1. Grants for *basic scientific research*, or for related activities, such as research conferences, construction of specialized research facilities, and travel to selected meetings of international scientific organizations of major importance. In addition, social science dissertation research grants provide funds for research expenses (not stipends) in order to improve the quality and significance of dissertations and reduce the time required for their completion. All of these programs seek basic scientific understanding of behavioral and social processes and improved research methods. Support is provided for research which seeks to discover and test scientific generalizations.

2. Programs in *science education*. Sociologists are eligible for support in fellowship programs ranging from graduate through senior postdoctoral. In addition, departments of sociology may apply for graduate traineeships for award to their full-time students. Various programs designed to identify and train promising scientists from secondary school students to senior scientists include institutes for retraining school or college teachers, science course content improvement efforts, and participation in research by students and teachers. All grants and fellowships are awarded on the basis of merit without quotas for any field of science, institution, or geographic area.

3. *Institutional programs*. NSF programs which assist universities and colleges in upgrading their science competence include University Science Development, Graduate Science Facilities, Departmental Science Development, and College Science Improvement.

4. *Computing activities* in education and research. Innovative uses of computers by sociologists in instruction and research are supported by the Office of Computing activities.

5. In the area of *science policy and management*, the foundation contracts for studies or surveys of certain topics, such as communication among scientists, funding of U.S. science, and science manpower resources.

6. *Research Applied to National Needs (RANN)*. The foundation considers proposals for support of basic and applied research related to selected problems of society. Proposals for support under the RANN program are evaluated for their potential relevance to important national problems as well as for their scientific merit.

7. *Construction or Renovation of Graduate-Level Training and Research Facilities*. The foundation may support up to half of the cost of facilities for research and training of graduate students and postdoctoral personnel. Facilities may include any kind of space for research and training, except classrooms. Funds may also be requested for half the cost of movable and general-purpose laboratory apparatus, provided the cost does not exceed 15 percent of the total grant. For further information, write the Division of Institutional Programs, National Science Foundation.

Detailed information on all foundation programs is available in the NSF publication *Guide to Programs* issued annually. This is probably available in your college business or research office. It may also be obtained for $1.70 from the Superintendent of Documents, U.S. Government Printing Office, Washington, D.C. 20402.

National Science Foundation Division of Social Sciences Sociology and Social Psychology Programs

The Division of Social Sciences supports basic research and related activities in anthropology, economic and social geography, economics, the history and philosophy of science, linguistics, political science, social psychology, and sociology.

Included in the sociology and social psychology programs are: sociology, social psychology, demography, psycholinguistics, and basic studies of research methodology applicable to these fields.

Research in physiological and experimental psychology and in animal behavior is supported by the foundation's Psychobiology Program, Division of Biological and Medical Sciences. Application procedures are similar for both programs. The foundation does not provide support for research in clinical psychology.

GRANTS FOR SCIENTIFIC RESEARCH

Application Procedures

Formal application blanks are not used in the research grants program. The foundation's guide for the submission of research proposals contains suggestions for the preparation of proposals. Each proposal should contain the following information:

1. Name and address of institution.
2. Name, address (if different), and department of principal investigator(s). Telephone numbers are helpful.
3. Title of proposed research project.
4. Desired starting date (the earliest date on which funds would be required).
5. Time period for which support is requested.
6. Abstract of description of proposed research project.
7. Description of proposed research project, including objectives and research design.
8. Bibliography of related research.
9. Description of facilities available for the research.
10. Biographical information for senior personnel, and for junior personnel when appropriate, including bibliographies.
11. Budget.
12. Statement of current support and pending applications for this and other research by the principal investigator(s).

Please use this as a check list when submitting an application. Twenty complete copies of the proposal should be submitted. One copy should be signed by the principal investigator, by the department head, and by an official authorized to sign for the institution. For more complete information, see NSF 73-12, *Grants for Scientific Research.*

Other Related Research Activities

Includes support for research conferences, construction of specialized research facilities, special projects such as data banks, and travel to selected international scientific meetings. Other support for training activities includes summer and academic year institutes for teachers, course content improvement efforts, research participation by students and teachers, advanced science seminars, etc.

Submission Dates

Proposals may be submitted at any time. Processing requires three to six months. To allow time for adequate planning, the following schedule is offered as a guide:

Proposals Should Arrive

In (or Before)	*For Funds Needed In*
January	June–July
April	September–October
September	January–February

For further information on the research grants program, write to: Program Director for Sociology, Donald R. Ploch, Ph.D., or Program Director for Social Psychology, Roland Radloff, Ph.D. For researchers interested in Social Indicators, Dr. Murray Aborn is Program Director; for Law and Social Sciences, Dr. Lawrence Ross is Program Director.

Division of Social Sciences
National Science Foundation
Washington, D.C. 20550

Fellowships and Other NSF Programs of Interest to Social Scientists

Programs in Science Education

Social scientists are eligible to apply for all science education activities. Of particular interest may be the fellowship programs that encompass all levels of advanced study from predoctoral through senior postdoctoral.

1. *Predoctoral*, for students studying for masters or doctorates
2. *Regular Postdoctoral*, doctoral degrees or equivalent required
3. *Senior Postdoctoral*, intended primarily for senior scientists five years or more past the doctoral degree or with equivalent experience and training
4. *Science Faculty*, for college and university teachers who have three years college teaching experience and who plan to continue teaching

Graduate Fellowship Program

It is expected that in fiscal year 1975 the nationally competitive Graduate Fellowship Program will provide approximately 500 new three-year fellowships, to be awarded to beginning graduate students. In addition, approximately 1000 prior-year awardees will be supported. The competition is open only to citizens or nationals of the United States. This competition is administered for the Foundation by the National Research Council.

For the program announcement (E-75-12) write to:

Fellowship Office
National Research Council
2101 Constitution Avenue, N.W.
Washington, D.C. 20418

Faculty Fellowships in Science Applied to Societal Problems

Approximately 90 fellowships for tenures of 3 to 9 months are planned for award in fiscal year 1975 to help faculty members in junior and community colleges, colleges, and universities broaden their perspectives in the applications of science to the problems of our society. The competition is open only to citizens or nationals of the United States who are at the time of application a member of the science teaching faculty of a U.S. institution of higher education.

For the program announcement (E–75–37) write to the Division of Higher Education in Science, National Science Foundation, Washington, D.C. 20550.

Postdoctoral Energy-Related Fellowships

Approximately 90 fellowships for tenures of 6 to 12 months are planned for award in fiscal year 1975 to recent postdoctorals who have demonstrated a special aptitude for research and who have an interest in energy-related problems. The competition is open only to citizens or nationals of the United States. For the program announcement (E–75–37) write to the National Research Council at the address given above.

Energy-Related Graduate Traineeship Program

Energy-related graduate traineeships are offered to help meet the nation's emerging needs for scientific and professional manpower especially trained in energy-related work. In 1975, approximately 80 new traineeships will be awarded for graduate study of energy-related problems.

Grants for Improving Doctoral Dissertation Research in the Social Sciences

These grants are intended to improve the scientific quality of doctoral dissertations in the social sciences by making possible the use of quantities of data, data of better quality from sources that otherwise could not be exploited, and technically more advanced means of acquiring and analyzing data than can ordinarily be afforded by the student or his department. It is also hoped that the time required for the completion of some dissertations can be reduced.

The dissertation must deal with matters of scientific concern. Originality and evidence that a grant will significantly increase the potential social scientific contribution of the research will be principal considerations in making awards.

Funds may be used for such items as travel to specialized libraries, museums, or field research locations; sample survey costs; costs of specialized equipment; purchase of computer time *only* where an appropriate machine is *not* available in the institution; purchase of microfilms and other forms of data; and payments to subjects or for field research expenses. Textbooks and journals cannot be purchased with dissertation research grant funds, and funds may not be used for typing or reproduction of the student's dissertation. These funds may not be used as a stipend. Support for living expenses while conducting the research should be sought from other sources. Requests for expense or per diem allowances for periods when the student is away from his home base for research purposes should be appropriately adjusted to take account of this rule, and must be carefully justified in terms of living costs. No funds can be provided for dependents of students.

Applications may be made on behalf of a student who is at an advanced stage in his graduate training at a U.S. institution for a doctorate in the social sciences or in science policy. (Psychobiology and clinical psychology are not included.) Proposals may be submitted prior to the student's completion of all requirements for the doctorate except the dissertation, although the actual awarding of grants ordinarily will be contingent on their completion.

The application should be submitted by the dissertation advisor, department chairman or chairman of the departmental committee on doctoral degrees. One application may be on behalf of several candidates provided the budget and other information relevant to each candidate are set out as separate parts of the proposal.

For information write the Division of Social Science, National Science Foundation, Washington, D.C. 20550.

National Institute of Mental Health
U.S. Department of Health, Education, and Welfare
5600 Fishers Lane
Rockville, Md. 20852

Programs of particular relevance to sociologists include:

Behavioral Sciences Research Branch, Social Sciences Section. Joyce B. Lazer, Executive Secretary. Stimulates and supports research in the behavioral sciences relevant to an understanding of behavior and mental health. Areas of support include culture and personality, cross-cultural factors, social perception and attitudes, socialization, social structure and dynamics, social change, sociolinguistics, and group behavior.

Applied Research Branch, Social Problems Section. Hubert H. Coburn, Executive Secretary. Supports applied research for studies dealing with mental health aspects of social problems, social systems, program evaluation methods, research utilization processes, mental retardation, and aging.

Applied Research Branch, Juvenile Problems Section. Joseph R. Marches, Acting Executive Secretary. Supports applied research in children and youth problems, school and college mental health, and primary prevention and maladjustive behavior.

Center for Studies of Metropolitan Problems. Joan Schulman, Acting Executive Secretary. Research, training, and demonstration grants. The range of proposals includes the different ways in which commonly recognized social groups perceive and experience urban life; the changing meaning and definition of work in urban settings; new town studies; emergent alternative social forms (e.g., communes, cooperatives, free schools); and mental health aspects of urban planning, environment, and technology.

National Institute of Child Health and Human Development (HEW)
Bethesda, Md. 20014

Center for Population Research, Population and Reproduction Branch. Sydney H. Newman, Ph.D., Behavioral Scientist Administrator.

The center is interested in research grant proposals on the behavioral-social science aspects of population, family planning, and reproductive behavior. An outline is available to suggest scope of interests.

National Institutes of Health
Pre- and Postdoctoral Fellowships

The National Research Service Award Act of 1974 (NRS) authorizes the National Institutes of Health (NIH) and the Alcohol, Drug Abuse, and Mental Health Administration (ADAMHA) to have predoctoral and postdoctoral research training programs—individual fellowships and institutional fellowships (training grants).

Although NIH has this authorization it has been determined (new legislation pending) that individual support would be available only at the postdoctoral level and that predoctoral support would be available only through the institutional fellowship program. Some institutional support at this level may possibly be available through existing NIH training grants and inquiries concerning this kind of support should be directed to the Graduate or Medical Dean of the institution where you would like to study.

INSTITUTIONAL NATIONAL RESEARCH SERVICE AWARDS

A domestic public or nonprofit private institution may apply for a grant for a research training program in a specified area of research from which a number of awards will be made to individuals selected by the training program director at the institution. Grants may also be made to Federal institutions which are eligible under Section 507 of the Public Health Service Act. Support for both predoctoral and postdoctoral trainees may be requested. Each applicant institution must submit an application according to instructions, using forms provided by NIH or ADAMHA.

The applicant institution must have or be able to develop the staff and facilities required for the proposed program. The training program director at the institution will be responsible for the selection and appointment of trainees and the overall direction of the training program. In selecting trainees, the program director must make certain that individuals receiving support meet the eligibility requirements set forth in these guidelines (see pages 2 and 3) and that they will submit a signed Payback Agreement at the time of appointment and prior to receiving any stipend or other allowance from the grant.

The stipends for predoctoral and postdoctoral trainees is the same as for the individual award. In addition to stipends, the applicant institution may request and be provided with tuition, fees, and travel costs for predoctoral trainees; an allowance of up to $1000 for each postdoctoral (in lieu of tuition, fees, and travel); actual indirect costs or 8 percent of the total award for related institutional costs such as salaries, equipment, supplies, etc.

A Statement of Appointment form (PHS–2271) and a Payback Agreement signed by the trainee indicating his or her intent to meet the service or payback requirements must be submitted to the awarding unit at the time the training begins for each appointment or reappointment of a trainee on the grant. Subsequent changes in the terms and conditions of appointments will require amended appointment forms. Any change in training status that will affect the payback requirement must be reported to the awarding unit by the grantee institution.

Applications and Receipt

Application kits containing forms, instructions, and related information may be obtained from Grants Inquiries, Division of Research Grants, NIH, Bethesda, Maryland 20014; from NIMH or NIAA, Grants Management Branch, both located at 5600 Fishers Lane, Rockville, Md. 20852; or NIDA Grants Management Branch, 11400 Rockville Pike, Rockville, Md. 20852. Applicants are encouraged to submit applications well in advance of the published application receipt dates to allow awarding units sufficient time to request any supplemental information which may be required. Application receipt dates will be widely distributed in NIH and ADAMHA announcements. Applications received too late for one review will be considered at the next review cycle.

The Alcohol, Drug Abuse, and Mental Health Administration Pre- and Postdoctoral Fellowships

The Alcohol, Drug Abuse, and Mental Health Administration (ADAMHA) of HEW has *predoctoral* national research service awards available for behavioral research. Awards are made to *individual applicants* selected as a result of national competition.

To be eligible, one must be a citizen or noncitizen national of the United States, or have a permanent visa at the time of application. Further, one must have completed two or more years of graduate work as of the proposed activation date of the award and have a doctoral prospectus.

The annual stipend for predoctoral individuals is $3900. Applications must be received by January and results will be announced in June.

Although fellowships are awarded for twelve-month periods, applicants may receive up to a total of three years' support under the national research service award. Upon completion of the award, recipients are expected to engage in biomedical or behavioral research or teaching for a period equal to the period of support. Individuals who fail to fulfill this obligation may be required to pay back an amount of the stipend received plus interest. All applicants are alerted to this payback agreement.

Given the decreasing level of support for institutional level training grants, graduate students are encouraged to consider the possibility of applying for these individual level fellowships.

The Alcohol, Drug Abuse, and Mental Health Administration also has *postdoctoral* support available. The level of the stipend varies, depending upon the amount of relevant postdoctoral experience one has had. The table which follows gives these levels of stipend for years of relevant experience at entry and for the year of the award:

Years of relevant experience at entry	Year of award		
	1st Year	2nd Year	3rd Year
0	$10,000	$10,400	$10,800
1	10,800	11,200	11,600
2	11,500	11,900	12,300
3	12,200	12,600	13,000
4	12,800	13,200	13,600
5 or more	13,200	13,600	14,000

Individual application kits must be obtained by writing to: Grants Management Officer, National Institute of Mental Health, 5600 Fishers Lane, Rockville, Md. 20852.

For additional information on the ADAMHA programs write to: Division of Extramural Research Training Programs, 5600 Fishers Lane, Rockville, Md. 20852.

Research Career Development Awards

Awards are made to institutions to increase the number of stable full-time career opportunities for scientists of superior potential and capability in the sciences related to health. Institutions may apply for awards on behalf of individuals who have had three or more years of relevant postdoctoral research or professional experience and who are in need of further research career development.

For additional information on the above programs write: Career Development Review Branch, Division of Research Grants, National Institute of Health, Bethesda, Md. 20014.

U.S. Department of Labor, Employment and Training Administration

The Department of Labor is currently spending approximately $13,000,000 a year for research and experimental demonstration projects through its Office of Research and Development in the Employment and Training Administration. These projects include experiments in criminal justice, employment studies, the National Longitudinal Surveys of Labor Force Behavior (as previously reported on page 123), and other areas of interest to sociologists.

For the sociologist on sabbatic leave who wishes to work intensively exploring the research possibilities within the DOL, there is the Intergovernmental Personnel Act (IPA) assignment, whereby DOL pays 49 percent of the academic salary of the professor for research within the Department for a period of a year or more. This program also provides the professor with an opportunity to serve as a participant observer within a large governmental bureaucracy.

For information regarding any of the above R&D areas or for employment opportunities within the R&D office under an IPA, write to: Dr. Howard Rosen, Director, Office of Research and Development, Employment and Training Administration, 601 D Street, NW, U.S. Department of Labor, Washington, D.C. 20213.

Grants for Research in Social Welfare and Social Security

Under the Cooperative Research Grants Program, serving the interests of both agencies, grants are awarded for research on a wide range of questions related to the income maintenance, medical care, and social service programs under the Social Security Act. Particular emphasis is placed on research closely related to important program and policy issues. For example, the major areas of research in the field of Income Maintenance are:

Studies of *alternative types of income-maintenance systems* and their effectiveness in providing adequate earnings replacement and preventing poverty among nonworking and low-income groups.

Analyses of the effects of alternative methods of *social security financing* upon fiscal stability, economic growth, employment, and income distribution.

Assessment of the financing policies and benefit provisions of *private pension and insurance programs* and their effects upon economic security, employment patterns, labor mobility, and earnings maximization.

Determination of alternative measures for the *definitation of income adequacy* applicable to populations of differing demographic characteristics.

Studies of *lifetime employment patterns*, including geographic and occupational mobility; *earnings histories*, asset accumulation and debt; and the allocation of work, training, education, leisure, and unemployment throughout the life cycle.

Studies of the factors affecting the social, psychological, occupational, and financial characteristics of *the aged*, the timing of retirement, and the adequacy of retirement income.

Examination of the immediate and long-range economic, social, and psychological impact of the *loss of a family head*, and associated needs for income, training, and social service support for young and middle-aged dependents.

Analyses of the needs for income support, health services, retraining or relocation assistance in relation to various types of *long- and short-term disability*.

Evaluation of *public knowledge and attitudes* concerning income-maintenance programs.

Comparative studies and in-depth analyses of social security concepts and *programs in other countries*.

Research on topics related to Health Insurance include:

Studies of the effect of Title XVIII Medicare (and related aspects of Title XIX Medicaid) programs on:
 —the *organization, administration, and financing* of health care services;
 —the *purchasing power, spending patterns, and level of living* of covered groups;
 —access to *quality care* for covered groups;
 —*utilization and costs* of alternative mixes of health services and facilities under *public and private programs;* and
 —*public attitudes and knowledge* about health care programs.

Analyses of the needs for the costs and benefits associated with alternative systems for:
 —*financing uncovered health services and products*, including prescription drugs; and
 —providing access to quality health care for *additional segments of the population.*

Studies of the factors associated with *rising health costs* and evaluation of *methods of reimbursement* designed to contain costs without reduction in the quality of care.

Grants may be made only to nonprofit organizations and may not be made to individuals; grantee organizations must pay part of the total cost of the research. Applications are reviewed by an Advisory Panel of nonfederal specialists which recommends applications for approval. Important factors considered in evaluating applications are the potential value and national significance of the knowledge to be gained, soundness of the research design, adequacy of resources to conduct the project, and the relationship of the research to similar work.

If in doubt whether a research proposal is within the scope of the Cooperative Research Program, potential applicants are encouraged to submit a draft of the proposal for review by agency staff. Application deadlines are January 5, May 10, and September 10 for projects that may begin no earlier than May 1, September 1, and January 1 respectively.

Application forms and additional information may be obtained from: Co-operative Research Branch, Office of Research and Demonstrations, Social and Rehabilitation Service, Department of Health, Education, and Welfare, Washington, D.C. 20201. *Or:* Chief, Research Grants Staff, Office of Research and Statistics, Social Security Administration, U.S. Department of Health, Education, and Welfare, 3-B-5 Meadows East Building, 6401 Security Boulevard, Baltimore, Md. 21235.

U.S. Department of Health, Education, and Welfare, Office of Education—Bureau of Research Washington, D.C.

The U.S. Office of Education administers funds for the support of educational research and development through its Bureau of Research. The Bureau is made up of five divisions which deal with elementary education, secondary and vocational education, higher education, information technology and dissemination, and research centers and regional laboratories. Each of the first four divisions handles basic research projects as well as those focused on the development of curricula, methods of teaching and learning, and organizational and administrative procedures in education.

The general purpose of basic research projects is to develop new knowledge about the educational process, thus providing a foundation for further developmental work. The content of basic studies draws primarily on the fields of psychology, for more information about learning and motivation; sociology and anthropology, to examine social and cultural factors related to education; and physiology to explore the relationships between physical and mental functions.

The Bureau of Research identifies, develops, and programs funds for priority areas, but it is always in a position to receive unsolicited proposals, and funds are reserved for this purpose. Also, "guideline" statements pertaining to particular areas are sometimes made available to stimulate their development, and occasional requests for proposals are issued in selected areas. It is always useful for those interested in specific projects to contact appropriate members of the Bureau staff before actually drafting a proposal in order to become acquainted with current directions as a guide to proposal development.

Persons interested in participating in the Office of Education research and development program should request a copy of the pamphlet "Support for Research and Related Activities" from the Bureau of Research, U.S. Office of Education, Washington, D.C. 20202. Those concerned with a project requiring less than $10,000 in federal funds should request information on the "Small Project" program. This program is operated in each of the nine HEW Regional Offices by an educational research advisor who may be contacted directly for information about possibilities for small projects in his region. (Regional offices are listed in the pamphlet mentioned above.)

The Bureau also operates the Educational Resources Information Center (ERIC) which provides direct access to research literature in behavioral sciences and education. Monthly issues of *Research in Education* (available from the Government Printing Office) abstract and index over 700 documents—the latter available from the ERIC Document Reproduction Service, National Cash Register Company, 4936 Fairmont Avenue, Bethesda, Md. 20014.

Research Costing

GUIDE TO RESEARCH COSTING*†   5.B.1

Activity	Total	Week ending ___	Week ending ___	Week ending ___	___

1. Total
   a) Man hours
   b) Cost ($)
   c) % of total completed					

2. Planning
   a) Man-hours
   b) Cost
   c) % completed					

3. Pilot Study and Pretests
   a) Man-hours
   b) Cost
   c) % completed					

4. Drawing Sample
   a) Man-hours
   b) Cost
   c) % completed					

5. Preparing Observational
   Materials
   a) Man-hours
   b) Cost
   c) % completed					

6. Selection and Training
   a) Man-hours
   b) Cost
   c) % completed					

*Source: Russell K. Ackoff, *Design for Social Research* (Chicago: University of Chicago, 1953), p. 347. By permission of the University of Chicago Press. Copyright 1953 by the University of Chicago.

†Suggested form for budget-time schedule summary. (There is nothing necessary or sufficient about this listing of activities, nor is the order absolute in any sense.)

GUIDE TO RESEARCH COSTING (*Continued*)

Activity	Total	Week ending ___	Week ending ___	Week ending ___	___

7. Trial Run
   a) Man-hours
   b) Cost
   c) % completed					

8. Revising Plans
   a) Man-hours
   b) Cost
   c) % completed					

9. Collecting Data
   a) Man-hours
   b) Cost
   c) % completed					

10. Processing Data
   a) Man-hours
   b) Cost
   c) % completed					

11. Preparing Final Report
   a) Man-hours
   b) Cost
   c) % completed					

5.B.2   GUIDE TO RESEARCH BUDGETING

This guide includes all items that are required in the NSF Research Grant Proposal Budget.* If the researcher has carefully followed the Guide to Research Costing, the preparation of the Grant Proposal Budget will be more accurate.

Budget Format

Proposals for research grants should include budgets in the following format for each year of support requested. It is important to note that the use of a budget summary does not eliminate the need for an itemized explanation of proposed costs when required in this booklet.

*National Science Foundation, Grants for Scientific Research, NSF73-12, Appendix III, pp. 34–39. For a copy write National Science Foundation, Washington, D.C. 20550.

RESEARCH GRANT PROPOSAL BUDGET
Year Beginning _____

Budget Category	NSF funded Man-months			Proposed amount
	Cal	Acad	Sum	
A. Salaries and Wages				
1. Senior personnel				
a. (Co) Principal investigator (list by name)	___	___	___	___
b. Faculty associates (list by name)	___	___	___	___
Subtotal				___
2. Other personnel (nonfaculty)				
a. Research associates (postdoctoral) (list separately by name if available, otherwise give numbers)				
. . . .	___	___	___	___
. . . .	___	___	___	___
b. Nonfaculty professionals (list separately, by category, giving number, e.g., one computer programmer)				
. . . .	___	___	___	___
c. (number) Grad. students (Res. Asst.)				___
d. (number) Prebaccalaureate students				___
e. (number) Secretarial-clerical				___
f. (number) Technical, shop, and other				
Total salaries and wages				
B. Staff Benefits				___
C. Total Salaries, wages and staff Benefits (A + B)				
D. Permanent Equipment (list as required)				
1.				___
2.				___
Total permanent equipment				
E. Expendable Supplies and Equipment . . .				
F. Travel				
1. Domestic				___
2. Foreign (list as required)				___
Total travel				
G. Publication Costs				___
H. Computer Costs (if charged as direct costs)				___
I. Other Costs (itemize by major type)				
1.				___
2.				___
3.				___
Total other costs				
J. Total Direct Costs (C through I)				
K. Indirect Costs				
1. On campus . . . . . .% of				___
2. Off campus . . . . .% of				___
Total indirect costs				
L. Total Costs (J plus K)				
M. Total Contributions from Other Sources				___
N. Total Estimated Project Cost				___

Research Reporting

Within the professional code, the reporting of research is one of the mores. Beyond the mundane pressures to publish, there is an underlying normative prescription: *Let the world know what you have found. Add to the storehouse of knowledge. Try to write so that you connect past research with your findings and so that other scholars may build upon your work in the future.*

In this section both oral and written reporting is described. Research reporting usually takes place in a rather closed world where professionals interact with one another either in professional meetings or through learned journals. Some important attributes of this subculture will be described.

SPECIFICATIONS FOR SOCIOLOGICAL REPORT RATING*

5.C.1

	Defective	Substandard	Standard	Superior
Statement of Problem:				
1. Clarity of Statement	Statement is ambiguous, unclear, biased, inconsistent, or irrelevant to the research.	Problem must be inferred from incomplete or unclear statement.	Statement is unambiguous and includes precise description of research objectives.	Statement is unambiguous and includes formal propositions, and specifications for testing them.
2. Significance of Problem	No problem stated, or problem is meaningless, unsolvable, or trivial.	Solution of the problem would be of interest to a few specialists.	Solution of the problem would be of interest to many sociologists.	Solution of the problem would be of interest to most sociologists.
3. Documentation	No documentation to earlier work, or documentation is incorrect.	Documentation to earlier work is incomplete or contains errors of citation or interpretation.	Documentation to earlier work is reasonably complete.	Documentation shows in detail the evolution of the research problem from previous research findings.
Description of Method:				
4. Appropriateness of Method	Problems cannot be solved by this method.	Only a partial or tentative solution can be obtained by this method.	Solution of the problem by this method is possible, but uncertain.	Problem is definitely solvable by this method.
5. Adequacy of Sample or Field	Sample is too small, or not suitable, or biased, or of unknown sampling characteristics.	The cases studied are meaningful, but findings can not be projected.	Findings are projectable, but with errors of considerable, or of unknown, magnitude.	Results are projectable with known small errors, or the entire universe has been enumerated.
6. Replicability	Not replicable.	Replicable in substance, but not in detail.	Replicable in detail with additional information from the author(s).	Replicable in detail from the information given.

*Source: Theodore Caplow designed this form. It was tested by the Committee on Research, American Sociological Society. See "Official Reports and Proceedings," *American Sociological Review* (December 1958), 704–11. Cf. Stuart C. Dodd and Louis N. Gray, "Scient-Scales for Measuring Methodology," Institute for Sociological Research, University of Washington, Seattle, 1962. Mimeograph copies available on request.

SPECIFICATIONS FOR SOCIOLOGICAL REPORT RATING* (Continued)

	Defective	Substandard	Standard	Superior
Presentation of Results:				
7. Completeness				
8. Comprehensibility	Results are incomprehensible, or enigmatic.	Comprehension of results requires special knowledge or skills.	Relevant results are presented, partly in detail, partly in summary form.	Relevant details are presented in detail.
9. Yield	No contribution to solution of problem.	Useful hints or suggestions toward solution of problem.	Tentative solution of problem.	Definitive solution of problem.
Interpretation:				
10. Accuracy	Errors of calculation, transcription, dictation, logic, or fact detected.	Errors likely with the procedures used. No major errors detected.	Errors unlikely with the procedures used. No errors detected.	Positive checks of accuracy included in the procedures.
11. Bias	Evident bias in presentation of results and in interpretation.	Some bias in interpretation, but not in presentation of results.	No evidence of bias.	Positive precautions against bias included in procedures.
12. Usefulness	Not useful.	Possible influence on some future work in this area.	Possible influence on some future work in this area.	Probable influence on all future work in this area.

FORM FOR SOCIOLOGICAL REPORT RATING*

Author _____

Title _____

Publication Reference _____

Rater _____

Date _____

Check (√) Appropriate Columns	Defective 0	Substandard 1	Standard 2	Superior 3
Statement of problem:				
1. Clarity of Statement	_____	_____	_____	_____
2. Significance of Problem	_____	_____	_____	_____
3. Documentation	_____	_____	_____	_____
Description of method:				
4. Appropriateness of Method	_____	_____	_____	_____
5. Adequacy of Sample or Field	_____	_____	_____	_____
6. Replicability	_____	_____	_____	_____
Presentation of results:				
7. Completeness	_____	_____	_____	_____
8. Comprehensibility	_____	_____	_____	_____
9. Yield	_____	_____	_____	_____
Interpretation:				
10. Accuracy	_____	_____	_____	_____
11. Bias	_____	_____	_____	_____
12. Usefulness	_____	_____	_____	_____

Enter number of checks in each column in appropriate blanks; weight as indicated, and add for Total Rating

_ X 0 = 0   _ X 1 = _   _ X 2 = _   _ X 3 = _

[*Total Rating*]
[ ]

*Theodore Caplow designed this rating form. Test reliabilities appear in "Official Reports and Proceedings," *American Sociological Review* 23 (December 1958): 704–11. See also the reports of the Educational Testing Service, Princeton, N.J., for ingenious rating scales on a large variety of subjects.

GUIDE TO SOCIOLOGICAL JOURNALS*

Acta Sociologica (Scandinavian Review of Sociology) Munksgaard, A.S. 47 Prags Boulevard, Copenhagen S., Denmark.

*This guide has been assembled from the work of Lawrence J. Rhoades, John Pease, and Joan Rytina Huber. When first published the guide was the revised work of John Pease. An earlier work was first presented by John Pease and Joan Rytina, "Sociological Journals," *American Sociologist* 3 (February 1968): 41–45. Lawrence Rhoades has now compiled *The Authors Guide to Selected Journals*, Professional Information Series No. 1 (1975), American Sociological Association, 1722 N Street N.W., Washington, D.C. 20036, $3 per copy. The published guide contains a much longer list because it includes all journals that expressed interest in receiving manuscripts from sociologists and social psychologists. Those journals not listed under this section are named in the section immediately following.

1955. Quarterly. Book reviews. Cumulative index for vols. 1–5. Text in English, French, German, and the Scandinavian languages.

The American Journal of Sociology. The University of Chicago Press, 5750 Ellis Avenue, Chicago, Ill. 60637.

1895. Bimonthly. Abstracts. Book reviews. Annual index. Cumulative index for vols. 1–70.

American Sociological Review. American Sociological Association, 1722 N Street N.W., Washington, D.C. 20036.

1936. Bimonthly. Abstracts. Book Reviews. Annual index. Cumulative index for vols. 1–25 and vols. 26–30. Official journal of the American Sociological Association and distributed free to members.

The American Sociologist. American Sociological Association, 1722 N Street N.W., Washington, D.C. 20036.

1966. Quarterly. Devoted primarily to discussion of professional concerns and includes employment bulletins and announcements of professional meetings. Official journal of the American Sociological Association and distributed free to members.

Annual Review of Sociology. American Sociological Association, 1722 N Street N.W., Washington, D.C. 20036.

1975. Bimonthly. Progress reports of developments in various fields of sociology. Official journal of the American Sociological Association.

Archives Européens de Sociologie (European Journal of Sociology). Musée de l'Homme, Palais de Chaillot, F.-75, Paris XVI, France.

1960. Semiannually. Annual index. Text in English, French, and German.

Australian Journal of Social Issues. Australian Council of Social Services, P.O. Box 388, Haymarket 200, Sydney, Australia.

1961. Four issues per year. Significant issues of social welfare, public interest, and social change.

The Australian and New Zealand Journal of Sociology. Department of Social Studies, University of Melbourne, Parkville, N. 2, Victoria, Austrialia.

1965. Semiannually. Abstracts. Book reviews. Annual index. Official journal of the Sociological Association of Australia and New Zealand.

Berkeley Journal of Sociology. 410 Barrows Hall, University of California, Berkeley, Calif. 94720.

1955–58, vols. 1–4 published as *Berkeley Publications in Society and Institutions.* 1959. Annually. Cumulative index for volumes 1–11. Official publication of the Graduate Sociology Club of the University of California at Berkeley.

The British Journal of Sociology. Routledge & Kegan Paul, Ltd., Broadway House, 68–74 Carter Lane, London E.C.4, England.

1950. Quarterly. Book reviews. Annual index. Cumulative index for volumes 1–10.

Canadian Review of Sociology and Anthropology. Department of Sociology, University of Toronto, Toronto M5S 1A1, Ontario, Canada.

1965. Quarterly.

Case Western Reserve Journal of Sociology. Department of Sociology, Case Western Reserve University, Cleveland, Ohio 44106.

1967. Annually. Book reviews.

The Commonwealth Sociologist. Department of Sociology, Penn State University, 206 Liberal Arts Tower, University Park, Pa. 16802.

1970. Semiannually. Provides forums for superior undergraduate and graduate work as well as professional papers.

Contemporary Sociology: A Journal of Review. American Sociological Association. 1722 N Street N.W., Washington, D.C. 20036.

1972. Bimonthly. Book reviews. Book notes. Letters. Official journal of the American Sociological Association.

Contributions to Indian Sociology. Mouton & Company, Herderstraat 5, The Hague, Netherlands.

1957. Irregularly. Book reviews. Annual index.

The Cornell Journal of Social Relations. Sociology Department, Uris Hall, Cornell University, Ithaca, N.Y. 14850.

1966. Semiannually. Publishes especially, but not exclusively, the work of young scholars.

Current Sociology. International Sociological Association. Publisher: Mouton and Company, 43 rue de Lille, Paris 7e, France. Business address: Department of Sociology, University of Warwick, Coventry, Warwickshire, England.

1952. Triannually. Each issue contains an analysis of trends in, and an annotated bibliography on, some aspect of sociology.

et. al. Sociological Corporations. P.O. Box 77951, Los Angeles, Calif. 90007.

1967. Triannually. Each issue is primarily about a single topic.

G.S.S. Journal. Columbia University Graduate Sociology Club, Department of Sociology, Columbia University, 605 West 115 Street, New York, N.Y. 10025.

1961. Triannually. Official journal of the Columbia University Graduate Sociology Club and distributed free to members.

Ghana Journal of Sociology. Department of Sociology, University of Ghana, Legon, Ghana, West Africa.

1963. Semiannually. Book reviews. Official publication of the Ghana Sociological Association.

Graduate Sociology Journal. The Graduate Sociology Club, The University of Pennsylvania, Philadelphia, Pa. 19104.

1960. Annually. Official publication of the Graduate Sociology Club of the University of Pennsylvania and distributed free to members.

Indian Journal of Social Research. Singhal House, Shivaji Road, Meirut (U.P.), India.

1960. Triannually.

The Insurgent Sociologist. Department of Sociology, University of Oregon, Eugene, Ore. 97403.

1970. Quarterly. Devoted to development of new sociology with Marxist orientation.

International Journal of Comparative Sociology. E. J. Brill, Leiden, Netherlands, publisher. Manuscript address: Department of Sociology and Anthropology, York University, Downsview, Ontario M3J 1P3, Canada.

International Journal of Contemporary Sociology (Indian Sociological Bulletin). Rakesh Marg, Pili Kothi, G. T. Road, Ghaziabad, U.P., India.

1963. Quarterly. Book reviews. Annual index.

International Review of Modern Sociology. International Journals, Inc., Department of Sociology, Northern Illinois University, Dekalb, Ill. 60115.

1971. Semiannually.

The Jewish Journal of Sociology. 55 New Cavendish Street, London, W.I, England.

1959. Semiannually. Book reviews. Annual index.

Journal of Health and Social Behavior. American Sociological Association, 1722 N Street N.W., Washington, D.C. 20036.

1960–66 vols. 1–7 published as the *Journal of Health and Human Behavior.* 1967. Quarterly. Book reviews. Annual index. Official publication of the American Sociological Association.

Journal of Mathematical Sociology. Gordon and Breach, Science Publishers, Inc., Department of Social Relations, Carnegie-Mellon University, Pittsburgh, Pa. 15213.

1971. Biannually.

International Journal of Sociology. International Arts and Science Press, Inc. 901 N. Broadway, White Plains, N.Y. 10603.

1971. Quarterly.

International Journal of Sociology of the Family. Department of Sociology, Northern Illinois University, DeKalb, Ill. 60115.

1971. Semiannually.

International Review of Modern Sociology. Department of Sociology, Northern Illinois University, DeKalb, Ill. 60115.

1971. Semiannually.

Journal of Political and Military Sociology. Department of Sociology, Northern Illinois University, DeKalb, Ill. 60115.

1972. Semiannually.

Journal of Sociology and Social Welfare. Department of Sociology, California State University, Northridge, Calif. 91324.

1973. Quarterly.

The Kansas Journal of Sociology. Department of Sociology, The University of Kansas, Lawrence, Kans. 66045.

The Pacific Sociological Review. Sage Publications with Pacific Sociological Association, 275 South Beverly Drive, Beverly Hills, Calif. 90212.

1958. Semiannually. Annual index. Cumulative index for vols. 1–6. Official journal of the Pacific Sociological Association and distributed free to members.

Philippine Sociological Review. Philippine Sociological Society, Central Subscriptions Service, Box 655, Greenhills, Rizal D738, Philippines.

1953. Quarterly. Cumulative index for vols. 1–13. Official journal of the Philippine Sociological Society and distributed free to members.

The Polish Sociological Bulletin. RUCH Export and Import Enterprise, P.O. Box 154, Warsaw I, Poland.

1961. Semiannually. Official publication of the Polish Sociological Association.

Rivista Di Sociologia. Instituto Di Sociologia, Libera Universita, Viale Pola, 12, Roma, Italy.

1963. Quarterly.

The Review of Social Theory. Department of Sociology, University of Missouri, Columbia, Mo. 65207.

1972. Semiannually.

Revista Latino Americana de Sociologia. Instituto Torcuato Di Tella, Virrey del Pino 3230, Buenos Aires, Argentina.

1970. Triannually.

Revista Mexicana de Sociologia. Facultad de Ciencias Politicas y Sociales, Ciudad Universitaria, Mexico 20, D.F.

1938. Quarterly.

Revista de Sociologia. Departamento de Sociologia de la Universidad Nacional Mayor de San Marcos de Lima, Lima, Peru.

1963. Biannually.

Romanian Journal of Sociology. Publishing House of the Romanian People's Republic, Cartimex, Str. 13 Decemvrie 3-5, P.O. Box 134135, Bucharest, Romania.

1962. Volume 1 published as *Rumanian Journal of Sociology.* 1963. Annually. Book reviews. Text in English, French, and Romanian.

Rural Sociology. 206 Weaver Building, Penn State University, University Park, Pa. 16802.

1936. Quarterly. Abstracts. Book reviews. Annual index. Cumulative indexes for vols. 1-20 and vols. 21-30. Official journal of Rural Sociological Society and distributed to members free.

Social Forces. University of North Carolina Press with Southern Sociological Society, 168 Hamilton Hall, University of North Carolina, Chapel Hill, N.C. 27514.

1922-25, vols. 1-3 published as the *Journal of Social Forces.* 1925. Quarterly. Abstracts. Book reviews. Annual index.

Social Problems. Post Office Box 190, Kalamazoo, Mich. 49005.

1953. Quarterly. Book reviews. Annual index. Official journal of the Society for the Study of Social Problems and distributed free to members.

Social Research. New School for Social Research, 65 Fifth Avenue, New York, N.Y. 10003.

1953. Quarterly.

Social Studies: Irish Journal of Sociology. St. Patricks College, Maynooth, Co. Kildare, Ireland.

1972. Bimonthly.

Sociologia. Fundacao Escola de Sociologia e Politica, Rua General Jardin, 522 Sao Paula, SP, Brazil.

1939. Quarterly. Abstracts. Book reviews. Annual index. Text in English and Portuguese.

Sociologia Internationalis. Verlagsbuchhandlung, Duncker and Humblot, 1000 Berlin 41 (Steglitz), Dietrich-Schäfer-Weg 9, Postfact 330, Germany.

1963. Semiannually. Book reviews. Text in English, French, German, and Spanish.

Sociologia Neerlandica. Royal VanGorcum, Limited, Assen, Netherlands.

1962. Semiannually. Book reviews. Official publication of the Netherlands Sociological Society.

Sociologia Ruralis. Royal VanGorcum, Limited, Assen, Netherlands.

1960. Quarterly. Abstracts. Book reviews. Annual index. Text in English, French, and German. Official journal of the European Society for Rural Sociology and distributed to members free.

Sociological Bulletin. Indian Sociological Society, Department of Sociology, Delhi School of Economics, University of Delhi, Delhi-7, India.

1952. Semiannually. Official publication of the Indian Sociological Society.

Sociological Focus. North Central Sociological Association, Department of Sociology, University of Akron, Akron, Ohio 44325.

1967. Quarterly. Official journal of the Ohio Valley Sociological Society and distributed free to members.

Sociological Inquiry. O.I.E.S., 252 Bloor Street West, Toronto, Ontario, Canada M56 1V6.

1930-60, vols. 1–30 published as *Alpha Kappa Deltan.* 1961. Semiannually. Annual index. Each issue devoted to a single topic. Official journal of Alpha Kappa Delta and distributed free to members for the first two years.

Sociological Methods and Research. Sage Publications, 275 South Beverly Drive, Beverly Hills, Calif. 90212.

1972. Quarterly.

The Sociological Quarterly. 1004 Elm Street, Columbia, Mo. 65201.

1953. Quarterly. Book reviews. Annual index. Official journal of the Midwest Sociological Society and distributed free to members.

Sociological Review Monographs. University of Keele, Keele, Staffordshire ST5 5BG, England.

1958. Annually. Each issue is devoted to a single topic.

The Sociological Review. University of Keele, Keele, Staffordshire, ST5 5BG, England.

1953. Triannually. Book reviews. Annual index.

Sociological Studies. Cambridge University Press, 32 East 57 Street, New York N.Y. 10022.

1968. Annually. Each issue is devoted to a single topic.

Sociologie et Societes. Department de Sociologie, Universite de Montreal, Montreal, Canada.

1969. Semiannually. Cross-cultural journals in sociology in French.

Sociological Symposium. Virginia Polytechnic Institute and State University, 660 McBridge Hall, Virginia Polytechnic and State University, Blacksburg, Va. 24061.

1968. Semiannually. Each issue is devoted to a single topic.

Sociologiske Meddelelser. Sociological Institute, University of Copenhagen, Rosenborggrade 15, Copenhagen K, Denmark.

1952. Semiannually. Book reviews. Annual index. Cumulative index for vols. 1–10. Text in Danish (and occassionally in other Scandinavian languages) and English.

Sociologus: New Series. Duncker and Humblot, Dietrich-Schäfer-Weg 9, Berlin 41, Germany.

1951. Semiannually. Abstracts. Book reviews. Text in English and German.

Sociology. British Sociological Association. Publisher: Oxford University Press, Press Road, Neasden, London N.W. 10, ODD, England.

1967. Triannually. Official publication of the British Sociological Association.

Sociology of Education. American Sociological Association, 1722 N Street N.W., Washington, D.C. 20036.

1927–62, vols. 1–36 published as the *Journal of Educational Sociology.* 1963. Quarterly. Abstracts. Annual index. Official publication of the American Sociological Association.

Sociology and Social Research. University of Southern California, 703 West 34 Street, Los Angeles, Calif. 90007.

1916–21, vols. 1–5 published as *Studies in Sociology;* 1921–27, volumes 6–11 published as *Journal of Applied Sociology.* 1927. Quarterly. Abstracts. Book reviews. Annual index. Cumulative index for volumes 1–30.

Sociology of Work and Occupations: An International Journal. Sage Publications, 275 South Beverly Drive, Beverly Hills, Calif. 90212.

1974. Quarterly.

Sociometry. American Sociological Association, 1722 N Street N.W., Washington, D.C. 20036.

1937. Quarterly. Abstracts. Annual index. Official publication of the American Sociological Association.

Soviet Sociology. International Arts and Sciences Press, 108 Grand Street, White Plains, N.Y. 10701.

1962. Quarterly. Book reviews. Annual index. A journal of translations.

Summation. Department of Sociology, Michigan State University, East Lansing, Mich. 48824.

1968. Semiannually. Abstracts. Book reviews. Official journal of the Michigan State University Sociological Association and distributed free to members.

Teaching Sociology. Sage Publications, 275 South Beverly Drive, Beverly Hills, Calif. 90212.

1973. Semiannually.

Theory and Society. Elsevier Scientific Publishing Co., P.O. Box 330, Amsterdam, Netherlands. Renewal and critique in social theory. Editor: Alvin W. Gouldner, Sociologist Instituut, University van Amsterdam, Korte Spinhulsstegg 3, Amsterdam, Netherlands.

The Wisconsin Sociologist: New Series. Department of Sociology, University of Wisconsin-Milwaukee, Milwaukee, Wis. 53211.

1962. Quarterly. Book reviews. Official journal of the Wisconsin Sociological Association and distributed free to members.

Guide to Related Sociological Journals

These journals were identified by Lawrence J. Rhoades as those expressing interest in receiving manuscripts from Sociologists and Social Psychologists. See his *The Authors Guide to Selected Journals*. Cf. *Directory of Scholarly and Research Opportunities* (Los Angeles: Academic Media, 1975).

JOURNAL

Academy of Management Journal
Acta Criminologica
Administration & Society
Administration in Mental Health
Administrative Science Quarterly
Administrative Science Review
Adolescence
Africa Today
African Studies Review
Altered States of Consciousness
Journal of American Folklore
American Educational Research Journal
Journal of the American Geriatrics Society
Journal of the American Institute of Planners
American Journal of Economics and
  Sociology
American Journal of Political Science
American Journal of Psychology
American Psychologist
The American Statistician
Journal of Applied Communications Research
Journal of Applied Social Psychology
Asian Survey
AV Communication Review
Journal of Black Studies
Behavior Research Methods &
  Instrumentation
Behavior Science Research
Journal of Broadcasting
California Journal of Educational Research
Catalyst
Character Potential: A Record of Research
Child Care Quarterly
Child Psychiatry and Human Development
Child Welfare
The Cleveland State Law Review
Clinical Social Work Journal
Cognition
The Colorado Quarterly
Journal of Communication
Communication Research

Community College Social Science Quarterly
Journal of the Community Development
  Society
Community Mental Health Journal
Comparative Political Studies
Compensation Review
Journal of Conflict Resolution
Journal of Consumer Affairs
Journal of Criminal Law & Criminology
Criminology
Journal of Cross-Cultural Psychology
Cybernetica
Cycles
Day Care and Early Education
Demography
The Journal of Developing Areas
Drug Forum
Economic and Social Review
Education and Urban Society
Journal of Educational Psychology
Journal of Educational Thought
The Journal of Emotional Education
Environment and Behavior
et al.
ETC. A Review of General Semantics
The Journal of Ethnic Studies
European Journal of Social Psychology
Ethnicity
Evaluation
Exceptional Children
The Family Coordinator
Family Planning Digest
Family Planning Perspectives
Family Process
Federal Probation
The Futurist
The Journal of General Psychology
Georgia Social Science Journal
The Gerontologist
The Green Revolution
Group Psychotherapy & Psychodrama

Growth and Change
Handbook of International Sociometry
Harvard Business Review
Health Services Research
Journal of Higher Education
Journal of the Assoc. for the Study of
  Perception
Journal of Homosexuality
Hospital Administration
Milbank Memorial Fund Quarterly/Health
  and Society
Human Behavior Magazine
The Human Context
Human Mosaic
Journal of Human Resources
Human Resource Management
Humanitas
Improving College & University Teaching
The Indian Historian
Industrial and Labor Relations Review
Industrial Relations: A Jrnl. of Economy &
  Society
Intellect
Journal of Interamerican Studies & World
  Affairs
International Development Review
International Interactions
International Journal of the Addictions
International Journal of Cooperative
  Development
International Journal of Ethnic Studies
International Journal of Offender Therapy &
  Comparative Criminology
International Journal of Symbology
International Migration Review
International Review of Administrative
  Sciences
International Studies Quarterly
Issues in Criminology
Law & Society Review
Journal of Leisure Research
Life-Threatening Behavior
Manpower
Journal of Marketing Research
Journal of Marriage and the Family
Methods of Information in Medicine
Multivariate Behavioral Research
Journal of Negro Education
The New Scholar

Opinion
Peace and Change, a Journal of Peace
  Research
People Watching
Journal of Personality & Social Psychology
Journal of Personality Assessment
Personnel
The Personnel Administrator
Personnel and Guidance Journal
Political Science Quarterly
Journal of Popular Culture
Population Review
Population Studies
Public Opinion Quarterly
The Prison Journal
Psychiatry
Psychological Bulletin
The Psychological Record
Psychological Review
Psychology
The Journal of Psychology
Psychometrika
Public Administration Review
Public Welfare
Quarterly Journal of Economics
Quarterly Journal of Speech
Race
Journal for the Scientific Study of Religion
Review of Religious Research
Religious Humanism
Journal of Research in Crime & Delinquency
Research on Consumer Behavior
Review of Educational Research
Review of Public Data Use
The Review of Social Theory
Rocky Mountain Social Science Journal
S.A.M. Advanced Management Journal
The Journal of Sex Research
Journal of School Psychology
Science & Society
Simulation and Games
Small Group Behavior
Social Action
Social Biology
Social Compass
Social Policy
Journal of Social Issues
Journal of Social Policy
The Journal of Social Psychology

Social Science Quarterly
Social Work
Journal of Socio-Economic Planning Sciences
Sociological Analysis
Soundings: An Interdisciplinary Journal
Southeastern Review
Southern Speech Communication Journal
Studies in Family Planning
Technology Assessment
Technology and Culture
Journal of Thought
Trans-Action

Journal of Vocational Behavior
Town Planning Review
University of Chicago School Review
Urban Affairs Quarterly
Urban and Social Change Review
Urban Education
Urban Life and Culture
War on Hunger
War/Peace Report
Women's Studies
World Politics
Youth and Society

New Journals

Signs: Journal of Women in Culture and Society. The University of Chicago Press, 11030 Langley Ave., Chicago, Ill. 60628. Editor, Box 20, 307 Barnard Hall, Barnard College, New York, N.Y. 10027.

1975. Quarterly, International journal devoted to status of and research about women.

Armed Forces and Society: An Interdisciplinary Journal. Editor, Box 46, Social Science Building, University of Chicago, Chicago, Ill. 60637.

1974. Devoted to research and analysis of military organization, civilian relations, arms control, and peacekeeping.

The Journal of Consumer Research. 222 South Riverside Plaza, Chicago, Ill. 60606. Editor: Ronald E. Frank, Journal of Consumer Research, The Wharton School—W253 University of Pennsylvania, Philadelphia, Pa. 19174.

1974. An interdisciplinary journal co-sponsored by ten professional organizations including the American Sociological Association.

The International Journal of Critical Sociology. Editor: T. K. N. Unnithan, Department of Sociology, Jaipur, India.

1975. Biannual publication of Jaipur Institute of Sociology. Publishes articles critical of present type of sociology and critical appraisals of social issues and policies.

Social Science Research. Editors: Robert K. Leik and Peter H. Rossi, University of Massachusetts, Amherst, Mass. Publisher: Academic Press, 111 Fifth Avenue, New York, N.Y. 10003.

1975. Quarterly. Multidisciplinary journal emphasizing quantitative and methodological techniques.

Evaluation: A Forum for Human Service Decision Centers. Minneapolis, Minnesota.

1974. Experimental magazine supported by a collaborative research grant from National Institute of Health.

Sociological Methods and Research. Editors: Edgar F. Borgatta and George W. Bohrnstedt, Sage Publications, Inc., P.O. Box 776, Beverly Hills, Calif. 90213.

1974. Quarterly. Devoted to sociology as a cumulative empirical science, focused on the assessment of the scientific status of sociology.

Sociological Practice. Edited by Donald E. Gelfand and Bernard Phillips. Human Services Press, 72 Fifth Ave., New York, N.Y. 10011.

1976. Semiannually. Review Articles on relevance of sociological subfields to practice. Purpose of journal is to put sociology to work by transforming knowledge into social action.

Focus on Poverty Research. Institute for Research on Poverty. 3412 Social Science Building. University of Wisconsin-Madison. Madison, Wisconsin 53706.

1976. Quarterly. Purpose is to acquaint a wide audience with the work of the Institute for Research on Poverty.

Current Information about Published Work

Current Contents in the Social and Behavioral Sciences is a weekly listing of the contents of journals and some books in the social and behavioral sciences. It also includes an index by first author and principal words in the titles of articles.

The Educational Resources Information Center (ERIC) of the National Institute of Education (NIE) publishes a monthly abstract journal, *Resources in Education* (RIE), which announces research reports and other nonjournal literature of interest to the educational community. These documents are cataloged, abstracted, and indexed by subject, author or investigator, and responsible institution.

Resources in Education started publication in November 1966 and can be purchased in single copies or on subscription from the Superintendent of Documents, U.S. Government Printing Office, Washington, D.C. 20402. Annual cumulative sets have been reprinted and can be obtained from Macmillan Information, 216R Brown Street, Riverside, N.J. 08075.

Macmillan Information also publishes *Current Index to Journals in Education* (CIJE), which indexes articles in over 700 journals. These journals represent the core of the periodical/serial literature in the field of education.

Individual monthly volumes and yearly cumulations of *Resources in Education* and *Current Index to Journals in Education* are available in many college and university libraries, as well as some special libraries. Most of these libraries are open to the public for on-site reference and many also have complete ERIC microfiche collections. *Resources in Education* is also available in the offices of many school systems at the state and local level. All routine searches for documentary material should begin with *Resources in Education.*

ERIC was originally conceived in the U.S. Office of Education in the mid-1960s as a system of providing ready access to recent educational research and other education related literature. The ERIC Processing and Reference Facility is a centralized information processing facility serving Central ERIC and sixteen decentralized clearinghouses, each specializing in a branch of knowledge. For further information, write ERIC Processing and Reference Facility, 4833 Rugby Avenue, Suite 303, Bethesda, Md. 20014. Telephone (301) 656-9723.

WHERE SOCIOLOGISTS PUBLISH; WHERE PRESTIGIOUS SOCIOLOGISTS PUBLISH AND WHY

5.C.4

Sociologists publish research monographs with numerous publishing companies and university presses and research articles in 300 or more journals. A directory of publishers lists more than 260 publishing outlets in the United States. The

Guide to Sociological Journals includes 72 journals and the list of *Related Sociological Journals* extends to almost 200. Other outlets include many well-known journals that print sociological articles including *Harpers Magazine, Atlantic Monthly, Commentary, New Republic*, and so on. Sociologists write in newspapers, prepare pamphlets, and distribute mineograph and printed materials to selected audiences.[1] They write to secure tenure and promotion, gain merit increases, increase their status, and because they just like to write and "get their work out." They are driven by an ethic that impels them to "make their work known" so that their knowledge will be preserved and transmitted.

Of all the motives that drive the scholar to write, the most universal and persistent is the desire for status. This is expressed first as a desire to become "known" and then to rank even higher in prestige. It is appropriate therefore to find out which journals rank high in prestige.

Where Do the Prestigious Sociologists Publish and Why?

Ideally, every writer would be judged by the intrinsic worth of his research in whatever journal it appeared. In fact, no scholar, no matter how thorough, can read all or even a substantial part of the available journals. The result is that each sociologist who publishes is evaluated in part (in large part?) by the reputations of the journals in which he publishes. The degree to which most articles are noticed, read, used, and cited depends to a great extent on the kinds of journals in which the articles are published.

Norval D. Glenn undertook investigations of American sociologists' evaluations of 63 journals in which sociologists frequently publish.[2] In February 1970, he mailed a questionnaire to a randomly drawn sample of 250 professors and associate professors in departments with Sociology Ph.D. programs listed in the *Guide to Graduate Departments of Sociology, 1969*. He asked his respondents to assign weights to the list of 63 journals in accordance with their judgment of the average importance of their contributions to the field. They were asked to use articles in the *American Sociological Review* as a standard for reference, using a weight of 10 to an article in that journal.[3] A publication judged only half as important was to be assigned a weight of 5. Using relative weights in this manner, judges produce mean weights that are shown in table 1.

Glenn describes some of his conclusions to the findings as each column is analyzed:

"The data in the first column of table 1 indicate two major dimensions of the reputations of the journals. The mean weight is essentially an indicator of the *intensity* of prestige, whereas the number of respondents who assigned weights (shown in parentheses) is a rough indicator of how well the journal was known among the respondents, or of the *extensity* of the journal's prestige. The extent of being known and the extensity of prestige are not the same, of course, unless all of those who know an object grant it some prestige."[4]

"If the measure of extensity were exact, total prestige could be arrived at by multiplying the measure of extensity by the measure of intensity. However, since no measure of total prestige can be derived from the data at hand, and since the measures of intensity and extensity are imperfectly correlated ($r = +.73$), the journals can be only partially ordered as to their prestige."[5]

"The reader must be cautioned that citation data indicate that the prestige of the journals does not closely correspond with the average impact their articles

Table 1. *Means of the Weights Assigned to 63 Journals by a Sample of American Sociologists*

				Category of respondent			
				Had published in journal		Relevant specialists[a]	
Journal	Mean weight	(N)	Standard deviation	Mean	(N)[b]	Mean	(N)[b]
American Sociological Review	10.0[c]	—	—	—	—		
American Journal of Sociology	9.6	(129)	1.2	9.6	(35)	—	—
Social Forces	8.1	(127)	1.9	8.1	(41)	—	—
Sociometry	7.8	(119)	2.2	8.6	(8)	8.1	(34)
British Journal of Sociology	7.8	(115)	2.1	—	—	—	—
American Anthropologist	7.7	(118)	2.3	—	—	—	—
Social Problems	7.6	(113)	2.2	8.7	(15)	—	—
American Political Science Review	7.5	(110)	2.2	—	—	8.0	(9)
Demography	7.4	(90)	2.2	8.8	(5)	9.1	(13)
Annals of the American Academy of Political and Social Science	7.2	(126)	2.3	8.1	(10)	—	—
Public Opinion Quarterly	7.1	(116)	2.1	7.4	(14)	7.2	(14)
American Economic Review	7.1	(99)	2.9	—	—	—	—
Journal of Personality and Social Science	7.1	(81)	2.2	—	—	7.1	(26)
European Journal of Sociology	6.9	(69)	2.4	—	—	—	—
Behavioral Science	6.8	(87)	2.3	—	—	—	—
Rural Sociology	6.7	(109)	2.2	7.2	(18)	7.8	(8)
Human Organization	6.7	(104)	2.0	7.4	(5)	—	—
Journal of Social Psychology	6.7	(102)	2.1	5.3	(6)	6.8	(33)
Administrative Science Quarterly	6.7	(98)	2.4	6.5	(5)	—	—
Milbank Memorial Fund Quarterly	6.7	(97)	2.4	—	—	7.1	(14)
International Journal of Comparative Sociology	6.7	(77)	2.4	—	—	—	—
American Behavioral Scientist	6.6	(110)	2.4	—	—	—	—
Journal of Social Issues	6.6	(108)	2.0	—	—	—	—
Social Research	6.6	(88)	2.2	—	—	—	—
Daedalus	6.5	(111)	2.8	—	—	—	—
Human Relations	6.5	(91)	2.2	6.4	(5)	—	—
Population Studies	6.5	(74)	2.2	—	—	7.3	(12)
Harvard Educational Review	6.4	(93)	2.9	—	—	6.0	(7)
Current Sociology	6.4	(78)	2.4	—	—	—	—
Canadian Review of Sociology and Anthropology	6.4	(77)	2.1	—	—	—	—
Sociological Review	6.3	(68)	2.0	—	—	—	—
International Social Science Journal	6.3	(65)	2.2	—	—	—	—
American Sociologist	6.2	(123)	2.4	7.9	(8)	—	—
Journal of Marriage and the Family	6.2	(108)	2.4	6.4	(14)	6.5	(21)
Journal of Conflict Resolution	6.2	(86)	2.6	—	—	—	—
Journal of Health and Social Behavior	6.2	(83)	2.4	8.8	(6)	8.3	(12)
Sociology of Education	6.1	(93)	2.0	6.4	(5)	6.1	(8)
Sociological Quarterly	6.1	(83)	1.9	6.6	(11)	—	—
Acta Sociologica	6.1	(71)	2.1	—	—	—	—
Social Science Quarterly	6.0	(64)	2.0	—	—	—	—
Southwestern Journal of Anthropology	6.0	(54)	2.2	—	—	—	—
Sociology and Social Research	5.9	(107)	1.9	6.0	(10)	—	—

Table 1. *Continued*

Journal	Mean weight	(N)	Standard deviation	Had published in journal		Relevant specialists[a]	
				Mean	(N)[b]	Mean	(N)[b]
Sociology	5.9	(33)	2.0	—	—	—	—
Sociological Inquiry	5.8	(86)	1.9	6.7	(13)	—	—
Transaction	5.7	(118)	2.7	5.0	(8)	—	—
Pacific Sociological Review	5.7	(94)	2.2	5.7	(7)	—	—
Law and Society Review	5.7	(62)	2.3	—	—	8.0	(5)
Sociological Analysis	5.7	(57)	1.7	6.2	(5)	5.7	(7)
Journal of Gerontology	5.4	(51)	2.2	6.5	(6)	—	—
Journal of Research in Crime and Delinquency	5.4	(46)	1.9	—	—	6.6	(14)
American Journal of Economics and Sociology	5.3	(96)	2.0	—	—	—	—
British Journal of Criminology	5.3	(61)	1.8	—	—	6.7	(14)
Gerontologist	5.3	(57)	2.1	—	—	—	—
Crime and Delinquency	5.2	(58)	1.9	—	—	5.6	(16)
Science and Society	5.2	(51)	2.1	—	—	—	—
Journal of Criminal Law, Criminology, and Police Science	5.1	(64)	1.9	—	—	5.9	(15)
Phylon	5.0	(82)	2.1	5.4	(8)	5.4	(12)
Eugenics Quarterly[d]	5.0	(51)	2.3	—	—	—	—
Jewish Journal of Sociology	4.9	(43)	1.8	—	—	—	—
American Journal of Correction	4.8	(73)	2.0	—	—	5.3	(15)
Eugenics Review	4.7	(41)	2.2	—	—	—	—
Journal of Negro Education	4.5	(57)	2.2	—	—	5.5	(11)
New Society	4.5	(37)	2.0	—	—	—	—
Federal Probation	3.8	(57)	1.8	—	—	4.5	(15)

Source: Norval D. Glenn, "American Sociologists Evaluation of 63 Journals," *TAS* 6 (November 1971): 300–301. Used with permission of American Sociological Association.

[a] The relevant specialists for a specialized journal are the respondents with a specialty in the same area as that of the old journal.
[b] Means are shown only where the N is five or more.
[c] The weight for the *ASR* was given on the questionnaire and was not assigned by the respondents.
[d] This journal is now called *Social Biology*.

have on the discipline. For instance, Lin and Nelson (1969) found substantial differences in the frequency of citation of articles in the *ASR*, the *AJS*, and *Social Forces*; yet my data indicate that those three journals were very similar in prestige. A major reason for this discrepancy may be that variation in circulation of the three journals (16,584 for the *ASR*, 9335 for the *AJS*, and about 4000 for *Social Forces* in 1969 or 1970); authors probably are more likely to cite an article if the journal is in their personal library."[6]

It is important to direct the reader's attention to the considerable dissensus in the evaluations of the journals, as roughly indicated by the standard deviations in table 1, column 2.

"These data, plus data not shown, make it clear that there is not a highly integrated system of prestige in sociology. Therefore, the best outlets for the writings of a particular sociologist depend on who are his or her significant others and who is likely to judge and reward him or her. Only the highest-prestige general journals seem to be very good outlets for almost any sociologist."[7]

One might suspect that a respondent would tend to overevaluate journals in which he had published or with which he was otherwise identified, but in the case of the general journals, the means of the weights given by respondents who had and who had not published in them were invariably similar and in some cases identical (table 1, column 3). There was, however, a tendency for persons to assign unusually high weights to the lower-prestige journals if they had published in them but not in the higher-prestige journals.

Although articles in prestigious journals rank high, the highest weights are given to Research and Theoretical Monographs (mean weight = 33.8), Textbooks (18.1), and Edited Books (11.2).[8]

Notes

1. For a comprehensive guide to publishing opportunities, see *Directory of Publishing Opportunities* (3rd ed.; Chicago, Ill.: Marquis Who's Who, 1975).

2. Norval D. Glenn, "American Sociologists' Evaluations of Sixty-Three Journals," *American Sociologist* 6 (November 1971): 298–303.

3. The *American Sociological Review* is the official journal of the American Sociological Association and is received by all members.

4. Glenn, "American Sociologists' Evaluations of Sixty-Three Journals," p. 300.

5. Ibid., p. 301.

6. Ibid., 302.

7. Ibid.

8. Glenn and Villemez have derived a weighting scheme for the different types of publications. It yields a useful index of "importance to the discipline." The Glenn-Villemez Comprehensive Index (GUCI) generates six distinct indices of publication productivity: number of articles, number of books, total publications (articles plus books), article points, book points, and total points. See Norval D. Glenn and Wayne Villemez, "The Productivity of Sociologists at 45 American Universities," *American Sociologist* 5 (August 1970): 244–52.

HOW SOCIOLOGISTS GET PUBLISHED   *5.C.5*

Few academics know all the ins and outs of publishing because the rules governing this activity are not a few, easily learned principles, but rather a multitude of various considerations any one of which can work for or against you. Each form of publishing has its own set of particular requirements.

Finding a Publisher for Articles

Each journal has its own goals and its own preferred style. It may have its own definition of appropriate length. And most important will be the standards of quality that the editors impose upon their acceptance of articles received. The extent to which the writer gauges these considerations accurately, the greater will be his or her chance of acceptance. The way to gain such a background is to become thoroughly familiar with the journal in which you hope to publish. If you want to publish in the most prestigious journals you should not send them any work that fails to meet the standards exhibited in those journals. You must be aware that the competition is intense and that the acceptance rate ranges each year between 10 and 20 percent of the articles received. And this rate includes articles often rejected until substantial revisions have been made to meet editors' criticisms. Each article is read by two or more professional readers, whose evaluations are subsequently weighed by the editor.

The younger scholar might be advised to choose among journals where the competition is less intense. Specialized journals in the area of interest may more readily accept an article if it conforms to their interest pattern. Many journals look for theoretical or opinion material and do not impose patterns of design and statistical rigor. They are more interested in well-written material that treats of concerns to their journal readers.

The writer who gets published usually makes tentative drafts and asks for the advice of colleagues. He or she is willing to accept criticism and willing to re-write, rewrite, and rewrite if necessary. The final draft is a perfect copy as far as possible. This means good paper, clear and correct typing, with footnoting and all style requirements matched against the format of the given journal.

Whatever the fate of the papers submitted, it must be remembered that writing is an art even for scientific work. The writer who wants to be published keeps writing and submitting work. There are numerous journals, and most work of reasonable quality can be published somewhere. This is a wonderful opportunity that is offered. In the exercise of the art the writer learns the ins and outs both of writing and the placement of work. If a writer seeks prestige, he or she will aim for the prestigeful journals only when the work merits it and when the writing commends it.

Finding a Publisher for Books

It will be recalled that Norvall Glenn reported that "although articles in presti-gious journals rank high, the highest weights are given to Research and Theoretical Monographs (mean weight = 33.8), Textbooks (18.1), and Edited Books (11.2)." In addition to gaining the writer higher prestige, books may make money. Royalties for best-selling texts and books of readings can be very rewarding. All books have the prospect of making some money, but research monographs ordinarily yield only prestige. But the monograph has a long and durable life, and the writer may be remembered for it long after his other writings are for-gotten. The decision as to publishing monographs, texts, or readings is one that requires a balancing of motives and skills—all timed according to appropriate stages in the professional career. A few general rules for finding a publisher for books has been set forth by Carolyn Mullins:

When and How?

The ideal time to begin interesting publishers in a research monograph is when you begin the research or receive funds to support it. If a text or trade book is on your mind, start looking for a publisher as soon as you get the idea for it.

Texts are usually intended for classroom use only. Rarely do they have scholarly interest. Trade books—e.g., Vance Packard's books and Riesman's *The Lonely Crowd*—have a nonacademic market in addition to whatever student or professional market they may have. Monographs are usually in-tended for faculty use; many have some utility in graduate seminars, and a few are useful in advanced undergraduate courses. Publishers, naturally, are de-lighted when a genuine research monograph also has obvious text and/or trade markets. Publishers (some university presses excepted) usually show greater interest in texts and trade books than in monographs because the former are more likely to make money. It follows, then, that competition is more likely to develop if you are trying to interest publishers in a text or trade book than if a monograph is your intended product.

Edited collections—whether of previously published papers or of unpublished papers—can fall into any category. They present many different and specialized problems. These have to do with obtaining permissions, pricing, keeping them within reasonable size limits, getting several contributors to cooperate and meet deadlines, trying to set contract obligations and rewards equitably, and so forth. They are also less popular now than they used to be, partly because of the high permission cost that is often involved.[1]

Note

1. Carolyn J. Mullins, "Everything You Always Wanted to Know About Book Publishing" (Paper given at Indiana University, February 1, 1975), pp. 2–3. Quote used by permission of author. Writing books and finding a publisher for monographs and textbooks is discussed more fully in C. J. Mullins, *Writing and Publishing in the Social and Behavioral Sciences* (New York: Wiley-Interscience, 1977).

PROFESSIONAL COMMUNICATION AND REPORTING   5.C.6

A professional research life is an ongoing process of research investigation, reading of research journals, preparing scientific papers and reading them before professional audiences of various learned societies, and finally publishing by article and monograph. In order to command attention, it is necessary for researchers to make themselves and their work known to colleagues in local, state, regional, national and international circles.

The North American sociologist who wishes to be known in national and international circles will join the American Sociological Association and may affiliate with one or both of the leading international sociological associations: International Sociological Association and Institut International de Sociologie.

Of all the many circles in which the researcher may move and find outlets, no forums are more important than reports at annual meetings of the American Sociological Association and publication in the *American Sociological Review*. If you are a young sociologist you should join the American Sociological Association as soon as you make a commitment to professional life. You should begin reading the *ASR*, which will provide research examples of high-quality work as well as names of leaders in the field. For the aspiring sociologist, the *ASR* should stimulate participation in the annual meetings and encourage growth of research interests. One of the first steps to professionalization is to know the research in your fields of interest and the leading researchers who are at the cutting edge of the discipline. The second and most important step is to join this circle by participation, achievement, and recognition.

The American Sociological Association is a voluntary association of individual members. Many categories of membership exist. Full membership in the ASA requires the holding of a Ph.D. degree in sociology or in some related field, or the completion of three years of graduate study in such field. There were 14,654 members of all categories in 1974; of this total, 6988 (48 percent) were full members. Approximately eight out of ten numbers are employed in sociology departments in colleges and universities, another 12 percent have appointments in academic units outside of sociology, and 9 percent work in nonacademic settings.

Of the total membership, 12,861 come from the 50 states and 1683 come from 79 countries outside the United States.

Approximately 25 percent of the total members are women. Growth of the Association is indicated by a membership of 115 in 1906, the first year of the founding, to 14,654 in 1974.

Regional associations are part of the contact and communication pattern and often represent the first professional experience of the young scholar. Regional meetings are smaller, the competition for acceptance of papers is less intense. This is a good place for the young scholar to start becoming a professional. There are associations in every region; their names are listed in section C.7.

5.C.7 **ANNUAL MEETINGS HELD BY VARIOUS SOCIOLOGICAL AND KINDRED SOCIETIES WITH COMMON SECTION TOPICS IN SOCIOLOGY, PSYCHOLOGY, AND ANTHROPOLOGY**

For information about annual meetings of the American Sociological Association and the other sociological societies write:

American Sociological Association
1722 N Street, N.W.
Washington, D.C. 20036
Telephone: 202/833-3410

Meetings of the American Sociological Association:

1977 Chicago, September 5-8
1978 San Francisco, August 28-31
1979 Boston, August 27-30
1980 Atlanta, August 25-28

Other Major Sociological Associations:

American Catholic Sociological Society
District of Columbia Sociological Society
Eastern Sociological Society
International Sociological Association
Institut International de Sociologie
Midwest Sociological Society
North Central Sociological Association
Pacific Sociological Association
Rural Sociological Society
Society for the Study of Social Problems
Southern Sociological Society
Southwestern Sociological Association

Annual Meetings Held by Kindred Social Science and Allied Societies:
American Anthropological Association. Executive Offices, American Anthropological Association, 3700 Massachusetts Avenue, N.W., Washington, D.C. 20005.

American Association for the Advancement of Science. American Association for the Advancement of Science, 1515 Massachusetts Avenue, N.W., Washington, D.C. 20005.

American Political Science Association. American Political Science Association, 1527 New Hampshire Avenue, N.W., Washington, D.C. 20036.

American Psychological Association. American Psychological Association, 1200 17th Street, N.W., Washington, D.C. 20036.

American Public Health Association. American Public Health Association, Inc., 1740 Broadway, New York, N.Y. 10019

American Statistical Association. Executive Director, American Statistical Association, 810 18th Street, N.W., Washington, D.C. 20036.

Canadian Sociology and Anthropology Association. Canadian Sociology and Anthropology Association, Postal Box 878, Montreal, P.Q., Canada.

Population Association of America. Population Association of America, P.O. Box 14182, Benjamin Franklin Station, Washington, D.C. 20044.

Annual sociological meetings are commonly organized in sections around the following topics:

METHODOLOGY AND RESEARCH TECHNOLOGY
- Methodology (Social Science and Behavioral)
- Research Technology
- Statistical Methods

SOCIOLOGY: HISTORY AND THEORY
- Of Professional Interest
- History and Present State of Sociology
- Theories, Ideas and Systems

SOCIAL PSYCHOLOGY
- Personality and Culture
- Interaction Within (Small) Groups
- Leadership

GROUP INTERACTIONS
- Interaction Between (Large) Groups (Race Relations, Group Relations, etc.)

CULTURE AND SOCIAL STRUCTURE
- Social Organization
- Culture (Evolution)
- Social Anthropology (and Ethnology)

COMPLEX ORGANIZATIONS (MANAGEMENT)
- Industrial Sociology (Labor)
- Military Sociology
- Bureaucratic Structures

SOCIAL CHANGE AND ECONOMIC DEVELOPMENT
- Social Change and Economic Development
- Market Structures and Consumer Behavior

MASS PHENOMENA
- Social Movements
- Public Opinion
- Communication
- Collective Behavior
- Sociology of Leisure
- Mass Culture

POLITICAL INTERACTIONS
- Interactions Between Societies, Nations and States
- Political Sociology

SOCIAL DIFFERENTIATION
- Social Stratification
- Sociology of Occupations and Professions

RURAL SOCIOLOGY AND AGRICULTURAL ECONOMICS
- Rural Sociology (Village, Agriculture)

URBAN STRUCTURES AND ECOLOGY
- Urban Sociology and Ecology

SOCIOLOGY OF THE ARTS
- Sociology of Language and Literature
- Sociology of Art (Creative and Performing)

SOCIOLOGY OF EDUCATION
  Sociology of Education
SOCIOLOGY OF RELIGION
  Sociology of Religion
SOCIAL CONTROL
  Sociology of Law
  Penology and Correctional Problems
SOCIOLOGY OF SCIENCE
  Sociology of Science and
    Technology
DEMOGRAPHY AND HUMAN
BIOLOGY
  Demography (Population Study)
  Human Biology
THE FAMILY AND
SOCIALIZATION
  Sociology of the Child and Socializa-
    tion
  Adolescence and Youth
  Sociology of Sexual Behavior
  Sociology of the Family

SOCIOLOGY   OF   HEALTH   AND
MEDICINE
  Sociology of Medicine (Public
    Health)
  Social Psychiatry (Mental Health)
SOCIAL PROBLEMS AND
SOCIAL WELFARE
  Social Gerontology
  Social Disorganization (Crime)
  Applied Sociology (Social Work)
  Delinquency
SOCIOLOGY OF KNOWLEDGE
  Sociology of Knowledge
  History of Ideas
COMMUNITY DEVELOPMENT
  Sociology of Communities and
    Regions
PLANNING, FORECASTING,
AND SPECULATION
  Planning, Forecasting, and
    Speculation

Meetings of the International Sociological Association are developed around 34 research committee sections. These divisions of interest represent a good statement of what modern sociologists are doing around the world.

01 Armed Forces and Society
02 Aspirations, Needs and Development
03 Community Research
04 Sociology of Education
05 Ethnic, Race and Minority Relations
06 Family Research
07 Futures Research
08 History of Sociology
09 Innovative Processes in Social Change
10 Sociology of International Relations
11 Sociology of Aging
12 Sociology of Law
13 Sociology of Leisure
14 Sociology of Mass Communications
15 Sociology of Medicine
16 Sociology of National Movements and Imperialism
17 Sociology of Organization
18 Political Sociology
19 Sociology of Poverty, Social Welfare and Social Policy
20 Sociology of Mental Health
21 Regional and Urban Development
22 Sociology of Religion
23 Sociology of Science

24 Social Ecology
25 Sociolinguistics
26 Sociotechnics
27 Sociology of Sport
28 Social Stratification
29 Deviance and Social Control
30 Sociology of Work
31 Sociology of Migration
32 Sex Roles in Society
33 Logic and Methodology in Sociology
34 Sociology of Youth

COMMON SECTION TOPICS FOR PSYCHOLOGY AND ANTHROPOLOGY AT ANNUAL MEETINGS*

PSYCHOLOGY
Clinical Psychology
  Behavior problems
  Community mental health
  Crime and delinquency
  Experimental psychopathology
  Group therapy
  Individual diagnosis
  Mental deficiency
  Objective tests
  Projective techniques
  Psychotherapy
  Speech pathology
Counseling and Guidance
  Educational counseling
  Nondirective therapy
  Personal adjustment
  Rehabilitation
  Vocational counseling
Developmental Psychology
  Childhood and adolescence
  Infancy
  Maturity and old age
  Nursery and pre-school
Personality
  Development
  Measurement
  Personality and body
  Personality and learning
  Personality and perception
  Personality theory
  Structure and dynamics
School Psychology

Educational Psychology
  Educational measurement
  Programmed learning
  School adjustment
  School learning
  Special education
  Student personnel
  Teacher personnel
Engineering Psychology
General Psychology
  History and biography
  Theory and systems
Industrial and Personnel Psychology
  Employee and executive training and
    development
  Employee morale and attitudes
  Job analysis and position
    classification
  Labor-management relations
  Market research, advertising
  Organizational behavior
  Performance evaluation, criterion
    development
  Recruiting, selection, placement
  Safety research and training
  Salary and pay plans

ANTHROPOLOGY
Major Divisions
  Archeology
  Ethnology
  History of anthropology
  Methodology

*The classification shown is used by the National Science Foundation in its Register of Social Scientists.

Anthropological linguistics	Economic anthropology
Physical anthropology	Ethnomusicology
Social/Cultural anthropology	Human paleontology
Specialties	Museology
Anthropological folklore	Primatology
Cultural ecology	Psychological anthropology

5.C.8 **GUIDE TO THE JOURNALS SPONSORED BY THE AMERICAN SOCIOLOGICAL ASSOCIATION**

American Sociological Review is the official journal of the American Sociological Association publishing articles of major concern to social scientists. New trends and developments in theory and research are reported. Comments from readers and authors are printed relevant to articles previously published. The *Review* is sent to all members and is the journal most widely read by sociologists. Bimonthly.

Sociometry is a journal of research in social psychology. It is genuinely interdisciplinary in the publication of works by both sociologists and psychologists. Quarterly.

Contemporary Sociology: A Journal of Reviews. This journal is devoted entirely to book reviews and is designed to give new thrust and style to book reviewing. Besides reviews of specific books it features survey essays, symposium essays, review essays, and letters. Bimonthly.

The American Sociologist contains major articles analyzing sociology as a profession and as a discipline. Included are reports on standards and practices in teaching, research, publication, and the application of sociological knowledge. Short notes and letters are accepted. Quarterly.

Journal of Health and Social Behavior is distinctive for a sociological approach to the definition and analysis of problems bearing on human welfare. Articles range from drugs and smoking to health care organizations and costs, professional and nonprofessional role conflicts, and various topics related to women. Bimonthly.

Sociology of Education is a forum for educators and social scientists seeking to advance sociological knowledge about education. The journal serves as a significant medium for the application of this knowledge to major issues of educational policy and practice. Quarterly.

Other Important Publications

ASA Footnotes is the organ for the official reports and proceedings of the Association. It invites opinion on such matters as the state of undergraduate education, the future employment of sociologists, the status of women and minorities in sociology, the linkage of sociology to social policy, alternative modes of graduate training, broadening the world perspective of American sociology, and adding to the knowledge base of the discipline.

Arnold Rose Monograph Series provides an opportunity for members and student members of the ASA to publish short research monographs (100–300 typed pages) in any subject matter field in sociology that normally is beyond the scope of publication in regular academic journals. Numerous volumes have been published since its establishment in 1968.

Sociological Methodology. An official publication of ASA published by Jossey-Bass, Inc., is an annual volume exploring new ventures to advance the knowledge of research methodology in various realms of sociological inquiry.

ASA Reader Series: Issues and Trends in Sociology, founded in 1968, includes volumes devoted to topics of salient theoretical and substantive interest that emphasize the development and progressive refinement over time of the issue in question. A number of volumes have been published. Terminated 1976.

Annual Review of Sociology summarizes progress of development in various fields, of sociology. Established in 1975. Bimonthly.

GUIDE TO THE JOURNALS SPONSORED BY THE AMERICAN PSYCHOLOGICAL ASSOCIATION

5.C.9

American Psychologist

The *American Psychologist* is the official journal of the American Psychological Association, publishing both the official papers of the association and substantive articles on psychology. The May issue contains the highlights of the annual convention to be held the following September and the December issue contains a list of all the papers presented at the convention. In addition, once each year the *American Psychologist* devotes an entire issue (normally the November issue) to the extensive coverage and analysis of a single topic of current concern to the social sciences.

The broad scope of this publication makes it of interest to a wide and varied audience.

Published monthly.

Contemporary Psychology

A journal of reviews—critical reviews—of books, films, and other material in the field of psychology. It provides a means by which the reader may keep abreast of current psychological thought and opinion. Reviews of approximately 380 books are published annually.

Published monthly.

Journal of Abnormal Psychology

The *Journal of Abnormal Psychology* is devoted to basic research and theory in the broad area of abnormal behavior.

Published bimonthly.

Journal of Applied Psychology

This journal gives primary consideration to original quantitative investigation of value to those people interested in the following broad areas: personnel research; industrial working conditions, research on opinion and morale factors; job analysis and classification research; marketing and advertising research; and vocational and educational prognosis, diagnosis, and guidance at the secondary and college levels.

Published bimonthly.

Journal of Comparative and Physiological Psychology

This journal publishes original research reports in the field of comparative and physiological psychology, including animal learning, conditioning, and sensory processes. Editorial policies favor articles reporting studies of substantial scope, usually involving series of related experiments. Supplementary reports provide for short articles describing replications of or advances in techniques used in previously published researches.

Published bimonthly, 2 vols. per year.

Journal of Consulting and Clinical Psychology

This publication is devoted to the area of clinical psychology, both child and adult. Its range of content reflects the many facets of this area, including such topics as personality assessment and diagnosis, theories and techniques of behavior modification, community mental health concepts and techniques, etiology of behavior, structure and dynamics of personality, and clinical psychopathology.

Published bimonthly.

Journal of Educational Psychology

The *Journal of Educational Psychology* publishes original investigations and theoretical papers dealing with problems of learning and teaching, and with the psychological development, relationships, and adjustment of the individual.

Published monthly, 3 vols. per year.

Psychological Abstracts

Psychological Abstracts publishes concise abstracts of the world's literature in psychology and pertinent allied subjects. All titles and abstracts of foreign material are translated into English.

Published monthly.

Psychological Bulletin

The *Psychological Bulletin* is concerned with research reviews and methodological contributions in the field of psychology. One of the principal functions of this journal is to publish critical, evaluative summaries of research. The methodological articles are directed toward people who might or do make practical use of such information, and are intended to bridge the gap between the technical statistician and the typical research psychologist. Articles feature the application of new methodology as well as the creative application of more familiar methodology.

Published monthly, 2 vols. per year.

Journal of Counseling Psychology

The *Journal of Counseling Psychology* serves as a primary publication medium for research on counseling theory and practice.

Published bimonthly.

Psychological Review

The Psychological Review is the major psychological journal of articles of theoretical significance to any area of scientific endeavor in psychology. It contains original articles which propose theoretical ideas and developments, and offers critical discussions of theoretical issues.

Published bimonthly.

Journal of Personality and Social Psychology

This journal is devoted to basic research and theory in the broad areas of social interaction and group processes. Specifically, it deals with interpersonal perception and attitude change, the psychological aspects of formal social systems and less structured collective phenomena, the socialization process at both child and adult levels, social motivation and personality dynamics, the structure of personality, and the relation of personality to group process and social systems.

Published monthly, 3 vols. per year.

GUIDE TO MAJOR JOURNALS IN POLITICAL SCIENCE AND PUBLIC ADMINISTRATION

5.C.10

American Political Science Review. American Political Science Association, 1726 Massachusetts Avenue, N.W., Washington, D.C. 20036.

Official journal of the American Political Science Association. Offers scientific studies, essays, bibliographies, and news and notes on contemporary matters in the profession. Founded 1903. Circulation 13,000.

Political Science Quarterly. Academy of Political Science, Fayerweather Hall, Columbia University, New York, N.Y. 10027.

Studies in the field of political science and economics of interest to scholars and laymen. Founded 1886. Circulation 9000.

Annals of the American Academy of Political and Social Science, 3397 Chestnut Street, Philadelphia, Pa. 19104.

Founded 1890. Circulation 17,000.

Journal of Politics. Southern Political Science Association, University of Florida, Gainesville, Fla. 32601.

Interpretative articles covering all of the various subfields of political science by leading United States and foreign scholars. Scholarly review of new publications. Founded 1938.

Midwest Journal of Political Science. Wayne State University Press, 5980 Cass Avenue, Detroit, Mich. 48202.

Scholarly publication of Midwest Conference of Political Science. Founded 1957. Circulation 800.

Public Administration Review. American Society for Public Administration, 1225 Connecticut Ave., N.W., Washington, D.C. 20036.

Publishes material representative of all interests and opinions among practitioners, teachers, researchers, and students of public administration. Founded 1939. Bimonthly.

The Review of Politics. University of Notre Dame, Notre Dame, Ind. 46556.

Political theory, contemporary social movements, international relations, cultural developments, and politics. Founded 1939. Circulation 2500.

Foreign Affairs. Council on Foreign Relations, Inc., 58 East 68 Street, New York, N.Y. 10021.

A nonpartisan review of current ideas and policies affecting United States relations in all parts of the world, including international, political, commercial, and business communities. Founded 1922. Circulation 58,000.

Social Research. Graduate Faculty of New School for Social Research, 66 West 12 Street, New York, N.Y. 10011.

International quarterly of political and social science. Founded 1934. Circulation 1700.

World Politics. Center of International Studies, Princeton University, Crown Hall, Princeton, N.J. 08540.

Problems of international relations of a general and theoretical nature, emphasizing social change and employing multidisciplinary methods and concepts. Founded 1948. Circulation 2300.

Other journals to which political scientists contribute and read are the *Western Political Quarterly*, *Public Interest*, and *Commentary*. A great number of specialized journals exist.

5.C.11   GUIDE TO MAJOR JOURNALS IN ANTHROPOLOGY

There are many specialized fields and journals in anthropology to be found in physical anthropology, ethnology, archeology, and linguistics. The three journals of most general interest to social scientists generally are probably the following:

American Anthropologist. American Anthropological Association, 1530 P Street N.W., Washington, D.C. 20005.

Founded 1899. Circulation 6000.

Current Anthropology. University of Chicago Press, 5750 Ellis Avenue, Chicago, Ill. 60637.

Founded 1953. Circulation 8000.

Human Organization. Society for Applied Anthropology, Lafferty Hall, University of Kentucky, Lexington, Ky. 40506.

Founded 1941. Circulation 3000.

5.C.12   GUIDE TO MAJOR RESEARCH JOURNALS IN EDUCATION

Education represents a field of breadth and scope since it extends from nursery school to adult education and encompasses a wide variety of subject matter. The journals listed below are research journals that have the broadest scope.

American Educational Research Journal
Journal of Experimental Education
Educational and Psychological Measurement
Journal of Educational Psychology
Review of Educational Research
Child Development
Journal of Educational Measurement

Other more specialized research journals include *Journal of Research in Science Teaching*, *American Journal of Mental Deficiency*, *Journal of Reading Behavior*, *Reading Research Quarterly*, *The Educational Psychologist*.

GUIDE TO MAJOR JOURNALS USED BY ORGANIZATIONAL AND BEHAVIORAL RESEARCHERS IN BUSINESS *5.C.13*

Administrative Science Quarterly
Journal of Applied Psychology
Organizational Behavior and Human Performance
Academy of Management Journal
Organization and Administrative Sciences
Decision Sciences
Human Relations
Sociometry

There are hundreds of journals in anthropology, economics, education, law, business, social work, etc. Directories of world journals include:

INTERNATIONAL COMMITTEE FOR SOCIAL SCIENCES: *Documentation in the Social Sciences: World List of Social Science Periodicals*. 3rd ed. Paris: UNESCO, 1966.
The Standard Periodical Directory. 4th ed. New York: Oxbridge, 1973.

Index